MW00331735

Windows Server 2016 Automation with PowerShell Cookbook

Second Edition

Powerful ways to automate and manage Windows administrative tasks

Thomas Lee

BIRMINGHAM - MUMBAI

Windows Server 2016 Automation with PowerShell Cookbook

Second Edition

Copyright © 2017 Packt Publishing

All rights reserved. No part of this book may be reproduced, stored in a retrieval system, or transmitted in any form or by any means, without the prior written permission of the publisher, except in the case of brief quotations embedded in critical articles or reviews.

Every effort has been made in the preparation of this book to ensure the accuracy of the information presented. However, the information contained in this book is sold without warranty, either express or implied. Neither the author, nor Packt Publishing, and its dealers and distributors will be held liable for any damages caused or alleged to be caused directly or indirectly by this book.

Packt Publishing has endeavored to provide trademark information about all of the companies and products mentioned in this book by the appropriate use of capitals. However, Packt Publishing cannot guarantee the accuracy of this information.

First published: October 2015

Second edition: September 2017

Production reference: 1190917

Published by Packt Publishing Ltd.
Livery Place
35 Livery Street
Birmingham
B3 2PB, UK.

ISBN 978-1-78712-204-8

www.packtpub.com

Credits

Author
Thomas Lee

Reviewer
Mike F Robbins

Acquisition Editor
Meeta Rajani

Content Development Editor
Abhishek Jadhav

Technical Editor
Mohd Riyan Khan

Copy Editors
Safis Editing
Juliana Nair

Project Coordinator
Judie Jose

Proofreader
Safis Editing

Indexer
Aishwarya Gangawane

Graphics
Kirk D'Penha

Production Coordinator
Aparna Bhagat

About the Author

Thomas Lee is a consultant/trainer/writer from England and has been in the IT business since the late 1960's. After graduating from Carnegie Mellon University, Thomas joined ComShare where he was a systems programmer building the Commander II time-sharing operating system, a forerunner of today's Cloud computing paradigm. He moved to Comshare UK in 1975 and later went to work for ICL, again developing operating systems. After a sabbatical in 1980/81, he joined Arthur Andersen Management Consultants (now known as Accenture). He left in 1988 to run his own consulting and training business, which is still active today.

Thomas holds numerous Microsoft certifications, including MCSE (one of the first in the world) and later versions, MCT (22 years), and was awarded Microsoft's MVP award 17 times. He is also a Fellow of the British Computer Society. He has written extensively for the UK trade press, including PC Pro.

Today, Thomas writes and talks mainly on PowerShell and Azure. He currently works for a number of clients to deliver training and to build training courses. Having traveled the world, he entered semi-retirement in 2016 and is spending more time at his cottage in the English countryside, along with his wife, Susan, and their daughter, Rebecca. He continues to give back to the community and spends a lot of time as group administrator for the PowerShell forum on Spiceworks, where he is also a Moderator.

Acknowledgment

I'd first like to thank Jeffrey Snover of Microsoft for the invention of PowerShell. I was lucky enough to be in the room the very first time he presented what was then called Monad. His enthusiasm was infectious, and 15 years later I am still excited.

Also, a shout out to the author of the first edition, Ed Goad. His first edition was a great base to work on although all the recipes in this edition are reworked totally.

A huge thank you has to go to the Packt team: Meeta Rajani, Abhishek Jadhav, Mohd Riyan Khan, and Judie Jose. You guys did a great job getting this book out of the door and dealing with the crises that arose during the writing. And thanks too to our most excellent tech reviewer Mike Robbins. Your reviews were always excellent.

When I began this project, I had a co-author, David Cobb. Sadly, for personal reasons, he had to drop out, but I thank him for the chapters he was able to write.
We had a large number of volunteer reviewers who read through the various chapters. I appreciate all the work you folks did to try to make this a better book.

As each recipe evolved, I would sometimes hit problems. I got a lot of help from the Spiceworks community. Their PowerShell forum is a great source of information and encouragement. If you have problems with PowerShell, this is a great place to get a solution.

And finally, I have to thank my wonderful wife, Susan. She has been patient as things progressed, she put up with my bad moods when progress was not as smooth as desirable, and kept me sane when all around me was craziness.

About the Reviewer

Mike F. Robbins is a Microsoft MVP on Windows PowerShell and a SAPIEN Technologies MVP. He is a co-author of *Windows PowerShell TFM 4th Edition* and is a contributing author of a chapter in the *PowerShell Deep Dives* book. Mike has written guest blog articles for the Hey, Scripting Guy! blog, PowerShell Magazine, and PowerShell.org. He is the winner of the advanced category in the 2013 PowerShell Scripting Games. Mike is also the leader and co-founder of the Mississippi PowerShell User Group. He blogs at mikefrobbins.com and can be found on Twitter at @mikefrobbins.

www.PacktPub.com

For support files and downloads related to your book, please visit www.PacktPub.com.

Did you know that Packt offers eBook versions of every book published, with PDF and ePub files available? You can upgrade to the eBook version at www.PacktPub.comand as a print book customer, you are entitled to a discount on the eBook copy. Get in touch with us at service@packtpub.com for more details.

At www.PacktPub.com, you can also read a collection of free technical articles, sign up for a range of free newsletters and receive exclusive discounts and offers on Packt books and eBooks.

https://www.packtpub.com/mapt

Get the most in-demand software skills with Mapt. Mapt gives you full access to all Packt books and video courses, as well as industry-leading tools to help you plan your personal development and advance your career.

Why subscribe?

- Fully searchable across every book published by Packt
- Copy and paste, print, and bookmark content
- On demand and accessible via a web browser

Customer Feedback

Thanks for purchasing this Packt book. At Packt, quality is at the heart of our editorial process. To help us improve, please leave us an honest review on this book's Amazon page at https://www.amazon.com/dp/1787122042.

If you'd like to join our team of regular reviewers, you can email us at customerreviews@packtpub.com. We award our regular reviewers with free eBooks and videos in exchange for their valuable feedback. Help us be relentless in improving our products!

Table of Contents

Preface

PowerShell was first introduced to the world at the Professional Developer's conference in Los Angles in 2003 by Jeffrey Snover. Code named Monad, it represented a complete revolution in management. A white paper written around that time, *The Monad Manifesto* (refer to `http://www.jsnover.com/blog/2011/10/01/monad-manifesto/`) remains an amazing analysis of the problem at the time of managing large number of Windows systems. A key takeaway—the GUI does not scale, whereas PowerShell does.

PowerShell has transformed managing of complex, network-based Windows infrastructure and increasingly non-Windows infrastructure. Knowledge of PowerShell and how to get the most from PowerShell is now obligatory for any IT Pro job—the adage being *Learn PowerShell or learn Golf.*

This book takes you through the use of PowerShell in a variety of scenarios using many of the rich set of features included in Windows Server 2016. This preface provides you with an introduction to what is in the book and some tips on how to get the most out of the content.

What this book covers

Chapter 1, *What's New in PowerShell and Windows Server,* looks at some of the key new features in Windows Server 2016 and in the latest version of PowerShell.

Chapter 2, *Implementing Nano Server,* shows you how to set up and use Nano Server—a new server installation option for Windows Server 2016. Nano Server provides a great platform for running roles with a vastly reduced attack and patch surface.

Chapter 3, *Managing Windows Updates,* helps you get to grips with managing updates via Windows Update. With the importance of keeping all your Windows servers fully patched, managing WSUS is a key take in almost any size organization.

Chapter 4, *Managing Printers,* shows you how to manage printers, printer queues, and printer drivers, including deploying printers via Group Policy. This chapter also looks at branch office printing.

Chapter 5, *Managing Server Backup*, examines the use of Windows Server Backup and covers both backup (and restore) via cmdlet and via the console application. Windows Server Backup is a nice feature you can use either on its own in a small organization or to augment an enterprise wide third-party service.

Chapter 6, *Managing Performance*, shows you how to measure and monitor the performance of a server. There are several recipes that demonstrate how to get specific performance measurements and how to create graphs of performance for further analysis.

Chapter 7, *Troubleshooting Windows Server 2016*, looks at a number of aspects of both reactive and proactive troubleshooting. This includes getting events from the event log and forwarding event logs to a central server. This chapter also looks at the Best Practice Analyzer features baked into Windows Server.

Chapter 8, *Managing Windows networking services*, looks at various aspects of networking. Networks are today central to almost every organization and this chapter looks at a variety of network-related tasks, including looking at new ways (with PowerShell) to do old things, setting up DNS, DHCP, and Active directory, as well as building a multi-tier certificate authority infrastructure.

Chapter 9, *Managing Network Shares*, looks at sharing data between systems, including building a scaled out clustered file server based on iSCSI and using the DFS Namespace and DFS Replication features of Windows Server.

Chapter 10, *Managing Internet Information Server*, shows you how to conduct a variety of IIS-related tasks, including IIS installation and configuration, setting up SSL and managing cipher suites, as well as configuring Network Load Balancing.

Chapter 11, *Managing Hyper-V*, demonstrates the use of Hyper-V. This chapter shows you how to build and deploy VMs with Hyper-V. This includes nested Hyper-V running a Hyper-V VM inside another Hyper-V VM (which is useful for a number of scenarios).

Chapter 12, *Managing Azure*, looks at managing IaaS resources in Azure using PowerShell. To test the recipes in this chapter, you need access to Azure. This chapter describes how to get a trial subscription.

Chapter 13, *Using Desired State Configuration*, shows how to use this important feature to ensure a server is setup correctly and continues to remain so. This covers setting up a pull server and configuring partial configurations.

What you need for this book

To get the most out of this book, you need to experiment with the code contained in the recipes. To avoid errors impacting live production servers, you should instead use virtualization to create a test lab, where mistakes do not cause any serious damage. This book uses a variety of servers within a single `Reskit.Org` domain containing multiple servers, and using an IP address block of `10.10.10/24` described in *Getting the most from this book*.

Ideally, you should have a Windows 10 or Windows Server 2016 host with virtualization capabilities and use a virtualization solution. If you have access to a cloud computing platform, then you could perform most of the recipies in cloud-hosted virtual machines although that has not been tested. You can use any virtualization.

The book was developed using Hyper-V and nested Hyper-V on Windows 10 Creator's Update and Windows Server 2016. More details of the servers are contained in the preface and each recipe.

Who this book is for

This book is aimed at IT Pros, including system administrators, system engineers, as well as architects and consultants who need to leverage PowerShell to simplify and automate their daily tasks.

Getting the most from this book

This book was written based on some assumptions and with some constraints. You will need to read this section to understand how I intended the book to be used and what I have assumed about you. This should help you to get the most from this book.

1. The first assumption I made in writing this book is that you know the basics of PowerShell. This is not a PowerShell tutorial. The recipes do make use of a wide range of PowerShell features, including WMI, Remoting, AD and so on, but you will need to know the basics of PowerShell. The book uses PowerShell language, syntax, and cmdlets that come with Windows Server 2016 and Windows 10 (CU).

2. The recipes provide the basics—you adopt and adapt. The recipes are designed to show you the basics of how to manage certain aspects of Windows Server 2016 using PowerShell (and in some cases Windows Console Applications). In many cases, a recipe stresses that you can improve it for your environment. The recipe is meant to show you how some features work, so you can leverage and extend it for your environment.

3. Start by running the recipes step by step. The recipes were built and tested step by step. Once you have it working, re-factor them into your own reusable functions. In some cases, we build simple functions as a guide to richer scripts you could build.

4. Writing PowerShell scripts for publication in a book is a layout nightmare. To get around this, I have made extensive use of the various ways in which you can create multiline commands within PowerShell. This involves using the back tick (`) line continuation as well as using the Pipe character at the end of the line. I also sometimes specify an array of values across multiple lines with a comma at the end of the continuing line. Hopefully, the screenshots more or less match up. So, read the text carefully and pay attention particularly to the back tick. In all too many places and to save lots of extra blank space, code spills over a page break, or where a figure and related text are split across a page boundary. I hope there are not too many issues with layout!

5. Many of the cmdlet or object methods used in this book produce output that may not be all that helpful or useful. In some cases, the output generates a lot of pages of little value. For this reason, many recipes pipe to Out-Null. Feel free to remove this where you want to see more details. In some cases, I have adjusted the output to avoid wasted white space. Thus, if you test a recipe, you may see the output that is laid out a bit differently, but it should contain the same information. Of course, the specific output you see may be different based on your environment and the specific values you use in each step.

6. To write this book, I have used a large VM farm consisting of over 20 Windows 2016 servers and Windows 10 clients. All the hosts used in this book are a combination of some physical hardware (running almost entirely on Windows 10 Creators Update and a large set of VMs, including the following:
   - Domain Controllers (DC1, DC2)—also hosts DHCP Server, IIS, and other roles).
   - File Servers (FS1, FS1)
   - Network Load Balanced IIS servers (NLB1, NLB2)
   - Print Server (PSrv)

- General purpose servers (SRV1, SRV2)
- Client computers (CL1, SG-BR-CL1)
- Certificate servers (root, CA)
- Hyper-V Servers (HV1, HV1), including an embedded VM, VM1.

Each recipe notes the servers in use. Feel free to change things to suit your needs and based on your own naming conventions.

7. In building the VM farm, I have used an IP address block of 10.10.10.0/24. The recipes show specific addresses in use, but you can adapt these to fit your environment. The IP addresses used are assigned as follows:

IP address	Server name
10.10.10.10	DC1 (DC, DHCP, DNS, IIS, and so on)
10.10.10.11	DC2 (DC, DHCP, and DNS)
10.10.10.20	Root (CA offline root)
10.10.10.21	CA.Reskit.Org—issuing CA
10.10.10.50	SRV1 (server with numerous roles)
10.10.10.51 10.10.10.55	SRV2 (server with numerous roles) ReskitNLB (NLB Virtual Server)
10.10.10.60	PSRV (print server)
10.10.10.61	Sales.Reskit.Org—a network printer
10.10.10.62	Sales2.reskit.org—a printer at as remote office
10.10.10.100	FS.Reskit.Org (Cluster address)
10.10.10.101/102	FS1 (file server cluster node—with 2 nics)
10.10.10.105/106	FS2 (file server cluster node—with w nics)
10.10.10.131	Nano1
10.10.10.132	Nano2
10.10.10.141	SG-CL1 (client computer in the Sales Group)
10.10.10.146	SG-BR-CL1 (sales group branch office client)
10.10.10.201	HV1 (Hyper-V server)

`10.10.10.202`	HV2 (Hyper-V server)
`10.10.10.251`	WSUS1 (WSUS Server)
`10.10.10.254`	Default gateway

The full set of VMs, at the end of this writing, took up around 725 GB of storage. Fortunately, storage is cheap!

8. PowerShell provides great feature coverage—you can manage most of the functions and features of Windows Server 2016 using PowerShell, but by no means all. In some cases, you can dip down into WMI using the CIM cmdlets to get to object properties and methods not exposed by any cmdlet. The advent of CDXML-based cmdlets has increased the number of networking and other cmdlets that are WMI-based. But even then, there are still a number of places where you need to use a Windows console application or invoke an unmanaged DLL. The bottom line is that to manage some aspects of Windows, such as event forwarding or performance logging, you will need to use older tools. We try to avoid these, but in many cases the recipe demonstrates how to use the console applications within PowerShell.

9. I have avoided where possible using external, third-party modules and have focused on what comes in the box. But, in some cases, such as Azure, you have to add code and in other cases such as DSC you benefit greatly from third-party code. The book shows that there is a wealth of tools, add-ins, and tips/tricks that you can leverage (even if we do not use all that much of it). One thing to keep in mind, integrating various add-ons (and keeping them up to date and working well) can be a challenge.

10. All the code provided in this book has been tested; it worked and did what it says (at least during the writing stage). The production process is complex and it's possible that errors in code creep in during the production stages. Some of the more complex steps may have errors introduced during production. If any step fails for you, please contact PACKT and we'll help. Feel free to post issues to the Spiceworks PowerShell forum for quick resolution.

11. In writing this book, we set out to create content around a number of features of Windows Server 2016. As the book progressed, we quickly hit (and broke) several content limits. In order to publish the book, it was necessary to remove some content, which we did most reluctantly. Coverage of Storage and Containers had to be dropped. To paraphrase Jeffrey Snover, *To ship is to choose. I hope I chose well.*

12. In writing the recipes, we use full cmdlet names with no aliases and with all parameter names spelled out in full (so, this means no abbreviated parameter names or positional parameters). This makes the text a bit longer, but hopefully easier to read and understand.

13. Some recipes in this book rely on other recipes being completed. These related recipes worked well when we wrote them and hopefully will work for you as well. Each depending recipe is noted.

14. There is a fine line between PowerShell and a Windows feature. To use PowerShell to manage a Windows feature, you need to understand the feature itself. The chapters describe each feature although in the space limited, thus I can't provide complete details of every feature. I have provided links to help you get more information. And as ever, Bing and Google are your friends.

Sections

In this book, you find several headings that appear frequently (Getting ready, How to do it, How it works, There's more).

To give clear instructions on how to complete a recipe, we use these sections as follows:

Chapter and Recipe Headings

Every chapter and every recipe introduces some part of Windows which the recipes help you to manage. I've attempted to summarize the key points about each feature - but as ever there is more detail you can discover using your favorite search engine.

Getting ready

This section tells you what to expect in the recipe, and describes how to set up any software or any preliminary settings required for the recipe. It also indicates the hosts (VMs) you need for the recipe and any files, folders, or other resources you need to complete the recipe successfully.

How to do it...

This section contains the steps required to follow the recipe. We show the PowerShell code you use to perform each step

How it works...

This section contains a detailed explanation of what happened in the previous section along with screen shots to show you the results of the recipe.

There's more...

This section consists of additional information about the recipe in order to make the reader more knowledgeable about the recipe.

Conventions

In this book, you find a number of text styles that distinguish between different kinds of information. Here are some examples of these styles and an explanation of their meaning.

Code words in text, database table names, folder names, filenames, file extensions, pathnames, URLs, and so on are shown as follows:

"A great PowerShell cmdlet is Get-Help"

A block of code is set as follows:

```
If (-Not (Get-WindowsFeature -Name PowerShell))
  {
    'PowerShell Not installed'
  }
```

Any command-line input or output is written as follows (Note the back tick at the end of the second line):

```
#  Copy ISO image
 Copy-Item -Path c:\Image\Server2016.iSO `
           -TargetPath c:\VM\ISO\Server2016.ISO
```

New terms and **important words** are shown in bold. Words that you see on the screen, for example, in menus or dialog boxes, appear in the text like this: "Clicking the **Next** button moves you to the next screen."

Warnings or important notes appear in a box like this.

 Tips and tricks appear like this.

Reader feedback

Feedback from our readers is always welcome. Let us know what you think about this book-what you liked or disliked. Reader feedback is important for us as it helps us develop titles that you can really get the most out of.

To send us general feedback, simply e-mail feedback@packtpub.com, and mention the book's title in the subject of your message.

If there is a topic that you have expertise in and you are interested in either writing or contributing to a book, see our author guide at www.packtpub.com/authors.

Customer support

Now that you are the proud owner of a Packt book, we have a number of things to help you to get the most from your purchase.

Downloading the color images of this book

We also provide you with a PDF file that has color images of the screenshots/diagrams used in this book. The color images will help you better understand the changes in the output. You can download this file from https://www.packtpub.com/sites/default/files/downloads/WindowsServer2016AutomationwithPowerShellCookbookSecondEdition_ColorImages.pdf.

Errata

Although we have taken every care to ensure the accuracy of our content, mistakes do happen. If you find a mistake in this book-maybe a mistake in the text or the code-we would be grateful if you could report this to us. By doing so, you can save other readers from frustration and help us improve subsequent versions of this book. If you find any errata, please report them by visiting http://www.packtpub.com/submit-errata, selecting your book, clicking on the **Errata Submission Form** link, and entering the details of your errata. Once your errata are verified, your submission is accepted and the errata uploaded to our website or added to any list of existing errata under the Errata section of that title.

To view the previously submitted errata, go to https://www.packtpub.com/books/content/support and enter the name of the book in the search field. The required information appears under the **Errata** section.

If you find issues, feel free to reach out to the author via the Spiceworks forum.

Piracy

Piracy of copyrighted material on the Internet is an ongoing problem across all media. At Packt, we take the protection of our copyright and licenses very seriously. If you come across any illegal copies of our works in any form on the Internet, please provide us with the location address or website name immediately so that we can pursue a remedy.

Please contact us at copyright@packtpub.com with a link to the suspected pirated material.

We appreciate your help in protecting our authors and our ability to bring you valuable content.

Questions

If you have a problem with any aspect of this book, you can contact us at questions@packtpub.com, and we do our best to address the problem.

Help and assistance

If you want help on any of the recipes, or want to discover more information about any of the steps, come over to the PowerShell forum at Spiceworks. Navigate to: https://community.spiceworks.com/programming/powershell and ask away. Note you do need to register to be able to ask questions and participate.

1

What's New in PowerShell and Windows Server

This chapter covers the following recipes:

- Exploring Remote Server Administration Tools (RSAT)
- Discovering new cmdlets in PowerShell 4 and Windows Server 2012 R2
- Discovering new cmdlets in PowerShell 5/5.1 and Windows Server 2016
- Exploring PowerShellGet
- Exploring PackageManagement
- Creating an internal PowerShell repository

Introduction

Windows Server changes quickly, with a new release about every two years. Since the publication of the last edition of this book, Microsoft has delivered both Windows Server 2012 R2 and Windows Server 2016 (as well as client OS versions: Windows 8.1 and Windows 10).

PowerShell evolved alongside the server OS with a release of both PowerShell version 4, version 5, and version 5.1. This chapter reviews the changes in both the OS and PowerShell and highlights the biggest and most useful changes and new cmdlets.

This chapter also explores PowerShellGet and `PackageManagement` modules, perhaps the most interesting and useful new features released in PowerShell 5 and PowerShell 5.1.

Exploring Remote Server Administration Tools (RSAT)

Remote Server Administration Tools (**RSAT**) are tools available on both servers and client systems to manage server services. RSAT tools are available in Windows desktop and server versions. Most of the RSAT tools are not installed by default but are easily added.

RSAT includes GUI tools, like **Microsoft Management Console** (**MMC**) and MMC snap-ins (for example the DNS or DHCP MMC snap-ins) as well as command-line tools and additional PowerShell modules. You have the option of installing the Windows feature including the tools (most useful on a server), or just the tools to manage the feature (most useful on a workstation).

The recipe that follows is run from DC1, a Windows Server 2016 with Desktop Experience installation. If you try to use Server Core for this recipe, note that Out-GridView, for example in step 3, is not available in the Server Core version, as it lacks the graphical user interface. For Server Core installations, use Format-Table instead.)

How to do it...

1. You use the Get-Command, and Tee-Object cmdlets to retrieve both the collection of PowerShell commands and the number of cmdlets into PowerShellvariables before installing the **RSAT**:

```
$CountOfCommandsBeforeRSAT = Get-Command |
    Tee-Object -Variable 'CommandsBeforeRSAT' |
        Measure-Object
'{0} commands' -f $CountOfCommandsBeforeRSAT.count
```

2. Examine the objects returned by Get-Command:

```
$CommandsBeforeRSAT | Get-Member |
 Select-Object -ExpandProperty TypeName -Unique
```

3. View commands in Out-GridView:

```
$CommandsBeforeRSAT |
    Select-Object -Property Name, Source, CommandType |
        Sort-Object -Property Source, Name |
            Out-GridView
```

`Out-GridView` is not available in the *Server Core* version, as it lacks the graphical user interface. For Server Core installations, use Format-Table instead.

4. Store the collection of PowerShell modules and a count into variables as well:

```
$CountOfModulesBeforeRSAT = Get-Module -ListAvailable |
    Tee-Object -Variable 'ModulesBeforeRSAT' |
        Measure-Object
            '{0} commands' -f $CountOfModulesBeforeRSAT.count
```

5. View modules in `Out-GridView`:

```
$ModulesBeforeRSAT |
    Select-Object -Property Name -Unique |
        Sort-Object -Property Name |
            Out-GridView
```

6. Review the RSAT Windows Features available and their installation status:

```
Get-WindowsFeature -Name RSAT*
```

`Get-WindowsFeature` only works on Windows Server operating systems.

7. Install RSAT with sub features and management tools:

```
Install-WindowsFeature -Name RSAT -IncludeAllSubFeature `
                        -IncludeManagementTools
```

8. Now that RSAT features are installed, see what commands are available:

```
$CountOfCommandsAfterRSAT = Get-Command |
    Tee-Object -Variable 'CommandsAfterRSAT' |
        Measure-Object
 '{0} commands' -f $CountOfCommandsAfterRSAT.count
```

9. View commands in `Out-GridView`:

```
$CommandsAfterRSAT |
    Select-Object -Property Name, Source, CommandType |
        Sort-Object -Property Source, Name |
            Out-GridView
```

10. Now check how many modules are available:

```
$CountOfModulesAfterRSAT = Get-Module -ListAvailable |
    Tee-Object -Variable 'ModulesAfterRSAT' |
        Measure-Object
'{0} commands' -f $CountOfModulesAfterRSAT.count
```

11. View modules in `Out-GridView`:

```
$ModulesAfterRSAT | Select-Object -Property Name -Unique |
    Sort-Object -Property Name |
        Out-GridView
```

12. Store the list of commands into an XML file for later research:

```
$CommandsAfterRSAT |
    Export-Clixml `
        -Path $env:HOMEPATH\Documents\WS2016Commands.XML"
```

How it works...

In *step 1*, you use `Get-Command` to enumerate all the commands available in PowerShell. This includes functions and aliases. It is useful to store the result of such commands into a variable, `$CommandsBeforeRSAT` in this case, so you are able to investigate the commands without making the request again. Using `Tee-Object`, you store the array of commands in that variable while continuing to use the pipeline to `Measure-Object` to store the count of commands, then display the result using the PowerShell string formatting function: `'{0} commands' -f $CountOfCommandsBeforeRSAT`

In *step 2*, you pipe the `$CommandsBeforeRSAT` variable to `Get-Member` to examine the `TypeName` of the objects returned, as shown in the following screenshot:

```
PS C:\Windows\system32> $CommandsBeforeRSAT | Get-Member | Select-Object -ExpandProperty  TypeName -Unique
System.Management.Automation.AliasInfo
System.Management.Automation.FunctionInfo
System.Management.Automation.FilterInfo
System.Management.Automation.CmdletInfo
```

As you see, these commands are objects of the AliasInfo, FunctionInfo, and CmdletInfo types in the System.Management.Automation namespace (plus a FilterInfo type, which provides information about a filter that is stored in the session state.) PowerShell commands returned by Get-Command include aliases, functions, and cmdlets.

In *step 3*, you use Select-Object to show the useful properties, and pipe that to a Sort-Object, then pipe to Out-GridView to search and filter the PowerShell commands, as you see in the following screenshot:

In *step 4*, you use `Get-Module` just like `Get-Command`, but use the `-ListAvailable` parameter to see all the installed modules, not just those loaded into the current session. Again you use `Tee-Object` to store the array of modules into a variable, `$ModulesBeforeRSAT`, while passing the result down the pipeline to `Measure-Object` to calculate the count which you then display.

In *step 5*, you pipe the variable to a `Select-Object` for the interesting columns, `Sort-Object`, then pipe that to `Out-GridView` again to review the available modules as shown here:

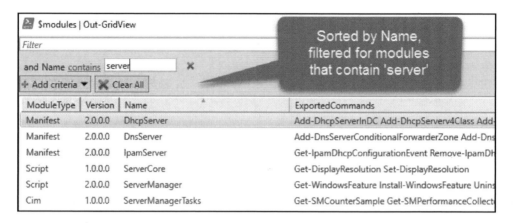

In *step 6*, you view the RSAT features available in your server with `Get-WindowsFeature -Name RSAT*`, as shown in the following screenshot:

```
PS C:\Windows\system32> Get-WindowsFeature -Name RSAT*

Display Name                                     Name                      Install State
------------                                     ----                      -------------
[X] Remote Server Administration Tools           RSAT                      Installed
    [X] Feature Administration Tools             RSAT-Feature-Tools        Installed
        [X] SMTP Server Tools                    RSAT-SMTP                 Installed
        [X] BitLocker Drive Encryption Administratio... RSAT-Feature-Tools-B...  Installed
            [X] BitLocker Drive Encryption Tools RSAT-Feature-Tools-B...  Installed
            [X] BitLocker Recovery Password Viewer RSAT-Feature-Tools-B... Installed
        [X] BITS Server Extensions Tools         RSAT-Bits-Server          Installed
        [X] DataCenterBridging LLDP Tools        RSAT-DataCenterBridg...  Installed
        [X] Failover Clustering Tools            RSAT-Clustering           Installed
            [X] Failover Cluster Management Tools RSAT-Clustering-Mgmt    Installed
            [X] Failover Cluster Module for Windows ... RSAT-Clustering-Powe... Installed
            [X] Failover Cluster Automation Server RSAT-Clustering-Auto... Installed
            [X] Failover Cluster Command Interface RSAT-Clustering-CmdI... Installed
        [X] Network Load Balancing Tools         RSAT-NLB                  Installed
        [X] Shielded VM Tools                    RSAT-Shielded-VM-Tools    Installed
        [X] SNMP Tools                           RSAT-SNMP                 Installed
        [X] Storage Replica Module for Windows Power... RSAT-Storage-Replica Installed
        [X] WINS Server Tools                    RSAT-WINS                 Installed
    [X] Role Administration Tools                RSAT-Role-Tools           Installed
        [X] AD DS and AD LDS Tools               RSAT-AD-Tools             Installed
            [X] Active Directory module for Windows ... RSAT-AD-PowerShell    Installed
            [X] AD DS Tools                      RSAT-ADDS                 Installed
                [X] Active Directory Administrative ... RSAT-AD-AdminCenter   Installed
                [X] AD DS Snap-Ins and Command-Line ... RSAT-ADDS-Tools      Installed
            [X] AD LDS Snap-Ins and Command-Line Tools RSAT-ADLDS           Installed
        [X] Hyper-V Management Tools             RSAT-Hyper-V-Tools        Installed
        [X] Remote Desktop Services Tools        RSAT-RDS-Tools            Installed
            [X] Remote Desktop Gateway Tools     RSAT-RDS-Gateway          Installed
            [X] Remote Desktop Licensing Diagnoser T... RSAT-RDS-Licensing-D... Installed
        [X] Active Directory Certificate Services Tools RSAT-ADCS          Installed
            [X] Certification Authority Management T... RSAT-ADCS-Mgmt       Installed
            [X] Online Responder Tools           RSAT-Online-Responder     Installed
        [X] Active Directory Rights Management Servi... RSAT-ADRMS          Installed
        [X] DHCP Server Tools                    RSAT-DHCP                 Installed
        [X] DNS Server Tools                     RSAT-DNS-Server           Installed
        [X] Fax Server Tools                     RSAT-Fax                  Installed
        [X] File Services Tools                  RSAT-File-Services        Installed
            [X] DFS Management Tools             RSAT-DFS-Mgmt-Con         Installed
            [X] File Server Resource Manager Tools RSAT-FSRM-Mgmt          Installed
            [X] Services for Network File System Man... RSAT-NFS-Admin      Installed
        [X] Network Controller Management Tools  RSAT-NetworkController    Installed
        [X] Network Policy and Access Services Tools RSAT-NPAS             Installed
        [X] Print and Document Services Tools    RSAT-Print-Services       Installed
        [X] Remote Access Management Tools       RSAT-RemoteAccess         Installed
            [X] Remote Access GUI and Command-Line T... RSAT-RemoteAccess-Mgmt Installed
            [X] Remote Access module for Windows Pow... RSAT-RemoteAccess-Po... Installed
        [X] Volume Activation Tools              RSAT-VA-Tools             Installed
```

Get-WindowsFeature presents an information dense tree view of the RSAT tools available. Note the many sub-features under Remote Server Admin Tools and under Role Administration Tools. Each feature may be installed individually by name, or all features installed with one command as in this example.

In *step 7*, install all the RSAT features with the `-IncludeAllSubFeature` and `-IncludeManagementTools` parameters. You may limit what is installed by changing the first parameter to a comma separated list of desired feature names.

In *steps 8-11*, once the RSAT features are installed, repeat the `Get-Command` and `Get-Modules` code to see all the additional cmdlets and modules.

In *step 12* you use `Export-CliXML` to store the array to an XML file. If you want to compare what is available in different OS and PowerShell versions, you use the array of objects saved to this file and compare it with an XML file generated under some other PowerShell or Windows versions.

There's more...

Jose Barreto, a Principal Program Manager, Applications and Services Group at Microsoft, reviewed the new Windows Server 2016 cmdlets (based on Windows Server 2016 CTP). This post shows you how to use `Export-CliXML` to see what has changed between PowerShell versions:

```
https://blogs.technet.microsoft.com/josebda/2015/05/26/new-powershell-cmdlets-
in-windows-server-2016-tp2-compared-to-windows-server-2012-r2/.
```

Discovering new cmdlets in PowerShell 4 and Windows Server 2012 R2

PowerShell V4 and Server 2012 R2 added many new features to existing cmdlets but did not add many new cmdlets. A notable exception is **Desired State Configuration** (**DSC**) feature that debuted in PowerShell V4.

DSC is a set of language extensions that enable you to define computer configurations in a declarative fashion then apply that configuration to managed computers. DSC is a tool to provision or manage servers and to ensure those systems stay configured correctly. DSC provides a solution to the problem of configuration drift—computer configurations that change, often incorrectly, over time.

Get more information on DSC in `Chapter 13`, *Using Desired State Configuration*.

New cmdlets

Two other useful cmdlets included in PowerShell V4 are:

- `Get-FileHash`: Creates a hash value from a given file or binary value. This is useful for quickly determining whether files have changed or for finding duplicate files (that have different file names)
- `Test-NetConnection`: Diagnoses a network connection and provides helpful troubleshooting information. This cmdlet is described in more detail in `Chapter 8`, *Managing Windows Network Services*.

How to do it...

1. You use the `Show-Command` to investigate the `Get-FileHash` cmdlet:

   ```
   Show-Command -Name Get-FileHash
   ```

`Show0-Command` is not available in the Server Core version, as it lacks the graphical user interface.

2. In the dialog that pops up, the **Path** tab corresponds to one of three parameter sets for this command. For the **Path** tab, enter `$Env:windirnotepad.exe` or any other valid file path.
3. Choose an algorithm like **SHA512** from the drop-down menu.
4. Click the **Copy** button then paste the command into your PowerShell ISE and press *Enter* to run it. Note the hash value that is returned.
5. Use `Show-Command` to investigate `Test-NetConnection`:

   ```
   Show-Command -Name Test-NetConnection
   ```

6. In the dialog box, the **CommonTCPPort** tab corresponds to the default parameter set, the first of four. Choose **HTTP** from the **CommonTCPPort** drop-down, and choose **Detailed** for **InformationLevel**. Then click **Copy**, and paste the script into your editor below the `Show-Command` line, then close the `Show-Command` window. Select this line and press *F8* to run this line.

7. Repeat your call to `Show-Command -Name Test-NetConnection`. Choose the **ICMP** tab and enter a valid internet hostname like `Windows.Com` in the **ComputerName** field, or leave it blank, and choose **Detailed** for **InformationLevel**.

8. Click the **Copy** button then paste the command into your PowerShell ISE below the previous command, then close the `Show-Command` window and select the line and press *F8* to run it.

9. Repeat your call to `Show-Command Name Test-NetConnection`. Choose the **NetRouteDiagnostics** tab, check the box for **DiagnoseRouting,** and click **Run**.

10. Repeat your call to `Show-Command -Name Test-NetConnection`. Choose the **RemotePort** tab, enter `443` for the **Port**, and choose **Detailed** for **InformationLevel**, and click **Run**.

How it works...

In *step 1*, you use `Show-Command` to provide a graphical interface to explore new commands like `Get-FileHash` or new ways to use commands you know. It is the same interface that displays in the **Commands** tab in PowerShell ISE, and the interface is programmatically generated from the parameter definitions in the cmdlet or function, so it works with commands you create or install from outside sources.

In *steps 2 and 3*, choosing the **Path** tab corresponds to a parameter set defined in the command; each parameter set may have different required and optional parameters, represented by check boxes, drop-down menus, or text fields. This parameter set requires the **Path** and **Algorithm** parameters.

In *step 4*, the **Copy** button puts a syntax-correct command on our clipboard, either to be run as is or added to a script and modified. This is a very useful feature for new PowerShell scripters or those working with unfamiliar commands. The result of the command displays in the console, but it could be stored into a variable for comparison with other hash values to look for duplicate or changed files:

In *steps 5 and 6*, you use `Show-Command` to explore the `Test-NetConnection` cmdlet. This is a flexible and useful troubleshooting command with four parameter sets to use. First, test the connection to a web host over HTTP port `80`. Note the `-InformationLevel Detailed` parameter provides additional troubleshooting information on the connectivity.

In *steps 7 and 8*, you use the ICMP parameter set with the `-InformationLevel Detailed` parameter to ping, using ICMP echo request, a web server. This is different to the earlier steps—here you are just determining whether the target server is responding to echo requests. Some web servers turn off returning of pings, so you may see a server that doesn't respond to a ping but does allow a port `80` HTTP connection.

In *step 9*, you use the `NetRouteDiagnostics` parameter set with the `-DiagnoseRouting` parameter, which was introduced in PowerShell 5.1, to get routing information. Here when you click the **Run** button, the result displays in the console window.

In *step 10*, you specify a `RemotePort` parameter set with a specified `Port` and `ComputerName` to test:

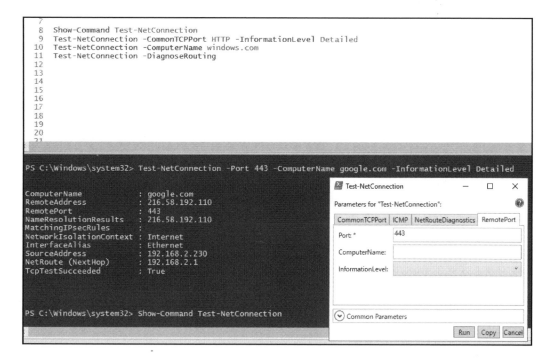

There's more...

Both Server 2012 R2 and PowerShell V4 introduced many new features and added enhancements to existing features. This included the Hyper-V, *SmbShare*, and *BranchCache* features, all of which were improved. These features came with PowerShell modules that enable you to leverage these features using PowerShell. Get more information on the modules that support the 2012 R2 features at `https://technet.microsoft.com/en-us/library/dn249523.aspx`.

Discovering new cmdlets in PowerShell 5/5.1 and Windows Server 2016

PowerShell V5, PowerShell V5.1, and Windows Server 2016 also added new features.

Getting ready

Run the commands in the following recipe on a Windows Server 2016 with *Desktop Experience* version.

PowerShellGet module

PowerShellGet, formerly known as **OneGet**, is a module that provides you with a simple way to discover, install, and update PowerShell modules and scripts. It has dependencies on the PackageManagement module, which relies on NuGet. It is an open source project, located at https://github.com/powershell/powershellget.

Refer to *Explore PowerShellGet* recipe.

PackageManagement module

The cmdlets in the PackageManagement module provide a single interface for software publication, discovery, installation, and inventory.

Refer to the following recipe:

- *Explore PackageManagement*
- *Create a PackageManagement repository*

Microsoft.PowerShell.Archive module

The Microsoft.Powershell.Archive module contains two useful functions: Compress-Archive and Expand-Archive. These enable you to create and extract ZIP files. With previous versions of PowerShell versions, you managed archives by using the System.IO.Compression namespace from the .Net framework, the Shell.Application com object or software like 7-Zip.

Microsoft.PowerShell.Utility module

The Microsoft.PowerShell.Utility module contains several new cmdlets useful for debugging interactively and within runspaces.

Debugging and runspace Cmdlets include: `Get-Runspace`, `Debug-Runspace`, `Get-RunspaceDebug`, `Enable-RunspaceDebug`, **and** `Disable-RunspaceDebug`, `Wait-Debugger`, `Debug-Job`.

These cmdlets enable debugging PowerShell scripts within runspaces and jobs and add additional debugging features for debugging production PowerShell interactively.

Other new modules

Other new modules in this version of PowerShell (and where to find more information about each module) include:

Module	Description	Documentation
`ConfigCI`	Manage the configurable code integrity policy for Windows	https://technet.microsoft.com/en-us/library/mt634481.aspx
`Defender`	Manage Windows defender	https://technet.microsoft.com/en-us/library/dn433280.aspx
`EventTracingManagement`	Manage event tracing for Windows providers and sessions	https://technet.microsoft.com/en-us/library/dn919247.aspx
`HgsClient`, `ShieldedVMDataFile`, and `ShieldedVMTemplate`	Manage the host guardian service, for shielded Hyper-V guest machines.	https://technet.microsoft.com/en-us/library/dn914505.aspx https://technet.microsoft.com/en-us/library/mt791280.aspx https://technet.microsoft.com/en-us/library/mt282520.aspx
`IISAdministration`	Manage IIS replaces WebAdministration cmdlets	https://technet.microsoft.com/en-us/library/mt270166.aspx
`NetworkController`	Manage the new network controller role in Server 2016	https://technet.microsoft.com/en-us/library/dn859239.aspx
`NetworkSwitchManager`	Manage supported network switches in Server 2016	https://technet.microsoft.com/en-us/library/mt171434.aspx
`Pester`	Manage unit tests for PowerShell modules and cmdlets	https://github.com/pester/Pester/wiki
`PnpDevice`	Cmdlets for managing plug and play devices	https://technet.microsoft.com/en-us/library/mt130251.aspx
`StorageQoS` and `StorageReplica`	Support new storage functionality in Server 2016.	https://technet.microsoft.com/en-us/library/mt608557.aspx https://technet.microsoft.com/en-us/library/mt744543.aspx

Other new cmdlets

Some other useful cmdlets included are:

- `Write-Information`: A replacement for the `Write-Host` cmdlet that is consistent with the other `Write-*` cmdlets in the `Microsoft.PowerShell.Utility` namespace. See https://blogs.technet.microsoft.com/heyscriptingguy/2015/07/04/weekend-scripter-welcome-to-the-powershell-information-stream/.

- `ConvertFrom-String` and `Convert-String`: The new string parsing functions that create structured data from strings, or parse out string data into structured data. See https://blogs.msdn.microsoft.com/powershell/2014/10/31/convertfrom-string-example-based-text-parsing/.

- `Format-Hex`: This cmdlet formats information into hexadecimal.

- `Get-Clipboard` and `Set-Clipboard`: A cmdlet to simplify working with the clipboard, replacing piping to `clip.exe`.

- `Clear-RecycleBin`: This cmdlet empties the **Recycle Bin**.

- `New-TemporaryFile`: Simplifies the creation of temporary files within PowerShell scripts.

- `New-Guid`: A wrapper for `[GUID]::NewGuid()` to simplify the creation of **Globally Unique Identifiers (GUIDs)**. A GUID is an identifier, unique in space and time, that you use in a variety of scenarios. *System Center Virtual Machine Manager*, for example, uses GUIDs in jobs created by the UI.

- `Enter-PSHostProcess` and `Exit-PSHostProcess`: These enable you to debug PowerShell processes outside the current host process.

- `Export-ODataEndpointProxy`: This cmdlet generates a wrapper module for working with an OData endpoint. See https://msdn.microsoft.com/en-us/powershell/reference/5.1/microsoft.powershell.odatautils/microsoft.powershell.odatautils.

Explore some of these cmdlets here and in later chapters as well.

How to do it...

1. Investigate `Write-Information` by looking at the `Write-*` commands, and help for the `about_Redirection` topic:

```
Get-Command -Verb Write -Module *Utility
Get-Help about_Redirection -ShowWindow
```

2. Use `Write-Information`:

```
Write-Information "Test"
```

3. This produces no output. To resolve, you should inspect and change the `$InformationPreference` variable:

```
Get-Variable "InformationPreference"
Set-Variable -Name "InformationPreference" -Value "Continue"
```

4. Use `Write-Information` again:

```
Write-Information "Test"
```

5. Next, set `$InformationPreference` back to default value:

```
$InformationPreference = "SilentlyContinue"
```

6. Review the information-related options in the *CommonParameters* of each command:

```
Show-Command Get-Item
```

7. Use `ConvertFrom-String` to get objects from strings; `NoteProperties` are created with default names:

```
"Here is a sentence!" | ConvertFrom-String
"Here is a sentence!" | ConvertFrom-String | Get-Member
```

8. Use `-PropertyNames` to control the names:

```
"Here is a sentence!" |
   ConvertFrom-String -PropertyNames First,Second,
                                  Third,Fourth
```

9. Use `-Delimiter` to get items from a list:

```
"Here,is,a,list!" |
   ConvertFrom-String -PropertyNames First,Second,
                                  Third,Fourth `
                    -Delimiter ','
```

10. You next test the template capabilities of `ConvertFrom-String`:

```
$TextToParse = @'
Animal, Bird
Shape like Square
Number is 42
Person named Bob
'@$Template1 = @'
{[string]Category*:Animal}, {[string]Example:Bird}
'@ConvertFrom-String -TemplateContent $Template1 `
                  -InputObject $TextToParse
```

11. `ConvertFrom-String` recognizes only one line from the text—the template needs more examples to *train* the function, so add a second example to the template and test:

```
$Template2 = @'
{[string]Category*:Animal}, {[string]Example:Bird}
{[string]Category*:Country} like {[string]Example:Italy}
'@
ConvertFrom-String -TemplateContent $Template2 `
                  -InputObject $TextToParse
```

12. Note three lines are recognized, even the last line that is unusual. Adding another example to our template trains the function enough to recognize all four lines:

```
$Template3 = @'
{[string]Category*:Animal}, {[string]Example:Bird}
{[string]Category*:Country} like {[string]Example:Italy}
{[string]Category*:Number} like {[int]Example:99}
'@
ConvertFrom-String -TemplateContent $Template3 `
                  -InputObject $TextToParse
```

13. Experiment with `Format-Hex` to output values in hexadecimal:

```
$TestValue =
@"
This is line 1
and line 2
"@
$TestValue | Format-Hex
```

14. Experiment with `Get-ClipBoard` and `Set-Clipboard` by selecting some text, then press *Ctrl+C* to copy to clipboard, then inspect the clipboard:

```
#Select this line and press Control-C to copy to clipboard
$Value = Get-Clipboard
$Value
```

15. Use `Set-Clipboard` to replace the clipboard value, then *Ctrl+V* to paste that new value:

```
$NewValue = "#Paste This!"
$NewValue | Set-Clipboard
#Press Control-V to paste!
```

How it works...

In *step 1*, you get the commands with the `Write` verb in the `Microsoft.PowerShell.Utility` module. `Write-Information` is an addition to this module that writes out to a new information stream, which the `about_Redirection` help topic describes in detail:

```
PS C:\Windows\system32> Get-Command -Verb Write -Module *Utility

CommandType     Name                    Version    Source
-----------     ----                    -------    ------
Cmdlet          Write-Debug             3.1.0.0    Microsoft.PowerShell.Utility
Cmdlet          Write-Error             3.1.0.0    Microsoft.PowerShell.Utility
Cmdlet          Write-Host              3.1.0.0    Microsoft.PowerShell.Utility
Cmdlet          Write-Information       3.1.0.0    Microsoft.PowerShell.Utility
Cmdlet          Write-Output            3.1.0.0    Microsoft.PowerShell.Utility
Cmdlet          Write-Progress          3.1.0.0    Microsoft.PowerShell.Utility
Cmdlet          Write-Verbose           3.1.0.0    Microsoft.PowerShell.Utility
Cmdlet          Write-Warning           3.1.0.0    Microsoft.PowerShell.Utility
```

In *steps 2-5*, note that messages from `Write-Information` are not displayed by default. The `$InformationPreference` variable controls this behaviour within your PowerShell session.

In *step 6*, you'll see the CommonParameters now include `InformationAction` and `InformationVariable`

More information is available in `Get-Help about_CommonParameters`:

In *step 7* you create a `PSCustomObject` using `ConvertFrom-String` with `NoteProperties` named `P1`, `P2`, `P3`, and `P4` that correspond to words separated by whitespace from the input text, with `string` or `char` data types:

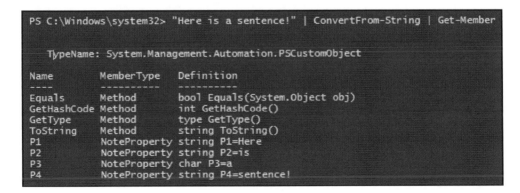

In *step 8*, you control the names of the `NoteProperties`. In *step 9* you change the delimiter from the default of whitespace to a comma, thus parsing a comma separated list:

```
PS C:\Windows\system32> "Here,is,a,list!" | ConvertFrom-String -PropertyNames First,Second,Third,Fourth -Delimiter ',' | Get-Member


   TypeName: System.Management.Automation.PSCustomObject

Name        MemberType   Definition
----        ----------   ----------
Equals      Method       bool Equals(System.Object obj)
GetHashCode Method       int GetHashCode()
GetType     Method       type GetType()
ToString    Method       string ToString()
First       NoteProperty string First=Here
Fourth      NoteProperty string Fourth=list!
Second      NoteProperty string Second=is
Third       NoteProperty char Third=a
```

In *step 10*, you investigate the `-TemplateObject` parameter to parse inconsistently formatted data. Here you provide one or more patterns by example in the `TemplateObject` and provide the template along with the text to parse. The template starts with one line as an example, and initially recognizes only one line out of four in the text to match:

```
PS C:\Windows\system32> $TextToParse = @'
Animal, Bird
Shape like Square
Number is 42
Person named Bob
'@

$Template1 = @'
{[string]Category*:Animal}, {[string]Example:Bird}
'@
ConvertFrom-String -TemplateContent $Template1 -InputObject $TextToParse

Category
--------
Animal
```

In *steps 11* and *steps 12*, you improve the template with each attempt, achieving complete matching results from the `Convert-FromString`:

```
PS C:\Windows\system32> $TextToParse = @'
Animal, Bird
Shape like Square
Number is 42
Person named Bob
'@

PS C:\Windows\system32> $Template3 = @'
{[string]Category*:Animal}, {[string]Example:Bird}
{[string]Category*:Country} like {[string]Example:Italy}
{[string]Category*:Number} like {[int]Example:99}
'@

PS C:\Windows\system32> ConvertFrom-String -TemplateContent $Template3 -InputObject $TextToParse

Category Example
-------- -------
Animal   Bird
Shape    Square
Number   42
Person   Bob
```

In *step 13*, you use `Format-Hex` on a `here` string that contains two lines of text. Note the `0D` `0A` bytes corresponding to carriage return and line feed (CRLF) between lines:

```
PS C:\Windows\system32> $TestValue =
@"
This is line 1
and line 2
"@

PS C:\Windows\system32> $TestValue
This is line 1
and line 2

PS C:\Windows\system32> $TestValue | Format-Hex

           00 01 02 03 04 05 06 07 08 09 0A 0B 0C 0D 0E 0F

00000000   54 68 69 73 20 69 73 20 6C 69 6E 65 20 31 0D 0A   This is line 1..
00000010   61 6E 64 20 6C 69 6E 65 20 32                     and line 2
```

In *step 14* and *step 15*, you work with `Set-Clipboard` and `Get-Clipboard`. By copying any text with *Ctrl+C*, you then capture that value into a variable with `Get-Clipboard`. You use `Set-Clipboard` to change that value, and use *Ctrl+V* to verify the change.

There's more...

Each PowerShell release comes with release notes that dive into the details of changes introduced with that version. These pages are updated with community contributions, as PowerShell is now partially open source:

- **WMF 5.0 Release Notes**:
  https://msdn.microsoft.com/en-us/powershell/wmf/5.0/releasenotes
- **WMF 5.1 Release Notes**:
  https://msdn.microsoft.com/en-us/powershell/wmf/5.1/release-notes

The documentation is published on GitHub and accepts contributions from users via pull-requests so users may help improve the documentation. You'll find PowerShell documentation on GitHub at https://github.com/PowerShell/PowerShell-Docs.

Complete documentation is available on TechNet, see the Windows 10 and Server 2016 PowerShell module reference at https://technet.microsoft.com/en-us/library/mt156917.aspx.

Exploring PowerShellGet

The PowerShellGet module enables you to work with repositories, sites which contain scripts and modules to download and use. If you have a Linux background, you are familiar with repositories and tools like apt-get (On Ubuntu Linux) and RPM (on Red Hat Linux). PowerShellGet delivers similar functionality within PowerShell.

Ensure you're running with administrator privileges so you can update PowerShellGet to the latest version.

How to do it...

1. You begin by reviewing the commands available in the PowerShellGet module:

```
Get-Command -Module PowerShellGet
```

2. Before moving on, you should update to the latest NuGet to get the PackageManagement module current, then update the PowerShellGet module per the GitHub instructions at https://github.com/powershell/powershellget. PowerShellGet has a dependency on PackageManagement, which in turn relies on NuGet. PowerShellGet and PackageMangagement both come within Windows 10 and Server 2016, but Windows updates are less frequent than releases at the PowerShell gallery. Updating ensures you have the latest versions of all the dependencies. To update NuGet:

```
Install-PackageProvider -Name NuGet -Force -Verbose
```

3. Close your PowerShell session by running Exit and open a new PowerShell session.

4. Check the version of the NuGet PackageProvider:

```
Get-PackageProvider -Name NuGet |
    Select-Object Version
```

5. Update PowerShellGet:

```
Install-Module -Name PowerShellGet -Force
```

6. Close your PowerShell session by running Exit and reopen it again.

7. Check the version of PowerShellGet:

```
Get-Module -Name PowerShellGet |
    Select-Object -ExpandProperty Version
```

8. View the default PSGallery repository for PowerShellGet:

```
Get-PSRepository
```

9. Review the various providers in the repository:

```
Find-PackageProvider |
  Select-Object -Property Name, Source, Summary |
  Format-Table -Wrap -AutoSize
```

10. View available providers with packages in PSGallery:

```
Find-PackageProvider -Source PSGallery |
    Select-Object -Property Name, Summary |
        Format-Table -Wrap -AutoSize
```

11. Use the Get-Command cmdlet to find cmdlets in PowerShellGet:

```
Get-Command -Module PowerShellGet -Verb Find
```

12. Request all the commands in the PowerShellGet module, store them in a variable, and store the count as well:

```
$CommandCount = Find-Command |
    Tee-Object -Variable 'Commands' |
        Measure-Object
"{0} commands available in PowerShellGet" `
                        -f $CommandCount.Count
```

13. Review the commands in Out-GridView and note the module names:

```
$Commands | Out-GridView
```

14. Request all the available PowerShellGet modules, store them in a variable and store the count as well:

```
$ModuleCount = Find-Module |
    Tee-Object -Variable 'Modules' |
        Measure-Object
"{0} Modules available in PowerShellGet" -f $ModuleCount.Count
```

15. Review the modules in Out-GridView:

```
$Modules | Out-GridView
```

16. Request all available DSC resources, store them in a variable, and view them in Out-GridView:

```
$DSCResourceCount = Find-DSCResource |
    Tee-Object -Variable 'DSCResources' |
        Measure-Object
"{0} DSCResources available in PowerShellGet" -f `
                        $DSCResourceCount.Count
$DSCResources | Out-GridView
```

17. Find the available scripts and store them in a variable. Then view them using `Out-GridView`:

```
$ScriptCount = Find-Script |
   Tee-Object -Variable 'Scripts' |
      Measure-Object
"{0} Scripts available in PowerShellGet" -f $ScriptCount.Count
 $Scripts | Out-GridView
```

18. When you discover a module you would like to simply install the module. This functionality is similar for `Scripts`, `DSCResources`, and so on:

```
Get-Command -Module PowerShellGet -Verb Install
```

19. Install the `TreeSize` module, as an example, or choose your own. As this is a public repository, Windows does not trust it by default, so you must approve the installation:

```
Install-Module -Name TreeSize -Verbose
```

20. If you choose to trust this repository, set the `InstallationPolicy` to `Trusted`, and you'll no longer need to confirm each installation: *Use at your own risk, you are responsible for all software you install on servers you manage*:

```
Set-PSRepository -Name PSGallery  -InstallationPolicy Trusted
```

21. Review and test the commands in the module:

```
Get-Command -Module TreeSize
Get-Help Get-TreeSize -Examples
Get-TreeSize -Path $env:TEMP -Depth 1
```

22. Remove the module just as easily:

```
Uninstall-Module -Name TreeSize -Verbose
```

23. If you would like to inspect the code before installation, download and review the module code:

```
New-Item -ItemType Directory `
         -Path $env:HOMEDRIVE\downloadedModules
Save-Module -Name TreeSize `
         -Path $env:HOMEDRIVE\downloadedModules" +
              "$env:windirexplorer.exe"
$env:HOMEDRIVE\downloadedModules
```

24. Import the downloaded module:

```
$ModuleFolder = "$env:HOMEDRIVE\downloadedModules\TreeSize"
Get-ChildItem -Path $ModuleFolder -Filter *.psm1 -Recurse |
    Select-Object -ExpandProperty FullName -First 1 |
        Import-Module -Verbose
```

25. When you are done with discovering the new module, you can remove it from your system:

```
Remove-Module -Name TreeSize
$ModuleFolder | Remove-Item -Recurse -Force
```

How it works...

In *step 1*, you start by reviewing the cmdlets in the `PowerShellGet` module:

```
PS C:\Windows\system32> Get-Command -Module PowerShellGet


CommandType     Name                        Version    Source
-----------     ----                        -------    ------
Function        Find-Command                1.1.2.0    PowerShellGet
Function        Find-DscResource            1.1.2.0    PowerShellGet
Function        Find-Module                 1.1.2.0    PowerShellGet
Function        Find-RoleCapability         1.1.2.0    PowerShellGet
Function        Find-Script                 1.1.2.0    PowerShellGet
Function        Get-InstalledModule         1.1.2.0    PowerShellGet
Function        Get-InstalledScript         1.1.2.0    PowerShellGet
Function        Get-PSRepository            1.1.2.0    PowerShellGet
Function        Install-Module              1.1.2.0    PowerShellGet
Function        Install-Script              1.1.2.0    PowerShellGet
Function        New-ScriptFileInfo          1.1.2.0    PowerShellGet
Function        Publish-Module              1.1.2.0    PowerShellGet
Function        Publish-Script              1.1.2.0    PowerShellGet
Function        Register-PSRepository       1.1.2.0    PowerShellGet
Function        Save-Module                 1.1.2.0    PowerShellGet
Function        Save-Script                 1.1.2.0    PowerShellGet
Function        Set-PSRepository            1.1.2.0    PowerShellGet
Function        Test-ScriptFileInfo         1.1.2.0    PowerShellGet
Function        Uninstall-Module            1.1.2.0    PowerShellGet
Function        Uninstall-Script            1.1.2.0    PowerShellGet
Function        Unregister-PSRepository     1.1.2.0    PowerShellGet
Function        Update-Module               1.1.2.0    PowerShellGet
Function        Update-ModuleManifest       1.1.2.0    PowerShellGet
Function        Update-Script               1.1.2.0    PowerShellGet
Function        Update-ScriptFileInfo       1.1.2.0    PowerShellGet
```

In *steps 2-7*, you ensure `PowerShellGet` and its dependency `PackageManagement` are up to date by updating the `NuGet` provider, verifying the version, then restarting your PowerShell session and updating `PowerShellGet` and verifying its version.

```
PS C:\Windows\system32> Install-PackageProvider Nuget -force -Verbose
VERBOSE: Using the provider 'Bootstrap' for searching packages.
VERBOSE: Finding the package 'Bootstrap::FindPackage' 'Nuget'.
VERBOSE: Performing the operation "Install Package" on target "Package 'nuget' version '2.8.5.208' from 'https://oneget.org/nuget-2.8.5.208.package.swidtag'.".
VERBOSE: Installing the package 'https://oneget.org/nuget-2.8.5.208.package.swidtag'.
VERBOSE: Installed the package 'nuget' to 'C:\Program Files\PackageManagement\ProviderAssemblies\nuget\2.8.5.208\Microsoft.PackageManagement.NuGetProvider.dll'.
VERBOSE: Skipping previously processed assembly: C:\Program Files\PackageManagement\ProviderAssemblies\nuget\2.8.5.208\Microsoft.PackageManagement.NuGetProvider
.dll.

Name                      Version         Source          Summary
----                      -------         ------          -------
nuget                     2.8.5.208       https://onege... NuGet provider for the OneGet meta-package manager
VERBOSE: Importing the package provider Nuget
VERBOSE: The provider 'NuGet' has already been imported. Trying to import it again.
VERBOSE: Loading an assembly 'C:\Program Files\PackageManagement\ProviderAssemblies\nuget\2.8.5.208\Microsoft.PackageManagement.NuGetProvider.dll'.
VERBOSE: Acquiring providers for assembly: C:\Program Files\PackageManagement\ProviderAssemblies\nuget\2.8.5.208\Microsoft.PackageManagement.NuGetProvider.dll
VERBOSE: Imported provider 'C:\Program Files\PackageManagement\ProviderAssemblies\nuget\2.8.5.208\Microsoft.PackageManagement.NuGetProvider.dll'.
```

The `-Verbose` flag gives you more details on the installation, but it is not required. Note that you must `Exit` your session after running this command and reopen to continue with the latest version.

Check our `NuGet` provider version after reopening our PowerShell session:

```
PS C:\Windows\system32> Get-PackageProvider -Name NuGet | Select-Object Version

Version
-------
2.8.5.208
```

In *step 6-7*, you update the `PowerShellGetmodule`:

```
PS C:\Windows\system32> Install-Module -Name PowerShellGet -Force
WARNING: The version '1.1.1.0' of module 'PackageManagement' is currently in use. Retry the operation after closing the applications.
PS C:\Windows\system32>
```

Note that you must exit your session after running this command and reopen to continue with the latest version.

In *step 8*, check your `PowerShellGet` version after reopening your PowerShell session:

```
PS C:\Windows\system32> Get-Module -Name PowerShellGet | Select-Object Version

Version
-------
1.1.2.0


PS C:\Windows\system32>
```

In *step 9*, you use `Get-PSRepository`. `PowerShellGet` starts with a single repository `PSGallery` installed by default:

```
PS C:\Windows\system32> Get-PSRepository

Name            InstallationPolicy   SourceLocation
----            ------------------   --------------
PSGallery       Trusted              https://www.powershellgallery.com/api/v2/
```

In *step 10*, review the package providers available:

```
Find-PackageProvider | Select Name, Source, Summary | Format-Table -Wrap -AutoSize

Name            InstallationPolicy   SourceLocation
----            ------------------   --------------
PSGallery       Trusted              https://www.powershellgallery.com/api/v2/


Name                   Source                                                       Summary
----                   ------                                                       -------
nuget                  https://oneget.org/nuget-2.8.5.208.package.swidtag           NuGet provider for the OneGet meta-package manager
ps1                    https://oneget.org/ps1-1.0.0.210.package.swidtag             ps1 provider for the OneGet meta-package manager
chocolatey             https://oneget.org/ChocolateyPrototype-2.8.5.130.package.swidtag  ChocolateyPrototype provider for the OneGet meta-package manager
PowerShellGet          PSGallery                                                    PowerShell module with commands for discovering, installing, updating and
                                                                                    publishing the PowerShell artifacts like Modules, DSC Resources, Role
                                                                                    Capabilities and Scripts.
GistProvider           PSGallery                                                    Gist-as-a-Package - PackageManagement  PowerShell Provider to interop with
                                                                                    Github Gists
GitHubProvider         PSGallery                                                    GitHub-as-a-Package - PackageManagement PowerShell Provider to interop
                                                                                    with Github
TSDProvider            PSGallery                                                    PowerShell PackageManager provider to search & install TypeScript
                                                                                    definition files from the community DefinitelyTyped repo
ChocolateyGet          PSGallery                                                    An PowerShell OneGet provider that discovers packages from
                                                                                    https://www.chocolatey.org.
MyAlbum                PSGallery                                                    MyAlbum provider discovers the photos in your remote file repository and
                                                                                    installs them to your local folder.
ContainerImage         PSGallery                                                    This is a PackageManagement provider module which helps in discovering,
                                                                                    downloading and installing Windows Container OS images.

                                                                                    For more details and examples refer to our project site at
                                                                                    https://github.com/PowerShell/ContainerProvider.
Docker.MsftProvider    PSGallery                                                    PowerShell module with commands for discovering, installing, and updating
                                                                                    Docker images.
NanoServerPackage      PSGallery                                                    A PackageManagement provider to  Discover, Save and Install Nano Server
                                                                                    Packages on-demand
OfficeProvider         PSGallery                                                    OfficeProvider allows users to install Microsoft Office365 ProPlus from
                                                                                    Powershell.
GitLabProvider         PSGallery                                                    GitLab PackageManagement provider
WSAProvider            PSGallery                                                    Provider to Discover, Install and inventory windows server apps
0install               PSGallery                                                    Zero Install is a decentralized cross-platform software-installation
                                                                                    system.
```

Note the source column; the first three providers listed correspond to `NuGet`, `OneGet`, and `Chocolatey` providers. `NuGet` is a repository devoted to developer libraries. `OneGet` was the name of this module (and repository) but has been deprecated and replaced by `PackageManagement`. You explore `Chocolatey` in a later recipe. The remaining rows are the available providers in the `PSGallery` repository.

In *step 11*, you limit your repository search with Find-PSRepository by specifying the -Source PSGallery parameter:

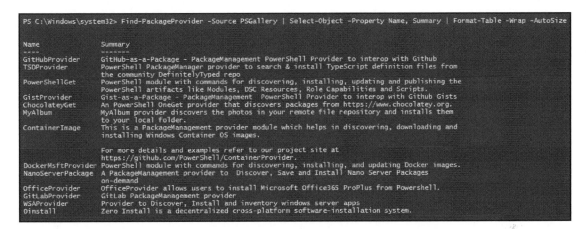

In *step 12*, you discover the PowerShellGet commands containing the verb Find:

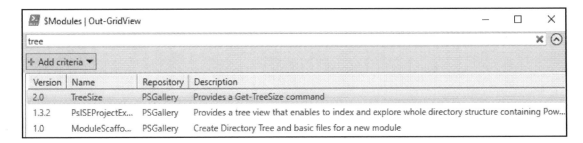

In *steps 13 - 18*, you use the Find-* commands to store the available commands, modules, DSC resources, and scripts into variables, then explore what is available using Out-GridView (including using the built-in filter capability to search for a module), for example:

Version	Name	Repository	Description
2.0	TreeSize	PSGallery	Provides a Get-TreeSize command
1.3.2	PsISEProjectEx...	PSGallery	Provides a tree view that enables to index and explore whole directory structure containing Pow...
1.0	ModuleScaffo...	PSGallery	Create Directory Tree and basic files for a new module

In *step 19*, you review the install commands in the `PowerShellGet` module. Their functions are very similar:

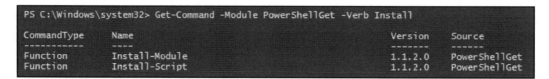

In *step 20*, the `TreeSize` module looks like an interesting tool to inspect folders and their sizes. Install it by using the `Install-Module` cmdlet. You use the `-Verbose` switch to get more information about what the cmdlet is doing:

After confirming the **Untrusted repository** pop up dialog, PowerShell installs the module.

In *step 21*, you see that the code available on `PSGallery`, as well as other public repositories, is just that, public. You must choose to trust the code you download from the internet to take advantage of the functionality provided by that code. To trust this repository and disable prompting, use the command (**at your own risk and responsibility**):

```
Set-PSRepository -Name PSGallery -InstallationPolicy Trusted
```

In *step 22*, you evaluate and test the module:

```
PS C:\Windows\system32> Get-Help Get-TreeSize -Examples

NAME
    Get-TreeSize

SYNOPSIS
    Recursively lists provider items and sums their lengths


    --------------------- EXAMPLE 1 ---------------------

    PS C:\>Get-Treesize

    Localization\ 12021
    |-- En-US\     2025
    |-- En\        1339




    --------------------- EXAMPLE 2 ---------------------

    PS C:\>Get-Treesize -ShowFiles

    Localization\             12021
    |-- Localization.psd1      6698
    |-- En-US\                 2025
       |-- UserSettings.psd1 1000
       |-- Localization.psd1 958
       |-- numbers.psd1        67
    |-- UserSettings.psd1     1959
    |-- En\                   1339
       |-- UserSettings.psd1 1253
       |-- numbers.psd1        86




    --------------------- EXAMPLE 3 ---------------------

    PS C:\>Get-Treesize | Format-Custom
```

In *step 23*, uninstalling a module is simple:

```
PS C:\Windows\system32> Uninstall-Module dbatools -Verbose
VERBOSE: Performing the operation "Uninstall-Module" on target "Version '0.8.692' of module 'dbatools'".
VERBOSE: Successfully uninstalled the module 'dbatools' from module base 'C:\Program Files\WindowsPowerShell\Modules\dbatools\0.8.692'.

PS C:\Windows\system32>
```

In *step 24*, if you prefer, download code and inspect it before installing, using `Save-Module`, then browse the module's files in *Windows Explorer*:

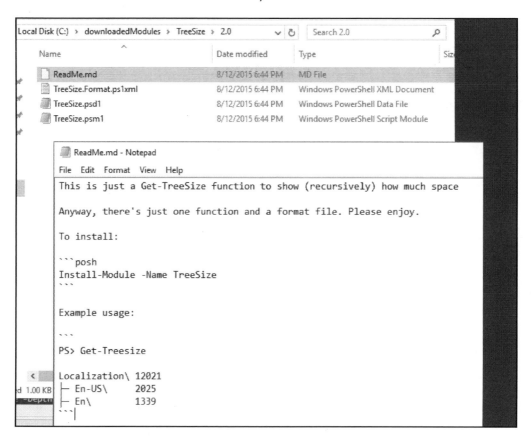

In *step 25*, after reviewing the code, import the module by locating the `.psm1` file which defines the module, using `Get-ChildItem`, then piping that filename to `Import-Module`:

```
PS C:\Windows\system32> $ModuleFolder = "$env:HOMEDRIVE\downloadedModules\TreeSize"
Get-ChildItem -Path $ModuleFolder -Filter *.psm1 -Recurse |
Select -ExpandProperty FullName -First 1 |
Import-Module -Verbose
VERBOSE: Loading module from path 'C:\downloadedModules\TreeSize\2.0\TreeSize.psm1'.
VERBOSE: Exporting function 'Get-TreeSize'.
VERBOSE: Exporting alias 'TreeSize'.
VERBOSE: Importing function 'Get-TreeSize'.
VERBOSE: Importing alias 'TreeSize'.
```

In *step 26*, you uninstall the module from your session and delete the module's folder. You may, of course, wish to keep the module!

There's more...

There are a wealth of other resources in the `PSGallery`—you use the `Find-*` cmdlets to explore the online resources you can download and use:

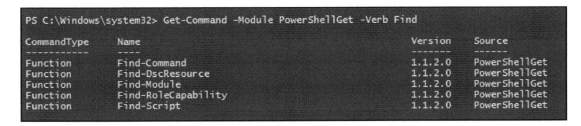

```
PS C:\Windows\system32> Get-Command -Module PowerShellGet -Verb Find

CommandType     Name                                 Version    Source
-----------     ----                                 -------    ------
Function        Find-Command                         1.1.2.0    PowerShellGet
Function        Find-DscResource                     1.1.2.0    PowerShellGet
Function        Find-Module                          1.1.2.0    PowerShellGet
Function        Find-RoleCapability                  1.1.2.0    PowerShellGet
Function        Find-Script                          1.1.2.0    PowerShellGet
```

The `PowerShellGet` module enables search for commands, DSC resources, modules, role capabilities, a feature of **Just Enough Administration (JEA)**, and scripts. You can download and use these various tools, or leverage them to build your own custom scripts.

Exploring PackageManagement

`PowerShellGet` is a powerful resource for PowerShell, built on top of the core `PackageManagement` capabilities of PowerShell 5. It is one of many `PackageManagment` providers available, as shown here:

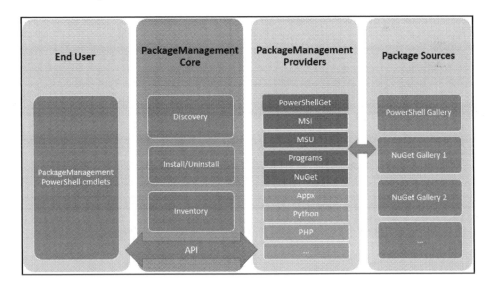

Image Source: https://blogs.technet.microsoft.com/packagemanagement/2015/04/28/introducing-packagemanagement-in-windows-10/

PackageManagement is a unified interface for software package management systems, a tool to manage package managers. You use the PackageManagement cmdlets to perform **software discovery, installation, and inventory (SDII)** tasks. PackageManagement involves working with package providers, package sources, and the software packages themselves.

Within the PackageManagement architecture, PackageManagement providers represent the various software installers that provide a means to distribute software via a standard plug-in model using the PackageManagement APIs. Each PackageManagement provider manages one or more package sources or software repositories. Providers may be publicly available or can be created within an organization to enable developers and system administrators to publish or install propriety or curated software packages.

PackageManagement Core is effectively an API. The core includes a set of PowerShell cmdlets that enable you to discover available software packages, as well as to install, uninstall, update, and inventory packages using PackageManagement.

Each PackageManagement provider is a different installer technology or package manager that plugs-in via the PackageManagement API. PowerShellGet, NuGet, and Chocolatey are examples of PackageManagement providers.

Each provider is made up of one or more sources, which may be public or private. For example, NuGet has a public source, but your organization may add private sources for the NuGet provider, enabling curation of approved software to make it available to corporate developers.

How to do it...

You use the cmdlets within the PackageManagement module to explore the capabilities it provides.

1. Review the cmdlets in the PackageManagement module:

   ```
   Get-Command -Module PackageManagement
   ```

2. Review the installed providers with Get-PackageProvider:

   ```
   Get-PackageProvider | Select-Object -Property Name, Version
   ```

3. The provider list includes msi, msu, and Programs package providers. These providers expose applications and updates installed on your computer which you can explore:

```
Get-Package -ProviderName msi |
    Select-Object -ExpandProperty Name
Get-Package -ProviderName msu |
    Select-Object -ExpandProperty Name
Get-Package -ProviderName Programs |
    Select-Object -ExpandProperty Name
```

4. The NuGet source contains developer library packages. This functionality is outside the scope of this book, but worth exploring if you do Windows or web development:

```
Get-PackageProvider -Name NuGet
```

5. There are also other package providers you can explore:

```
Find-PackageProvider |
    Select-Object -Property Name,Summary |
        Format-Table -Wrap -AutoSize
```

6. Notice Chocolatey, which is a very useful tool for Windows administrators and power users. Those with some Linux background may think of Chocolatey as apt-get for Windows. You cannot use this provider until you install it and confirm the installation:

```
Install-PackageProvider -Name Chocolatey -Verbose
```

7. Verify Chocolatey is now in the list of installed providers:

```
Get-PackageProvider | Select-Object Name,Version
```

8. Look for available software packages from the Chocolatey package provider. Store these in a variable so you don't request the collection more than once, and explore it:

```
$AvailableChocolateyPackages = `
    Find-Package -ProviderName Chocolatey
# How many software packages are available at Chocolatey?
$AvailableChocolateyPackages | Measure-Object
```

9. Pipe to `Out-GridView` to search for interesting software packages from Chocolatey:

```
$AvailableChocolateyPackages |
   Sort-Object Name,Version |
      Select-Object Name, Version, Summary |
         Out-GridView
```

10. Install one or more packages. `sysinternals` is a good example to use. Use `-Verbose` to get details on the installation:

```
Install-Package -ProviderName Chocolatey `
                 -Name sysinternals `
                 -Verbose
```

11. Review installed Chocolatey packages, stored to `C:\chocolatey\` by default, this path is stored in the `$env:ChocolateyPath` environment variable. Then review the executable files included with the `sysinternals` package:

```
Get-ChildItem -Path $env:ChocolateyPath\lib |
   Select-Object -Property Name
Get-ChildItem -Path `
   $env:ChocolateyPath\lib\sysinternals.2016.11.18\tools `
              -Filter *.exe |
   Select-Object -Property Name
```

12. Run any installed command included with `sysinternals`:

```
$PSInfoCommand = `
'C:\Chocolatey\lib\sysinternals.2016.11.18\tools\PsInfo.exe'
Invoke-Expression -Command $PSInfoCommand
```

13. Installed packages are enumerated with `Get-Package` and updated using the same command to install them, `Install-Package`:

```
Get-Package -ProviderName Chocolatey |
   Install-Package -Verbose
```

How it works...

In *step 1*, you review the cmdlets available in the `PackageManagement` module:

```
PS C:\foo> Get-Command -Module PackageManagement

CommandType     Name                          Version    Source
-----------     ----                          -------    ------
Cmdlet          Find-Package                  1.1.1.0    PackageManagement
Cmdlet          Find-PackageProvider          1.1.1.0    PackageManagement
Cmdlet          Get-Package                   1.1.1.0    PackageManagement
Cmdlet          Get-PackageProvider           1.1.1.0    PackageManagement
Cmdlet          Get-PackageSource             1.1.1.0    PackageManagement
Cmdlet          Import-PackageProvider        1.1.1.0    PackageManagement
Cmdlet          Install-Package               1.1.1.0    PackageManagement
Cmdlet          Install-PackageProvider       1.1.1.0    PackageManagement
Cmdlet          Register-PackageSource        1.1.1.0    PackageManagement
Cmdlet          Save-Package                  1.1.1.0    PackageManagement
Cmdlet          Set-PackageSource             1.1.1.0    PackageManagement
Cmdlet          Uninstall-Package             1.1.1.0    PackageManagement
Cmdlet          Unregister-PackageSource      1.1.1.0    PackageManagement
```

In *step 2*, you use the `Get-PackageProvider` cmdlets to display the currently installed package providers:

```
PS C:\foo> Get-PackageProvider | Select-Object -Property Name, Version

Name          Version
----          -------
Chocolatey    2.8.5.130
msi           3.0.0.0
msu           3.0.0.0
NuGet         2.8.5.208
PowerShellGet 1.1.2.0
Programs      3.0.0.0
```

In *step 3*, you use `Get-Package` with the `-ProviderName` parameter to review packages installed via the `msi`, `msu`, and `Programs` package providers:

```
PS C:\foo> Get-Package -ProviderName msu | Select Name

Name
----
Definition Update for Windows Defender - KB2267602 (Definition 1.233.3763.0)
Definition Update for Windows Defender - KB2267602 (Definition 1.233.3794.0)
Definition Update for Windows Defender - KB2267602 (Definition 1.233.3735.0)

Definition Update for Windows Defender - KB2267602 (Definition 1.233.
Definition Update for Windows Defender - KB2267602 (Definition 1.233.1099.0)
Definition Update for Windows Defender - KB2267602 (Definition 1.233.897.0)
```

In *step 4*, review the `NuGet` provider:

```
PS C:\foo> Get-PackageProvider -Name NuGet | Select-Object -Property Name, Version

Name   Version
----   -------
NuGet  2.8.5.208
```

In *step 5*, search for other package providers:

In *step 6*, you use `Install-PackageProvider` to install the `Chocolatey` provider. Since it is untrusted as a public source, you must approve the installation (**at your own risk and responsibility**):

In this example, you run `Install-PackageProvider` from within the ISE. By default, this pops up a confirmation dialog. If you run this cmdlet from the PowerShell console, you see a prompt there. You can suppress these confirmation requests by including the parameter – `Confirm:$False`.

In *step 7*, you verify `Chocolatey` is now installed as a package provider:

```
PS C:\foo> Get-PackageProvider | Select-Object -Property Name,Version

Name            Version
----            -------
Chocolatey      2.8.5.130
msi             3.0.0.0
msu             3.0.0.0
NuGet           2.8.5.208
PowerShellGet   1.1.2.0
Programs        3.0.0.0
```

In *step 8*, retrieve a list of available software packages from the
`ChocolateyPackageProvider`, store as a variable, and count the available packages:

```
PS C:\foo> $AvailableChocolateyPackages = Find-Package -ProviderName Chocolatey
#How many software packages are available?
$AvailableChocolateyPackages | Measure-Object


Count    : 4504
Average  :
Sum      :
Maximum  :
Minimum  :
Property :
```

In *step 9*, pipe the variable to `Out-GridView` and use the filter feature to explore what is available. This example is filtering for the `Sysinternals` package:

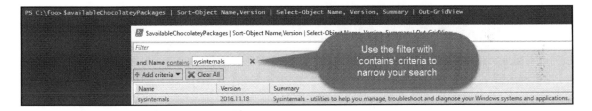

In *step 10*, you install this package (or any package you choose):

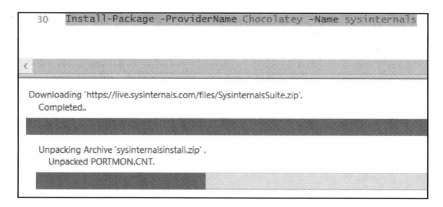

In *step 11*, you review the installed Chocolatey packages, and the files contained within the sysinternals package folder:

```
PS C:\foo> Get-ChildItem -Path $env:ChocolateyPath\lib\sysinternals.2016.11.18\tools -Filter *.exe | Select-Object -Property Name

Name
----
accesschk.exe
accesschk64.exe
```

In *step 12*, run any Sysinternals command, for example, PsInfo.Exe:

```
PS C:\foo> $PSInfoCommand = "C:\Chocolatey\lib\sysinternals.2016.11.18\tools\PsInfo.exe"
Invoke-Expression -Command $PSInfoCommand

PsInfo v1.78 - Local and remote system information viewer
Copyright (C) 2001-2016 Mark Russinovich
Sysinternals - www.sysinternals.com

Querying information for SVR2016...

System information for \\SVR2016:
Uptime:                     0 days 6 hours 20 minutes 12 seconds
Kernel version:             Windows Server 2016 Datacenter, Multiprocessor Free
Product type:               Standard Edition
Product version:            6.3
Service pack:               0
Kernel build number:        14393
Registered organization:
Registered owner:           Windows User
IE version:                 9.0000
System root:                C:\Windows
Processors:                 1
Processor speed:            2.4 GHz
Processor type:             Intel(R) Core(TM) i7-4710HQ CPU @
Physical memory:            4 MB
Video driver:               Microsoft Hyper-V Video
```

In *step 13*, you enumerate the installed packages with `Get-Package`. As time goes by, packages can be updated with bug fixes, new features, and so on. You can update all the installed packages if any updates exist, as follows:

```
PS C:\foo> Get-Package -ProviderName Chocolatey | Install-Package -Verbose
VERBOSE: Skipping installed package sysinternals 2016.11.18.
```

There's more...

Details of `NuGet` package and its functionality are outside the scope of this book, but worth exploring if you do Windows or web development. More information on `NuGet` packages is available from `https://www.nuget.org/Packages`.

`Chocolatey` has both a command-line interface and a `PowerShell` module. The command line interface offers functionality comparable to the `PackageManagement` module, targeted toward end users and system administrators. `Chocolatey` is supported on any Windows PC running Windows 7 or later. You can get more information on installing and using `Chocolatey` via the command line from `https://chocolatey.org/install`.

`Sysinternals` is a must-have toolkit for Windows administrators. You can find additional training on the `Sysinternals` tools on the Channel 9 website at `https://channel9.msdn.com/Series/sysinternals`.

Creating an internal PowerShell repository

It is useful to create your own PowerShell repository for personal or corporate use. The tools to enable you to build your own repository are not included in PowerShell. There are three main approaches available that enable you to build a repository:

- Using Visual Studio's `NuGet` package manager to download and install the `Nuget.Server` package into a new web project, and deploy to your own IIS Server. This option is free. However, you need to use Visual Studio 2015 (Either the full version or the free community edition) to create your own web project, download the `Nuget` server software, and deploy it into your environment. More information is available at `https://www.nuget.org/packages/NuGet.Server`.

- Using a third-party NuGet host's SAAS platform. This is the simplest solution, but software licensing fees may apply, and some organizations might have reservations about keeping the code on external servers. Choices for this approach include Visual Studio Team Services, http://myget.org/, and ProGet.

- Installing a 3rd-party NuGet software repository on your server. This simplifies the setup process for hosting your own software repository, but software licensing fees may apply.

> More information is available on hosting from the NuGet site at https://docs.nuget.org/ndocs/hosting-packages/overview.

The simplest approach to setting up your own software repository is to install and configure the free or trial version of ProGet. Do so via a GUI installation—the steps are described at https://inedo.com/support/documentation/proget/installation/installation-guide.

You have the choice of using an existing SQL Server instance or installing SQL Express as part of the installation. SQL is used to hold the repository's data. You may also choose to install your repository to an existing IIS Server or install ProGet with its own internal web server.

Inedo also provides a PowerShell script to perform the installation, which you may customize. For the script based installation, you need to register for a free license key at https://my.inedo.com.

> You can find more information on using ProGet from the Inedo web site at https://inedo.com/support/kb/1088/using-powershell-to-install-and-configure-proget.

How to do it...

1. Once you have installed ProGet using either the GUI or PowerShell script approach, log in to the ProGet application home page using the default admin account until you create a username and password:

2. From **Feeds** page, click **Create New Feed**:

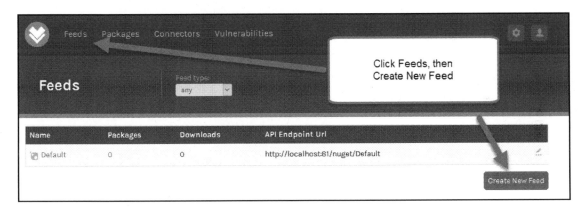

3. A list of supported feed types is displayed. Choose **PowerShell**:

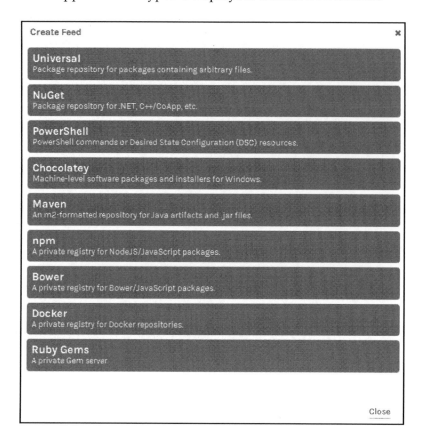

4. Enter a feed name of your choice: (for example, `MyPowerShellPackages`) and click the **Create New PowerShell Feed** button:

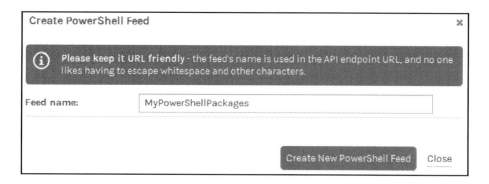

5. Review the properties of your new feed:

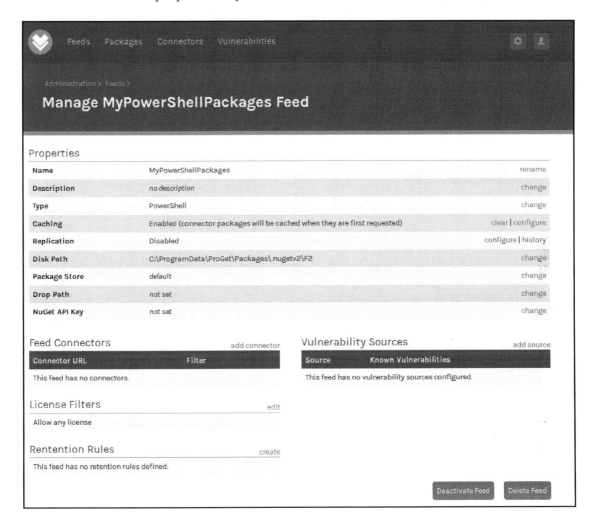

6. Open the PowerShell ISE or console, and register your new repository:

```
$RepositoryURL = `
  "http://localhost:81/nuget/MyPowerShellPackages/"
Register-PSRepository -Name MyPowerShellPackages `
    -SourceLocation $RepositoryURL`
    -PublishLocation $RepositoryURL `
    -InstallationPolicy Trusted
```

7. Publish a module you already have installed (`Pester`, for example):

```
Publish-Module -Name Pester -Repository MyPowerShellPackages `
               -NuGetApiKey "Admin:Admin"
```

8. Download a module from `PSGallery`, save it to the `C:\Foo folder`, and publish to your new repository (for example, `Carbon`):

```
Find-Module -Name Carbon -Repository PSGallery
New-Item -ItemType Directory -Path 'C:\Foo'
Save-Module -Name Carbon -Path C:\foo
Publish-Module -Path C:\Foo\Carbon `
               -Repository MyPowerShellPackages `
               -NuGetApiKey "Admin:Admin"
```

9. Find all the modules available in your newly created and updated repository:

```
Find-Module -Repository MyPowerShellPackages
```

How it works...

There are various options for setting up a NuGet-based repository for `PowerShell`. `ProGet` is a universal package manager from Inedo (See `https://inedo.com/proget` for more information on ProGet). ProGet is a very simple choice as it is easy to get started and offers the ability to scale to enterprize level. ProGet has both a free and a paid subscription version available. The ProGet installer creates a NuGet web server backed by a SQL Express database.

In *step 1*, you visit the server web administration page and optionally review the functionality available.

In *steps 2-5*, you use ProGet to create a new repository for your PowerShell modules. As you see, you use the ProGet GUI to create this new repository.

In *step 6*, you register your new repository in your PowerShell session. You need to know the repository URL and have a NuGet API key, using the default username/password of Admin /Admin.

In *step 7*, you publish a module to the repository—you are using a module that is installed in your PowerShell session, `Pester`.

In *step 8*, you locate and download an additional module from the PSGallery, and publish this module to your local repository.

In *step 9*, you see the modules available from your local repository:

There's more...

ProGet is a rich product. It provides both automatic failover and scalability which are needed features for PowerShell repositories in large organization's repository. ProGet is one option you have for creating your own organization specific repository. To learn more about ProGet, visit http://inedo.com/support/documentation/proget.

NuGet is a free, open source package management system provided by the Microsoft ASP.NET development platform and is provided as a Visual Studio extension. To learn more about NuGet, visit https://docs.nuget.org/ndocs/api/nuget-api-v3.

2
Implementing Nano Server

This chapter contains the following recipes:

- Deploying a Nano Server in a VM
- Connecting to and managing a Nano Server
- Installing features with Nano Server packages

Introduction

Nano Server is a new installation mode of Windows Server 2016. It is a minimal implementation of Windows Server with no desktop, and no default features or services. Nano Server has a minimal disk, memory, and CPU footprint to reduce attack surface and patching requirements.

Deploying a Nano Server in a VM

Deploying a Nano Server is a simple and customizable process. This recipe focuses on the most straightforward implementation which is deploying a Nano Server in a virtual machine. With Nano Server you have several customization options:

- **Network address**: By default, Nano Server uses DHCP to acquire an IP address. You can configure the IP address, subnet, gateway, and DNS both before or after deployment.
- **Domain membership**: By default, Nano Server is not domain joined. You can configure domain membership both before or after deployment.

As this book was going to press, Microsoft has announced that, going forward, Nano Server is only available as a container base OS image. Refer to: `https://docs.microsoft.com/en-us/windows-server/get-started/nano-in-semi-annual-channel` for more information.

Getting ready

You need Windows Server 2016 installation ISO file and a Windows Server 2016 system running Hyper-V (`HV1`). This recipe assumes the path to the ISO file is `D:\iso\WinServer2016.iso`.

This recipe assumes you have Hyper-V setup and have at least one switch defined.

You also need a folder for storing the base image files (`C:\NanoBase` in this recipe) and a folder for storing the virtual machine file and VHDX files (`C:\VMs` in this recipe).

How to do it...

1. On the VM host, mount Server 2016 installation ISO:

```
$Server2016ISOPath = 'D:\iso\WinServer2016.iso'
$MountResult = Mount-DiskImage -ImagePath $Server2016ISOPath `
                              -PassThru
$MountResult | Select-Object -Property *
```

2. Determine the drive letter(s) of mounted ISO(s), including the colon (:):

```
$Server2016InstallationRoot = ($MountResult |
    Get-Volume |
        Select-object -ExpandProperty Driveletter) + ':'
$Server2016InstallationRoot
```

3. Get the path of the `NanoServerImageGenerator` module within the server installation disk:

```
$NanoServerFolder = `
    Join-Path -Path $Server2016InstallationRoot `
            -ChildPath 'NanoServer'
$NsigFolder = Join-Path -Path $NanoServerFolder `
                      -ChildPath 'NanoServerImageGenerator'
```

4. Review the contents of the `NanoServerImageGenerator` module folder:

```
$NsigFolder
Get-ChildItem -Path $NsigFolder -Recurse
```

5. Import the `NanoServerImageGenerator` module and review the commands it contains:

```
Import-Module -Name $NanoServerImageGeneratorModuleFolder
Get-Command -Module NanoServerImageGenerator
```

6. Designate the folder for the base Nano Server images:

```
$NanoBaseFolder = 'C:\NanoBase'
```

7. Designate the folder for the VM images:

```
$VMFolder = 'D:\VMs'
```

8. Define the Nano Server computer name and file paths for your Nano Server VM:

```
$NanoComputerName = 'NANO1'
$NanoVMFolder     = Join-Path -Path $VMFolder
                             -ChildPath $NanoComputerName
$NanoVMPath       = Join-Path -Path $NanoVMFolder `
                             -ChildPath "$NanoComputerName.vhdx"
```

9. Create a Nano Server VM image, as a guest VM within Hyper-V and prompt for the administrator password:

```
New-NanoServerImage -DeploymentType Guest -Edition Datacenter
                    -MediaPath  $Server2016InstallationRoot `
                    -BasePath   $NanoBaseFolder `
                    -TargetPath $NanoVMPath `
                    -ComputerName $NanoComputerName
```

10. Define a VM switch for your Nano Server:

```
$SwitchName = Get-VMSwitch |
   Select-Object -ExpandProperty Name -First 1
```

11. Create a new VM in Hyper-V using the Nano Server VM image:

```
New-VM -VHDPath $NanoVMPath -Name $NanoComputerName `
    -Path $NanoVMFolder `
    -SwitchName $SwitchName `
    -Generation 2 -Verbose
```

12. Start your new Nano Server VM:

```
Start-VM -Name $NanoComputerName -Verbose
```

How it works...

In *step 1*, you mount the Windows Server installation ISO file:

```
PS C:\foo> $Server2016ISOPath = 'D:\iso\WinServer2016.iso'
$MountResult = Mount-DiskImage -ImagePath $Server2016ISOPath -PassThru
$MountResult | Select-Object -Property *


Attached                 : False
BlockSize                : 0
DevicePath               :
FileSize                 : 5653628928
ImagePath                : D:\iso\WinServer2016.iso
LogicalSectorSize        : 2048
Number                   :
Size                     : 5653628928
StorageType              : 1
PSComputerName           :
CimClass                 : ROOT/Microsoft/Windows/Storage:MSFT_DiskImage
CimInstanceProperties    : {Attached, BlockSize, DevicePath, FileSize...}
CimSystemProperties      : Microsoft.Management.Infrastructure.CimSystemProperties
```

In *step 2*, you store the drive letter for the mounted ISO file:

```
PS C:\foo> $Server2016InstallationRoot = ($MountResult |
        Get-Volume |
            Select-object -ExpandProperty Driveletter) + ':'
$Server2016InstallationRoot
E:
```

In *step 3* and *step 4*, you get the path to the `NanoServerImageGenerator` module folder within the installation media and review the contents:

```
PS C:\foo> $NanoServerFolder = Join-Path -Path $Server2016InstallationRoot -ChildPath 'NanoServer'
$NsigFolder = Join-Path -Path $NanoServerFolder -ChildPath 'NanoServerImageGenerator'
$NsigFolder
E:\NanoServer\NanoServerImageGenerator

PS C:\foo> Get-ChildItem -Path $NsigFolder  -Recurse


    Directory: E:\NanoServer\NanoServerImageGenerator


Mode                LastWriteTime         Length Name
----                -------------         ------ ----
d-r---        2016-09-12   8:19 AM                en-US
--r---        2016-09-12   8:19 AM         163433 Convert-WindowsImage.ps1
--r---        2016-09-12   8:19 AM            478 NanoServerImageGenerator.psd1
--r---        2016-09-12   8:19 AM         101216 NanoServerImageGenerator.psm1


    Directory: E:\NanoServer\NanoServerImageGenerator\en-US


Mode                LastWriteTime         Length Name
----                -------------         ------ ----
--r---        2016-09-12   8:19 AM          13302 nanoserverimagegenerator.strings.psd1
```

In *step 5*, you import the module and view the commands it contains:

```
PS C:\foo> Import-Module -Name $NsigFolder
Get-Command -Module NanoServerImageGenerator

CommandType     Name                                    Version    Source
-----------     ----                                    -------    ------
Function        Edit-NanoServerImage                     1.0.0.0    NanoServerImageGenerator
Function        Get-NanoServerPackage                    1.0.0.0    NanoServerImageGenerator
Function        New-NanoServerImage                      1.0.0.0    NanoServerImageGenerator
```

In *step 6* to *step 8* you define the variables and paths for the new Nano Server VM:

```
PS C:\> $NanoBaseFolder = 'C:\NanoBase'
PS C:\> $VMFolder = 'D:\VMs'
PS C:\> $NanoComputerName = 'NANO1'
PS C:\> $NanoVMFolder = Join-Path -Path $VMFolder -ChildPath $NanoComputerName
PS C:\> $NanoVMPath = Join-Path -Path $NanoVMFolder -ChildPath $("{0}.vhdx" -f $NanoComputerName)
```

In *step 9*, you create the Nano Server image, and you provide the administrator password when prompted.

```
PS C:\> New-NanoServerImage -DeploymentType Guest -Edition Datacenter
-MediaPath $Server2016InstallationRoot -BasePath $NanoBaseFolder `
-TargetPath $NanoVMPath -ComputerName $NanoComputerName
```

Monitor the progress bar as the cmdlet builds the image:

```
Converting image....
   Processing.


Operation.
   Running.
```

In *step 10*, you store the name of the Hyper-V switch to which you connect your new Nano Server. If you have defined more than one switch, this recipe returns the first switch found—you may need to adjust this step depending on your configuration. The output looks like this::

```
PS C:\foo> $SwitchName = Get-VMSwitch | Select-Object -ExpandProperty Name -First 1
```

In *step 11*, you create the VM in Hyper-V, referring to the newly created VHDX file.

```
PS C:\foo> New-VM -VHDPath $NanoVMPath -Name $NanoComputerName -Path $NanoVMFolder `
     -SwitchName $SwitchName -Generation 2 -Verbose
VERBOSE: New-VM will create a new virtual machine "NANO1".

Name   State CPUUsage(%) MemoryAssigned(M) Uptime   Status             Version
----   ----- ----------- ----------------- ------   ------             -------
NANO1  Off   0           0                 00:00:00 Operating normally 8.0
```

In *step 12*, you start your new VM.

```
PS C:\foo> Start-VM -Name $NanoComputerName -Verbose
VERBOSE: Start-VM will start the virtual machine "NANO1".

PS C:\foo>
```

There's more...

This recipe uses the default settings for networking based on DHCP and only applies the guest package to your new VM. You can define networking and packages at deployment time. Review online documentation for `New-NanoServerImage`: `https://technet.microsoft.com/en-us/library/mt791180.aspx`.

In *step 4*, you import the `NanoServerImageGenerator` module explicitly. You could also copy the module to your local module store. You can use any folder contained in `$PSModulePath`. Adding the module to your module store removes the need to import the module explicitly.

In *step 7*, you define the path to the VHD file. You should use the `.vhdx` extension for a VM generation 2 image, or the `.vhd` extension for a VM generation 1 image.

In *step 10*, you create the Nano Server VM. You store the VM file configuration files in the same folder as the VM disk. Additionally, the generation specified in this command needs to correspond to the choice of file extension in *step 7*. For a generation 1 VM use `.vhd`, and for a generation 2 VM use `.vhdx`. You may find yourself creating various Nano Servers in your learning process. To clean up a Nano Server VM, run the following commands:

```
Stop-VM -Name $NanoComputerName
Remove-VM -Name $NanoComputerName
Dismount-DiskImage -ImagePath $Server2016ISOPath
```

You use this VM in the later recipes of this chapter.

Connecting to and managing a Nano Server

Nano Server is designed to be managed remotely without the use of remote desktop services or local console access. You can connect directly to your Nano Server or use other tools to carry out management functions.

Nano Server lacks a desktop experience and remote desktop capability. You use the **Nano Server Recovery Console** to do some basic network management and to view operating system information. You perform most configuration and management remotely.

Perhaps the simplest way to connect to and configure **virtual machines (VMs)** is for you to use PowerShell Direct, a new feature introduced in Windows Server 2016. PowerShell Direct enables PowerShell remoting to VMs via the hypervisor instead of using the network, without the need to access the recovery console or configure networking for the VM.

Getting ready

Your Nano Server should be running in Hyper-V, and you should have administrator access on the Hyper-V host and know the VM Name and administrator password for the Nano Server.

You should decide on how to set up networking for the Nano Server VM. You can use DHCP (the default) or implement Static IP address details for your Nano Server. If you choose a static address, know the desired address, subnet, gateway, and DNS Server. In this recipe for Reskit.org, use the following:

- IPAddress: `10.10.10.131`
- Subnet Mask: `255.255.255.0`
- Gateway: `10.10.10.254`
- DNS: `10.10.10.10/10.10.10.11`

How to do it...

Method 1, using the **Nano Server Recovery Console**:

1. Launch Hyper-V management console, and locate the VM running Nano Server.
2. Double-click the VM to bring up the recovery console.
3. Enter the username administrator and the password that you defined when you created the VM.
4. Nano Server then display basic information about the server with a menu of options. Choose **Networking** from this menu by pressing *Enter*, then press *Enter* again to choose the default adapter.
5. Your Nano Server's IP configuration is displayed, with key navigation options displayed at the bottom of the screen. Note your IP address to use to connect later in this recipe.

6. Press *F11* at this screen to configure your IP address, if desired. Then press *F4* to change from DHCP to static IP, and use the *Tab* key to move between the **IP Address**, **Subnet Mask**, and **Default Gateway** fields, and enter the desired values.

Method 2, using PowerShell Direct:

1. From the Hyper-V host, open PowerShell ISE. List the VMs:

```
Get-VM -Name N*
```

2. Store the Nano Server VM name and administrator credential in variables:

```
$NanoComputerName = 'NANO1'
$Credential = Get-Credential `
    -Message "Enter administrator password for target VM:" `
    -UserName administrator
```

3. Get the running processes using `Invoke-Command` via PowerShell Direct:

```
Invoke-Command -VMName $NanoComputerName -Credential $Credential
                            -ScriptBlock { Get-Process }
```

4. Enter an interactive PowerShell remoting session via PowerShell Direct:

```
Enter-PSSession -VMName $NanoComputerName -Credential $Credential
```

5. You are connected just like that in a PowerShell remoting session! Create and use a test folder in your Nano server:

```
New-Item -ItemType Directory -Path C:\foo `
        -ErrorAction SilentlyContinue
Set-Location C:\foo
```

6. Gather information about your server using the new `Get-ComputerInfo` cmdlet:

```
Get-ComputerInfo -Property CsName, WindowsEditionId,
                        OSServerLevel, `
    OSType, OSVersion, WindowsBuildLabEx, BiosBIOSVersion
```

7. Examine `$PSVersionTable`, noting the value of the `PSEdition` property:

```
$PSVersionTable
```

8. Get the IP Address of your Nano Server, noting it for later recipe steps:

```
Get-NetIPAddress -AddressFamily IPV4 -InterfaceAlias Ethernet |
      Select-Object -ExpandProperty IPAddress
```

9. If required, change the IP Address of your Nano Server, and display the new IP:

```
New-NetIPAddress -InterfaceAlias 'Ethernet' `
                 -IPAddress 10.10.10.131 `
                 -PrefixLength 24 `
                 -DefaultGateway 10.10.10.254
Get-NetIPAddress -InterfaceAlias 'Ethernet' -AddressFamily IPv4
```

10. If required, set the DNS of your Nano Server, and display the DNS information:

```
Set-DnsClientServerAddress -InterfaceAlias 'Ethernet' `
                           -ServerAddresses 10.10.10.10,
                                            10.10.10.11
Get-DnsClientServerAddress
```

11. Exit your remoting session:

```
Exit-PSSession
```

Method 3, Using PowerShell Remoting:

1. PowerShell remoting requires that the remoting target computer IP should be among the TrustedHosts defined on your computer. Add the IP Address of the Nano Server to our computer's TrustedHosts and verify the value:

```
$NanoServerIP = '10.10.10.131'
Set-Item -Path WSMan:\localhost\Client\TrustedHosts `
         -Value $NanoServerIP -Force
Get-Item -Path WSMan:\localhost\Client\TrustedHosts
```

2. Verify WSMan connectivity to the Nano Server:

```
Test-WSMan -Path $NanoServerIP
```

3. Connect via PowerShell remoting to the Nano Server:

```
Enter-PSSession -ComputerName $NanoServerIP `
                -Credential $Credential
```

4. Use `Get-ComputerInfo` to inspect the Nano Server:

```
Get-ComputerInfo -Property CsName, WindowsEditionId,
                     OSServerLevel, OSType, OSVersion,
                     WindowsBuildLabEx, BiosBIOSVersion
```

5. Exit your remoting session:

```
Exit-PSSession
```

Method 4, Using WMI with the CIM cmdlets:

1. Create a new CIM session on the Nano Server, and view the `$CimSession` object:

```
$CimSession = New-CimSession -Credential $Credential `
                              -ComputerName $NanoServerIP
$CimSession
```

2. Examine the properties of the `Win32_ComputerSystem` CIM class:

```
Get-CimInstance -CimSession $CimSession `
           -ClassName Win32_ComputerSystem |
               Format-List -Property *
```

3. Count the CIM classes available:

```
Get-CimClass -CimSession $CimSession | Measure-Object
```

4. View the running processes using the `CIM_Process` WMI class and a WMI query:

```
Get-CimInstance -CimSession $CimSession `
           -Query "SELECT * from CIM_Process"
```

5. Remove your CIM Session:

```
Get-CimSession | Remove-CimSession
```

How it works...

In *Method 1*, you use the **Nano Server Recovery Console** from the Hyper-V manager. This technique is useful when the Nano Server has an invalid Ethernet configuration or an unknown IP address.

In *step 1* and *step 2*, from Hyper-V manager, double-click on the NANO1 virtual machine to bring up the **Nano Server Recovery Console**.

In *step 3*, you log in with the username administrator and the password you provided during the creation of the VM:

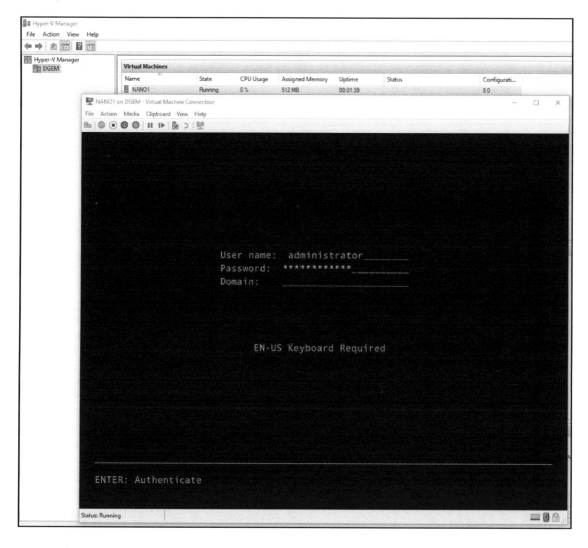

In *step 4*, you view the summary information on your Nano Server and navigate through the screens using the keyboard, with the menu options displayed at the bottom:

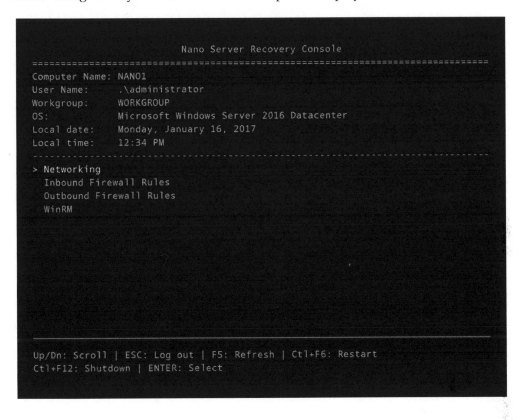

When you select **Networking** from the initial screen, you see the Network Settings folder, like this:

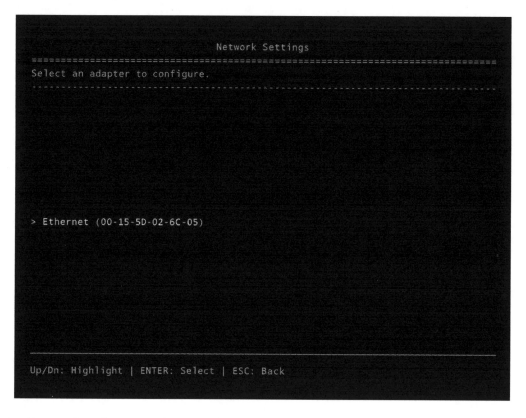

In *step 5*, you view the networking configuration of your server, noting the IP address so you can access it later.

In *step 6*, you can modify your IP address. The default configuration uses DHCP. If your scenario requires it, disable DHCP and define a valid static **IP Address**, **Subnet Mask**, and **Default Gateway**:

```
                              IP Configuration
==============================================================================
Ethernet
Microsoft Hyper-V Network Adapter
00-15-5D-02-6C-05
------------------------------------------------------------------------------




                    DHCP            [          Disabled          ]
                    IP Address      ....................................
                    Subnet Mask     _____
                    Default Gateway _____






..............................................................................
 ESC: Cancel | ENTER: Save | F4: Toggle
```

In *Method 2*, you use PowerShell Direct. PowerShell Direct is a new feature introduced in Hyper-V in Windows Server 2016 (and Windows 10). PowerShell Direct enables PowerShell scripting against Windows Server 2016 and Windows 10 virtual machines directly through the hypervisor, without requiring network, firewall, or remoting configuration. PowerShell Direct simplifies deployment and automation scripting for Hyper-V hosted virtual machines.

In *step 1*, you get the list of VM names from the local Hyper-V server:

```
PS C:\foo> Get-VM -Name N*

Name   State   CPUUsage(%) MemoryAssigned(M) Uptime                  Status             Version
----   -----   ----------- ----------------- ------                  ------             -------
NANO1  Running 0           512               1.06:49:21.5540000 Operating normally 8.0


PS C:\foo>
```

In *step 2*, you store the VM name and credential in a variable for later use in the recipe:

```
PS C:\foo> $Credential = Get-Credential -Message "Enter password for administrator user on target VM:" -UserName administrator
```

In *step 3*, you view the running processes from the VM using `Invoke-Command` with a script block of `Get-Process`. Note that the `-VMName` parameter indicates the use of PowerShell Direct:

```
PS C:\foo> Invoke-Command -VMName $NanoComputerName -Credential $Credential `
  -ScriptBlock { Get-Process }
```

Handles	NPM(K)	PM(K)	WS(K)	CPU(s)	Id	SI	ProcessName	PSComputerName
0	6	748	1828	0.03	292	0	csrss	NANO1
0	5	892	3512	0.02	284	0	EMT	NANO1
0	0	0	4		0	0	Idle	NANO1
0	19	3792	10460	0.16	348	0	lsass	NANO1
0	42	27980	52264	2.47	2016	0	powershell	NANO1
0	8	1640	4704	0.08	332	0	services	NANO1
0	2	316	1036	0.02	208	0	smss	NANO1
0	8	1628	5040	0.09	440	0	svchost	NANO1
0	14	1720	5620	0.05	472	0	svchost	NANO1
0	14	9212	12944	0.38	556	0	svchost	NANO1
0	7	1404	5448	0.02	584	0	svchost	NANO1
0	9	1572	5456	0.03	600	0	svchost	NANO1
0	19	12508	22068	4.70	648	0	svchost	NANO1
0	14	2212	7060	0.08	712	0	svchost	NANO1
0	28	5708	12496	0.19	748	0	svchost	NANO1
0	28	4012	8968	0.02	836	0	svchost	NANO1
0	16	5060	12844	0.13	992	0	svchost	NANO1
0	0	80	68	0.92	4	0	System	NANO1
0	7	724	3264	0.02	316	0	wininit	NANO1
0	6	1296	5984	0.03	1600	0	WMIADAP	NANO1
0	8	5764	11376	1.50	1640	0	WmiPrvSE	NANO1

In *step 4*, you enter an interactive PowerShell remoting session through PowerShell Direct using the `-VMName` parameter:

```
PS C:\foo> Enter-PSSession -VMName $NanoComputerName -Credential $Credential

[NANO1]: PS C:\Users\administrator\Documents>
```

In *step 5,* you connect to the VM, note the VM name in the prompt and that your current directory is in the default `Documents` folder. Create and use a test folder in your Nano Server:

```
[NANO1]: PS C:\Users\administrator\Documents> New-Item -ItemType Directory -Path c:\foo `
    -ErrorAction SilentlyContinue
Set-Location c:\foo

[NANO1]: PS C:\foo>
```

In *step 6,* you gather computer information using a new cmdlet in PowerShell 5.1, `Get-ComputerInfo`:

```
[NANO1]: PS C:\> Get-ComputerInfo -Property CsName, WindowsEditionId, OSServerLevel, `
    OSType, OSVersion, WindowsBuildLabEx, BiosBIOSVersion


CsName             : NANO1
WindowsEditionId   : ServerDatacenterNano
OsServerLevel      : NanoServer
OsType             : WINNT
OsVersion          : 10.0.14393
WindowsBuildLabEx  : 14393.693.amd64fre.rs1_release.161220-1747
BiosBIOSVersion    : {VRTUAL - 1, Hyper-V UEFI Release v1.0, EDK II - 10000}
```

In *step 7,* `$PSVersionTable` has a `PSEdition` of `Core` rather than `Desktop`. The Core version supports a subset of the features of the full Desktop edition of PowerShell:

```
[NANO1]: PS C:\Users\administrator\Documents> $PSVersionTable

Name                           Value
----                           -----
WSManStackVersion              3.0
PSRemotingProtocolVersion      2.3
SerializationVersion           1.1.0.1
PSEdition                      Core
PSVersion                      5.1.14368.1000
BuildVersion                   10.0.14368.1000
PSCompatibleVersions           {1.0, 2.0, 3.0, 4.0...}
CLRVersion
```

In *step 8,* you get the `IPAddress` property from the `Get-NetIPAddress` cmdlet:

```
[NANO1]: PS C:\Users\administrator\Documents> Get-NetIPAddress -AddressFamily IPV4 -InterfaceAlias Ethernet |
    Select-Object -ExpandProperty IPAddress
169.254.232.208
```

In *step 9*, you can set your IP address:

```
[NANO1]: PS C:\foo> New-NetIPAddress -InterfaceAlias 'Ethernet' -IPAddress 10.10.10.151 `
    -PrefixLength 24 -DefaultGateway 10.10.10.254


IPAddress           : 10.10.10.151
InterfaceIndex      : 3
InterfaceAlias      : Ethernet
AddressFamily       : IPv4
Type                : Unicast
PrefixLength        : 24
PrefixOrigin        : Manual
SuffixOrigin        : Manual
AddressState        : Tentative
ValidLifetime       : Infinite ([TimeSpan]::MaxValue)
PreferredLifetime   : Infinite ([TimeSpan]::MaxValue)
SkipAsSource        : False
PolicyStore         : ActiveStore
```

In *step 10*, you set your DNS:

```
[NANO1]: PS C:\foo> Set-DnsClientServerAddress -InterfaceAlias 'Ethernet' `
    -ServerAddresses 10.10.10.10, 10.10.10.11
Get-DnsClientServerAddress

InterfaceAlias             Interface Address ServerAddresses
                           Index     Family
--------------             --------- ------- ---------------
Ethernet                         3 IPv4    {10.10.10.10, 10.10.10.11}
Ethernet                         3 IPv6    {}
Loopback Pseudo-Interface 1       1 IPv4    {}
Loopback Pseudo-Interface 1       1 IPv6    {}
```

In *step 11*, exit your remoting session. Note the change in the prompt:

```
[NANO1]: PS C:\foo> Exit-PSSession

PS C:\foo>
```

With *Method 3*, you use regular PowerShell remoting. In *step 1*, you connect to the Nano Server VM. Before you can do so, you need to add the VMs IP address to your `TrustedHosts` on your Windows 2016 server. Note that you can set this value to an asterisk (*) which enables you to connect to any remoting capable computer:

```
[NANO1]: PS C:\foo> $NanoServerIP = '10.10.10.151'
Set-Item WSMan:\localhost\Client\TrustedHosts $NanoServerIP -Force
Get-Item WSMan:\localhost\Client\TrustedHosts


   WSManConfig: Microsoft.WSMan.Management\WSMan::localhost\Client

Type            Name               SourceOfValue   Value
----            ----               -------------   -----
System.String   TrustedHosts                       10.10.10.151
```

In *step 2*, you test your remoting connectivity to the VM using `Test-WSMan`:

```
PS C:\foo> Test-WSMan $NanoServerIP


wsmid           : http://schemas.dmtf.org/wbem/wsman/identity/1/wsmanidentity.xsd
ProtocolVersion : http://schemas.dmtf.org/wbem/wsman/1/wsman.xsd
ProductVendor   : Microsoft Corporation
ProductVersion  : OS: 0.0.0 SP: 0.0 Stack: 3.0
```

In *step 3*, you remote into the VM with PowerShell remoting:

```
PS C:\foo> Enter-PSSession -ComputerName $NanoServerIP -Credential $Credential

[10.10.10.151]: PS C:\Users\administrator\Documents>
```

In *step 4*, as you gather computer information. Note that the `-Property` is optional, leave it out or pass in an asterisk (*) to display a great deal of useful information about the target computer:

```
[10.10.10.151]: PS C:\> Get-ComputerInfo -Property CsName, WindowsEditionId, OSServerLevel,
    OSType, OSVersion, WindowsBuildLabEx, BiosBIOSVersion


CsName            : NANO1
WindowsEditionId  : ServerDatacenterNano
OsServerLevel     : NanoServer
OsType            : WINNT
OsVersion         : 10.0.14393
WindowsBuildLabEx : 14393.693.amd64fre.rs1_release.161220-1747
BiosBIOSVersion   : {VRTUAL - 1, Hyper-V UEFI Release v1.0, EDK II - 10000}
```

In *step 5*, you end your remoting session:

```
[10.10.10.151]: PS C:\foo> Exit-PSSession
PS C:\foo>
```

In *Method 4*, you use **Windows Management Instrumentation (WMI)** and the cmdlets in the CimCmdlets module to work with your Nano Server. WMI is an open standard that describes managed IT elements as objects with properties and relationships. The CIMCmdlets module contains the preferred cmdlets you use to manage Windows Servers via WMI. PowerShell in Windows Server 2016 supports both the older WMI cmdlets (contained in the Microsoft.PowerShell.Management module) and the newer CIMCmdlets module. Nano Server ships with CIMCmdlets, not WMI.

In *step 1*, you create a CIM session to the Nano Server using the credential and IP address you defined earlier, and you store it in the variable $CimSession:

```
PS C:\foo> $CimSession = New-CimSession -Credential $Credential -ComputerName $NanoServerIP
$CimSession

Id          : 1
Name        : CimSession1
InstanceId  : c8a93c75-c063-4d49-ba07-7b682b7b11a4
ComputerName : 10.10.10.151
Protocol    : WSMAN


PS C:\foo>
```

In *step 2*, within this CIM session, you access an instance of the Win32_ComputerSystem class to view information about the Nano Server:

```
PS C:\foo> Get-CimInstance -CimSession $CimSession -ClassName Win32_ComputerSystem | Format-List *

PSShowComputerName      : True
AdminPasswordStatus     : 3
BootupState             :
ChassisBootupState      : 3
KeyboardPasswordStatus  : 3
              rdStatus



PSComputerNa            : 192.168.
CimClass                : root/cimv2:Win32_ComputerSystem
CimInstanceProperties   : {Caption, Description, InstallDate, Name...}
CimSystemProperties     : Microsoft.Management.Infrastructure.CimSystemProperties
```

In *step 3*, you gather a count of the classes:

```
PS C:\foo> Get-CimClass -CimSession $CimSession | Measure-Object


Count     : 838
Average   :
Sum       :
Maximum   :
Minimum   :
Property  :
```

In *step 4*, you query the CIM_Process class:

```
PS C:\foo> Get-CimInstance -CimSession $CimSession -Query "SELECT * from CIM_Process"

ProcessId Name                 HandleCount WorkingSetSize VirtualSize     PSComputerName
--------- ----                 ----------- -------------- -----------     --------------
0         System Idle Process  0           4096           65536           10.10.10.151
4         System               323         57344          1974272         10.10.10.151
212       smss.exe             46          688128         2199029833728   10.10.10.151
296       csrss.exe            110         1970176        2199035736064   10.10.10.151
320       wininit.exe          76          3928064        2199042248704   10.10.10.151
336       services.exe         179         5058560        2199041740800   10.10.10.151
352       lsass.exe            728         10661888       2199064793088   10.10.10.151
436       svchost.exe          192         6164480        2199056437248   10.10.10.151
468       svchost.exe          269         6688768        2199057764352   10.10.10.151
572       svchost.exe          127         5861376        2199052247040   10.10.10.151
588       svchost.exe          319         8515584        2199073071104   10.10.10.151
604       svchost.exe          135         3604480        2199054733312   10.10.10.151
648       svchost.exe          482         21643264       2199139741696   10.10.10.151
684       svchost.exe          287         6873088        2199066492928   10.10.10.151
720       svchost.exe          710         22839296       2199128432640   10.10.10.151
796       svchost.exe          291         8560640        2199066771456   10.10.10.151
960       svchost.exe          311         12668928       2199105224704   10.10.10.151
268       EMT.exe              66          3862528        2199043854336   10.10.10.151
1208      WmiPrvSE.exe         159         8671232        2199059148800   10.10.10.151
1256      WmiPrvSE.exe         202         11505664       2199062700032   10.10.10.151
1664      WmiApSrv.exe         134         6787072        2199051653120   10.10.10.151
```

In *step 5*, you remove your CIM session:

```
PS C:\foo> Get-CimSession | Remove-CimSession
```

There's more...

`Get-ComputerInfo` is a new cmdlet introduced in PowerShell 5.1. `Get-ComputerInfo` returns an object of type `Microsoft.PowerShell.Commands.ComputerInfo` that contains a wealth of information from the target computer including hardware, bios, OS, driver, and networking data. The documentation is available and updateable on github: `https://github.com/PowerShell/PowerShell-Docs/blob/staging/reference/5.1/Microsoft.PowerShell.Management/Get-ComputerInfo.md`.

PowerShell Direct is a useful new feature for Hyper-V in Windows Server 2016. It simplifies PowerShell scripting for VMs. For more information on this feature, see: `https://docs.microsoft.com/en-us/virtualization/hyper-v-on-windows/user-guide/powershell-direct`.

PowerShell remoting is a powerful feature that has security implications, this is why the `TrustedHosts` setting is empty by default, and the administrator must explicitly add addresses of servers to manage, or may add an asterisk (*) to allow remoting to any server. More information about remoting is available within the PowerShell documentation:

```
Get-Help about_Remote*
```

PowerShell on Nano Server contains the Core edition of PowerShell. PowerShell Core implements a subset of the full Desktop edition features. The cmdlets provided should be enough for you to configure networking to allow you to manage Nano Server remotely.

Learn about what is and what is not supported with PowerShell in Nano Server: `https://technet.microsoft.com/en-us/windows-server-docs/get-started/powershell-on-nano-server`.

WMI is a key aspect of PowerShell scripting, using either the WMI or CIM cmdlets. The latter are preferred if only because they are a little quicker. Learn more about `CIMCmdlets` in PowerShell: `https://technet.microsoft.com/en-us/library/jj553783.aspx`.

You use WMI via the CIM cmdlets to manage and apply Windows updates to your Nano Servers: `https://technet.microsoft.com/en-us/windows-server-docs/get-started/manage-nano-server#managing-updates-in-nano-server`.

Installing features with Nano Server packages

Nano Server is a minimal implementation of a Windows Server 2016. You can customize it to include only the desired features and roles you require. You customize Nano Servers using the `PackageManagement` module along with the `NanoServerPackage` provider. The `NanoServerPackage` provider can search, download, or install packages that implement features and roles for Nano Server from an online gallery. This provider enables you to install useful server features and roles which you will explore in this recipe.

In Nano Server, packages replace the **Add Roles & Features** functionality in other editions of Windows. For example, if you need a web server, in other editions of Windows you would install the Web Server (IIS) role, but in Nano server, you would install the `Microsoft-NanoServer-IIS-Package` package. Instead of installing the **File Services** role, you would install the `Microsoft-NanoServer-Storage-Package` package.

You can deploy a Nano Server in a workgroup, which is the default. You can also join the Nano Server to your domain. Nano Servers must join to the domain to utilize certain Windows features like Windows Clusters. In this recipe, you will deploy a domain joined Nano Server. To achieve this, you need to obtain a domain blob file which you create using the `djoin` console command. You transfer this blob file to the Nano Server to join it to the domain. You also review the available Nano Server packages and install the selected packages to support the file server role, web server role, and the **Desired State Configuration (DSC)** support.

Getting ready

Before starting, you should ensure that the pre-requisites for using `PowerShellGet` are installed and are updated. See recipe in `Chapter 1`, *What's New in PowerShell and Windows Server*, *Exploring PowerShellGet* recipe for how you can achieve this.

To enable the Nano Server to join the domain, you first create a domain join blob file. Run the following command with an account in Domain Admins group, from a virtual machine on the domain as follows:

```
djoin.exe /provision /domain RESKIT /machine NANO2
   /savefile .\NANO2.djoin
```

The `djoin` command creates the domain join blob as `.\NANO2.djoin`. Copy the newly created `NANO2.djoin` file to a folder on your Hyper-V host (`C:\foo` in this recipe.)

You also need the Windows Server 2016 installation ISO mounted (You use `E:` in this recipe as the location of this ISO image.)

A Nano Server can use DHCP or static IP addresses. In this recipe for provisioning `NANO2` on the `Reskit.org` domain, you use the following settings:

- IPAddress: `10.10.10.132`
- Subnet Mask: `255.255.255.0`
- Gateway: `10.10.10.254`
- DNS: `10.10.10.10/10.10.10.11`

How to do it...

1. From your Hyper-V host, view the currently installed package providers:

   ```
   Get-PackageProvider
   ```

2. View the available package providers online, noting the `NanoServerPackage` provider:

   ```
   Find-PackageProvider | Select-Object -Property Name, Summary |
       Format-Table -AutoSize -Wrap
   ```

3. Install the `NanoServerPackage` provider:

   ```
   Install-PackageProvider -Name NanoServerPackage -Verbose
   ```

4. View the commands included with the provider:

   ```
   Get-Command -Module NanoServerPackage
   ```

5. View the available Nano Server packages:

   ```
   $NanoPackages = Find-NanoServerPackage |
                   Select-Object -Property Name, Description
   $NanoPackages | Format-Table -AutoSize -Wrap
   ```

6. Determine which of the available packages you wish to install, store them as an array in the `$Installpackages` variable and then display that array:

```
$InstallPackages = @('Microsoft-NanoServer-Storage-Package',
                     'Microsoft-NanoServer-IIS-Package',
                     'Microsoft-NanoServer-DSC-Package')
$InstallPackages
```

7. Define the path to the Windows Server 2016 installation media:

```
$Server2016InstallationRoot = 'E:\'
```

8. Define the path of the `NanoServerImageGenerator` folder:

```
$NanoServerFolder = Join-Path -Path $Server2016InstallationRoot
                                    -ChildPath 'NanoServer'
$NsigFolder = Join-Path -Path $NanoServerFolder
                              -ChildPath 'NanoServerImageGenerator'
$NsigFolder
```

9. Import the `NanoServerImageGenerator` module and review the commands contained in that module:

```
Import-Module -Name $NsigFolder
Get-Command -Module NanoServerImageGenerator
```

10. Define the folders for the base Nano Server images and the VM images:

```
$NanoBaseFolder = 'C:\NanoBase'
$VMFolder = 'D:\VMs'
```

11. Define paths for the Nano Server VM:

```
$NanoComputerName = 'NANO2'
$NanoVMFolder = Join-Path -Path $VMFolder
                                -ChildPath $NanoComputerName
$NanoVMPath = Join-Path -Path $NanoVMFolder
                              -ChildPath "$NanoComputerName.vhdx"
```

12. Define the networking parameters:

```
$IPV4Address = '10.10.10.132'
$IPV4DNS = '10.10.10.10','10.10.10.11'
$IPV4Gateway = '10.10.10.254'
$IPV4SubnetMask = '255.255.255.0'
```

13. Build a hash table $NanoServerImageParameters to hold parameters for the New-NanoServerImage cmdlet:

```
$NanoServerImageParameters = @{
    DeploymentType = 'Guest'
    Edition = 'DataCenter'
    TargetPath = $NanoVMPath
    BasePath = $NanoBaseFolder
    DomainBlobPath = $DomainJoinBlobPath
    Ipv4Address = $IPV4Address
    Ipv4Dns = $IPV4DNS
    Ipv4Gateway = $IPV4Gateway
    IPV4SubnetMask = $IPV4SubnetMask
    Package = $InstallPackages
}
```

14. Create a new Nano Server image, passing in configuration parameters using splatting:

```
New-NanoServerImage @NanoServerImageParameters
```

15. Once complete, review the VM switches available, and define the Hyper-V switch to use:

```
Get-VMSwitch | Select-Object -ExpandProperty Name
$SwitchName = 'Internal'
```

16. Create the Nano virtual machine from the newly created VM disk, and start the VM:

```
New-VM -VHDPath $NanoVMPath `
    -Name $NanoComputerName `
    -Path $NanoVMFolder `
    -SwitchName $SwitchName `
    -Generation 2 -Verbose |
        Start-VM
```

How it works...

To get ready for this recipe, create the computer account for NANO2 in the RESKIT domain using the djoin command to create the domain blob file. You store this blob in the blob file NANO2.djoin.

In *step 1*, you review the installed package providers. Note that if `NanoServerPackage` provider is missing, you need to install this package provider to continue:

```
PS C:\foo> Get-PackageProvider

Name              Version      DynamicOptions
----              -------      --------------
msi               3.0.0.0      AdditionalArguments
msu               3.0.0.0
NuGet             2.8.5.208    Destination, ExcludeVersion, Scope, SkipDependencies, Headers, Filter...
PowerShellGet     1.0.0.1      PackageManagementProvider, Type, Scope, AllowClobber, SkipPublisherCh...
Programs          3.0.0.0      IncludeWindowsInstaller, IncludeSystemComponent
```

In *step 2* and *step 3*, you list the available `PackageManagement` package providers, noting the `NanoServerPackage` package, then install this package provider:

```
PS C:\foo> Find-PackageProvider | Select-Object Name, Summary | Format-Table -AutoSize -Wrap

Name               Summary
----               -------
nuget              NuGet provider for the OneGet meta-package manager
psl                psl provider for the OneGet meta-package manager
chocolatey         ChocolateyPrototype provider for the OneGet meta-package manager
PowerShellGet      PowerShell module with commands for discovering, installing, updating and publishing the
                   PowerShell artifacts like Modules, DSC Resources, Role Capabilities and Scripts.
ContainerImage     This is a PackageManagement provider module which helps in discovering, downloading and
                   installing Windows Container OS images.

                   For more details and examples refer to our project site at
                   https://github.com/PowerShell/ContainerProvider.
DockerMsftProvider PowerShell module with commands for discovering, installing, and updating Docker images.
NanoServerPackage  A PackageManagement provider to Discover, Save and Install Nano Server Packages on-demand
GitHubProvider     GitHub-as-a-Package - PackageManagement PowerShell Provider to interop with Github
GistProvider       Gist-as-a-Package - PackageManagement  PowerShell Provider to interop with Github Gists
ChocolateyGet      An PowerShell OneGet provider that discovers packages from https://www.chocolatey.org.
TSDProvider        PowerShell PackageManager provider to search & install TypeScript definition files from the
                   community DefinitelyTyped repo
MyAlbum            MyAlbum provider discovers the photos in your remote file repository and installs them to your
                   local folder.
OfficeProvider     OfficeProvider allows users to install Microsoft Office365 ProPlus from Powershell.
WSAProvider        Provider to Discover, Install and inventory windows server apps
GitLabProvider     GitLab PackageManagement provider
0install           Zero Install is a decentralized cross-platform software-installation system.

PS C:\foo> Install-PackageProvider -Name NanoServerPackage -Verbose
VERBOSE: Using the provider 'Bootstrap' for searching packages.
VERBOSE: Finding the package 'Bootstrap::FindPackage' 'NanoServerPackage','','',''.
VERBOSE: Using the provider 'PowerShellGet' for searching packages.
VERBOSE: The -Repository parameter was not specified.  PowerShellGet will use all of the registered repositories.
VERBOSE: Getting the provider object for the PackageManagement Provider 'NuGet'.
VERBOSE: The specified Location is 'https://www.powershellgallery.com/api/v2/' and PackageManagementProvider is 'NuGet'.
VERBOSE: Searching repository 'https://www.powershellgallery.com/api/v2/FindPackagesById()?id='NanoServerPackage'' for ''.
VERBOSE: Total package yield:'1' for the specified package 'NanoServerPackage'.
VERBOSE: Skipping installed package NanoServerPackage 1.0.1.0.
```

In *step 4*, you view the commands associated with the `NanoServerPackage`. While these commands are specific to this package, they are wrapper cmdlets for similarly named `PackageManagement` cmdlets that can be viewed with `Get-Command -Noun Package`:

```
PS C:\foo> Get-Command -Module NanoServerPackage

CommandType     Name                       Version     Source
-----------     ----                       -------     ------
Function        Find-NanoServerPackage     1.0.1.0     NanoServerPackage
Function        Install-NanoServerPackage  1.0.1.0     NanoServerPackage
Function        Save-NanoServerPackage     1.0.1.0     NanoServerPackage
```

In *step 5*, you view the available packages for Nano Server. Note that some of these packages are installed using switch parameters in the `New-NanoServerImage` cmdlet, for example, the `-DeploymentType Guest` switch installs the `Microsoft-NanoServer-Guest-Package`:

```
PS C:\foo> $NanoPackages = Find-NanoServerPackage | Select-Object -Property Name, Description
$NanoPackages | Format-Table -AutoSize -Wrap

Name                                                    Description
----                                                    -----------
Microsoft-NanoServer-IPHelper-Service-Package           Provides tunnel connectivity using IPv6 transition
                                                        technologies (6to4, ISATAP, Port Proxy, and Teredo), and
                                                        IP-HTTPS.
Microsoft-NanoServer-SCVMM-Compute-Package              Includes services for monitoring a Hyper-V host using
                                                        System Center Virtual Machine Manager (SCVMM).
Microsoft-NanoServer-ShieldedVM-Package                 Includes Host Guardian Service and other features necessary
                                                        to provision shielded VMs on a Hyper-V server.
Microsoft-NanoServer-Compute-Package                    Includes Hyper-V and NetQoS which provide a virtualization
                                                        host platform and network services for creating and
                                                        managing virtual machines and their resources.
Microsoft-NanoServer-SecureStartup-Package              Includes support for BitLocker, Trusted Platform Module,
                                                        Secure Boot, and other services for supporting
                                                        hardware-based security features.
Microsoft-NanoServer-OEM-Drivers-Package                Includes basic drivers for a variety of network adapters
                                                        and storage controllers. This is the same set of drivers
                                                        included in a Server Core installation of Windows Server.
Microsoft-NanoServer-Storage-Package                    Includes services and tools for creating and managing file
                                                        system and storage resources.
Microsoft-NanoServer-Defender-Package                   Includes Windows Defender which provides real-time
                                                        protection against viruses, spyware, and other malicious
                                                        software. Also includes a default signature file containing
                                                        virus and spyware definitions.
Microsoft-NanoServer-DSC-Package                        Includes PowerShell Desired State Configuration which
                                                        provides a set of PowerShell language extensions, cmdlets,
                                                        and resources for declaratively configuring software
                                                        services and applications.
Microsoft-NanoServer-DNS-Package                        Includes Domain Name System (DNS) Server which provides
                                                        name resolution for TCP/IP networks.
Microsoft-NanoServer-IIS-Package                        Includes Internet Information Services (IIS) which provides
                                                        a reliable, manageable, and scalable Web application
                                                        infrastructure.
Microsoft-NanoServer-DCB-Package                        Includes Data Center Bridging (DCB) which is a suite of
                                                        IEEE standards that are used to enhance Ethernet local area
                                                        networks by providing hardware-based bandwidth guarantees
                                                        and transport reliability.
Microsoft-NanoServer-FailoverCluster-Package            Includes Failover Clustering which allows multiple servers
                                                        to work together to provide high availability of server
                                                        roles.
Microsoft-NanoServer-SoftwareInventoryLogging-Package   Includes services and tools for logging Microsoft asset
                                                        management data and forwarding this data periodically to a
                                                        collection server for aggregation.
Microsoft-NanoServer-Host-Package                       Includes drivers and services for running on a physical
                                                        machine.
Microsoft-NanoServer-SNMP-Agent-Package                 Simple Network Management Protocol (SNMP) is a popular
                                                        protocol for network management. It is used for collecting
                                                        information from, and configuring, network devices, such as
                                                        servers, printers, hubs, switches, and routers on an
                                                        Internet Protocol (IP) network.
Microsoft-NanoServer-SCVMM-Package                      Includes services for monitoring a physical or virtual
                                                        machine using System Center Virtual Machine Manager (SCVMM).
Microsoft-NanoServer-Guest-Package                      Includes drivers and integration services for running as a
                                                        guest virtual machine in Hyper-V.
Microsoft-NanoServer-Containers-Package                 Includes services and tools to create and manage Windows
                                                        Server Containers and their resources.
```

In *step 6*, you define `$InstallPackages` as an array of the desired packages:

```
PS C:\> $InstallPackages = @('Microsoft-NanoServer-Storage-Package',
                             'Microsoft-NanoServer-IIS-Package',
                             'Microsoft-NanoServer-DSC-Package')
$InstallPackages
Microsoft-NanoServer-Storage-Package
Microsoft-NanoServer-IIS-Package
Microsoft-NanoServer-DSC-Package
```

In *step 7* and *step 8*, you define the path to the server installation media, and to the `NanoServerImageGenerator` module folder:

```
PS C:\foo> $Server2016InstallationRoot = 'E:\'

PS C:\foo> $NanoServerFolder = Join-Path -Path $Server2016InstallationRoot -ChildPath 'NanoServer'
$NsigFolder = Join-Path -Path $NanoServerFolder -ChildPath 'NanoServerImageGenerator'
$NsigFolder
E:\NanoServer\NanoServerImageGenerator
```

In *step 9*, you import the `NanoServerImageGenerator` module and view the modules commands:

```
PS C:\foo> Import-Module -Name $NsigFolder
Get-Command -Module NanoServerImageGenerator

CommandType     Name                      Version    Source
-----------     ----                      -------    ------
Function        Edit-NanoServerImage      1.0.0.0    NanoServerImageGenerator
Function        Get-NanoServerPackage     1.0.0.0    NanoServerImageGenerator
Function        New-NanoServerImage       1.0.0.0    NanoServerImageGenerator
```

In *step 10* and *step 11*, you define paths required for the Nano Server base image, VM name, folder, and file path. There is no output from these steps.

In *step 12*, you define the path to the domain join file that you created in the *Getting ready* section:

```
PS C:\foo> $DomainJoinBlobPath = 'C:\foo\NANO2.djoin'
```

In *step 13*, define the networking configuration for the VM. Note the `$IPV4DNS` is an array with two values storing the primary and secondary DNS server IP addresses:

```
PS C:\foo> $IPV4Address = '10.10.10.152'
$IPV4DNS = '10.10.10.10','10.10.10.11'
$IPV4Gateway = '10.10.10.254'
$IPV4SubnetMask = '255.255.255.0'
```

In *step 14*, you define and view a hash table variable holding all the parameters required in the next step:

```
PS C:\foo> $NanoServerImageParameters = @{
    DeploymentType = 'Guest'
    Edition = 'DataCenter'
    TargetPath = $NanoVMPath
    BasePath = $NanoBaseFolder
    DomainBlobPath = $DomainJoinBlobPath
    Ipv4Address = $IPV4Address
    Ipv4Dns = $IPV4DNS
    Ipv4Gateway = $IPV4Gateway
    IPV4SubnetMask = $IPV4SubnetMask
    InterfaceNameOrIndex = 'Ethernet'
    Package  = $InstallPackages
}
$NanoServerImageParameters

Name                     Value
----                     -----
TargetPath               D:\VMs\NANO2\NANO2.vhdx
DeploymentType           Guest
Ipv4Dns                  {10.10.10.10, 10.10.10.11}
IPV4SubnetMask           255.255.255.0
InterfaceNameOrIndex     Ethernet
Edition                  DataCenter
BasePath                 C:\NanoBase
Ipv4Address              10.10.10.152
Ipv4Gateway              10.10.10.254
DomainBlobPath           C:\foo\NANO2.djoin
Package                  {Microsoft-NanoServer-Storage-Package, Microsoft-NanoServer-IIS-Package, Microso...
```

In *step 15*, you run the `New-NanoServerImage` using splatting to pass the required parameters. Answer the prompt for an administrator password, and review the progress of the creation of the new Nano Server image. Once complete, results are available for review in a time stamped folder under `C:\NanoBaseLogs`:

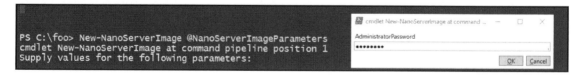

In *step 16*, view the available Hyper-V switch names, and choose the one to associate with your new VM:

```
PS C:\foo> Get-VMSwitch | Select-Object -ExpandProperty Name
Public-Wifi
Internal

PS C:\foo> $SwitchName = 'Internal'
```

In *step 17*, you create the new VM, and pipe it to `Start-VM` to start it:

```
PS C:\foo> New-VM -VHDPath $NanoVMPath -Name $NanoComputerName -Path $NanoVMFolder `
    -SwitchName $SwitchName -Generation 2 -Verbose |
    Start-VM
VERBOSE: New-VM will create a new virtual machine "NANO2".
```

There's more...

Creating a domain joined Nano Server simplifies Nano Server management. From any domain server with RSAT tools installed, you can manage this Nano Server VM using the Server Manager.

From the Server Manager, right click on **All Servers**, and choose **Add Servers**:

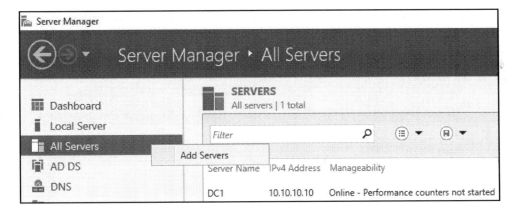

Enter the name of the server to manage in the **Name (CN)** field, click **Find Now**, then click the triangle(Add) button, then click **OK**:

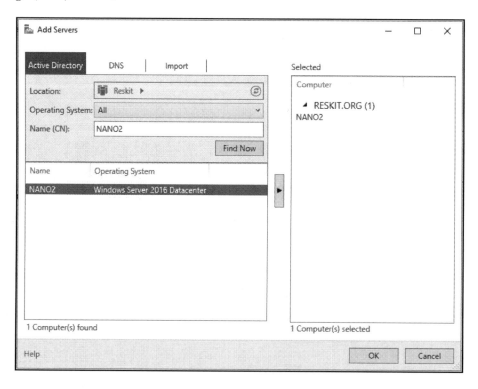

You can now manage your new Nano Server like any other Windows Server.

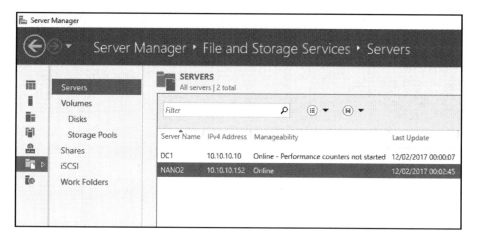

This recipe uses the `djoin` tool to create a domain blob file and passes the path in the `-DomainBlobPath` parameter. If the host server is a member of the domain, use the `-DomainName` and `-ComputerName` parameters instead.

To discover more about offline domain join, see the *Offline Domain Join (Djoin.exe) Step-by-Step Guide*: `https://technet.microsoft.com/en-us/library/offline-domain-join-djoin-step-by-step(WS.10).aspx`.

Nano packages can be installed either at deployment time or after deployment. You can add packages after deploying the Nano Server in either an offline or online mode. As a best practice, in keeping with Jeffrey Snover's cattle not pets server philosophy, it is usually better to start over and deploy a new Nano Server that's properly configured than to modify the configuration of an existing Nano server.

For more information on various deployment scenarios for Nano Server: `https://technet.microsoft.com/en-us/windows-server-docs/get-started/deploy-nano-server`.

There are Nano server packages you can download from GitHub. See the NanoServerPackage on GitHub site at: `https://github.com/OneGet/NanoServerPackage`.

3
Managing Windows Updates

In this chapter, we will cover the following recipes:

- Installing Windows Server Update Services
- Configuring WSUS update synchronization
- Configuring the Windows Update client
- Creating computer target groups
- Configuring WSUS auto-approvals
- Managing updates

Introduction

Windows administrators must manage Windows updates to ensure that the operating systems and software running on their computers are patched to resolve known bugs and are protected from known security vulnerabilities. **Windows Server Update Services (WSUS)** was a feature that was added in 2016 that enables the system administrators to manage the download and distribution of updates to the organization's computers.

Windows Software Update Services could be better named as Microsoft Software Update Services. WSUS manages not only Windows operating system updates but also updates for most Microsoft software products. Updates may apply to the Windows OS or any Microsoft software.

This chapter covers the installation and configuration of the WSUS server, the configuration of WSUS client computers, the management, approval, and installation of updates, and how to report on the status of the update installation.

Installing Windows Server Update Services

To use WSUS, you first install the Windows feature for update services, then perform the initial configuration. WSUS has dependencies that include the IIS web server and ASP.NET 4.6, so these dependencies are installed automatically if they are not present.

Getting ready

To follow this recipe, open a PowerShell session on server **WSUS1**. WSUS1 is a domain-joined server with internet access.

How to do it...

The steps for the recipe are as follows:

1. Install the Windows Update feature and tools, with `-Verbose` for additional feedback:

   ```
   Install-WindowsFeature -Name 'UpdateServices' `
   -IncludeManagementTools -Verbose
   ```

2. Review the features that are installed on your server, noting that not only has **Windows Software Update Services** been installed, but **Web Server (IIS)**, **ASP.Net 4.6**, and **Windows Internal Database** have as well:

   ```
   Get-WindowsFeature |
   Where-Object -FilterScript {($psitem.Installed)}
   ```

3. Create a folder for WSUS update content:

   ```
   $WSUSContentDir = 'C:\WSUS'
   New-Item -Path $WSUSContentDir -ItemType Directory
   ```

4. Perform post-installation configuration using `WsusUtil.exe`:

   ```
   & "$env:ProgramFiles\Update Services\Tools\WsusUtil.exe" `
       postinstall
                   CONTENT_DIR=$WSUSContentDir
   ```

5. Once configuration completes, the output includes a line stating `Log file is located at`, followed by a path to a `.tmp` file in the user's temp directory. Review this log file to see what was done in the configuration (adjust the file name as necessary):

```
Get-Content -Path "$env:TEMP\1tmp234.tmp"
```

6. View some websites on this machine, noting the WSUS website:

```
Get-Website
```

7. View the cmdlets in the `UpdateServices` module:

```
Get-Command -Module UpdateServices
```

8. Inspect the `TypeName` and properties of the object created with `Get-WsusServer`:

```
$WSUSServer = Get-WsusServer
$WSUSServer.GetType().Fullname
$WSUSServer | Select-Object -Property *
```

9. The object is of type `UpdateServer` in the `Microsoft.UpdateServices.Internal.BaseApi` namespace, and is the main object you interact with to manage WSUS from PowerShell. Inspect the methods of the object:

```
$WSUSServer | Get-Member -MemberType Method
```

10. Inspect some of the configuration values of the `UpdateServer` object:

```
$WSUSServer.GetConfiguration() |
    Select-Object -Property SyncFromMicrosoftUpdate,LogFilePath
```

11. Product categories are the various operating systems and programs for which updates are available. See what product categories are included by WSUS after the initial install:

```
$WSUSProducts = Get-WsusProduct -UpdateServer $WSUSServer
$WSUSProducts.Count
$WSUSProducts
```

12. Your `$WSUSServer` object contains a subscription object with properties and methods useful for managing the synchronization of updates. Access the `Subscription` object in the `$WSUSServer` object and inspect it, noting that it is also in the `Microsoft.UpdateServices.Internal.BaseApi` namespace:

```
$WSUSSubscription = $WSUSServer.GetSubscription()
$WSUSSubscription.GetType().Fullname
$WSUSSubscription | Select-Object -Property *
$WSUSSubscription | Get-Member -MemberType Method
```

13. Before you choose which product updates you want, you need to know what product categories are available. Get the latest categories of products available from Microsoft Update servers, and use a while loop to wait for completion:

```
$WSUSSubscription.StartSynchronizationForCategoryOnly()

Do {
Write-Output $WSUSSubscription.GetSynchronizationProgress()
Start-Sleep -Seconds 5
}
While ($WSUSSubscription.GetSynchronizationStatus() -ne `
'NotProcessing')
```

14. Once synchronization is complete, check the results of the synchronization:

```
$WSUSSubscription.GetLastSynchronizationInfo()
```

15. Again, review the categories of the products available:

```
$WSUSProducts = Get-WsusProduct -UpdateServer $WSUSServer
$WSUSProducts.Count
$WSUSProducts
```

How it works...

In *step 1*, you install WSUS by installing the `UpdateServices` feature. Note the link for additional configuration instructions:

```
PS C:\> Install-WindowsFeature -Name 'UpdateServices' -IncludeManagementTools -Verbose
VERBOSE: Installation started...
VERBOSE: Continue with installation?
VERBOSE: Prerequisite processing started...
VERBOSE: Prerequisite processing succeeded.

Success Restart Needed Exit Code      Feature Result
------- -------------- ---------      --------------
True    No             Success        {ASP.NET 4.6, HTTP Activation, Remote Serv...
WARNING: Additional configuration may be required. Review the article Managing WSUS Using PowerShell at TechNet Library (http://go.microsoft.
com/fwlink/?LinkId=235499) for more information on the recommended steps to perform WSUS installation using PowerShell.
VERBOSE: Installation succeeded.
```

In *step 2*, you review what has been installed on your server by piping the results of `Get-WindowsFeature` to `Where-Object`, which filters the object passed in the pipeline. This object is referenced by the `$PSItem` variable (or the shorter `$_`) variable, returning only those that are installed—that is, those whose `Installed` property is `$true`. Installing the `UpdateServices` Windows feature installed the prerequisites, such as `Web Server (IIS)`, automatically:

```
PS C:\> Get-WindowsFeature | Where-Object -FilterScript {$PSItem.Installed}

Display Name                                    Name                        Install State
------------                                    ----                        -------------
[X] File and Storage Services                   FileAndStorage-Services         Installed
    [X] File and iSCSI Services                 File-Services                   Installed
        [X] File Server                         FS-FileServer                   Installed
    [X] Storage Services                        Storage-Services                Installed
[X] Web Server (IIS)                            Web-Server                      Installed
    [X] Web Server                              Web-WebServer                   Installed
        [X] Common HTTP Features                Web-Common-Http                 Installed
            [X] Default Document                Web-Default-Doc                 Installed
            [X] Static Content                  Web-Static-Content              Installed
        [X] Performance                         Web-Performance                 Installed
            [X] Dynamic Content Compression     Web-Dyn-Compression             Installed
        [X] Security                            Web-Security                    Installed
            [X] Request Filtering               Web-Filtering                   Installed
            [X] Windows Authentication          Web-Windows-Auth                Installed
        [X] Application Development             Web-App-Dev                     Installed
            [X] .NET Extensibility 4.6          Web-Net-Ext45                   Installed
            [X] ASP.NET 4.6                     Web-Asp-Net45                   Installed
            [X] ISAPI Extensions                Web-ISAPI-Ext                   Installed
            [X] ISAPI Filters                   Web-ISAPI-Filter                Installed
    [X] Management Tools                        Web-Mgmt-Tools                  Installed
        [X] IIS Management Console              Web-Mgmt-Console                Installed
        [X] IIS 6 Management Compatibility      Web-Mgmt-Compat                 Installed
            [X] IIS 6 Metabase Compatibility    Web-Metabase                    Installed
            [X] IIS 6 Management Console        Web-Lgcy-Mgmt-Console           Installed
```

In *steps 3* and *4*, you create a folder to hold the WSUS update content, and then perform the post-installation configuration for WSUS:

```
PS C:\> $WSUSContentDir = 'C:\WSUS'
PS C:\> New-Item -Path 'C:\WSUS' -ItemType Directory


    Directory: C:\


Mode                LastWriteTime         Length Name
----                -------------         ------ ----
d-----        28/02/2017     17:31               WSUS

PS C:\> & "$env:ProgramFiles\Update Services\Tools\WsusUtil.exe"WsusUtil.exe" postinstall CONTENT_DIR=$WSUSContentDir
Log file is located at C:\Users\Administrator\AppData\Local\Temp\2\tmp1AF8.tmp
Post install is starting
Post install has successfully completed
```

In *step 5*, you review the log file written by `WsusUtil.exe` in the previous command. This
log is useful for troubleshooting or for verifying a successful configuration:

```
Get-Content C:\Users\Administrator\AppData\Local\Temp\2\tmp1AFB.tmp
2017-02-28 17:33:56  Postinstall started
2017-02-28 17:33:56  Detected role services: Api, UI, WidDatabase, Services
2017-02-28 17:33:56  Start: LoadSettingsFromParameters
2017-02-28 17:33:56  Content local is: True
2017-02-28 17:33:56  Content directory is: C:\WSUS
2017-02-28 17:33:56  SQL instname is:
2017-02-28 17:33:56  End: LoadSettingsFromParameters
2017-02-28 17:33:56  Start: Run
2017-02-28 17:33:56  Fetching WsusAdministratorsSid from registry store
2017-02-28 17:33:56  Value is S-1-5-21-564364657-173954772-155622663-1000
2017-02-28 17:33:56  Fetching WsusReportersSid from registry store
2017-02-28 17:33:56  Value is S-1-5-21-564364657-173954772-155622663-1001
2017-02-28 17:33:56  Configuring content directory...
2017-02-28 17:33:56  Configuring groups...
2017-02-28 17:33:56  Starting group configuration for WSUS Administrators...
2017-02-28 17:33:56  Found group in regsitry, attempting to use it...
2017-02-28 17:33:56  Writing group to registry...
2017-02-28 17:33:56  Finished group creation
2017-02-28 17:33:56  Starting group configuration for WSUS Reporters...
2017-02-28 17:33:56  Found group in regsitry, attempting to use it...
2017-02-28 17:33:56  Writing group to registry...
2017-02-28 17:33:56  Finished group creation
2017-02-28 17:33:56  Configuring permissions...
2017-02-28 17:33:56  Fetching content directory...
2017-02-28 17:33:56  Fetching ContentDir from registry store
2017-02-28 17:33:56  Value is C:\WSUS
2017-02-28 17:33:56  Fetching group SIDs...
```

In *step 6*, you view the websites on the WSUS1 server, noting the `WSUS` website, bound to
HTTP on port `8530`:

```
PS C:\> Get-Website

Name                ID    State    Physical Path                  Bindings
----                --    -----    -------------                  --------
Default Web Site    1     Started  %SystemDrive%\inetpub\wwwroot  http *:80:
WSUS                6668  Started  C:\Program Files\Update        http :8530:
Administration      363            Services\WebServices\Root\     https :8531: sslFlags=0
```

In *step 7*, you review the commands in the `UpdateServices` module, which you investigate
in later recipes:

```
PS C:\> Get-Command -Module UpdateServices

CommandType     Name                                Version     Source
-----------     ----                                -------     ------
Cmdlet          Add-WsusComputer                    2.0.0.0     UpdateServices
Cmdlet          Add-WsusDynamicCategory             2.0.0.0     UpdateServices
Cmdlet          Approve-WsusUpdate                  2.0.0.0     UpdateServices
Cmdlet          Deny-WsusUpdate                     2.0.0.0     UpdateServices
Cmdlet          Get-WsusClassification              2.0.0.0     UpdateServices
Cmdlet          Get-WsusComputer                    2.0.0.0     UpdateServices
Cmdlet          Get-WsusDynamicCategory             2.0.0.0     UpdateServices
Cmdlet          Get-WsusProduct                     2.0.0.0     UpdateServices
Cmdlet          Get-WsusServer                      2.0.0.0     UpdateServices
Cmdlet          Get-WsusUpdate                      2.0.0.0     UpdateServices
Cmdlet          Invoke-WsusServerCleanup            2.0.0.0     UpdateServices
Cmdlet          Remove-WsusDynamicCategory          2.0.0.0     UpdateServices
Cmdlet          Set-WsusClassification              2.0.0.0     UpdateServices
Cmdlet          Set-WsusDynamicCategory             2.0.0.0     UpdateServices
Cmdlet          Set-WsusProduct                     2.0.0.0     UpdateServices
Cmdlet          Set-WsusServerSynchronization       2.0.0.0     UpdateServices
```

In *steps 8* and *9*, you use `Get-WsusServer` to create your `$WSUSServer` object and inspect the properties and methods:

```
PS C:\> $WSUSServer = Get-WsusServer
$WSUSServer | Select *

WebServiceUrl                     : http://WSUS1:8530/ApiRemoting30/WebService.asmx
BypassApiRemoting                 : False
IsServerLocal                     : True
Name                              : WSUS1
Version                           : 10.0.14393.0
IsConnectionSecureForApiRemoting  : True
PortNumber                        : 8530
PreferredCulture                  : en
ServerName                        : WSUS1
UseSecureConnection               : False
ServerProtocolVersion             : 1.20

PS C:\> $WSUSServer | Get-Member -MemberType Method


   TypeName: Microsoft.UpdateServices.Internal.BaseApi.UpdateServer

Name                        MemberType   Definition
----                        ----------   ----------
AddDynamicCategories        Method       void AddDynamicCategories(System.Collections.Generic.IEnumera...
AddDynamicCategory          Method       void AddDynamicCategory(Microsoft.UpdateServices.Administrati...
CancelAllDownloads          Method       void CancelAllDownloads(), void IUpdateServer.CancelAllDownlo...
CreateComputerTargetGroup   Method       Microsoft.UpdateServices.Administration.IComputerTargetGroup ...
CreateDynamicCategory       Method       Microsoft.UpdateServices.Administration.IDynamicCategory Crea...
CreateInstallApprovalRule   Method       Microsoft.UpdateServices.Administration.IAutomaticUpdateAppro...
CreateObjRef                Method       System.Runtime.Remoting.ObjRef CreateObjRef(type requestedType)
DeleteDynamicCategory       Method       void DeleteDynamicCategory(string name, Microsoft.UpdateServi...
DeleteInstallApprovalRule   Method       void DeleteInstallApprovalRule(int ruleId), void IUpdateServe...
DeleteUpdate                Method       void DeleteUpdate(guid updateId), void IUpdateServer.DeleteUp...
Equals                      Method       bool Equals(System.Object obj)
ExpirePackage               Method       void ExpirePackage(Microsoft.UpdateServices.Administration.Up...
ExportPackageMetadata       Method       void ExportPackageMetadata(Microsoft.UpdateServices.Administr...
ExportUpdates               Method       void ExportUpdates(string packagePath, string logPath)
```

In *step 10*, you use `Get-WsusProduct` to create and view the default collection of available product categories. Sadly, this list is out of date:

```
PS C:\> $WSUSProducts = Get-WsusProduct
$WSUSProducts

Title                                    ID
-----                                    --
Exchange 2000 Server                     83a83e29-7d55-44a0-afed-aea164bc35e6
Exchange Server 2003                     3cf32f7c-d8ee-43f8-a0da-8b88a6f8af1a
Exchange                                 352f9494-d516-4b40-a21a-cd2416098982
Local Publisher                          7c40e8c2-01ae-47f5-9af2-6e75a0582518
Locally published packages               5cc25303-143f-40f3-a2ff-803a1db69955
Microsoft Corporation                    56309036-4c77-4dd9-951a-99ee9c246a94
Office 2003                              1403f223-a63f-f572-82ba-c92391218055
Office XP                                6248b8b1-ffeb-dbd9-887a-2acf53b09dfe
Office                                   477b856e-65c4-4473-b621-a8b230bb70d9
SQL Server                               7145181b-9556-4b11-b659-0162fa9df11f
SQL                                      0a4c6c73-8887-4d7f-9cbe-d08fa8fa9d1e
Windows 2000 family                      3b4b8621-726e-43a6-b43b-37d07ec7019f
Windows Server 2003 family               dbf57a08-0d5a-46ff-b30c-7715eb9498e9
Windows Server 2003, Datacenter Edition  7f44c2a7-bc36-470b-be3b-c01b6dc5dd4e
Windows XP 64-Bit Edition Version 2003   a4bedb1d-a809-4f63-9b49-3fe31967b6d0
Windows XP family                        558f4bc3-4827-49e1-accf-ea79fd72d4c9
Windows                                  6964aab4-c5b5-43bd-a17d-ffb4346a8e1d
```

In *step 11*, you make your product categories current by synchronizing from the Microsoft Update servers, using a while loop to wait for the synchronization to complete. This can take several minutes when doing this for the first time:

```
PS C:\> $WSUSSubscription.StartSynchronizationForCategoryOnly()

Do {
    Write-Output $WSUSSubscription.GetSynchronizationProgress()
    Start-Sleep -Seconds 5
}
While ($WSUSSubscription.GetSynchronizationStatus() -ne 'NotProcessing')

$WSUSSubscription.GetLastSynchronizationInfo() | Select-Object -Property

TotalItems ProcessedItems      Phase
---------- --------------      -----
     3139              0 Categories
     3139              5 Categories
```

```
     3139           3139 NotProcessing
```

In *step 12*, you check the result of the synchronization:

```
PS C:\> $WSUSSubscription.GetLastSynchronizationInfo()

Id                : 9d673e1d-1a48-4d99-9033-6df613089a87
StartTime         : 28/02/2017 19:58:25
EndTime           : 28/02/2017 20:08:15
StartedManually   : True
Result            : Succeeded
Error             : NotApplicable
ErrorText         :
UpdateErrors      : {}
```

There's more...

This recipe describes a single-server WSUS deployment, but WSUS also runs on multiple servers to support large networks, can synchronize from other WSUS servers on the network, can use web proxies, and can work with SQL Server instead of the Windows Internal Database.

> WSUS server requirements and deployment scenarios are documented on technet at
> https://technet.microsoft.com/en-us/library/hh852344(v=ws.11).as px#BKMK_1.1.

While the UpdateServices module is very useful, most of the tasks you perform in PowerShell to administer WSUS involve accessing the UpdateServer and Subscription objects directly.

MSDN contains documentation on these objects under the Microsoft.UpdateServices.Administration namespace.

> Explore the documentation at
> https://msdn.microsoft.com/en-us/library/windows/desktop/microso ft.updateservices.administration(v=vs.85).aspx to understand the available methods and properties.

Configuring WSUS update synchronization

Once you have completed the installation of WSUS, you configure the update services by choosing the product updates your organization requires, and which classifications of updates to download and make available to the computers on your network. Once these are defined, you can synchronize updates manually or on a schedule, and your WSUS server will download the updates for the product categories and update classifications you have selected from the Microsoft Update servers to make available to the computers on your network. The first synchronization can take hours, depending on your selections, and then subsequent synchronizations will pull only the newest updates since the last synchronization.

Getting ready

For this recipe, you will download updates for the following products to your WSUS server:

- Windows Server 2016
- SQL Server 2016
- Windows 10

You will also choose which types of windows updates to download. In this recipe, you will select the following classifications:

- Critical updates
- Definition updates
- Security updates
- Service packs
- Update roll-ups
- Updates

How to do it...

The steps for the recipe are as follows:

1. Locate the products you want to download to your WSUS server using `Get-WsusProduct` to search the product titles:

```
Get-WsusProduct -TitleIncludes 'Server 2016'
Get-WsusProduct -TitleIncludes 'Windows 10'
```

2. Build a list of software product titles you wish to include:

```
$ChosenProducts = @('Windows Server 2016',
            'Microsoft SQL Server 2016',
            'Windows 10' )
```

3. Assign the desired products to include in Windows Update:

```
Get-WsusProduct |
Where-Object {$PSItem.Product.Title -in $ChosenProducts} |
  Set-WsusProduct
```

4. Updates are classified into distinct categories; a view which classifications of updates are available:

```
Get-WsusClassification
```

5. Build a list of desired update classifications to make available on your WSUS server and view the list:

```
$ChosenClassifications = @('Critical Updates',
              'Definition Updates',
              'Security Updates',
              'Service Packs',
              'Update Rollups',
              'Updates')
$ChosenClassifications
```

6. Set our list of desired update classifications in WSUS:

```
Get-WsusClassification |
Where-Object {$PSItem.Classification.Title -in
$ChosenClassifications} |Set-WsusClassification
```

7. Create a variable for the Subscription object, start synchronizing Windows Updates, and watch the progress in a loop:

```
$WSUSServer = Get-WsusServer
$WSUSSubscription = $WSUSServer.GetSubscription()
#Start synchronizing available
updates$WSUSSubscription.StartSynchronization()
$IntervalSeconds = 1
#Wait for synchronizing to start
Do {
    Write-Output $WSUSSubscription.GetSynchronizationProgress()
    Start-Sleep -Seconds $IntervalSeconds
    }
```

```
While ($WSUSSubscription.GetSynchronizationStatus() -eq `
'NotProcessing')
#wait for all phases of process to end
Do {
    Write-Output $WSUSSubscription.GetSynchronizationProgress()
    Start-Sleep -Seconds $IntervalSeconds
    }
Until ($WSUSSubscription.GetSynchronizationStatus() -eq `
'NotProcessing')
```

8. Synchronization takes a few moments to start with, and then takes a long time to complete, depending on the number of products chosen. Wait for the process to start in a do-while loop, then wait for the process to complete in a do-until loop:

```
$WSUSSubscription.StartSynchronization()
 $IntervalSeconds = 1
#Wait for synchronizing to start
Do {
   Write-Output $WSUSSubscription.GetSynchronizationProgress()
   Start-Sleep -Seconds $IntervalSeconds
   }
While ($WSUSSubscription.GetSynchronizationStatus()
-eq ` 'NotProcessing')
#Wait for all phases of process to end
Do {
   Write-Output $WSUSSubscription.GetSynchronizationProgress()
   Start-Sleep -Seconds $IntervalSeconds
   }
 Until ($WSUSSubscription.GetSynchronizationStatus()
 -eq ` 'NotProcessing')
```

9. When the final loop is complete, check the results of the synchronization:

```
$WSUSSubscription.GetLastSynchronizationInfo()
```

10. Configure automatic synchronization to run once per day:

```
$WSUSSubscription = $WSUSServer.GetSubscription()
 $WSUSSubscription.SynchronizeAutomatically = $true
 $WSUSSubscription.NumberOfSynchronizationsPerDay = 1
 $WSUSSubscription.Save()
```

How it works...

In this recipe, you see how to configure WSUS updating.

In *step 1*, you use `Get-WsusProduct` to perform searches for products supported by Windows Update by title:

```
PS C:\> Get-WsusProduct -TitleIncludes 'Server 2016'
Get-WsusProduct -TitleIncludes 'Windows 10'

Title                                                              ID
-----                                                              --
Exchange Server 2016                                               49c3ddde-4df2-4534-980c-83f4e27b23b5
Microsoft SQL Server 2016                                          93f0b0bc-9c20-4ca5-b630-06eb4706a447
Windows Server 2016                                                569e8e8f-c6cd-42c8-92a3-efbb20a0f6f5
Windows 10 and later drivers                                       05eebf61-148b-43cf-80da-1c99ab0b8699
Windows 10 and later upgrade & servicing drivers                  34f268b4-7e2d-40e1-8966-8bb6ea3dad27
Windows 10 Anniversary Update and Later Servicing Drivers         bab879a4-c1af-4b52-9617-0f9ae1286fb6
Windows 10 Anniversary Update and Later Upgrade & Servicing Drivers 0ba562e6-a6ba-490d-bdce-93a770ba8d21
Windows 10 Anniversary Update Server and Later Servicing Drivers  3c54bb6c-66d1-4a79-884c-8a0c96fa20d1
Windows 10 Dynamic Update                                          e4b04398-adbd-4b69-93b9-477322331cd3
Windows 10 Feature On Demand                                       e104dd76-2895-41c4-9eb5-c483a61e9427
Windows 10 GDR-DU LP                                               6111a83d-7a6b-4a2c-a7c2-f222eebcabf4
Windows 10 GDR-DU                                                  abc45868-0c9c-4bc0-a36d-03d54113baf4
Windows 10 Language Interface Packs                                7d247b99-caa2-45e4-9c8f-6d60d0aae35c
Windows 10 Language Packs                                          fc7c9913-7a1e-4b30-b602-3c62fffd9b1a
Windows 10 LTSB                                                     d2085b71-5f1f-43a9-880d-ed159016d5c6
Windows 10                                                         a3c2375d-0c8a-42f9-bce0-28333e198407
```

In *step 2*, you store a list of the chosen product titles in a variable:

```
PS C:\>$ChosenProducts = @('Windows Server 2016'
        ,'Microsoft SQL Server 2016'
        ,'Windows 10' )
```

In *step 3*, you use `Get-WsusProduct` to retrieve the `WsusProduct` objects with titles that match your list and pipe these to `Set-WsusProduct` to enable the synchronization of updates for these products in WSUS:

```
PS C:\> Get-WsusProduct |
    Where-Object {$PSItem.Product.Title -in $ChosenProducts} |
        Set-WsusProduct
```

In *step 4*, you use `Get-WsusClassification` to review which classifications of updates are available from Windows Update:

```
PS C:\> Get-WsusClassification

Title               ID
-----               --
Applications        5c9376ab-8ce6-464a-b136-22113dd69801
Critical Updates    e6cf1350-c01b-414d-a61f-263d14d133b4
Definition Updates  e0789628-ce08-4437-be74-2495b842f43b
Driver Sets         77835c8d-62a7-41f5-82ad-f28d1af1e3b1
Drivers             ebfc1fc5-71a4-4f7b-9aca-3b9a503104a0
Feature Packs       b54e7d24-7add-428f-8b75-90a396fa584f
Security Updates    0fa1201d-4330-4fa8-8ae9-b877473b6441
Service Packs       68c5b0a3-d1a6-4553-ae49-01d3a7827828
Tools               b4832bd8-e735-4761-8daf-37f882276dab
Update Rollups      28bc880e-0592-4cbf-8f95-c79b17911d5f
Updates             cd5ffd1e-e932-4e3a-bf74-18bf0b1bbd83
Upgrades            3689bdc8-b205-4af4-8d4a-a63924c5e9d5
```

In *step 5*, you store the list of desired update classifications in a variable and view it:

```
PS C:\> $ChosenClassifications = @('Critical Updates'
    ,'Definition Updates'
    ,'Security Updates'
    ,'Service Packs'
    ,'Update Rollups'
    ,'Updates')
$ChosenClassifications
Critical Updates
Definition Updates
Security Updates
Service Packs
Update Rollups
Updates
```

In *step 6*, you use `Get-WsusClassification` to retrieve the `WsusClassification` objects with titles that match your list and pipe these to `Set-WsusClassification` to enable the synchronization of these categories of updates in WSUS:

```
PS C:\> Get-WsusClassification |
    Where-Object {$PSItem.Classification.Title -in $ChosenClassifications} |
        Set-WsusClassification
```

In *step 7*, you use `Get-WsusServer` to create a `$WSUSServer` object. Use the `GetSubscription` method on that object to create a `Subscription` object:

```
PS C:\>
$WSUSServer = Get-WsusServer
$WSUSSubscription = $WSUSServer.GetSubscription()
$WSUSSubscription.StartSynchronization()
```

In *step 8*, you use the `StartSynchronization` method on the `UpdateServer` object to begin synchronization, and use a `do-while` loop to wait for the synchronization process to start by waiting until the result of the `GetSynchronizationProgress` method changes from `NotProcessing`. The `$IntervalSeconds` variable determines the time between checks. You can increase this value to 60 to check every minute. Once started, you use a `do-until` loop to watch the value of the same method as it returns the progressive stages of the synchronization, and wait for the process to complete and return `NotProcessing` once more:

```
PS C:\> $WSUSServer = Get-WsusServer
$WSUSSubscription = $WSUSServer.GetSubscription()
$WSUSSubscription.StartSynchronization()
$IntervalSeconds = 1
#Wait for synchronizing to start
Do {
    Write-Output $WSUSSubscription.GetSynchronizationProgress()
    Start-Sleep -Seconds $IntervalSeconds
}
While ($WSUSSubscription.GetSynchronizationStatus() -eq 'NotProcessing')
#wait for all phases of process to end
Do {
    Write-Output $WSUSSubscription.GetSynchronizationProgress()
    Start-Sleep -Seconds $IntervalSeconds
}
Until ($WSUSSubscription.GetSynchronizationStatus() -eq 'NotProcessing')
#When complete, check result of synchronization
Start-Sleep $IntervalSeconds
$WSUSSubscription.GetLastSynchronizationInfo()

TotalItems ProcessedItems          Phase
---------- --------------          -----
         0              0 NotProcessing
         0              0    Categories
         0              0    Categories
        16              0       Updates
        16              2       Updates
         6              U
```

In *step 9*, you use the `GetLastSynchronizationInfo` method on the `Subscription` object to review the results of the synchronization:

In step 10, if you want your WSUS server to download updates from Microsoft automatically, you use the `Subscription` object to configure automatic synchronization once daily and save the configuration:

```
PS C:\> $WSUSSubscription.SynchronizeAutomatically = $true
$WSUSSubscription.NumberOfSynchronizationsPerDay = 1
$WSUSSubscription.Save()
```

There's more...

In *step 3*, you used the $PSItem mechanism to represent an object in the pipeline. You could have used $_ instead. Either works.

To understand the various categories of updates, review the descriptions available and refer to the online documentation:

```
$WSUSServer.GetUpdateClassifications() | Select-Object -Property
Title,Description
```

> Documentation of the terminology that defines the software updates is available at
> https://support.microsoft.com/en-us/help/824684/description-of-t
> he-standard-terminology-that-is-used-to-describe-microsoft-
> software-updates.

Configuring the Windows Update client

Windows computers download updates from Microsoft servers by default. To override this behavior, you can either configure the Windows Update client using GPO settings or manually update the registry of each client.

Getting ready

Run this recipe from WSUS1 with RSAT installed for working with Group Policy Objects.

```
$FeatureName = 'RSAT'
Install-WindowsFeature $FeatureName -IncludeAllSubFeature
```

How to do it...

The steps for the recipe are as follows:

1. Define and view the WSUS server URL using the properties returned from Get-WsusServer:

```
$WSUSServer = Get-WsusServer
$WSUSServerURL = "http{2}://{0}:{1}" -f `
                $WSUSServer.Name,
                $WSUSServer.PortNumber,
```

```
                    ('','s')[$WSUSServer.UseSecureConnection]
$WSUSServerURL
```

2. Create a **Group Policy Object** (GPO) and link it to your domain:

```
$PolicyName = "WSUS Client"
New-GPO -Name $PolicyName
New-GPLink -Name $PolicyName -Target "DC=RESKIT,DC=Org"
```

3. Add registry key settings to the group policy to assign the WSUS server:

```
$key = 'HKLM\Software\Policies\Microsoft\Windows\WindowsUpdate\AU'
Set-GPRegistryValue -Name $PolicyName `
                -Key $key `
                -ValueName 'UseWUServer'`
                -Type DWORD -Value 1
$key = 'HKLM\Software\Policies\Microsoft\Windows\WindowsUpdate\AU'
Set-GPRegistryValue -Name $PolicyName `
                -Key $key `
                -ValueName 'AUOptions' `
                -Type DWORD `
                -Value 2
$key = 'HKLM\Software\Policies\Microsoft\Windows\WindowsUpdate'
Set-GPRegistryValue -Name $PolicyName `
                -Key $key `
                -ValueName 'WUServer' `
                -Type String `
                -Value $WSUSServerURL
$key = 'HKLM\Software\Policies\Microsoft\Windows\WindowsUpdate'
Set-GPRegistryValue -Name $PolicyName `
                -Key $key `
                -ValueName 'WUStatusServer' `
                -Type String -Value $WSUSServerURL
```

4. Each PC on the domain then begins using the WSUS server once the group policy is updated. To make this happen immediately, on each PC, run the following commands:

```
Gpupdate /force
Wuauclt /detectnow
```

How it works...

In *step 1*, you use `Get-WsusServer` to create the `$WSUSServer` object and use its properties to define the Windows Update server URL in the `$WSUSServerURL` variable. This URL is not stored in a single property, so the variable is built with a format string using the `Name`, `PortNumber`, and `UseSecureConnection` properties.

The portion of code that inspects the `UseSecureConnection` property appends an *s* to the HTTP of the URL only if the `UseSecureConnection` property is set to `$true`. This statement is similar to an **if and only if (IIF)** function in other languages:

```
PS C:\> $WSUSServer = Get-WsusServer
$WSUSServerURL = "http{2}://{0}:{1}" -f
                    $WSUSServer.Name,
                    $WSUSServer.PortNumber,
                    ('','s')[$WSUSServer.UseSecureConnection]
$WSUSServerURL
http://WSUS1:8530
```

In *step 2*, you create a new group policy object entitled `WSUS Client` with `New-GPO` and link the group policy to the RESKIT.org domain with `New-GPLink`:

```
PS C:\> $PolicyName = "WSUS Client"
New-GPO -Name $PolicyName
New-GPLink -Name $PolicyName -Target "DC=RESKIT,DC=Org"
```

In *step 3*, you define four registry key values and associate them with the group policy object using `Set-GPRegistryValue`:

```
PS C:\>
$key = 'HKLM\Software\Policies\Microsoft\Windows\WindowsUpdate\AU'
Set-GPRegistryValue -Name $PolicyName
                    -Key $key
                    -ValueName 'UseWUServer'
                    -Type DWORD -Value 1
$key = 'HKLM\Software\Policies\Microsoft\Windows\WindowsUpdate\AU'
Set-GPRegistryValue -Name $PolicyName
                    -Key $key
                    -ValueName 'AUOptions'
                    -Type DWORD
                    -Value 2
$key = 'HKLM\Software\Policies\Microsoft\Windows\WindowsUpdate'
Set-GPRegistryValue -Name $PolicyName
                    -Key $key
                    -ValueName 'WUServer'
                    -Type String
                    -Value $WSUSServerURL
$key = 'HKLM\Software\Policies\Microsoft\Windows\WindowsUpdate'
Set-GPRegistryValue -Name $PolicyName
                    -Key $key
                    -ValueName 'WUStatusServer'
                    -Type String -Value $WSUSServerURL
```

In *step 4*, you force a group policy update on any Windows computer in the domain and start the Windows Update client immediately:

```
PS C:\Users\Administrator> Gpupdate /force
Wuauclt /detectnow
Updating policy...
```

There's more...

The AUOptions value's Value 2 is **Notify for download and notify for install**. For an explanation of the available options see
https://technet.microsoft.com/en-us/library/cc512630.aspx.

For non-domain computers to use your WSUS server, you may update their registry manually. The minimum settings are:

```
# Define registry settings
$key = 'HKLM:Software\Policies\Microsoft\Windows\WindowsUpdate'
New-ItemProperty -PropertyType String `
                -Path $key `
                -Name WUServer -Value 'http://WSUS1:8530'
New-ItemProperty -PropertyType String `
                -Path $key `
                -Name WUStatusServer -Value 'http://WSUS1:8530'
New-ItemProperty -PropertyType DWord `
                -Path "$key\AU" `
                -Name UseWUServer -Value 1
# Start looking for updates immediately
Wuauclt /detectnow
```

> You can get full documentation for WSUS registry keys at
> https://technet.microsoft.com/en-us/library/dd939844(v=ws.10).as
> px

Creating computer target groups

Different types of computers in your organization require different approaches to software updating. Employee workstations run software that application servers do not. Some servers are mission critical and must only be updated after you test the updates thoroughly. Sometimes critical updates are released that must be applied immediately, while some may be optional.

To manage the distribution software updates, define computer target groups on your WSUS server and assign computers these target groups. Each computer target group can be configured to apply updates differently. You create a target group for the Domain Controllers in this recipe.

Getting ready

WSUS must be installed and configured on the update server, and clients must be configured to use the WSUS server to apply this recipe.

How to do it...

The steps for the recipe are as follows:

1. Create a WSUS computer target group for the Domain Controllers:

```
$WSUSServer = Get-WsusServer
$WSUSServer.CreateComputerTargetGroup('Domain Controllers')
```

2. Add a computer to the new computer target group:

```
Get-WsusComputer -NameIncludes DC1 |
Add-WsusComputer -TargetGroupName 'Domain Controllers'
```

3. List the clients in the computer target group:

```
$DCGroup = $WSUSServer.GetComputerTargetGroups() |
Where-Object -Property Name -eq 'Domain Controllers'
  Get-WsusComputer |
Where-Object -Property ComputerTargetGroupIDs
  -Contains $DCGroup.Id
```

How it works...

In *step 1*, you create the $WSUSServer object and use the CreateComputerTargetGroup method to define a new computer target group on your WSUS server:

```
PS C:\> $WSUSServer = Get-WsusServer
$WSUSServer.CreateComputerTargetGroup("Domain Controllers")

UpdateServer                                            Id                                        Name
------------                                            --                                        ----
Microsoft.UpdateServices.Internal.BaseApi.UpdateServer b76f8295-29c3-468c-9eac-311cfb0d2d67 Domain Controllers
PS D:\Google Drive\Book Authoring\Content First Drafts\ch3\result logs>
```

In *step 2*, you use `Get-WsusComputer` to retrieve the `WsusComputer` object for the `DC1` server and pipe this object to the `Add-WsusComputer` method, which adds it to the new WSUS computer target group:

```
PS C:\> Get-WsusComputer -NameIncludes DC1 |
    Add-WsusComputer -TargetGroupName "Domain Controllers"
```

In *step 3*, you use the `GetComputerTargetGroups` method of the `$WSUSServer` object, filtered with `Where-Object`, to retrieve the new `'Domain Controllers'` computer target group, and store it in the variable `$DCGroup`:

```
PS C:\> $DCGroup = $WSUSServer.GetComputerTargetGroups() |
    Where-Object Name -eq "Domain Controllers"
```

In *step 4*, you use `Get-WsusComputer` and inspect the `ComputerTargetGroupIDs` property, looking for a match to the `$DCGroup.Id` property from the previous step to show that the `DC1` computer is a member of this `ComputerTargetGroup`:

```
PS C:\> Get-WsusComputer |
    Where-Object ComputerTargetGroupIDs -Contains $DCGroup.Id

Computer        IP Address   Operating System                Last Status Report
--------        ----------   ----------------                ------------------
dc1.reskit.org 10.10.10.10 Windows Server 2016 Datacenter 03/03/2017 22:38:47
```

There's more...

Rather than assigning computers to computer target groups on the WSUS server, you can assign computers to computer target groups in WSUS using the Group Policy with a feature called client-side targeting.

A group policy object is created and linked to the OU that contains the computers. This group policy object is then associated with one or more WSUS computer target groups. When the computer connects to the WSUS server, it declares these groups to the server and receives the updates assigned to those groups.

To learn more, see the client-side documentation at
https://technet.microsoft.com/en-us/library/dd252762.aspx

Configuring WSUS auto-approvals

WSUS organizes Windows updates under different classifications. You can view these classifications by using the `Get-WsusClassification` cmdlet. Two particularly important classifications you should check regularly are `Critical Updates` and `Definition Updates`. The `Critical Updates` classification includes updates that address severe security flaws and zero-day vulnerabilities. The `Definition Updates` classification includes definition files for Windows Defender to identify and remove malware.

These two classifications are important enough to approve them automatically. Auto-approval ensures WSUS installs these updates on client computers as soon as possible. In this recipe, you will create an auto-approval rule for these updates.

Getting ready

Run this recipe on the WSUS1 server.

How to do it...

Run this recipe to configure auto-approval of WSUS update:

1. Create the auto-approval rule:

```
$WSUSServer = Get-WsusServer
$ApprovalRule = $WSUSServer.CreateInstallApprovalRule('Critical
Updates')
```

2. Define a deadline for the rule:

```
$type = 'Microsoft.UpdateServices.Administration.
          AutomaticUpdateApprovalDeadline'
$RuleDeadLine = New-Object -Typename $type
$RuleDeadLine.DayOffset = 3
$RuleDeadLine.MinutesAfterMidnight = 180
$ApprovalRule.Deadline = $RuleDeadLine
```

3. Add update classifications to the rule:

```
$UpdateClassification = ` $ApprovalRule.
                          GetUpdateClassifications()
$UpdateClassification.Add(($WSUSServer.
                          GetUpdateClassifications() |
```

```
        Where-Object -Property Title -eq 'Critical Updates'))
    $UpdateClassification.Add(($WSUSServer.
                            GetUpdateClassifications() |
        Where-Object -Property Title -eq 'Definition Updates'))
    $ApprovalRule.SetUpdateClassifications($UpdateClassification)
```

4. Assign the rule to a computer target group:

```
    $TargetGroups = New-Object `
      Microsoft.UpdateServices.Administration.
              ComputerTargetGroupCollection
    $TargetGroups.Add(($WSUSServer.GetComputerTargetGroups() |
      Where-Object -Property Name -eq "Domain Controllers"))
  $ApprovalRule.SetComputerTargetGroups($TargetGroups)
```

5. Enable and save the rule:

```
    $ApprovalRule.Enabled = $true
    $ApprovalRule.Save()
```

How it works...

In *step 1*, you create the $WSUSServer object using Get-WsusServer, then use the CreateInstallApprovalRule method to create a new AutomaticUpdateApprovalRule object, and store them in the $ApprovalRule variable:

```
PS C:\> $WSUSServer = Get-WsusServer
$ApprovalRule = $WSUSServer.CreateInstallApprovalRule("Critical Updates")
```

In *step 2*, you define $RuleDeadline, a new AutomaticUpdateApprovalDeadline object, configured to install automatically with a three-day grace period after becoming available and the scheduled installation time of 3 am. You associate this deadline object with your approval rule:

```
PS C:\> # Define a deadline:
$RuleDeadLine = New-Object
Microsoft.UpdateServices.Administration.AutomaticUpdateApprovalDeadline
$RuleDeadLine.DayOffset = 3
$RuleDeadLine.MinutesAfterMidnight = 180
$ApprovalRule.Deadline = $RuleDeadLine
```

In *step 3*, you use the `GetUpdateClassifications` method of the `$ApprovalRule` object and store the resulting object in the `$UpdateClassification` variable. The object initially contains no update classifications. You then use the `Add` method of this object to add in the two desired update classifications filtered by `Title` and associate these with the `$ApprovalRule` object using the `SetUpdateClassifications` method:

```
PS C:\> $UpdateClassification = $ApprovalRule.GetUpdateClassifications()
$UpdateClassification.Add(($WSUSServer.GetUpdateClassifications() |
    Where-Object -Property Title -eq 'Critical Updates'))
$UpdateClassification.Add(($WSUSServer.GetUpdateClassifications() |
    Where-Object -Property Title -eq 'Definition Updates'))
$ApprovalRule.SetUpdateClassifications($UpdateClassification)
0
1
```

In *step 4*, you define `$TargetGroups` and set it to contain the computer target group named `'Domain Controllers'` using the `GetComputerTargetGroups` method of `$WSUSServer`, filtered by `Where-Object`. You then associate `$TargetGroups` with the new `$ApprovalRule` using the `SetComputerTargetGroups` method:

```
PS C:\> $TargetGroups = New-Object `
Microsoft.UpdateServices.Administration.ComputerTargetGroupCollection
$TargetGroups.Add(($WSUSServer.GetComputerTargetGroups() |
    Where-Object -Property Name -eq "Domain Controllers"))
$ApprovalRule.SetComputerTargetGroups($TargetGroups)
0
```

In *step 5*, you set the Enabled property of the `$ApprovalRule` object, and use the `Save` method to complete the configuration:

```
PS C:\> $ApprovalRule.Enabled = $true
$ApprovalRule.Save()
```

There's more...

You can view your approved updates using the `GetUpdates` method of the `$WSUSServer` object and filter on the `IsApproved` property:

```
$WSUSServer.GetUpdates() |
    Where-Object -Property IsApproved -eq $true |
        Select-Object -Property Title, CreationDate, `
UpdateClassificationTitle
```

Managing updates

The WSUS administrator performs several tasks to manage update distribution. These tasks begin with the awareness of which updates are available, approved, installed or marked to be installed for each computer target group. For the available updates, the administrator must approve or reject the updates to control which updates are made available. This recipe covers listing installed updates, listing available updates, approving updates, and declining updates.

Getting ready

In this recipe, you manage updates using PowerShell. You should open a PowerShell session on WSUS1 to perform this recipe.

How to do it...

In this recipe you manage WSUS updates:

1. Open a PowerShell session, and view the overall status of all Windows updates on WSUS1:

```
$WSUSServer = Get-WsusServer
$WSUSServer.GetStatus()
```

2. View the computer targets:

```
$WSUSServer.GetComputerTargets()
```

3. View the installed updates on DC1 using Get-Hotfix and Get-SilWindowsUpdate:

```
Get-HotFix -ComputerName DC1
$CimSession = New-CimSession -ComputerName DC1
Get-SilWindowsUpdate -CimSession $CimSession
$CimSession | Remove-CimSession
```

4. Search the WSUS server for updates with titles containing *Windows Server 2016* that are classified as security updates, newest to oldest, and store them in a variable. Examine the variable using `Get-Member`, reviewing the properties and methods of the `Microsoft.UpdateServices.Internal.BaseApi.Update` object:

```
$SecurityUpdates = $WSUSServer.SearchUpdates( `
"Windows Server 2016") |
Where-Object -Property UpdateClassificationTitle `
-eq 'Security Updates' |
    Sort-Object -Property CreationDate -Descending
$SecurityUpdates | Get-Member
```

5. View the matching updates:

```
$SecurityUpdates |
    Select-Object -Property CreationDate, Title
```

6. Select one of the updates to approve based on the KB article ID:

```
$SelectedUpdate = $SecurityUpdates |
Where-Object -Property KnowledgebaseArticles -eq 4019472
```

7. Define the computer target group where you will approve this update:

```
$DCTargetGroup = $WSUSServer.GetComputerTargetGroups() |
    Where-Object -Property Name -eq 'Domain Controllers'
```

8. Approve the update for installation in the target group:

```
$SelectedUpdate.Approve('Install',$DCTargetGroup)
```

9. Select one of the updates to decline based on the KB article ID:

```
$DeclinedUpdate = $SecurityUpdates |
  Where-Object -Property KnowledgebaseArticles -eq 4020821
```

10. Decline the update:

```
$DeclinedUpdate.Decline($DCTargetGroup)
```

How it works...

In *step 1*, you create the `$WSUSServer` object using `Get-WsusServer` and use the `GetStatus` method to view the status of Windows updates on the WSUS server:

```
PS C:\> $WSUSServer = Get-WsusServer

#See overall update status
$WSUSServer.GetStatus()

UpdateCount        DeclinedUpdateCount  ApprovedUpdateCount  NotApprovedUpdateCount  ComputerTargetCount
-----------        -------------------  -------------------  ----------------------  -------------------
10448              82                   24                   10342                   6
```

In *step 2*, you review the computer targets configured in WSUS with the `GetComputerTargets` method:

```
PS C:\> $WSUSServer.GetComputerTargets()

FullDomainName      IPAddress        ClientVersion       LastSyncTime        OSDescription
--------------      ---------        -------------       ------------        -------------
dc1.reskit.org      10.10.10.10      10.0.14393.594      12/05/2017 01:31:17 Windows Server 2016 Datacenter
dg                  10.10.10.254     10.0.14393.594      12/05/2017 04:34:07 Windows Server 2016 Datacenter
sg-cli1.reskit.org  10.10.10.141     10.0.10240.1...     02/04/2017 19:49:01 Windows 10 Pro
wsus1.reskit.org    ::1              10.0.14393.594      12/05/2017 03:52:08 Windows Server 2016 Datacenter
srv1.reskit.org     10.10.10.50      10.0.14393.594      12/05/2017 01:29:02 Windows Server 2016 Datacenter
srv2.reskit.org     10.10.10.51      10.0.14393.0        13/03/2017 01:51:16 Windows Server 2016 Datacenter
```

In *step 3*, you use two different methods to view the installed updates. The first is `Get-Hotfix`, and the second is `Get-SilWindowsUpdate`, which is one of the `SoftwareInventoryLogging` module cmdlets introduced in PowerShell version 5. These cmdlets use CIM sessions to connect to computers and gather inventory information:

```
PS C:\> Get-HotFix -ComputerName DC1

$CimSession = New-CimSession DC1
Get-SilWindowsUpdate -CimSession ($CimSession) | Format-Table -AutoSize
$CimSession | Remove-CimSession


Source     Description       HotFixID      InstalledBy            InstalledOn
------     -----------       --------      -----------            -----------
DC1        Update            KB3192137     NT AUTHORITY\SYSTEM    12/09/2016
DC1        Update            KB3211320     NT AUTHORITY\SYSTEM    07/03/2017
DC1        Update            KB4013418     NT AUTHORITY\SYSTEM    19/03/2017
DC1        Security Update   KB3213986     NT AUTHORITY\SYSTEM    07/03/2017


ID         InstallDate PSComputerName
--         ----------- --------------
KB3192137  12/09/2016  DC1
KB3211320  07/03/2017  DC1
KB4013418  19/03/2017  DC1
KB3213986  07/03/2017  DC1
```

In *step 4*, you use the `SearchUpdates` method on the `$WSUSServer` to search the available updates by title, then use `Where-Object` to filter on the `UpdateClassificationTitle` property for security updates and then sort them from newest to oldest. You then use `Get-Member` to examine the `Update` object, noting the many methods and properties:

```
PS C:\> $SecurityUpdates = $WSUSServer.SearchUpdates("Windows Server 2016") |
    Where-Object -Property UpdateClassificationTitle -EQ 'Security Updates' |
        Sort-Object -Property CreationDate -Descending

$SecurityUpdates | Get-Member


   TypeName: Microsoft.UpdateServices.Internal.BaseApi.Update

Name                              MemberType   Definition
----                              ----------   ----------
AcceptLicenseAgreement            Method       void AcceptLicenseAgreement(), void IUpdate.AcceptLicenseAgreement()
Approve                           Method       Microsoft.UpdateServices.Administration.IUpdateApproval Approve(Microsoft.UpdateServices.Administr...
ApproveForOptionalInstall         Method       Microsoft.UpdateServices.Administration.IUpdateApproval ApproveForOptionalInstall(Microsoft.Update...
CancelDownload                    Method       void CancelDownload(), void IUpdate.CancelDownload()
CreateObjRef                      Method       System.Runtime.Remoting.ObjRef CreateObjRef(type requestedType)
Decline                           Method       void Decline(), void Decline(bool failIfReplica), void IUpdate.Decline()
Equals                            Method       bool Equals(System.Object obj)
ExpirePackage                     Method       void ExpirePackage(), void IUpdate.ExpirePackage()
ExportPackageMetadata             Method       void ExportPackageMetadata(string fileName), void IUpdate.ExportPackageMetadata(string fileName)
GetCh...       PreviousRevision   M...         Microsoft.UpdateServices.A...    on.RevisionChanges GetChange...    Revision(), Microsof...
                                               GetHashCode()
...
...cyName                                      ...;}
MsrcSeverity                      Property     Mic...          ices.Administration.Msr...        verity {get;set;}
ProductFamilyTitles               Property     System.Collections.Specialized.StringCollection ProductFamilyTitles {get;}
ProductTitles                     Property     System.Collections.Specialized.StringCollection ProductTitles {get;}
PublicationState                  Property     Microsoft.UpdateServices.Administration.PublicationState PublicationState {get;set;}
ReleaseNotes                      Property     string ReleaseNotes {get;set;}
RequiresLicenseAgreementAcceptance Property    bool RequiresLicenseAgreementAcceptance {get;set;}
SecurityBulletins                 Property     System.Collections.Specialized.StringCollection SecurityBulletins {get;}
```

In *step 5*, you view the security updates that matched your search. Note that each displays a knowledge base (KB) ID that is useful for identifying and researching individual updates:

```
PS C:\> $SecurityUpdates | Select CreationDate, Title

CreationDate          Title
------------          -----
09/05/2017 18:45:42   Cumulative Update for Windows Server 2016 Technical Preview 5 for x64-based Systems (KB3207296)
09/05/2017 18:45:10   Cumulative Update for Windows Server 2016 Technical Preview 5 for x64-based Systems (KB3195038)
09/05/2017 18:43:48   Security Update for Adobe Flash Player for Windows Server 2016 Technical Preview 5 (for x64-based Systems) (KB3209498)
09/05/2017 18:43:38   Security Update for Adobe Flash Player for Windows Server 2016 Technical Preview 5 (for x64-based Systems) (KB3202790)
09/05/2017 18:43:27   Security Update for Adobe Flash Player for Windows Server 2016 Technical Preview 5 (for x64-based Systems) (KB3194343)
09/05/2017 18:43:25   Security Update for Adobe Flash Player for Windows Server 2016 Technical Preview 5 (for x64-based Systems) (KB3201860)
09/05/2017 17:00:05   2017-05 Security Update for Adobe Flash Player for Windows Server 2016 for x64-based Systems (KB4020821)
09/05/2017 17:00:03   2017-05 Cumulative Update for Windows Server 2016 for x64-based Systems (KB4019472)
09/05/2017 06:54:45   Cumulative Update for Windows Server 2016 Technical Preview 5 for x64-based Systems (KB3199442)
17/04/2017 18:25:47   Security Update for Adobe Flash Player for Windows Server 2016 Technical Preview 5 (KB3188128)
17/04/2017 18:25:17   Security Update for Adobe Flash Player for Windows Server 2016 Technical Preview 4 for x64-based Systems (KB3188128)
17/04/2017 18:24:57   Security Update for Windows Server 2016 Technical Preview 5 (KB3172729)
17/04/2017 18:23:09   Cumulative Update for Windows Server 2016 Technical Preview 3 (KB3097877)
17/04/2017 17:07:23   Cumulative Update for Windows Server 2016 Technical Preview 5 for x64-based Systems (KB3172989)
17/04/2017 17:03:59   Cumulative Update for Windows Server 2016 Technical Preview 5 for x64-based Systems (KB3188966)
17/04/2017 16:57:40   Cumulative Update for Windows Server 2016 for x64-based Systems (KB3193494)
11/04/2017 17:00:05   Security Update for Adobe Flash Player for Windows Server 2016 (for x64-based Systems) (KB4018483)
11/04/2017 17:00:03   Cumulative Update for Windows Server 2016 for x64-based Systems (KB4015217)
03/04/2017 18:27:04   Cumulative Update for Windows Server 2016 for x64-based Systems (KB3176495)
03/04/2017 18:26:21   Cumulative Update for Windows Server 2016 Technical Preview 5 for x64-based Systems (KB3176494)
03/04/2017 17:46:22   Cumulative Update for Windows Server 2016 Technical Preview 5 for x64-based Systems (KB3163016)
14/03/2017 17:00:05   Security Update for Adobe Flash Player for Windows Server 2016 (for x64-based Systems) (KB4014329)
13/12/2016 18:00:01   Security Update for Adobe Flash Player for Windows Server 2016 Technical Preview 5 (for x64-based Systems) (KB3209498)
13/12/2016 18:00:01   Cumulative Update for Windows Server 2016 Technical Preview 5 for x64-based Systems (KB3207296)
08/11/2016 18:00:00   Security Update for Windows Server 2016 Technical Preview 5 (KB3198389)
13/09/2016 17:00:00   Security Update for Adobe Flash Player for Windows Server 2016 Technical Preview 4 for x64-based Systems (KB3188128)
24/08/2016 17:00:00   Security Update for Windows Server 2016 Technical Preview 5 (KB3172729)
13/07/2016 21:00:00   Cumulative Update for Windows Server 2016 Technical Preview 5 for x64-based Systems (KB3172989)
10/11/2015 18:00:00   Cumulative Update for Windows Server 2016 Technical Preview 3 (KB3097877)
```

In *step 6*, you filter the selected updates for a single update that you wish to approve using `Where-Object` to match on the `KnowledgebaseArticles` property:

```
$SelectedUpdate = $SecurityUpdates |
    Where-Object -Property KnowledgebaseArticles -EQ 4019472
```

In *step 7*, you define the computer target group for the `Domain Controllers` using the `GetComputerTargetGroups` method of the `$WSUSServer` object, filtered by `Where-Object`:

```
$DCTargetGroup = $WSUSServer.GetComputerTargetGroups() |
    Where-Object -Property Name -eq 'Domain Controllers'
```

In *step 8*, you use the `Approve` method of the `$SelectedUpdate` object-which takes two parameters:, an `UpdateApprovalAction` and a `TargetGroup`-and approve the selected update for the `Domain Controllers` target group:

```
PS C:\> $SelectedUpdate.Approve("Install",$DCTargetGroup)

UpdateTitle          GoLiveTime           Deadline             AdministratorName     TargetGroup
-----------          ----------           --------             -----------------     -----------
2017-05 Cumulativ... 12/05/2017 18:48:34  31/12/9999 23:59:59  RESKIT\Administrator  Domain Controllers
```

In *step 9*, you select an update to decline, using `Where-Object` to filter the selection to a single update using the `KnowledgebaseArticles` property:

```
PS C:\> $DeclinedUpdate = $SecurityUpdates |
    Where-Object -Property KnowledgebaseArticles -EQ 4020821
```

In *step 10*, you use the `Decline` method of the update object, and provide the `TargetGroup` object as a parameter to decline this update for the `Domain Controllers` target group computers:

```
PS C:\> $DeclinedUpdate.Decline($DCTargetGroup)
```

There's more...

Two community PowerShell modules available via the `Install-Module` or the PowerShell Gallery website are useful for working with Windows Update.

`PoshWSUS` simplifies the management of the WSUS server, wrapping up the interaction with the various objects and enumerations with easy-to-use cmdlets. For example, this command would decline updates for all non-English LanguagePack updates (note the `-WhatIf` parameter support):

```
Get-PSWSUSUpdate -IncludeText 'LanguagePack' -ExcludeText 'English' Deny-
PSWSUSUpdate -WhatIf
```

`PSWindowsUpdate` enables the management and installation of Windows updates provided from a WSUS server, Windows Update, or Microsoft Update. For example, this command will install the newly approved update on DC1 and reboot if required:

```
Get-WUInstall -AcceptAll -AutoReboot
```

4
Managing Printers

In this chapter, we cover the following recipes:

- Installing and sharing printers
- Publishing a printer
- Changing the spool directory
- Changing printer drivers
- Printing a test page on a printer
- Reporting on printer security
- Modifying printer security
- Deploying shared printers
- Enabling Branch Office Direct Printing
- Creating a printer pool
- Reporting on printer usage

Introduction

Printing is a feature that has been incorporated into Windows operating systems, and has evolved over the years. Printing in Windows Server 2016 has not changed much from earlier versions, and provides you with the ability to create print servers that you can share with users in your organization.

With Windows printing, the physical device that renders output onto paper is a print device. A printer is, in effect, the queue for one or more print devices. A print server can support multiple printers (as can individual client workstations). The print device has a driver that converts your documents to the printed form on a given print device. Some drivers come with Windows—others you need to obtain from the printer vendor.

You use both the printers—that is, the printing device and printer port—when you create a new printer on your print server. In many organizations, printers are often stand-alone devices with just a TCP/IP connection. You can also connect a print device to your server using the server's local USB, parallel, or serial port.

Microsoft did not change the basic print architecture in Windows Server 2016. Windows Server 2012 introduced a new driver architecture, version 4, which Windows Server 2016 supports. This driver model enables two different driver types: printer class drivers and model-specific drivers. The former provides a single driver for a variety of specific printing device models, whereas latter is used for just a single model. Increasingly, print device manufacturers are implementing more generic drivers that can simplify organizational roll-out for printer drivers.

Another change in Windows Server 2012, carried over into Windows Server 2016, is that you no longer use the print server to distribute printer drivers. Clients can use the point and print feature to send print jobs to the server. Additionally, you can use tools such as the System Center Configuration Manager or Group Policies to distribute print drivers to clients.

This chapter covers installing, managing, and updating printers, print drivers, and printer ports on a Windows Server 2016 print server. You may find that some of the administration tools used in this chapter are not available on Windows Server Core. To enable full management, you need to have the full GUI (including the *Desktop Experience* for any GUI utilities).

Installing and sharing printers

The first step in creating a print server for your organization involves installing the print server feature, then installing printer ports and printer drivers, and finally creating printers.

Getting ready

In this recipe, you are going to set up a print server, PSRV, and then set up a TCP/IP printer for the Sales Group. This process involves installing the print server feature in Windows Server 2016. Then you create a port for a new printer and install the driver for the Sales Group group's new printer, an NEC Color MultiWriter. Finally, you create and then share the printer. Once complete, you can review what you have accomplished.

How to do it...

1. Install the `Print-Server` feature on `PSRV`, along with the print management tools:

```
Install-WindowsFeature -Name Print-Server,
                            RSAT-Print-Services
```

2. Add a `PrinterPort` for a new printer:

```
Add-PrinterPort -Name Sales_Color `
    -PrinterHostAddress 10.10.10.61
```

3. Add a `PrinterDriver` for this printer server:

```
Add-PrinterDriver -Name
  'NEC Color MultiWriter Class Driver'
                -PrinterEnvironment 'Windows x64'
```

4. Add the printer:

```
Add-Printer -Name SGCP1 `
        -DriverName 'NEC Color MultiWriter
                                Class Driver' `
        -Portname 'Sales_Color'
```

5. Share the printer:

```
Set-Printer -Name SGCP1 -Shared $True
```

6. Review what you have done:

```
Get-PrinterPort -Name SGCP1 |
    Format-Table -Property Name, Description,
                    PrinterHostAddress, PortNumber
                    -Autosize
Get-PrinterDriver -Name NEC* |
    Format-Table -Property Name, Manufacturer,
                    DriverVersion, PrinterEnvironment
 Get-Printer -ComputerName PSRV -Name SGCP1 |
        Format-Table -Property Name, ComputerName,
        Type, PortName, Location, Shared
```

How it works...

In *step 1*, you add the `Print-Server` feature and the management tools to `PSRV`. To do this, open a PowerShell window on the `PSRV` host and install the `Print-Server` feature. You can either do this directly or remotely, and you can use the PowerShell console or the ISE directly from the `Print-Server`. The output looks like this:

```
PS C:\> Install-WindowsFeature -Name Print-Server,
                               RSAT-Print-Services

Success Restart Needed Exit Code     Feature Result
------- -------------- ---------     --------------
True    No             Success       {Print Server, Print and Document Services...
```

In *step 2*, you add a new port for the color printer you wish to add. In *step 3*, you add the `PrinterDriver` for the printer (in our case, an `NEC Color MultiWriter Class Driver`). In *step 4*, you add a new printer, `SGCP1`, to the system. You use the `PrinterDriver` and printer port you created for this new printer. In *step 5*, you share the printer. A shared printer enables users to connect to the printer and print to the associated print device. Windows bases permissions for the printer on the **Discretionary Access Control List (DACL)**, which you set up when you create the printer. Another recipe later in this chapter shows you how you can view and update the `DACL` for a printer. There is no output for *step 2*, *step 3*, *step 4*, and *step 5*.

Once you have created and shared the printer, you can view the results. In *step 6*, you view the printer port, printer driver, and printer. Note that the printer is shared in the following output:

```
PS C:\> Get-PrinterPort -Name Sales_Color |
    Format-Table -Property Name, Description, PrinterHostAddress, Portnumber

Name        Description        PrinterHostAddress Portnumber
----        -----------        ------------------ ----------
Sales_Color Standard TCP/IP Port 10.10.10.61             9100


# Look at printer drivers added
PS C:\> Get-PrinterDriver -Name NEC* |
    Format-Table -Property Name, Manufacturer, DriverVersion, PrinterEnvironment

Name                               Manufacturer   DriverVersion PrinterEnvironment
----                               ------------   ------------- ------------------
NEC Color MultiWriter Class Driver NEC            2814750710366208 Windows x64


# Get Printer Details
PS C:\> Get-Printer -ComputerName Psrv  -Name SGCP1 |
        Format-Table -Property Name, ComputerName, Type, PortName,
                      Location, Published, Shared

Name  ComputerName Type PortName    Location Published Shared
----  ------------ ---- --------    -------- --------- ------
SGCP1 Psrv         Local Sales_Color          False     True
```

Publishing a printer

Once you create and share a printer, as shown in the previous recipe, you can additionally publish it to the Active Directory. When you publish a printer, you can also specify a location for the printer that enables your users to search for published printers based on location and capabilities. End users can search AD to find printers and to find the printers near to them. In this recipe, you publish the printer you created in the previous recipe and examine the results.

Getting ready

In this recipe, you publish the printer that you created in the preceding recipe, *Installing and sharing printers*.

How to do it...

1. Get the printer to publish and store the returned object in $Printer:

   ```
   $Printer = Get-Printer -Name SGCP1
   ```

2. Observe the publication status:

   ```
   $Printer | Format-Table -Property Name, Published
   ```

3. Publish the printer to AD:

   ```
   $Printer | Set-Printer -Published $true `
                          -Location '10th floor 10E4'
   ```

4. View the updated publication status:

   ```
   Get-Printer -Name SGCP1 |
       Format-Table -Property Name, Published, Location
   ```

How it works...

In *step 1*, you get the printer details for the `Sales Group` group's printer, `SGCP1`, and store it in `$Printer`. There is no output from this step.

In *step 2*, you output the printer details to see that you have not yet published the printer:

```
PS C:\> $Printer | Format-Table -Property Name, Published


Name  Published
----  ---------
SGCP1      True
```

In *step 3*, you publish the printer by piping the `Printer` object to `Set-Printer`, specifying that you wish to publish the printer. In *step 4*, you can see the results of publishing the printer:

```
PS C:\> Get-Printer -Name SGCP1 |
           Format-Table -Property Name, Published, Location


Name   Published Location
----   --------- --------
SGCP1       True 10th floor 10E4
```

As you can see, you have now published the printer and set the location to the `10th floor`, area `10E4`.

There's more...

When you publish a printer to the Active Directory, users need to be able to find it. One way is to use the **Find Printers** dialog to search for published printers.

To use this (in Windows Server 2016 and Windows 10), you click **Start | Settings | Devices | Printers & scanners** to bring up the **Add printers & scanners** dialog. From this dialog box, click **Add a printer or scanner**. Wait until the searching is complete, then click on **The printer that I want isn't listed**, which brings up the **Add Printer** dialog:

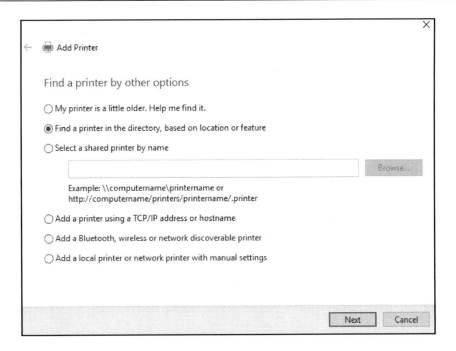

Select **Find a printer in the directory, based on location or feature**, then click **Next**. You now see the **Find Printers** dialog:

You, or your users, can use the **Printers** tab to search for printers by **Name**, **Location**, and **Model**, and use the **Features** tab to search for printers with specific features (for example, the ability to print in color).

Changing the spool directory

By default, Windows uses the folder `%SystemRoot%\System32\spool\PRINTERS` to store spooled jobs. On our print server, `PSRV`, this folder is `C:\Windows\System32\spool\PRINTERS`. In some cases, particularly when your users generate large amounts of printed output, this folder and the volume could become full, which is not a good thing. To help you avoid issues, you can move the default `spool` directory to a different folder (for example, `C:\Spool`), or you could move the spool folder to a folder on another volume (for example, `E:\Spool`).

Getting ready

There are two ways you can change the `spool` directory. The first way is to use the classes inside the .NET Framework's `System.Printing` namespace to update the folder name. The second, and probably the simplest, way is to update the registry with the folder to use for spooling. This recipe shows both methods.

How to do it...

First, let's look at how you change the `spool` folder using the .NET Framework:

1. Load the `System.Printing` namespace and classes:

   ```
   Add-Type -AssemblyName System.Printing
   ```

2. Define the required permissions—that is, the ability to administrate the server:

   ```
   $Permissions =
    [System.Printing.PrintSystemDesiredAccess]::
     AdministrateServer
   ```

3. Create a `PrintServer` object with the required permissions:

```
$Ps = New-Object
        -TypeName System.Printing.PrintServer `
                -ArgumentList $Permissions
```

4. Update the default `spool` folder path:

```
$Newpath = 'C:\Spool'
$Ps.DefaultSpoolDirectory = $Newpath
```

5. Commit the change:

```
$Ps.Commit()
```

6. Restart the `Spooler` to accept the new folder:

```
Restart-Service -Name Spooler
```

7. Once the `Spooler` has restarted, view the results:

```
New-Object -TypeName System.Printing.PrintServer |
    Format-Table -Property Name,
        DefaultSpoolDirectory
```

Another way to set the `Spooler` directory is by directly editing the registry as follows:

1. First stop the `Spooler` service:

```
Stop-Service -Name Spooler
```

2. Set the `spool` directory registry setting:

```
PS C:\foo> $RPath    = 'HKLM:\SYSTEM\CurrentControlSet\Control\ +
                        Print\Printers'
$Spooldir = 'C:\SpoolViaRegistry'
Set-ItemProperty -Path $RPath `
                -Name DefaultSpoolDirectory `
                -Value 'C:\SpoolViaRegistry'
```

3. Restart the `Spooler`:

    ```
    Start-Service -Name Spooler
    ```

4. View the results:

    ```
    New-Object -TypeName System.Printing.PrintServer |
        Format-Table -Property Name,
            DefaultSpoolDirectory
    ```

How it works...

The .NET Framework's `System.Printing` namespace contains some useful printing-related classes and enums, some of which you use in this recipe. PowerShell does not load this namespace by default. You load it in *step 1*, using the `Add-Type` cmdlet, which produces no output.

In *step 2*, you create a `variable`, `$Permissions`, that holds the print permissions you need-namely the ability to administer the print server. In *step 3*, you instantiate a `PrintServer` object with the permission to administer the print server. These permissions are separate from normal administrative privileges. Even running the commands in an elevated PowerShell console requires you to create permissions, as you can see here.

In *step 4*, you change the `Spool` folder to the in-memory `PrintServer` object, and then in *step 5*, you commit the update. In *step 6*, you restart the `Spooler`, and then, in *step 7*, observe the results from changing the `Spooler` folder. The output from *step 6* and *step 7* looks like this:

```
PS C:\> Restart-Service -Name Spooler
WARNING: Waiting for service 'Print Spooler (Spooler)' to start...

PS C:\> New-Object System.Printing.PrintServer   |
        Format-Table Name, DefaultSpoolDirectory

Name    DefaultSpoolDirectory
----    ---------------------
\\PSRV  C:\spool
```

The second and simpler method involves just updating the registry value entry that holds the `spool` folder name (and restarting the `Spooler`). To do this, in *step 8*, you stop the `Spooler`, and in *step 9*, you update the registry value that the `Spooler` system uses for its `spool` folder. Note that you do *not* have to do *steps 1-7* to use the second method!

In *step 10*, you restart the `Spooler` service, which now uses the new `Spool` folder. Finally, in *step 11*, you view the results of changing the `Spool` folder, which looks like this:

```
PS C:\> New-Object -TypeName System.Printing.PrintServer |
          Format-Table -Property Name, DefaultSpoolDirectory

Name    DefaultSpoolDirectory
----    ---------------------
\\PSRV  C:\SpoolViaRegistry
```

Note that the two methods you use in this recipe use different folder names for illustration. The folder name may not be appropriate for your installation. In production, you should also consider moving the `Spool` folder to a separate volume to avoid running out of space on the system volume.

This recipe makes use of the underlying .NET `System.Printing` namespace instead of just commands from the `PrintManagement` modules. This approach has value in many other places inside Windows. In general, the advice is to use cmdlets where/when you can and only then dip down into either the .NET Framework or the CIM/WMI namespaces and classes.

Changing printer drivers

Once you set up a printer, as shown in the recipe *Installing and sharing a printer*, users can use the printer and its associated driver to print their documents. You may need to change the driver to change the printer model or to update the driver. In the *Installing and sharing a printer* recipe, you installed an `NEC Color MultiWriter Class Driver`, which works with many NEC color printers. But suppose you decide to replace this printer with a different printer model from a different vendor, say an HP color laser printer.

In this recipe, you change the driver for the printer. The assumption behind this recipe is that the printer name and printer port (the printer's IP address and port number) remains constant. You might need to change the printer driver for a printer, should you replace an old printer for a newer or different printer (for example, replacing an NEC printer with an HP printer). In this case, the printing device and its driver changes, but everything else remains the same.

Getting ready

In this recipe, you change the driver for the printer you created in the *Installing and sharing a printer recipe*.

How to do it...

1. Add the print driver for the new printing device:

    ```
    Add-PrinterDriver -Name
                'HP LaserJet 9000 PS Class Driver'
    ```

2. Get the `Sales Group` printer object and store it in `$Printer`:

    ```
    $Printer = Get-Printer -Name SGCP1
    ```

3. Update the driver using the `Set-Printer` cmdlet:

    ```
    Set-Printer -Name $Printer.Name
                -DriverName 'HP LaserJet 9000
                            PS Class Driver'
    ```

4. Observe the results:

    ```
    Get-Printer -Name SGCP1 `
                -ComputerName PSRV
    ```

How it works...

In the first step in this recipe, you install the driver for the new print device, an HP
LaserJet 9000 PS Class Driver. You do this by using the `Add-PrinterDriver`
command. If the printer driver is not one provided by Windows (and can be added using
`Add-PrinterDriver`), you may need to run manufacturer-supplied driver software to
install the driver.

Once you have the driver installed, in *step 2*, you retrieve the printer details for the Sales
Group object's color printer. In *step 3*, you update the drivers used for this printer by using
the `Set-Printer` command. In *step 4*, you see the results, which look like this:

```
PS C:\> Get-Printer -Name SGCP1 `
                -ComputerName PSRV

Name   ComputerName Type  DriverName                      PortName    Shared Published DeviceType
----   ------------ ----  ----------                      --------    ------ --------- ----------
SGCP1  PSRV         Local HP LaserJet 9000 PS Class Driver Sales_Color True   True      Print
```

Printing a test page on a printer

From time to time, you may wish to print a test page on a printer, for example, after changing toner or printer ink, or after changing the print driver (as shown in the *Changing printer drivers* recipe). In those cases, the test page helps you to ensure that the printer is working properly.

Getting ready

For this recipe, you print a test page on the Sales Group object's LaserJet printer, as updated by the *Changing printer drivers* recipe.

How to do it...

1. Get the printer objects from WMI:

   ```
   $Printers = Get-CimInstance -ClassName
               Win32_Printer
   ```

2. Display the number of printers defined:

   ```
   '{0} Printers defined on this system' `
       -f $Printers.Count
   ```

3. Get the Sales Group printer:

   ```
   $Printer = $Printers |
               Where-Object Name -eq "SGCP1"
   ```

4. Display the printer's details:

   ```
   $Printer | Format-Table -AutoSize
   ```

5. Print a test page:

   ```
   Invoke-CimMethod -InputObject $Printer `
                   -MethodName PrintTestPage
   ```

How it works...

In *step 1*, you use `Get-CimInstance` to return all the printers defined on this system. In *step 2*, you display the total printers defined:

```
PS C:\> '{0} Printers defined on this system' -f $Printers.Count
7 Printers defined on this system
```

In *step 3*, you get the printer object corresponding to the `Sales Group` LaserJet printer. In *step 4*, you display the details of this printer:

```
PS C:\> $Printer | Format-Table -AutoSize

Name  ComputerName Type  DriverName              PortName             Shared Published DeviceType
----  ------------ ----  ----------              --------             ------ --------- ----------
SGCP1              Local HP LaserJet 9000 PS Class Driver Sales_Color,Sales_Color2 True   False     Print
```

In *step 5*, you invoke the `PrintTestPage` method on the `Sales Group` LaserJet printer, which then generates a test page on the printer. If you are using the printer MMC snap-in, the printer test page looks like this:

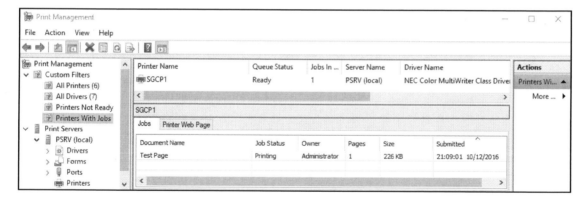

Reporting on printer security

In the Windows operating system, all objects secured by the OS have four key properties:

- The owner
- The primary group
- **Discretionary Access Control List (DACL)**
- **System Access Control List (SACL)**

The DACL contains a set of individual permissions, known as **Access Control Entries (ACEs)**, that define a particular permission. Each ACE contains properties that describe the permission, including a trustee (the security principal to whom you are giving this permission), a permission mask (what permission is being allowed or disallowed), and an ACE type (what type is allowed, disallowed). You can find details of the permission masks on the MSDN.

Getting ready

This recipe displays the DACL for the Sales Group printer, SGCP1, created by the *Installing and sharing printers* recipe and later updated by the *Changing printer drivers* recipe. You could easily convert this recipe into an advanced function (for example, Get-PrinterSecurity) with a parameter to tell the function which printer to examine.

How to do it...

1. Create a hash table containing printer permissions:

```
$Permissions = @{
    ReadPermissions     = [uint32] 131072
    Print               = [uint32] 131080
    PrintAndRead        = [uint32] 196680
    ManagePrinter       = [uint32] 983052
    ManageDocuments     = [uint32] 983088
    ManageChild         = [uint32] 268435456
    GenericExecute      = [uint32] 536870912
    ManageThisPrinter   = [uint32] 983116
}
```

2. Get a list of all printers and select the `Sales Group` color printer:

```
$Printer = Get-CimInstance -Class Win32_Printer `
                            -Filter "Name = 'SGCP1'"
```

3. Get the `SecurityDescriptor` and `DACL` for each printer:

```
$SD = Invoke-CimMethod -InputObject $Printer `
                    -MethodName
                         GetSecurityDescriptor
$DACL = $SD.Descriptor.DACL
```

4. For each `Ace` in the `DACL`, look to see what permissions you have set, and report accordingly:

```
ForEach ($Ace in $DACL) {
```

5. Look at each permission that can be set and check to see if the `Ace` is set for that permission:

```
Foreach ($Flag in ($Permissions.GetEnumerator() ) ) {
# Is this flag set in the access mask?
If ($Flag.value -eq $Ace.AccessMask) {
```

6. If this permission is set, then get the `AceType`:

```
$AceType = switch ($Ace.AceType)
{
  0 {'Allowed'; Break}
  1 {'Denied'; Break}
  2 {'Audit'}
}
```

7. Get the permission type, nicely formatted:

```
$PermType = $flag.name
              -Csplit '(?=[A-Z])' -ne '' -join ' '
```

8. Finally, display the results (and end the loops and `If` statement):

```
'Account: {0}{1} - {2}: {3}' -f $ace.Trustee.Domain,
                                $Ace.Trustee.Name,
                                $PermType, $AceType
} # End of If $flag,Value
} # End Foreach $Flag loop
} # End Each $Ace
```

How it works...

This recipe begins, in *step 1*, by defining a hash table of the permissions that you can use in a printer's DACL. In *step 2*, you use the Get-CimInstance cmdlet to retrieve the WMI object relating to the Sales Group color printer.

In step 3, you use the GetSecurityDescriptor method of the printer object to get the DACL for this printer. The DACL, which you store in the $DACL variable, is an array of individual Win32_ACE objects.

In *steps 4* you examine each Ace in the DACL to get, decode, and display the details of the permission expressed by this Ace entry. In *step 5*, you iterate through the permissions (as defined in *step 1*). In *step 6*, you check to see if the flag matches the AccessMask property of the Ace. If the entry matches, you determine the ace type in *step 6*. In *step 7*, you get the permission type nicely formatted. Finally, in *step 8*, you display the particular permissions. The output from the final step in this recipe looks like this:

```
ACE Trustee: Administrator
   Account: RESKIT\Administrator - Manage Printer: Allowed
ACE Trustee: Administrator
   Account: RESKIT\Administrator - Manage Documents: Allowed
ACE Trustee: CREATOR OWNER
   Account: \CREATOR OWNER - Manage Child: Allowed
ACE Trustee: ALL APPLICATION PACKAGES
   Account: APPLICATION PACKAGE AUTHORITY\ALL APPLICATION PACKAGES - Manage Child: Allowed
ACE Trustee: Everyone
   Account: \Everyone - Print: Allowed
ACE Trustee: Everyone
   Account: \Everyone - Generic Execute: Allowed
ACE Trustee: ALL APPLICATION PACKAGES
   Account: APPLICATION PACKAGE AUTHORITY\ALL APPLICATION PACKAGES - Print: Allowed
ACE Trustee: ALL APPLICATION PACKAGES
   Account: APPLICATION PACKAGE AUTHORITY\ALL APPLICATION PACKAGES - Generic Execute: Allowed
ACE Trustee: Administrators
   Account: BUILTIN\Administrators - Manage This Printer: Allowed
ACE Trustee: Administrators
   Account: BUILTIN\Administrators - Manage Child: Allowed
```

Modifying printer security

As you saw in the previous recipe, *Reporting on printer security*, the DACL for a printer defines what access Windows allows to the printer. To change the set of permissions, you need to change the DACL. You could, for example, update the DACL on the Sales Group printer to just allow members of the Sales Group to print on the printer. This recipe updates the DACL to enable the AD Sales Group to print to the Sales Group printer.

Getting ready

Before you can run this recipe, you need to create a group in the AD. In this recipe, you use a group, Sales Group, contained in the Sales OU. To create the OU, the domain local group, do the following:

```
# Creating the OU and Group
$SB = { New-ADOrganizationalUnit -Name 'Sales'
                                 -Path 'DC=Reskit,DC=Org'
        New-ADGroup -Name 'Sales Group'
                    -Path 'OU=Sales,DC=Reskit,DC=Org'
                    -GroupScope DomainLocal
}
Invoke-Command -ComputerName DC1 -ScriptBlock $SB
```

How to do it...

1. Define the user who is to be given access to this printer and get the group's security principal details:

```
$GroupName = 'Sales Group'
$Group = New-Object -Typename
                    Security.Principal.NTAccount `
                    -Argumentlist $GroupName
```

2. Next, get the group's SID:

```
$GroupSid = $Group.Translate([Security.Principal.
                        Securityidentifier]).Value
```

3. Now define the SDDL that gives this user access to the printer:

```
$SDDL = 'O:BAG:DUD:PAI(A;OICI;FA;;;DA)' +
        '(A;OICI;0x3D8F8;;;$GroupSid)'
```

4. Display the details:

```
'Group Name : {0}' -f $GroupName
'Group SID : {0}'  -f $GroupSid
'SDDL : {0}'       -f $SDDL
```

5. Get the `Sales Group` printer object:

```
$SGPrinter = Get-Printer -Name SGCP1
```

6. Set the `Permissions`:

```
$SGPrinter | Set-Printer -Permission $SDDL
```

How it works...

In *step 1*, you use `New-Object` to get the security principal details for the `Sales Group` from the Active Directory. In *step 2*, you use this object's `Translate` method to retrieve the SID for the group.

In *step 3*, you define the `SDDL` that is used to set permissions. In this step, as a sanity check, you can see the information you use to set the `DACL`. The output looks like this:

```
Group Name          : Accounting Group
Group SID           : S-1-5-21-715049209-2702507345-667613206-1118
SDDL                : O:BAG:DUD:PAI(A;OICI;FA;;;DA)(A;OICI;0x3D8F8;;;S-1-5-21-715049209-2702507345-667613206-1118)
```

In *step 5*, you get the printer object for the `Sales Group` printer, and in *step 6*, you update the printer with the `SDDL` string you created in *step 3*. That sets the `Sales Group` printer's `DACL`. You can verify the results by rerunning the *Reporting on printer security* recipe.

Deploying shared printers

Traditionally, you used scripting to deploy printers. With this method, you create a logon or startup script and deploy this logon script via Group Policies. When machines start up or users log on, the logon script automatically sets up printers.

Once you have set up a shared printer, such as the shared `Sales Group` color printer, as shown in this chapter, you can deploy it. There are several ways to automate local client printer deployment, including using PowerShell, WMI, the `Printui.dll` utility, and the `Wscript.Network` COM object. All of these methods have been in use for a long time and are quite efficient, although PowerShell is the preferred way, naturally.

Getting ready

To deploy a printer to a client, you first need a client computer system. Our demo lab includes a Windows 10 Enterprise client (SG-CL1), which we use in this recipe. To test this recipe, you need the client computer, the print server (PSVR), and the domain controller (DC1).

Once you create the client, you can run the following commands to add it to the domain in the Sales OU (created separately):

```
$Cred = Get-Credential 'Reskit\administrator'
# you enter the password
$OUPath = 'OU=Sales, DC=Reskit,DC=Org'
Add-Computer -DomainName 'Reskit' `
             -DomainCredential $cred
```

Next, you need a Group Policy object that deploys the logon script. The easiest way to create this **Group Policy Object (GPO)** is to use the GUI-there are no PowerShell cmdlets (or WMI/.NET objects) that can help.

To create the GPO, you use the **Group Policy Management Console (GPMC)** tool. This tool is part of the management tools for Active Directory, and is also part of the **Remote Server Admin Tools (RSAT)** that you can download for client systems. Once you install the GPMC, you can run it and expand the domain to make our **Sales** OU visible:

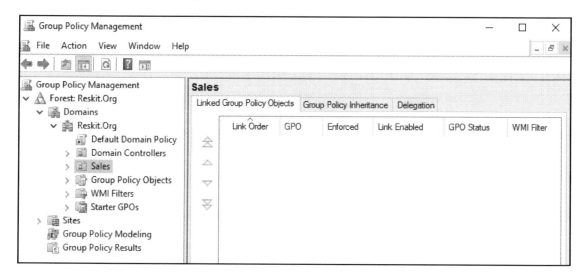

Next, you right-click the **Sales** OU, specify the Group Policy **Name**, and click **OK**:

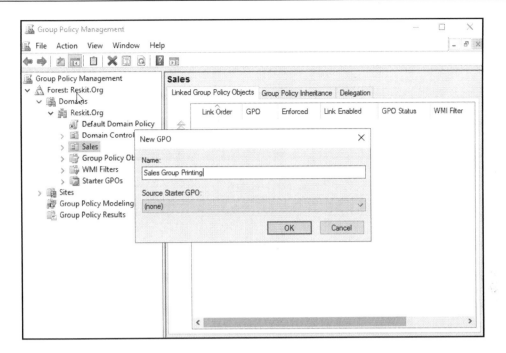

With the GPO created, right-click the GPO and select **Edit**:

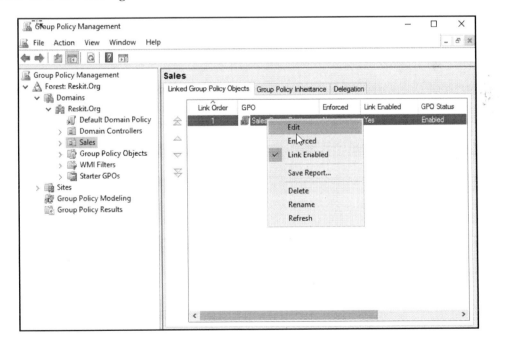

This brings up the **Group Policy Management Editor**. Select the **User Configuration** |
Windows Settings | **Scripts (Logon/Logoff)**:

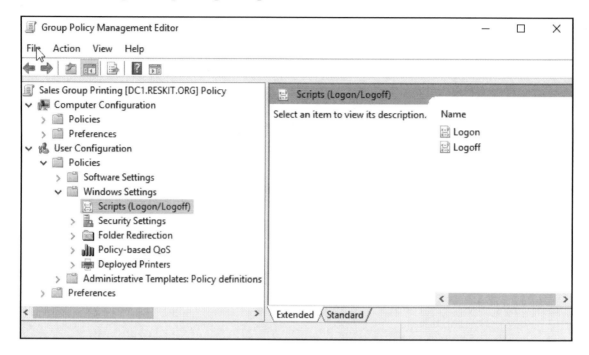

Then double-click **Logon** to bring up the **Logon Properties** dialog, and then click on the
PowerShell Scripts tab:

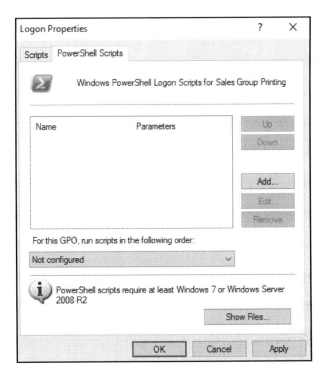

From this dialog, click on **Add** to bring up the **Add a Script** dialog:

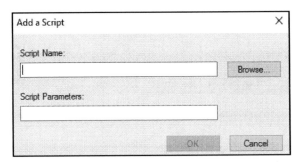

From this dialog, enter the **Script Name** `Sales Group Logon Script.ps1`, then click on **OK**, which brings up the **Logon Properties** box with the script shown here:

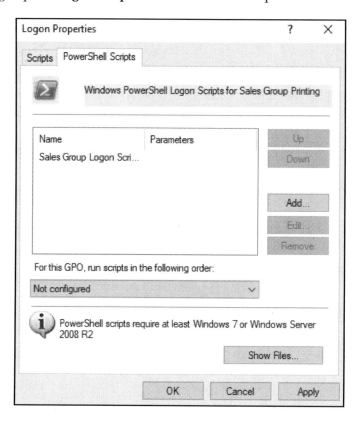

Note the file name in this dialog box. This file (`Sales Group Logon Script.ps1`) is a file within the `Logon Script` folder inside the GPO object in your `SYSVOL` folder on your domain controller. The path for the `Logon Script` folder was `Reskit.Org\SysVol\Reskit.Org\Policies\{CF4F8264-0FD7-4D21-8267-8F36D7CE 3DCF}\UserScripts\Logon`. If you are testing this, you should see a different GUID in this path.

From the **Logon Properties** dialog, click **OK** to close the dialog, then close the GPMC editor. These steps have created an empty logon script. You can add the content for this logon script by going through the following recipe.

How to do it...

Once you have created the logon script GPO, as shown previously, it's time to create the script:

1. Using the ISE, open the script file you created in the introduction to this recipe and enter the logon script:

```
# Sales Group Logon Script.ps1
# Logon Script for Sales Group to add printer
# 1. Start transcript
Start-Transcript -Path C:\transcript\transcript.txt
                    -Append
# 2. Log information to the transcript
'*** Logon script - Sales GVroup Logon Script.ps1'
'*** Date/time: [{0}]' -f (Get-Date)
# 3. Setup up printer connection then try to connect
$Connection = 'PSRV\SGCP1'
Try {
     $Printer = Get-Printer -Name $Connection
     If ($Printer)
     {
         '*** Sales group printer found'
          $Printer
     }
     Else
         {Throw "Printer not found"}
}
Catch {
     '*** SG Printer does not exist'
     '*** Date/time: [{0}]' -f (Get-Date)
     '*** Adding SG Printer '
     Add-Printer -ConnectionName $connection -Verbose
     Get-Printer -Name $Connection
     '******';''
}
# 5. And stop the transcript
Stop-Transcript
```

2. Once you create and save the script, you can test it by logging onto the `SG-CL1` computer and displaying the file `C:\Transcript\Transcript.txt`, which on the first logon looks like this:

```
***********************
Windows PowerShell transcript start
Start time: 20161214142529
Username: RESKIT\tfl
RunAs User: RESKIT\tfl
Machine: SG-CL1 (Microsoft Windows NT 10.0.14393.0)
Host Application:   -ExecutionPolicy ByPass -File Sales Group Logon Script.ps1
Process ID: 3604
PSVersion: 5.1.14393.0
PSEdition: Desktop
PSCompatibleVersions: 1.0, 2.0, 3.0, 4.0, 5.0, 5.1.14393.0
BuildVersion: 10.0.14393.0
CLRVersion: 4.0.30319.42000
WSManStackVersion: 3.0
PSRemotingProtocolVersion: 2.3
SerializationVersion: 1.1.0.1
***********************
Transcript started, output file is C:\transcript\transcript.txt
*** Logon script - Sales Group Logon Script.ps1
*** Date/time: [14/12/2016 14:25:30]
*** Sales group printer does not exist
*** Date/time: [14/12/2016 14:25:32]
*** Adding SG Printer

Name                          ComputerName   Type        DriverName              PortName
----                          ------------   ----        ----------              --------
\\PSRV\SGCP1                  PSRV           Connection  NEC Color MultiWriter ... Sales_Color...
***********************
Windows PowerShell transcript end
End time: 20161214142533
***********************
```

3. Once the logon script has installed the printer, subsequent logon scripts create a transcript entry that looks like this:

```
***********************
Windows PowerShell transcript start
Start time: 20161215173403
Username: RESKIT\tfl
RunAs User: RESKIT\tfl
Machine: SG-CL1 (Microsoft Windows NT 10.0.14393.0)
Host Application:   -ExecutionPolicy ByPass -File Sales Group Logon Script.ps1
Process ID: 2964
PSVersion: 5.1.14393.0
PSEdition: Desktop
PSCompatibleVersions: 1.0, 2.0, 3.0, 4.0, 5.0, 5.1.14393.0
BuildVersion: 10.0.14393.0
CLRVersion: 4.0.30319.42000
WSManStackVersion: 3.0
PSRemotingProtocolVersion: 2.3
SerializationVersion: 1.1.0.1
***********************
Transcript started, output file is C:\transcript\transcript.txt
*** Logon script - Sales Group Logon Script.ps1
*** Date/time: [15/12/2016 17:34:03]
*** Sales group printer found

Name            ComputerName   Type        DriverName              PortName      Shared  Published
----            ------------   ----        ----------              --------      ------  ---------
\\psrv\SGCP1    psrv           Connection  NEC Color MultiWriter ... Sales_Colour... True    True
***********************
Windows PowerShell transcript end
End time: 20161215173418
***********************
```

How it works...

The recipe creates a GPO to distribute a logon script to users whose user accounts are in the Sales OU. You set up the logon script by following the steps in the introduction to this recipe. Then, you create and save the actual logon script. Finally, you edit the empty script file to add the logon script details.

Once you have this logon script created, the printer is automatically added to the Sales Group users' systems. New users in the Sales Group just need to log off and log on again to get the printer setup.

There's more...

This recipe showed you one way to deploy a printer through the use of a logon script. This method is one that has been used by IT professionals for decades. It is also a very flexible approach for many organizations-you can do quite a lot with the logon script.

Another way to deploy printers to client systems would be to use **Group Policy preferences (GPP)**. The use of GPP adds flexibility to the process, but it is essentially an all-GUI administration experience. Windows Server 2016 does not provide cmdlets that would enable you to automate printer management fully via GPP or GPO.

 See https://technet.microsoft.com/en-us/library/cc754699(v=ws.11).aspx for more details on how to deploy printers using Group Policies.

Enabling Branch Office Direct Printing

Branch Office Direct Printing (BODP) is a feature introduced in Windows Server 2012 that is designed to reduce print traffic across your WAN. With BODP, a user in a branch office sends the print job directly to a branch office printer. There is no need to send the print job from the client to a centralized print server and then back to the branch office printer. Print jobs can be quite large, so this can improve printing and reduce print job-related WAN traffic.

Getting ready

This recipe needs a second shared printer, SGBRCP1, set up as follows:

```
$PtrName = 'Sales_Branch_Color'
$PtrIP = '172.16.1.61'
$DrvName = 'NEC Color MultiWriter Class Driver'
Add-PrinterPort -Name $ptrname `
                -PrinterHostAddress $PtrIP
Add-PrinterDriver -Name $DrvName `
                  -PrinterEnvironment 'Windows x64'
Add-Printer -Name 'SGBRCP1' `
            -DriverName $DrvName `
            -Portname 'Sales_Branch_Color'
Set-Printer -Name 'SGBRCP1' -Shared $true `
            -Published $true
```

This second printer is a branch office printer for which you enable BODP printing.

How to do it...

1. Set the SGBRCP1 printer for Branch Office Direct Printing:

```
$Printer = SGBRCP1
$PServer = 'PSRV'
Set-Printer -Name $Printer -ComputerName $PServer `
            -RenderingMode BranchOffice
```

2. Get the printing mode:

```
$Key = 'HKLM:\SYSTEM\CurrentControlSet\Control\ +
        Print\Printers\SGBRCP1\Printer\DriverData'
$BROPrint = (Get-ItemProperty
            $Key).EnableBranchOfficePrinting
```

3. Now display the value of the RenderingMode:

```
Get-Printer $Printer -Full |
    Format-Table Name, RenderingMode
```

4. Now reset to default:

```
Set-Printer -Name $printer 1 `
-ComputerName $PServer `
-RenderingMode SSR
```

5. Redisplay the RenderingMode property for the remote printer:

```
Get-Printer $Printer -Full |
    Format-Table -Property Name, RenderingMode
```

How it works...

This recipe is relatively straightforward, with a bit of a twist. In *step 1*, you set BODP for printer SGBRCP1 using the Set-Printer command.

In *step 2*, you look into the registry for details about the shared printer. At the time of writing, using the cmdlet Get-Printer does not return the RenderingMode by default. You can either specify the -FULL switch to Get-Printer, or you can get the details from the registry. Using the -FULL switch takes additional time, so it's not done by default-accessing this setting from WMI should be faster. Also, the RenderingMode property is not returned, by default.

In *step 3*, you use the Get-Printer command, specifying the -Full parameter, to return the following:

```
PS C:\> Get-Printer $Printer -Full |
            Format-Table Name, RenderingMode

Name      RenderingMode
----      -------------
SGBRCP1   BranchOffice
```

Finally, in *steps 4* and *5*, you reset the value of Branch Office Direct Printing to default, then re-redisplay the value:

```
PS C:\> Get-Printer $Printer -Full |
        Format-Table Name, RenderingMode

Name      RenderingMode
----      -------------
SGBRCP1             SSR
```

There's more...

BODP is straightforward to set up—the printers need to be networked (TCP/IP based) and support **client-side rendering (CSR)**. Traditionally, rendering is server-side (RenderingMode set to SSR). See
https://technet.microsoft.com/en-us/library/jj134152(v=ws.11).aspx for deeper technical details of Branch Office Direct Printing, including some important limitations you should be aware of before deploying branch office printing.

You use the Set-Printer cmdlet to set BODP. However, the Get-Printer cmdlet does not return the Branch Office Printing mode by default. The -Full switch on the Get-Printer command returns both the Branch Office Printing mode and the object's security descriptor in SDDL format.

Creating a printer pool

On Windows, a printer pool is a single named printer with two or more print devices (printer ports). Windows sends a given print job to any of the printers in the pool. This feature is very useful in environments where users do a lot of printing and need the speed that additional printers can provide, without having to ask the user to choose which specific print device to use.

There are no PowerShell cmdlets to enable you to create a printer pool. Older printer features—the use of PrintUI.DLL and RunDLL32, which have been features in Windows for several versions. These tools are another example of making use of console applications where you need them.

Getting ready

You run this recipe on the PSRV. Additionally, this recipe assumes you have created the printer, as per the *Install and share printers recipe*.

How to do it...

1. Add a new port for this printer:

```
Add-PrinterPort -Name Sales_Color2  `
                -PrinterHostAddress   10.10.10.62
```

2. Create a printer pool for printer SGCP1:

```
$printer = 'SGCP1'
Rundll32 PrintUi.dll,PrintUIEntry /Xs /n
"$Printer"  Portname 'Sales_Color2,Sales_Color'
```

3. To see the results, get the printer details and display them as a nice table:

```
Get-Printer SGCP1 |
    Format-Table -Property Name, Type,
                    DriverName, PortName
```

How it works...

As noted earlier, you use PrintUI.dll to set up a printer pool. You invoke this DLL by using the RunDLL32.exe console application. The DLL contains the functions that the printer management GUI dialog use to perform their actions. RunDLL32.exe enables you to use scripting to perform the necessary printer configuration operations.

In *step 1* of the recipe, you add a second printer port. In this case, we are adding a second network port. You could use a parallel, serial, or USB port if that is appropriate in your environment. In most organisations, the print server is in a server room, with networked printers nearer to the users.

In *step 2*, you use PrintUI.DLL to set the SGCP1 printer to have two printer ports, thus creating a printer pool. In *step 3*, after you create the printer pool, you can view the results by using Get-Printer, which shows the following:

```
PS C:\> Get-Printer SGCP1 |
          Format-Table Name, Type, DriverName, PortName

Name    Type DriverName                      PortName
----    ---- ----------                      --------
SGCP1 Local HP LaserJet 9000 PS Class Driver Sales_Color,Sales_Color2
```

You can also look at the GUI entry for the printer on the print server, PSRV:

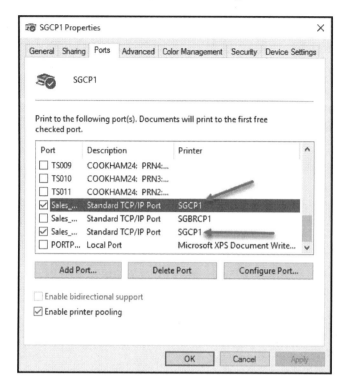

Reporting on printer usage

Printer usage information is useful for capacity planning, and possibly budgeting, for your shared printers. By default, printer usage details are unmonitored, but you can turn logging on (and off!). When you enable printer usage monitoring, the Windows Spooler service writes a record to the event log for each print job containing critical usage information.

This recipe shows you how to turn on printer usage reporting and shows how to create a function to return printer usage information. This recipe creates a function that returns printer usage information as objects. Objects are easier as they enable you to process the output specifically for your environment-for example, counting the total number of pages printed, reporting on who is using the printer, and so on.

Getting ready

Run this recipe on PSRV where you have already set up a printer. This recipe assumes you have set up a printer. You also need to use the printer a bit to generate some event log entries on which you report, otherwise the recipe may return errors when you try to get event log entries.

How to do it...

1. Run `webtutil` to turn on printer monitoring:

```
$log = 'Microsoft-Windows-PrintService'
webtutil.exe sl $log /operational /Enabled:true
```

2. Define a `Function`:
    1. Specify the `Function` header for an advanced function:

    ```
    Function Get-PrinterUsage {
    [CmdletBinding()]
    Param()
    ```

    2. Get the events from the `PrintService` event log:

    ```
    $Dps = Get-WinEvent -LogName
    Microsoft-Windows-PrintService/Operational |
        Where-Object ID -eq 307
    ```

    3. Create a hash table for each event log record:

    ```
    Foreach ($Dp in $Dps) {
        $Document = [Ordered] @{}
    ```

    4. Populate the hash table with properties from the event log entry:

    ```
    $Document.Id       = $dp.Properties[0].value
    $Document.Type     = $dp.Properties[1].value
    $Document.User     = $dp.Properties[2].value
    $Document.Computer = $dp.Properties[3].value
    $Document.Printer  = $dp.Properties[4].value
    $Document.Port     = $dp.Properties[5].value
    $Document.Bytes    = $dp.Properties[6].value
    $Document.Pages    = $dp.Properties[7].value
    ```

5. Create an object for this printer usage entry:

```
$UEntry = New-Object -Type PSObject
  -Property $Document
```

6. Give it a better type name:

```
$UEntry.PsTypeNames.Clear()
$UEntry.PsTypeNames.Add("Packt.PrintUsage")
```

7. Output the entry:

```
$UEntry
} # End of foreach
} # End of function
```

3. Set and use an alias to get the printer usage:

```
Set-Alias -Name GPRU
          -Value Get-PrinterUsage
GPRU | Format-Table
```

How it works...

In the first step of the recipe, you use the utility `wevtutil.exe` to tell the `Spooler` to start recording printer usage details to the event log. Printer usage event logging is not turned on by default, and at present, there is no PowerShell cmdlet to turn on event logging.

In the first sub-step in *step 2*, you create an advanced function by decorating the `Param()` block with the `CmdletBinding()` attribute. In the second sub-step, you get all the printer event log entries that relate to usage reporting (`ObjectID 307`). In the third sub-step in *step 2*, the function iterates through each entry in the log. In the fourth sub-step, for each entry, you create a hash table that holds the information returned from the event log. In *sub-step 5* and *sub-step 6*, you create a `PSObject` for the event log entry and change the object type name from `PSObject` to `Packt.PrintUsage`. Finally, in *sub-step 7*, you also close out the `foreach` loop and the advanced function.

Finally, in *step 3*, you define an alias for this new function. Then you use the function, via its alias, and pipe the output objects to `Format-Table` to produce a nice output like this:

There's more...

By creating a function that returns an object for each event log entry, you get significant flexibility in using the output of the function. The `Get-PrinterUsage` function changes the type name of the returned object. With a custom type name, you could create a customized display XML that creates an output that suits your requirements. You can also use the objects returned and filter out the usage of specific printers by user. You can also use `Measure-Object` to get the total number of pages printed, the average pages per job, and the maximum print job length.

5

Managing Server Backup

This chapter covers the following recipes:

- Configure and set backup policy
- Examine the results of a backup
- Initiate a backup manually
- Restore files and folders from a backup
- Backup and restore a Hyper-V virtual machine
- Backup and perform bare metal recovery
- Restore the registry from a backup
- Create a daily backup report
- Create an Azure backup

Introduction

The ability to backup and restore a Windows Server has been a feature of Windows since the first version of Windows NT, released in 1993. In the early days, you used NTBackup (via a GUI) to carry out backup and restore activities. With Server 2008, Windows Server Backup replaced NTBackup and offered 15 cmdlets (provided in an old-school PS Snap-in) to augment the GUI. The Snap-in was replaced with a module, `WindowsServerBackup`, and was improved with Server 2012. The module remains unchanged in Server 2016 and provided 49 cmdlets.

Windows Server Backup (WSB) provides a set of features to enable you to backup and restore files, folders, and Hyper-V VMs as well as an entire system. These features are more than adequate for many organizations and come for free with Windows Server 2016. Nevertheless, some organizations need more functionality. There is a rich third party backup industry with a variety of competing products that deliver more than the in-box Windows Server Backup offers. This chapter concentrates on Windows Server Backup and Azure backup.

Windows Server Backup backs up both entire volumes as well as specific files and folders. You can tell WSB both to include and to exclude specific files/folders from the backup (include C: Data, C: HyperV, C: foo; exclude *.tmp, *.bak, and C: Foobin). And WSB makes it simple to backup and restore a Hyper-V **Virtual Machine (VM)**. What you backup, you can restore: you can restore entire volumes, individual files or folders, restore a VM, and restore the system state to a new machine (aka bare metal recovery).

The recipes in this chapter show how to setup your backup policy, to configure what/where/when/how to backup and how to recover.

With the growth in cloud computing, an increasing number of organizations utilize cloud backup as an alternative to or in addition to using on-premises (and private cloud) resources. Azure Backup is an Azure service that backs up your on-premises systems to the cloud and enables file/folder/volume/system restores. Our final recipe in this chapter shows how you can do a backup to Azure and how to restore.

The recipes in this chapter make use of the PSRV server which you set up in Chapter 4, *Managing Printers* and other servers in the Reskit.Org domain—each recipe indicates the specific servers to use. But feel free to use other server names, different disk layouts, and so on—adjusting the recipes accordingly.

Most of the recipes in this chapter rely on cmdlets in the WindowsServerBackup module. We also make use of the console application Wbadmin and the Azure Resource Management cmdlets. In some cases, such as backing up and restoring Hyper-V, you may find it easier to use the Wbadmin console application—you have choices! And as icing on the cake, the final recipe used both the AzureRM cmdlets and the Azure backup cmdlets and the recovery agent.

You have choices! And as icing on the cake, the final recipe used both the AzureRM cmdlets and the Azure backup cmdlets and the recovery agent.

Configure and set backup policy

With WSB, you create a backup policy that describes what you want to backup from your server (backup source), where you want to put the backup (backup target), and when you want the backup to take place (the backup schedule). You first create an empty policy in memory or get an editable copy of the active backup policy. You then configure the policy object with a backup source and backup to your requirements. You then either save the policy as the (new!) active policy or use it to run a one-off backup. Once you have set an active policy, WSB runs the backup automatically based on the schedule you define when you populate the backup policy.

In this recipe, you create and configure a policy that backs up the C: drive every morning at 06:00. This policy object is the starting point for examining backup with WSB. Later recipes enable you to perform, explicitly, system state backup, one-off backup, selective file backup, and VM backup (and restores)—all of which are variations on this recipe.

Getting ready

This recipe assumes you have loaded the Windows Server Backup feature and that you have no active WSB backup policy on the printer server PSRV. To install the Windows Server Backup feature, do this:

```
Install-WindowsFeature -Name Windows-Server-Backup
```

You also need to ensure you have no active backup policy set on this server. To ensure this is the case, do this:

```
If (Get-WBPolicy) { Remove-WBPolicy -All -Force }
```

This code fragment first tests to see if there is an active policy, and if so, removes it. By using the -Force parameter, Remove-WBPolicy does not prompt you to complete the operation, which is what you want if you are automating setting up backup on one or more computers.

This recipe also assumes you have two physical disks in the PSRV computer. You should set the first to C:, and you should create a second disk with just a single volume. Give this new volume a drive letter set to E:. For testing, you can always use a virtual hard drive for the E: volume.

In a production environment, backup up to a second volume or a virtual hard disk stored on a single physical disk is not a good idea. For production, always ensure the backup target is on a separate physical disk.

How to do it...

The steps for the recipe are as follows:

1. Once you load the Windows Server Backup feature and ensure there is no active policy, create a new (in memory) backup policy:

```
$Pol = New-WBPolicy
```

2. View the new policy:

```
$Pol
```

3. Add a schedule to the backup policy:

```
$Schedule = '06:00'
Set-WBSchedule -Policy $POL -Schedule $Schedule
```

4. View disks to be backed up:

```
Get-WBDisk |
    Format-Table -Property DiskName, DiskNumber,
                            FreeSpace, Properties
```

5. Use Disk 1 as the backup target and set it in policy:

```
$TargetDisk = Get-WBDisk |
    Where-Object Properties -Match 'ValidTarget' |
        Select-Object -First 1
$Target = New-WBBackupTarget -Disk $TargetDisk
                            -Label 'Recipe 6-1'
                            -PreserveExistingBackups $true
Add-WBBackupTarget -Policy $Pol -Target $Target
```

6. Add details of what to backup (the C: drive) to the backup policy:

```
$DisktoBackup = Get-WBDisk | Select-Object -First 1
$Volume       = Get-WBVolume -Disk $DisktoBackup |
                    Where-Object FileSystem -eq NTFS
Add-WBVolume -Policy $Pol -Volume $Volume
```

7. View the policy:

```
$Pol
```

8. Make policy active (NOTE THIS FORMATS THE TARGET DISK!):

```
Set-WBPolicy -Policy $Pol -Force
```

9. Add a drive letter to Disk 1 to enable you to view the results subsequently:

```
$Drive = Get-CimInstance -Class Win32_Volume |
         Select -Last 1 |
             Where-Object {-not ($_.DriveLetter)}
Set-CimInstance -InputObject $Drive
                -Property @{DriveLetter='Q:'}|
                    Format-Table Name,DriveLetter
```

10. View the active policy:

```
Get-WBPolicy
```

11. Review the summary of the backup:

```
Get-WBSummary
```

How it works...

In *step 1*, you create a new editable policy and save it to $Pol. This empty policy is not yet ready to be used for an actual backup, but it is in an editable state. You use other cmdlets to populate the policy with backup details before either using it ad hoc or setting the policy as your active backup policy. In Windows Server 2016, you can have only one currently active backup policy.

In *step 2*, you view the newly created policy. As you can see, there are several items that you need to add before you can set this policy to active. The empty policy looks like this:

```
PS C:> $Pol

Schedule              :
BackupTargets         :
VolumesToBackup       :
FilesSpecsToBackup    :
FilesSpecsToExclude   :
ComponentsToBackup    :
BMR                   : False
SystemState           : False
OverwriteOldFormatVhd : False
VssBackupOptions      : VssCopyBackup
```

In *step 3*, you use `Set-WBSchedule` to set a time for the backup to occur. You define the backup time in this recipe as 06:00 (that is, 6:00 in the morning). Specifying the time as 06:00 means the WSB starts a backup job at 6:00 every morning. The `Set-SBSchedule` returns a `DateTime` object in which you can see the time of the next backup. The output shows the date of the backup as of today's date—but WSB ignores the date. The output of this step looks like this:

```
PS C:\> $Schedule = '06:00'
PS C:\> Set-WBSchedule -Policy $POL -Schedule $Schedule

20 March 2017 06:00:00
```

With *step 4* you use the `Get-WBDisk` and then pipe the output to Format-Table which displays a list of volumes that are potential backup targets. Disks that WSB can backup to have the `ValidTarget` property set. The output from *step 4* is shown in the following screenshot :

```
PS C:\> Get-WBDisk |
            Format-Table -Property DiskName, DiskNumber,
                              FreeSpace, Properties

DiskName               DiskNumber    FreeSpace              Properties
--------               ----------    ---------              ----------
Virtual HD ATA Device           0 121787637760 ContainsCriticalVolume
Microsoft Virtual Disk          1  95086919168             ValidTarget
```

In *step 5*, you specify that WSB should use a specific disk to hold the backup(s). In this case, you are going to have WSB store the individual backup files onto the second disk (shown as `DiskNumber 1` in the preceding output. You need to get a `WBDisk` object for your destination and use this when configuring the target set in the backup policy. The output from `Add-WBBackupTarget` shows how the policy has evolved as follows:

```
PS C:\> $TargetDisk = Get-WBDisk |
            Where-Object Properties -match 'ValidTarget' |
              Select-Object -First 1
PS C:\> $Target = New-WBBackupTarget -Disk $TargetDisk `
                   -Label 'Recipe 6-1' `
                   -PreserveExistingBackups $true
PS C:\> Add-WBBackupTarget -Policy $Pol -Target $Target -Force

Label                   : Recipe 6-1
WBDisk                  : Microsoft Virtual Disk
WBVolume                :
Path                    :
TargetType              : Disk
InheritAcl              : False
PreserveExistingBackup  : True
```

In *step 6*, you add the source volume(s) you want to backup. In this recipe, you are just backing up the C: drive (DiskNumber 0) which is the first volume on the first disk as shown in the following screenshot:

```
PS C:\> $DisktoBackup = Get-WBDisk | Select-Object -First 1
PS C:\> $Volume = Get-WBVolume -Disk $DisktoBackup |
           Where-Object FileSystem -eq 'NTFS'
PS C:\> Add-WBVolume -Policy $Pol -Volume $Volume

VolumeLabel : System Volume
MountPath   : C:
MountPoint  : \\?\Volume{0da61551-0000-0000-0000-100000000000}
FileSystem  : NTFS
Property    : Critical, ValidSource
FreeSpace   : 121785053184
TotalSpace  : 137436856320
```

In *step 7*, you display the final policy:

```
PS C:\> $Pol

Schedule               : {20/03/2017 06:00:00}
BackupTargets          : {Recipe 6-1}
VolumesToBackup        : {System Volume (C:)}
FilesSpecsToBackup     :
FilesSpecsToExclude    :
ComponentsToBackup     :
BMR                    : False
SystemState            : False
OverwriteOldFormatVhd  : False
VssBackupOptions       : VssCopyBackup
```

With *step 8*, you make this policy active. There are two implications to this: First, the E: drive is formatted and made available for backup. Second, WSB takes over the entire disk and destroys any volumes you have on this disk. You also lose any existing drive letters on the disk. **BE VERY CAREFUL WHEN TESTING OR USING THIS RECIPE ESPECIALLY ON A PRODUCTION SERVER!**

In *step 9*, you give the second disk a drive letter, Q:, which you can then to view the results of backup operations carried out on your system. Note that you could get an error here if Windows has already created a drive letter for you. You can use the Q: drive from both PowerShell and Windows Explorer to view backup files, but at this point in the recipe no backup has run yet, and the drive is empty. The output from *step 9* looks like this:

```
PS C:\> $Drive = Get-CimInstance -Class Win32_volume |
            Where-Object Label -eq 'Recipe 6-1'
PS C:\> Set-CimInstance -InputObject $Drive -Property @{DriveLetter='Q:'}
PS C:\> Get-CimInstance -Class Win32_Volume |
            Where-Object Label -eq 'Recipe 6-1' |
                Format-Table -Property Driveletter, Label

Driveletter Label
----------- -----
Q:          Recipe 6-1
```

In *step 10* and *step 11*, you see the currently active policy and the backup summary, something like this:

```
PS C:> Get-WBPolicy

Schedule            : {20/03/2017 06:00:00}
BackupTargets       : {Recipe 6-1}
VolumesToBackup     : {System Volume (C:)}
FilesSpecsToBackup  : {}
FilesSpecsToExclude : {}
ComponentsToBackup  : {}
BMR                 : False
SystemState         : False
OverwriteOldFormatVhd : False
VssBackupOptions    : VssCopyBackup


PS C:> Get-WBSummary

NextBackupTime                : 21/03/2017 06:00:00
NumberOfVersions              : 36
LastSuccessfulBackupTime      : 20/03/2017 13:18:54
LastSuccessfulBackupTargetPath  : \\?\Volume{303f5cce-4450-45e0-b268-8f2de40de561}
LastSuccessfulBackupTargetLabel : Recipe 6-1
LastBackupTime                : 20/03/2017 13:18:54
LastBackupTarget              : Q:
DetailedMessage               :
LastBackupResultHR            : 0
LastBackupResultDetailedHR    : 0
CurrentOperationStatus        : NoOperationInProgress
```

As you can see from the above screenshot, there are numerous backups on the Q: drive, and the next backup is at 6:00 in the morning.

There's more...

This recipe creates and activates a basic backup policy for the PSRV server. Once you set the policy, WSB creates a backup of the *C*: volume daily at 6:00. Once WSB has run your backup job, WSB sets the next backup time to be 24 hours later. You can see this in the next recipe.

In step 5, you used the -match operator to select a target backup disk. This ensures that the string ValidTarget is somewhere inside the Properties property. You could have used -eq as well, assuming that the valid target string always contains just ValidTarget. Using -match is a somewhat more liberal approach.

At the end of this recipe, you have set a backup policy. At that point, WSB has not created a backup. The backup occurs when WSB runs the job at 06:00 tomorrow. You can also trigger off a manual backup using the policy file you created in this recipe.

To perform a manual backup, after *step 12*, type:

```
$MBPol = Get-WBPolicy -Editable
          Start-WBBackup -Policy $MBPol
```

The output looks like this:

```
PS C:\> $MBPol = Get-WBPolicy -Editable
PS C:\> Start-WBBackup -Policy $MBPol
Creating a shadow copy of the volumes in the backup...
Creating a shadow copy of the volumes in the backup...
Creating a shadow copy of the volumes in the backup...
Updating the backup for deleted items...
Volume 1 (0%) of 1 volume(s).
   .... multiple lines deleited for brevity
Volume 1 (100%) of 1 volume(s).
Creating a shadow copy of the backup storage location(s)...
The backup operation completed.
```

The Start-WBBackup cmdlet creates a large number of output lines, most of which are not contained in this screenshot (for brevity).

Examine the results of a backup

In the previous recipe, you created a basic backup policy that runs a full backup of the *C*: volume every day at 6:00. This recipe examines the results of the backup and helps you understand the details of the resulting backup.

Getting ready

Before carrying out this recipe, you need to have had a backup job completed. In the recipe *Configure and set backup policy*, you created a backup job that would run every morning. Thus, you can wait until the day after you set up this daily backup, or you can run a once-off job as shown at the end of that recipe.

How to do it...

The steps for the recipe are as follows:

1. Retrieve and view the current WSB backup policy:

   ```
   Get-WBPolicy
   ```

2. View an overview of what is on the target disk:

   ```
   Get-ChildItem -Path Q: -Recurse -Depth 3 -Directory
   ```

3. View the details of a backup:

   ```
   $Backup = (Get-ChildItem -Path Q:\WindowsImageBackup\Psrv `
                      -Directory |
                          Select-Object -First 1).FullName
   explorer.exe $Backup
   ```

4. Mount the VHD, change its drive letter to T:, then look inside the VHD:

   ```
   $BFile = Get-ChildItem -Path $Backup*.vhdx
   Mount-DiskImage -ImagePath $BFile.FullName
   $Drive = Get-CimInstance -Class Win32_Volume |
               Where-Object DriveType -eq 3 |
               Select-Object -Last 1
   Set-CimInstance -InputObject $Drive
                   -Property @{DriveLetter='T:'}
   Explorer T:
   ```

5. Get details of the last backup job:

   ```
   Get-WBJob -Previous 1
   ```

How it works...

In *step 1*, you use the `Get-WBPolicy` to retrieve the current backup policy. Depending on when the backup ran, the policy looks something like this:

```
PS C:\> Get-WBPolicy

Schedule                : {20/03/2017 06:00:00}
BackupTargets           : {Recipe 6-1}
VolumesToBackup         : {System Volume (C:)}
FilesSpecsToBackup      : {}
FilesSpecsToExclude     : {}
ComponentsToBackup      : {}
BMR                     : False
SystemState             : False
OverwriteOldFormatVhd   : False
VssBackupOptions        : VssCopyBackup
```

Notice that this policy looks like the one you saw at the end of the previous recipe. If the scheduled backup job has run, then the `Schedule` property would show the next backup has changed. Assuming no changes to the policy, you get a backup automatically every day.

In *step 2*, you see what WSB has written to the backup target, the `Q:` drive. If this is the first time you have run through this recipe and created a backup, your `Q:` drive is most probably empty at this point. When WSB runs it creates a folder structure, and with that done, the step looks like this:

```
PS Q:\> Get-ChildItem -Path Q: -Recurse -Depth 3 -Directory


    Directory: Q:\


Mode                LastWriteTime         Length Name
----                -------------         ------ ----
d-----        22/12/2016     06:00               WindowsImageBackup


    Directory: Q:\WindowsImageBackup


Mode                LastWriteTime         Length Name
----                -------------         ------ ----
d-----        22/12/2016     06:08               PSRV


    Directory: Q:\WindowsImageBackup\PSRV


Mode                LastWriteTime         Length Name
----                -------------         ------ ----
d-----        22/12/2016     06:08               Backup 2016-12-22 060006
d-----        22/12/2016     06:08               Catalog
d-----        22/12/2016     06:08               Logs
d-----        22/12/2016     06:08               SPPMetadataCache
```

WSB creates a folder `WindowsImageBackup` at the root of the disk, with a subfolder for the server that WSB backs up. Below this subfolder folder, there are three further folders containing backup information and logs, plus folder(s) for the backup. Each backup has a separate folder beneath `<drive>:\WindowsImageBackpup<ServerName>` as you can see in *step 3*:

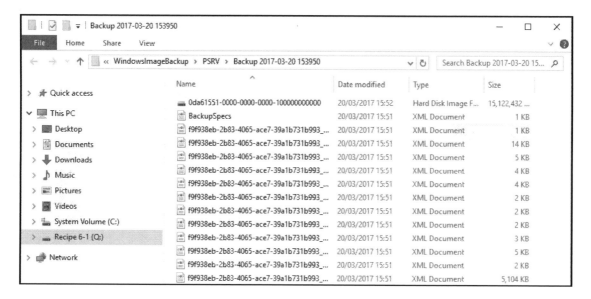

The backup folder contains some XML files that describe the backup, plus a VHDX hard drive image that contains the backup. In *step 4*, you mount that VHDX, then open Windows Explorer to view the contents of this virtual hard drive, as shown in the following screenshot:

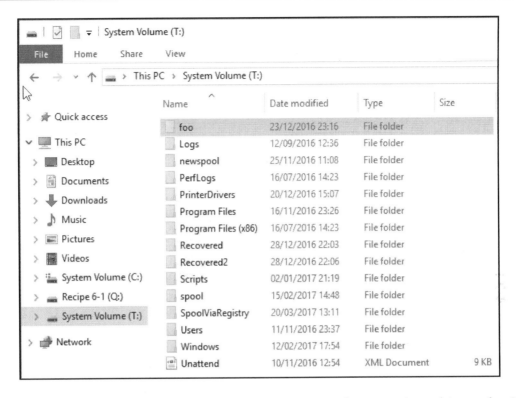

As you can see, this VHD contains all the files that were on the system's C: drive at the time of the backup. When you mount the VHD, Windows can assign a different drive letter for the newly mounted VHDX, other than T:. If so, then you need to change the recipe accordingly. Likewise, when Windows mounts the drive, it happens without a resulting drive letter. In addition to using WMI, you can also use the disk management snap-in inside the compmgmt.msc MMC console and add a drive letter before proceeding.

In *step 5*, you use the Get-WBJob cmdlet to examine the last Windows backup job to run. This cmdlet gets details of the backup job including the start and end times and the job state. This cmdlet also returns two file paths: the first for details of files and folders backed up and the second for errors encountered by WSB. These can help you to diagnose a failure in the backup job.

There's more...

In this recipe, you mounted a VHDX that was the target of the backup. This virtual disk file contains all the files and folders on the backup source, PSRV's C: volume, at the time of the backup. Once you have mounted the backup VHDX, you can retrieve individual files and folders should you wish to.

In *step 4*, you obtained volumes where the Drivetype was equal to 3. In WMI, many properties use coded values. For Win32_Volume objects, a drive type of 3 indicates a local drive. For a full list of the drive type values, see https://msdn.microsoft.com/en-us/library/aa394515(v=vs.85).aspx.

Initiate a backup manually

In most cases, your server's backup policy is fire and forget. You create and set the backup policy, and from then on backup just happens at the time you specify in the backup schedule. In other cases, perhaps before and after a major system change, you may want to initiate a one-off backup and not wait for WSB to create a scheduled backup. Additionally, you may just want to create a backup of key files. In those cases, you can run a backup based on a one-off policy.

Getting ready

To perform this recipe, you may find it helpful to remove the existing backup policy. This ensures the one-off policy you create in this recipe does not overlap with earlier/later recipes. If you perform this recipe on a live production server, make sure reinstate the backup policy after you have completed your testing.

Removing the policy is straightforward:

```
If (Get-WBPolicy) { Remove-WBPolicy -All -Force }
```

This recipe also uses a folder C:\Foo. If this does not exist on your system, create the folder and create two files in the folder, as follows:

```
New-Item -Path C:\Foo -ItemType Directory
Get-Date | Out-File -Path C:\Foo\d1.txt
Get-Date | Out-File -Path C:\Foo\d2.txt
```

How to do it...

1. Create and populate a new one-off backup policy to backup just two folders:

```
$OOPol = New-WBPolicy
$FSpec1 = New-WBFileSpec -FileSpec 'C:\Foo'
$FSpec2 = New-WBFileSpec `
          -FileSpec 'C:\Users\administrator\Documents'
Add-WBFileSpec -Policy $OOPol -FileSpec $FSpec1, $FSpec2
$Volume = Get-WBVolume -VolumePath Q:
$Target = New-WBBackupTarget -Volume $Volume
Add-WBBackupTarget -Policy $OOPol -Target $Target
```

2. Start the backup using the one-off backup policy:

```
Start-WBBackup -Policy $OOpol
```

3. Find the `.vhdx` backup file and mount it:

```
$ImagePath = 'Q:*.vhdx'
$BUFile = Get-ChildItem $ImagePath -Recurse
$ImageFilename = $BUFile.FullName
$MountResult = Mount-DiskImage -StorageType VHDX `
                              -ImagePath $ImageFilename `
                              -PassThru
```

4. If there is a volume label, get it, otherwise set it to `T:` as follows:

```
$Vol = Get-Ciminstance -Classname Win32_Volume |
          Where-Object {(-Not $_.DriveLetter) `
 -and ($_.Label -NotMatch 'Recipe')}
If ($Vol.DriveLetter)
  {$DriveLetter = $Vol.DriveLetter}
Else
    {$DriveLetter = 'T:'
    $Vol | Set-CimInstance -Property
                @{DriveLetter=$Driveletter}
}
```

5. Now view it in Explorer:

```
Explorer $Driveletter
```

How it works...

In the *Getting ready* section, you cleared the existing policy—this ensures any existing backup policy does not affect how this recipe works. To remove your policy, you check to see if one exists and if so, you invoke the Remove-WBPolicy with the -ALL parameter to remove the currently active backup policy (that is, the policy you set in the *Configure and set backup policy* recipe).

In *step 1*, you start by creating a new one-off policy, $OOPOL. Then you create two backup file specifications (that tell WSB what to backup and anything to exclude) and attach those file specification objects to the backup policy. Next, you create a backup target and add this to the one-off policy. Once you add the backup target to the one-off policy, you see the backup target details:

```
#      STEP 1

PS C:\> $OOPol        = New-WBPolicy
PS C:\> $FSpec1       = New-WBFileSpec -FileSpec 'C:\Foo'
PS C:\> $FSpec2       = New-WBFileSpec -FileSpec 'C:\Users\administrator\Documents'
PS C:\> Add-WBFileSpec -Policy $OOPol -FileSpec $FSpec1,$FSpec2
PS C:\> $Volume       = Get-WBVolume -VolumePath Q:
PS C:\> $Target       = New-WBBackupTarget -Volume $Volume
PS C:\> Add-WBBackupTarget -Policy $OOPol -Target $Target

Label                 : Recipe 6-1
WBDisk                :
WBVolume              : Recipe 6-1 (Q:)
Path                  : \\?\Volume{303f5cce-4450-45e0-b268-8f2de40de561}
TargetType            : Volume
InheritAcl            : False
PreserveExistingBackup : False
```

In *step 2*, you run the one-off policy to create the one-off backup. The output, truncated for brevity, looks similar to this:

```
PS C:\> Start-WBBackup -Policy $OOPol
Initializing the list of items to be backed up...
Creating a shadow copy of the volumes in the backup...
Updating the backup for deleted items...
Scanning the file system...
Volume 1 (79%) of 1 volume(s).
Compacting the virtual hard disk for volume C:, 33% completed.
Creating a shadow copy of the backup storage location(s)...
The backup operation completed.
```

In *step 3*, you find the VHDX file that WSB wrote to, and mount it. In *step 4*, you check to see if Windows has used a drive letter for this mounted virtual hard drive. If so you use that drive letter, but if not, you assign the drive letter *T:* to the mounted VHDX. These two steps do not produce output to the PowerShell Window, but you can bring up the Disk Management tool and see the new *T:* drive, like this:

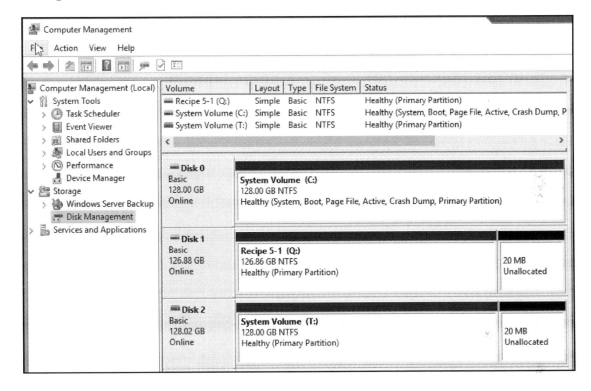

In *step 5*, you bring the newly mounted drive into Explorer which (when you expand the tree in the left pane!), looks like this:

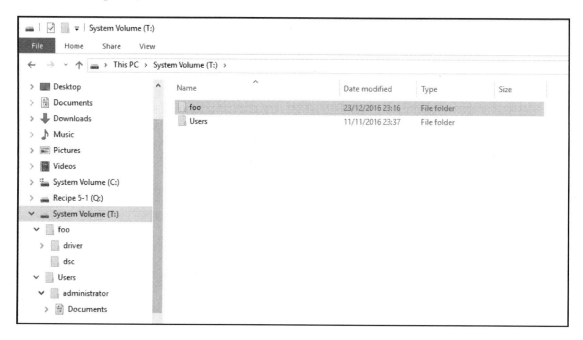

As you can see above, this backup file (The VHDX is now the T: drive) contains just two folders which are the ones you specified in *step 1*.

There's more...

Mounting the backup VHDX file and adding a drive letter if needed is a bit complex since the individual classes and cmdlets do not work together as well as you might like. If you have a large number of volumes on a server you are backing up, you may need to adjust *step 4* to accommodate your particular set of volumes.

Restore files and folders

Performing backups is great, but backups are only useful if you can use them to restore files and folders. The reasons for restoring include recovering from a major system disaster, recovering from a single disk failure, or just restoring a file a user has inadvertently deleted.

In the previous recipe, you saw how you could mount the VHDX that WSB created for you and give it a drive letter. So one way to recover the file is just to mount the backup VHDX and then use Explorer or other tools to copy files from the backup to a new home. This recipe uses the WSB cmdlets to recover to a separate folder. You would do this if you wanted to recover some particular files and did not want to overwrite anything.

Getting ready

In this recipe, you first create a new backup policy and start it to create a backup. This script, which is derived from the recipe *Configure and set a backup policy*, is as follows:

```
If (Get-WBPolicy) {Remove-WBPolicy -All}
If (-NOT (Test-Path C:food1.txt)) {
  'D1' | Out-File C:food1.txt}
$FullBUPol = New-WBPolicy
$Schedule  = '06:00'
Set-WBSchedule -Policy $FullBUPol -Schedule $Schedule | Out-Null
$TargetDisk = Get-WBDisk |
  Where-Object Properties -match 'ValidTarget' |
      Select-Object -First 1
$Target = New-WBBackupTarget -Disk $TargetDisk `
                             -Label 'Recipe 6-4' `
                             -PreserveExistingBackups $true
Add-WBBackupTarget -Policy $FullBUPol -Target $Target -Force |
      Out-Null
$DisktoBackup = Get-WBDisk | Select-Object -First 1
$Volume = Get-WBVolume -Disk $DisktoBackup
Add-WBVolume    -Policy $FullBUPol -Volume $Volume | Out-Null
Set-WBPolicy    -Policy $FullBUPol -Force
Start-WBBackup -Policy $FullBUPol -Force | Out-Null
$Drive = Get-CimInstance -Class Win32_Volume |
            Where-Object Label -Match 'Recipe'
Set-CimInstance -InputObject $Drive `
                -Property @{DriveLetter='Q:'}
```

Compared with earlier recipes, the above script fragment contains additional syntax to remove the output generated by some of the WSB cmdlets. If you are adapting this recipe to your own organization's needs, you may find the removed output of value from an auditing point of view—just remove the pipe to `Out-Null`. You then see more output which can be helpful as you tune the recipe in practice, or if you are using a transcript to create an audit trail of operations.

This code also ensures a file,C:\foo\d1.txt; exists. You may have created this file with earlier recipes, but if not, this starting point ensures this file exists in the backup.

If this is the first backup you have created, your system may not have been setup to give you the necessary access permissions on your drive. When testing any recipes in this book, you may need to adjust the recipe to cater for your specific system and system settings.

How to do it...

1. Get the most recent backup job and view the job's items:

```
$Job = Get-WBJob -Previous 1
$Job
$Job | Select-Object -ExpandProperty JobItems
```

2. Get and display the Backup set information for this job:

```
$BUSet = Get-WBBackupSet | Where-Object Versionid -EQ
$Job.VersionId
$BUSet
```

3. Recover a single file:

```
If (-Not (Test-Path C:\Recovered))
  {New-Item -Path C:\Recovered -ItemType Directory}
$File       = 'C:\Foo\d1.txt'
$TargetPath = 'C:\Recovered'
Start-WBFileRecovery -BackupSet $BUSet -SourcePath $File `
    -TargetPath $TargetPath -Option CreateCopyIfExists `
    -Force
Get-ChildItem -Path $TargetPath
```

4. Recover an entire folder structure:

```
If (-Not (Test-Path C:\Recovered2))
  {New-Item -Path C:\Recovered2 -ItemType Directory}
$SourcePath = 'C:\Foo'
$TargetPath = 'C:\Recovered2'
Start-WBFileRecovery -BackupSet $BUSet `
                     -SourcePath $SourcePath  `
                     -TargetPath $TargetPath `
                     -Recursive -Force
Get-ChildItem -Path $TargetPathfoo
```

How it works...

In *step 1*, you use the `Get-WBJob` cmdlet to retrieve details about the most recent backup job. You also use the output from `Get-WBJob` to view the job's items. The job details look like the following:

```
PS C:\> $Job = Get-WBJob -Previous 1
PS C:\> $Job

JobType          : Backup
StartTime        : 21/03/2017 16:10
EndTime          : 21/03/2017 16:29
JobState         : Completed
CurrentOperation :
HResult          : 0
DetailedHResult  : 0
ErrorDescription :
JobItems         : {VolumeList}
VersionId        : 03/21/2017-16:10
SuccessLogPath   : C:\Windows\Logs\WindowsServerBackup\Backup-21-03-2017_16-10-04.log
FailureLogPath   : C:\Windows\Logs\WindowsServerBackup\Backup_Error-21-03-2017_16-10-04.log

PS C:\> $Job | Select-Object -ExpandProperty JobItems

Name             : VolumeList
Type             : VolumeList
State            : Completed
HResult          : 0
DetailedHResult  : 0
ErrorDescription :
BytesProcessed   : 13802864640
TotalBytes       : 13802864640
CurrentItem      :
SubItemProcessed : 1
SubItemFailed    : 0
TotalSubItem     : 1
SubItemList      : {C:}
```

As you can see in this case, the previous job has completed successfully. WSB backed up the C: volume as the policy requested. Although the `$Job` variable shows log files with both a `Success` and `Failure` log file, there is little useful information contained in those text files.

In *step 2*, you retrieve the backup set that you are going to use to retrieve a backed-up file and a backed up folder. The Backup set information looks like this:

```
PS C:\> $BUSet = Get-WBBackupSet | Where-Object Versionid -eq $Job.VersionId
PS C:\> $BUSet

VersionId        : 03/21/2017-16:10
BackupTime       : 21/03/2017 16:10:04
BackupTarget     : \\?\Volume{303f5cce-4450-45e0-b268-8f2de40de561}
RecoverableItems : Volumes, SystemState, Applications, Files, BareMetalRecovery
Volume           : {System Volume (C:)}
Application      : {Registry}
VssBackupOption  : VssCopyBackup
SnapshotId       : 1bad2a5f-64cb-4b55-b3a0-10669839c80c
BackupSetId      : bc6a2dfc-610d-4ba6-81e9-f7e671b6eaab
```

In *step 3*, you recover a single file (`C:\Foo\D1.txt`). To avoid potential data loss, you restore to a new folder (`C:\Recovered`). Once WSB has recovered the file, you can see the recovered file in the folder `C:\Recovered`. It looks like this:

```
PS C:\> If (-Not (Test-Path C:\Recovered))
    {New-Item -Path C:\Recovered -ItemType Directory}
PS C:\> $File       = 'C:\Foo\D1.txt'
PS C:\> $TargetPath = 'C:\Recovered\'
PS C:\> Start-WBFileRecovery -BackupSet $BUSet -SourcePath $File `
        -TargetPath $TargetPath -Option CreateCopyIfExists `
        -Force
Recovering files from C:\Foo\D1.txt :
Completed.

PS C:\> Get-ChildItem -Path $TargetPath

    Directory: C:\Recovered

Mode                LastWriteTime         Length Name
----                -------------         ------ ----
-a----         20/03/2017     19:00          62 d1.txt
```

In *step 4*, you recover an entire backed up folder (`C:\Foo`) and any subfolders to a new folder `C:\Recovered2`. When the recovery is complete and depending on what you stored in `C:\Foo`, you see something like this:

```
PS C:\> If (-Not (Test-Path C:\Recovered2))
    {New-Item -Path C:\Recovered2 -ItemType Directory}

PS C:\> $SourcePath = 'C:\Foo\'
PS C:\> $TargetPath = 'C:\Recovered2\'
PS C:\> Start-WBFileRecovery -BackupSet $BUSet -SourcePath $SourcePath `
        -TargetPath $TargetPath -Recursive -Force
Recovering files from C:\Foo\ :
Recovering files from C:\Foo\ : 88% of files recovered.
Completed.

PS C:\> Get-ChildItem -Path C:\Recovered2\foo

    Directory: C:\recovered2\foo

Mode                LastWriteTime         Length Name
----                -------------         ------ ----
d-----         13/11/2016     00:02                driver
d-----         09/12/2016     10:17                dsc
-a----         20/03/2017     19:00          62 d1.txt
-a----         20/03/2017     19:00          62 d2.txt
```

There's more...

The backup job results you looked at has a job type of backup. As you saw in *steps 3* and *4*, you can use WSB to recover files and folders from a backup. You can look at the results of earlier file recovery jobs you just ran by using `Get-WBJob` to get the previous two jobs. The most recent previous job was the recovery of a single file you performed in *step 4* and the second most recent represented the recovery you carried out in *step 3*.

Backup and restore a Hyper-V Virtual Machine

There are many ways to back up a Hyper-V VM. You could, of course, use the recipes in this chapter inside the VM to back up your VM's hard drive contents to a network drive. As an alternative, you could use WSB to backup an entire VM and restore it.

Regarding the WSB commands to use when backing up a Hyper-V VM, you have options. You can use the WSB cmdlets, as you have done so far in this chapter. Or, you can use the Wbadmin console application. Wbadmin is a Windows command line tool that pre-dates the PowerShell module. It has the advantage of being higher ranked in search engines—useful if you wish to learn more. You may also find `Wbadmin` simpler to use in practice. This recipe shows how to use `Wbadmin` to create a backup of your VM and then restore it.

Getting ready

For this recipe, you need a Windows Server 2016 system with Hyper-V installed plus a working VM. In this recipe, you use the Windows Server 2016 host, `HV1`, that runs the `DC1.Reskit.Org` domain controller which you backup and then restore.

How to do it...

This recipe is in two parts. In the first part, you create a backup of a running Hyper-V VM, as follows:

1. On your Hyper-V host, look at the `DC1` VM and check the VM is up and running:

```
Get-VM -Name DC1
```

2. Create the backup using `Wbadmin`:

```
Wbadmin Start Backup -BackupTarget:C: -HyperV:'DC1'
```

3. Examine the log files created by Wbadmin:

```
$Logfile = Get-ChildItem `
  -Path $env:windirLogsWindowsServerBackup*.log |
    Sort-Object -Property LastWriteTime -Descending |
       Select-Object -First 1
Get-Content -Path $Logfile
```

4. Look at the files created in the backup target:

```
Get-ChildItem -Path C:WindowsImageBackup
Get-ChildItem -Path C:WindowsImageBackupHV1
```

The preceding steps create the backup. In the next part of this recipe, you restore the VM from the backup. To demonstrate a worst case scenario recovery, you remove the original VM completely from Hyper-V. Then you restore it from the backup, as follows:

1. Look at VM to see that the VM exists as do key components of the Hyper-V VM:

```
$Vm        = Get-VM -Name DC1
$VmCfgLoc = $Vm.ConfigurationLocation
$VmCfgOK  = Test-Path -Path $VmCfgLoc
$vmDskLoc = ($Vm.HardDrives).Path
$VmDskOK  = Test-Path -Path $VmDskLoc
"Location of Config Information: {0}" -f $VmCfgLoc
"Exists: {0}" -f $VmCfgOK
"Location of DC1 Hard Drive : {0}" -f $VmDskLoc
"Exists: {0}" -f $VmDskOK
```

2. Remove the VM from Hyper-V and observe the results:

```
Stop-VM    -Name DC1 -TurnOff -Force
Remove-VM -Name DC1 -Force
Get-VM     -Name DC1
```

3. Now restore the VM from backup:

```
$Version = $Backupversions |
    Select-String 'Version identifier' |
        Select-Object -Last 1
$VID = $Version.Line.Split(' ')[2]
$Cmd =  "& Wbadmin Start Recovery -Itemtype:Hyperv -Items:DC1 "
$Cmd += "-Version:$vid -AlternateLocation
        -RecoveryTarget:C:Recovery"
Invoke-Expression -Command $Cmd
```

4. And observe the results:

```
Start-VM -Name DC1
Get-VM -Name DC1
$Vm        = Get-VM -Name DC1
$VmCfgLoc = $Vm.ConfigurationLocation
$VmCfgOK  = Test-Path -Path $VmCfgLoc
$VmDskLoc = ($Vm.HardDrives).path
$VmDskOK  = Test-Path -Path $VmDskLoc
"Location of Config Information: {0}" -f $VmCfgLoc
"Exists: {0}" -f $VmCfgOK
"Location of DC1 Hard Drive : {0}" -f $vmDskLoc
"Exists: {0}" -f $VmDskOK
```

How it works...

In *step 1*, you examine the Hyper-V host to check to see the status of the VM DC1. This VM is the VM that serves as the first Domain Controller in the Reskit.Org's Active Directory forest. You create this domain controller in the recipe *Installing domain controllers* in Chapter 8, *Managing Windows Network Services*. As you can see from *step 1*, your DC1 virtual machine is up and running:

```
PS C:\> Get-VM -Path DC1

Name State  CPUUsage(%) MemoryAssigned(M) Uptime              Status             Version
---- -----  ----------- ----------------- ------              ------             -------
DC1  Running 0          4000              00:29:30.8490000 Operating normally 8.0
```

With *step 2*, you use `Wbadmin` to back up the `DC1` virtual machine. The output looks like this:

```
PS C:\> Wbadmin Start Backup -BackupTarget:C: -HyperV:'DC1'
wbadmin 1.0 - Backup command-line tool
(C) Copyright 2013 Microsoft Corporation. All rights reserved.

Retrieving volume information...
Any virtual machines included in the backup might be temporarily placed into a
saved state when the backup runs.
This will back up HyperV\DC1 to C:.                    ⟵
Do you want to start the backup operation?
[Y] Yes [N] No Y

The backup operation to C: is starting.
Creating a shadow copy of the volumes specified for backup...

Starting application backup...
Copying files for DC1(Online)... 4% done.
Backup of DC1(Online) succeeded.
Application backup succeeded.
Backup of DC1(Online) succeeded.

Summary of the backup operation:
------------------
The backup operation successfully completed.
Backup of DC1(Online) succeeded.

Application backup succeeded.

Log of files successfully backed up:
C:\WINDOWS\Logs\WindowsServerBackup\Backup-22-03-2017_22-07-49.log
```

The arrow in the above screenshot points to the line that reads *This will backup HyperV\DC1 to C:*. Directly after, notice that Wbadmin seems to request permission to start the backup operation, but then answers itself and continues. This is normal operation for `Wbadmin`. The developers probably could have taken those lines out of `Wbadmin`, but they didn't.

Note that the `-HyperV` switch you use in *step 2* is not available under Windows 10. You need to run this recipe, therefore, on the Windows Server 2016 server system hosting Hyper-V.

In *step 3*, you look at the log file generated by `Wbadmin`:

```
PS C:\> Get-Content C:\WINDOWS\Logs\WindowsServerBackup\Backup-29-12-2016_23-56-53.log
Backed up D:\
Backed up D:\DC1\
Backed up D:\DC1\DC1-AutoRecovery.avhdx
Backed up D:\DC1\DC1.vhdx
Backed up D:\DC1\Ref2016.vhdx
Backed up D:\hyper-v\
Backed up D:\hyper-v\DC1
Backed up D:\hyper-v\DC1\New Virtual Machine\
Backed up D:\hyper-v\DC1\New Virtual Machine\Snapshots\
Backed up D:\hyper-v\DC1\New Virtual Machine\Snapshots\FC35EC6C-021C-4A9C-BB86-010A59E22DF7.vmcx
Backed up D:\hyper-v\DC1\New Virtual Machine\Snapshots\FC35EC6C-021C-4A9C-BB86-010A59E22DF7.VMRS
Backed up D:\hyper-v\DC1\New Virtual Machine\Virtual Machines\
Backed up D:\hyper-v\DC1\New Virtual Machine\Virtual Machines\6501E155-A138-48E0-8392-683FF6F26759.VMRS
Backed up D:\hyper-v\DC1\New Virtual Machine\Virtual Machines\6501E155-A138-48E0-8392-683FF6F26759.vmcx
Application backup
Writer Id: {66841CD4-6DED-4F4B-8F17-FD23F8DDC3DE}
   Component: 6501E155-A138-48E0-8392-683FF6F26759
   Caption    : Online\DC1
   Logical Path:
```

As you can see, WSB backed up the `DC1` VHDX and the *Ref2016* base disk. The DC1 VM and the other VMs in the `Reskit.Org` VM farm make use of differencing disks—so backing up both disks is vital if you are to restore the VM to a working state.

In *step 4*, you look inside the `C:\WindowsImageBackup\` folder on the backup target drive. For this recipe, you created it in HV1's `C:` drive. The files in that folder are as shown in the following screenshot:

```
PS C:\> Get-ChildItem -Path C:\WindowsImageBackup\

    Directory: C:\WindowsImageBackup

Mode                LastWriteTime         Length Name
----                -------------         ------ ----
d-----        3/22/2017  10:09 PM                HV1

PS C:\> Get-ChildItem -Path C:\WindowsImageBackup\HV1

    Directory: C:\WindowsImageBackup\HV1

Mode                LastWriteTime         Length Name
----                -------------         ------ ----
d-----        3/22/2017  10:20 PM                Backup 2017-03-22 220749
d-----        3/22/2017  10:20 PM                Catalog
d-----        3/22/2017  10:20 PM                Logs
d-----       12/29/2016   3:03 PM                SPPMetadataCache
-a----       12/29/2016   3:00 PM             16 MediaId
```

You have now backed up the DC1 virtual machine. With this backup, you can restore the VM back to Hyper-V. To test this, you first remove the VM from Hyper-V. In *step 5*, you display where Hyper-V has stored DC1 virtual machine's configuration information and the VHDX file for the virtual machine, which looks like this:

```
Location of Config Information: D:\DC1
Exists: True
Location of DC1 Hard Drive : D:\DC1\Virtual Hard Disks\DC1.vhdx
Exists: True
```

In *step 6*, you stop then remove the DC1 VM. The result is that the VM is no longer available, as you can see:

```
PS C:\> Stop-VM    -Name DC1 -TurnOff -Force
PS C:\> Remove-VM -Name DC1 -Force
PS C:\> Get-VM     -Name DC1
Get-VM : Hyper-V was unable to find a virtual machine with name "DC1".
At line:1 char:1
+ Get-VM     -Name DC1
+ ~~~~~~~~~~~~~~~~~~~~~
    + CategoryInfo          : InvalidArgument: (DC1:String) [Get-VM], VirtualizationException
    + FullyQualifiedErrorId : InvalidParameter,Microsoft.HyperV.PowerShell.Commands.GetVM
```

With the VM removed, you restore it from the backup taken earlier in *step 2*. To do this, you need to get the backup version details. For this, you construct a string expression with those details embedded. To restore the VM, you then invoke the constructed expression. The result is that the restoration process commences. You can see these operations here:

```
PS C:\> $Backupversions = Wbadmin.Exe Get Versions -Backuptarget:C:
PS C:\> $Version = $Backupversions | Select-String 'Version identifier' |
                   Select-Object -Last 1
PS C:\> $VID = $Version.Line.Split(' ')[2]
PS C:\> $Cmd = "& Wbadmin.exe Start Recovery -Itemtype:Hyperv -Items:DC1 "
PS C:\> $Cmd += "-Version:$vid -AlternateLocation -RecoveryTarget:C:\Recovery"
PS C:\> Invoke-Expression -Command $Cmd

wbadmin 1.0 - Backup command-line tool
(C) Copyright 2013 Microsoft Corporation. All rights reserved.

Warning: If a Virtual Machine you are trying to recover to alternate location
was backed up from this host, this will delete and overwrite the original
virtual machine if it still exists.

You have chosen to recover the application HyperV. The files for the
following components will be recovered to C:\Recovery.

Warning: If a Virtual Machine you are trying to recover to alternate location
was backed up from this host, this will delete and overwrite the original
virtual machine if it still exists.

Warning: The virtual machines might not start if their network settings are
different after recovery. After recovery is complete use Hyper-V Manager to
verify the network settings of the virtual machines before they are started.

VM name: DC1
VM caption: Online\DC1
VM identifier: DD8F6DE3-5F65-4990-B0DD-BF328BFB47BE

Do you want to recover the application HyperV?
[Y] Yes [N] No Y

Preparing the component DC1(Online) for recovery...
Recovering the files for the component DC1(Online), copied (1%).
Recovering the files for the component DC1(Online), copied (100%).
Recovering the component DC1(Online).
The component DC1(Online) was successfully recovered.
The recovery operation completed.
Log of files successfully recovered:
C:\WINDOWS\Logs\WindowsServerBackup\ApplicationRestore-22-03-2017_22-35-29.log

Summary of the recovery operation:
--------------------
The component DC1(Online) was successfully recovered.
```

In *step 8*, you can see that the VM has been restored:

```
PS C:\> Start-VM -Name DC1
PS C:\> Wait-Vm  -Name DC1 -For IPAddress
PS C:\> Get-VM -Name DC1

Name State   CPUUsage(%) MemoryAssigned(M) Uptime              Status             Version
---- -----   ----------- ----------------- ------              ------             -------
DC1  Running 0           4000              00:01:28.9540000    Operating normally 8.0
```

After starting the DC1 VM, Get-VM shows that the VM is running. In the final part of *step 8*, you look at where Hyper-V now stores the VM configuration information and the VM's hard drive, like this:

```
Location of Config Information: C:\Recovery\DC1\D_\Book - DC1
Exists: True
Location of DC1 Hard Drive : C:\Recovery\DC1\D_\Book - DC1\Virtual Hard Disks\DC1.vhdx
Exists: True
```

Note that the VM's configuration information and the DC1. VHDX file is in `C:\Recovery`, rather than from the `D:\DC1` folder used before the backup (and before the removal of the VM). In operation, once WSB restores the VM, you may wish to move the VM to a different location rather than leave it in the recovery location. A very quick and easy way would be to copy the VHDX files to the new Hyper-V server and create a new VM on that server.

There's more...

In *steps 2* and *step 3*, you perform a VM backup and examine the resulting log file. In *step 3*, you hardcoded the name of the log file. You could have run *step 2*, assigning the output to a variable and then used string manipulation to get the last line to get the actual file name. As a Windows console application, `Wbadmin` emits a set of strings rather than objects (which are so much easier to manipulate).

In *step 2*, you use `Wbadmin`. This console mode application does not play well in a one-to-many remoting session. You need to run these scripts directly on the server.

In *step 6*, you remove a VM from Hyper-V. This action does not delete any VHDs that the VM use. To clean up the old VM, you should also remove the VHD storage. You could also create a new VM and attach the older virtual hard drives.

In *step 7*, you use some string manipulation to create command string to run `Wbadmin` to restore the DC1 VM. You get the backup version by doing some string parsing on the output of `Wbadmin`. You get the version information of the last backup, insert it into a command string, then execute the command string. In practice, you may need to change the logic in this recipe to reflect the nature of the VM to restore. Another option is to present `-ALL` the backup versions on the Hyper-V Server with `Out-Gridview`, and ask the user to select the backup.

Using `Wbadmin` or any older console application can be useful. In some cases, you need these console applications since there is no PowerShell cmdlet for that particular operation. When you use older console applications in your PowerShell scripts, you may need to do some string manipulation to extract the necessary information from the application's output.

Backup and perform bare metal recovery

The **Bare metal recovery (BMR)** is the process of restoring a backup onto a new machine. Suppose your file server, **FS1**, has a catastrophic failure and has to be replaced by a new server computer. To get this new host up and running, you could manually run through the setup of the OS, add relevant print drivers, re-define the printers, and then restore the data. Or you could just do a BMR from a backup. This recipe shows how to do bare metal recovery using the PowerShell cmdlets in the `WindowsServerBackup` module and then the bare metal recovery feature of Windows Setup.

Getting ready

To enable you to see BMR in action on a server, you must first install the Windows backup feature loaded on the server you wish to back up. You run the first part of this recipe on your server to create a backup capable of being restored using BMR. Then, after replacing the hardware, you perform a recovery onto to a new server based on the backup previously taken. This recipe uses a server, `FS1` which backs up and restores, across the network, to/from another server `SRV1`. You create a second server, `FS1A` and perform BMR onto it.

How to do it...

In the first part of this recipe, you run commands to create a backup of `FS1`, over the network, to `SRV1` as follows:

1. Ensure you have `Windows-Server-Backup` installed on FS1:

```
Install-WindowsFeature –Name Windows-Server-Backup
```

2. Setup backup policy, create a backup share, and take a backup with the backup
   file stored on a newly created network share:

```
# Remove any old policy
   If (Get-WBPolicy)  {Remove-WBPolicy -All -Force}
# Create new policy
   $FullBUPol = New-WBPolicy
   $Schedule = '06:00'
# Set schedule
   Set-WBSchedule -Policy $FullBUPol -Schedule
   $Schedule | Out-Null
# Create a credential
   $U = 'administrator@reskit.org'
   $P = ConvertTo-SecureString -String 'Pa$$w0rd'
     -AsPlainText -Force
   $Cred = New-Object -TypeName
   System.Management.Automation.PSCredential `
         -ArgumentList $U,$P
 # Create target and add to backup policy
    Invoke-Command -ComputerName SRV1 -Credential $cred `
    -ScriptBlock {
    New-Item -Path 'C:Backup' `
      -ItemType Directory
     New-SmbShare -Name Backup -Path 'C:Backup' `
        -FullAccess "$Env:USERDOMAINdomain admins"
         }
$Target = New-WBBackupTarget -NetworkPath 'SRV1Backup' `
                           -Credential $Cred
Add-WBBackupTarget -Policy $FullBUPol -Target $Target `
                 -Force | Out-Null
# Get and set volume to backup
   $DisktoBackup = Get-WBDisk | Select-Object -First 1
   $Volume = Get-WBVolume -Disk $DisktoBackup
   Add-WBVolume -Policy $FullBUPol -Volume
                $Volume | Out-Null
# Add BMR to policy
   Add-WBBareMetalRecovery -Policy $FullBUPol
# Set policy
   Set-WBPolicy -Policy $FullBUPol -Force
# Start the backup
   Start-WBBackup -Policy $FullBUPol -Force
```

Once you have the backup created, you can restore it using the rest of this recipe:

1. Using the Hyper-V MMC console on your Hyper-V host, create a new Hyper-V VM, and call it FS1A. Create a new disk and attach the Windows Server 2016 DVD ISO image into the DVD drive of the VM. Once completed, open a PowerShell window on your Hyper-V host and type:

   ```
   Get-VM -Name FS1A
   Get-VM -Name FS1A | Select-Object -ExpandProperty HardDrives
   Get-VM -Name FS1A | Select-Object -ExpandProperty DVDDrives
   ```

2. Start the VM using Start-VM and observe the VM status:

   ```
   Start-VM -Name FS1A
   Get-VM -Name FS1A
   ```

3. Using the MMC Console on your Hyper-V Host, open up a connection to the new FS1A VM. You see the start of the Windows Server setup process.

4. From the Windows Setup dialog, select your required language and input device, then click **Next**.

5. From the next dialog, click **Repair your computer**.

6. Setup then prompts you for an option—click **Troubleshoot**.

7. From the **Advanced Options** page, click on **System Image Recovery**.

8. From the **Re-image Your Computer** pop-up, click **Cancel**.

9. From the **Select a system image backup** window, click **Next**.

10. From the **Select the location of the backup for the computer you want to restore Windows**, click **Advanced**.

11. From the **Re-Image Your Computer** popup, click **Search for a system image on the network**.

12. From the **Are you sure you want to connect to the network?** dialog box, click **Yes**.

13. From the **Specify the location of the system image** window, enter the location where you stored the backup (in step 2), SRV1Backup, then click **Next**.

14. From the **Enter network credentials** box, enter credentials that will enable you to access SRV1Backup. Then click **OK**.

15. Once Windows connects to the remote machine and displays the location of backups, select the right share, and then click **Next**.

16. Click on the backup from which WSB should restore (in the case here, there is only one), and click `Next`.

17. From the **Re-image your computer** window, ensure that the details shown are correct, then click **Finish**.

18. Windows setup displays a warning to tell you that all disks to be restored are going to be re-formatted. Click **Yes** to continue.

19. Once the FS1A computer has finished the recovery operation and has rebooted, you can logon to the newly restored computer. Open a PowerShell console and verify you have recovered the host by the recovery by typing:

```
HostName
Get-NetIPConfiguration
```

How it works...

In *step 1*, you install the backup feature. If you or someone else has previously loaded the feature, then you will see this:

```
PS C:\> Install-WindowsFeature -Name Windows-Server-Backup

Success Restart Needed Exit Code        Feature Result
------- -------------- ---------        --------------
True    No             Success          {Windows Server Backup}
```

On the other hand, if you haven't loaded the Windows server and the backup feature is not loaded, then this step loads the feature, like this:

```
PS C:\> Install-WindowsFeature -Name Windows-Server-Backup

Success Restart Needed Exit Code        Feature Result
------- -------------- ---------        --------------
True    No             NoChangeNeeded {}
```

With the backup feature loaded, in *step 2* you create a bare metal recovery based full backup of FS1's C: drive. The approach is similar to that shown in the *Configure and set backup policy* recipe earlier in this chapter. Note that in *step 2*, you may get an error adding the volume to the policy if using a Generation 2 VM—you need to adjust the recipe accordingly.

```
PS C:\> If (Get-WBPolicy)  {Remove-WBPolicy -All -Force}
# Create new policy
$FullBUPol = New-WBPolicy
$Schedule = '06:00'
# Set schedule
Set-WBSchedule -Policy $FullBUPol -Schedule $Schedule | Out-Null
# Create a credential
$U = 'administrator@reskit.org'
$P = ConvertTo-SecureString -String 'Pa$$w0rd' -AsPlainText -Force
$Cred = New-Object -TypeName System.Management.Automation.PSCredential `
                   -ArgumentList $U,$P
# Create target and add to backup policy
Invoke-Command -ComputerName SRV1 -Credential $cred `
   -ScriptBlock {
     New-Item -Path 'C:\Backup' `
              -ItemType Directory
     New-SmbShare -Name Backup -Path 'C:\Backup' `
                  -FullAccess "$Env:USERDOMAIN\domain admins" |
         Out-Null


   }
$Target = New-WBBackupTarget -NetworkPath '\\SRV1\Backup' -Credential $Cred
Add-WBBackupTarget -Policy $FullBUPol -Target $Target -Force | Out-Null
# Get and set volume to backup
$DisktoBackup = Get-WBDisk | Select-Object -First 1
$Volume = Get-WBVolume -Disk $DisktoBackup
Add-WBVolume -Policy $FullBUPol -Volume $Volume | Out-Null
# Add BMR to policy
Add-WBBareMetalRecovery -Policy $FullBUPol
# Set policy
Set-WBPolicy -Policy $FullBUPol -Force
PS C:\> Start-WBBackup -Policy $FullBUPol -Force
Creating a shadow copy of the volumes in the backup...
Volume 1 (0%) of 1 volume(s).
Volume 1 (100%) of 1 volume(s).
The backup operation completed.
```

The backup itself generates no messages showing progress as you piped many commands
to Out-Null. Feel free to test this recipe, remove the pipes to Out-Null, and see far more
messages when you test this recipe!

In this step, when you create the target on a remote system, SRV1 in this case, you should
get no output if the folder and SMB share do not exist. If on the other hand, these items do
exist, you should see the following:

```
An item with the specified name C:\Backup already exists.
    + CategoryInfo          : ResourceExists: (C:\Backup:String) [New-Item], IOException
    + FullyQualifiedErrorId : DirectoryExist,Microsoft.PowerShell.Commands.NewItemCommand
    + PSComputerName        : SRV1

The name has already been shared.
    + CategoryInfo          : NotSpecified: (MSFT_SMBShare:ROOT/Microsoft/Windows/SMB/MSFT_SMBShare) [New-SmbShare], CimException
    + FullyQualifiedErrorId : Windows System Error 2118,New-SmbShare
    + PSComputerName        : SRV1
```

After the backup has completed, you simulate a disaster so you can use the backup to recover from that disaster. Using Hyper-V makes easy for you to simulate the disaster. With Hyper-V, just create a brand new VM with a VM name of FS1A. This VM has a new, empty disk, and the Windows Server 2016 DVD loaded into the VMs DVD drive.

You can then start the VM, and once the server is up and running, connect to the VM using Hyper-V's VM Connect. The initial screens show Windows setup's progress. Once setup completes its initialization, it displays a dialog box allowing you to set the language, time and currency format, and keyboard or input keyboard:

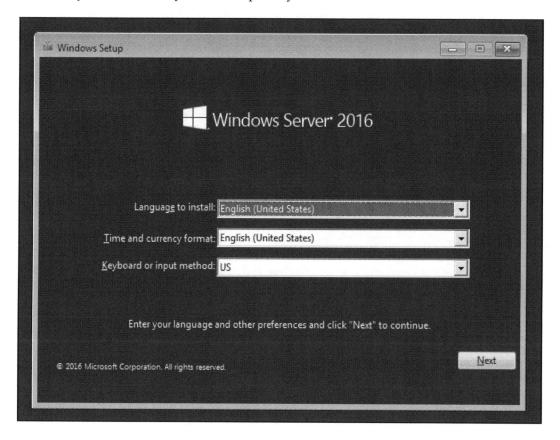

After clicking **Next**, in *step 7*, you see the next dialog box:

In *step 8*, you see the option to troubleshoot your PC:

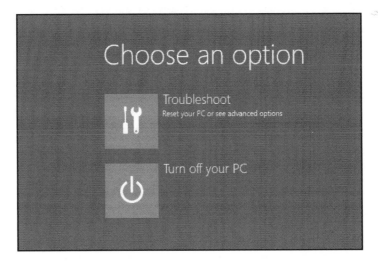

After clicking on **Troubleshoot**, in *step 9*, you see the **Advanced Options** window, where you select **System Image Recovery**:

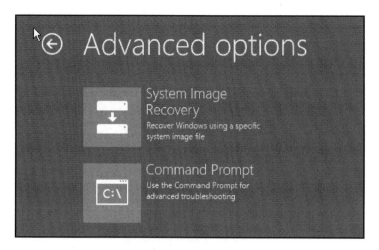

The **System Image Recovery** option first attempts to find a backup system image on the computer (FS1A), but of course, this does not exist. Clicking **Cancel** moves on to enabling setup to find a backup on the network.

In *step 11*, you see the **Select a system image backup** dialog, where you click on **Next**.

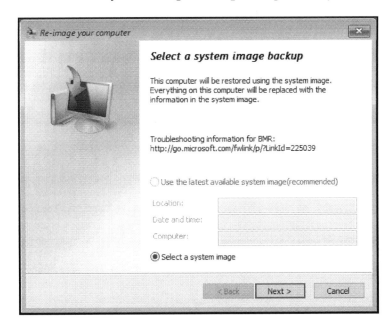

In *step 12*, you see a dialog box showing you no local images; here you click **Advanced...** :

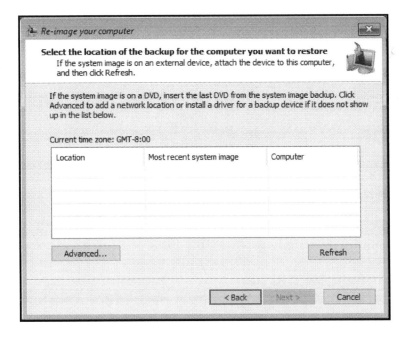

In *step 13*, you click on **Search for a system image on the network**.

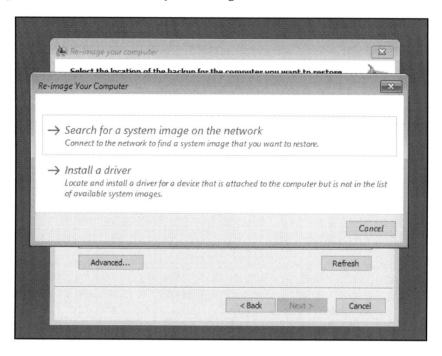

In *step 14*, you tell Windows that you want to connect to the network. Sensibly, the dialog box warns you that there are some risks involved with starting the network before security updates, and so on, are all installed.

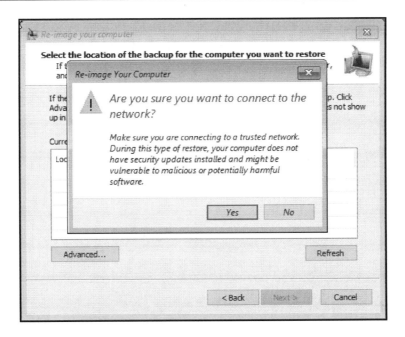

In *step 15*, you enter the details of where the system can find a backup to restore. In *step 2*, you saved the backup to SRV1Backup, so you enter that as the **Network folder**:

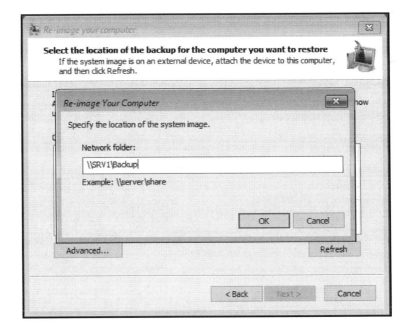

In *step 16*, you enter the credentials that Windows is to use to access the remote server and access a backup image stored on that system. Use the Domain Administrator account or another account that is a member of either the Local Administrators or the Backup Operators groups.

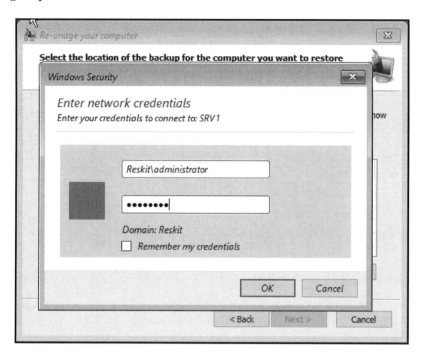

Once Windows setup connects to the remote system, it displays details of the backup location:

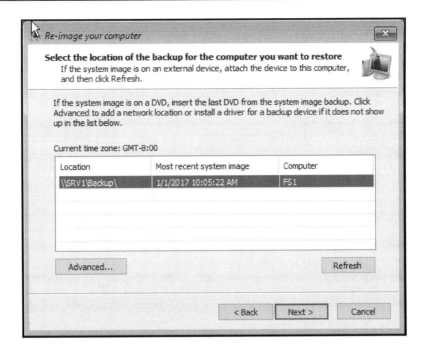

In *step 17*, Windows setup presents you with details of the backup it has found on SRV1:

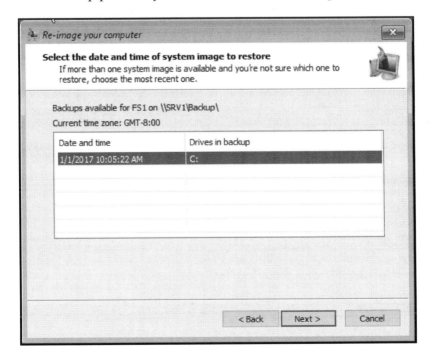

Step 18 provides you with additional restore operations. In most cases you can just click **Next**:

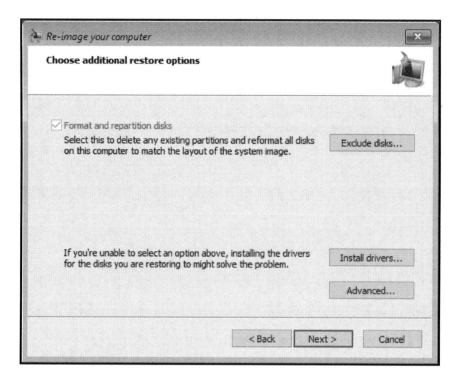

In *step 19*, setup provides details of the backup that it proposes to restore. Clicking on **Finish** starts off the restoration process.

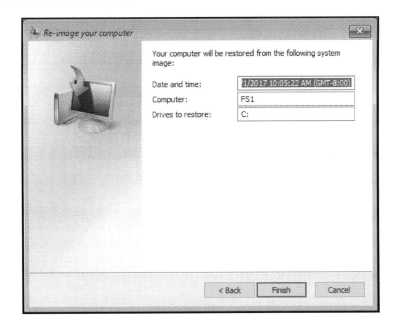

Step 20 provides another safety opportunity, setup warns you that all the disks to be restored are going to be re-formatted and replaced. Reformatting the disk is the is you want in this recipe, but it's sensible for the GUI to double check that you are restoring to the correct disk:

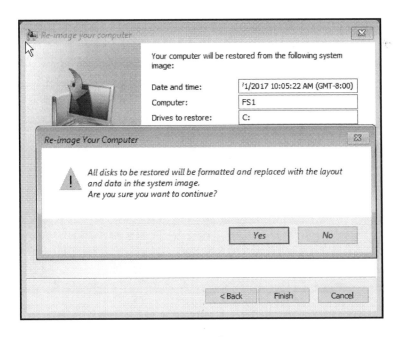

Once the restoration process starts, you see a progress dialog box showing progress:

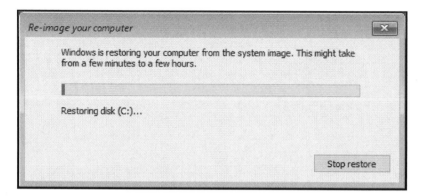

Once Windows completes the process of restoring the system, it reboots. After the reboot, you can logon and examine the restored server:

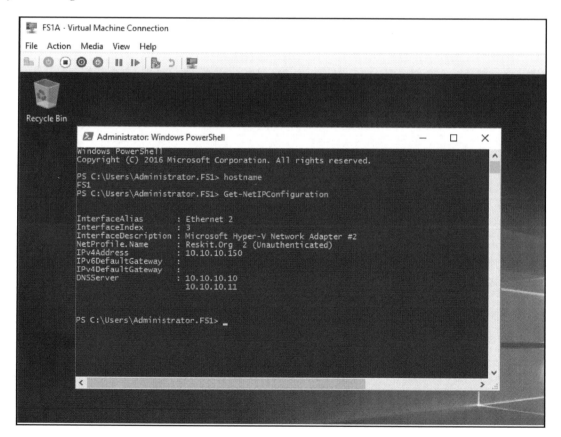

As you can see, the new VM, FS1A, is now running the restored FS1 host. The FS1A VM has the same IP address that FS1 had (when it was backed up). But as you can see, Windows has now applied the IP address to a new network interface (Ethernet 2). Effectively the new VM has a different NIC and thus gets a new Interface—but WSB applies the old IP address onto this new host. It may be the same make and model as the NIC in the old system (the old VM), but this NIC has a different serial number. It's important that you check the IP address details after you recover the VM and adjust if needed.

There's more...

Once your restored server is up and running, it has the same configuration as the original server. This configuration includes the machine name, IP Address, server certificates, and so on. As part of the overall restoration process, you may need to move the VM to another Hyper-V host so you may need to adjust this recipe to suit your requirements.

In *step 14*, Windows setup asks you if you want to connect to the network. In some environments, when you are restoring a VM, your network may be considered hostile (until you get the restored VM fully patched). Asking you whether you want to access the network is a great precaution. But since you are going to perform a bare metal restore from the network, connecting to the network is appropriate. If your network is that hostile, you may need to implement a different recovery and backup approach.

Restore the registry from a backup

In Windows, applications such as the registry can register with WSB. These applications contain a **Volume Shadow Copy Service** (**VSS**) writer. WSB uses that writer in the backup process to ensure application data is consistent when WSB takes the backup. The feature enables WSB to restore the application from the backup. In this recipe, you create a backup of a system including the registry and restore the registry from a backup to view the recovered hive.

Getting ready

This recipe uses the application server SRV1. Ensure the server has the WSB feature added, as shown in the *Configure and set backup policy* recipe. Your VM needs to have a second VHD added and setup as the E: drive. You use this second drive as the backup target. If you are creating a new virtual hard drive to test this recipe, ensure you bring the drive online, initialize it, and format it.

How to do it...

The steps for the recipe are as follows:

1. You begin this recipe by creating keys/values in the registry:

```
$TopKey  = 'HKLM:SoftwarePackt'
$SubKey  = 'Recipe6-7'
$RegPath = Join-Path -Path $TopKey -ChildPath $SubKey
New-Item -Path $TopKey
New-Item -Path $RegPath
Set-ItemProperty -Type String -Name RecipeName
                 -Path $RegPath `
                 -Value 'Recipe 6-7'
Get-Item -Path $RegPath
```

2. Create a full backup of this server by first removing any existing backup policy then creating a new backup policy with a schedule:

```
If (Get-WBPolicy) { Remove-WBPolicy -All -Force
$FullBUPol = New-WBPolicy
$Schedule = '06:00'
```

3. Create and set the backup schedule:

```
Set-WBSchedule -Policy $FullBUPol -Schedule
$Schedule | Out-Null
```

4. Set the backup target:

```
$BuDisk = Get-WBDisk |
    Where-Object Properties -eq 'ValidTarget'
$BuVol = $BuDisk | Get-WBVolume
$Target = New-WBBackupTarget -Volume $BuVol | Out-Null
Add-WBBackupTarget -Policy $FullBUPol -Target $Target -Force |
    Out-Null
```

5. Set the disk to backup and specify full metal recovery:

```
$DisktoBackup = Get-WBDisk |
    Select-Object -First 1
$Volume = Get-WBVolume -Disk $DisktoBackup
Add-WBVolume -Policy $FullBUPol -Volume $Volume |
    Out-Null
Add-WBBareMetalRecovery -Policy $FullBUPol
Add-WBSystemState -Policy $FullBUPol
```

6. Start the backup:

```
Start-WBBackup -Policy $FullBUPol -Force
```

7. Examine applications that were backed up and can be restored:

```
$Backup = Get-WBBackupSet |
    Where-Object BackupTarget `
                    -Match 'E:' |
        Select -Last 1
$Backup.Application
```

8. Restore the registry:

```
$Version = $Backup.VersionId
Wbadmin Start Recovery -Version:$Ver `
    -ItemType:App `
    -Items:Registry `
    -Recoverytarget:E:
```

9. See what WSB restored:

```
Get-ChildItem -Path E:RegistryRegistry
```

10. Once the recovery is complete, you can mount the recovered registry. Start by opening Regedit and click on the HKEY_LOCAL_MACHINE in the left pane:

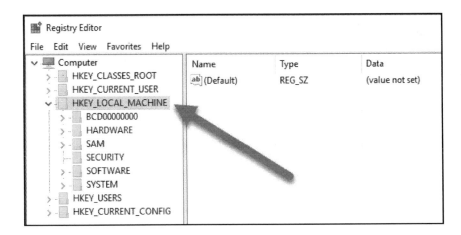

11. Then click on **File, Load Hive**. From the **Load Hive** dialog, enter a file name of `E:RegistryRegistrySOFTWARE`, then click **Open**:

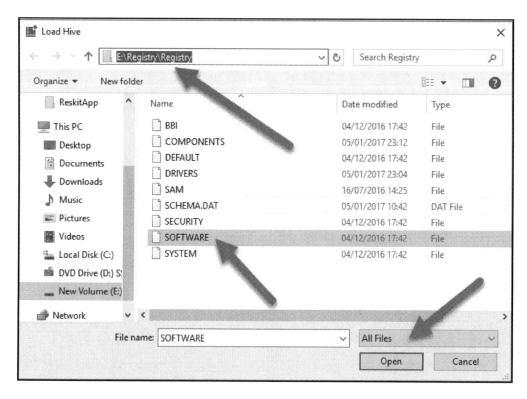

12. In The **Load Hive** dialog, enter a key name of `OldSoftwareHive` and then click **OK**:

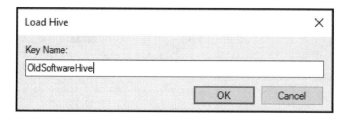

13. You can then expand the `OldSoftware` key; open `Packt` and you see the key added at the start of this recipe.

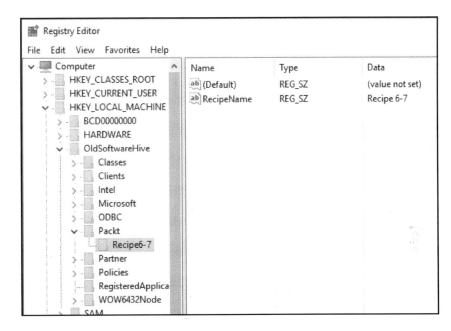

14. Once you have loaded the hive, open up a new PowerShell console and view the restored hive:

```
Get-ChildItem HKLM:\OldSoftwareHive\Packt
```

How it works...

In *step 1*, you add a new key HKEY_LOCAL_MACHINESoftwarePackt, and under that, another sub-key, Recipe 6-7. You then add a new value entry called RecipeName with a value of Recipe 6-7. This step demonstrates adding a key and a value entry to the registry and looks like this:

```
PS C:\> $TopKey  = 'HKLM:\Software\Packt'
PS C:\> $SubKey  = 'Recipe6-7'
PS C:\> $RegPath = Join-Path -Path $TopKey -ChildPath $SubKey
PS C:\> New-Item -Path $TopKey

    Hive: HKEY_LOCAL_MACHINE\Software

Name                            Property
----                            --------
Packt

PS C:\> New-Item -Path $Regpath

    Hive: HKEY_LOCAL_MACHINE\Software\Packt

Name                            Property
----                            --------
Recipe6-7

PS C:\> Set-ItemProperty -Type String -Name RecipeName -Path $regpath -Value "Recipe 6-7"
PS C:\> Get-Item -Path $Regpath

    Hive: HKEY_LOCAL_MACHINE\Software\Packt

Name                            Property
----                            --------
Recipe6-7                       RecipeName : Recipe 6-7
```

In *step 2* through *step 6*, you use the PowerShell cmdlets to create a full backup of the system and the C: volume to the E: volume:

```
PS C:\> If (Get-WBPolicy) {Remove-WBPolicy -All -Force}
PS C:\> $FullBUPol    = New-WBPolicy
PS C:\> $Schedule     = '06:00'
PS C:\> Set-WBSchedule -Policy $FullBUPol -Schedule $Schedule | Out-Null
PS C:\> $BuDisk       = Get-WBDisk | Where-Object Properties -Match 'ValidTarget'
PS C:\> $BuVol        = $BuDisk | Get-WBVolume | Where-Object MountPath -eq 'E:'
PS C:\> $Target       = New-WBBackupTarget -Volume $BuVol
PS C:\> Add-WBBackupTarget -Policy $FullBUPol -Target $Target -Force | Out-Null
PS C:\> $DisktoBackup = Get-WBDisk | Where-Object Disknumber -eq 0
PS C:\> $Volume       = Get-WBVolume -Disk $DisktoBackup
PS C:\> Add-WBVolume   -Policy $FullBUPol -Volume $Volume | Out-Null
PS C:\> Add-WBBareMetalRecovery -Policy $FullBUPol
PS C:\> Add-WBSystemState -Policy $FullBUPol
PS C:\> Start-WBBackup -Policy $FullBUPol -Force
Creating a shadow copy of the volumes in the backup...
Creating a shadow copy of the volumes in the backup...
Volume 1 (0%) of 1 volume(s).
Volume 1 (100%) of 1 volume(s).
Compacting the virtual hard disk for volume C:, 98% completed.
Creating a shadow copy of the backup storage location(s)...
The backup operation completed.
```

If you are using Generation 2 VMs to test this recipe, you may need to change this step to ensure you pick up the right volume. In these steps, you create a new backup policy then run the backup operation.

Once WSB has completed backing up the system, in `step 7` you get the backup details to show that WSB has backed up the Registry:

```
PS C:\> $Backup = Get-WBBackupSet | Where-Object BackupTarget -Match 'E:' |
            Select -Last 1
PS C:\> $Backup.Application

Identifier WriterId                                Component
---------- --------                                ---------
Registry   afbab4a2-367d-4d15-a586-71dbb18f8485   {Registry\}
```

In *step 8*, you restore the registry, and as you can see, the restoration was successful:

```
PS C:\>     wbadmin Start Recovery -Version:$Version -ItemType:App -Items:Registry -Recoverytarget:E:\
wbadmin 1.0 - Backup command-line tool
(C) Copyright 2013 Microsoft Corporation. All rights reserved.

You have chosen to recover the application Registry. The files for the
following components will be recovered to E:\.
Note: Recovering the files to an alternate location without involving writer will not recover the
application.

Component = Registry (\Registry)

Do you want to recover the application Registry?
[Y] Yes [N] No Y

Preparing the component Registry for recovery...
Recovering the files for the component Registry, copied (20%).
Recovering the files for the component Registry, copied (100%).
Recovering the component Registry.
The component Registry was successfully recovered.
The recovery operation completed.
Log of files successfully recovered:
C:\Windows\Logs\WindowsServerBackup\ApplicationRestore-26-03-2017_20-26-36.log

Summary of the recovery operation:
--------------------
The component Registry was successfully recovered.
```

And in *step 9*, you use `Get-ChildItem` to discover the registry hives recovered:

```
PS C:\> Get-ChildItem -Path E:\Registry\Registry\

    Directory: E:\Registry\Registry

Mode                LastWriteTime         Length Name
----                -------------         ------ ----
-a----        04/12/2016     17:42         65536 BBI
-a----        05/01/2017     23:12      41943040 COMPONENTS
-a----        04/12/2016     17:42        524288 DEFAULT
-a----        05/01/2017     23:04       5242880 DRIVERS
-a----        16/07/2016     14:25         65536 SAM
-a----        05/01/2017     10:42      11796480 SCHEMA.DAT
-a----        04/12/2016     17:42         32768 SECURITY
-a----        04/12/2016     17:42      66846720 SOFTWARE
-a----        04/12/2016     17:42      13893632 SYSTEM
```

In *steps 10-13*, you use Regedit to load the hive, and in *step 13* you view the hive.

Once you load the hive using Regedit, you can then view the hive and the hive's contents using PowerShell, as shown in *step 14*:

```
PS C:\> Get-ChildItem -Path HKLM:\OldSoftwareHive\Packt

    Hive: HKEY_LOCAL_MACHINE\OldSoftwareHive\Packt

Name                           Property
----                           --------
Recipe6-7                      RecipeName : Recipe 6-7
```

There's more...

This chapter (and this recipe) was written to be part of Chapter 6. However late in the production process, this chapter was re-numbered, however some artifacts of the old chapter number remain, such as the Recipe Name. Feel free to substitute different names.

When you restored the registry, WSB wrote the backed-up registry hives to a new location, the `E:` volume. Regedit enables you to mount a restored hive and view the contents. A neat feature is that after mounting the hive in Regedit, you can manipulate that hive directly from PowerShell. Support staff can use this approach to compare a hive in the currently active registry against a backup copy from some time past. An admin might have accidentally removed an application and you need to determine the registry settings requires to resurrect the application. As a forensic tool, you could use this technique to report on all changes made to some of all of the registry.

When using Generation 2 VMs, note that the available volumes are different from what you see using Generation VMs. You may need to adjust the recipe to ensure you pick up the correct volume to backup.

Create a daily backup report

Most backup jobs are fire and forget. You set them up, and they run. In such an environment, it is easy to forget about backups until the time when you need them (that is to recover a file, folder or entire server). One thing you can do is to generate a daily report on the state of backup on a critical server. You can run this report early every morning, and email it to one or more people in your organization to notify them of any issues that may have arisen with processing backups on critical servers.

This recipe creates a scheduled task which sends an email containing a summary of backup operations on your server, in this case: you use the file server FS1. This recipe is in two parts: the first part is a simple script that creates a backup report (on FS1) and the used email to send you the backup report. The second part of this recipe sets up the scheduled task that runs the backup report script. This second script also summarizes the results of setting up the scheduled task.

Getting ready

The idea of this recipe is that you have a scheduled job that sends you an email every day on the status of backup activities on a server. So before we can run this recipe, you need to ensure you have loaded the backup features onto that server, as shown in the *Configure and set backup policy* recipe.

How to do it...

The first part of this recipe is the script that creates the backup report and emails it via SendGrid, as follows:

1. Create a credential for SendGrid:

```
Function Get-MailCred {
$User = 'apikey'
$Pw = <your api key>
$Password = ConvertTo-SecureString -String $Pw
                                   -AsPlainText -Force
```

```
        New-Object -Typename System.Management.
                Automation.PSCredential `
                -ArgumentList $User,$password
    }
```

2. Start building the backup report:

```
$Now = Get-Date
$StartTime = $Now.AddDays(-7)
$Report = "Backup Report for $Env:COMPUTERNAME at [$now] `n"
$Report += '--------------------------------------------`n`n'
```

3. Query and report on the backup sets available:

```
$Report += '*** Backup Sets *** `n'
$Report += Get-WBBackupSet |
  Where-Object BackupTime -gt $startTime |
    Format-Table Versionid, BackupTime,
                Application, BackupTarget |
                Out-String
$Report += '`n'
```

4. Create an array of key backup event IDs:

```
$Report += '*** Event Log Messages'
$EvtArray = (100, 224, 227, 517, 518, 521, 527, 528, 544, 545)
$EvtArray += (546, 561, 564, 612)
```

5. Search the Windows event logs for events and add to the report:

```
$Report += Get-WinEvent -LogName 'Microsoft-Windows-Backup' |
  Where-Object {($_.TimeCreated -ge $StartTime) -and
    ($EvtArray -contains $_.ID)} |
      Format-Table -Property TimeCreated,
      LevelDisplayName, ID,     Message |
          Out-String
$Report += '`n'
```

6. Search the backup logs for errors and include filenames, then save the report away:

```
$Report += '*** Backup Error logs ***'
$Logs = Get-ChildItem -Path
        'C:WindowsLogsWindowsServerBackup*.log' |
        Sort-Object -Property LastWriteTime |
        Where-Object LastWriteTime -GE $StartTime
$Report += ($Logs | Where-Object Name -match 'Error'
            | Out-String)
$Report += ' `n'
 If (-NOT Test-Path -Path C:Reports)
     {New-Item -Path C:Reports -Directory}
$Report | Out-File -FilePath C:ReportsReport.txt
```

7. Send the report via e-mail:

```
$MailCred = Get-MailCred
$From       = 'BackupReport@Reskit.Org'
$To         = 'PowerShellbook@Gmail.Com'
$Body       = 'Daily backup report - contained
                in the attachment'
$SMTPServer = 'Smtp.SendGrid.Net'
$Subject    = "Backup Report for $Env:COMPUTERNAME
                at: [$Now]"
Send-MailMessage -From $From -To $To `
                 -Attachments C:ReportsReport.txt `
                 -SmtpServer  $SMTPServer `
                 -Body        $Report `
-Subject      $Subject `
-Credential   $Mailcred
```

8. Save the above part of this recipe (step 1 through step 7) as C: ScriptsBackupReport.ps1.

In the next part of this recipe, you setup up the C:\Scripts\BackupReport.ps1 as a regular task and finally observe the output. Before performing the second part, double check to ensure that the report script is in the right place:

```
$ReportScript = 'C:\Scripts\BackupReport.ps1'
 If ( -NOT (Test-Path $ReportScript) )
     {Throw 'Report script not found - exiting'}
```

9. Schedule the script using the task scheduler:

```
# Assume steps 1-6 are saved in c:scriptsbackupreport.ps1
$Name      = 'Daily Backup Report'
$Action    = New-ScheduledTaskAction -Execute `
'%SystemRoot%\system32\WindowsPowerShell\v1.0\powershell.exe" `
           -Argument $ReportScript
$Trigger   = New-ScheduledTaskTrigger -Daily -At 6am
$User      = 'ReskitBUAdministrator'
$Password  = 'Pa$$w0rd'
$Task      = Register-ScheduledTask -TaskName $Name -Action
           $Action `
                 -Trigger $Trigger `
                 -User $User `
                 -Password $Password
```

How it works...

In *step 1*, you create a simple function, `Get-MailCred`, that provides the credentials you need to send mail via `SendGrid.Net`. Before you run this recipe and this function, you need to add your API key which you get from `SendGrid`. Effectively, the user id for `SendGrid` is `apikey` and the password is your API key.

 Note: You should be very careful about exposing the API Key. If you plan on using this recipe, you are going to need to determine whether you need to pass credentials to your mail server, and how to achieve it for your environment. In general, leaving plain text credentials in any production script is a not good idea.

The first part of this script is where you create and mail the report; you save this locally on FS1, then you use the second part of this script to create the scheduled task.

In *step 2*, you start by creating a report with a header. In *step 3*, you get all the backup sets available and add these details to the report. In *steps 4* and *5*, you look at the Windows Backup event log, and pull out any relevant event log entries, and add them to the report. In *step 6*, you look for any backup error log and add information to the report.

Finally, in *step 7*, you use `SendGrid` to send mail on to a user. In this recipe, you used Gmail as your mail target, although you could have used any other mail server in `step 8`. From Gmail's web interface, the mail and report look like this:

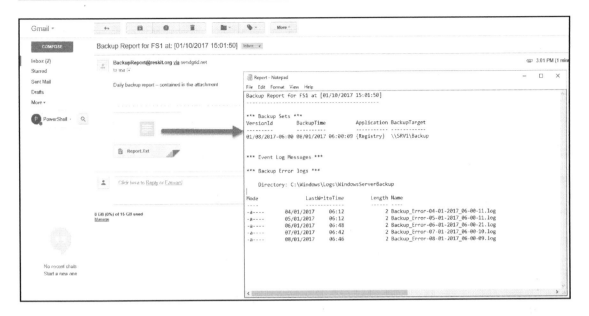

To turn this script into a scheduled task, you start with *step 8* and create a scheduled task. Providing you specified the parameters correctly, you get no output from this task. In *step 9*, you find and display the details of the scheduled task:

```
Task Name             State    Action                      Start                        Frequency
Daily Backup Report   Ready    c:\Scripts\BackupReport.ps1  2017-01-10T06:00:00+00:00 1
```

Once you set up this scheduled task, the task runs every morning at 06:00 and generates a report. Needless to say, if you are going to be creating a regular report, you could easily add more details to the report. You could improve the report script to produce HTML as output. You could then either set the body to this HTML document or just attach it to the mail.

There's more...

This recipe used `Sendgrid.com` as an SMTP Server. In the first part of this recipe, you created the backup report which you sent as an email message. SendGrid has a free account that enables you to send up to 100 emails per day, which is more than enough for the testing of scripts that send mail. In this recipe, the `Get-MailCred` function is used to return a credential object for SendGrid. To test this recipe, navigate to `https://SendGrid.Com` and sign up for a free account and get your API Key.

Backup and restore using Microsoft Azure

The recipes in this chapter, thus far, have been focused on Windows Server Backup. An alternative to performing backups is backing up to the cloud. This recipe demonstrates using Azure Backup as an alternative to the Windows Server Backup product.

Getting ready

For this recipe to succeed, you need a computer to backup from, an Azure account, and you need to have the Azure cmdlets loaded. You also need to load the online backup cmdlets (which you do in this recipe).

In this recipe, you use SRV2 as the server to backup (and restore). You can run this recipe on any server.

To load the Azure cmdlets, you use the Install-Module cmdlet, as demonstrated in the Explore PowerShellGet recipe in Chapter 1, *What's new in PowerShell and Windows Server*. You use this cmdlet on SRV2 to find and load the Azure Resource Manager cmdlets that you use in this recipe. Then, you can view the newly installed module, as follows:

```
Install-Module -Name AzureRm -Repository PSGallery
Get-Module -Name AzureRM -ListAvailable
```

If this is the first module you have installed using Install-Module, you also see a pop-up requesting permission to install NuGet. This is normal.

How to do it...

The steps for the recipe are as follows:

1. Login to Azure:

   ```
   Login-AzureRmAccount
   ```

2. Get Azure Subscription details:

   ```
   $Sub = Get-AzureRmSubscription
   Select-AzureRmSubscription -SubscriptionId
   $Sub[0].SubscriptionId
   ```

3. Register with Azure recovery services provider:

```
Register-AzureRmResourceProvider
        -ProviderNamespace 'Microsoft.RecoveryServices `
```

4. Create an ARM Resource Group:

```
$RGName   = 'Recipe'
$Location = 'WestEurope'
New-AzureRmResourceGroup -Name $RGName -Location $Location
```

5. Create Azure Recovery Vault:

```
$VaultName = 'RecipeVault'
New-AzureRmRecoveryServicesVault -Name $VaultName `
-ResourceGroupName $RGName `-Location $Location
```

6. Set Recovery Vault properties:

```
$Vault = Get-AzureRmRecoveryServicesVault -Name $VaultName
Set-AzureRmRecoveryServicesBackupProperties -Vault $Vault `
                -BackupStorageRedundancyLocallyRedundant
```

7. Examine the backup vault:

```
Get-AzureRmRecoveryServicesVault
```

8. Get MARS Agent installer and install it:

```
New-Item C:\Foo -ItemType Directory -Force `
                -ErrorAction SilentlyContinue | Out-Null
$MarsURL = 'Http://Aka.Ms/Azurebackup_Agent'
$WC = New-Object -TypeName System.Net.WebClient
$WC.DownloadFile($MarsURL,'C:\FOO\MarsInstaller.EXE')
C:FooMarsInstaller.EXE /q
```

9. Import the Azure Backup Module:

```
Import-Module `
'C:\Program\FilesMicrosoft Azure Recovery Services
Agent\bin\Modules\MSOnlineBackup'
```

10. Get and display the credentials for the recovery vault:

```
$CredPath = 'C:\Foo
$CredsFile = Get-AzureRmRecoveryServicesVaultSettingsFile `
                -Backup -Vault $Vault `
                -Path $CredPath
"Credential File Path: [{0}]" -f $CredsFile.FilePath
```

11. Register this computer with the recovery vault:

```
Start-OBRegistration -VaultCredentials $Credsfile.FilePath `
                    -Confirm:$false
```

12. Set network details:

```
Set-OBMachineSetting -NoProxy
Set-OBMachineSetting -NoThrottle
```

13. Set encryption:

```
$PassPhrase = ConvertTo-SecureString `
    -String 'Cookham!JerryGarcia$123_Rebecca' -AsPlainText -Force
$PassCode = 'BWROCKS!0'
Set-OBMachineSetting -EncryptionPassphrase $PassPhrase
                    -SetPasscode $Passcode
```

14. Create and view a backup policy:

```
$APolicy = New-OBPolicy
$APolicy
```

15. Configure and set backup schedule:

```
$Sched = New-OBSchedule -DaysofWeek Tuesday, Saturday `
                        -TimesofDay    04:00
Set-OBSchedule -Policy $APolicy -Schedule $Sched
```

16. Set retention policy:

```
$RetentionPolicy = New-OBRetentionPolicy -RetentionDays 7
Set-OBRetentionPolicy -Policy $APolicy -RetentionPolicy
$RetentionPolicy
```

17. Specify files to backup and files to exclude:

```
$Inclusions = New-OBFileSpec -FileSpec 'C:'
$Exclusions = New-OBFileSpec -FileSpec 'C:Windows' -Exclude
Add-OBFileSpec -Policy $APolicy -FileSpec $Inclusions
Add-OBFileSpec -Policy $APolicy -FileSpec $Exclusions
```

18. Remove existing policy and set a new one:

```
If (Get-OBPolicy) {Remove-OBPolicy -Force
Set-OBPolicy -Policy $APolicy -Confirm:$false
```

19. Get and display the Azure backup schedule:

```
Get-OBPolicy | Get-OBSchedule
```

20. Perform a one-off backup based on the currently active backup policy:

```
Get-OBPolicy | Start-OBBackup
```

Having used the Azure Backup cmdlets to backup a server (SRV2 in this case), you can also recover files and folders using the following:

21. Set source volume to recover from:

```
$Source = Get-OBRecoverableSource
```

22. Get the recovery points from which you can restore (that is, the most recent):

```
$RPs = Get-OBRecoverableItem -Source $Source |
    Select-Object -First 1
```

23. Choose what to restore:

```
$FilesFolders = Get-OBRecoverableItem -RecoveryPoint $RP `
                                -Location "C:Foo\"
$Item = Get-OBRecoverableItem -RecoveryPoint $RP `
                        -Location "C:Foo\" `
                        -SearchString "MarsInstaller.EXE "
```

24. Examine a file that was explicitly NOT backed up:

```
Get-OBRecoverableItem -RecoveryPoint $RP `
                        -Location 'C:\Windows' `
                        -SearchString 'mib.bin'
```

25. Recover specified files and folders:

```
$RecoveryOption =New-OBRecoveryOption `
    -DestinationPath 'C:\temp' `
    -OverwriteType Skip
Start-OBRecovery -RecoverableItem $Item -RecoveryOption
$RecoveryOption
```

26. See what OBRecovery recovered:

```
Get-ChildItem C:\AzRecover\C_vol
Get-ChildItem C:\AzRecover\C_vol\Foo
```

How it works...

After you install the Azure cmdlets, the first thing to do is logon to Azure. If you are using an AAD account to logon, you can pass credentials directly the cmdlet. If you are using a Microsoft Live account to logon, you see two dialog boxes:

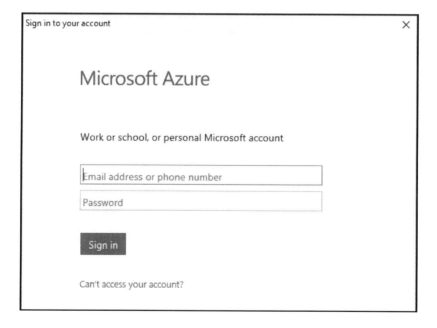

From this dialog, you enter your Live ID and click on **Sign in**. Azure takes you to a second dialog box where you enter your password:

After a successful logon in *step 1*, the cmdlet outputs details about your account, like this:

```
PS C:\> Login-AzureRmAccount

Environment           : AzureCloud
Account               : AzureAdmin@Reskit.Org
TenantId              : 53746561-6c20-596f-7572-204661636521
SubscriptionId        : 4a6572727-9207-26f6-36b7-32069742121
SubscriptionName      : Reskit.Org
CurrentStorageAccount :
```

In *step 2*, you obtain (and display) the subscription object that relates to your Azure Subscription. Depending on how many subscriptions you have, you may need to adjust *step 2* to ensure you select the correct Azure subscription to use for the rest of this recipe. Select-AzureRmSubscription cmdlet directs Azure PowerShell to use the chosen subscription. This step looks like this:

```
PS C:\> $Sub = Get-AzureRmSubscription
PS C:\> Select-AzureRmSubscription -SubscriptionId $Sub[0].SubscriptionId

Environment           : AzureCloud
Account               : AzureAdmin@Reskit.Org
TenantId              : 53746561-6c20-596f-7572-204661636521
SubscriptionId        : 4a6572727-9207-26f6-36b7-32069742121
SubscriptionName      : Reskit.Org
CurrentStorageAccount :
```

In *step 3*, which you only need do once, you register your currently active subscription with the Azure Recovery Services. The result of registering are details about what resource types you can access, like this:

```
PS C:\> Register-AzureRmResourceProvider -ProviderNamespace 'Microsoft.RecoveryServices'

ProviderNamespace : Microsoft.RecoveryServices
RegistrationState : Registered
ResourceTypes     : {vaults, operations, locations, locations/backupStatus...}
Locations         : {West US, East US, North Europe, West Europe...}
```

Once you have your subscription registered, you create the resource group in *step 4*. Resource groups hold all ARM resources:

```
PS C:\> $RGName    = 'Recipe'
PS C:\> $Location  = 'WestEurope'
PS C:\> New-AzureRmResourceGroup -Name $RGName -Location $Location

ResourceGroupName : Recipe
Location          : westeurope
ProvisioningState : Succeeded
Tags              :
ResourceId        : /subscriptions/4a6572727-9207-26f6-36b7-32069742121/resourceGroups/Recipe
```

Next, in *step 5*, you create the Azure Recovery Vault:

```
PS C:\> $VaultName = 'RecipeVault'
PS C:\> New-AzureRmRecoveryServicesVault -Name $VaultName -ResourceGroupName $RGName `
                                          -Location $Location

Name              : RecipeVault
ID                : /subscriptions/4a6572727-9207-26f6-36b7-32069742121/resourceGroups/Recipe/providers/Microsoft.RecoveryServices/vaults/RecipeVault
Type              : Microsoft.RecoveryServices/vaults
Location          : westeurope
ResourceGroupName : Recipe
SubscriptionId    : 4a6572727-9207-26f6-36b7-32069742121
Properties        : Microsoft.Azure.Commands.RecoveryServices.ARSVaultProperties
```

In *step 6*, you set the recovery vault to use Azure's Locally Redundant store option. There is no output from this step.

Next, in *step 7*, you examine the Recovery Vault:

```
PS C:\> Get-AzureRmRecoveryServicesVault

Name              : RecipeVault
ID                : /subscriptions/4a6572727-9207-26f6-36b7-32069742121/resourceGroups/Recipe/providers/Microsoft.RecoveryServices/vaults/RecipeVault
Type              : Microsoft.RecoveryServices/vaults
Location          : westeurope
ResourceGroupName : Recipe
SubscriptionId    : 4a6572727-9207-26f6-36b7-32069742121
Properties        : Microsoft.Azure.Commands.RecoveryServices.ARSVaultProperties
```

In *step 8*, you use the `System.Net.Webclient` .NET class to download the **Microsoft Azure Recovery Services** (**MARS**) Agent installer, which you then run. The MARS installer installs the backup cmdlets on your system. There is no output from *step 8*.

In *step 9*, you install the Online Backup module manually. There is no output from this step.

In *step 10*, you use the `Get-AzureRMRecoveryServicesVaultSettingsFile` to download the Vault settings file and display the location where you stored it. This file is, in effect, a certificate that enables the computer to access Azure Recovery Services and it looks like this:

```
PS C:\> $CredPath    = 'C:\Foo'
PS C:\> $CredsFile    = Get-AzureRmRecoveryServicesVaultSettingsFile -Backup -Vault $Vault -Path  $CredPath
PS C:\> "Credential File Path: [{0}]" -f $CredsFile.FilePath

Credential File Path: [C:\Foo\RecipeVault_Mon Mar 27 2017.VaultCredentials]
```

With *step 11*, you register this computer with Azure Recovery Services with your recovery vault in Azure's Western Europe region, as follows:

```
PS C:\> Start-OBRegistration -VaultCredentials $Credsfile.FilePath -Confirm:$false
Vault credentials validation succeeded. Below are the backup vault details.

CertThumbprint      : a94630f92e3320846484b64c61b4f421f7579131
SubscriptionID      : 4a6572727-9207-26f6-36b7-32069742121
ServiceResourceName : RecipeVault
Region              : westeurope

Machine registration succeeded.
```

In *step 12*, you set backup details for this system, including a proxy setting (no proxy), a throttle setting (no throttling). This step produced no output.

In *step 13*, you set the encryption passphrase and security pin to use for this vault. Note without these items, you cannot recover your data. You need to keep these credentials (and the scripts that contain them) carefully protected. The output of this step is as follows:

```
PS C:\> $PassPhrase = ConvertTo-SecureString -String 'Cookham!JerryGarcia£123_Rebecca' -AsPlainText -Force
PS C:\> $PassCode   = 'BWROCKS!0'
PS C:\> Set-OBMachineSetting -EncryptionPassphrase $PassPhrase -SecurityPIN $Passcode
Server properties updated successfully.
```

This step completes the installation and setup of Azure backup, and you are now ready to create a backup. With Azure Recovery Services, any backups of a Windows server/client to Azure Backup are governed by a backup policy (similar to on-premises WSB backup). The online backup policy has three key components

- A backup schedule that specifies when backups need to be taken and synchronized with the service.
- A retention schedule that specifies how long to retain the recovery points in Azure.
- A file inclusion/exclusion specification that states what should be (and should not be) backed up.

In *step 14*, you create and display a new empty Azure Online Backup policy:

```
PS C:\> $APolicy = New-OBPolicy
PS C:\> $APolicy

BackupSchedule  :
DsList          :
PolicyName      :
RetentionPolicy :
State           : New
PolicyState     : Valid
```

In *step 15*, you create a backup schedule and assign it to your backup. This sets up Azure recovery to perform a backup at 4:00 every Tuesday and Saturday:

```
PS C:\> $Sched = New-OBSchedule -DaysofWeek Tuesday, Saturday -TimesofDay 04:00
PS C:\> Set-OBSchedule -Policy $APolicy -Schedule $Sched

BackupSchedule  : 14:00
                  Wednesday, Saturday,
                  Every 1 week(s)
DsList          :
PolicyName      :
RetentionPolicy :
State           : New
PolicyState     : Valid
```

With *step 16*, you set a retention period of seven days:

```
PS C:\> $RetentionPolicy = New-OBRetentionPolicy -RetentionDays 7
PS C:\> Set-OBRetentionPolicy -Policy $APolicy -RetentionPolicy $RetentionPolicy

BackupSchedule   : 04:00
                   Tuesday, Saturday,
                   Every 1 week(s)
DsList           :
PolicyName       :
RetentionPolicy  : Retention Days : 7
                   WeeklyLTRSchedule :
                   Weekly schedule is not set
                   MonthlyLTRSchedule :
                   Monthly schedule is not set
                   YearlyLTRSchedule :
                   Yearly schedule is not set
State            : New
PolicyState      : Valid
```

In *step 17*, you specify the files that WSB should include in the backup (all of `C:`) and the files that should you wish to exclude from the backup (i.e. the contents of the `C:\ Windows folders`). There is no output from this step.

Finally, in *step 18*, you set *$Apolicy* as the currently active policy. If there was an existing policy, you should remove it first before setting a new policy. This new policy produces details of what you want WSB to back up (and to omit) and looks like this:

```
PS C:\> If (Get-OBPolicy) {Remove-OBPolicy -Confirm:$false}
PS C:\> Set-OBPolicy -Policy $APolicy -Confirm:$false

BackupSchedule   : 04:00
                   Tuesday, Saturday,
                   Every 1 week(s)
DsList           : {DataSource
                   DatasourceId:140738999491858
                   Name:C:\
                   FileSpec:FileSpec
                   FileSpec:C:\
                   IsExclude:False
                   IsRecursive:True
                   ,FileSpec
                   FileSpec:C:\Windows
                   IsExclude:True
                   IsRecursive:True
                   }
PolicyName       : 419dbee5-603c-4bad-9f56-e95e2db06099
RetentionPolicy  : Retention Days : 7
                   WeeklyLTRSchedule :
                   Weekly schedule is not set
                   MonthlyLTRSchedule :
                   Monthly schedule is not set
                   YearlyLTRSchedule :
                   Yearly schedule is not set
State            : Existing
PolicyState      : Valid
```

With *step 19*, you display the schedule for Azure Backup, based on the policy you set earlier:

```
PS C:\> Get-OBPolicy | Get-OBSchedule

SchedulePolicyName    : 3b1abde1-f223-42e1-bc04-32e3691547ca
ScheduleRunDays       : {Tuesday, Saturday}
ScheduleRunTimes      : {04:00:00}
ScheduleWeeklyFrequency : 1
State                 : Existing
OfflineSeedingParams  :
```

As the screenshot shows, you have created an Azure backup policy that backs up twice a week at 04:00 on Tuesday and Saturday. Needless to say, you are likely to need to adjust the details of this policy before putting it into operation. Once you have a policy set, you perform a one-off backup based on the policy, as you see in *step 20*:

```
PS C:\> Get-OBPolicy | Start-OBBackup

Taking snapshot of volumes...
Preparing storage...
Generating backup metadata information and preparing the metadata VHD...
Data transfer is in progress. It might take longer since it is the first backup and all data needs to be transferred...
Data transfer completed and all backed up data is in the cloud. Verifying data integrity...
Data transfer completed
Job completed.
The backup operation completed successfully.
```

After you back up (at least once), you can recover files and folders from the backup. You restore to a folder on your local system. In *steps 21*, *22*, *23*, and *24* you set the items you wish to recover and to where you want Azure Backup to recover them. In *step 25*, you look at a file that was not backed up (and you see no actual output). These steps generate no output.

In *step 26*, you set the recovery options then commence the backup:

```
PS C:\> $RecoveryOption = New-OBRecoveryOption -DestinationPath 'C:\AzRecover' `
                          -OverwriteType Skip
PS C:\> Start-OBRecovery -RecoverableItem $Item -RecoveryOption $RecoveryOption

Job is in pre restore step...
Estimating size of backup items...
Estimating size of backup items...
Job completed.
The recovery operation completed successfully.
```

Once the backup has completed, in *step 27*, you view the files that Azure Backup restored from an earlier backup, as follows:

```
PS C:\AzRecover\C_vol> Get-ChildItem  C:\AzRecover\C_vol

    Directory: C:\AzRecover\C_vol

Mode                LastWriteTime         Length Name
----                -------------         ------ ----
d-----        28/03/2017     01:50                Foo

PS C:\AzRecover\C_vol> Get-ChildItem  C:\AzRecover\C_vol\Foo

    Directory: C:\AzRecover\C_vol\Foo

Mode                LastWriteTime         Length Name
----                -------------         ------ ----
-a----        28/03/2017     00:21       39912192 MarsInstaller.EXE
```

As you can see, by performing this recipe you backed up server SRV2, then restored a backed up file from the Azure's recovery vault onto SRV2.

There's more...

In *step 4*, the recipe sets the Azure region to Western Europe. With the growth of Azure data centers around the world, there may be an Azure region closer to you. Check on the Microsoft Azure Regions page at https://azure.microsoft.com/en-gb/regions/

In *step 15*, you set the time for the backup (04:00). Azure backup only starts backup jobs on the hour or half hour, starting at midnight (00:00). If you set the time to, say, 16:20, this will generate an error later, in *step 18*, when you set the policy using Set-OBPolicy.

6
Managing Performance

In this chapter, we are going to cover the following recipes:

- Exploring performance counters with Get-Counter
- Exploring performance counters using CIM cmdlets
- Configuring and use Data Collector Sets
- Reporting on performance data
- Generating performance monitoring graph
- Creating a system diagnostics report

Introduction

Managing performance has been a challenge since the earliest days of computing. Windows NT 3.1 came with a marvelous tool, **Performance Monitor (Perfmon)**, that allowed you to see what the OS and applications are doing and what resources they are consuming.

This chapter shows you how you can use PowerShell to obtain and display performance information. The recipes in this chapter show you how you can use a cmdlet and WMI to get and report the performance information. This chapter shows how you can generate performance graphs and reports for management. And of course, you can leverage the various recipes in this chapter to conduct your performance monitoring and reporting.

The Windows performance monitoring framework is known as **Performance Logging and Alerting (PLA)**. PLA is built into Windows and uses COM and DCOM to obtain performance and diagnosis information from both local and remote computers.

PLA enables you to obtain a variety of performance data from running systems. PLA provides graphic tools such as *Performance Monitor* and *Task Manager* to help bring the data to life. These tools utilize the performance monitoring framework built into Windows.

You can also use PowerShell to obtain performance information from the PLA. While you can use a GUI tool for looking at one system, with PowerShell you can obtain the performance information across your entire IT infrastructure.

In PLA, a counter set is a performance object that provides performance information about some aspect of your systems such as memory, disk devices, or network components. Counter sets are built by Microsoft as well as third parties and are implemented as DLLs in your system.

A counter set contains one or more counters, each of which provides one measurement of an aspect of the counter type. For example, the `Memory` counter set on Windows Server 2016 has 36 counters, such as `PagesperSecond`, `PageFaultsperSecond`, and `AvailableBytes`.

Counter sets have a counter set type: single-instance or multi-instance. Counters like `\Memory\Page/Sec` are single-instance where each sample contains just one measurement. Other counters, such as `\Processor(*)\% Processor Time` are multi-instance. This counter returns a counter sample for each processor in the server, plus one for the total (nicely named `_total`). The multi-instance counters in the `Processor` counter set return one measurement for each processor core, plus one for the total. This counter returns one measurement for each core (or two measurements if hyper-threading is available and enabled. For example, for each processor core on a dual-processor hex-core system with hyper-threading, you would have 24 measurements.

A counter sample is a specific measurement of a counter at some point in time. To get a counter sample, you use the `Get-Counter` cmdlet and specify the counter name (that is, the path) to the counter set. The path is formatted as `\\<servername\<counterset name>\CounterName`, for example `\\DC1\Memory\Page Faults/sec`. If you are getting counters on the local machine, you can omit the computer name prefix and just specify `\Memory\Page Faults/sec`. Note that the counter set and counter names can be long and can have spaces in the names. You need to specify paths using PowerShell string quoting.

You use the `Get-Counter` cmdlet to obtain details of available counter sets, the counters with each set, and get counter samples. The `Get-Counter` cmdlet utilizes PLA to get counter set, counter and counter sample information from both local and remote computers.

The `PerformanceCounterSampleSet` object, returned by `Get-Counter`, contains a `CounterSamples` property. This property contains one measurement of the counter (for single-instance counters) or an array of samples (for each instance with multi-instance counters).

Another way to surface performance information is with WMI. WMI holds performance objects, and you can use either the WMI cmdlets or the CIM cmdlets. The latter are slightly faster, and more firewall friendly.. If you are conducting remote performance monitoring on a constant basis, or opening up a CIM Session to the monitored server, then using the CIM cmdlets gives improved performance.

In the first recipe of this chapter, you explore counter sets, and counter set samples using `Get-Counter`. The next recipe looks at getting performance information using the CIM cmdlets.

This recipe uses several servers to simulate a normal organization. Consider using fewer servers.

Explore performance counters with Get-Counter

`Get-Counter` is the cmdlet you use both to discover the counter sets available on a machine, and to obtain performance samples from a local or remote server. In this recipe, you use a Windows Server 2016 server, `SRV1`, to examine performance counter sets and counters on local and remote computers.

Getting ready

This recipe uses several remote machines: `DC1`, `CA`, `SRV1`, `FS1`, `FS2`, and `PSRV`. Adjust the recipe to reflect the computers in your testing or production environment.

This recipe uses several servers to simulate a normal organization. Consider using fewer servers.

How to do it...

1. You start by using `Get-Counter` to discover performance counter sets on the local machine:

```
$CounterSets = Get-Counter -ListSet *
  "There are {0} counter sets on [{1}]" `
                              -f $CounterSets.count, (hostname)
```

2. Discover performance counter sets on remote systems:

```
$Machines = 'DC1', 'CAa', 'SRV1', 'FS1', 'FS2', 'PSRV'
  foreach ($Machine in $Machines)
  {
      $RCounters = Get-Counter -ListSet * -ComputerName $machine
      "There are {0} counters on [{1}]" -f $RCounters.count,
                                           ($machine)
  }
```

3. Use `Get-Counter` to explore key performance counter sets:

```
Get-Counter -ListSet Processor, Memory, Network*,*Disk* |
        Select-Object -Property countersetname, Description |
            Format-Table -Wrap
```

4. You now look at two counters: `Memory` and `Processor`. Get and display counters in these two counter sets:

```
$Counters = (Get-Counter -ListSet Memory).counter
"Memory counter set has [{0}] counters" -f $counters.Count
$counters = (Get-Counter -ListSet Processor).counter
"Processor counter set has [{0}] counters" -f $counters.Count
Get a sample from each counter in the memory counter set:
$Counters = (Get-Counter -ListSet Memory).counter
"{0,-19} {1,-50} {2,10}" -f 'At', 'Counter', 'Value'
foreach ($Counter in $Counters)
  {
      $C = Get-Counter -Counter $Counter
      $T = $C.Timestamp # Time
      $N = $C.CounterSamples.Path.Trim() # Couner Name
      $V = $C.CounterSamples.CookedValue # Value
      "{0,-15} {1,-59} {2,20}" -f $t, $n, $v
  }
```

5. Next you discover the sample set types for key performance counters:

```
Get-Counter -ListSet Processor, Memory, Network*, *Disk* |
Select-Object -Property CounterSetName, CounterSetType
```

6. Explore two performance counter sample sets using examples of both counter set types:

```
$Counter1 = '\Memory\Page Faults/sec'
$PFS      = Get-Counter -Counter $Counter1
$PFS
$Counter2 = '\Processor(*)\% Processor Time'
$CPU = Get-Counter -Counter $Counter2
$CPU
```

7. Look at the properties of the performance counter sample set object:

```
$PFS | Get-Member -MemberType *Property |
        Format-Table -Wrap
```

8. Now look at what counters the samples contain and the way they look :

```
$CPU.CounterSamples | Get-Member -MemberType *Property |
        Format-Table -Wrap
$CPU.CounterSamples | Format-List -Property *
```

How it works...

The `Get-Counter` cmdlet is the tool you use both to discover the performance counter sets and counters, as well as, to get specific the counter samples. In *step 1*, you get all the performance counter sets on the local system and display the results. The results you obtain vary depending on the specific features you install on your computers. On the SRV1 VM, *step 1* looked like this:

```
PS C:> $CounterSets = Get-Counter -ListSet *
PS C:> "There are {0} counter sets on [{1}]" -f $CounterSets.count, (hostname)
There are 167 counter sets on [SRV1]
```

In *step 2*, you expand the scope a bit to return the number of counter sets in multiple machines in the network. The domain controllers and other servers have different features loaded. Therefore you see different number of counter sets on each machine:

```
There are 165 counters on [dc1]
There are 147 counters on [ca]
There are 193 counters on [dg]
There are 167 counters on [srv1]
There are 175 counters on [fs1]
There are 174 counters on [fs2]
There are 147 counters on [psrv]
```

In *step 3*, you explore some of the most useful counters in Windows Server 2016, which are as follows:

```
CounterSetName          Description
--------------          -----------
Processor               The Processor performance object consists of counters that measure aspects of processor
                        activity. The processor is the part of the computer that performs arithmetic and logical
                        computations, initiates operations on peripherals, and runs the threads of processes.  A
                        computer can have multiple processors.  The processor object represents each processor as an
                        instance of the object.
Memory                  The Memory performance object  consists of counters that describe the behavior of physical
                        and virtual memory on the computer.  Physical memory is the amount of random access memory on
                        the computer.  Virtual memory consists of the space in physical memory and on disk.  Many of
                        the memory counters monitor paging, which is the movement of pages of code and data between
                        disk and physical memory.  Excessive paging, a symptom of a memory shortage, can cause delays
                        which interfere with all system processes.
Network QoS Policy      This counter set consists of flow statistics specific to a network QoS policy.
Network Interface       The Network Interface performance object consists of counters that measure the rates at which
                        bytes and packets are sent and received over a network connection.  It includes counters that
                        monitor connection errors.
Network Adapter         The Network Adapter performance object consists of counters that measure the rates at which
                        bytes and packets are sent and received over a physical or virtual network connection.  It
                        includes counters that monitor connection errors.
FileSystem Disk Activity The FileSystem Disk Activity performance counter set consists of counters that measure the
                        aspect of filesystem's IO Activity.  This counter set measures the number of bytes filesystem
                        read from and wrote to the disk drive.
LogicalDisk             The Logical Disk performance object consists of counters that monitor logical partitions of a
                        hard or fixed disk drives.  Performance Monitor identifies logical disks by their a drive
                        letter, such as C.
PhysicalDisk            The Physical Disk performance object consists of counters that monitor hard or fixed disk
                        drive on a computer.  Disks are used to store file, program, and paging data and are read to
                        retrieve these items, and written to record changes to them.  The values of physical disk
                        counters are sums of the values of the logical disks (or partitions) into which they are
                        divided.
```

With *step 4* you use `Get-Counter` to return and display a count of how many counters exist in the `Memory` and `Processor` counter sets, as you see here:

```
Memory counter set has [36] counters
Processor counter set has [15] counters
```

Now that you have found the counter sets and looked inside a few, you get counter samples in *step 5*. In this case, you retrieve a counter sample for each counter in the Memory counter set:

```
At                        Counter                                            Value
14/01/2017 00:30:00       \\srv1\memory\page faults/sec          12.0078471280982
14/01/2017 00:30:01       \\srv1\memory\available bytes                 1257881600
14/01/2017 00:30:02       \\srv1\memory\committed bytes                 4254994432
14/01/2017 00:30:03       \\srv1\memory\commit limit                   5827514368
14/01/2017 00:30:04       \\srv1\memory\write copies/sec                         0
14/01/2017 00:30:05       \\srv1\memory\transition faults/sec    1.99866808758643
14/01/2017 00:30:06       \\srv1\memory\cache faults/sec                         0
14/01/2017 00:30:07       \\srv1\memory\demand zero faults/sec                   0
14/01/2017 00:30:08       \\srv1\memory\pages/sec                                0
14/01/2017 00:30:09       \\srv1\memory\pages input/sec                          0
14/01/2017 00:30:10       \\srv1\memory\page reads/sec                           0
14/01/2017 00:30:11       \\srv1\memory\pages output/sec                         0
14/01/2017 00:30:12       \\srv1\memory\pool paged bytes                 137068544
14/01/2017 00:30:13       \\srv1\memory\pool nonpaged bytes               42594304
14/01/2017 00:30:14       \\srv1\memory\page writes/sec                          0
14/01/2017 00:30:15       \\srv1\memory\pool paged allocs                   108561
14/01/2017 00:30:16       \\srv1\memory\pool nonpaged allocs                 76393
14/01/2017 00:30:17       \\srv1\memory\free system page table entries   12311148
14/01/2017 00:30:18       \\srv1\memory\cache bytes                       31903744
14/01/2017 00:30:19       \\srv1\memory\cache bytes peak                  97136640
14/01/2017 00:30:20       \\srv1\memory\pool paged resident bytes        101056512
14/01/2017 00:30:21       \\srv1\memory\system code total bytes            3825664
14/01/2017 00:30:22       \\srv1\memory\system code resident bytes         3547136
14/01/2017 00:30:23       \\srv1\memory\system driver total bytes         13737984
14/01/2017 00:30:24       \\srv1\memory\system driver resident bytes      12300288
14/01/2017 00:30:25       \\srv1\memory\system cache resident bytes              0
14/01/2017 00:30:26       \\srv1\memory\% committed bytes in use  73.0534822617316
14/01/2017 00:30:27       \\srv1\memory\available kbytes                   1224696
14/01/2017 00:30:28       \\srv1\memory\available mbytes                      1197
14/01/2017 00:30:29       \\srv1\memory\transition pages repurposed/sec          0
14/01/2017 00:30:30       \\srv1\memory\free & zero page list bytes      879222784
14/01/2017 00:30:31       \\srv1\memory\modified page list bytes          42606592
14/01/2017 00:30:32       \\srv1\memory\standby cache reserve bytes      182726656
14/01/2017 00:30:33       \\srv1\memory\standby cache normal priority bytes 193556480
14/01/2017 00:30:34       \\srv1\memory\standby cache core bytes                 0
14/01/2017 00:30:35       \\srv1\memory\long-term average standby cache lifetime (s)  14400
```

As noted earlier, counters can be either single or multi-instance. In *step 6*, you use Get-Counter to explore the counter set types of a few key counters. The Processor counter set is multi-instance whereas the Memory counter set is single-instance as you can see here:

```
CounterSetName              CounterSetType
--------------              --------------
Processor                   MultiInstance
Memory                      SingleInstance
Network QoS Policy          SingleInstance
Network Interface           MultiInstance
Network Adapter             MultiInstance
FileSystem Disk Activity    SingleInstance
LogicalDisk                 MultiInstance
PhysicalDisk                MultiInstance
```

In *step 7* you explore a single-instance and a multi-instance counter. As you can see here, the `Processor` object returns a sample for each processor in your computer plus one for the total CPU time across all cores. If you are using `Get-Counter` on a computer with hyper-threaded processors, you would see two measurements for each processor core. Our VM, which is not hyper-threaded and only has one processor assigned results in what you see here:

```
Timestamp                    CounterSamples
---------                    --------------
14/01/2017 00:42:44          \\srv1\memory\page faults/sec :
                             0.999193451046316


14/01/2017 00:42:45          \\srv1\processor(0)\% processor time :
                             1.62150741984958

                             \\srv1\processor(_total)\% processor time :
                             1.62150741984958
```

With *step 8*, you examine the `PerformanceCounterSampleSet` object and view the properties on this object:

```
   TypeName: Microsoft.PowerShell.Commands.GetCounter.PerformanceCounterSampleSet

Name            MemberType      Definition
----            ----------      ----------
CounterSamples  Property        Microsoft.PowerShell.Commands.GetCounter.PerformanceCounterSample[] CounterSamples
                                {get;set;}
Timestamp       Property        datetime Timestamp {get;set;}
Readings        ScriptProperty  System.Object Readings {get=$strPaths = ""
                                    foreach ($ctr in $this.CounterSamples)
                                    {
                                        $strPaths += ($ctr.Path + " :" + "`n")

                                        $strPaths += ($ctr.CookedValue.ToString() + "`n`n")
                                    }
                                    return $strPaths;}
```

The `CounterSamples` property contains the counter samples taken at the time in the `TimeStamp`. In *step 9*, you look at the values and properties of two counter samples:

```
    TypeName: Microsoft.PowerShell.Commands.GetCounter.PerformanceCounterSample

Name                 MemberType  Definition
----                 ----------  ----------
CookedValue          Property    double CookedValue {get;set;}
CounterType          Property    System.Diagnostics.PerformanceCounterType CounterType {get;set;}
DefaultScale         Property    uint32 DefaultScale {get;set;}
InstanceName         Property    string InstanceName {get;set;}
MultipleCount        Property    uint32 MultipleCount {get;set;}
Path                 Property    string Path {get;set;}
RawValue             Property    uint64 RawValue {get;set;}
SecondValue          Property    uint64 SecondValue {get;set;}
Status               Property    uint32 Status {get;set;}
TimeBase             Property    uint64 TimeBase {get;set;}
Timestamp            Property    datetime Timestamp {get;set;}
Timestamp100NSec     Property    uint64 Timestamp100NSec {get;set;}



Path                 : \\srv1\processor(0)\% processor time
InstanceName         : 0
CookedValue          : 0
RawValue             : 3159552968750
SecondValue          : 131289666340986025
MultipleCount        : 1
CounterType          : Timer100NsInverse
Timestamp            : 15/01/2017 15:10:34
Timestamp100NSec     : 131289666340980000
Status               : 0
DefaultScale         : 0
TimeBase             : 10000000

Path                 : \\srv1\processor(_total)\% processor time
InstanceName         : _total
CookedValue          : 0
RawValue             : 3159552968750
SecondValue          : 131289666340986025
MultipleCount        : 1
CounterType          : Timer100NsInverse
Timestamp            : 15/01/2017 15:10:34
Timestamp100NSec     : 131289666340980000
Status               : 0
DefaultScale         : 0
TimeBase             : 10000000
```

There's more...

In *step 4* of this recipe, you used a separate call for Get-Counter to retrieve each counter.
As you can see from the screenshot, it took 35 seconds to gather all these counters. Using
Get-Counter is convenient if you just want one counter (for example, CPU utilization). If
you need to get all the counters in a counter set, there are more efficient techniques for
getting multiple counters.

In *step 6* of this recipe, you should notice that the $PFS variable contains the readings script property. The Get-Sample cmdlet returns the $PFS a variable. This variable is an object of the type PerformanceCounterSampleSet. PowerShell added this property to the underlying .NET object through the magic of the extensible type system. This script property returns a simple array of the counter path and the cooked value for the sample. You can use this as an alternative delving into the PerformanceCounterSampleSet object itself. Note that the first member of the array has a trailing. You may need to remove if you wish to use it as a counter path value in some other cmdlet. If you do use the readings script property, the code that results is more complex than just using the properties on the sample set object directly. If you are interested, the script is defined in the file $PSHome\getevent.types.ps1xml. Of course, you can update this extended type information if that is appropriate.

Explore performance counters using CIM cmdlets

Another way to access performance information is via WMI. You can use either the WMI or the CIM cmdlets to access a large number of performance counters, as an alternative to using Get-Counter. The naming structure is different from using Get-Counter. With WMI, each counter is a separate WMI class.

With WMI, each performance counter set is a WMI class. The WMI performance counters are found in the ROOT\CimV2 namespace and have a name that begins with Win32_Perf. For example, the Memory performance counter set contains 36 separate counters. The WMI class Win32_PerfFormattedData_PerfOS_Memory contains 46 properties including all of the individual performance counters. With WMI, you get all the measurements back in one call to Get-CimInstance, whereas you would need to call Get-Counter for each sample. There are other ways to collect counters as shown in later recipes.

In this recipe, you get performance counters from local and remote machines using the CIM cmdlet set. The CIM cmdlet set is preferable to the older WMI commands as it is a little faster. And it can make use of WinRM for remote sessions.

Getting ready

You run this recipe on SRV1, but you could use any server. This recipe uses the CIM cmdlets, so you need at least PowerShell 3.0. You could revise this recipe to make use of the WMI cmdlets. Using the WMI cmdlets might be useful in the case where you are communicating with an older system that does not have PowerShell remoting up and running.

How to do it...

1. Find Performance related counters in Root\CimV2:

   ```
   Get-CimClass -ClassName Win32*perf* | Measure-Object
   Get-CimClass -ClassName Win32*perfFormatted* | Measure-Object
   Get-CimClass -ClassName Win32*perfraw* | Measure-Object
   ```

2. Find key performance classes:

   ```
   Get-CimClass "Win32_PerfFormatted*perfos*" |
   Select-Object -Property CimClassName
   Get-CimClass "Win32_PerfFormatted*disk*" |
                       Select-Object -Property CimClassName
   ```

3. Get Memory counter samples:

   ```
   Get-CimInstance -ClassName Win32_PerfFormattedData_PerfOS_Memory
   ```

4. Get CPU counter samples:

   ```
   Get-CimInstance
       -ClassName Win32_PerfFormattedData_PerfOS_Processor|
               Where-Object Name -eq '_Total'
   Get-CimInstance
       -ClassName Win32_PerfFormattedData_PerfOS_Processor |
               Select-Object -Property Name, PercentProcessortime
   ```

5. Get Memory counter samples from a remote system:

   ```
   Get-CimInstance -ClassName Win32_PerfFormattedData_PerfOS_Memory
                   -ComputerName DC1
   ```

How it works...

In this recipe, you use Get-CimClass to discover WMI performance classes within the Root/CimV2 namespace. You also use the Get-CimInstance cmdlet to retrieve performance information.

In *step 1*, you use the Get-CimClass to find the performance counter classes implemented on your system. You look at the general performance classes, then the formatted and raw classes as you discover the total number of performance classes and the number that are either raw or formatted (cooked). For the performance counters supported in WMI, there are two classes for each counter: a raw class and a cooked class. The former returns raw counter values and the latter returns cooked counter values as shown:

```
PS C:\> Get-Cimclass -ClassName Win32*perf* | Measure-Object


Count    : 343
Average  :
Sum      :
Maximum  :
Minimum  :
Property :




PS C:\> Get-Cimclass -ClassName Win32*perfFormatted* | Measure-Object


Count    : 171
Average  :
Sum      :
Maximum  :
Minimum  :
Property :




PS C:\> Get-Cimclass -ClassName Win32*perfraw* | Measure-Object


Count    : 171
Average  :
Sum      :
Maximum  :
Minimum  :
Property :
```

In *step 2*, you look at some of the most relevant WMI performance classes, those related to the OS performance and those related to the disk. These are just a few of the many performance classes in WMI, and looks like:

```
PS C:\> Get-cimclass "win32_PerfFormatted*perfos*" | Select-Object -Property CimClassName

CimClassName
------------
Win32_PerfFormattedData_PerfOS_Cache
Win32_PerfFormattedData_PerfOS_Memory
Win32_PerfFormattedData_PerfOS_NUMANodeMemory
Win32_PerfFormattedData_PerfOS_Objects
Win32_PerfFormattedData_PerfOS_PagingFile
Win32_PerfFormattedData_PerfOS_Processor
Win32_PerfFormattedData_PerfOS_System


PS C:\> Get-cimclass "win32_PerfFormatted*disk*" | Select-Object -Property CimClassName

CimClassName
------------
Win32_PerfFormattedData_Counters_FileSystemDiskActivity
Win32_PerfFormattedData_PerfDisk_LogicalDisk
Win32_PerfFormattedData_PerfDisk_PhysicalDisk
```

In *step 3*, you retrieve memory related performance counters. There are a large number of
properties returned, some of which may be helpful while others less so. Regarding the
Memory counter set, the AvailableBytes, CommittedBytes and PagesperSecond are
ones on which need to focus. Here's the output:

```
PS C:\> Get-CimInstance -ClassName Win32_PerfFormattedData_PerfOS_Memory


Caption                                    :
Description                                :
Name                                       :
Frequency_Object                           :
Frequency_PerfTime                         :
Frequency_Sys100NS                         :
Timestamp_Object                           :
Timestamp_PerfTime                         :
Timestamp_Sys100NS                         :
AvailableBytes                             : 688861184
AvailableKBytes                            : 672716
AvailableMBytes                            : 656
CacheBytes                                 : 55291904
CacheBytesPeak                             : 124846080
CacheFaultsPersec                          : 0
CommitLimit                                : 2652426240
CommittedBytes                             : 1655054336
DemandZeroFaultsPersec                     : 19
FreeAndZeroPageListBytes                   : 50941952
FreeSystemPageTableEntries                 : 12310378
LongTermAverageStandbyCacheLifetimes       : 14400
ModifiedPageListBytes                      : 4993024
PageFaultsPersec                           : 27
PageReadsPersec                            : 0
PagesInputPersec                           : 0
PagesOutputPersec                          : 0
```

In the case of memory samples, many of the measurements are in bytes. You can always get one of the properties, for example, `CommittedBytes`, and divide it by 1 GB (a neat feature of PowerShell) to convert the value into megabytes. You can even format the value to remove some of the digits. You could get the value of `CommittedBytes` into a variable (for example, `$CB`) and the expression: `($CB/1Gb).ToString('n2')` turns committed bytes into 1.54 gigabytes.

In *step 4*, you get the CPU related performance counters. The first statement gets the full set of counter information for the `_Total` occurrence. The second returns the CPU utilization both for the total and for each of the CPUs, it is shown as follows:

```
PS C:\> Get-CimInstance -ClassName Win32_PerfFormattedData_PerfOS_Processor |
    Where Name -eq '_Total'


Caption                  :
Description              :
Name                     : _Total
Frequency_Object         :
Frequency_PerfTime       :
Frequency_Sys100NS       :
Timestamp_Object         :
Timestamp_PerfTime       :
Timestamp_Sys100NS       :
C1TransitionsPersec      : 15
C2TransitionsPersec      : 73
C3TransitionsPersec      : 0
DPCRate                  : 1
DPCsQueuedPersec         : 81
InterruptsPersec         : 163
PercentC1Time            : 22
PercentC2Time            : 73
PercentC3Time            : 0
PercentDPCTime           : 0
PercentIdleTime          : 96
PercentInterruptTime     : 0
PercentPrivilegedTime    : 0
PercentProcessorTime     : 2
PercentUserTime          : 0
PSComputerName           :



PS C:\> Get-Ciminstance -ClassName Win32_PerfFormattedData_PerfOS_Processor |
    Select -Property Name, PercentProcessortime

Name    PercentProcessortime
----    --------------------
_Total                     0
0                          0
```

In the last step in this recipe, you retrieve CPU counters from a remote machine, DC1. Using Get-CimInstance leverages WSMan to communicate with the remote machine. If you needed to, you could create a CIM session over DCOM and invoke the cmdlet over the CIM session. As WinRM is much more firewall friendly, this should not be necessary. The output of the Memory class looks identical to the output returned from a local CIM instance as follows:

```
PS C:\> Get-CimInstance -ClassName Win32_PerfFormattedData_PerfOS_Memory -ComputerName DC1


Caption                              :
Description                          :
Name                                 :
Frequency_Object                     :
Frequency_PerfTime                   :
Frequency_Sys100NS                   :
Timestamp_Object                     :
Timestamp_PerfTime                   :
Timestamp_Sys100NS                   :
AvailableBytes                       : 562872320
AvailableKBytes                      : 549680
AvailableMBytes                      : 536
CacheBytes                           : 66990080
CacheBytesPeak                       : 130334720
CacheFaultsPersec                    : 0
CommitLimit                          : 2549665792
CommittedBytes                       : 1793781760
DemandZeroFaultsPersec               : 7
FreeAndZeroPageListBytes             : 34189312
FreeSystemPageTableEntries           : 12309607
LongTermAverageStandbyCacheLifetimes : 14400
ModifiedPageListBytes                : 1671168
PageFaultsPersec                     : 19
PageReadsPersec                      : 0
PagesInputPersec                     : 0
PagesOutputPersec                    : 0
PagesPersec                          : 0
PageWritesPersec                     : 0
PercentCommittedBytesInUse           : 70
```

There's more...

In this recipe, you discovered how to find the WMI performance classes as well as looking at a few of the classes. WMI is huge and contains a large number of classes. You could usefully spend time looking at the various classes provided. There is a tremendous amount of information available from both WMI and from Get-Counter, which are both build on the PLA platform.

With so many classes, it's easy to get overwhelmed and spend inordinate amounts of time looking at counters which yield little useful information. With performance management, you need to work out when you have adequate information to help resolve any performance issues.

If you are going to be working a lot with WMI to manage performance information, you could consider using type and display XML to customize the objects to suit your needs. You could add alias properties to provide shorter name aliases (for example, adding a property CB as an alias to `CommittedBytes`. You could also add format XML to improve the default output of values from the various classes. The details of type and format XML are outside the scope of this book, but there are plenty of references on the internet that you can leverage.

Configuring and using Data Collector Sets

The first two recipes in this chapter used different techniques (`Get-Counter` and WMI) to retrieve specific counters and counter sets. As you seen, getting a large number of counter values for detailed analysis can be very slow with these mechanisms. These techniques are ideal for retrieving one or two bits of information (CPU utilization for example, or pages/second). If you want to get a larger number of statistics (for example, all of the networking statistics including TCP, UDP, IP, and ICMP) the techniques do not scale well.

A better approach to gathering large number of counters is to use the Data Collector Sets and have Windows do the work for you. To do this, you first create and configure a collector set. When you start the set, Windows starts collecting the data you have configured the collector set to return. Finally, when the collection has been completed, you use Performance Monitor to view the results.

This approach is very much easier. You just define the collector sets, create a schedule telling Windows when to collect the data and let Windows do the rest. You could easily deploy counter sets to all your key servers. Once deployed, you use them to help resolve performance issues. With the data collection process deployed, you improve your ability to respond to most of the performance issues.

Getting ready

This recipe runs on SRV1. As with all recipes in this book, feel free to use different servers to test this recipe.

How to do it...

1. Create and populate a new performance data collector:

```
$Name = 'SRV1 Collector Set'
$SRV1CS = New-Object -COMObject PLA.DataCollectorSet
$SRV1CS.DisplayName = $Name
$SRV1CS.Duration = 12*3600 # 12 hours - 19:00
$SRV1CS.SubdirectoryFormat  = 1
$SRV1CS.SubdirectoryFormatPattern = 'yyyy\-MM'
$SRV1CS.RootPath = Join-Path -Path "$Env:SystemDrive" `
                             -Childpath "\PerfLogs\Admin\$Name"
$SRV1Collector = $SRV1CS.DataCollectors.CreateDataCollector(0)
$SRV1Collector.FileName = "$Name_"
$SRV1Collector.FileNameFormat = 3
$SRV1Collector.FileNameFormatPattern = "yyyy\-MM\-dd"
$SRV1Collector.SampleInterval = 15
$SRV1Collector.LogFileFormat  = 3    # BLG format
$SRV1Collector.LogAppend = $true
```

2. Define counters of interest:

```
$Counters = @(
    '\Memory\Pages/sec',
    '\Memory\Available MBytes',
    '\Processor(_Total)\% Processor Time',
    '\PhysicalDisk(_Total)\% Disk Time',
    '\PhysicalDisk(_Total)\Disk Transfers/sec' ,
    '\PhysicalDisk(_Total)\Avg. Disk Sec/Read',
    '\PhysicalDisk(_Total)\Avg. Disk Sec/Write',
    '\PhysicalDisk(_Total)\Avg. Disk Queue Length'
)
```

3. Add the counters to the collector:

```
$SRV1Collector.PerformanceCounters = $Counters
```

4. Create a schedule—start tomorrow morning at 07:00:

```
$StartDate = Get-Date -Day $((Get-Date).Day+1) `
                      -Hour 7 -Minute 0 -Second 0
$Schedule = $SRV1CS.Schedules.CreateSchedule()
$Schedule.Days = 127
$Schedule.StartDate = $StartDate
$Schedule.StartTime = $StartDate
```

5. Create, add, and start the collector set:

```
Try
  {
      $SRV1CS.Schedules.Add($Schedule)
      $SRV1CS.DataCollectors.Add($SRV1Collector)
      $SRV1CS.Commit("$Name" , $null , 0x0003) | Out-Null
      $SRV1CS.Start($false)
  }
Catch [Exception]
  {
      Write-Host "Exception Caught: " $_.Exception
                                  -ForegroundColor Red
      return
  }
```

6. Once you have created the collector set, you may want to totally remove it, you can do so as follows:

```
$DCStRemote = New-Object -COMObject PLA.DataCollectorSet
$Name = 'SRV1 Collector Set'
$DCstRemote.Query($Name,'LocalHost')
$DCstRemote.Stop($true)
$DCstRemote.Delete()
```

7. If you have not removed the collector set and it's stopped, you can easily restart it:

```
$DCStRemote = New-Object -COMObject PLA.DataCollectorSet
$Name = 'SRV1 Collector Set'
$DCstRemote.Query($Name,'LocalHost')
$DCstRemote.Start($true)
```

How it works...

This recipe produces no output as you configure the collector set. In *step 1*, you begin by creating the COM object `PLA.DataCollectorSet`. You then configure the display name, the collection period, and details of where to store the performance data that the data collection process collects. Then you create the data collector object and configure the details of the output files generated by the data collection process.

With *step 1*, you set the $SRV1Collector object's LogFileFormat property to 3. This file format value specified an output file type of binary log (.blg). The advantage of this format is that you can use it with Perfmon to graph the collected output. You have other options, including:

- Tab separated .tsv file
- Comma separated .csv file

In *step 2*, you create an array of the names of the counters for which you want Windows to collect counter samples. The collector set collects performance information, so the counter paths you use do not need the machine name. The counter paths you specify here were the ones you discover with Get-Cmdlet -List.

In *step 3*, you assign these counters to the data collector set. In the recipe, you used a simple code-generated array of counter names. You could have stored the desired counters in a text file (accessed by Get-Content).

In *step 4*, you create a schedule when Windows performs the requested data collection. In this case, it starts at 07:00, and collects data for 127 days.

Finally, in *step 5*, you add the schedule to the job, add the new data collector to the OS, and start the collection process. The performance data collection set is scheduled to run every day. Starting it means Windows starts the collection process immediately and does not wait until the next morning. After running this step, you can utilize the data collected.

Using the `.blg` format, as this recipe does, once you stop the data collector, you can see the results in Perfmon as follows:

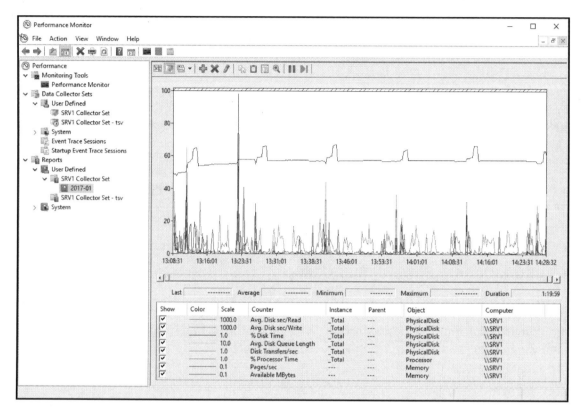

Step 6 shows the actions that you need to take to remove this data collector. Note that you need to stop the collector, if it's active, before removing it. If the collection is not currently active, the STOP method will generate an error message, but the code does remove the collector.

In `step 7`, you start a collector by creating the COM object, then querying for the appropriate data collection set and once you find it, you can start it as shown.

There's more...

This recipe makes use of COM and a COM object (`PLA.XXX`). As a result, there is rather less output to look at—as you run the recipe, you notice there is no output to the screen. You can use your discovery skills to examine the COM objects.

The performance collection process makes use, under the covers, of an XML to describe the monitoring you wish to carry out. Fortunately, you do not have to edit the XML since the statements in this recipe do what is necessary. You can take a look at the XML as you run the steps in this recipe if you are interested.

There are different types of output files that you can configure, then you create a data collector set. This recipe used the default format of binary log (the files have an extension .blg). You can use the tab and comma separated value file formats, but if you do, those are not directly usable by Perfmon as shown in this recipe. TSV files are, on the other hand, useful as we demonstrate later in this chapter.

Reporting on performance data

In the first three recipes in this chapter, you have seen different ways to collect performance information. In this recipe, you create a report on this gathered performance information based on the CSV files output by the data collection process.

Getting ready

This recipe was written to use SRV1. As with any recipe, you can use any server in your infrastructure, but you would need to adjust the details of all steps to reflect the changes you are making. This recipe also used CSV files, as created by the PLA infrastructure. As noted earlier, it is simple and straightforward to adjust the counter output file to be CSV.

Use the recipe *Configuring and using Data Collector Sets*, change the counter output file to CSV and generate CSV output in the folder C:\PerfLogs\ADMIN.

How to do it...

1. Import the performance counters:

```
$Folder = 'C:\PerfLogs\Admin'
$File = Get-ChildItem -Path $Folder\*.csv -Recurse
```

2. Import the performance counters:

```
$Counters = Import-Csv -Path $File.FullName
```

3. Fix the issue with the first row in the counters:

```
$Counters[0] = $counters[1]
```

4. Next you calculate an overall average, minimum and maximum CPU times:

```
$CN = '\\SRV1\Processor(_Total)\% Processor Time'
$HT = @{
 Name = 'CPU'
 Expression = {[system.double] $_.$cn}
}
$Stats = $counters |
    Select-Object -Property *,$ht |
Measure-Object -Property CPU `
              -Average -Minimum -Maximum
```

5. Add the 95th percent value of CPU:

```
$CN = '\\srv1\Processor(_Total)\% Processor Time'
$Row = [int]($Counters.Count * .95 )
$Cpu = ($counters.$CN | Sort-Object)
$Cpu95 = $CPU[$Row]
Add-Member -InputObject $stats -Name CPU95 `
          -MemberType NoteProperty -Value $cpu95
```

6. Combine the results into a single report:

```
$Stats.Cpu95   = $Stats.Cpu95.tostring('n2')
$Stats.Average = $Stats.Average.ToString('n2')
$Stats.Maximum = $Stats.Maximum.ToString('n2')
$Stats.Minimum = $Stats.Minimum.ToString('n2')
$Stats | Format-Table -Property Property,Count, Maximum,
                                        Cpu95, Minimum
```

How it works...

In *step 1*, you get the details of the CSV file that contained the performance data with which you create a simple report. You created this CSV file based on the configure and use Data Collector Sets recipe, with the file type set to comma separated value, indicated by setting the file type to 0 (zero).

In *step 2*, you import the CSV files into the $Counters variable (which becomes an array). You may need to adjust *step 1* and *step 2* to use different folder names and to cater for having multiple results files.

A feature of using CSV files as we do here is that the first row in the returned counter samples is not valid. The feature is that some values are not returned correctly, in particular, the first row that was returned. This issue has been present in Windows for some considerable time but is simple to work around. As you can see in *step 3*, you just copy the second row of the results over the first. Without this, the later steps may not work due to missing data.

With *step 4*, you calculate the average, minimum, and maximum CPU usage and then store that information in the `$Stats` variable.

In *step 5*, you work out an approximation of the 95th percentile CPU time. This is a good number to track, as it is a measure of how high, in general, the CPU load is on the computers that you are monitoring. It eliminates the very occasional, but high CPU using events. You calculate this by first counting the total number of rows returned. Then you get an index value which you calculate as 0.95 times the number of rows. You then use this index to get that row from a list of sorted CPU values. So with 100 rows of data returned, this calculation would return row 95. Assuming you have an adequate number of samples, this approach gets you a row that is a good approximation of the 95th percentile CPU time measurement. At the end of this step, you add the value as a note property (CPU95).

In the last step, *step 6*, you re-format three counters to display only CPU usage to just two decimal points, then you output this as a nice table, which looks like this:

```
Property                                   Count Maximum CPU95 Minimum
--------                                    ----- ------- ----- -------
\\SRV1\Processor(_Total)\% Processor Time   2881   35.06  0.86   35.06
```

There's more...

In this recipe, we reported on just one counter, the total CPU time on a system. You can always change the data collection process to include more counters (for example, networking counters, storage counters, and so on). Then, you can adjust this recipe to report on these additional values. And of course, you can expand the basics of this recipe to report on multiple systems in one report. By doing both of these, you can generate useful performance reports that can provide input for capacity planning.

Generating performance monitoring graph

In the previous recipe, you created a simple text based report which you could expand to cover not just the CPU on the SRV1 server, but more counters across multiple machines. But they would be pure text. You could use performance monitor and the binary log files to create Perfmon graphs you could cut/paste into a report.

In this recipe, you use the data generated using the data collector mechanism to draw a graph using classes from the Windows.Forms.DataVisualization namespace.

Getting ready

Like the *Reporting on performance data* recipe, this recipe uses CSV files from the data collection process noted earlier.

How to do it...

1. Load the System.Windows.Forms and System.Windows.Forms.DataVisulization assemblies:

   ```
   Add-Type -AssemblyName System.Windows.Forms
   Add-Type -AssemblyName System.Windows.Forms.DataVisualization
   ```

2. Import the CSV data from earlier, and fix row 0:

   ```
   $CSVFile = Get-childitem -Path C:\PerfLogs\Admin\*.csv `
                            -Recurse
   $Counters = Import-Csv $CSVFile
   $Counters[0] = $Counters[1]
   ```

3. Create a chart object:

   ```
   $CpuChart = New-Object -TypeName `
           System.Windows.Forms.DataVisualization.Charting.Chart
   ```

4. Define the chart dimensions:

   ```
   $CpuChart.Width = 600
   $CpuChart.Height = 400
   $CpuChart.Titles.Add('SRV1 CPU Utilization') | Out-Null
   ```

5. Create and define the chart area:

```
$ChartArea = New-Object -TypeName `
    System.Windows.Forms.DataVisualization.Charting.ChartArea
$ChartArea.Name = 'SRV1 CPU Usage'
$ChartArea.AxisY.Title = '% CPU Usage'
$CpuChart.ChartAreas.Add($ChartArea)
```

6. Identify the date/time column to get its name:

```
$Name = ($Counters[0] | Get-Member |
Where-Object MemberType -EQ 'NoteProperty')[0].Name
```

7. Add the data points to the chart:

```
$CpuChart.Series.Add('CPUPerc') | Out-Null
$CpuChart.Series["CPUPerc"].ChartType = 'Line'
$Counters | ForEach-Object{
$CPUChart.Series["CpuPerc"].Points.AddXY($_.$Name,
$_."\\SRV1\Processor(_Total)\% Processor Time") |
Out-Null
}
```

8. Save and display the chart image using `MSPaint`:

```
$CPUChart.SaveImage('C:\Perflogs\SRV1_CpuUtil.Png','png')
MSPaint.Exe C:\Perflogs\SRV1\CpuUtil.png
```

How it works...

This recipe utilizes features in the .NET Framework's `System.Forms.DataVisualization` namespace. PowerShell does not load this namespace by default. For this reason, in *step 1*, you explicitly add the namespace, and its parent namespace, `System.Windows.Forms`.

In *step 2*, you use `Import-CSV` to import the data file. You may need to adjust this step depending on what collector set output files you are using.

In *step 3*, you create a new chart object using `New-Object`. As there are no native cmdlets to assist in creating a chart, you need to dip down and utilize the .NET objects directly. Our starting point is the chart.

In *step 4*, you set the chart's height and width, and use the Chart's Add method to add the title. This method calls outputs the charts Titles object which is not of much use in production so just pipe it to Out-Null. As you work with this recipe, test this step with full output to gain a deeper understanding of the objects involved in data charting.

In *step 5*, you create the chart area. A chart area is a control that is added to a chart and contains, in this case, for example, the CPU graph for SRV1.

When you turn a counter set captured by PLA into a CSV, PowerShell converts each counter sample into a custom object, where the first field is the time/date of the sample. So in *step 6*, you work out that the name of that first note property.

In *step 7*, you add a new data series to the chart and define it as a line graph. Then you loop through each counter and add an XY point onto the graph (the current time and the CPU use). Once all the counter values are read and graphed, in *step 8*, you save the chart to a **Portable Network Graphic (PNG)** file and view it using Paint. The resulting graph looks like this:

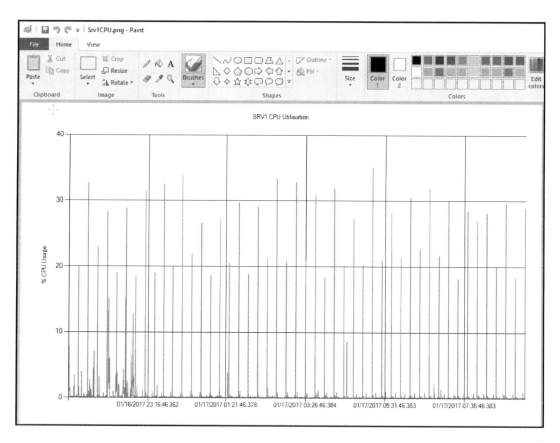

There's more...

This recipe showed you how to create a simple report graphing one counter, CPU utilization, across several hours of monitoring. You could add a second series, for example, memory pages per second, and so on. The result could be one or more customized graphs that are similar to what you see in Performance Monitor. You can use this recipe to automate the creation of the counter samples and creation of customized graphs. You could even create a scheduled task that created the graph or graphs, then email the resulting graph or graphs.

Creating a system diagnostics report

The PLA subsystem that you have been working with in this chapter has an additional kind of report that the PLA and PowerShell can generate, a System Diagnostic report. This report is simple to create and makes use of some of the approaches used in this chapter.

Getting ready

You run this recipe on server SRV1.

How to do it...

1. Start the data collector on the local system:

```
$PerfReportName="System\System Diagnostics"
$DataSet = New-Object -ComObject Pla.DataCollectorSet
$DataSet.Query($PerfReportName,$null)
$DataSet.Start($true)
```

2. Wait for the data collector to finish:

```
Start-Sleep -Seconds $Dataset.Duration
```

3. Get the report and view it:

```
$Dataset.Query($PerfReportName,$null)
$PerfReport = $Dataset.LatestOutputLocation + "\Report.html"
  & $PerfReport
```

How it works...

In *step 1*, you create a `PLA.DataCollectorSet` object and use it to query then start the Systems Diagnostics report. This report comes built into Windows, but you update it (or create customized reports if you so desire). This step is a part of the patterns that you adopt when using `PLA.DataCollectorSet` objects. You instantiate the object, then use the `Query` method to return details of this report.

In *step 2*, you sleep for the length of time it should take Windows to create the report, which by default is 600 seconds (10 minutes). Depending on how you are adapting this recipe, you may wish to update the time value.

Finally, in *step 3*, you re-query the report, which should have finished. After the query, you retrieve the filename that PLA used to store the report. You then execute this report (`Report.HTML`) to view the performance report. The report looks like this:

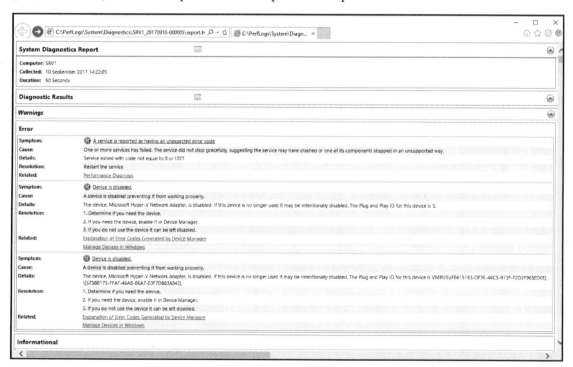

There's more...

In *step 3*, you just execute the report which brings the HTML file up into your browser. As an alternative to viewing it, you could turn this recipe into a script and run the script using a scheduled task. The scheduled task script could then create the report and mail it to you. You could also improve on this, for example, storing the reports to a central location and just email the location to other IT admins. Or possibly only email the report if there is an issue. Alternatively, you could send an everything is just fine email and let the mail recipients know where they can get the report should they need or want to examine it in more detail.

7
Troubleshooting Windows Server 2016

In this chapter, we cover the following recipes:

- Checking network connectivity
- Using troubleshooting packs
- Using best practice analyzer
- Managing Windows event logs
- Forwarding event logs

Introduction

Troubleshooting is the art and science of discovering the cause of some problem in your organization's computing estate and providing a solution that overcomes the problem. Troubleshooting encompasses a variety of tasks.

One common issue to begin this chapter with is troubleshooting network connectivity. With applications and services increasingly being networked and with the proliferation of wireless devices, network connectivity can be a problem in many organizations. In the first recipe, you look at some commands that can help you to troubleshoot this area.

Microsoft has built a troubleshooting framework into both Windows 10 and into Server 2016. These troubleshoots enable common problems to be resolved by an IT pro just running the troubleshooter. And for the really adventurous ones, you could even build your own troubleshooter, but such details are outside the scope of this book.

Troubleshooting is not just what you do when an issue arises. It also involves being proactive to avoid small issues becoming major problems. Often it also means ensuring that your systems and services are setup by way of accepted best practice.

The *Exchange* and *Office Communications Server* (now known as Skype For Business) teams both produced **best practice analyzer (BPA)** tools. These were applications that examined your Exchange or OCS (Skype for Business) environment and showed you places where you have not configured your application base on best practice. With Windows Server, many of the Windows features have their own BPA tools built around a common framework and are powered by PowerShell. The BPA tools can help you to ensure that the features installed on your Windows servers are operating according to best practice.

A great feature of Windows and Windows applications, roles, and services is the sheer amount of information logged. Windows NT (which is the basis for both Windows 10 and Windows Server 2016) initially came with a number of base event logs. In Windows Vista, Microsoft extended the amount of logging with the addition of application and service logs. These logs contain a wealth of additional information and along with the base logs can be invaluable in terms of both troubleshooting after the fact, and being proactive.

It is certainly the case that getting information out of these logs is a bit like looking for a needle in a hay stack. PowerShell has some great features for helping you to find the information you need quickly and easily. Learning how to get event log information from the logs takes time. To simplify the managing events across multiple hosts, you can also forward event log entries to a central host.

Checking network connectivity

One of the first troubleshooting tasks is checking the network connectivity between a client (or server) computer and another server computer. The client and server computers can be on the same physical subnet, or thousands of miles away and separated by routers. In order to provide a successful service to a client, your infrastructure needs to enable clients to connect to.

Traditionally, you might have used tools including `Ping`, `Tracert`, and `Pathping`. You can continue to use these Windows console applications within PowerShell—they work the way they have always worked. You may find even more useful, two newer cmdlets available with Windows Server 2016 which have additional useful features. The cmdlets also return output as objects which makes it easier to utilize the cmdlets on a PowerShell script.

This recipe uses one console command (Ping.exe, or just Ping in PowerShell) and two cmdlets, Test-Connection and Test-NetConnection. The Test-Connection is an older cmdlet and part of the Microsoft.PowerShell.Management module, while Test-NetConnection is a bit newer and is contained in the NetTCPIP module.

Getting ready

In this recipe, you check for connectivity from a server, SRV1, to its domain controllers (DC1 and DC2). The two DCs are domain controllers in the Reskit.Org domain, and SRV1 is a domain joined server. All the systems are running Server 2016.

How to do it...

Here is how you check the basic network connectivity:

1. Use Ping to test connectivity from CL1 to DC1:

   ```
   Ping DC1
   ```

2. Use Test-NetConnnection to test connection to DC1:

   ```
   Test-Connection -ComputerName DC1
   ```

3. Test with a simple true/false return:

   ```
   Test-Connection -ComputerName DC1 -Quiet
   ```

4. Test multiple systems at once:

   ```
   Test-Connection -ComputerName 'DC1','DC2','SRV1' -Count 1
   ```

5. Test connectivity to DC1 for SMB traffic:

   ```
   Test-NetConnection -ComputerName DC1 -CommonTCPPort SMB
   ```

6. Get a detailed connectivity check, using DC1 with HTTP:

   ```
   Test-NetConnection -ComputerName DC1 -CommonTCPPort HTTP `
                      -InformationLevel Detailed
   ```

7. Check connectivity to a port (LDAP on DC1):

```
Test-NetConnection -ComputerName DC1 -Port 445
```

8. Check connectivity to a system that is up and running but for a port that does not exist or is not open:

```
Test-NetConnection -ComputerName DC1 -PORT 9999
```

9. Finally, test for a system that does not exist:

```
Test-NetConnection -ComputerName DC99 -PORT 9999
```

How it works...

In *step 1*, you use the familiar Windows console command `Ping` (`Ping.exe`), Windows console command to check connectivity from `CL1` to `DC1`. The `Ping` command sends four **Internet Control Message Protocol (ICMP)** echo request messages to the remote server, `DC1` which should respond. Assuming connectivity is possible and that firewalls are not getting in the way, you should get four responses that show how long the `Ping` took and how many hops were involved. The output looks like this:

```
PS C:\> Ping DC1

Pinging DC1.Reskit.Org [10.10.10.10] with 32 bytes of data:
Reply from 10.10.10.10: bytes=32 time<1ms TTL=128
Reply from 10.10.10.10: bytes=32 time<1ms TTL=128
Reply from 10.10.10.10: bytes=32 time<1ms TTL=128
Reply from 10.10.10.10: bytes=32 time<1ms TTL=128

Ping statistics for 10.10.10.10:
    Packets: Sent = 4, Received = 4, Lost = 0 (0% loss),
Approximate round trip times in milli-seconds:
    Minimum = 0ms, Maximum = 0ms, Average = 0ms
```

In *step 2*, you use the `Test-Connection` cmdlet to ping `DC1` just using a cmdlet. The cmdlet itself issues the necessary ICMP messages but creates a nice object to return the results. The output looks like this:

```
PS C:\> Test-Connection -ComputerName DC1

Source  Destination  IPV4Address   IPV6Address   Bytes  Time(ms)
------  -----------  -----------   -----------   -----  --------
SRV1    DC1          10.10.10.10                 32     0
SRV1    DC1          10.10.10.10                 32     0
SRV1    DC1          10.10.10.10                 32     0
SRV1    DC1          10.10.10.10                 32     0
```

A useful feature of `Test-Connection` is the `-Quiet` parameter. This tells the cmdlet to test the connection but only return a Boolean response—true if the cmdlet could connect to the remote system or false if the connection was not successful. You see the results in *step 3* like this:

```
PS C:\> Test-Connection -ComputerName DC1 -Quiet
True
```

Another nice feature of `Test-Connection` is it allows you to test multiple connections in a single call to the cmdlet. The `-ComputerName` property accepts either a single computer name as you seen in the previous step, or as you see in *step 4*, multiple computers, with output that looks like this:

```
C:\> Test-Connection -computer 'DC1','DC2','SRV1' -Count 1

Source  Destination  IPV4Address   IPV6Address                  Bytes  Time(ms)
------  -----------  -----------   -----------                  -----  --------
SRV1    DC1          10.10.10.10                                32     0
SRV1    DC2          10.10.10.11                                32     0
SRV1    SRV1         10.10.10.50   fe80::b8df:5252:3cf6:b0b7%2  32     0
```

In *step 5*, you use the `Test-NetConnection` to not only test simple connectivity, but to test that a particular application is active and accepting network connections via some port. In this case, the port is a *well known* one (SMB or port 445).

The output of this step looks like this:

```
PS C:\> Test-NetConnection -ComputerName DC1 -CommonTCPPort SMB

ComputerName     : DC1
RemoteAddress    : 10.10.10.10
RemotePort       : 445
InterfaceAlias   : Ethernet
SourceAddress    : 10.10.10.50
TcpTestSucceeded : True
```

In *step 6*, you use `Test-NetConection` along with its `-Detailed` switch to get a bit more information about the tested connection. In this step which you run on SRV1, you test the connection from SRV1 to the HTTP port (port 80) on DC1. Assuming you have DC1 up and running and you have the `Web-Server` feature loaded, you see an output like this:

```
PS C:\> Test-NetConnection -ComputerName DC1 -CommonTCPPort HTTP
                         -InformationLevel Detailed


ComputerName            : DC1
RemoteAddress           : 10.10.10.10
RemotePort              : 80
NameResolutionResults   : 10.10.10.10
MatchingIPsecRules      :
NetworkIsolationContext : Private Network
InterfaceAlias          : Ethernet
SourceAddress           : 10.10.10.50
NetRoute (NextHop)      : 0.0.0.0
TcpTestSucceeded        : True
```

In *step 7*, you check a port using the port number. In this case, you check for SMB connectivity to DC1, with an output like this:

```
PS C:\> Test-NetConnection -ComputerName DC1 -Port 445

ComputerName     : DC1
RemoteAddress    : 10.10.10.10
RemotePort       : 445
InterfaceAlias   : Ethernet
SourceAddress    : 10.10.10.50
TcpTestSucceeded : True
```

In *step 8*, you see the results of a port that does not exist on DC1 (port 999), with output like this:

```
WARNING: Ping to 10.10.10.123 failed -- Status: DestinationHostUnreachable

ComputerName            : 10.10.10.123
RemoteAddress           : 10.10.10.123
InterfaceAlias          : Ethernet
SourceAddress           : 10.10.10.50
PingSucceeded           : False
PingReplyDetails (RTT)  : 0 ms
```

In *step 9*, you see the results of testing for a connection to a host that is online, but using a port that is not open on the host. Output looks like this:

```
C:\> Test-NetConnection -ComputerName DC1 -PORT 9999
WARNING: TCP connect to DC1:9999 failed

ComputerName            : DC1
RemoteAddress           : 10.10.10.10
RemotePort              : 9999
InterfaceAlias          : Ethernet
SourceAddress           : 10.10.10.50
PingSucceeded           : True
PingReplyDetails (RTT)  : 0 ms
TcpTestSucceeded        : False
```

There's more...

In *step 1*, you use an older tool, Ping. In the rest of the recipe, you use two cmdlets which have some features that are not available with Ping. One key feature is that both cmdlet return structured objects and not raw string blobs.

With *step 4*, you see the ability of Test-Connection to test multiple systems at once. This may have advantages if you are testing a large number of systems as part of a regular report.

In *step 5*, you tested for connectivity from SRV1 to DC1 over SMB, using port 445. In the earlier versions of windows, SMB transport used NetBIOS over TCP and made use of Ports 137, 138, and 139. The cmdlet checks over port 445 for SMB.

In *step 8* and *step 9*, you use the `Test-NetConnection` cmdlet to observe the results of a port (on a working server) not available and on a non-working server. In *step 8*, you see the impact of testing a working server with a particular port not open, and in *step 9* a computer that is not online. Because a nice object is returned from the two `Test-` cmdlets, you can easily issue the cmdlets and then test the result whereas with `Ping`, you could check the results but it would involve string parsing. All in all, `Ping` is better and faster than the command line, but less easy to manipulate programmatically.

Using troubleshooting packs

Windows includes a number of troubleshooting packs. These are tools that you can use to diagnose and resolve common errors.

Getting ready

You run this recipe on `SRV1`, a domain joined server in the `Reskit.Org` domain.

How to do it...

In this recipe, you see how to use the troubleshooting packs:

1. Get troubleshooting packs:

```
$TSPackfolders = Get-ChildItem `
                -Path C:\Windows\diagnostics\system -Directory
$TSPacks = Foreach ($TSPack in $TSPackfolders) {
        Get-TroubleshootingPack -Path $TSPack.FullName}
```

2. Display the packs:

```
$TSPacks | Format-Table -Property Name, Version,
        MinimumVersion, Description `
                -Wrap -Autosize
```

3. Get a troubleshooting pack for Windows Update:

```
$TsPack = $TSPacks | Where-Object `
                  id -eq 'WindowsUpdateDiagnostic'
```

4. Look at the problems this troubleshooting pack addresses:

```
$TSPack.RootCauses
```

5. Look at the solutions to these issues:

```
$TSPack.RootCauses.Resolutions
```

6. Run this troubleshooting pack (answering questions from the command line):

```
$TsPack | Invoke-TroubleshootingPack
```

7. Use the `Get-TroubleshootingPack` cmdlet to create an `AnswerFile`:

```
Get-TroubleshootingPack -Path $TSPack.path `
                  -AnswerFile c:\Answers.xml
```

8. Display the `AnswerFile`:

```
Get-Content -Path C:\Answers.xml
```

9. Run WU pack using `AnswerFile`:

```
$TsPack | Invoke-TroubleshootingPack `
          -AnswerFile C:\Answers.xml `
          -Unattend
```

How it works...

In *step 1*, you get a list of the troubleshooting packs available on SRV1. and store that in the $TSPacks variable. There is no output from this step.

In *step 2*, you display the `$TSPacks` variable to display the troubleshooting packs available, with output like this:

```
PS C:\Windows\system32> $TSPacks | Format-Table -Property Name, Version,
                                MinimumVersion,
                                Description
                        -Wrap -AutoSize

Name                                         Version MinimumVersion Description
----                                         ------- -------------- -----------
Aero                                         1.0     6.1            Find and fix problems with the Aero desktop experience.
Windows Store Apps                           4.0     6.1            Troubleshoot problems that may prevent Windows Store Apps from working properly
Sound                                        4.1     6.1            Troubleshoot problems that prevent your computer from playing or recording sound.
Background Intelligent Transfer Service      3.5     6.0            Find and fix problems that may prevent background downloads from working
Blue Screen                                  1.0     6.1            Troubleshoot errors that cause Windows to stop or restart unexpectedly
Hardware and Devices                         4.0     6.1            Find and fix problems with devices and hardware.
Devices and Printers                         3.0     6.1            Troubleshoot problems with devices and printers.
HomeGroup                                    1.2     6.1            Find and fix problems with viewing computers or shared files in a homegroup.
Internet Explorer Performance                1.2     6.1            Find and fix problems with Internet Explorer performance.
Internet Explorer Safety                     1.1     6.1            Find and fix problems with security and privacy features in Internet Explorer.
Keyboard                                     1.0     6.1            Find and fix problems with your computer's keyboard settings.
Windows Network Diagnostics                  4.0     6.1            Detects problems with network connectivity.
Program Compatibility Troubleshooter         2.0     6.1            Find and fix problems with running older programs on this version of Windows.
Performance                                  1.0     6.1            Find and fix problems to help optimize Windows speed and performance.
Power                                        1.0     6.1            Find and fix problems with your computer's power settings to conserve power and extend battery life.
Printer                                      4.0     6.1            Find and fix problems with printing.
Search and Indexing                          1.0     6.1            Find and fix problems with Windows Search.
Speech                                       1.0     6.1            Get your microphone ready and fix problems that may prevent Windows from hearing you
USB                                          1.0     6.2            Troubleshoot problems with a USB device
Video Playback                               3.0     6.1            Find and fix problems playing movies, television, and video
Windows Media Player Settings                1.1     6.1            Find and fix problems with Windows Media Player settings.
Windows Media Player Library                 1.1     6.1            Find and fix problems with the Windows Media Player Library.
Windows Media Player DVD                     1.1     6.1            Find and fix problems with playing DVDs in Windows Media Player.
Windows Update                               9.1     6.1            Resolve problems that prevent you from updating Windows.
```

In *step 3*, you search the list of troubleshooting packs available on `SRV1` and select the `Windows Update Diagnostic` troubleshooting pack, which produces no output.

With *step 4* and *step 5*, you examine the root cause conditions the troubleshooting pack checks for and the details of what the troubleshooting pack does to resolve each of these root cause conditions. The first issue involves the default Windows Update data locations are corrupt or invalid. One solution is to repair the default locations by changing these locations back to Windows default settings.

The list of root cause issues, which you produced in *step 4* looks like this:

```
PS C:\Windows\system32> $TSPack.RootCauses

Name
----
Default Windows Update data locations have changed
Potential Windows Update Database error detected
Windows Update components must be repaired
System date and time aren't correct
```

The solutions provided by the troubleshooting pack to resolve these issues, which you created in *step 5*, looks like this:

```
PS C:\> $TSPack.RootCauses.Resolutions

Name                                         Manual  Elevation  Interactive
----                                         ------  ---------  -----------
Repair default Windows Update locations      False   True       False
Repair Windows Update Database Corruption    False   True       True
Repair Windows Update components             False   True       True
Set the correct date and time               False   True       False
```

In *step 6*, you run the Windows Update Diagnostic troubleshooting pack interactively. The initial output looks like this:

```
PS C:\> $TsPack = $TSPacks | where id -eq 'WindowsUpdateDiagnostic'
PS C:\> $TsPack | Invoke-TroubleshootingPack

Please select the resolutions to apply
The following resolutions are available to address problems that were found

Potential Windows Update Database error detected
[1] Repair Windows Update Database Corruption

Windows Update components must be repaired
[2] Repair Windows Update components

[?] Help
[x] Exit
:
```

To just check for a single issue, say the first one to repair a Windows Update Database Corruption, just enter 1 and return. When you do this, you first find the results, like this:

```
Running resolution 'Repair Windows Update components'...
Stopping Bits service
Stopping CryptSvc service
Clearing Bits queue
Starting CryptSvc service
Starting Bits service


The selected resolutions have been run.
Please select whether you wish to run additional resolutions or exit.

[1] Run additional resolutions

[?] Help
[x] Exit
:
```

Finally enter X to complete the troubleshooter which produces no additional output.

In *step 7*, you use the `Get-Troubleshootingpack` to create an `AnswerFile`. The cmdlet is meant to ask for the same answers to the same questions you saw in *step 6*. Instead of performing the resolution, the cmdlet then creates an `AnswerFile`.

In *step 8*, you view the output from *step 7*, which looks like this:

```
PS C:\> Get-Content -Path C:\Answers.xml

<?xml version="1.0" encoding="UTF-8"?>
<Answers Version="1.0">
  <Interaction ID="INT_AggressiveMode">
     <Value>1</Value>
  </Interaction>
</Answers>
```

Finally, in *step 9*, you run this troubleshooter using the `AnswerFile` in an unattended mode. There is no output from this step.

There's more...

With `Get-TroubleshootingPack`, the cmdlet relies on you entering a file system path. The cmdlet does not know the default address. This cmdlet looks in the path supplied and returns a `DiagPack` object. You then pass that object to `Invoke-TroubleshootingPack` to run the pack.

In *step 7* through *step 9*, the recipe creates an `AnswerFile` then uses it. However, at the time of writing, some of the troubleshooting pack do not produce a correct `AnswerFiles`. When you generate the `AnswerFile`, you may be offered different questions, and the resultant `AnswerFile` may not be totally complete. This is a known issue and awaits a fix. For now, at least, the best idea is to run the troubleshooting pack interactively.

Use best practice analyzer

In IT, the term *best practices* refers to guidelines setting out the best way to configure a server or application as defined in subject matter experts (such as the application's development and support teams). Some best practice recommendations may not apply or be relevant. Following best practice can both solve existing issues and avoid future ones, but a bit of common sense is needed to ensure you are following the advice that is relevant for you and your organization.

A best practice model is a set of specific guidelines. A BPA is an automated tool that analyzes your infrastructure and points out areas where it the environment is not compliant with the best practice model.

Windows provides a built in BPA framework, complete with PowerShell support for managing the BPA process. Windows and applications come with a number of BPA models. The PowerShell cmdlets let you find the BPA models, invoke them, and then view the results.

Since not all BPA model guidelines are relevant for all situations, the BPA feature also lets you ignore specific recommendations that are not relevant for you.

Getting ready

This recipe runs on server SRV1, an application server you use in several of the recipes in this book, plus the DC1 domain controller.

How to do it...

1. Get all BPA models on SRV1:

   ```
   Get-BpaModel | Format-Table -Property Name, Id
   ```

2. Invoke BPA model for file services:

   ```
   Invoke-BpaModel -ModelId Microsoft/Windows/FileServices
   ```

3. Get BPA results for this scan:

   ```
   $Results = Get-BpaResult `
                  -ModelId Microsoft/Windows/FileServices
   ```

4. Display how many tests/results in the BPA model:

   ```
   $Results.count
   ```

5. Discover how many errors were found:

   ```
   ($Results | Where-Object Severity -eq 'Error').count
   ```

6. Discover how many warnings were found:

```
$Warnings = $Results | Where-Object Severity -eq 'Warning'
$Warnings.count
```

7. Examine the first three warnings:

```
$Warnings | Select-Object -First 3 |
Format-List -Property Category, Problem, Impact, Resolution
```

8. Use BPA remotely—check what models exist on DC1:

```
Invoke-Command -ComputerName DC1 -ScriptBlock {Get-BpaModel} |
    Format-Table -Property Name, Id
```

9. Run BPA Analyzer for AD on DC1:

```
$SB = {Invoke-BpaModel -ModelId `
                Microsoft/Windows/DirectoryServices}
 Invoke-Command -ComputerName DC1 -ScriptBlock $SB
```

10. Get the BPA results for this scan from DC1:

```
$SB = {Get-BpaResult -ModelId `
            Microsoft/Windows/DirectoryServices}
$RRESULTS = Invoke-Command -ComputerName DC1 -ScriptBlock $SB
```

11. How many checks were made and results found:

```
$RResults.count
$RResults | Group-Object -Property SEVERITY |
                Format-Table -Property Name, Count
```

12. Look at an error:

```
$RResults | Where-Object Severity -EQ 'Error' |
Format-List -Property Category,Problem,Impact,Resolution
```

How it works...

In *step 1*, you retrieve and display the BPA models on SRV1 with output that looks like this:

```
PS C:\> Get-BpaModel | Format-Table -Property Name, Id

Name                                                    Id
----                                                    --
RightsManagementServices                                Microsoft/Windows/ADRMS
CertificateServices                                     Microsoft/Windows/CertificateServices
Cluster-Aware Updating                                  Microsoft/Windows/ClusterAwareUpdating
Microsoft DHCP Server Configuration Analysis Model      Microsoft/Windows/DHCPServer
DirectoryServices                                       Microsoft/Windows/DirectoryServices
Microsoft DNS Server Configuration Analysis Model       Microsoft/Windows/DNSServer
File Services                                           Microsoft/Windows/FileServices
Hyper-V                                                 Microsoft/Windows/Hyper-V
LightweightDirectoryServices                            Microsoft/Windows/LightweightDirect...
Network Policy and Access Services (NPAS)               Microsoft/Windows/NPAS
Microsoft Remote Access Server Configuration An...      Microsoft/Windows/RemoteAccessServer
TerminalServices                                        Microsoft/Windows/TerminalServices
Windows Server Update Services                          Microsoft/Windows/UpdateServices
Microsoft Volume Activation Configuration Analy...      Microsoft/Windows/VolumeActivation
WebServer                                               Microsoft/Windows/WebServer
```

In *step 2*, you invoke a specific model, the BPA model for file services. The output from this step looks like this:

```
PS C:\> Invoke-BpaModel -ModelId Microsoft/Windows/FileServices

ModelId            : Microsoft/Windows/FileServices
SubModelId         :
Success            : True
ScanTime           : 21/07/2017 11:21:59
ScanTimeUtcOffset  :
Detail             : {SRV1, SRV1}
```

In *step 3*, you get the BPA results for the scan that you ran in *step 2*, and you store this in the $Results variable. There is no output from this step.

In *step 4*, you display the number or checks carried out and the number of results returned, with output like this:

```
PS C:\> $Results.count
116
```

With *step 6*, you view how many errors were found—the output looks like this:

```
PS C:\> ($Results | Where-Object Severity -eq 'Error').count
0
```

There were eleven warnings returned as you can see in the previous screen capture. In *step 7*, you display the first three warnings, with output like this:

```
PS C:\> $Warnings | Select -First 3 |
    Format-List Category, Problem, Impact, Resolution


Category    : Configuration
Problem     : In addition to the normal file names, the server is creating short, eight-character
              file names with a three-character file extension (8.3 file names) for all files.
Impact      : Creating short file names in addition to the normal, long file names can
              significantly decrease file server performance.
Resolution  : Disable short file name creation unless short file names are required by legacy
              applications.

Category    : Configuration
Problem     : Srv.sys is not set to start on demand.
Impact      : Client computers will not be able to access file shares and other Server Message
              Block (SMB)-based network services on this computer.
Resolution  : Set Srv.sys to start on demand.

Category    : Configuration
Problem     : AsynchronousCredits doesn't have the recommended value on this server.
Impact      : SMB not in a default configuration, which could lead to less than optimal behavior.
Resolution  : Set AsynchronousCredits to the recommended value, 64.
```

In *step 8* through *step 12*, you look at the BPA models then run the `DirectoryServices` BPA model on your domain controller, `DC1`, remotely. In *step 8*, you discover the models that exist on `DC1` and the output from this step looks like this:

```
PS C:\> Invoke-Command -ComputerName DC1 -ScriptBlock {Get-BpaModel} |
    Format-Table -Property Name, Id

Name                                                          Id
----                                                          --
RightsManagementServices                                      Microsoft/Windows/ADRMS
CertificateServices                                           Microsoft/Windows/CertificateServices
Microsoft DHCP Server Configuration Analysis Model            Microsoft/Windows/DHCPServer
DirectoryServices                                             Microsoft/Windows/DirectoryServices
Microsoft DNS Server Configuration Analysis Model             Microsoft/Windows/DNSServer
File Services                                                 Microsoft/Windows/FileServices
Hyper-V                                                       Microsoft/Windows/Hyper-V
LightweightDirectoryServices                                  Microsoft/Windows/LightweightDirect...
Network Policy and Access Services (NPAS)                     Microsoft/Windows/NPAS
Microsoft Remote Access Server Configuration Analysis Model   Microsoft/Windows/RemoteAccessServer
TerminalServices                                              Microsoft/Windows/TerminalServices
Windows Server Update Services                                Microsoft/Windows/UpdateServices
Microsoft Volume Activation Configuration Analysis Model      Microsoft/Windows/VolumeActivation
WebServer                                                     Microsoft/Windows/WebServer
```

In *step 9*, you run `DirectoryServices` BPA model remotely which creates output that looks like this:

```
PS C:\> $SB = {Invoke-BpaModel -ModelId `
                   Microsoft/Windows/DirectoryServices}
PS C:\> Invoke-Command -ComputerName DC1 -ScriptBlock $sb

ModelId           : Microsoft/Windows/DirectoryServices
SubModelId        :
Success           : True
ScanTime          : 21/07/2017 11:24:58
ScanTimeUtcOffset :
Detail            : {DC1, DC1}
```

In *step 10*, you retrieve the results and store them in the variable `$RResults` for later use. There is no output from this step.

In *step 11*, you look at the number of results and you show how many of each type of result was returned from the BPA model invocation. The output looks like this:

```
PS C:\> $RResults.count
43

PS C:\> $RResults | Group-Object SEVERITY |
              Format-Table -Property Name, Count

Name          Count
----          -----
Information    35
Error           1
Warning         7
```

Finally, in *step 12*, you look at one specific error returned with output that looks like this:

```
PS C:\> $RRResults | Where-Object Severity -EQ 'Error' |
    Format-List -Property Category,Problem,Impact,Resolution


Category     : Configuration
Problem      : The primary domain controller (PDC) emulator operations master in this forest is not
               configured to correctly synchronize time from a valid time source.
Impact       : If the PDC emulator master in this forest is not configured to correctly synchronize
               time from a valid time source, it might use its internal clock for time
               synchronization. If the PDC emulator master in this forest fails or otherwise
               becomes unavailable (and if you have not configured a reliable time server
               (GTIMESERV) in the forest root domain), other member computers and domain
               controllers in the forest will not be able to synchronize their time.
Resolution   : Set the PDC emulator master in this forest to synchronize time with a reliable
               external time source. If you have not configured a reliable time server (GTIMESERV)
               in the forest root domain, set the PDC emulator master in this forest to synchronize
               time with a hardware clock that is installed on the network (the recommended
               approach). You can also set the PDC emulator master in this forest to synchronize
               time with an external time server by running the w32tm /config
               /computer:DC1.Reskit.Org /manualpeerlist:time.windows.com /syncfromflags:manual
               /update command. If you have configured a reliable time server (GTIMESERV) in the
               forest root domain, set the PDC emulator master in this forest to synchronize time
               from the forest root domain hierarchy by running w32tm /config
               /computer:DC1.Reskit.Org /syncfromflags:domhier /update.
```

There's more...

In *step 1*, you display the BPA models which exist on SRV1. And in *step 8*, you view, remotely, the BPA models on DC1. In both cases, you may see different models available depending on which features you have added to each machine. The domain controller DC1 has a BPA model for AD, while SRV1 does not.

In *step 2* through *step 7*, you are carrying out a BPA scan against the file server feature on SRV1. In this model, there are 116 individual checks carried out by the model. Running this model on SRV1, you can see that there were no errors and eleven warnings. The first three warnings (shown in *step 7*) show some of the issues the BPA model found. Warning 1 shows that you can improve the performance of the file server feature by eliminating short name support. The second warning suggests setting Srv.sys to start on demand while the final warning suggests a configuration change that can lead to improved performance.

Running the AD BPA model on DC1 has 43 configuration checks which result in one error and 7 warnings. The error, which you can see in *step 12*, is caused by the forest root DC, which is DC1, it has no external time source. Since DC1 is the time master for the Reskit.org domain, you need to ensure the time on DC1 is synchronized with an external source otherwise domain joined hosts could experience time drift that could lead to other issues. The BPA model results set out clearly the problem, it's impact and a good and focused solution.

Managing event logs

Windows computers maintain a set of event logs that document events that occur on a given machine. Any time an event occurs, the application or service can log events which can then be used to help in the debugging process.

In Windows, there are two types of event logs: Windows logs and application and services logs. Windows logs began with Windows NT 3.1 and continue in Windows Server 2016 and are important components in troubleshooting and system monitoring.

Windows Vista added a new category of logs, application and services logs. These logs contain events that are within a single application, service, or other Windows component. Windows comes by default with a set of application and service logs—adding components such as new Windows features or roles often results in additional application and service logs.

These logs give you a great picture of what your system is actually doing. Additionally, you can also add new event logs and enable scripts to log events which occur while the script is running.

PowerShell provides you with several useful cmdlets to help you comb the event log looking for key events. The `Get-EventLog` enables you to get details of the logs that exist as well as retrieving log events from the Windows logs. With `Get-WinEvent`, you can examine both the classic Windows logs and the new application and services logs. You use both these cmdlets in this recipe.

Getting ready

This recipe uses two Windows Server 2016 systems. You run the recipe on a domain attached server, `SRV1` and the `Reskit.Org` domain's domain controller (`DC1`). `SRV1` is used in a number of recipes in this book as is the `DC1` domain controller. You run this recipe on `SRV1`.

 Depending on which recipes you have attempted using `SRV1` and `DC1`, you may see different results to those shown in this recipe. You may see more or less event logs and more or less events.

How to do it...

1. Get any Windows event logs which exist on SRV1:

```
Get-EventLog -LogName *
```

2. Get Windows event logs remotely from DC1:

```
Get-EventLog -LogName * -ComputerName DC1
```

3. Clear application log on DC1:

```
Clear-EventLog -LogName Application -ComputerName DC1
```

4. Examine the types of events on SRV1:

```
Get-EventLog -LogName application |
  Group-Object -property EntryType |
      Format-Table -Property Name, Count
```

5. Examine which area created the events in the Windows System log:

```
Get-EventLog -LogName System |
  Group-Object -Property Source |
      Sort-Object -Property Count -Descending |
          Select-Object -First 10 |
              Format-Table -Property name, count
```

6. Examine all local event logs using Get-WinEvent:

```
$LocEventLogs = Get-WinEvent -ListLog *
$LocEventLogs.count
$LocEventLogs |
      Sort-Object -Property RecordCount -Descending |
          Select-Object -First 10
```

7. Examine all of the event logs on DC1:

```
$RemEventLogs = Get-WinEvent -ListLog * -ComputerName DC1
$RemEventLogs.count
$RemEventLogs |
Sort-Object -Property RecordCount -Descending |
Select-Object -First 10
```

8. Look at Windows Update application and services log and discover which updates have been found and downloaded:

```
$Updates = Get-WinEvent `
-LogName 'Microsoft-Windows-WindowsUpdateClient/Operational' |
Where-Object ID  -EQ 41
$out = Foreach ($Update in $Updates) {
$ht = @{}
$ht.Time = $Update.TimeCreated
$ht.update = ($Update.Properties | Select -First 1).Value
New-Object -TypeName PSObject -Property $HT }
$out |
Sort-Object -Property TimeCreated |
        Format-Table -Wrap
```

How it works...

In *step 1* which you run on SRV1, you view the Windows logs existing on SRV1 by executing the Get-EventLog cmdlet. Depending on which features and applications you have added to SRV1, you should see something looking like this:

```
PS C:\> Get-EVentLog -LogName *

  Max(K) Retain OverflowAction          Entries Log
  ------ ------ --------------          ------- ---
  20,480      0 OverwriteAsNeeded        19,919 Application
  15,168      0 OverwriteAsNeeded          138 DFS Replication
  20,480      0 OverwriteAsNeeded            0 HardwareEvents
     512      7 OverwriteOlder              0 Internet Explorer
  20,480      0 OverwriteAsNeeded            0 Key Management Service
  20,480      0 OverwriteAsNeeded        29,373 Security
  20,480      0 OverwriteAsNeeded        61,889 System
  15,360      0 OverwriteAsNeeded        15,454 Windows PowerShell
```

In *step 2*, you retrieve the Windows events logs which exist on DC1, which looks like this:

```
PS C:\> Get-EventLog -LogName * -ComputerName DC1

Max(K) Retain OverflowAction        Entries Log
------ ------ --------------        ------- ---
   512      7 OverwriteOlder            320 Active Directory Web Services
20,480      0 OverwriteAsNeeded      21,312 Application
15,168      0 OverwriteAsNeeded       1,324 DFS Replication
   512      0 OverwriteAsNeeded       3,186 Directory Service
02,400      0 OverwriteAsNeeded         336 DNS Server
20,480      0 OverwriteAsNeeded           0 HardwareEvents
   512      7 OverwriteOlder              0 Internet Explorer
20,480      0 OverwriteAsNeeded           0 Key Management Service
31,072      0 OverwriteAsNeeded     188,206 Security
20,480      0 OverwriteAsNeeded      17,112 System
15,360      0 OverwriteAsNeeded      15,825 Windows PowerShell
```

In step 3, you clear a remote event log—in this case the application log on DC1. There is no output from this step.

In *step 4*, you examine the types of events in the application event log on SRV1. There are a large number of information type events, most of which you can usually simply ignore. With Windows Server 2016, some events have an entry type of 0, a value that is not documented. The output looks like this:

```
PS C:\> Get-EventLog -LogName application |
            Group-Object -property EntryType |
              Format-Table -Property Name, Count

Name        Count
----        -----
Information 19549
0             246
Error         103
Warning        21
```

In step 5, you investigate the source of the events in the Windows System event log. For brevity, the recipe just examines the more common sources, with output that looks like this:

```
PS C:\> Get-EventLog -LogName System |
    Group-Object -Property Source |
        Sort-Object -Property Count -Descending |
            Select -First 10 |
                Format-Table -Property name, count

Name                                  Count
----                                  -----
Service Control Manager               57343
WAS                                     653
Microsoft-Windows-Kernel-General        508
Microsoft-Windows-Hyper-V-Netvsc        469
Microsoft-Windows-Time-Service          418
Microsoft-Windows-FilterManager         317
EventLog                                278
Microsoft-Windows-Kernel-Boot           192
HTTP                                    179
Microsoft-Windows-DNS-Client            171
```

With *step 6*, you use `Get-WinEvent` to first get basic details of each of the existing logs (including both the classic Windows logs and the applications and services logs). Then, you display the total number of logs, as well as top 10 busiest event logs, with output like this:

```
PS C:\> $LocEventLogs = Get-WinEvent -ListLog *
PS C:\> $LocEventLogs.count
385

PS C:\> $LocEventLogs |
        Sort-Object -Property RecordCount -Descending |
            Select-Object -First 10
LogMode    MaximumSizeInBytes RecordCount LogName
-------    ------------------ ----------- -------
Circular            20971520        61837 System
Circular            20971520        27148 Security
Circular            20971520        19979 Application
Circular            20000000        19253 Microsoft-Windows-Store/Operational
Circular            10485760        17476 Microsoft-Windows-TaskScheduler/Operational
Circular            15728640        15487 Windows PowerShell
Circular             4194304         8245 Microsoft-Windows-GroupPolicy/Operational
Circular             8388608         4898 Microsoft-Windows-SmbClient/Security
Circular             1052672         2566 Microsoft-Client-Licensing-Platform/Admin
Circular             1052672         2524 Microsoft-Windows-Kernel-IO/Operational
```

In *step 7*, you repeat these commands to discover how many total event logs exist on DC1 and the busiest ten logs, with output like this:

```
PS C:\> $RemEventLogs = Get-WinEvent -ListLog * -ComputerName DC1
PS C:\> $RemEventLogs.count
407

PS C:\> $RemEventLogs |
          Sort-Object -Property RecordCount -Descending |
            Select-Object -First 10

LogMode    MaximumSizeInBytes RecordCount LogName
-------    ------------------ ----------- -------
Circular          134217728      187690 Security
Circular           20000000       29766 Microsoft-Windows-Store/Operational
Circular           10485760       17463 Microsoft-Windows-TaskScheduler/Operational
Circular           20971520       16648 System
Circular           15728640       15819 Windows PowerShell
Circular            4194304        7485 Microsoft-Windows-GroupPolicy/Operational
Circular           15728640        3146 Microsoft-Windows-PowerShell/Operational
Circular            1052672        3012 Directory Service
Circular            1052672        2483 Microsoft-Windows-Kernel-IO/Operational
Circular            1052672        2424 Microsoft-Client-Licensing-Platform/Admin
```

Finally, in step, you investigate the event entries in the Windows Update Operational log. In particular, you look at the events with an event ID of 41—these events are logged whenever Windows Update discovers and downloads an update that is to be applied (once the update is complete). Depending on how you have SRV1 setup, you may see output for this step similar to the following:

```
PS C:\> $Updates = Get-WinEvent -LogName 'Microsoft-Windows-WindowsUpdateClient/Operational' |
          Where-Object ID  -EQ 41
PS C:\> $out = Foreach ($Update in $Updates) {
          $ht = @{}
          $ht.Time = $Update.TimeCreated
          $ht.update = ($Update.Properties | Select -First 1).Value
          New-Object -TypeName PSObject -Property $HT }
PS C:\> $out |
          Sort-Object -Property TimeCreated |
            Format-Table -Wrap


Time                   update
----                   ------
24/07/2017 19:40:22 Definition Update for Windows Defender - KB2267602 (Definition 1.249.158.0)
24/07/2017 17:56:28 Definition Update for Windows Defender - KB2267602 (Definition 1.249.155.0)
23/07/2017 17:42:55 Definition Update for Windows Defender - KB2267602 (Definition 1.249.118.0)
23/07/2017 16:28:32 Definition Update for Windows Defender - KB2267602 (Definition 1.249.116.0)
23/07/2017 15:53:03 2017-07 Cumulative Update for Windows Server 2016 for x64-based Systems
                       (KB4025339)
23/07/2017 15:53:03 Microsoft .NET Framework 4.7 for Windows 10 Version 1607 and Windows Server
                       2016 for x64 (KB3186568)
23/07/2017 15:53:03 2017-06 Update for Windows Server 2016 for x64-based Systems (KB3150513)
23/07/2017 14:57:00 2017-06 Update for Windows Server 2016 for x64-based Systems (KB4023834)
23/07/2017 13:43:12 Definition Update for Windows Defender - KB2267602 (Definition 1.249.113.0)
23/07/2017 13:42:56 Windows Malicious Software Removal Tool for Windows 8, 8.1, 10 and Windows
                       Server 2012, 2012 R2, 2016 x64 Edition - July 2017 (KB890830)
```

There's more...

In *step 1* and *step 2*, you examine the Windows event logs that exist on two systems (SRV1 and DC1). As you can see, the logs available differ—on DC1, you see the Active Directory Web Services log which does not exist on SRV1.

In *step 3*, you clear the application log on DC1. As a best practice for event logs, you should only clear a log once you have copied the log elsewhere for safe keeping. Naturally, mileage varies on this point since the vast majority of event logs entries are not of very much use in day to day operations.

In *step 4*, you seen the different classifications of events, including one with a name of 0. In this case, the property containing the event log entry type is based on an enum, and this enum was not updated so PowerShell is unable to display the entry name for this event log entry type.

In *step 6* and *step 7*, you examine the service and application logs that exist on SRV1. These steps demonstrate how additional features or applications can result in additional event logs.

Step 8 shows you how to dive into a specific event in a specific event log. In this case, you examine the Software Update service's operational log to discover events with an event ID of 41. In general, when retrieving information from your event logs, you need to know which log and which event ID to look for.

Forward event logs to a central server

By default, every Windows computer in your organization keeps its own local event logs. You examined these logs in the *Searching event logs for specific events* recipe. The logs on SRV1, for example, are separate from the logs on DC1. In larger environments, analyzing event logs across large number of servers is complex. With 100 servers, you would need to run a script on each of those 100 servers, which could become quite complex. Having each server forward events to a central computer can simplify this task greatly.

Also consider what happens if a server is compromised. Hackers often clear event logs after doing naughty things on a hacked machine. This helps to cover the hacker's tracks. A best security practice is to get the event details sent to a central and hopefully more secure server as quickly as possible. With Windows, you can use using event forwarding to achieve this.

Forwarding event logs to a central server allows you to centralize your log file analysis and reporting and also to reduce the risk of a malign actor damaging a server but covering his tracks and hoping to avoid detection.

Getting ready

In this recipe which you run on DC1, you forward failed logon events from SRV1 to the domain controller, DC1. This is a simple and convenient configuration for testing using private virtual machines. In production, you should consider forwarding to a separate host.

This recipe uses two hosts, DC1 (a domain controller in the reskit.org domain) and SRV1 (a domain joined server in the same domain). You run the recipe on DC1.

How to do it...

This recipe shows you how to forward events.

1. Configure event collection on each server—first on DC1 (locally) then remotely to SRV1:

```
wecutil qc /quiet | Out-Null
Invoke-Command -ComputerName SRV1 `
                -ScriptBlock {wecutil qc /quiet} | Out-Null
```

2. Create the collector security group, add DC1:

```
$ECGName='Event Collector Group'
New-ADGroup -Name $ECGName -GroupScope Global `
            -Path 'OU=IT,DC=Reskit,DC=Org'
Add-ADGroupMember -Identity $ECGName -Members'DC1$'
```

3. Display membership of this new group:

```
Get-ADGroupMember -Identity $ECGName
```

4. Create a new GPO to configure event collection:

```
$GPOName = 'Event Collection'
$ECGName = 'Event Collector Group'
$gpo  = New-GPO -Name $GPOName
$link = New-GPLink -Name $GPOName `
                    -Target "DC=Reskit,DC=Org"
$p1 = Set-GPPermission -Name $GPOName `
```

```
                            -TargetName "$ECGName" `
                            -TargetType Group `
                            -PermissionLevel GpoApply
    $p2 = Set-GPPermission -Name $GPOName `
                            -TargetName 'Authenticated Users' `
                            -TargetType Group `
                            -PermissionLevel None
```

5. Set GPO permissions:

```
Set-GPPermission -Name $GPOName `
                 -TargetName 'Authenticated Users' `
                 -TargetType Group `
                 -PermissionLevel None
```

6. Apply the settings to the new GPO object:

```
$WinRMKey=
'HKLM\Software\Policies\Microsoft\Windows\WinRM\Service'
  Set-GPRegistryValue -Name $GPOName -Key $WinRMKey `
                      -ValueName 'AllowAutoConfig'
                      -Type DWORD -Value 1 |
                      Out-Null
  Set-GPRegistryValue -Name $GPOName -Key $WinRMKey `
                      -ValueName "IPv4Filter" -Type STRING `
                      -Value "*" |
                      Out-Null
  Set-GPRegistryValue -Name $GPOName -Key $WinRMKey `
                      -ValueName "IPv6Filter" `
                      -Type STRING -Value "*" |
                        Out-Null
```

7. Create XML for the subscription, and save it to a file:

```
$xmlfile = @'
<Subscription xmlns="http://schemas.microsoft.com/2006/03/
  windows/events/subscription">
    <SubscriptionId>FailedLogins</SubscriptionId>
      <SubscriptionType>SourceInitiated</SubscriptionType>
      <Description>Source Initiated Subscription</Description>
      <Enabled>true</Enabled>
<Uri>http://schemas.microsoft.com/wbem/
wsman/1/windows/EventLog</Uri>
      <ConfigurationMode>Custom</ConfigurationMode>
      <Delivery Mode="Push">
          <Batching>
              <MaxItems>1</MaxItems>
                <MaxLatencyTime>1000</MaxLatencyTime>
```

```
        </Batching>
         <PushSettings>
            <Heartbeat Interval="60000"/>
         </PushSettings>
         </Delivery>
      <Expires>2018-01-01T00:00:00.000Z</Expires>
      <Query>
         <![CDATA[
            <QueryList>
               <Query Path="Security">
                  <Select>Event[System/EventID='4625']</Select>
               </Query>
            </QueryList>]]>
      </Query>
         <ReadExistingEvents>true</ReadExistingEvents>
      <TransportName>http</TransportName>
      <ContentFormat>RenderedText</ContentFormat>
      <Locale Language="en-US"/>
     <LogFile>ForwardedEvents</LogFile>
   <AllowedSourceNonDomainComputers>
  </AllowedSourceNonDomainComputers>
<AllowedSourceDomainComputers>O:NSG:NSD:(A;;GA;;;DC)(A;;GA;;;NS)
 </AllowedSourceDomainComputers>
 </Subscription>
'@
 $xmlfile | Out-File -FilePath C:\Event.xml
```

8. Create a subscription on DC1 for this event:

```
wecutil cs Event.xml
```

9. Create the source security group:

```
New-ADGroup -Name 'Event Source' -GroupScope Global
Add-ADGroupMember -Identity "Event Source" -Members 'SRV1$'
```

10. Create the GPO for the event source systems:

```
New-GPO -Name 'Event Source'
New-GPLink -Name 'Event Source' `
           -Target 'DC=Reskit,DC=Org'
 Set-GPPermission -Name 'Event Source' `
                  -TargetName 'Event Source' `
                  -TargetType Group `
                  -PermissionLevel GpoApply
 Set-GPPermission -Name 'Event Source' `
                  -TargetName 'Authenticated Users' `
                  -TargetType Group `
```

```
                     -PermissionLevel None
```

11. Apply the settings for the source GPO to point to DC1:

```
$EventKey='HKLM\Software\Policies\Microsoft\
 Windows\EventLog\EventForwarding\SubscriptionManager'
$TargetAddress=
'Server=http://DC1.reskit.org:5985/wsman/SubscriptionManager/WEC'
Set-GPRegistryValue -Name 'Event Source; -Key $EventKey `
                    -ValueName '1' `
                    -Type STRING `
                    -Value $TargetAddress
```

12. Restart SRV1:

```
Restart-Computer -ComputerName SRV1 `
                 -Wait -For PowerShell `
                 -Force
```

13. Once SRV1 has rebooted, attempt to login using incorrect credentials.

14. View the result of invalid logins:

```
$badlogins = Get-WinEvent -LogName ForwardedEvents
 Foreach ($badlogin in $badlogins)
 {
   $obj = [Ordered] @{}
   $obj.time   = $badlogin.TimeCreated
   $obj.logon  = ($badlogin |
      Select-Object -ExpandProperty properties).value |
         Select-Object -Skip 5 -First 1
   New-Object -TypeName PSobject -Property $obj
 }
```

How it works...

In *step 1*, you enable the Windows event collector on both DC1 and SRV1. In *step 2*, You create a new global group, Event Collection, which defines the event collector computer—in this case DC1. There is no output from these two steps.

In *step 3*, you use the `Get-ADGroupMember` cmdlet to confirm the membership if the `Event Collector` global group. The output looks like this:

```
PS C:> Get-ADGroupMember -Identity $ECGName

distinguishedName : CN=DC1,OU=Domain Controllers,DC=Reskit,DC=Org
name              : DC1
objectClass       : computer
objectGUID        : cf557bc7-45e3-407a-8fb2-4a14d0d6537a
SamAccountName    : DC1$
SID               : S-1-5-21-715049209-2702507345-667613206-1000
```

In *step 4*, you create a new GPO, `Event Collection` to configure event collection. There is no output from this step. With *step 5*, you set permissions on the GPO with output like this:

```
PS C:\> Set-GPPermission -Name $GPOName `
                 -TargetName 'Authenticated Users' `
                 -TargetType Group `
                 -PermissionLevel None

DisplayName      : Event Collection
DomainName       : Reskit.Org
Owner            : RESKIT\Domain Admins
Id               : 0023d350-09ee-428d-8013-b5c617f97bd9
GpoStatus        : AllSettingsEnabled
Description      :
CreationTime     : 03/09/2017 23:57:47
ModificationTime : 03/09/2017 23:58:00
UserVersion      : AD Version: 0, SysVol Version: 0
ComputerVersion  : AD Version: 0, SysVol Version: 0
WmiFilter        :
```

In *step 6*, you apply detailed settings on the `Event Collection` GPO which produces no output.

In *step 7*, you create the XML for the source initiated event collection and save it to file store. There is no output from this step. In *step 8*, you register the event collection details with Windows. There is also no output from this step.

In *step 9*, you create a new group to hold the computers which forward events (the systems acting as an event source). In this case you just specify `SRV1` as an event source. There is no output from this step.

In *step 10*, you create a new GPO to configure the systems acting as an event source, in this case just `SRV1`. There is no output from this step.

In *step 11* you specify details of the event source GPO with output like this:

```
PS C:\> $EventKey='HKLM\Software\Policies\Microsoft\Windows\EventLog\EventForwarding\SubscriptionManager'
PS C:\> $TargetAddress="Server=http://DC1.reskit.org:5985/wsman/SubscriptionManager/WEC"
PS C:\> Set-GPRegistryValue -Name "Event Source" -Key $EventKey
                            -ValueName '1'  `
                            -Type STRING  `
                            -Value $TargetAddress
                            DisplayName      : Event Source

DomainName        : Reskit.Org
Owner             : RESKIT\Domain Admins
Id                : 83da9e1d-ea48-4a78-a2b1-27095aee808e
GpoStatus         : AllSettingsEnabled
Description       :
CreationTime      : 04/09/2017 14:34:23
ModificationTime  : 05/09/2017 15:45:38
UserVersion       : AD Version: 0, SysVol Version: 0
ComputerVersion   : AD Version: 5, SysVol Version: 5
WmiFilter         :
```

In *step 12*, you reboot the machine, then in *step 13* you attempt to logon using invalid credentials. Finally, in *step 14*, you use `Get-WinEvent` to retrieve the forwarded bad login events, then output the details of the bad logon, with output like this:

```
PS C:\> $badlogins = Get-WinEvent -LogName ForwardedEvents
PS C:\> Foreach ($badlogin in $badlogins) {
            $obj = [Ordered] @{}
            $obj.Time   = $badlogin.TimeCreated
            $obj.Logon  = ($badlogin |
                Select-Object -ExpandProperty properties).value | select -skip 5 -first 1
            New-Object -TypeName PSobject -Property $obj
        }

Time                    Logon
----                    -----
06/09/2017 09:30:12 EvilHacker
05/09/2017 19:01:11 hacker420X@mahkooc.com
04/09/2017 19:00:39 NiceHacker@ReallyBadplace.com
04/09/2017 19:00:14 administrator
```

There's more...

In many of the steps in this recipe, you pipe cmdlet to `Out-Null` to avoid extra output. This is a useful approach for production scripts—you may choose to remove the calls to `Out-Null` and view the output of some of the commands to gain more familiarity.

In this recipe, you created and configured two GPOs. You use the first GPO, `Event Collection`, to target the computer to be used for collecting events. This is `DC1` for simplicity—but in production you would most likely setup a separate system to be the event collector. The second GPO, `Event Source`, is used to define the collection.

In *step 7*, you create an XML file containing details of the event subscription. You have considerable flexibility in terms of the configuration of event collection, but you do need to define it in XML. Mistakes in the XML can be very difficult to troubleshoot.

In *step 9*, you added one host, `SRV1`, to the global `Event Source` group. This group defines the systems that are to be the source of the events defined in *step 8*.

In *step 14*, you use `Get-WinEvent` to retrieve the forwarded bad login events. Depending on what invalid credentials you provide, you get different results. Also, in *step 14*, you create an object for each bad logon. You could extend that object in production—for example you could add the host where the invalid login was attempted.

8
Managing Windows Networking Services

This chapter contains the following recipes:

- New ways to do old things
- Configuring IP addressing
- Converting IP address from static to DHCP
- Installing domain controllers and DNS
- Configuring zones and resource records in DNS
- Installing and authorizing a DHCP server
- Configuring DHCP scopes
- Configuring DHCP server failover and load balancing
- Building a public key infrastructure
- Creating and managing AD users, groups, and computers
- Adding users to AD using a CSV file
- Reporting on AD users
- Finding expired computers in AD
- Creating a privileged user report

Introduction

PowerShell has provided useful improvements in our ability to manage networking. Windows Server has some features built in such as DHCP failover, DNS, and AD, you manage these with cmdlets. Windows Server 2016 includes comprehensive cmdlets that replaces the host of arcane and incompatible configuration and troubleshooting console applications.

The focus of this chapter is the core networking services contained in Windows Server 2016. These services include DHCP, DNS, Active Directory, and Certificate Services. The recipes in this chapter look at how to manage these features using PowerShell. We also note the few remaining things you cannot do with a PowerShell cmdlet.

In the *New ways to do old things* recipe, you look at some of the Windows console applications that you might have used for network troubleshooting and their updated PowerShell equivalents. You should find that everything you could do with a console application you can also do with a native cmdlet and more. This recipe only looks at few of the key networking related cmdlets versus their console application equivalents. There are over 300 console applications (and Visual Basic scripts) in Windows Server 2016. Some of those many console applications (but not all) have cmdlet equivalents; this chapter cannot cover them all.

With Windows Server 2016, networking means TCP/IP. In the *Configuring IP addressing* recipe, you look at how to set up and manage IP addresses on a computer, while in the *Converting IP Address from static to DHCP* recipe, you change a computer having a static IP configuration to have a dynamic DHCP based IP configuration. IP configuration via DHCP tends to be used for client computers and devices, while you use static IP configuration for your servers.

A central piece of your IT infrastructure is your **Active Directory (AD)** and AD **domain controllers (DCs)**. You use the *Installing domain controllers* recipe to install an AD forest and to add a second DC to the domain. You also install a DNS server as part of the installation of the first AD server. When you create these two domain controllers using the recipe, you also add DNS servers to both DCs. By default, Windows creates the necessary zone and resource records and ensures that Active Directory replicates the DNS records to the second DC/DNS server.

In the *Configuring DNS zones and resource records*, you configure DNS server zones and DNS resource records. You can use this recipe to manage the zones and resource records and to test whether your DNS servers are working.

The **Dynamic Host Control Protocol (DHCP)** network protocol enables a DHCP client to request and obtain IP configuration details from a DHCP server. For the DHCP server to provide IP configuration information to a DHCP client, you need to configure the DHCP scopes (sets of IP addresses to offer to DHCP clients), and DHCP options (details of the IP configuration such as default gateway and DNS server.

In the *Installing and configuring DHCP* recipe, you install and set up the DHCP service and prepare it for use in your network. Once this is complete, you make use of the *Configure DHCP scope* recipe to implement a DHCP service in your network. Finally, with the *Configure DHCP server failover and load balancing* recipe, you install a second DHCP server in the domain. Then you configure the two DHCP servers to do both load balancing and failover.

Managing the objects in your AD environment is straightforward. In the *Creating and managing AD users, groups, and computers* recipe, you use cmdlets to create, update, and remove users and security groups (and manage the members of a group). The *Reporting on AD users* recipe shows how you can find users in your AD and generate reports. The *Finding expired computers* recipe helps you to find domain computers that have expired.

An important aspect of many of the networking cmdlets used here is that they utilize WMI and the use of **cmdlet definition XML (CDXML)** to define each cmdlet. CDXML is a feature of PowerShell that lets you write XML that converts a WMI class into a cmdlet. For example, the cmdlet `Get-NetAdapter` returns details of each network adapter in your system. You could get the same information by using the command `Get-CimInstance -Namespace ROOT/StandardCimv2 -class MSFT_NetAdapter`. The CDXML based cmdlets do more than just retrieve information. They also allow you to update and remove the underlying WMI instances. All in all, this makes managing network-related objects much simpler. With CDXML, Microsoft was able to provide PowerShell cmdlets to unlock all that greatness that is hidden in the depths of WMI.

There are two consequences of this approach. The first is performance. Using WMI can be slower than using older Windows console applications based on the native Win32 API. Second, the error messages that CDXML cmdlets return can be less helpful than those returned by other core cmdlets. It can be difficult to understand some of the messages that can result. The big advantage of course, is the ease of scripting. You have cmdlets that utilize objects that make scripting easier and more consistent.

A final thing to be aware of, which is, there are a lot of WMI classes each of which are related. For example, in the namespace ROOT/StandardCimv2, you have two related classes: MSFT_NetIPInterface and MSFT_NetAdapter. The classes overlap. And since CDXML just converts a single class to cmdlets, the resultant cmdlets also overlap. To get a complete picture of a network link, you may need to use both classes/cmdlet. If you are doing a lot of networking troubleshooting, you could roll-your-own functions to produce a single object for each interface that combines multiple WMI classes.

New ways to do old things

Networking IT pros have used a small set of console applications for decades to carry out basic troubleshooting activities. These help you to manage all manner of networking components. Tools such as Ipconfig, Tracert, and NSlookup are used by IT pros all over the world. The **network shell (netsh)** is another veritable treasure chest of tools to configure and manage your networking components.

The latest versions of PowerShell within the latest versions of the Windows operating system provide a wealth of new network-focused cmdlets that overlap with those old command-line tools. These tools represent new ways of doing old things.

Naturally, you shouldn't just use the new commands because you can. This recipe shows you that the new commands are often better and can be sufficiently different as compared to the older console (and a lot more useful). This recipe helps you to re-equip your networking tool belt!

Getting ready

This recipe uses the DC1 domain controller in the Reskit.Org domain and SRV1, a domain joined server in the Reskit domain. But you can execute this recipe on any system, assuming you have the latest versions of Windows and PowerShell loaded.

How to do it...

In this recipe, you use both the old command and explore some of the options available with the new ones. You can see the expected output in the *How it works...* section. Naturally, you may need to adapt some of these steps to accord with your environment.

1. From the DC1 server, retrieve IP address configuration:

```
# Two variations on the old way
ipconfig.exe
ipconfig.exe /all
# The new Way with Get-NetIPConfiguration
Get-NetIPConfiguration
```

Run the remainder of this recipe on server SRV1.

2. From SRV1, ping the DC1 computer (using both FQDN and hostname):

```
# Ping a remote machine two ways
Ping DC1.Reskit.Org -4
Test-NetConnection DC1.Reskit.Org
# And explore some new things Ping does not do
Test-NetConnection DC1.Reskit.Org -Port 389 `
                                -InformationLevel Detailed
Test-NetConnection DC1 -CommonTCPPort SMB
```

3. Use and share folders:

```
# Map a local drive letter to a network share
net use X: \\DC1\c$
New-SMBMapping -LocalPath 'Y:' -RemotePath \\SRV1\c$
# Find out what has been used/mapped
net use
Get-SMBMapping
# Share a folder for others to use
net share foo=c:\
New-SmbShare -Path C:\ -Name FooNew
# Discover what folders are shared
net share
Get-SmbShare
Share a folder: # share the old way
net share Foo=c:\
# and the new way
New-SmbShare -Path C:\ -Name Foo2
# And see what has been shared the old way
net share
# and the new way
```

```
Get-SmbShare
```

4. Perform DNS lookups:

```
# Lookup a DNS record for a host
nslookup -querytype=all DC1.Reskit.Org
# The new way
Resolve-DnsName -Name DC1.Reskit.Org -Type ALL
```

5. Examine the DNS client cache:

```
# The old way
ipconfig /displaydns
# The new way
Get-DNSClientCache
```

6. Flush the DNS client cache:

```
# The old way
ipconfig /Flushdns
# Vs the new way
Clear-DnsClientCache
```

How it works...

In *step 1*, you compare the ipconfig.exe Windows console command with the (newer) Get-NetIPConfiguration cmdlet. Both output the basic IP configuration. ipconfig does not, by default, return the details of the configured DNS Server. You have to use the /all switch to view that. Get-NetIPConfiguration returns more information as you can see here:

```
PS C:\> ipconfig.exe

Windows IP Configuration

Ethernet adapter Ethernet:
   Connection-specific DNS Suffix  . :
   Link-local IPv6 Address . . . . . : fe80::7c02:98f1:76b5:d1f%3
   IPv4 Address. . . . . . . . . . . : 10.10.10.10
   Subnet Mask . . . . . . . . . . . : 255.255.255.0
   Default Gateway . . . . . . . . . : 10.10.10.254
Tunnel adapter isatap.{C056D004-9A93-4155-8654-1EDC8DE8509E}:
   Media State . . . . . . . . . . . : Media disconnected
   Connection-specific DNS Suffix  . :

PS C:\> ipconfig.exe /all

Windows IP Configuration

   Host Name . . . . . . . . . . . . : DC1
   Primary Dns Suffix  . . . . . . . : Reskit.Org
   Node Type . . . . . . . . . . . . : Hybrid
   IP Routing Enabled. . . . . . . . : No
   WINS Proxy Enabled. . . . . . . . : No
   DNS Suffix Search List. . . . . . : Reskit.Org

Ethernet adapter Ethernet:

   Connection-specific DNS Suffix  . :
   Description . . . . . . . . . . . : Microsoft Hyper-V Network Adapter
   Physical Address. . . . . . . . . : 00-15-5D-01-71-39
   DHCP Enabled. . . . . . . . . . . : No
   Autoconfiguration Enabled . . . . : Yes
   Link-local IPv6 Address . . . . . : fe80::7c02:98f1:76b5:d1f%3(Preferred)
   IPv4 Address. . . . . . . . . . . : 10.10.10.10(Preferred)
   Subnet Mask . . . . . . . . . . . : 255.255.255.0
   Default Gateway . . . . . . . . . : 10.10.10.254
   DHCPv6 IAID . . . . . . . . . . . : 50337117
   DHCPv6 Client DUID. . . . . . . . : 00-01-00-01-20-10-56-CC-00-15-5D-01-71-39
   DNS Servers . . . . . . . . . . . : ::1
                                       127.0.0.1
   NetBIOS over Tcpip. . . . . . . . : Enabled

Tunnel adapter isatap.{C056D004-9A93-4155-8654-1EDC8DE8509E}:

   Media State . . . . . . . . . . . : Media disconnected
   Connection-specific DNS Suffix  . :
   Description . . . . . . . . . . . : Microsoft ISATAP Adapter
   Physical Address. . . . . . . . . : 00-00-00-00-00-00-00-E0
   DHCP Enabled. . . . . . . . . . . : No
   Autoconfiguration Enabled . . . . : Yes

PS C:\> Get-NetIPConfiguration

InterfaceAlias       : Ethernet
InterfaceIndex       : 3
InterfaceDescription : Microsoft Hyper-V Network Adapter
NetProfile.Name      : Reskit.Org
IPv4Address          : 10.10.10.10
IPv6DefaultGateway   :
IPv4DefaultGateway   : 10.10.10.254
DNSServer            : ::1
                       127.0.0.1
```

Step 2 looks at ways you can check that a remote system is up and running. Traditionally, you would have used `ping.exe`. The `ping.exe` uses ICMP echo request and echo request to implement ping. However, some routers, gateway devices, and hosts turn off ICMP, making ping less than useful. By comparison, the `Test-NetConnection` is more flexible. You can check whether a port, besides ICMP, is open on a host, for example, port `389` for LDAP. You could find that the ping might fail, whereas the `Test-NetConfiguration` succeeds. In *step 2*, you test, from `SRV1`, the connections to `DC1`, as follows:

```
PS C:\> Ping DC1.Reskit.Org -4
Pinging DC1.Reskit.Org [10.10.10.10] with 32 bytes of data:
Reply from 10.10.10.10: bytes=32 time<1ms TTL=128
Reply from 10.10.10.10: bytes=32 time<1ms TTL=128
Reply from 10.10.10.10: bytes=32 time<1ms TTL=128
Reply from 10.10.10.10: bytes=32 time<1ms TTL=128

Ping statistics for 10.10.10.10:
    Packets: Sent = 4, Received = 4, Lost = 0 (0% loss),
Approximate round trip times in milli-seconds:
    Minimum = 0ms, Maximum = 0ms, Average = 0ms

PS C:\> Test-NetConnection DC1.Reskit.Org
ComputerName             : DC1.Reskit.Org
RemoteAddress            : 10.10.10.10
InterfaceAlias           : Ethernet
SourceAddress            : 10.10.10.50
PingSucceeded            : True
PingReplyDetails (RTT)   : 0 ms

PS C:\> Test-NetConnection DC1.Reskit.Org -Port 389 -InformationLevel Detailed

ComputerName             : DC1.Reskit.Org
RemoteAddress            : 10.10.10.10
RemotePort               : 389
NameResolutionResults    : 10.10.10.10
MatchingIPsecRules       :
NetworkIsolationContext  : Private Network
InterfaceAlias           : Ethernet
SourceAddress            : 10.10.10.50
NetRoute (NextHop)       : 0.0.0.0
TcpTestSucceeded         : True

[SRV1]: PS C:\> Test-NetConnection DC1.Reskit.Org -CommonTCPPort SMB
ComputerName      : DC1.Reskit.Org
RemoteAddress     : 10.10.10.10
RemotePort        : 445
InterfaceAlias    : Ethernet
SourceAddress     : 10.10.10.50
TcpTestSucceeded  : True
```

With *step 3*, you look at folder sharing. You look at using the `net` command and the cmdlets in the `SMBShare` module. Comparing the two methods looks like this:

```
#  STEP  3. SMB Folder sharing/using

PS C:\> net use X:  \\SRV1\c$
The command completed successfully.

PS C:\> New-SMBMapping -LocalPath 'Y:' -RemotePath \\SRV1\c$
Status Local Path Remote Path
------ ---------- -----------
OK     Y:         \\SRV1\c$

PS C:\> net use
New connections will be remembered.
Status      Local      Remote                Network

-------------------------------------------------------------------------------
OK          X:         \\SRV1\c$             Microsoft Windows Network
OK          Y:         \\SRV1\c$             Microsoft Windows Network
The command completed successfully.

PS C:\> Get-SMBMapping
Status Local Path Remote Path
------ ---------- -----------
OK     X:         \\SRV1\c$
OK     Y:         \\SRV1\c$
```

In *step 4* you create two shared folders as follows:

```
PS C:\> net share Foo=c:\
Foo was shared successfully.

PS C:\> New-SmbShare -Path C:\ -Name Foo2
Name ScopeName Path Description
---- --------- ---- -----------
Foo2 *         C:\

PS C:\> net share
Share name    Resource                        Remark
-------------------------------------------------------------------------------
ADMIN$        C:\Windows                      Remote Admin
I$            I:\                             Default share
C$            C:\                             Default share
E$            E:\                             Default share
IPC$                                          Remote IPC
H$            H:\                             Default share
Foo           c:\
Foo2          C:\
The command completed successfully.


[SRV1]: PS C:\> Get-SmbShare

Name          ScopeName Path                  Description
----          --------- ----                  -----------
ADMIN$        *         C:\Windows            Remote Admin
C$            *         C:\                   Default share
E$            *         E:\                   Default share
Foo           *         c:\
Foo2          *         C:\
H$            *         H:\                   Default share
I$            *         I:\                   Default share
IPC$          *                               Remote IPC
```

With *step 5*, you perform DNS lookups the old and new way:

```
PS C:\> nslookup -querytype=all DC1.Reskit.Org
Server:  DC1.Reskit.Org
Address:  10.10.10.10
DC1.Reskit.Org  internet address = 10.10.10.10

PS C:\> Resolve-DnsName -Name DC1.Reskit.Org -Type ALL
Name                                     Type  TTL   Section   IPAddress
----                                     ----  ---   -------   ---------
DC1.Reskit.Org                           A     3600  Answer    10.10.10.10
```

In *step 6*, you examine the DNS client cache. The client cache content always depends on the prior lookups, so you may see more addresses in your client cache. On SRV1, the cache is as follows:

```
PS C:\> ipconfig /displaydns
Windows IP Configuration
    dc2.reskit.org
    ----------------------------------------
    Record Name . . . . . : DC2.Reskit.Org
    Record Type . . . . . : 1
    Time To Live  . . . . : 3120
    Data Length . . . . . : 4
    Section . . . . . . . : Answer
    A (Host) Record . . . : 10.10.10.11

    dc1.reskit.org
    ----------------------------------------
    Record Name . . . . . : DC1.Reskit.Org
    Record Type . . . . . : 1
    Time To Live  . . . . : 3026
    Data Length . . . . . : 4
    Section . . . . . . . : Answer
    A (Host) Record . . . : 10.10.10.10


PS C:\> Get-DnsClientCache
Entry             RecordName      Record Status  Section TimeTo Data   Data
                                  Type                   Live   Length
-----             ----------      ------ ------  ------- ------ ------ ----
dc2.reskit.org    DC2.Reskit.Org  A      Success Answer  3114   4 10.10.10.11
dc1.reskit.org    DC1.Reskit.Org  A      Success Answer  3020   4 10.10.10.10
```

There's more...

Using aliases for frequently used cmdlets is a great feature when using PowerShell directly from the command line (but best practice says avoid aliases in production code). In *step 1*, the cmdlet Get-NetIpConfiguration has the easy to remember alias GIP. Some IT pros find it easy to memorize the alias even if they do not recall the name of the aliased cmdlet.

In the first step of this recipe, you looked at your IP configuration. When diagnosing networking faults, there are some other cmdlets that you might find handy. One useful cmdlet is `Get-NetIPInterface`, which gets the IP interface and associated address information. The cmdlet returns the interface name (although on the returned object it's called `InterfaceAlias`), MTU, whether the address is static or DHCP allocated, and the connection state. A second cmdlet is `Get-NetAdapter` which returns basic information about network adapters, including a name, `ifIndex` (used for many networking commands to refer to an IP interface), the MAC address, and the link speed. Depending on the issue, these two cmdlets may provide more useful information.

With so many routers and ingress gateways disabling ICMP, using the cmdlet `Test-NetConnection` is a better troubleshooting command that you can use to check on connections to a server. The command enables you to check not only basic network connectivity but also to ensure that a particular port is open for business.

In this (and other) recipe, you used CDXML based cmdlet sets. Various teams at Microsoft created the CDXML for these cmdlets. If you are using WMI classes that do not currently have CDXML based cmdlets, you can use the approach and develop roll-your-own cmdlets.

Richard Siddaway wrote a short blog article on this subject. You can find this article at `https://blogs.technet.microsoft.com/heyscriptingguy/2015/02/03/registry-cmdlets-first-steps-with-cdxml/`.

Additionally, Microsoft issued a longer document during the beta phase of PowerShell V3 that describes this feature of PowerShell in more detail. This document can be found at `http://csharpening.net/wp-content/uploads/2012/05/Creating-Native-PowerShell-using-the-new-WMI-Developer-Platform-Draft.docx`.

Configuring IP addressing

Most IT pros are very familiar with setting and using the Windows **Control Panel**, and more lately the Windows **Settings** to configure a system's IP configuration (IP address, subnet mask, default gateway and DNS server) and to change a statically configured system to one that gets its configuration from DHCP. Savvy admins also were able to use the network shell, `Netsh.exe` to set the IP configuration details. In this recipe, we show how you do it with PowerShell and native cmdlets.

Getting ready

You run this recipe on server DC2. Server DC2 is a newly installed VM (or physical machine) whose NICs are default to DHCP. When DC2 boots up, it attempts to contact the DHCP server for IP address configuration. If there is no DHCP server on your subnet, running Get-NetIPConfiguration reveals that the server has an **Automatically Provided IP Address (APIPA)** in the 169.254/16 range. You use this recipe to provide a static IP configuration to this server.

How to do it...

1. Get the existing IP address information:

```
$IPType = 'IPv4'$Adapter = Get-NetAdapter |
    Where-Object {Status -eq 'up'}
$Interface = $Adapter |
 Get-NetIPInterface -AddressFamily $IPType
$IfIndex = $Interface.ifIndex
$IfAlias = $Interface.Interfacealias
Get-NetIPAddress -InterfaceIndex $Ifindex
                  -AddressFamily $IPType
```

2. Remove the existing IP address and default gateway, then set the IP address for DC2:

```
Remove-NetRoute -InterfaceIndex $IfIndex `
                -DestinationPrefix 0.0.0.0/0 `
                -Confirm $false
Remove-NetIPAddress -InterfaceIndex $ifindex `
                    -AddressFamily IPv4 `
                    -Confirm $false
```

3. Set the IP address for DC2:

```
Set-NetIPAddress -InterfaceAlias $IfAlias `
                -PrefixLength    24 `
                -IPAddress       '10.10.10.11'  `
                -DefaultGateway  '10.10.10.254' `
                -AddressFamily   $IPType
```

4. Set the DNS server details:

```
Set-DnsClientServerAddress -InterfaceIndex 3 `
                         -ServerAddresses 10.10.10.10
```

5. Test the new configuration:

```
Get-NetIPConfiguration
Test-NetConnection -ComputerName DC1 -Port 389
Resolve-DnsName -Name dc2.reskit.org -Server DC1
```

How it works...

In *step 1*, you obtain the IP address information using `Get-NetIPAddress`, as follows:

```
PS C:\> Get-NetIPAddress -InterfaceIndex $Ifindex -AddressFamily $IPType


IPAddress         : 10.10.10.150
InterfaceIndex    : 3
InterfaceAlias    : Ethernet
AddressFamily     : IPv4
Type              : Unicast
PrefixLength      : 24
PrefixOrigin      : Dhcp
SuffixOrigin      : Dhcp
AddressState      : Preferred
ValidLifetime     : 7.23:53:49
PreferredLifetime : 7.23:53:49
SkipAsSource      : False
PolicyStore       : ActiveStore
```

This address comes from a DHCP scope somewhere on your network. You can tell based on the values of `PrefixOrigin` and `SuffixOrigin` plus a limited lifetime. Manually configured IP addresses have an infinite lease time.

In *step 2*, you remove any old IP address and any old default gateway. As WMI stores configuration information separate from details of the default gateway, you need to remove both separately. In production scripts, to avoid WMI exceptions, you should wrap the cmdlets in a `Try`/`Catch` block. There is no output from this step.

Next, in *step* 3, you set the new IP address, subnet mask, and default gateway address as follows:

```
PS C:\> New-NetIPAddress -InterfaceAlias $IfAlias `
                -PrefixLength  24 `
                -DefaultGateway '10.10.10.254' `
                -IPAddress     '10.10.10.11' `
                -DefaultGateway '10.10.10.254' `
                -AddressFamily  $IPType


IPAddress          : 10.10.10.11
InterfaceIndex     : 3
InterfaceAlias     : Ethernet
AddressFamily      : IPv4
Type               : Unicast
PrefixLength       : 24
PrefixOrigin       : Manual
SuffixOrigin       : Manual
AddressState       : Tentative
ValidLifetime      : Infinite ([TimeSpan]::MaxValue)
PreferredLifetime  : Infinite ([TimeSpan]::MaxValue)
SkipAsSource       : False
PolicyStore        : ActiveStore
```

With the IP address, subnet mask, and default gateway set, in *step 4*, you set the DNS server address. There is no output generated by the `Set-DnsClientServerAddress` cmdlet.

With *step 2* through *step 4* in the recipe, you set a static IP configuration. To test it, in *step 5*, you check on the configuration by using `Get-NetIPConfiguration`, `Test-NetConnection`, and `Resolve-DnsName` cmdlets. These return the address, test the connection from this server to our primary domain controller (DC1), and then resolve address records for DC2. Running these commands looks like this:

```
PS C:\> Get-NetIPConfiguration

InterfaceAlias       : Ethernet
InterfaceIndex       : 3
InterfaceDescription : Microsoft Hyper-V Network Adapter
NetProfile.Name      : Reskit.Org
IPv4Address          : 10.10.10.11
IPv6DefaultGateway   :
IPv4DefaultGateway   : 10.10.10.254
DNSServer            : 10.10.10.10


PS C:\> Test-NetConnection -ComputerName DC1 -port 389

ComputerName     : DC1
RemoteAddress    : 10.10.10.10
RemotePort       : 389
InterfaceAlias   : Ethernet
SourceAddress    : 10.10.10.11
TcpTestSucceeded : True


PS C:\> Resolve-DnsName -Name dc2.reskit.org -Server DC1

Name                                   Type  TTL   Section   IPAddress
----                                   ----  ---   -------   ---------
DC2.Reskit.Org                         AAAA  1200  Question  fe80::6455:fbff:194b:fe9b
DC2.Reskit.Org                         A     1200  Question  10.10.10.11
```

There's more...

If you are going to be doing a lot of networking troubleshooting, it might be a good idea to create some scripts and functions that make it clearer and simpler. You can find one example at `http://techibee.com/powershell/powershell-get-ip-address-subnet-gateway-dns-serves-and-mac-address-details-of-remote-computer/1367`. That blog page describes a script that you could use. The script could easily be converted into a function and added to your troubleshooting module(s).

In *step 2* of this recipe, you remove the default gateway and any existing IP address. Both the `Remove-NetRoute` and `Remove-NetIPAddress` cmdlets generate an exception if there is no route, or IP address respectively. To get around this, you can wrap the calls to these cmdlets with `Try/Catch`. However there appears to be a bug with the `Remote-NetIpAddress` cmdlet. Even when you wrap the cmdlet in a PowerShell `Try/Catch` block, it does not catch the exception in the way you would expect.

In *step 5*, you check the IP configuration using `Get-NetIPConfiguration` to show the IP address, subnet mask, default gateway, and the DNS server configuration. Then you test the network connection from `DC2` to port `389` on `DC1`. Port `389` is the LDAP port. Setting up `DC2` as a domain controller requires the ability to connect to `DC1` domain controller's LDAP port. This cmdlet tests both, that network connectivity is available and that port `389` is reachable, which is more useful than the information returned from the `ping.exe` command.

Converting IP address from static to DHCP

In some cases, you may need to switch your server's IP address from static, as you did in the *Configuring IP addressing* recipe, back to DHCP. You might need to do this to re-purpose a server. You may have given it a static IP address to perform a role, but you plan to re-purpose this server and want to configure the server to obtain IP configuration from DHCP.

Getting ready

Run this recipe on the `DC2` server. Of course, after running and testing this recipe, you may need to re-run the Configure IP address recipe to ensure `DC2` remains correctly configured.

How to do it...

1. Get the existing IP address information:

```
$IPType = 'IPv4'
$Adapter = Get-NetAdapter | ? {$_.Status -eq 'up' }
$Interface = $Adapter |
    Get-NetIPInterface -AddressFamily $IPType
$IfIndex = $Interface.ifIndex
$IfAlias = $Interface.Interfacealias
Get-NetIPAddress -InterfaceIndex $Ifindex `
                 -AddressFamily $IPType
```

2. Set the interface to get its address from DHCP:

```
Set-NetIPInterface -InterfaceIndex `
$IfIndex -DHCP Enabled
```

3. Test the results:

```
Get-NetIPAddress -InterfaceIndex $Ifindex `
                 -AddressFamily $IPType
```

How it works...

In *step 1*, you get the network adapter details and display the configured IP address. Since this system has just one NIC, and you previously configured a static address, the IP address details reflect that as follows:

```
Get-NetIPAddress -InterfaceIndex $Ifindex -AddressFamily $IPType


IPAddress         : 10.10.10.11
InterfaceIndex    : 3
InterfaceAlias    : Ethernet
AddressFamily     : IPv4
Type              : Unicast
PrefixLength      : 24
PrefixOrigin      : Manual
SuffixOrigin      : Manual
AddressState      : Preferred
ValidLifetime     : Infinite ([TimeSpan]::MaxValue)
PreferredLifetime : Infinite ([TimeSpan]::MaxValue)
SkipAsSource      : False
PolicyStore       : ActiveStore
```

In *step 2*, you enable DHCP on the network interface, but there is no output.

Then, you use `Get-NetIPaddress` to return the IP address. It is the same DHCP address you saw in *step 1* of the *Configuring IP Addressing* recipe:

```
PS C:\> Get-NetIPAddress -InterfaceIndex $Ifindex -AddressFamily $IPType

IPAddress         : 10.10.10.150
InterfaceIndex    : 3
InterfaceAlias    : Ethernet
AddressFamily     : IPv4
Type              : Unicast
PrefixLength      : 24
PrefixOrigin      : Dhcp
SuffixOrigin      : Dhcp
AddressState      : Preferred
ValidLifetime     : 7.23:59:54
PreferredLifetime : 7.23:59:54
SkipAsSource      : False
PolicyStore       : ActiveStore
```

There's more...

Using WMI directly, or using CDXML-based cmdlets to obtain the source of IP address configuration works well, but can be slower than using `ipconfig.exe`.

Installing domain controllers and DNS

At the heart of mostof the corporate and organizational networks is **Active Directory** (**AD**). You use AD as an authentication and authorization platform. AD first debuted with Windows 2000. Microsoft improved it with each successive release of Windows Server.

In the early days of AD, you promoted a server computer to act as a domain controller by using the `DCPromo.exe` utility. In Server 2016, this command no longer exists. Instead of `DCPromo`, you could either use **Server Manager** or PowerShell.

This recipe shows how you use PowerShell to upgrade systems to be domain controllers. This recipe creates two servers (`DC1` and a replica DC, `DC2`) in the `Reskit.Org` domain. After you complete this recipe, your forest has only one domain, but you could easily extend this recipe to create multi-domain forests.

Getting ready

In this recipe, you use two domain controllers, DC1 and DC2. Before running this recipe, you should configure both DC1 and DC2 to have static IP address configurations. You can use the *Configuring IP addressing* recipe to show you how to set up the static address.

You run this recipe directly on both DC1 and DC2. As an alternative, you could wrap this recipe with a call to Invoke-Command and run this recipe from a client computer, as shown in *Installing and configuring Hyper-V feature* recipe in Chapter 11, *Managing Hyper-V*.

How to do it...

Run the first part of this recipe on DC1:

1. Install the AD-Domain-Services components plus the ManagementTools:

```
Install-WindowsFeature AD-Domain-Services
        -IncludeManagementTools
```

2. Now install the AD to DC1:

```
$PasswordSS = ConvertTo-SecureString `
                  -String 'Pa$$w0rd' `
                  -AsPlainText -Force
Install-ADDSForest -DomainName 'Reskit.Org' `
                  -SafeModeAdministratorPassword
$PasswordSS -Force -InstallDNS -NoReboot
```

3. Now you manually reboot DC1:

```
Restart-Computer -Force
```

Run the next part of this recipe on the second domain controller, DC2. You could alternatively run these steps remotely on another system by using the Invoke-Command cmdlet.

1. Check that DC1 is reachable on ports 445 and 389:

```
Resolve-DnsName -Name dc1.reskit.org `
                -Server DC1.Reskit.Org `
                -Type A
Test-NetConnection -ComputerName DC1.Reskit.Org `
                   -port 445
Test-NetConnection -ComputerName DC1.Reskit.Org `
                   -port 389
```

2. Add the AD DS features on DC2:

```
Install-WindowsFeature AD-Domain-Services, DNS,
                       RSAT-DHCP, Web-Mgmt-Tools
```

Promote DC2 to be a DC in the Reskit.Org domain:

```
$PasswordSS = ConvertTo-SecureString -String 'Pa$$w0rd'
                                     -AsPlainText -Force
Install-ADDSDomainController -DomainName 'Reskit.org' `
   -SafeModeAdministratorPassword $PasswordSS `
   -SiteName 'Default-First-Site-Name' `
   -NoRebootOnCompletion -Force
```

How it works...

Promoting any Windows Server 2016 computer to be a domain controller begins with you installing the AD-Domain-Services feature, which you carry out in *step 1*, like this:

```
PS C:\> Install-WindowsFeature AD-Domain-Services -IncludeManagementTools

Success Restart Needed Exit Code    Feature Result
------- -------------- ---------    --------------
True    No             Success      {Active Directory Domain Services, Group P...
```

With *step 2*, you promote DC1 to be a domain controller and install the DNS service on DC1:

```
PS C:\> $PasswordSS = ConvertTo-SecureString -string 'Pa$$w0rd' -AsPlainText -Force
PS C:\> Install-ADDSForest -DomainName 'Reskit.Org' `
          -SafeModeAdministratorPassword $PasswordSS -Force `
          -InstallDNS -NoReboot
WARNING: Windows Server 2016 domain controllers have a default for the security settin
g named "Allow cryptography algorithms compatible with Windows NT 4.0" that prevents w
eaker cryptography algorithms when establishing security channel sessions.

For more information about this setting, see Knowledge Base article 942564 (http://go.
microsoft.com/fwlink/?LinkId=104751).


WARNING: A delegation for this DNS server cannot be created because the authoritative
parent zone cannot be found or it does not run Windows DNS server. If you are integrat
ing with an existing DNS infrastructure, you should manually create a delegation to th
is DNS server in the parent zone to ensure reliable name resolution from outside the d
omain "Reskit.Org". Otherwise, no action is required.


WARNING: Windows Server 2016 domain controllers have a default for the security settin
g named "Allow cryptography algorithms compatible with Windows NT 4.0" that prevents w
eaker cryptography algorithms when establishing security channel sessions.

For more information about this setting, see Knowledge Base article 942564 (http://go.
microsoft.com/fwlink/?LinkId=104751).


WARNING: A delegation for this DNS server cannot be created because the authoritative
parent zone cannot be found or it does not run Windows DNS server. If you are integrat
ing with an existing DNS infrastructure, you should manually create a delegation to th
is DNS server in the parent zone to ensure reliable name resolution from outside the d
omain "Reskit.Org". Otherwise, no action is required.


Message                                              Context          RebootRequired  Status
-------                                              -------          --------------  ------
You must restart this computer to complete the operation... DCPromo.General.4                True Success
```

This step generates four warning messages. In most cases these are benign, and you can ignore them. In *step 3*, you reboot DC1. There is no output as such, the system restarts as the first domain controller in your forest.

In *step 4*, which you run over on DC2, you first check your network to ensure that the domain controller operation can be successful. You check that the DNS name exists for the current domain controller in the RESKIT domain, and ensure that DC2 can reach DC1 on ports 389 (LDAP) and 445 (SMB-based file/printer sharing). The output from *step 4* looks like this:

```
PS C:\> Resolve-DnsName -Name dc1.reskit.org -Server DC1.Reskit.Org -Type A

Name                                              Type   TTL   Section    IPAddress
----                                              ----   ---   -------    ---------
dc1.reskit.org                                    A      3600  Answer     10.10.10.10

PS C:\> Test-NetConnection -ComputerName DC1.Reskit.Org -port 445

ComputerName     : DC1.Reskit.Org
RemoteAddress    : 10.10.10.10
RemotePort       : 445
InterfaceAlias   : Ethernet
SourceAddress    : 10.10.10.11
TcpTestSucceeded : True

PS C:\> Test-NetConnection -ComputerName DC1.Reskit.Org -port 389

ComputerName     : DC1.Reskit.Org
RemoteAddress    : 10.10.10.10
RemotePort       : 389
InterfaceAlias   : Ethernet
SourceAddress    : 10.10.10.11
TcpTestSucceeded : True
```

With those three tests, you can see that DC1 and DC2 are in communication and that DC2 is ready for promotion. In *step 5*, which is not dissimilar to *step 1*, you add roles to the computer that enables you to promote this machine at some later date to be a DC. Installing these features looks this:

```
PS C:\> Install-WindowsFeature AD-Domain-Services, DNS, RSAT-DHCP, Web-Mgmt-Tools

Success Restart Needed Exit Code    Feature Result
------- -------------- ---------    --------------
True    No             Success      {Active Directory Domain Services, DNS Ser...
```

Note that you explicitly add DNS and some additional tools. You have options as to how and whether you add a second DNS server to the domain, and what (if any) management tools you add.

Now you are ready to promote `DC2` to be a domain controller in the `Reskit.org` network, in *step 6*. *Step 6* is very similar to *step 2*, except in *step 6* you are adding a domain controller to the existing `Reskit` domain/forest, which looks like this:

```
PS C:\> $PasswordSS = ConvertTo-SecureString -string 'Pa$$w0rd' -AsPlainText -Force
PS C:\> Install-ADDSDomainController -DomainName 'Reskit.org' `
            -SafeModeAdministratorPassword $PasswordSS `
            -SiteName 'Default-First-Site-Name' `
            -NoRebootOnCompletion -Force

WARNING: Windows Server 2016 domain controllers have a default for the security setting
named "Allow cryptography algorithms compatible with Windows NT 4.0" that prevents
weaker cryptography algorithms when establishing security channel sessions.

For more information about this setting, see Knowledge Base article 942564
(http://go.microsoft.com/fwlink/?LinkId=104751).

WARNING: A delegation for this DNS server cannot be created because the authoritative
parent zone cannot be found or it does not run Windows DNS server. If you are integrating
with an existing DNS infrastructure, you should manually create a delegation to this
DNS server in the parent zone to ensure reliable name resolution from outside
the domain "Reskit.Org". Otherwise, no action is required.

WARNING: Windows Server 2016 domain controllers have a default for the security setting
named "Allow cryptography algorithms compatible with Windows NT 4.0" that prevents
weaker cryptography algorithms when establishing security channel sessions.

For more information about this setting, see Knowledge Base article 942564
(http://go.microsoft.com/fwlink/?LinkId=104751).

WARNING: A delegation for this DNS server cannot be created because the authoritative
parent zone cannot be found or it does not run Windows DNS server. If you are integr
ating with an existing DNS infrastructure, you should manually create a delegation to
this DNS server in the parent zone to ensure reliable name resolution from outside t
he domain "Reskit.Org". Otherwise, no action is required.


Message                                              Context         RebootRequired Status
-------                                              -------         -------------- ------
You must restart this computer to complete the operation... DCPromo.General.4        True Success
```

There's more...

In *step 2*, you upgrade `DC1` to be a domain controller. Once the installation process has completed, you must reboot `DC1` before it can function as a DC which you do in *step 3*. If you run the step remotely, you could restart `DC1` using a command like this:

```
Restart-Computer  -Computer DC1 -Wait -For PowerShell
```

In *step 4*, you checked for connectivity on ports `445` and `389`. Port `445` is used for SMB file sharing, while port `389` is the port for LDAP. Domain joined systems need access to these ports on the domain controller for Group Policy.

After you reboot DC2, after *step 6*, DC2 is a domain controller and a DNS server. Using DNS tools, you can see that AD replicates the Reskit.org zone created on DC2 in an earlier recipe. When you create a zone as AD integrated, the AD replicates DNS zone information and resource records to other DCs in the domain. Also notice DC2 DC's network configuration. Before the promotion, DC2 had one DNS Server address (10.10.10.10-DC1). Since you added DNS to DC2, the promotion process adds a DNS server to DC2 DC's network configuration (127.0.0.1).

Configuring zones and resource records in DNS

DNS configuration using PowerShell is straightforward. You first add the DNS service. Then you create the zones you need and finally you create the resource records for those zones.

When you install an AD, as you did in the *Installing domain controllers* recipe, the AD installation process also installs the DNS service on the DC and configures both the necessary forward lookup zone and the AD-related resource records.

This recipe looks at the actions you may need to take once your DC is up and running. You can create new zones (for example, a reverse look zone), add an additional A and Mx records for mail, and set **Extended DNS** (**EDNS**). You also should test the DNS Server to ensure it is all up and working.

Getting ready

This recipe assumes you have the domain controller up and running as a DC, and that you have a DNS Administrator user created. You create the user as follows:

```
$PasswordSS = ConvertTo-SecureString `
                -String 'Pa$$w0rd' `
                -AsPlainText -Force
$NewUserHT = @{
  AccountPassword = $PasswordSS
  Enabled = $true
  PasswordNeverExpires = $true
  ChangePasswordAtLogon = $false}

New-ADUser @NewUserHT `
  -SamAccountName DNSADMIN `
```

```
          -UserPrincipalName 'DNSADMIN@reskit.org' `
          -Name 'DNSADMIN' `
          -DisplayName 'DNS Admin'
# Add to Enterprise and Domain Admin groups
Add-ADPrincipalGroupMembership `
 -Identity `
  'CN=DNSADMIN,CN=Users,DC=reskit,DC=org' `
-MemberOf `
 'CN=Enterprise Admins,CN=Users,DC=reskit,DC=org',
 'CN=Domain Admins,CN=Users,DC=reskit,DC=org'
# Ensure the user has been added
Get-ADUser -LDAPFilter '(Name=DNSADMIN)'
```

How to do it...

1. Create a new primary forward DNS zone:

```
Add-DnsServerPrimaryZone -Name foo.bar `
                         -ReplicationScope   Forest `
                         -DynamicUpdate      Secure `
                         -ResponsiblePerson  'DNSADMIN.reskit.org'
```

2. Create a new primary reverse lookup domain (for IPv4), and view both new DNS zones:

```
Add-DnsServerPrimaryZone
        -Name  '10.10.10.in-addr.arpa' `
        -ReplicationScope       Forest `
        -DynamicUpdate          Secure `
        -ResponsiblePerson      'DNSADMIN.reskit.org.'
Get-DNSServerZone
        -Name 'foo.bar', '10.10.10.in-addr.arpa'
```

3. Add an A resource record to foo.bar and get results:

```
Add-DnsServerResourceRecord -ZoneName 'foo.bar' `
                            -A `
                            -Name home `
                            -AllowUpdateAny `
                            -IPv4Address    '10.42.42.42' `
                            -TimeToLive     (30 * (24*60*60))
Get-DnsServerResourceRecord -ZoneName foo.bar `
                            -Name 'home'
```

4. Add `A` and `Mx` resource records to the `reskit.org` zone and display the results:

```
Add-DnsServerResourceRecord -ZoneName 'reskit.org' `
                            -A `
                            -Name            'mail' `
                            -CreatePtr `
                            -AllowUpdateAny `
                            -IPv4Address '    10.10.10.42' `
                            -TimeToLive      21:00:00
Add-DnsServerResourceRecordMX -Preference 10 `
                            -Name '.' `
                            -TimeToLive      (30 * (24*60*60)) `
                            -MailExchange    'mail.reskit.org' `
                            -ZoneName        'reskit.org'
Get-DnsServerResourceRecord -ZoneName 'reskit.org' `
                            -name '@' `
                            -RRType Mx
```

5. Set up EDNS on the server with a timeout 30 minutes:

```
Set-DNSServerEDns -CacheTimeout     '0:30:00' `
                  -Computername     DC1 `
                  -EnableProbes     $true `
                  -EnableReception $true
```

6. Test the DNS service on `DC1`:

```
Test-DnsServer -IPAddress 10.10.10.10 `
               -Context DnsServer
```

How it works...

This recipe makes use of the cmdlets in the `DnsServer` module to create zones, create resource records, retrieve resource records, and test the DNS server.

In *step 1*, you create a new DNS primary zone called `foo.bar`. You specify that this zone should replicate to all AD domain controllers in the forest and that local updates are to be secure only. You also specify the responsible person for queries is `DNSADMIN@Reskit.Org`. For internal DNS servers, this is probably not all that useful. But if you need to talk to the person responsible for some distant DNS server, for example, your ISPs server, then it can be useful to know who to contact. Creating a zone generates no output.

In *step 2*, you add another primary zone, this time a reverse lookup zone for the IP address block `10.10.10.0/24`. Reverse lookup zones allow DNS to resolve an IP address, for example, `10.10.10.10`, to a fully qualified name (`DC1.Reskit.Org`). The other settings are the same as for the `foo.bar` zone created in *step 1*. This step also retrieves the zone details for both zones, as follows:

```
PS C:\> Get-DNSServerZone -name 'foo.bar', '10.10.10.in-addr.arpa'

ZoneName                     ZoneType    IsAutoCreated   IsDsIntegrated   IsReverseLookupZone   IsSigned
--------                     --------    -------------   --------------   -------------------   --------
foo.bar                      Primary     False           True             False                 False
10.10.10.in-addr.arpa        Primary     False           True             True                  False
```

After adding zones, in *step 3*, you add a resource record—a host (`A`) record for the host `home.foo.bar`. You set the IP address to `10.42.42.42`, and the time to live is calculated to be 30 days (specified in this case in seconds). After adding the record, you retrieve the `A` record for `home.foo.bar`. Retrieving the record looks like this:

```
PS C:\> Get-DnsServerResourceRecord -ZoneName foo.bar -name 'home'

HostName         RecordType Type   Timestamp         TimeToLive      RecordData
--------         ---------- ----   ---------         ----------      ----------
home             A          1      0                 30.00:00:00     10.42.42.42
```

In *step 4*, you prepare for the addition of a new SMTP server, `Mail.Reskit.Org`. You first create the host's `A` record, then you create the **mail exchanger (MX)** record. There is no output from adding these two resource records. Then you retrieve the `MX` record, which looks like this:

```
PS C:\> Get-DnsServerResourceRecord -zonename 'reskit.org' -name '@' -RRType Mx

HostName         RecordType Type   Timestamp         TimeToLive      RecordData
--------         ---------- ----   ---------         ----------      ----------

@                MX         15     0                 00:00:00        [10][mail.reskit.org.]
```

With *step 5*, you specify EDNS settings and retrieve them. These settings enable your DNS server to probe other servers to determine if they support EDNS and to cache that information for 30 minutes. You also set your DNS server to accept queries that contain an EDNS record and to respond accordingly. These days, it's sensible to set up EDNS, especially for internet-facing DNS servers. The last command in this step retrieves and displays the EDNS settings, as follows:

```
Get-DnsServerEDns

CacheTimeout EnableProbes EnableReception
------------ ------------ ---------------
00:30:00     True         True
```

Once you have set up your DNS Server, and anytime you make changes to the configuration, it makes sense to test it. In *step 5*, you use the Test-DnsServer cmdlet to test the DNS server. The output looks like this:

```
PS C:\> Test-DnsServer -IPAddress 10.10.10.10 -Context DnsServer

IPAddress    Result  RoundTripTime TcpTried UdpTried
---------    ------  ------------- -------- --------
10.10.10.10  Success 00:00:11      True     True
```

There's more...

The DnsServer module leverages CDXML to build the cmdlets. As a result, the objects returned are WMI data wrapped in a .NET object. If you pipe the output of, for example, Get-DNSServerZone, the objects returned are of the type Microsoft.Management.Infrastructure.CimInstance#root/Microsoft/Windows/DNS/DnsServerPrimaryZone. The default output, specified by display XML loaded with the module, hides some of the details of each zone, such as whether a DNS server notifies any secondary servers of any change (NotifyServers), or whether WINS integration is enabled. If the default XML is insufficient, you can either pipe the output through Format-Table or Select-Object to select the properties you wish to view. And you could always update the default display XML to adapt the default output to suit your needs.

In *step 3*, you used the Add-DNSServerResourceRecord with the A switch to add an A resource record. You could have also used another cmdlet, Add-DnsServerResourceRecordA. Some of the more common resource records have specific cmdlets to enable you to add them.

In *step 5*, you setup EDNS. EDNS is an extension mechanism that extends the DNS protocol in a backwards compatible way. EDNS, among other things, enable bigger DNS replies. RFC 6891 (https://tools.ietf.org/html/rfc6891) specifies EDNS.

With *step 7*, you tested the basic working of the server. You can also test that the server has root hints created and whether it can resolve a specific zone.

In *step 1* and *step 2*, you create zones and resource records. The code in these steps creates the zones as AD integrated. The AD replicates both the zones and the records they contained to other DCs in the domain. After you complete the steps in this recipe on DC1, you see the replication of zones is you look at the DNS service on DC2.

One feature this recipe did not examine is **DNS Security Extensions (DNSSec)**. These extensions provide cryptographic assurance that the resource records you retrieve from DNS are correct, came from the server you think you did, and that a man-in-the-middle attack has not interfered with the resource record information. The details of DNSSec and how it works are outside the scope of this book.

> For more details about DNSSec, see the internet society's DNSSec page at `http://www.internetsociety.org/deploy360/dnssec/basics/?gclid=Cj0KEQiAzsvEBRDEluzk96e4rqABEiQAezEOoN2hUV3waJAgC8nU_2llDQjwosymcdEjKEr9OKPnsCoaAr4b8P8HAQ`.

> With that said, adding DNSSec security to a zone on your DNS server is simple. For example, to sign the `reskit.org` zone that you created on DC1, use the `Set-DnsServerDnsSecZoneSetting` cmdlet. For more details on using DNSSec, see the TechNet article at `https://technet.microsoft.com/en-us/library/hh831411(v=ws.11).aspx` (although the demonstration on that page is based on Windows Server 2012 and uses the GUI).

Installing and authorizing a DHCP server

Installing and authorizing a DHCP server is easy and straightforward. You can use the GUI, Server Manager to achieve this. Server Manager, though, is a GUI layered on top of PowerShell. The GUI gathers the details, and PowerShell does the rest. In this recipe, you carry out the installation and basic configuration using just the native cmdlets.

Getting ready

This recipe installs a DHCP server on DC1. You need that system up and running.

How to do it...

1. Login to DC1, and add the DHCP server feature to your system:

    ```
    Install-WindowsFeature -Name DHCP `
                            -IncludeManagementTools
    ```

2. Add the DHCP server's security groups:

    ```
    Add-DHCPServerSecurityGroup -Verbose
    ```

3. Let DHCP know it's all configured:

    ```
    Set-ItemProperty `
        -Path HKLM:\SOFTWARE\Microsoft\ServerManager\Roles\12 `
        -Name ConfigurationState `
        -Value 2
    ```

4. Authorize the DHCP server in Active Directory:

    ```
    Add-DhcpServerInDC -DnsName DC1.Reskit.Org
    ```

5. Restart DHCP:

    ```
    Restart-Service -Name DHCPServer -Force
    ```

How it works...

In *step 1*, you use the `Install-WindowsFeature` cmdlet to add the DHCP server and the DHCP `ManagementTools`, which looks like this:

```
PS C:\> Install-WindowsFeature -Name DHCP `
                            -IncludeManagementTools


Success Restart Needed Exit Code      Feature Result
------- -------------- ---------      --------------
True    No             Success        {DHCP Server, DHCP Server Tools}
```

In *step 2*, you add the necessary DHCP security groups. By default, this cmdlet does not produce any output. If you want to see some additional output, you can use the `-Verbose` switch. If you do, the cmdlet produces a bit of output, like this:

```
PS C:\> Add-DHCPServerSecurityGroup -Verbose

VERBOSE: Adds DHCP users and DHCP administrators security groups on the DHCP server DC1
```

In *step 3*, you tell Windows that the configuration of DHCP is complete. This step produces no output but is needed to let DHCP know that the necessary security groups are complete

Before a DHCP server is able to provide IP address information to client systems, you need to authorize it in AD. You perform this in *step 4*, and the output looks like this:

```
PS C:\> Add-DhcpServerInDC -DnsName DC1.Reskit.Org

WARNING: The DHCP server dc1.reskit.org with IP address 10.10.10.10 is
already authorized in Active Directory. The authorization check on the
DHCP server has been initiated.
```

With the last step, *step 5*, you restart the service. Once you restart the DHCP service, the newly authorized server can hand out IP addresses. You configure the DHCP addresses and DHCP options in the *Configuring DHCP scopes* recipe.

There's more...

In *step 1*, you install the DHCP server service on your system. If you use the Windows Server Manager GUI tool, DHCP is a server role versus a server feature. You need to know which is which to find and add the feature or role that provides the DHCP service. With PowerShell there is no difference between a feature and a role—you add both with the `Install-WindowsFeature` cmdlet.

In earlier versions of the `ServerManager` module, the cmdlet was named `Add-WindowsFeature`. In later versions of Windows Server, Microsoft renamed the cmdlet to `Install-WindowsFeatue`. That change did have the potential to break existing scripts. To avoid that, Microsoft sensibly added an alias of `Install-WindowsFeature`, namely, `Add-WindowsFeature`.

In *step 2*, you used the ‑Verbose switch. When you add the ‑Verbose switch to any cmdlet you can get some additional output that shows you what the cmdlet (or function) is doing. Some cmdlets are remarkably terse and provide little or no extra output. Other cmdlets provide more detailed verbose output.

In *step 5*, you authorize the DHCP server explicitly in the Active Directory. Authorization helps your organization avoid the potential for a rogue user setting up a DHCP server and handing out bad IP addresses. If you have multiple domain controllers, you may wish to force replication so that all DCs show this server as authorized. While the replication should occur pretty quickly, it never hurts to check the replication status before enabling the DHCP service.

Configuring DHCP scopes

In the previous recipe, *Installing and authorizing a DHCP server*, you installed and authorized a DHCP server. But before that server can begin to provide IP address configuration information to DHCP clients, you need to create a scope and options. The scope is the set of DHCP addresses DHCP can give out, while the options are specific configuration options your DHCP server provides along with an IP address.

Getting ready

Before you can configure DHCP scopes and options, you need to have completed the earlier *Installing and authorizing a DHCP server* recipe on DC1.

How to do it...

1. Create a DHCP scope:

```
Add-DhcpServerV4Scope -Name 'Reskit' `
                      -StartRange   10.10.10.150 `
                      -EndRange     10.10.10.199 `
                      -SubnetMask   255.255.255.0 `
                      -ComputerName DC1.Reskit.Org
```

2. Get scopes from the server:

```
Get-DhcpServerv4Scope -ComputerName DC1.Reskit.Org
```

3. Set DHCP `OptionValues`:

```
Set-DhcpServerV4OptionValue -DnsDomain Reskit.Org `
                            -DnsServer 10.10.10.10
```

4. View the options you have set:

```
Get-DhcpServerv4OptionValue `
   -ComputerName DC1.Reskit.Org
```

How it works...

This recipe used the DHCP server cmdlets to do basic DHCP scope configuration. In *step 1*, you create a new scope. This scope allows the server to offer up addresses in the address range 10.10.10.150 through to 10.10.10.199. There is no output from this step.

In *step 2*, you used the `Get-DhcpServerv4Scope` cmdlet to retrieve details of the scopes set on the named DHCP server, like this:

```
PS C:\> Get-DhcpServerv4Scope -ComputerName DC1.Reskit.Org

ScopeId      SubnetMask       Name     State    StartRange      EndRange        LeaseDuration
-------      ----------       ----     -----    ----------      --------        -------------
10.10.10.0   255.255.255.0    Reskit   Active   10.10.10.150    10.10.10.199    8.00:00:00
```

To enable the DHCP server to provide key IP configuration details, you add options to the scope. An option is a particular setting that the server can provide a client. For example, you set the DNS server address and the domain name for a DHCP client by using the options set in this step. As with *step 1*, adding options produces no output.

To view the options you set on the server, you can use the `Get-DHCPServerV4OptionValue` cmdlet, like this:

```
PS C:\> Get-DhcpServerv4OptionValue -ComputerName DC1.Reskit.Org

OptionId   Name               Type       Value            VendorClass
--------   ----               ----       -----            -----------
15         DNS Domain Name    String     {Reskit.Org}
6          DNS Servers        IPv4Add... {10.10.10.10}
```

There's more...

In *step 3*, you set an option and option value for the DNS server. An excellent feature of this cmdlet is that when setting a DNS server IP address, the cmdlet checks to see if the IP address provided is a DNS server. Although the cmdlet returns no output, if you run this step in the PowerShell ISE, you can see a progress bar showing the check. In this case, the test used an invalid IP address for the server that yields this result:

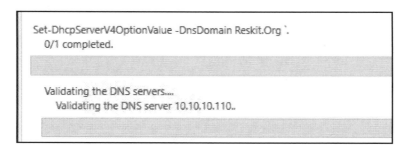

This recipe used a simple DHCP configuration. A single DHCP server, a single scope on a single subnet, and with only minimal options. There is more complexity you may encounter when scaling DHCP including scope versus server options and client classes which are outside the scope of this chapter. Nevertheless, the cmdlets used in this recipe form the core of what you might use in practice, just a few more options and the complexity is simplified even if we do not have space in this chapter to cover all that complexity.

Configuring DHCP server failover and load balancing

The basic installation and configuration of a single DHCP server, as shown in the two previous recipes, is straightforward. However, a single DHCP server represents a single point of failure. A standard solution to this shortcoming is to implement DHCP failover and load balancing. Microsoft added this to DHCP with Windows 2012. The feature and indeed DHCP is unchanged in Server 2016.

Getting ready

This recipe requires two servers, with one server (DC1) setup with a working and configured DHCP scope. You achieved this by using the *Configuring and authorizing a DHCP server, Configure DHCP scopes* recipes. The recipe needs a second, as of yet an unconfigured server, which in this case is the second DC, DC2.Reskit.Org.

How to do it...

1. Log in and install the DHCP feature on DC2:

   ```
   Install-WindowsFeature -Name DHCP,RSAT-DHCP `
                          -ComputerName DC2.Reskit.Org
   ```

2. Let DHCP know it's all configured:

   ```
   Invoke-Command -ComputerName DC2 `
   -ScriptBlock {Set-ItemProperty `
     -Path HKLM\:SOFTWARE\Microsoft\ServerManager\Roles\12 `
     -Name ConfigurationState `
     -Value 2}
   ```

3. Authorize the DHCP server in AD and view the results:

   ```
   Add-DhcpServerInDC -DnsName DC2.Reskit.Org
   Get-DhcpServerInDC
   ```

4. Configure failover and load balancing:

   ```
   Add-DhcpServerv4Failover `
       -ComputerName DC1.Reskit.Org `
       -PartnerServer DC2.Reskit.Org `
       -Name DC1-DC2 `
       -ScopeID 10.10.10.0 `
       -LoadBalancePercent 60 `
       -SharedSecret 'j3RryIsG0d!' `
       -Force
   ```

5. Observe the result:

```
'dc1', 'dc2' |
  ForEach {Get-DhcpServerv4Scope -ComputerName $_}
'dc1', 'dc2' |
  ForEach {Get-DhcpServerv4ScopeStatistics
            -ComputerName $_}
```

How it works...

In *step* 1, you install the DHCP feature on `DC2.Reskit.Org` remotely. Using the `Install-WindowsFeature` cmdlet, you can install features on any remote server. The results are:

```
PS C:\Windows\system32> Install-WindowsFeature -Name DHCP,RSAT-DHCP `
             -ComputerName DC2.Reskit.Org

Success Restart Needed Exit Code     Feature Result
------- -------------- ---------     --------------
True    No             Success       {DHCP Server}
```

With *step* 2, you set a registry value remotely. This value indicates that the configuration of `DC2` is complete. There is no output from this operation.

In *step 3*, you authorize `DC2` in the `DC2.Reskit.Org` server's AD. Once authorized, `DC2` can begin to hand out IP address leases from any configured scopes. The call to `Get-DHCPServerInDC` shows what servers you have authorized:

```
PS C:\Windows\system32> Get-DhcpServerInDC

IPAddress            DnsName
---------            -------
10.10.10.10          dc1.reskit.org
10.10.10.11          dc2.reskit.org
```

With both `DC1` and `DC2` set up and running DHCP, in *step 4*, you implement a load balancing failover relationship between `DC1` and `DC2`. You name the relationship `dc1-dc2`. You are setting the relationship to loadbalance the `10.10.10.0` scope you created earlier in the *Configuring DHCP scopes* recipe. By specifying the `-LoadBalancePercent` parameter, you tell `DC1` to issue 60% of the leases.

There's more...

This recipe showed building a load balancing and failover relationship between two DHCP servers. This relationship makes the scope highly available and provides for two servers to share the load. You can also set up DHCP to have a hot standby, rather than a load balancing relationship.

Building a public key infrastructure

In most organizations, you find a requirement for X.509 digital certificates. The organization might need an SSL certificate for a website, a server certificate for *Skype for Business*, or a code signing certificate as the basis for signing PowerShell scripts. Building a PKI for your organization is often an exercise in defense in depth.

A very simple design would be to make your DC an **AD Certificate Services** (**ADCS**) CA server. But that is not best practice. At a minimum, you need a single offline root CA, with a subordinate issuing CA. If you are more paranoid or have a bigger attack surface, you could consider an intermediate CA that, like the root, is offline with a third level CA that issues certificates. The richness and complexity of modern CA architecture are beyond the scope of this book.

This recipe creates a two-level CA architecture for the `Reskit.org` network. The root CA is `root`: a workgroup machine that you should keep offline. The second CA is `CA.Reskit.Org`, which you set up as an issuing CA. To complete this recipe, you need to create the root CA on the root computer, then create a CA certificate that you can use to create a CA on `CA.Reskit.Org`.

This recipe makes great use of the `certutil.exe` console application a Windows console program. Additionally, you need to be logged on as administrator and need to run this recipe in an elevated PowerShell console.

Getting ready

This recipe assumes you have two systems, `root` (a workgroup computer) and `CA.Reskit.Org` (a domain-joined server) both online and with no additional non-default services.

Once you have this recipe working, you can add the firewall, like this:

```
Get-NetFirewallRule -DisplayGroup 'File and Printer Sharing' |
```

```
Set-NetFirewallRule -Enabled True
```

 The following was checked during the drafting of this book. Errors may creep in during production especially with respect to line endings. E&OE!

How to do it...

1. Install ADCS features on the root computer:

```
Install-WindowsFeature -Name ADCS-Cert-Authority `
                       -IncludeManagementTools
```

2. Create CA policy file:

```
$CaInf = @"
 [Version]
 Signature="$Windows NT$"
 [Certsrv_Server]
 RenewalKeyLength=4096
 RenewalValidityPeriod=Years
 RenewalValidityPeriodUnits=20
 CRLPeriod=Weeks
 CRLPeriodUnits=26
 CRLDeltaPeriod=Days
 CRLDeltaPeriodUnits=0
 LoadDefaultTemplates=0
 AlternateSignatureAlgorithm=1
"@
$PathInf = Join-Path -Path $Env:SystemRoot `
                     -ChildPath 'capolicy.inf'
$CaInf | Out-File -FilePath $PathInf
```

3. Install a CertificateAuthority based on the capolicy.inf file you created in *step 2*:

```
Install-AdcsCertificationAuthority -CAType StandaloneRootCA `
-KeyLength 4096 -HashAlgorithmName SHA256 `
-ValidityPeriod Years -ValidityPeriodUnits 20 `
-CACommonName "Reskit Root CA" `
-CryptoProviderName "RSA#Microsoft Software Key Storage Provider"
-Force
```

4. Set **Certificate Revocation List** (**CRL**) validity and CRL publication point:

```
certutil.exe -setreg CACRLPublicationURLs `
'1:C:\Windows\System32\CertSrv\CertEnro\ll%3%8.crln2:http://ca
.reskit.org/pki/%3%8.crl'
certutil.exe -setreg CACACertPublicationURLs
 '2:http://ca.reskit.org/pki/%1_%3%4.crt'
certutil.exe -setreg CACRLPeriod 'Weeks'
certutil.exe -setreg CACRLPeriodUnits 26
certutil.exe -setreg CACRLDeltaPeriod 'Days'
certutil.exe -setreg CACRLDeltaPeriodUnits 0
certutil.exe -setreg CACRLOverlapPeriod 'Hours'
certutil.exe -setreg CACRLOverlapPeriodUnits 12
certutil.exe -setreg CAValidityPeriod 'Years'
certutil.exe -setreg CAValidityPeriodUnits 10
certutil.exe -setreg CADSConfigDN
'CN=Configuration,DC=reskit,DC=org'
```

5. Restart the CA with updated configuration:

```
Restart-Service -Name certsvc
```

6. Publish and view the `crl`:

```
certutil.exe -crl
$CEPath = 'C\:Windows\System32\CertSrv\Enroll'
Get-ChildItem -Path $CEPath
```

7. Copy CA certificate and (empty) CRL to subordinate CA:

```
$PathSCrl = Join-Path -Path `
 'C:\Windows\System32\CertSrv\CertEnroll' `
                -ChildPath 'Reskit Root CA.crl'
$PathDCrl = Join-Path -Path '\\ca\c$' `
                -ChildPath 'Reskit Root CA.crl'
Copy-Item $PathSCrl $PathDCrl -Destination $PathDCrl
$PathSCrt = Join-Path -Path `
 'C:\Windows\System32\CertSrv\CertEnroll' `
                -ChildPath 'ROOT_Reskit Root CA.crt'
$PathDCrt = Join-Path -Path 'cac$' `
                -ChildPath 'ROOT_Reskit Root CA.crt'
Copy-Item $PathSCrl $PathDCrl
```

Having set up the root CA, you next set up the intermediate subordinate issuing CA on CA.Reskit.Org. Do the next steps in this recipe on the issuing CA.

8. Create a `PKI` folder and move the CRT and CRL files to the folder:

```
New-Item C:\PKI -ItemType Directory
                -ErrorAction Ignore
Move-Item -Path         'C:\Reskit Root CA.crl' `
       -Destination 'C:\pki\Reskit Root CA.crl'
Move-Item -Path         'C:\ROOT_Reskit Root CA.crt' `
       -Destination 'C:\pki\ROOT_Reskit Root CA.crt'
```

9. Publish the CA details to the Active Directory and local certificate store:

```
cd C:\PKI
certutil.exe -dspublish -f 'ROOT_Reskit Root CA.crt' `
RootCA
certutil.exe -addstore -f root 'ROOT_Reskit Root `
CA.crt'
certutil.exe -addstore -f root 'Reskit Root CA.crl'
```

10. Create root CA certificate and CRL distribution endpoints:

```
New-SmbShare -Name PKI
             -FullAccess SYSTEM,'Reskit\Domain Admins' `
             -ChangeAccess 'Reskit\Cert Publishers' `
             -Path C:\PKI
```

11. Install a subordinate enterprise issuing CA:

```
Install-WindowsFeature ADCS-Cert-Authority,
                       ADCS-Web-Enrollment,
                       ADCS-Enroll-Web-Pol,
                       ADCS-Enroll-Web-Svc,
                       ADCS-Online-Cert,
                       Web-Mgmt-Console
       -IncludeManagementTools
```

12. Configure CRL endpoints in IIS:

```
New-WebVirtualDirectory -Site 'Default Web Site' `
                        -Name 'PKI' `
                        -PhysicalPath 'C:\PKI'
```

13. Install the subordinate issuing CA on `CA.Reskit.Org`:

```
# Create capolicy.inf
$CaInf = @'
[Version]
Signature="$Windows NT$"
```

```
[Certsrv_Server]
RenewalKeyLength=4096
RenewalValidityPeriod=Years
RenewalValidityPeriodUnits=5
LoadDefaultTemplates=0
AlternateSignatureAlgorithm=1
'@
# Save INF file
$PathInf = Join-Path -Path $Env:SystemRoot `
                     -ChildPath 'capolicy.inf'
$CaInf | Out-File -FilePath $PathInf
# Install CA
Install-AdcsCertificationAuthority `
            -CAType EnterpriseSubordinateCA `
            -CACommonName 'ReskitIssuing CA' `
            -CryptoProviderName 'RSA#Microsoft
                Software Key Storage Provider' `
            -KeyLength 4096 `
            -HashAlgorithmName SHA256 `
            -Confirm:$false
```

Run the next two steps on the root CA offline server.

14. Request CA certificate for `ca.reskit.org` from the root CA:

```
Set-Location -Path c:\
Copy-Item -Path '\\ca\c$\CA.Reskit.Org\
                _ReskitIssuing CA.req' `
          -Destination .
certreq.exe -submit 'C:\CA.Reskit.Org\
                _ReskitIssuing CA.req'
```

15. Use the Certificate Manager GUI tool to issue the requested certificate. After issuing, retrieve the certificate and copy back to the `ca.reskit.org` computer:

```
certreq.exe -retrieve 2 C:\CA.Reskit.Org.Crt
Copy-Item -Path c:\CA.Reskit.Org* -Destination \\Ca\C$
```

Run the remaining steps on the `CA.Reskit.Org` computer:

16. After copying cert from the `root` computer, install it on `CA.Reskit.Org`, then start and check the service:

```
Certutil.exe  -InstallCert C:\CA.Reskit.Org.Crt
Start-Service -Name CertSvc
Get-Service   -Name CertSvc
```

17. Set up CRL settings in the registry:

```
certutil.exe -setreg CACRLPeriod 'Weeks'
certutil.exe -setreg CACRLPeriodUnits 2
certutil.exe -setreg CACRLDeltaPeriod 'Days'
certutil.exe -setreg CACRLDeltaPeriodUnits 1
certutil.exe -setreg CACRLOverlapPeriod "Hours"
certutil.exe -setreg CACRLOverlapPeriodUnits 12
certutil.exe -setreg CAValidityPeriod "Years"
certutil.exe -setreg CAValidityPeriodUnits 5
```

18. Set up CRL distribution points:

```
$CrlList = Get-CACrlDistributionPoint
foreach ($Crl in $CrlList)
   {Remove-CACrlDistributionPoint -Uri $Crl.uri -Force}
$URI = 'C:\Windows\System32\CertSrv\CertEnroll\ReskitIssuing CA.crl'
Add-CACRLDistributionPoint -Uri $URI `
   -PublishToServer -PublishDeltaToServer -Force
Add-CACRLDistributionPoint
   -Uri http://ca.reskit.org/pki/reskit.crl `
   -AddToCertificateCDP -Force
Add-CACRLDistributionPoint
   -Uri file://ca.reskit.orgpki%3%8%9.crl `
   -PublishToServer -PublishDeltaToServer -Force
Restart-Service Certsvc
Start-Sleep -Seconds 15
certutil.exe -crl
```

19. Restart the service and publish the CRL:

```
# Step 19 - restart service then publish the CRL
Restart-Service -Name CertSvc
Start-Sleep -Seconds 15
Certutil.exe -crl
```

20. Test the CRL:

```
$WC = New-Object System.Net.WebClient
$Url = 'http://ca.reskit.org/pki/ReskitIssuing CA.crl'
$To = 'C:\ReskitIssuing CA.crl'
$WC.DownloadFile($URL, $to)
certutil -dump $to
```

How it works...

In *step 1*, you use `Install-WindowsFeature` to add the Certificate Services feature. As you can see, a reboot is not required:

```
PS C:\> Install-WindowsFeature -Name ADCS-Cert-Authority -IncludeManagementTools

Success Restart Needed Exit Code      Feature Result
------- -------------- ---------      --------------
True    No             Success        {Active Directory Certificate Services, Ce...
```

With *step 2*, you create here a string which you write to `capolicy.inf` in the folder (`C:\Windows`). Windows uses this policy file to define some aspects of the CA policy that relate to the certificate revocation list, an essential aspect of an enterprise PKI implementations.

You use the `Install-AdcsCertificationAuthority` cmdlet, specifying several other configuration items. These items include the common name for the CA, `Reskit Root CA`, the type of CA (a `StandaloneRootCA`), the key length of the CA root key, 4096 bits, the hash algorithm this CA is to use, `SHA256`, and a CA certificate validity period of 20 years. Setting the `-Confirm` parameter to `$false` eliminates a confirmation popup. There is a small bit of output indicating a successful installation:

```
PS C:\> Install-AdcsCertificationAuthority -CAType StandaloneRootCA `
                -KeyLength 4096  -HashAlgorithmName SHA256 `
                -ValidityPeriod Years -ValidityPeriodUnits 20 `
                -CACommonName "Reskit Root CA" `
                -CryptoProviderName "RSA#Microsoft Software Key Storage Provider" `
                -Confirm:$false

ErrorId ErrorString
------- -----------
      0
```

In *step 4*, you use the `certutil.exe` Windows console application to set details of where you plan to publish the CRL and details about how often you plan to update the CRL. `Certutil` sets these values in the system's registry. The certificate service retrieves the registry values at startup. Each time you call `Certutil` using the `-setreg` switch, `Certutil` displays both the old value and the new value for each registry item. The final call, for example, generates this output:

```
PS C:\> certutil.exe -setreg CA\DSConfigDN 'CN=Configuration,DC=reskit,DC=org'

HKEY_LOCAL_MACHINE\SYSTEM\CurrentControlSet\Services\CertSvc\Configuration\Reskit Root CA\DSConfigDN:

Old Value:
  DSConfigDN REG_SZ = cn=foo

New Value:
  DSConfigDN REG_SZ = CN=Configuration,DC=reskit,DC=org
CertUtil: -setreg command completed successfully.
The CertSvc service may need to be restarted for changes to take effect.
```

In *step 5*, you restart the `certsvc` service. `Restart-Service` produces no output from this step. In *step 6*, you publish the CRL details, and view the CRL files, as follows:

```
PS C:\> certutil.exe -crl
CertUtil: -CRL command completed successfully.

PS C:\> Get-ChildItem -Path C:\Windows\System32\CertSrv\CertEnroll


    Directory: C:\Windows\System32\CertSrv\CertEnroll


Mode                LastWriteTime         Length Name
----                -------------         ------ ----
-a----        01/02/2017     11:57           815 Reskit Root CA.crl
-a----        31/01/2017     21:22          1401 ROOT_Reskit Root CA.crt
```

To view the CRL information from the GUI execute the CRL file which displays the CRL GUI like this:

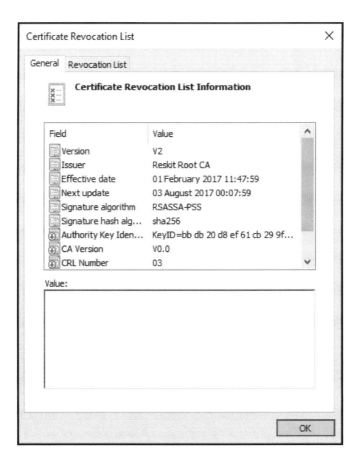

If you click on the **Revocation List** tab, you see the current revocation list which is empty. The CRL looks like this:

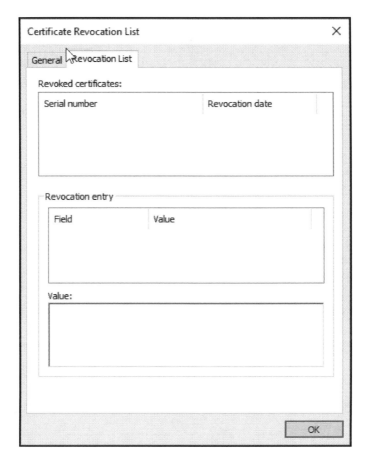

As you can see from this CRL GUI, there are currently no revoked certificates.

In *step 7*, you copy the CRL and the CA's certificate to the computer that is intended to become an intermediate subordinate issuing CA (CA.Reskit.Org). There is no output from this step. Once you complete this step, you can shut down the root server, you run the remainder of the steps in the recipe from CA.Reskit.Org.

In *step 8*, you move the certificate and CRL files into a new folder C:\PKI. When you are creating the files or moving them manually, you can always copy the files directly into the C:\PKI folder and avoid this step.

In *step 9*, you use `certutil.exe` to publish the offline root CA you created earlier into the Active Directory and add both the root CA certificate and the CRL into the certificate stores on the local machine.

```
PS C:\pki> certutil.exe -dspublish -f 'ROOT_Reskit Root CA.crt' RootCA
ldap:///CN=Reskit Root CA,CN=Certification Authorities,CN=Public Key Services,CN=Services,CN=Configuration,DC=Reskit,DC=Org?cACertificate

Certificate added to DS store.
ldap:///CN=Reskit Root CA,CN=AIA,CN=Public Key Services,CN=Services,CN=Configuration,DC=Reskit,DC=Org?cACertificate
Certificate added to DS store.
CertUtil: -dsPublish command completed successfully.

PS C:\pki> certutil.exe -addstore -f root 'ROOT_Reskit Root CA.crt'
root "Trusted Root Certification Authorities"
Signature matches Public Key
Certificate "Reskit Root CA" added to store.
CertUtil: -addstore command completed successfully.

PS C:\pki> certutil.exe -addstore -f root 'Reskit Root CA.crl'
root "Trusted Root Certification Authorities"
CRL "CN=Reskit Root CA" added to store.
CertUtil: -addstore command completed successfully.
```

In *step 10*, you create a share for the CA certificate and CRL distribution:

```
PS C:\> New-Item C:\PKI -ItemType Directory -ErrorAction Ignore

    Directory: C:\

Mode                LastWriteTime         Length Name
----                -------------         ------ ----
d-----        01/02/2017     16:10               PKI
```

With *step 11*, you install the Certificate Service components to the server. You also add the management tools to the server. If you plan to manage the server remotely, consider omitting the management tools. Note that this step only adds the Certificate Services components, you perform installation in a later step. Installing the components looks like this:

```
PS C:\> Add-WindowsFeature ADCS-Cert-Authority,
                    ADCS-Web-Enrollment,
                    ADCS-Enroll-Web-Pol,
                    ADCS-Enroll-Web-Svc,
                    ADCS-Online-Cert,
                    Web-Mgmt-Console
                    -IncludeManagementTools

Success Restart Needed Exit Code     Feature Result
------- -------------- ---------     --------------
True    No             Success       {Active Directory Certificate Services, Ce...
```

Although it may not be obvious, in *step 11*, you also installed IIS on the server (adding the `Web-Mgmt-Console` feature implies adding all the other web server features). So to setup the server to publish the CRL, in *step 12*, you need to add a new virtual directory to the IIS Server and configure IIS to allow double-escaping:

```
PS C:\PKI> New-WebVirtualDirectory -Site 'Default Web Site' `
                              -Name 'PKI' `
                              -PhysicalPath 'C:\PKI'

Name PhysicalPath
---- ------------
PKI  C:\PKI


PS C:\> C:\Windows\System32\inetsrv\appcmd.exe `
             set config /section:requestfiltering `
                        /allowdoubleescaping:true
Applied configuration changes to section
"system.webServer/security/requestFiltering" for
"MACHINE/WEBROOT/APPHOST" at configuration commit
path "MACHINE/WEBROOT/APPHOST"
```

In *step 13*, you create a `capolicy.inf` file, similarly to how you created this file on the root CA server. There is no output. You finish the step by using the `Install-ADDSCertificationAuthority` to make `ca.reskit.org` a subordinate issuing CA:

```
PS C:\> Install-AdcsCertificationAuthority -CAType EnterpriseSubordinateCA `
             -CACommonName 'ReskitIssuing CA' `
             -CryptoProviderName 'RSA#Microsoft Software Key Storage Provider' `
             -KeyLength 4096 `
             -HashAlgorithmName SHA256 `
             -Confirm:$false
WARNING: The Active Directory Certificate Services installation is incomplete. To ]
complete the installation, use the request file "C:\CA.Reskit.Org_ReskitIssuing CA.req"
to obtain a certificate from the parent CA. Then, use the Certification Authority snap-in
to install the certificate. To complete this procedure, right-click the node with the name
of the CA, and then click Install CA Certificate. The operation completed successfully. 0x0 (WIN32: 0)

ErrorId ErrorString
------- -----------
    398 The Active Directory Certificate Services installation is
        incomplete. To complete the installation, use the request
        file "C:\CA.Reskit.Org_ReskitIssuing CA.req" to obtain...
```

As you can see, installing the intermediate CA generated an error. This error message is normal when installing a subordinate CA. To complete the installation of the CA, you need to get the parent CA (the offline root CA) to issue a signed certificate for the subordinate CA. Installing the CA created a certificate request file, (`C:\CA.Reskit.Org_ReskitIssuing CA.req`). You next need to copy this certificate request file from the subordinate CA computer to the offline root CA. As before, there are many ways to get the request copied over to the root CA.

Once you have copied the certificate request to the root CA computer, you submit the request for the certificate using the certificate request you created in *step 13*.

```
PS C:\> certreq.exe -submit 'C:\CA.Reskit.Org_ReskitIssuing CA.req'
RequestId: 2
RequestId: "2"
Certificate request is pending: Taken Under Submission (0)
```

So having requested a certificate for CA.Reskit.ORG from the root CA, you need to issue the certificate and copy it back to the CA.Reskit.Org computer. You can request the certificate using the certreq command, but you need to use the GUI to issue the certificate, which you do in *step 15*:

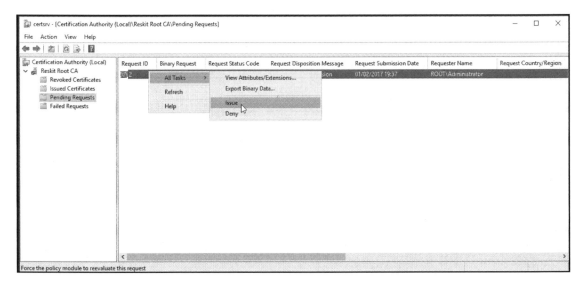

Once you issue and retrieve the certificate, you copy it to the subordinate issuing CA. There is no output from the copy command in *step 15*. In *step 16*, you complete the installation of your issuing CA by installing the just-issued and copied certificate, then starting the certsvc service then checking to ensure the service started:

```
PS C:\> certutil.exe -installcert C:\ca.reskit.org.crt
CertUtil: -installCert command completed successfully.
The CertSvc service may need to be restarted for changes to take effect.

PS C:\> Start-Service -Name CertSvc
PS C:\> Get-Service -Name CertSvc

Status    Name                 DisplayName
------    ----                 -----------
Running   CertSvc              Active Directory Certificate Services
```

In *step 17*, you use the `certutil.exe` command to set up the details of the CRL and the validity period for the certificates issued by the CA. Each call to `certutil` shows the old and new value for each registry settings. Here is what the first call to `certutil` looks like:

```
PS C:\> certutil.exe -setreg CA\CRLPeriod "Weeks"
HKEY_LOCAL_MACHINE\SYSTEM\CurrentControlSet\Services\CertSvc\Configuration\ReskitIssuing CA\CRLPeriod:

Old Value:
  CRLPeriod REG_SZ = Weeks

New Value:
  CRLPeriod REG_SZ = Weeks
CertUtil: -setreg command completed successfully.
The CertSvc service may need to be restarted for changes to take effect.
```

In *step 18*, you configure the certificate revocation lists details. In *step 19*, you restart the `certsvc` using the updated settings. It takes a few seconds after the service has started before you can publish the CA's certificate revocation list, which looks like this:

```
PS C:\pki> Restart-Service -Name CertSvc

PS C:\pki> Start-Sleep -Seconds 15

PS C:\pki> Certutil.exe -crl
CertUtil: -CRL command completed successfully.
```

And finally, you can test that the CA has issued the CRL and see what it contains. In *step 20,* you create a web client and download the CRL. Then you use `certutil.exe` to dump the CRL. The truncated output, with arrows pointing to key information (including the hashing algorithm, the issuing CA, and the number of CRL entries is zero). It looks like this:

```
PS C:\> certutil -dump $to
X509 Certificate Revocation List:          ◄─────────────────
Version: 2
Signature Algorithm:
    Algorithm ObjectId: 1.2.840.113549.1.1.10 RSASSA-PSS
    Algorithm Parameters:
    0000   30 34 a0 0f 30 0d 06 09  60 86 48 01 65 03 04 02
    0010   01 05 00 a1 1c 30 1a 06  09 2a 86 48 86 f7 0d 01
    0020   01 08 30 0d 06 09 60 86  48 01 65 03 04 02 01 05
    0030   00 a2 03 02 01 20
            2.16.840.1.101.3.4.2.1 sha256 (sha256NoSign)    ◄────────
            05 00
            1.2.840.113549.1.1.8 mgf1
                2.16.840.1.101.3.4.2.1 sha256 (sha256NoSign)
                05 00
            0x20 (32)
Issuer:
    CN=ReskitIssuing CA        ◄─────────────
    DC=Reskit
    DC=Org
  Name Hash(sha1): e232d9004c223e170f064c82b0a490bee2f20aaa
  Name Hash(md5): 97795df84f336ae126e69bacf9bf7e35

 ThisUpdate: 02/02/2017 00:16
 NextUpdate: 16/02/2017 12:36
CRL Entries: 0      ◄──────────────────────
CRL Extensions: 4
    2.5.29.35: Flags = 0, Length = 18
    Authority Key Identifier
        KeyID=60 84 26 cf 53 1b ee 96 e9 61 02 f7 d9 31 e1 ee f1 1e 93 11
```

There's more...

In *step 2,* you create a CA and configure some settings. At the time of writing, best practice seems to suggest that `SHA256` and a key length of 4096 bits are acceptable. But things change. Before deploying this recipe, research the latest best practice very carefully with regards to encryption algorithms and key lengths.

In *step 6,* you publish the root CA server certificate revocation list and view the file. The certificate and CRL files in the `CertEnroll` folder are binary so are not human readable. The output from this step looks like this:

```
PS C:\> Get-ChildItem -Path $CEPath


    Directory: C:\Windows\System32\CertSrv\CertEnroll


Mode                LastWriteTime         Length Name
----                -------------         ------ ----
-a----        01/02/2017     11:57           815 Reskit Root CA.crl
-a----        31/01/2017     21:22          1401 ROOT_Reskit Root CA.crt
```

In *step 7*, you copy the CA certificate and CRL from the root CA to the subordinate. That assumes network connectivity. In a production environment, you should always keep the root CA offline and off any network. In this situation, you need some means to move the two files to the subordinate CA computer such as a portable USB stick or drive.

In *step 12*, you did a basic setup of the CRL for your PKI. In production, you should consider hardening the setup. For example, you could change the permissions on the PKI folder to only all Reskit.Org administrators, or perhaps the certificate publishers group, to be the only accounts with permissions to write to this folder. You may also consider converting the PKI virtual directory into a separate IIS web application and run that application in a new and different web pool.

This recipe allowed you to implement a basic working two-level PKI. At present, you need to use a combination of PowerShell cmdlets, Windows console commands and the GUI. Perhaps later versions of Windows Server can provide better cmdlet coverage for setting up and managing certificates and certificate authorities.

Creating and managing AD users, groups, and computers

Your active directory, as created in the *Installing domain controllers and DNS* recipe authenticates users and computers. AD also makes use of group membership to simplify authorization. In this recipe, you add, remove, and update users and computers. You also create and remove groups and manage group membership as well as manage organizational units. This recipe uses the cmdlets in the ActiveDirectory module. You can use a more automated approach to adding users by following the *Adding users to the Active Directory using a CSV file* recipe.

Getting ready

This recipe uses two working domain controllers (DC1 and DC2) in the Reskit.Org domain.

How to do it...

1. Create a hash table for general user attributes:

```
$Password = 'Pa$$w0rd'
$PasswordSS = ConvertTo-SecureString `
              -String $Password `
              -AsPlainText -Force
$NewUserHT = @{}
$NewUserHT.AccountPassword = $PasswordSS
$NewUserHT.Enabled = $true
$NewUserHT.PasswordNeverExpires = $true
$NewUserHT.ChangePasswordAtLogon = $false
```

2. Create two new users:

```
New-ADUser @NewUserHT `
          -SamAccountName 'ThomasL' `
          -UserPrincipalName 'thomasL@reskit.org' `
          -Name 'ThomasL' `
          -DisplayName 'Thomas Lee (IT)'
New-ADUser @NewUserHT `
          -SamAccountName 'RLT' `
          -UserPrincipalName 'rlt@reskit.org' `
          -Name 'Rebecca Tanner' `
          -DisplayName 'Rebecca Tanner (IT)'
```

3. Create an OU and move users into it:

```
New-ADOrganizationalUnit -Name 'IT' `
                         -DisplayName 'Reskit IT Team' `
                         -Path 'DC=Reskit,DC=Org'
Move-ADObject `
 -Identity 'CN=ThomasL,CN=Users,DC=Reskit,DC=ORG' `
 -TargetPath 'OU=IT,DC=Reskit,DC=Org'
Move-ADObject `
 -Identity 'CN=Rebecca Tanner,CN=Users,DC=Reskit,DC=ORG' `
 -TargetPath 'OU=IT,DC=Reskit,DC=Org'
```

4. Create a third user in the IT OU:

```
New-ADUser @NewUserHT `
        -SamAccountName 'JerryG' `
        -UserPrincipalName 'jerryg@reskit.org' `
        -Description 'Virtualization Team' `
        -Name 'JerryGarcia' `
        -DisplayName 'Jerry Garcia (IT)' `
        -Path 'OU=IT,DC=Reskit,DC=Org'
```

5. Add and then remove users two ways:

```
New-ADUser @NewUserHT `
        -SamAccountName 'TBR' `
        -UserPrincipalName 'tbr@reskit.org' `
        -Name 'TBR' `
        -DisplayName 'User to be removed' `
        -Path 'OU=IT,DC=Reskit,DC=Org'
New-ADUser @NewUserHT `
        -SamAccountName 'TBR2' `
        -UserPrincipalName 'tbr2@reskit.org' `
        -Name 'TBR2' `
        -DisplayName 'User to be removed' `
        -Path 'OU=IT,DC=Reskit,DC=Org'
# Remove get | remove
Get-ADUser -Identity 'CN=TBR,OU=IT,DC=Reskit,DC=Org' |
        Remove-ADUser -Confirm:$false
# Remove directly
Remove-ADUser -Identity 'CN=TBR2,OU=IT,DC=Reskit,DC=Org' `
        -Confirm:$false
```

6. Update and display a user:

```
Set-ADUser -Identity ThomasL `
 -OfficePhone '44168555420' `
 -Office 'Cookham HQ' `
 -EmailAddress 'ThomasL@Reskit.Org' `
 -GivenName 'Thomas' `
 -Surname 'Lee' `
 -HomePage 'Https://tfl09.blogspot.com'
Get-ADUser -Identity ThomasL `
 -Properties Office,OfficePhone,EmailAddress
```

7. Create and populate a group:

```
New-ADGroup -Name 'IT Team' `
            -Path 'OU=IT,DC=Reskit,DC=org' `
            -Description 'All members of the IT Team' `
            -GroupScope DomainLocal
$ItUsers = Get-ADUser -Filter * `
            -SearchBase 'OU=IT,DC=Reskit,DC=Org'
Add-ADGroupMember -Identity 'CN=IT Team,OU=IT,DC=Reskit,DC=org' `
                  -Members $ItUsers
```

8. Add a computer to the AD:

```
New-ADComputer -Name 'Wolf' `
               -DNSHostName 'wolf.reskit.org' `
               -Description 'One for Jerry'`
               -Path 'OU=IT,DC=Reskit,DC=Org' `
               -OperatingSystemVersion 'Window Server 2016
                Data Center'
```

How it works...

This recipe uses some AD cmdlets contained in the `ActiveDirectory` module. The recipe shows how to do basic management of AD objects using PowerShell.

In *step 1*, you create a hash table of common user properties. You use this hash table to hold some of the common user properties. There is no output from this step.

In *step 2*, you add two users to the AD. Note that the parameters to `New-ADUser` include the properties set in the `$NewUserHT` hash table and the parameters you specify when you call `New-ADUser`. Note that, by default, the `Add-NewADUser` adds the new user into the the Users container in the root of the AD. There is no output from this step, although you can observe the two newly added users using the **Active Directory Users and Computers** MMC tool:

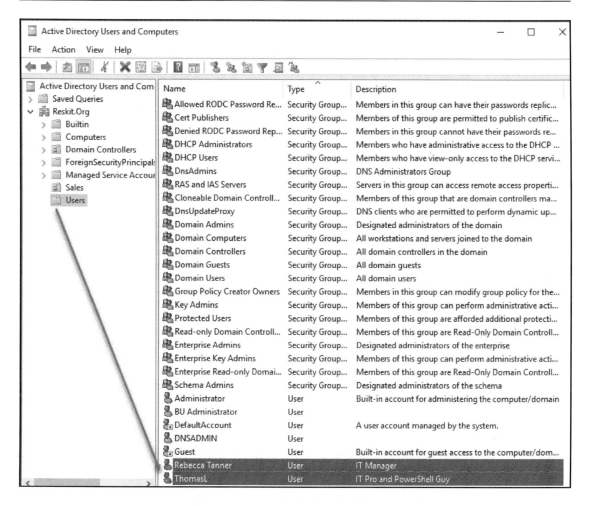

You do not need to create a user then move the user into the correct OU. Instead, you can use the -Path parameter to specify the OU in which you wish to create the user. In *step 4*, you create another user, this time directly in the IT organizational unit. As with previous steps, there is no output from adding this user. If you wish more output, specify the parameter -Passthru to New-ADuser.

Creating this third user with `-Passthru` looks like this:

```
PS C:\> New-ADUser @NewUserHT
            -SamAccountName     'JerryG'
            -UserPrincipalName 'jerryg@reskit.org'
            -Description        'Virtualization Team'
            -Name               'JerryGarcia'
            -DisplayName        'Jerry Garcia (IT)'
            -Path               'OU=IT,DC=Reskit,DC=Org'
            -PassThru


DistinguishedName : CN=JerryGarcia,OU=IT,DC=Reskit,DC=Org
Enabled           : True
GivenName         :
Name              : JerryGarcia
ObjectClass       : user
ObjectGUID        : 42d4820d-9281-45b3-bb02-2a98b165a5d5
SamAccountName    : JerryG
SID               : S-1-5-21-715049209-2702507345-667613206-1134
Surname           :
UserPrincipalName : jerryg@reskit.org
```

In *step 5*, you create two users that you then delete. *Step 5* shows two different ways you can remove a user. If you use the first pattern, you first get the object (the user to be removed) first, then delete it. Running this step from the console helps you to ensure you are deleting the correct user. The second approach works well if you are certain of no typos in the value you give to the `-Identity` parameter (the distinguished name of the user you wish to delete).

In *step 6*, you update a user's details specifying office and office phone, and so on. Then you retrieve the user's details from the AD:

```
PS C:\> Set-ADUser -Identity        ThomasL
            -OfficePhone    '44168555420'
            -Office         'Cookham HQ'
            -EmailAddress  'ThomasL@Reskit.Org'
            -GivenName      'Thomas'
            -Surname        'Lee'
            -HomePage       'Https://tf109.blogspot.com'

PS C:\> Get-ADUser -Identity        ThomasL
            -Properties    Office,OfficePhone,EmailAddress


DistinguishedName : CN=ThomasL,OU=IT,DC=Reskit,DC=Org
EmailAddress      : ThomasL@Reskit.Org
Enabled           : True
GivenName         : Thomas
Name              : ThomasL
ObjectClass       : user
ObjectGUID        : d8d326cb-0852-4099-a54b-47e78436c842
Office            : Cookham HQ
OfficePhone       : 44168555420
SamAccountName    : ThomasL
SID               : S-1-5-21-715049209-2702507345-667613206-1131
Surname           : Lee
UserPrincipalName : ThomasL@Reskit.Org
```

In *step 7*, you create a new domain local security group and populate it with the three users in the IT OU. There is no output from these commands. Once you have completed the first seven steps, you can observe the results using the **Active Directory Users and Computers** MMC console, like this:

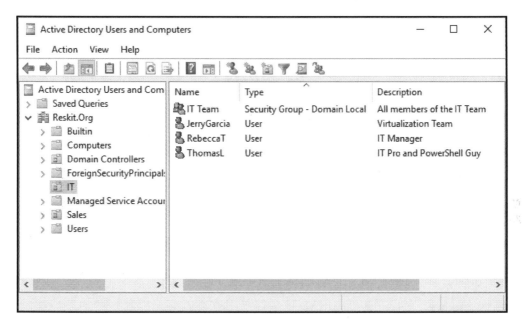

In *step 8*, you add a new computer, `Wolf`, to your AD. There is no output from this step.

There's more...

In *step 8*, you just added a computer to AD. You could also create a security group, say IT group computers and add the new computer to the group (and don't forget to add other IT group systems to the new security group).

Removing the computer from AD is also quite simple: you use the `Remove-ADComputer` cmdlet (Or use the `Get-ADComputer | Remove-ADComputer` pattern).

Adding users to AD using a CSV file

As mentioned several times in this book, `https://www.spiceworks.com/` has a busy PowerShell support forum (accessible at `https://community.spiceworks.com/ programming/powershell`). A frequently asked (and answered) question is: How do I add multiple users using an input file? This recipe does just that. You start with a simple CSV file containing the details of the users you wish to add. This script uses a CSV file and adds the users contained in the CSV.

Getting ready

This recipe assumes you have a domain setup and that you have created the IT organizational unit.

How to do it...

1. Import a CSV file containing the details of the users you want to add to AD:

   ```
   $Users = Import-CSV -Path C:\FooUsers.Csv
   ```

2. Add the users using the CSV:

   ```
   ForEach ($User in $Users) {
    $Prop = @{}
    $Prop.GivenName = $User.Firstname
    $Prop.Initials = $User.Initials
    $Prop.Surname = $User.Lastname
    $Prop.UserPrincipalName =
    $User.UserPrincipalName+"@reskit.org"
    $Prop.Displayname = $User.firstname.trim() + " " +
                        $user.lastname.trim()
    $Prop.Description = $User.Description
    $Prop.Name = $User.Alias
    $Prop.AccountPassword = $(ConvertTo-SecureString `
                -AsPlainText $user.password -Force)
    $Prop.ChangePasswordAtLogon = $true
    # Now create the user
    New-ADUser @Prop -Path 'OU=IT,DC=Reskit,DC=ORG' `
                    -Enabled:$true
    # Finally, display user created
   "Created $($Prop.Displayname)"
    }
   ```

How it works...

In *step 1*, you import the CSV file. The recipe imports the CSV file from the C:\ folder, adjust this step to accord with where you place the CSV file. The CSV file, which you can create using Excel or Notepad, looks like this:

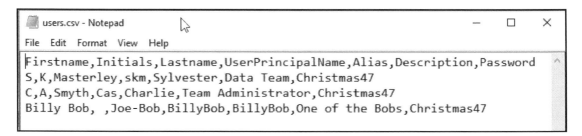

Importing the CSV file generates no output. In *step 2*, you iterate through the users in the CSV. For each user in the file, you generate a property hash table ($Prop) which you use as input to the New-ADUser cmdlet. After you add the user, you display a message logging that the script has added the requested user. If you run the entire recipe as a single script, saved as Recipe10-11.ps1, and using the users.csv file shown here, then the output looks like this:

```
PS C:\> Recipe10-11.ps1
Created S Masterley
Created C Smyth
Created Billy Bob Joe-Bob
```

There's more...

There are many variations on this theme. You can expand the data included in the CSV file to add more properties to the AD user. For example, you could include phone numbers, office details, and more. You could also extend the CSV to include lists of groups of which any user should be a member. You could also extend the script and create more objects for the new users to use: a personal folder on a server, some *SharePoint* server space, and an *Exchange* mailbox. If you have Skype for Business, you could enable the user, possibly by including some Skype for Business information for the user in the CSV.

Reporting on AD users

In this recipe, you generate a report on the users in your AD. Because the range of things you might wish to report on, the first step in this recipe defines a function: `Get-ReskitUser`. This function collects a range of information from the AD and returns it as a custom object. This approach allows you to customize this recipe further, for example reaching into Exchange, SharePoint, or Skype for Business and add additional properties to the object generated that `Get-Reskituser` returns. The recipe uses the `Get-ReskitUser` function and creates a report on aspects of the users in AD.

Getting ready

This recipe relies on having users defined and active. The users added using previous recipes serves as a good base. You should use a client system, have the users in your AD and log on to the computer. Also ensure that the `LastLogonDate` AD attribute for the computer is populated fully. Populating other fields, such as Office would also be useful to make the reporting a bit more realistic.

How to do it...

1. Define a function to return details on our AD Users:

```
Function Get-ReskitUser {
# Get PDC Emulator DC
$PrimaryDC = Get-ADDomainController -Discover `
                                    -Service PrimaryDC
# Get Users
$ADUsers = Get-ADUser -Filter * -Properties * `
                    -Server $PrimaryDC
# Iterate through them and create $Userinfo hash table:
Foreach ($ADUser in $ADUsers)
   {
     # Create a userinfo HT
     $UserInfo = [Ordered] @{}
     $UserInfo.SamAccountname =
                             $ADUser.SamAccountName
     $Userinfo.DisplayName = $ADUser.DisplayName
     $UserInfo.Office = $ADUser.Office
     $Userinfo.Enabled = $ADUser.Enabled
     $userinfo.LastLogonDate = $ADUser.LastLogonDate
     $UserInfo.ProfilePath = $ADUser.ProfilePath
```

```
        $userinfo.ScriptPath = $ADUser.ScriptPath
        $UserInfo.BadPWDCount = $ADUser.badPwdCount
        New-Object -TypeName PSObject -Property $UserInfo
    }
}
```

2. Get the users:

```
$RKUsers = Get-ReskitUser
```

3. Build the report header:

```
$RKReport = ''
$RkReport += "*** Reskit.Org AD Report`n"
$RKReport += "*** Generated [$(Get-Date)]`n"
$RKReport += "*******************************`n`n"
```

4. Report on `Disabled` users:

```
$RkReport += "*** Disabled Users`n"
$RKReport += $RKUsers |
             Where-Object {$_.Enabled -NE $true} |
             Format-Table `
             -Property SamAccountName, Displayname |
                Out-String
```

5. Report users who have not recently logged on:

```
$OneWeekAgo = (Get-Date).AddDays(-7)
$RKReport += "*** "Enabled users Not logged in" +
                   "in past 7 days`n"
$RkReport += $RKUsers |
        Where {$_.Enabled -and $_.LastLogonDate
                             -le $OneWeekAgo} |
            Sort-Object -Property LastlogonDate |
                Format-Table -Property Displayname,
                                        lastlogondate |
                Out-String
```

6. Users with high invalid password attempts:

```
$RKReport += "*** High Number of Bad
                   Password Attempts`n"
$RKReport += $RKUsers | Where-Object BadPwdCount -ge 5 |
    Format-Table `
            -Property SamAccountName, BadPwdCount |
             Out-String
```

7. Display the report:

$RKReport

How it works...

In *step 1*, you create the `Get-ReskitUser` function. This function gets all the users in the domain from the server acting as the PDC emulator. The function creates a hash table based on the what is returned from `Get-AdUser`. Finally, the function converts the hash table or each user into a `PSCustom` object which it returns to the caller.

In *step 2* through *step 6*, you construct the separate parts of the report: users who are disabled, users who have not recently logged on, and users who have had more than five failed attempts to enter a valid password. There is no output from these steps.

In *step 7*, you display the report, which looks like this:

```
*** Reskit.Org AD Report
*** Generated [02/03/2017 00:05:55]
**************************************

*** Disabled Users

SamAccountname DisplayName
-------------- -----------
Guest          Guest Account
DefaultAccount Default Account
krbtgt         krbtgt


*** Enabled users Not logged in the past 7 days

DisplayName      LastLogonDate
-----------      -------------
DNS Admin
BU Administrator 10/01/2017 15:38:21


*** High Number of Bad Password Attempts

SamAccountname BadPWDCount
-------------- -----------
ThomasL                  8
```

There's more...

You have scope to expand this basic reporting script. You could, for example, compare the user objects returned from each DC and report on any user object that AD has not replicated. You could also generate an email message and mail the report to key people in your organization.

Finding expired computers in AD

Expired computers, computers that have not logged on recently, can be something you need to investigate. A client computer that has not logged on to the domain for, say, a month, could have been stolen. Such a computer could also be an under-used asset that is a candidate for redeployment. If it's a server that has not logged in for a month, it could indicate a computer that is non-functioning and one you should investigate.

This recipe is a variation on the `Report on AD Users` recipe.

Getting ready

This recipe needs computer accounts in the AD.

How to do it...

1. Build the report header:

```
$RKReport = ''
$RkReport += "*** Reskit.Org AD Unused
            + "Computer Report`n"
$RKReport += "*** Generated [$(Get-Date)]`n"
$RKReport += "**********************************`n`n"
```

2. Report on computer accounts that have not logged in in past 14 days:

```
$RkReport += "*** Machines not logged on in past 14 days`n"
$FortnightAgo = (Get-Date).AddDays(-14)
$RKReport += Get-ADComputer `
    -Properties lastLogonDate `
    -Filter 'lastLogonDate -lt $FortnightAgo' |
        Sort-Object -Property lastLogonDate |
            Format-Table -PropertyName, lastLogonDate |
```

```
Out-string
```

3. Report on computer accounts that have not logged in the past month:

```
$RkReport += "*** Machines not logged on in past month`n"
$AMonthAgo = (Get-Date).AddMonths(-1)
$RkReport += Get-ADComputer `
    -Properties lastLogonDate `
    -Filter 'lastLogonDate -lt $AMonthAgo' |
        Sort-Object -Property lastLogonDate |
            Format-Table -Property Name, LastLogonDate |
                Out-String
```

4. Display the report:

```
$RKReport
```

How it works...

Generating this report involves several steps. In *step 1*, you create the report header. In *step 2* and *step 3* you report on computers that have not logged on for more than a fortnight (2 weeks) and those that have not logged on for more than a month. These steps generate no output.

In *step 3*, you display the report showing the computers that have not logged on for more than two weeks, and for more than a month. The first set might indicate people who are on holiday, or who may be working in another office or from home for that period. Machines that do not log on for more than a month are candidates for further investigation.

There's more...

There are many variations on this recipe. You could just report on computers that have not logged on for more than 90 days either as an alternative to the logging you are doing in this recipe or in addition to it. You might decide that computers not used a fortnight ago are not interesting to you and so you could drop that piece of the report.

When a computer logs on (and for that matter when a user logs on), the DC that performs the logon records the last logon time. By default, AD does not replicate this attribute to other DCs. Thus, it is entirely possible that a computer might never have recorded a logon against the DC you use to generate this report. If you have multiple DCs, consider extending this recipe to obtain computer logon details from all the domain controllers in the domain and report across all of them.

Creating a privileged user report

When you add a user to a group (and the user re-logs on), the user acquires additional permissions and rights. That may be a good thing! Group membership enables the user to perform job-related duties. However, adding the user to the Enterprise Admins group, for example, provides that user with rights over most of your forest. A user who acquires the membership to such high privilege groups may not have benign intentions and could represent a serious risk. The report you generate using this recipe shows the privileged users and any changes that someone has made to the group membership.

Getting ready

You need a DC on which to run this report.

How to do it...

1. Create an array for privileged users:

    ```
    $PUsers = @()
    ```

2. Query the Enterprise Admins/Domain Admins/Scheme Admins groups for members and add to the $Pusers array:

    ```
    # Enterprise Admins
    $Members = Get-ADGroupMember `
                  -Identity 'Enterprise Admins' -Recursive |
    Sort-Object -Property Name
    $PUsers += foreach ($Member in $Members) {
       Get-ADUser -Identity $Member.SID -Properties * |
              Select-Object
             -Property Name,
    @{Name='Group';expression={'Enterprise Admins'}},
    ```

```
WhenCreated, LastlogonDate
}
# Domain Admins
$Members = Get-ADGroupMember `
          -Identity 'Domain Admins' -Recursive|
              Sort-Object -Property Name
$PUsers += Foreach ($Member in $Members)
  {Get-ADUser -Identity $member.SID -Properties * |
          Select-Object -Property Name,
    @{Name='Group';expression={'Domain Admins'}}, `
    WhenCreated, Lastlogondate,SamAccountName
}
# Schema Admins
$Members = Get-ADGroupMember `
          -Identity 'Schema Admins' -Recursive |
Sort-Object Name
$PUsers += Foreach ($Member in $Members) {
    Get-ADUser -Identity $member.SID -Properties * |
          Select-Object -Property Name,
  @{Name='Group';expression={'Schema Admins'}}, `
  WhenCreated, Lastlogondate,SamAccountName
}
```

3. Create the basic membership report:

```
$Report = ""
$Report += "*** Reskit.Org AD Privileged
                        User Report`n"
$Report += "*** Generated [$(Get-Date)]`n"
$Report += "**********************************"
$Report += $PUsers| Format-Table -Property Name,
                    WhenCreated,
Lastlogondate `
-GroupBy Group |
Out-String
$Report += "`n"
```

4. Find out what has changed since last time this report ran

```
$ExportFile = "c:\Foop\users.clixml"
$OldFile = Try {Test-Path $ExportFile} Catch {}
if ($OldFile) # if the file exists, report
                    against changes
{
    # Import the results from the last time the
    # script was executed
    $OldUsers = Import-Clixml-Path -Path $ExportFile
    # Identify and report on the changes
```

```
          $Changes = "*** Changes to Privileges
                         User Membership`n"
          $Diff = Compare-Object
                      -ReferenceObject $OldUsers `
                             -DifferenceObject $PUsers
   If ($diff)
      {$Changes += $diff |
          Select-Object -Property @{Name='Name' ;expression=
          {$_.InputObject.Name}},
                        @{Name='Group';expression=
          {$_.InputObject.Group}},
                        @{Name='Side' ;expression=
          {If ($_.SideIndicator -eq '<=') `
                                   {'REMOVED'} Else
   {'ADDED'}}} | Out-String
   }
   Else
    {
      $LCT = (Get-Childitem
                  -Path $ExportFile).LastWriteTime
      $Changes += "No Changes since previous
                  Report [$LCT]"
    }
   }
   Else # Old file does not exist
   {
      $Changes += "EXPORT FILE NOT FOUND -
                      FIRST TIME EXECUTION?"
   }
   $Report += $Changes
```

5. Display the report

```
$Report
```

6. Save results from this execution (optional!)

```
Export-Clixml -InputObject $PUsers -Path $ExportFile
```

How it works...

This recipe works by first obtaining a set of privileged users. The recipe creates a report of the users who are members of certain groups that have high privilege levels. The recipe then compares the privileged users against an earlier set of users that you previously saved. After generating the report, this recipe saves the current list of privileged users.

In *step 1*, you create an array used later in this recipe.

With *step 2*, you query the AD to discover members of the some key groups (Enterprise Admins, Domain Admins, and Schema Admins) and add them to the array created in the prior step. This array contains members of those key groups.

In *step 3*, you use the list of now-privileged users to create a simple report of members of each of the three key groups.

With *step 4*, you retrieve the set of privileged users from some prior time and compare the set with users who are currently in those groups. You add the changes in privileged users to the report. Note that with this step, you convert the returned side indicator property into something more meaningful in this context (that is, a user has been ADDED or REMOVED to/from a sensitive group since the last time you ran this report.

The first four steps in this recipe generate no output. With *step 5*, you display the report to the console. The report looks like this:

There's more...

This recipe examined membership in three key groups: Enterprise Admins, Domain Admins, and Schema Admins. There are other groups that you could include in this report. These include Hyper-V Administrators, Storage Replica Administrators, Key Admins, Enterprise Key Admins, DNSAdmins, and DHCP Administrators. Applications such as Exchange, SharePoint, and Skype for Business also define application-specific administrative groups as the basis of **Role-Based Admin Control (RBAC)** for those applications. You may wish to add membership of these potentially sensitive groups to your report.

In *step 2*, you build up an array of privileged users in each of three groups. In the recipe, you do this group by group. Should you decide to expand this recipe to include more groups, you may wish to refactor *step 2* to be more general so as to cut down on the number of lines of PowerShell needed.

9
Managing Network Shares

This chapter covers the following recipes:

- Securing your SMB file server
- Creating and securing SMB shares
- Accessing SMB shares
- Creating an iSCSI target
- Using an iSCSI target
- Creating a scale-out SMB file server
- Configuring a DFS Namespace
- Configuring DFS Replication

Introduction

Sharing data across a network has been a feature of computer operating systems from the very earliest days of networking. This chapter looks at Windows Server 2016 features that enables you to share files and folders and to use the data that you have shared.

Microsoft's LAN Manager was the company's first network offering. It enabled client computers to create, manage, and share files in a secure manner. The protocol that LAN Manager used to provide this client/server functionality was an early version of the **Server Message Block (SMB)** protocol.

SMB is a file-level storage protocol that enables you to share files and folders securely and reliably. To increase reliability, you can install a cluster and cluster the file server role. This is an active-passive solution.

A **Scale-Out File Server (SOFS)** is a clustered file service where all nodes are active. With SMB 3, an SOFS provides continuous availability to files for any file-based application. Applications can include productivity applications (holding user documents, spreadsheets, and so on.) as well as both Hyper-V and SQL Server (to hold VHD/VHDX files, VM configuration details, and SQL databases).

This chapter shows you how you can implement and leverage the features of sharing data between systems, including SMB contained in Windows Server 2016. In the recipes in this chapter, you begin with creating and using basic SMB file sharing. Then you build an iSCSI infrastructure which you leverage in building an SOFS. You finish by looking at the **Distributed File System (DFS)**. With DFS, you can provide the means to connect to multiple shared folders, held on a variety of servers through DFS Namespace. A DFS Namespace is the virtual view of the files and folders with a DFS installation.

In the first recipe, *Securing your SMB file server*, you harden the security on your SMB file server. Then, in the recipes *Creating and securing SMB shares* and *Accessing SMB shares*, you set up simple file folder sharing and access the shared files.

With the *Creating an iSCSI target* recipe, you create an iSCSI target on server SRV1, while in the *Using an iSCSI target* recipe, you make use of that shared iSCSI disk from FS1. iSCSI is a popular **Storage Area Networking (SAN)** technology, and these recipes show you how to use the Microsoft iSCSI initiator and target features.

A key feature of Hyper-V in Windows Server 2016 and beyond is the use of SMB 3.x and SOFS. You can utilize an SOFS to hold Hyper-V virtual disks and VM configuration files as well as SQL databases. When combined with shared storage, SOFS provides you with good redundancy and improved performance. You can implement a SOFS as an inexpensive alternative to the fully-fledged SAN. In *Making SMB shares highly available* recipe, you set up a file sharing scale-out cluster (using servers FS1 and FS2) and show you can a file server using shared storage provided via iSCSI.

There are two separate features under the banner of the DFS. DFS Namespaces allows you to create a logical folder structure that you distribute across multiple computers. *DFS Replication* replicates data held on DFS target folders to provide a transparent fault tolerant and load balancing DFS implementation. In the *Configuring a DFS Namespace* recipe, you set up a domain-based DFS Namespace. And then you configure and set up DFS Replication in the *Configuring DFS Replication* recipe.

There are a number of servers involved in the recipes in this chapter—each recipe describes the specific serves you use for that recipe. As with other chapters, all the servers are members of the Reskit.Org domain.

Securing your SMB file server

The first step in creating a file server is to harden it. A file server can contain sensitive information, and you should take reasonable steps to avoid some of the common attack mechanisms and adopt best security practice. Security is a good thing but be careful! By locking down your SMB file server too hard, you can lock some users out of the server. SMB 1.0 has a number of weaknesses and in general should be removed. But, if you disable SMB 1.0, you may find that older computers (for example running Windows XP) lose the ability to access shared data.

Getting ready

This recipe helps you to harden a single file server, FS1, which has locally attached storage. The server is domain joined and has the full GUI. FS1 has only the default services, plus the FileServer feature loaded. To add the FileServer feature to Windows, you could do this:

```
Install-WindowsFeature -Name FS-FileServer `
                    -IncludeManagementTools
```

How to do it...

In this recipe, you harden the FS1 server.

1. Retrieve the SMB server settings:

   ```
   Get-SmbServerConfiguration
   ```

2. Turn off SMB1:

   ```
   Set-SmbServerConfiguration `
               -EnableSMB1Protocol $false `
               -Confirm:$false
   ```

3. Turn on SMB signing and encryption:

   ```
   Set-SmbServerConfiguration `
               -RequireSecuritySignature $true `
               -EnableSecuritySignature $true `
               -EncryptData $true `
               -Confirm:$false
   ```

4. Turn off default server and workstations shares:

```
Set-SmbServerConfiguration -AutoShareServer $false `
                           -AutoShareWorkstation $false `
                           -Confirm:$false
```

5. Turn off server announcements:

```
Set-SmbServerConfiguration -ServerHidden $true `
                           -AnnounceServer $false `
                           -Confirm:$false
```

6. Restart the server service with the new configuration:

```
Restart-Service -Name lanmanserver
```

How it works...

In *step 1*, you get the SMB server's configuration information. The `Get-SmbServerConfiguration` cmdlet in Windows Server 2016 returns 43 separate configuration properties. You can change some of these to harden your SMB server or to accommodate unique aspects of your infrastructure. Some of these properties, however, are relatively obscure—if you do not know what they do, consider leaving them at their default values.

In *step 2*, you use the `Get-SMBServerConfiguration` cmdlet and disable the SMB1 protocol. As Microsoft says (see `https://blogs.technet.microsoft.com/filecab/2016/09/16/stop-using-smb1/`), *SMB1 isn't safe.*

Improvements in SMB3 include pre-authentication integrity, encryption, and better message signing. In step 3, you set your SMB server to enable and require SMB signing and to require encryption of data transfer. SMB signing ensures that the SMB components sign every SMB data packet. SMB signing is particularly useful to reduce the risk of a man-in-the-middle attack. Requiring data encryption increases the security of your organization's data as it travels between server and client computers. A benefit of using SMB encryption versus something like IPSec is that deployment is just a matter of adjusting SMB server configuration. Once you find that you can safely turn off SMB1, consider removing the SMB1 feature from Windows, using `Remove-WindowsFeature -Feature FS-SMB1`.

Windows has a set of administrative shares it creates by default. In most cases, you can disable these. You turn off these default shares with *step 4*. With *step 5*, you also turn off server announcements which reduce the visibility of your file server to hackers. It's important to note that when setting up DFS Replication, the DFS Replication cmdlets require access to these administrative shares.

To make these changes effective, in *step 6*, you restart the server service, `lanmanserver`. Note that restarting the service closes any active connections. Ensure you restart during a scheduled maintenance outage or when you are certain the server is inactive.

There's more...

In this recipe, you hardened a full installation of Windows Server 2016. To further harden these various role servers, you should consider installing Server Core. Or if you did do a full installation, then once you have completed the setup of the server, remove the GUI elements and. In effect, revert back to a server core installation.

In *step 2*, you disabled `SMB1`. `SMB1` is an older and less secure version of the SMB protocol and could represent an attack vector. The downside to disabling is that older client computers only support `SMB1` and could cease to access shared data if you disable `SMB1`. Older clients include Windows XP and Windows Server 2003. Windows Vista/Server 2008 and later versions of Windows have build in support for `SMB2`. So as long as long as you are running fully supported clients and server systems, you should be able to turn off `SMB1`.

For large organizations, you should consider using the `AuditSmb1Access` configuration setting. This setting logs access to your server via `SMB1`. To discover any older SMB clients that would be affected by disabling `SMB1` you can search the SMB event log.

In *step 3*, you configured encryption for the file server. By default, `SMB3` uses the AES-CCM algorithm. This algorithm provides both encryption and packet signing for encrypted file shares. Note that you can set up encryption on an individual share or for all shares on the server. You may choose to not force encryption on all shares, rather on just shares that hold more sensitive data. Encrypting and signing packets requires additional CPU resource to carry out the hash calculation and to encrypt the packets. Packet signing and encryption decreases SMB performance but provides additional security.

Creating and securing SMB shares

For generations, administrators have used the `net.exe` command to set up shared folders and a lot more. These continue to work but you may find the new cmdlets easier to use, particularly if you are automating large-scale SMB server deployments.

This recipe looks at creating and securing shares on a Server 2016 platform using the PowerShell `SMBServer` module.

Getting ready

For this recipe, you use the file server (`FS1`) that you hardened in the recipe *Securing your SMB server*. On this server, you share out folders on the file server. Later, in the recipe *Accessing SMB shares*, you access the shared folders. Ensure you have created the `C:\Foo` folder on `FS1`. This recipe uses a security group, `IT Management` which you create in the `Reskit.Org` AD (or use a different group).

How to do it...

1. Discover the existing shares and access rights:

```
Get-SmbShare -Name * |
    Get-SmbShareAccess |
        Sort-Object -Property Name |
            Format-Table -GroupBy Name
```

2. Share a folder:

```
New-SmbShare -Name foo -Path C:\foo
```

3. Update the share's description:

```
Set-SmbShare -Name foo `
                -Description 'Foo share for IT' `
                -Confirm:$False `
```

4. Set the folder enumeration mode:

```
Set-SMBShare -Name foo `
         -FolderEnumerationMode AccessBased `
         -Confirm:$false
```

5. Set the encryption on the foo share:

```
Set-SmbShare -Name foo -EncryptData $true `
                 -Confirm:$false
```

6. Set and view share security:

```
Revoke-SmbShareAccess -Name foo `
                      -AccountName 'Everyone' `
                      -Confirm:$false | Out-Null
Grant-SmbShareAccess -Name foo -AccessRight Read `
                     -AccountName
                        'Reskit\ADMINISTRATOR' `
                     -ConFirm:$false | Out-Null
Grant-SmbShareAccess -Name foo -AccessRight Full `
                     -AccountName 'NT
                             Authority\SYSTEM' `
                     -Confirm:$False | Out-Null
Grant-SmbShareAccess -Name foo -AccessRight Full `
                     -AccountName 'CREATOR OWNER' `
                     -Confirm:$false | Out-Null
Grant-SmbShareAccess -Name foo -AccessRight Read `
                     -AccountName 'IT Team' `
                     -Confirm:$false | Out-Null
Grant-SmbShareAccess -Name foo -AccessRight Full `
                     -AccountName 'IT Management' `
                     -Confirm:$false | Out-Null
```

7. Review share access:

```
Get-SmbShareAccess -Name foo
```

How it works...

In *step 1*, you get all the current shares on `FS1` and it also displays the users/groups that have access to each share. Having turned off administrative shares in an earlier recipe, you see just two shares. A previous recipe created one of the shares (`Backup`). The other share is the `IPC$` share which Windows uses for RPC calls. The output looks like this:

```
PS C:\> Get-SmbShare -Name * |
    Get-SmbShareAccess |
        Format-Table -GroupBy Name

   Name: Backup

Name     ScopeName AccountName AccessControlType AccessRight
----     --------- ----------- ----------------- -----------
Backup   *         Everyone    Allow             Full


   Name: IPC$

Name ScopeName AccountName                 AccessControlType AccessRight
---- --------- -----------                 ----------------- -----------
IPC$ *         BUILTIN\Administrators       Allow             Full
IPC$ *         BUILTIN\Backup Operators     Allow             Full
IPC$ *         NT AUTHORITY\INTERACTIVE     Allow             Full
```

In *step 2*, you share the `C:\foo` folder, like this:

```
PS C:\> New-SmbShare -Name foo -Path C:\foo

Name ScopeName Path    Description
---- --------- ----    -----------
foo  *         C:\foo
```

In *steps 3*, *step 4*, and *step 5*, you set properties of the new share. You give the share a description, set the folder enumeration mode and set the server to encrypt any data transferred to/from this share. There is no output from these steps.

In *step 6*, you set the security permissions on the share. You begin by removing the default read permission granted to `Everyone`. Then you grant specific permissions to the share. These steps give read access to the share to all users in the `IT Team` group, and full access to the `IT Management` group members. There was no output from these four steps.

In *step 7*, you display the permissions on the `foo` share:

```
PS C:\> Get-SmbShareAccess -Name foo

Name ScopeName AccountName             AccessControlType AccessRight
---- --------- -----------             ----------------- -----------
foo  *         RESKIT\Administrator    Allow             Read
foo  *         NT AUTHORITY\SYSTEM     Allow             Full
foo  *         CREATOR OWNER           Allow             Full
foo  *         RESKIT\IT Team          Allow             Read
foo  *         RESKIT\IT Management    Allow             Full
```

There's more...

The IPC$ share, shown in *step 1*, is also known as the null session connection. This session connection enables anonymous users to enumerate the names of domain accounts and enumerate network shares. The lanmanserver service creates this share by default although you can turn it off. The IPC$ share is also used to support named pipe connections to your server.

 For details about IPC$ share, see https://support.microsoft.com/en-us/help/3034016/ipc-share-and-null-session-behavior-in-windows. Be careful should you chose to turn off the IPC$ share—test the resultant configuration very carefully.

In *step 6*, you set the share permissions. In this recipe, you create share permissions that mirror the permissions on the underlying folder. As ever when dealing with permissions, remove anything you do not explicitly need. At the same time, test all security settings very carefully. Small changes can have a significant impact.

Accessing SMB shares

In the recipe *Creating and securing SMB shares*, you set up the shared files on the FS1 server. In this recipe, you access and use the shared folders.

Getting ready

This recipe uses two servers—on one (FS1) you previously shared a few folders. In this recipe, you also utilize those shared files from server DC1. As with all recipes in this book, feel free to change the servers and folders being shared and used. Ensure you have a C:\Foo folder on FS1 created and populated with a few test files.

This recipe also uses a file on the C:\Foo folder on FS1—Marsinstaller.exe. This executable is created using the *Creating an Azure backup* recipe in Chapter 5, *Managing Server Backup* chapter. Feel free to use a different file and update *step 8* appropriately.

How to do it...

1. Examine the SMB client's configuration:

   ```
   Get-SmbClientConfiguration
   ```

2. You will require SMB signing from the client. You must run this command from an elevated console on the client computer:

   ```
   Set-SmbClientConfiguration `
           -RequireSecuritySignature $True `
                       -Confirm:$false
   ```

3. Examine SMB client's network interface:

   ```
   Get-SmbClientNetworkInterface | Format-Table
   ```

4. Examine the shares provided by FS1:

   ```
   net view \\FS1
   ```

5. Create a drive mapping, mapping the r: to the share on server FS1:

   ```
   New-SmbMapping -LocalPath r: `
                   -RemotePath \\FS1.Reskit.Org\foo
   ```

6. View the shared folder mapping:

   ```
   Get-SmbMapping
   ```

7. View the shared folder contents:

```
Get-ChildItem -Path r:
```

8. Run a program from the shared file:

```
R:\MarsInstaller.exe
```

9. View existing connections (Note: you need to run this in an elevated console):

```
Get-SmbConnection
```

10. What files are open on FS1? If any files are open you view them by doing this on FS1:

```
Get-SmbOpenFile
```

How it works...

In *step 1*, you get and examine the SMB client's configuration. The SMB client's configuration is similar to the SMB server's properties you explored in the first step of the *Securing your SMB server* recipe. There are fewer client-side properties, as you can see here:

```
C:\> Get-SmbClientConfiguration
ConnectionCountPerRssNetworkInterface : 4
DirectoryCacheEntriesMax              : 16
DirectoryCacheEntrySizeMax            : 65536
DirectoryCacheLifetime                : 10
DormantFileLimit                      : 1023
EnableBandwidthThrottling             : True
EnableByteRangeLockingOnReadOnlyFiles : True
EnableInsecureGuestLogons             : True
EnableLargeMtu                        : True
EnableLoadBalanceScaleOut             : True
EnableMultiChannel                    : True
EnableSecuritySignature               : True
ExtendedSessionTimeout                : 1000
FileInfoCacheEntriesMax               : 64
FileInfoCacheLifetime                 : 10
FileNotFoundCacheEntriesMax           : 128
FileNotFoundCacheLifetime             : 5
KeepConn                              : 600
MaxCmds                               : 50
MaximumConnectionCountPerServer       : 32
OplocksDisabled                       : False
RequireSecuritySignature              : False
SessionTimeout                        : 60
UseOpportunisticLocking               : True
WindowSizeThreshold                   : 8
```

With *step 2*, you modify the SMB client to require SMB signing. There is no output from this step. In *step 3*, you examine the network interfaces your client system uses to carry SMB traffic:

```
PS R:\> Get-SmbClientNetworkInterface |
            Format-Table -auto -wrap

If Idx RSS ? RDMA ? Speed     IpAddresses                    Friendly Name
----- ----- ------ -----     -----------                    -------------
2      True  False  10 Gbps   {fe80::458e:834a:e0a:479e,    10.10.10.150} Ethernet
3      False False  100 Kbps  {fe80::5efe:10.10.10.150}     isatap.{495B370B-020D-43D2-BEAF-A11390D3C902}
```

In *step 4*, you examine from the client the shares provided by the file server FS1. You use the net view command. There does not appear to be any cmdlet that can do this in the same way as the net command. The output from using the net command looks like this:

```
PS C:\> net view \\fs1

Shared resources at \\fs1

Share name  Type  Used as  Comment

-------------------------------------------------------------------------
Backup      Disk           Used in Recipe 5-7 to hold backup of SRV1
foo         Disk           Foo share for IT
The command completed successfully.
```

In *step 5*, you use New-SmbMapping to map a local drive (r:) to the \\fs1\.reskit.org\foo share, which looks like this:

```
PS C:> New-SmbMapping -LocalPath r: -RemotePath \\fs1.reskit.org\foo

Status Local Path Remote Path
------ ---------- -----------
OK     r:         \\fs1.reskit.org\foo
```

In *step 6*, you view the current drive mappings on the client computer, which looks like this:

```
PS C:\> Get-SmbMapping

Status Local Path Remote Path
------ ---------- -----------
OK     R:         \\fs1.reskit.org\foo
```

After creating the drive mapping, you can use all the normal cmdlets to access data on the r: drive. In *step 7*, you view the contents of r:.

```
PS C:\> Get-ChildItem -Path r:

    Directory: R:\

Mode                LastWriteTime         Length Name
----                -------------         ------ ----
-a----        09/01/2017     20:48       39075088 MarsInstaller.exe
-a----        09/01/2017     21:15           4458 VaultCredentials1
-a----        08/01/2017     22:56           4458 VaultCredentials2
-a----        09/01/2017     11:38             26 recovery.txt
-a----        05/02/2017     17:19             12 sss.txt
```

In *step 8*, you run a program on the shared drive. The details of this program (the *Mars* installer) are not the point here. In running a program, you have used a file.

In *step 9*, you then see the results of running the program. On the file server (FS1) you use the Get-SmbConnection cmdlet to see the files open on the server, which looks like this:

```
PS C:\> Get-SmbConnection

ServerName       ShareName UserName          Credential            Dialect NumOpens
----------       --------- --------          ----------            ------- --------
fs1.reskit.org   foo       RESKIT\JerryG     RESKIT.ORG\JerryG     3.1.1   0
fs1.reskit.org   foo       RESKIT\tf1        RESKIT.ORG\tf1        3.1.1   1
```

Knowing who connects to your file server can be useful, but even more useful is knowing what files they are accessing. In *step 10* you use the Get-SmbOpenFile cmdlet to show the open files:

```
PS C:\Users\Administrator> Get-SmbOpenFile

FileId        SessionId     Path     ShareRelativePath ClientComputerName        ClientUserName
------        ---------     ----     ----------------- ------------------        --------------
223338299757  223338299481  C:\foo\                    [fe80::458e:834a:e0a:479e] RESKIT\tf1
223338299765  223338299473  C:\foo\                    10.10.10.150               RESKIT\JerryG
```

There's more...

In *step 4*, you made use of net.exe to run the net view command. The cmdlet Get-SMBShare does not have a -ComputerName parameter that might enable you to retrieve shared folders from a remote computer. You could create a CIM session to fs1, and use Get-SMBShare against the CIM session to return the remote shares. However, doing that requires either the user to have administrative rights to the file server, or setting up a less-privileged end point on fs1 that non-privileged users can access. Using net.exe is another great example of where the old commands still have great value (and they perform a bit quicker) especially at the command line.

In *step 10*, you used Get-SmbOpenFile to see the files open on a file server. As you can see above, details of the open file and the computer making the connection, are not clearly shown. Instead of a file name, you get a FileId which is not clearly related to the actual file.

Creating an iSCSI target

iSCSI is an industry standard protocol which implements block storage over a TCP/IP network. Windows sees an iSCSI **Logical Unit Number** (**LUN**) as a locally attached disk. You can manage the disk just like locally attached storage.

Windows Server 2016 includes both iSCSI target (server) and iSCSI initiator (client) features. You set up an iSCSI target on a server and then use an iSCSI initiator on a client system to access the iSCSI target. You can use both Microsoft and 3rd party initiators and targets, although if you mix and match you need to test very carefully that the combination works in your environment.

With iSCSI, a target is a single storage unit (effectively a disk) that the client computer accesses using the iSCSI protocol. An iSCSI target server hosts one or more targets where each iSCSI target is equivalent to a LUN on a *Fiber Channel* SAN. The iSCSI initiator is a built-in component of Windows Server 2016 (and Windows 10). The iSCSI target feature is one you install optionally on Windows Server 2016.

You could use iSCSI in a cluster of Hyper-V servers for a **Cluster Shared Volume** (**CSV**). The servers in the cluster can use the iSCSI initiator to access an iSCSI target providing shared storage. For a SOFS, this share information can hold the virtual hard drives and configuration information for Hyper-V virtual machines as well as SQL Server databases. The shared iSCSI target is shared between nodes in a failover cluster enabling the VMs to be highly available.

Getting ready

In this recipe, you install the iSCSI target feature and set up a target on the server SRV1. SRV1 also requires an additional disk that you use to hold the target, the I: on the SRV1 server. A recipe in Chapter 4, *Managing Printers* made use of a second drive on SRV1 for backup purposes—the I: drive is a new and separate drive for this recipe.

How to do it...

1. Install the iSCSI target feature:

   ```
   Install-WindowsFeature FS-iSCSITarget-Server
   ```

2. Explore iSCSI target server settings:

   ```
   Get-IscsiTargetServerSetting
   ```

3. Create an iSCSI disk (that is a LUN):

   ```
   $LunPath = 'I:\SalesData.Vhdx'
   $LunName = 'SalesTarget'
   New-IscsiVirtualDisk -Path $LunPath `
                        -Description 'LUN For Sales' `
                        -SizeBytes 1.1GB
   ```

4. Create the iSCSI target:

   ```
   New-IscsiServerTarget -TargetName $LunName `
                         -InitiatorIds `
                             DNSNAME:FS1.Reskit.Org
   ```

5. Create iSCSI disk target mapping:

   ```
   Add-IscsiVirtualDiskTargetMapping `
                         -TargetName $LunName `
                         -Path $LunPath
   ```

How it works...

With *step 1,* you install the iSCSI target feature using `Install-WindowsFeature`, like this:

```
PS C:\> Install-WIndowsFeature FS-iSCSITarget-Server

Success Restart Needed Exit Code    Feature Result
------- -------------- ---------    --------------
True    No             Success      {iSCSI Target Server}
```

In *step 2,* you use the `Get-IscsiTargetServerSetting` cmdlet to explore the properties of the iSCSI target server:

```
PS C:\Windows\system32> Get-IscsiTargetServerSetting

ComputerName            : SRV1.Reskit.Org
IsClustered             : False
Version                 : 10.0
DisableRemoteManagement : False
```

In *step 3,* you create the VHDX that is to serve to hold a LUN as follows:

```
PS C:> New-IscsiVirtualDisk -Path  I:\Sales\SalesData.vhdx `
                            -Description 'LUN For Sales' `
                            -SizeBytes 1GB

ClusterGroupName    :
ComputerName        : SRV1.Reskit.Org
Description         : LUN For Sales
DiskType            : Dynamic
HostVolumeId        : {16A46190-ECA9-11E6-836B-00155D017120}
LocalMountDeviceId  :
OriginalPath        :
ParentPath          :
Path                : I:\Sales\SalesData.vhdx
SerialNumber        : 0F1AD0DD-B095-4616-83E2-3F65A220497F
Size                : 1073741824
SnapshotIds         :
Status              : NotConnected
VirtualDiskIndex    : 54770768
```

In *step 4*, you create the iSCSI target. In this step, you define an iSCSI target on the computer and specify which initiators can connect to this iSCSI target. In this case, you specified the initiator using a DNS name for the initiator and the computer name of the allowed initiator(s). In this case, you specify just one initiator (`fs1.reskit.org`). Creating the target looks like this:

```
PS C:\> New-IscsiServerTarget -TargetName $LunName `
                              -InitiatorIds DNSNAME:fs1.reskit.org

ChapUserName                  :
ClusterGroupName              :
ComputerName                  : SRV1.Reskit.Org
Description                   :
EnableChap                    : False
EnableReverseChap             : False
EnforceIdleTimeoutDetection   : True
FirstBurstLength              : 65536
IdleDuration                  : 00:00:00
InitiatorIds                  : {DnsName:fs1.reskit.org}
LastLogin                     :
LunMappings                   : {}
MaxBurstLength                : 262144
MaxReceiveDataSegmentLength   : 65536
ReceiveBufferCount            : 10
ReverseChapUserName           :
Sessions                      : {}
Status                        : NotConnected
TargetIqn                     : iqn.1991-05.com.microsoft:srv1-salestarget-target
TargetName                    : SalesTarget
```

Now that you have everything set up, you need to add the iSCSI virtual disk to the iSCSI target. You perform this in *step 5*, but the step generates no output. Once you have completed these steps, you have created an iSCSI target, with a LUN in place for use in an iSCSI initiator.

There's more...

If you are not familiar with iSCSI and iSCSI targets, see the TechNet article at `https://technet.microsoft.com/en-us/library/hh848272(v=ws.11).aspx` which presents an overview of iSCSI targets.

In *step 3*, you create the new LUN, using `New-IscsiVirtualDisk`. When using this command, you must specify a VHDX file extension. Windows Server 2016 does not support VHD files for new iSCSI targets. You can, however, add an old VHD file as an iSCSI virtual disk (you just can't create a new one).

When you create the virtual disk, it is uninitialized with no volumes or formatting. You use the initiator to mount and manage the drive as if it were local.

You can also increase security by using **Challenge Handshake Authentication Protocol (CHAP)** authentication. You can specify the CHAP username and password on both the initiator and the target to authenticate the connection to an iSCSI target. If the security of iSCSI traffic is an issue, you could consider securing iSCSI traffic using IPSec.

Using an iSCSI target

In the previous recipe, you created an iSCSI target. In this recipe, you will implement an iSCSI initiator that enables you to use the iSCSI target across the iSCSI network. You use the iSCSI feature included in Windows Server 2016 (and Windows 10) to access the target. Note that, by default, the iSCSI initiator does not start automatically. To use an initiator on an iSCSI client computer, you have to start the service (`msiscsi`) and enable the service to start on reboot automatically.

Getting ready

This recipe, which you run on server `FS1`, assumes you have created an iSCSI target as shown on the *Creating an iSCSI target* recipe.

How to do it...

1. Adjust the startup type and start the service:

```
Set-Service -Ma,e msiscsi -StartupType 'Automatic'
Start-Service =Name msiscsi
```

2. Add the iSCSI portal:

```
New-IscsiTargetPortal `
            -TargetPortalAddress Srv1.Reskit.Org `
            -TargetPortalPortNumber 3260
```

3. Find the `SalesTarget` iSCSI target on the portal:

```
$Target = Get-IscsiTarget |
    Where-Object NodeAddress -Match 'SalesTarget'
$Target
```

4. Connect to the target:

```
Connect-IscsiTarget -TargetPortalAddress Srv1 `
                    -NodeAddress $Target.NodeAddress
```

5. Set up the disk on the target and create a new volume with a drive letter:

```
$ISD = Get-Disk | Where-Object BusType -eq 'iscsi'
Set-Disk -InputObject $isd -IsOffline $False
Set-Disk -InputObject $isd -Isreadonly $False
$ISD | New-Volume -FriendlyName SalesData `
                  -FileSystem ReFS `
                  -DriveLetter S
```

6. Use the newly created `S:` drive, as follows:

```
Set-Location -Path S:
New-Item -Path S:\ -Name SalesData `
                   -ItemType Directory
'Testing 1-2-3' |
     Out-File -FilePath S:\SalesData\Test.txt
 Get-ChildItem -Path S:\SalesData
```

How it works...

The Microsoft iSCSI initiator is a service in Windows that Windows installs by default, but does not start automatically. In *step 1*, you set the iSCSI service, `msiscsi`, to automatically start on reboot. Then you start the service. This step provides some minimal output:

```
PS C:\> Set-Service msiscsi -StartupType 'Automatic'

PS C:\> Start-Service msiscsi
WARNING: Waiting for service 'Microsoft iSCSI Initiator Service (msiscsi)' to start...
```

In *step 2*, you tell Windows where to find the iSCSI portal. The iSCSI portal is a server address and a port number (the default port is 3260) on which the iSCSI initiator can find iSCSI targets. The output from New-IscsiTargetPortal shows details of the portal, like this:

```
PS C:\> New-IscsiTargetPortal -TargetPortalAddress Srv1.reskit.org `
                    -TargetPortalPortNumber 3260


InitiatorInstanceName  :
InitiatorPortalAddress :
IsDataDigest           : False
IsHeaderDigest         : False
TargetPortalAddress    : Srv1.reskit.org
TargetPortalPortNumber : 3260
PSComputerName         :
```

In *step 3*, you get a specific target by piping the output of Get-IscsiTarget to the Where-Object cmdlet to select the SalesTarget LUN that you created in the *Creating iSCSI target* recipe. You store the target in the $SalesTarget variable and then display it. The output from displaying the $SalesTarget variable looks like this:

```
PS C:\> $Target   = Get-IscsiTarget |
            Where-Object NodeAddress -Match 'SalesTarget'
PS C:\> $Target

IsConnected NodeAddress                                        PSComputerName
----------- -----------                                        --------------
      False iqn.1991-05.com.microsoft:srv1-salestarget-target
```

To connect the iSCSI target, in *step 4*, you use the Connect-IscsiTarget cmdlet, like this:

```
PS C:\> Connect-IscsiTarget -TargetPortalAddress Srv1 `
                    -NodeAddress $Target.NodeAddress

AuthenticationType     : NONE
InitiatorInstanceName  : ROOT\ISCSIPRT\0000_0
InitiatorNodeAddress   : iqn.1991-05.com.microsoft:fs1.reskit.org
InitiatorPortalAddress : 0.0.0.0
InitiatorSideIdentifier : 400001370000
IsConnected            : True
IsDataDigest           : False
IsDiscovered           : False
IsHeaderDigest         : False
IsPersistent           : True
NumberOfConnections    : 1
SessionIdentifier      : ffffda83afc10010-4000013700000028
TargetNodeAddress      : iqn.1991-05.com.microsoft:srv1-salestarget-target
TargetSideIdentifier   : 0100
PSComputerName         :
```

Now that you have connected to the iSCSI target, you have a new disk in your system. The disk is the LUN you created earlier. When you created the LUN you did not initialize it or format it. In step 5, you set up the disk for use. You set the disk to be online and make it read/write. Then you create a new volume on this disk, format it using the ReFS file system and give it the s: drive letter. Setting up the disk looks like this:

```
PS C:\> $ISD = Get-Disk | Where-Object BusType -eq 'iscsi'
PS C:\> Set-Disk -InputObject $isd -IsOffline $False
PS C:\> Set-Disk -InputObject $isd -Isreadonly $False
PS C:\> $ISD | New-Volume -FriendlyName SalesData -FileSystem ReFS -DriveLetter s

DriveLetter FileSystemLabel FileSystem DriveType HealthStatus OperationalStatus SizeRemaining     Size
----------- --------------- ---------- --------- ------------ ----------------- -------------     ----
S           SalesData       ReFS       Fixed     Healthy      OK                396.13 MB 1.06 GB
```

Now that you have connected to the disk, brought it online, and formatted it, the drive is ready for use. You can now perform all of the normal actions you might on a disk. In *step 6*, you set the location of the file system provider to your new s: drive, created a folder, and then created a file in that folder, as follows:

```
PS C:\> Set-Location -Path S:
PS S:\> New-Item -Path S:\  -Name SalesData -ItemType Directory

    Directory: s:\

Mode                LastWriteTime         Length Name
----                -------------         ------ ----
d-----        07/02/2017     22:32               SalesData

PS s:\> 'Testing 1-2-3' | Out-File -FilePath s:\SalesData\Test.txt
PS s:\> Get-ChildItem s:\SalesData

    Directory: s:\SalesData

Mode                LastWriteTime         Length Name
----                -------------         ------ ----
-a----        07/02/2017     22:33             32 Test.txt
```

There's more...

This recipe enabled you to use the Microsoft iSCSI initiator to connect to a Microsoft iSCSI-provided target. These built-in features work and are fine for simple use.

The iSCSI initiator and the iSCSI target features with Windows Server 2016 have seen little development or improvement since they were first released over a decade ago. You may find independent third party iSCSI vendors that are more appropriate depending on your requirements.

Creating a scale-out SMB file server

Windows clustering enables you to create a failover file server. When you cluster the file server role, one node in the cluster offers the SMB server features to the network based on shared storage. If that node fails, the cluster can fail over the file sharing service to another node and still access the shared storage. But the fail over can take some time and has some limitations.

An SOFS enables all nodes in the cluster to be active simultaneously. This provides for extra performance as well as improved fault tolerance. With an SOFS, you can hold Hyper-V virtual machine hard drives/configuration information and SQL databases. This recipe shows you how to set up an SOFS.

Getting ready

For this recipe, you need a two node cluster. The nodes are FS1 and FS2 each of which has already been set up with iSCSI targets that point to shared disks.

How to do it...

1. Add the `Failover-Clustering` feature to both servers:

```
Install-WindowsFeature -Name Failover-Clustering `
                       -ComputerName FS1 `
                       -IncludeManagementTools
Install-WindowsFeature -Name Failover-Clustering `
                       -ComputerName FS2 `
                       -IncludeManagementTools
```

2. Test the cluster nodes (run this on FS1):

```
$CheckOutput = 'c:\foo\clustercheck'
Test-Cluster -Node FS1, FS2 -ReportName "$CheckOutput.htm"
```

3. View cluster test results:

```
Invoke-Item -Path "$Checkoutput.htm"
```

4. Create the failover cluster:

```
New-Cluster -Name FS `
            -Node 'fs1.reskit.org',
                  'fs2.reskit.org' `
            -StaticAddress 10.10.10.100
```

5. Add the ClusterScaleOutFileServerRole:

```
Add-ClusterScaleOutFileServerRole -Name SalesFS
```

6. Add the target to the CSV:

```
Get-ClusterResource |
    Where-Object OwnerGroup -Match 'Available' |
        Add-ClusterSharedVolume -Name VM
```

7. Create a share:

```
$SdFolder = 'S:\SalesData'
New-SMBShare -Name SalesData `
             -Path $SdFolder `
             -Description 'SalesData'
```

8. Create a folder and add a continuously available share:

```
$HvFolder = 'C:\ClusterStorage\Volume1\HVData'
New-Item -Path $HvFolder -ItemType Directory |
    Out-Null
New-SMBShare -Name SalesHV -Path $HvFolder `
             -Description 'Sales HV (CA)' `
             -FullAccess 'Reskit\IT Team' `
             -ContinuouslyAvailable:$true
```

9. View the shared folders:

```
Get-SmbShare
```

How it works...

In *step 1*, you add the `Failover-Clustering` role to both `FS1` and `FS2`, which looks like this:

```
PS C:\> Install-WindowsFeature -Name Failover-Clustering `
                               -ComputerName FS1 `
                               -IncludeManagementTools

Success Restart Needed Exit Code     Feature Result
------- -------------- ---------     --------------
True    No             Success       {Failover Clustering}

PS C:\> Install-WindowsFeature -Name Failover-Clustering `
                               -ComputerName FS2 `
                               -IncludeManagementTools

Success Restart Needed Exit Code     Feature Result
------- -------------- ---------     --------------
True    No             Success       {Failover Clustering}
```

In *step 2*, you perform the cluster validation tests. These tests check to ensure that all the resources needed for the cluster are present and working properly. You should run the `Test-Cluster` cmdlet before creating a cluster and following any and all maintenance activities. If for any reason the cluster test fails, you need to check out why and correct the issue before proceeding. The output from the command looks like this:

```
PS C:\> $CheckOutput = 'c:\foo\clustercheck'
PS C:\> Test-Cluster  -Node FS1, FS2  -ReportName $CheckOutput

Mode                LastWriteTime         Length Name
----                -------------         ------ ----
-a----        08/02/2017     20:00        657770 clustercheck.htm
```

As you can see, the `Test-Cluster` does not provide much information returned to the console, aside from the pointer to the report file—in this case, `C:\Foo\ClusterCheck.Htm`.

In *step 3*, you view the output file generated by *step 2*. This output file is large, contains the results of the extensive tests performed by the Test-Cluster cmdlet, and looks like this:

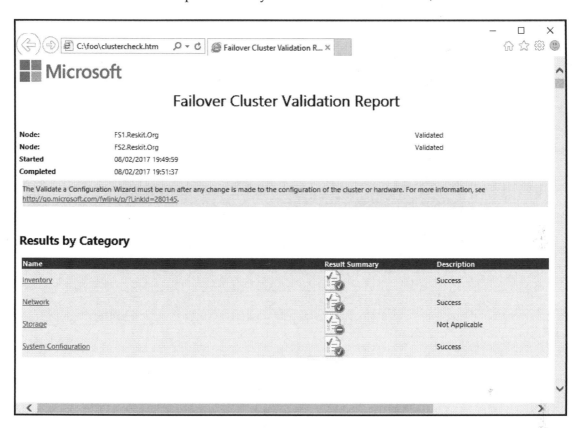

In *step 4*, you create the cluster using the New-Cluster cmdlet. The output is minimal and looks like this:

```
PS C:\ New-Cluster -Name FS `
                   -Node 'fs1.reskit.org', 'fs2.reskit.org' `
                   -StaticAddress 10.10.10.100

Name
----
FS
```

Once *step 5* has completed successfully, your cluster is up and running. In *step 5*, you add the `ClusterScaleOutFileServerRole` to the cluster. The output, also relatively minimal, looks like this:

```
PS C:\> Add-ClusterScaleOutFileServerRole -Name SalesFS

Name      OwnerNode State
----      --------- -----
SalesFS   FS1       Oneline
```

With the SOFS role added, you need to add the storage you wish to use for fail-over shares to a `ClusterSharedVolume`, which looks like this:

```
PS C:\> Get-ClusterResource |
            Where-Object OwnerGroup -Match 'Available'
            Add-ClusterSharedVolume -Name VM

Name            State  Node
----            -----  ----
Cluster Disk 1  Online FS1
```

With the cluster installed and the storage added to the CSV, you can now add shares to the file sharing cluster. First, in *step 7*, you add a normal active-passive share to the cluster, like this:

```
PS C:\> $SdFolder = 'S:\SalesData'
PS C:\> New-SMBShare -Name SalesData
                     -Path $SdFolder
                     -Description 'SalesData'

Name      ScopeName Path          Description
----      --------- ----          -----------
SalesData FS        S:\SalesData  SalesData
```

Now that you have the SOFS created, you create, in *step 8*, an active-active continuously available file share. Adding a continuously-available share looks like this:

```
PS C:\> $HvFolder = 'C:\ClusterStorage\Volume1\HVData'
PS C:\> New-Item -Path $HvFolder -ItemType Directory |
                 OUT-NULL
PS C:\> New-SMBShare -Name SalesHV -Path $HvFolder
                     -Description 'Sales HV (CA)'
                     -FullAccess 'Reskit\IT Team'
                     -ContinuouslyAvailable:$true

Name    ScopeName Path                             Description
----    --------- ----                             -----------
SalesHV SALESFS   C:\ClusterStorage\Volume1\HVDATA Sales HV (CA)
```

Now that you have finished these steps, with *step 9*, you view the shares created on the cluster, which looks like this:

```
PS C:\> Get-SmbShare

Name        ScopeName Path                              Description
----        --------- ----                              -----------
Backup      *         C:\Recipe 5-7 Restore applications Used in Recipe 5-7 to hold backup of SRV1
foo         *         C:\foo                            Foo share for IT
IPC$        *                                           Remote IPC
SalesData   FS        S:\SalesData                      SalesData
SalesHV     SALESFS   C:\ClusterStorage\Volume1\HVDATA  Sales HV (CA)
```

There's more...

In *step 1*, you added the clustering feature to both FS1 and FS2 independently. The `Install-WindowsFeature` cmdlet does not let you add the same feature (that is the clustering role) to multiple servers in a single command. To speed things up, you could run the installation on each server as background jobs that run in parallel (or use a workflow).

The preceding output shown for *step 3* is truncated but illustrates that the cluster validation has succeeded. At this point, the validation tests confirm that the elements required for the cluster are all present and correct. These tests are important in two ways. The test results verify that you have everything you need in place to create the cluster. Also, if the test is successful, then the cluster is supported by Microsoft. For large organizations running mission critical workloads, support can be critical.

Configuring a DFS Namespace

The **Distributed File System (DFS)** is a set of services in Windows that enables you to create a structured replicated file store on two or more servers within your organization. Microsoft first released DFS as an add-on to Windows NT 4.0. DFS has been improved significantly since then.

In Windows Server 2016, DFS has two separate components. The first is **DFS Namespace (DFSN)**. DFSN enables you to create a single contiguous namespace that refers to shares held on multiple servers. The second component, **DFS Replication (DFSR)**, performs replication of data between DFS nodes in the DFS Namespace.

With DFS Namespaces, you can make use of shared folders stored on computers throughout the organization to create a single logically structured namespace. This namespace appears to the user as a continuous and well-organized set of folders and subfolders even though the actual shared data may be in a variety of independently named shares on one or more computers in the organization.

Before you build your DFS Namespace, you need to create the shared folders that you wish to add to your DFS Namespace. The namespace design then determines which folder goes where within the namespace hierarchy. You also define the names of the folders in the namespace, and these can be different to the underlying file shares. When you view the DFS Namespace, the folders appear to reside on a single share that has multiple folders and subfolders. You navigate through the DFS Namespace and avoid needing to know the names of the actual servers and shares that physically hold your data.

DFSR replicates folders in the DFS Namespace between servers in your organization. DFSR utilizes the **Remote Differential Compression (RDC)** compression protocol to perform the replication. RDC just replicates blocks of data. Replication allows you to create multiple copies of your shared data and ensures that the changes you make to that data are quickly and efficiently replicated. This can be useful both for load balancing and for failover. Additionally, DFS is site aware, thus when you access folders in the DFS Namespaces, DFS attempts to find shared files within a site.

It is important to note that you can use DFSN without using DFSR. If you need to replicate data, there are a variety of tools available that may be more appropriate for your needs. For more information on file synchronization tools, look at `https://en.wikipedia.org/wiki/Comparison_of_file_synchronization_software`.

DFSN and DFSR each has a supporting PowerShell module. The `DFSN` module helps you to manage the DFS Namespaces in your DFS implementation. You manage DFSR replication using the `DFSR` module. With Server 2016, there are 23 cmdlets in the `DFSN` module and 45 cmdlets in the `DFSR` module.

In this recipe, you set up and configure a domain-based DFS Namespace on the servers `SRV1` and `SRV2`. You create additional DFS Namespace targets on other computers, add these to the DFS Namespace. In a later recipe, *Configuring DFS Replication*, you set up replication using DFSR.

Getting ready

This recipe assumes you have two servers: `SRV1` and `SRV2` with each server having a volume (`E:`) that you use as the location for the `DFS Root` If this drive does not exist, then create it on these two servers. Additionally, the recipe uses several folders shared on multiple computers as targets in our DFS Namespace.

In this recipe, you create a DFS Namespace, as set out in this table:

Namespace folder	Target SMB share
`\\ShareData` (DFS Namespace `Root`)	`\\Srv1\ShareData` and `\\Srv2\ShareData`
`\IT`	n/a
`\IT\ITData`	`\\fs1\ITData\`, `\\Fs2\ITData`
`\IT\ITManagement`	`\\Dc1\ITData, Dc2\ITData`
`\Sales`	n/a
`\SalesData`	`\\fs1\Sales, \\Fs2\Sales`
`\SalesHistorical`	`\\fs1\SalesHistorical` and `\\Fs2\SalesHistorical`

This recipe assumes you have not yet created the target folders involved in the DFS Namespace and therefore creates explicitly the folders and the SMB shares required.

How to do it...

1. Install DFS Namespace, DFS Replication, and the related management tools:

```
Install-WindowsFeature -Name FS-DFS-Namespace `
                       -IncludeManagementTools `
                       -ComputerName Srv1
Install-WindowsFeature -Name FS-DFS-Namespace `
                       -IncludeManagementTools `
                       -ComputerName Srv2
```

2. View the DFSN module and the DFSN cmdlets:

```
Get-Module -Name DFSN -ListAvailable
Get-Command -Module DFSN | Measure-Object
```

3. Create folders and shares for DFS Root:

```
$Sb = {
New-Item -Path E:\ShareData -ItemType Directory `
                            -Force | Out-Null
New-SmbShare -Name ShareData -Path E:\ShareData `
                            -FullAccess Everyone
}
Invoke-Command -ComputerName Srv1, Srv2 `
                -ScriptBlock $Sb
```

4. Create DFS Namespace Root pointing to ShareData:

```
New-DfsnRoot -Path \\Reskit.Org\ShareData `
             -TargetPath \\Srv1\ShareData `
             -Type DomainV2 `
             -Description 'Reskit Shared Data
                            DFS Root'
```

5. Add a second target and view results:

```
New-DfsnRootTarget -Path \\Reskit.Org\ShareData `
                   -TargetPath \\Srv2\ShareData |
                                            Out-Null
Get-DfsnRootTarget -Path \\Reskit.Org\ShareData
```

6. Create additional shares and populate:

```
# FS1 folders/shares
$Sb = {
New-Item -Path C:\IT2 -ItemType Directory | Out-Null
New-SmbShare -Name 'ITData' -Path C:\IT2 `
                            -FullAccess Everyone
New-Item -Path C:\Sales -ItemType Directory |
                                            Out-Null
New-SmbShare -Name 'Sales' -Path C:\Sales `
                            -FullAccess Everyone
New-Item -Path C:\OldSales -ItemType Directory |
                                            Out-Null
New-SmbShare -Name 'SalesHistorical' `
             -Path 'C:\OldSales'
# Add content to files in root
```

```
'Root' | Out-File -FilePath c:\it2\root.txt
'Root' | Out-File -FilePath c:\Sales\root.txt
'Root' | Out-File -FilePath c:\oldsales\root.txt
}
Invoke-Command -ScriptBlock $Sb -Computer FS1
# FS2 folders/shares
$Sb = {
New-Item -Path C:\IT2 -ItemType Directory | Out-Null
New-SmbShare -Name 'ITData' -Path C:\IT2 `
                              -FullAccess Everyone
New-Item -Path C:\Sales -ItemType Directory |
                                        Out-Null
New-SmbShare -Name 'Sales' -Path C:\Sales `
                         -FullAccess Everyone
New-Item -Path C:\OldSales -ItemType Directory |
                                        Out-Null
New-SmbShare -Name 'SalesHistorical' -Path C:\IT2
'Root' | Out-File -FilePath c:\it2\root.txt
'Root' | Out-File -FilePath c:\Sales\root.txt
'Root' | Out-File -FilePath c:\oldsales\root.txt
}
Invoke-Command -ScriptBlock $sb -Computer FS2
# DC1 folders/shares
$SB = {
New-Item -Path C:\ITM -ItemType Directory | Out-Null
New-SmbShare -Name 'ITM' -Path C:\ITM `
                         -FullAccess Everyone
'Root' | Out-File -Filepath c:\itm\root.txt
}
Invoke-Command -ScriptBlock $sb -Computer DC1
# DC2 folders/shares
$Sb = {
New-Item C:\ITM -ItemType Directory | Out-Null
New-SmbShare -Name 'ITM' -Path C:\ITM `
                         -FullAccess Everyone
'Root' | Out-File -FilePath c:\itm\root.txt
}
Invoke-Command -ScriptBlock $Sb -Computer DC2
```

7. Create DFS Namespace and set DFS targets:

```
New-DfsnFolder -Path '\\Reskit\ShareData\IT\ITData' `
               -TargetPath '\\fs1\ITData' `
               -EnableTargetFailback $true `
               -Description 'IT Data'
New-DfsnFolderTarget `
               -Path '\\Reskit\ShareData\IT\ITData' `
               -TargetPath '\\fs2\ITData'
New-DfsnFolder `
       -Path '\\Reskit\ShareData\IT\ITManagement' `
       -TargetPath '\\DC1\itm' `
       -EnableTargetFailback $true `
       -Description 'IT Management Data'
New-DfsnFolderTarget `
       -Path '\\Reskit\ShareData\IT\ITManagement' `
       -TargetPath '\\DC2\itm'
New-DfsnFolder `
       -Path '\\Reskit\ShareData\Sales\SalesData' `
       -TargetPath '\\fs1\sales' `
       -EnableTargetFailback $true `
       -Description 'SalesData'
New-DfsnFolderTarget `
       -Path '\\Reskit\ShareData\Sales\SalesData' `
       -TargetPath '\\fs2\sales'
New-DfsnFolder `
       -Path '\\Reskit\ShareData\Sales\SalesHistoric' `
       -TargetPath '\\fs1\SalesHistorical' `
       -EnableTargetFailback $true `
       -Description 'Sales Group Historical Data'
New-DfsnFolderTarget `
       -Path '\\Reskit\ShareData\Sales\SalesHistoric' `
       -TargetPath '\\fs2\SalesHistorical'
```

How it works...

Before you can use DFS to hold a DFS Namespace, you need to install the DFS Namespace feature. In *step 1*, you create a script block with the `Install-WindowsFeature` cmdlet, which looks like this:

```
Add-WindowsFeature -Name FS-DFS-Namespace `
                   -IncludeManagementTools `
                   -ComputerName 'Srv1'


Success Restart Needed Exit Code      Feature Result
------- -------------- ---------      --------------
True    No             Success        {{DFS Namespaces}

Add-WindowsFeature -NameFS-DFS-Namespace `
                   -IncludeManagementTools `
                   -ComputerName 'Srv1'


Success Restart Needed Exit Code      Feature Result
------- -------------- ---------      --------------
True    No             Success        {{DFS Namespaces}
```

In *step 2*, you look at the `DFSN` module and determine how many cmdlets the `DFSN` module contains, as follows:

```
PS C:\> Get-Module DFSN -ListAvailable

    Directory: C:\Windows\system32\WindowsPowerShell\v1.0\Modules

ModuleType Version   Name                 ExportedCommands
---------- -------   ----                 ----------------
Manifest   1.0       DFSN                 {Get-DfsnRoot, Remove-DfsnRoot, Set-DfsnRoot, New-DfsnRoot...}


PS C:\> Get-Command -Module DFSN | Measure-Object

Count    : 23
Average  :
Sum      :
Maximum  :
Minimum  :
Property :
```

In *step 3*, you create the folders and SMB shares on `Srv1` and `Srv2` that serve as the `DFS Root` as follows:

```
PS C:\> $Sb = {
  New-Item     -Path E:\ShareData -ItemType Directory -Force | Out-Null
  New-SmbShare -Name ShareData -Path E:\ShareData -FullAccess Everyone
}
Invoke-Command -ComputerName Srv1, Srv2 -ScriptBlock $Sb

Name         ScopeName Path         Description
----         --------- ----         -----------
ShareData    *         E:\ShareData
ShareData    *         E:\ShareData
```

With the `Root` shares created, in *step 4*, you create a new `DfsnRoot` folder on server `Srv1`:

```
PS C:\foo> New-DfsnRoot  -Path \\Reskit.Org\ShareData `
                         -TargetPath \\Srv1\ShareData `
                         -Type DomainV2 `
                         -Description 'Reskit Shared Data DFS Root'

Path                      Type       Properties TimeToLiveSec State  Description
----                      ----       ---------- ------------- -----  -----------
\\Reskit.Org\ShareData Domain V2                300           Online Reskit Shared Data DFS Root
```

In *step 5*, you create a second `DfsnRoot` folder, this time on `SRV2`. Then (despite the error message) you view the `DfsnRoot` targets:

```
#    STEP 5
PS C:\foo> New-DfsnRootTarget  -Path \\Reskit.Org\ShareData `
                               -TargetPath \\Srv2\ShareData
New-DfsnRootTarget : The requested object could not be found.
At line:1 char:1
+ New-DfsnRootTarget  -Path \\Reskit.Org\ShareData `
+ ─────────────────────────────────────────────────────
    + CategoryInfo       : ObjectNotFound: (MSFT_DfsNamespaceRootTarget:ROOT\Microsoft\...spaceRootTarget) [New-DfsnRootTarget], CimException
    + FullyQualifiedErrorId : MI RESULT 6,New-DfsnRootTarget

PS C:\foo> Get-DfsnRootTarget -Path \\Reskit.Org\ShareData

Path                    TargetPath                      State  ReferralPriorityClass ReferralPriorityRank
----                    ----------                      -----  --------------------- --------------------
\\Reskit.Org\ShareData \\Srv1.Reskit.Org\ShareData Online sitecost-normal       0
\\Reskit.Org\ShareData \\Srv2.Reskit.Org\ShareData Online sitecost-normal       0
```

Before you can create folders in the DFS Namespace, you need to create the underlying shares. In *step 6*, you create the shares (as noted in the earlier table), which looks like this:

```
PS C:\foo> $Sb = {
  New-Item       -Path C:\IT2  -ItemType Directory | Out-Null
  New-SmbShare   -Name 'ITData' -Path C:\IT2 -FullAccess Everyone
  New-Item       -Path C:\Sales -ItemType Directory | Out-Null
  New-SmbShare   -Name 'Sales' -Path C:\Sales -FullAccess Everyone
  New-Item       -Path C:\OldSales -ItemType Directory | Out-Null
  New-SmbShare -Name 'SalesHistorical' -Path 'C:\OldSales'
  'Root' | out-file c:\it2\root.txt
  'Root' | out-file c:\Sales\root.txt
  'Root' | out-file c:\oldsales\root.txt
}
Invoke-Command -ScriptBlock $Sb -Computer FS1

Name            ScopeName Path         Description PSComputerName
----            --------- ----         ----------- --------------
ITData          *         C:\IT2                   FS1
Sales           *         C:\Sales                 FS1
SalesHistorical *         C:\OldSales              FS1


PS C:\foo> $Sb = {
  New-Item       -Path C:\IT2 -ItemType Directory | Out-Null
  New-SmbShare   -Name 'ITData' -Path C:\IT2 -FullAccess Everyone
  New-Item       -Path C:\Sales  -ItemType Directory | Out-Null
  New-SmbShare   -Name 'Sales' -Path C:\Sales -FullAccess Everyone
  New-Item       -Path C:\OldSales -ItemType Directory | Out-Null
  New-SmbShare -Name 'SalesHistorical' -Path C:\IT2
  'Root' | out-file c:\it2\root.txt
  'Root' | out-file c:\Sales\root.txt
  'Root' | out-file c:\oldsales\root.txt
}
Invoke-Command -ScriptBlock $sb -Computer FS2

Name            ScopeName Path         Description PSComputerName
----            --------- ----         ----------- --------------
ITData          *         C:\IT2                   FS2
Sales           *         C:\Sales                 FS2
SalesHistorical *         C:\IT2                   FS2


PS C:\foo> $sb = {
  New-Item C:\ITM -ItemType Directory | Out-Null
  New-SmbShare -Name 'ITM' -Path C:\ITM -FullAccess Everyone
  'Root' | out-file c:\itm\root.txt
}
Invoke-Command -ScriptBlock $sb -Computer DC1

Name ScopeName Path    Description PSComputerName
---- --------- ----    ----------- --------------
ITM  *         C:\ITM              DC1


PS C:\foo> # DC2 folders/shares
$Sb = {
  New-Item C:\ITM -ItemType Directory | Out-Null
  New-SmbShare -Name 'ITM' -Path C:\ITM -FullAccess Everyone
  'Root' | out-file c:\itm\root.txt
}
Invoke-Command -ScriptBlock $Sb -Computer DC2

Name ScopeName Path    Description PSComputerName
---- --------- ----    ----------- --------------
ITM  *         C:\ITM              DC2
```

In *step 7*, you convert the shares held in different machines into your DFS Namespace, as follows:

```
PS C:\foo> New-DfsnFolder -Path '\\Reskit\ShareData\IT\ITData' `
                          -TargetPath '\\fs1\ITData\' `
                          -EnableTargetFailback $true `
                          -Description 'IT Data'

Path                            State  TimeToLiveSec Properties      Description
----                            -----  ------------- ----------      -----------
\\Reskit\ShareData\IT\ITData Online 300               Target Failback IT Data


PS C:\foo> New-DfsnFolderTarget -Path '\\Reskit\ShareData\IT\ITData' `
                                -TargetPath '\\fs2\ITData\'

Path                         TargetPath    State  ReferralPriorityClass ReferralPriorityRank
----                         ----------    -----  --------------------- --------------------
\\Reskit\ShareData\IT\ITData \\fs2\ITData\ Online sitecost-normal              0


PS C:\foo> New-DfsnFolder -Path '\\Reskit\ShareData\IT\ITManagement' `
                          -TargetPath '\\DC1\itm\' `
                          -EnableTargetFailback $true `
                          -Description 'IT Management Data'

Path                                State  TimeToLiveSec Properties      Description
----                                -----  ------------- ----------      -----------
\\Reskit\ShareData\IT\ITManagement Online 300             Target Failback IT Management Data

PS C:\foo> New-DfsnFolderTarget  -Path '\\Reskit\ShareData\IT\ITManagement' `
                                 -TargetPath '\\DC2\itm\'

Path                                TargetPath State  ReferralPriorityClass ReferralPriorityRank
----                                ---------- -----  --------------------- --------------------
\\Reskit\ShareData\IT\ITManagement \\DC2\itm\ Online sitecost-normal              0

PS C:\foo> New-DfsnFolder -Path '\\Reskit\ShareData\Sales\SalesData' `
                          -TargetPath '\\fs1\sales\' `
                          -EnableTargetFailback $true `
                          -Description 'SalesData'

Path                                State  TimeToLiveSec Properties      Description
----                                -----  ------------- ----------      -----------
\\Reskit\ShareData\Sales\SalesData Online 300             Target Failback SalesData

PS C:\foo> New-DfsnFolderTarget  -Path '\\Reskit\ShareData\Sales\SalesData' `
                                 -TargetPath '\\fs2\sales\'

Path                                TargetPath    State  ReferralPriorityClass ReferralPriorityRank
----                                ----------    -----  --------------------- --------------------
\\Reskit\ShareData\Sales\SalesData \\fs2\sales\ Online sitecost-normal              0


PS C:\foo> New-DfsnFolder -Path '\\Reskit\ShareData\Sales\SalesHistoric' `
                          -TargetPath '\\fs1\SalesHistorical\' `
                          -EnableTargetFailback $true `
                          -Description 'Sales Group Historical Data'

Path                                   State  TimeToLiveSec Properties      Description
----                                   -----  ------------- ----------      -----------
\\Reskit\ShareData\Sales\SalesHistoric Online 300             Target Failback Sales Group Historical Data


PS C:\foo> New-DfsnFolderTarget  -Path '\\Reskit\ShareData\Sales\SalesHistoric' `
                                 -TargetPath '\\fs2\SalesHistorical\'

Path                                   TargetPath           State  ReferralPriorityClass ReferralPriorityRank
----                                   ----------           -----  --------------------- --------------------
\\Reskit\ShareData\Sales\SalesHistoric \\fs2\SalesHistorical\ Online sitecost-normal              0
```

Now that you have the DFS Namespace created, you can examine it using the DFS MMC console:

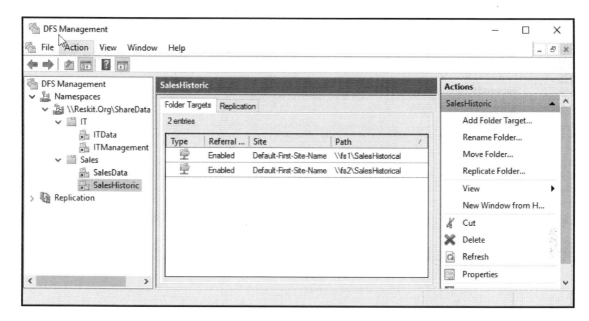

In the preceding screenshot, you can see that the DFS Namespace folder \\Reskit.Org\ShareData\Sales\SalesHistoric has two two targets, \\fs1\SalesHistorical and \\fs2\SalesHistorical. Those two targets are, thus far not synchronized using DFS. You set up synchronization in the next recipe.

There's more...

In creating your DFS Namespace, you created virtual folders without a target. The DNS folder \\Reskit.Org\ShareData\Sales, for example, has no target. This is a feature that enables you to create the logical hierarchy of folders that meets your needs, and only have the bottom most folders with folder targets.

In *step 1*, you add the DFS Namespace component on SRV1 and SRV2. You do this in two steps (first on SRV1, then on SRV2) since the Install-WindowsFeature cmdlet only accepts a single computer name (not an array of computer names).

The DFSN module, as shown in *step 2*, has 23 cmdlets. As with all PowerShell modules, you can use Get-Command as well as Get-Help to discover the cmdlets in the module and to get details on specific cmdlets. After installing the DFSN modules, ensure you use Update-Help to update your local help files with full details of the DFSN cmdlets.

In *step 5*, you both create a second DfsnRoot target and view the targets you have created. The New-DFNSRootTarget cmdlet produces an error message, but it is spurious. As you can see with the output from Get-DfsnRootTarget, both target folders are created correctly.

In *step 7*, you create the DFS Namespace. Once this is completed, you can use UNC Paths like \\Reskit.Org\Sales\SalesHistoric. However, the two targets are not synchronized. You can perform synchronization using DFS Replication or by a third-party tool.

For more information on DFS Namespaces and DFS Replication, see https://technet.microsoft.com/library/jj127250.aspx.

Configuring DFS Replication

DFSR is an efficient file replication engine built into Windows Server 2016. You can use DFS Replication to replicate DFSN targets in an efficient manner, especially across low-bandwidth connections.

In DFSR, a replication group is a collection of computers, knows as members. Each replication group member hosts replicated folders. Replicated folders are folders which DFSR ensures are synchronized. With DFS Replication groups, you can replicate the folders contained in your DFS Namespace.

A replicated folder is a folder that stays synchronized on each member. In the figure, there are two replicated folders: projects and proposals. As the data changes in each replicated folder, DFS replicates the changes across connections between the members of the replication group. The connections you set up between the members forms the replication topology.

Creating multiple replicated folders in a single replication group simplifies the process of deploying replicated folders because DFS applies the topology, schedule, and bandwidth throttling for the replication group to each replicated folder.

Each replicated folder has many properties. These include file and subfolder filters that enable you to filter out different files and subfolders for each replicated folder.

You can locate replicated folders on different volumes in the member. You do not need to have the replicated folders in a shared folder or part of a namespace.

DFS replication can support a variety of replication topologies to support a variety of requirements. For more information on the different replication topologies, see `https://www.petri.com/planning-dfs-architecture-part-two`.

Getting Ready

This recipe also sets up two DFS Replication groups as follows:

Replication group	Computers in RG	Content folders
FSShareRG	FS1, FS2	C:\IT2, C:\OldSales, C:\Sales
DCShareRG	DC1, DC2	C:\ITM

How to do it...

1. Install `DFS-Replication` feature on key servers:

```
$Sb = {Add-WindowsFeature -Name FS-DFS-Replication `
                         -IncludeManagementTools
}
Invoke-Command -ScriptBlock $Sb `
            -ComputerName DC1, DC2, FS1,
                          FS2, SRV1, SRV2 |
Format-Table -Property PSComputername,
                       FeatureResult, Success
```

2. Turn on administrative shares:

```
$Sb = {
        Set-SmbServerConfiguration `
                  -AutoShareServer $true `
                  -AutoShareWorkstation $true `
                  -Confirm:$false
}
Invoke-Command -ScriptBlock $Sb `
            -ComputerName DC1, DC2, FS2, FS2,
                          SRV1, SRV2
```

3. View DFS cmdlets:

```
Get-Module -Name DFSR -ListAvailable
Get-Command -Module DFSR | Measure-Object
```

4. Create and display replication groups:

```
New-DfsReplicationGroup `
    -GroupName FSShareRG `
    -DomainName Reskit.Org `
    -Description 'Replication Group for FS1,
                        FS2 shares' | Out-Null
New-DfsReplicationGroup `
    -GroupName DCShareRG `
    -DomainName Reskit.Org `
    -Description 'Replication Group for DC1,
                        DC2 shares' | Out-Null
Get-DfsReplicationGroup | Format-Table
```

5. Add replication group members for FSShareRG:

```
Add-DfsrMember -GroupName FSShareRG `
                -Description 'File Server members' `
                -ComputerName FS1,FS2 `
                -DomainName Reskit.Org | Out-Null
New-DfsReplicatedFolder -GroupName FSShareRG `
                        -FolderName ITData
                        -Domain Reskit.Org `
                        -Description 'ITData' `
                        -DfsnPath
        \\Reskit.Prg\ShareData\IT\ITData | Out-Null
New-DfsReplicatedFolder -GroupName FSShareRG `
                        -FolderName Sales
                        -Domain Reskit.Org `
                        -Description 'Sales' `
                        -DfsnPath
    \\Reskit.Org\ShareData\Sales\SalesData | Out-Null
New-DfsReplicatedFolder -GroupName FSShareRG `
                        -FolderName SalesHistorical
                        -Domain Reskit.Org `
                        -Description 'Sales history' `
                        -DfsnPath
\\Reskit.Org\ShareData\Sales\SalesHistoric | Out-Null
```

6. Add replication group members for `DCShareRG`:

```
Add-DfsrMember -GroupName DCShareRG `
               -Description 'DC Server members' `
               -ComputerName DC1,DC2 `
               -DomainName Reskit.Org |
                   Out-Null
New-DfsReplicatedFolder `
               -GroupName DCShareRG `
               -FolderName ITManagement `
               -Domain Reskit.Org `
               -Description 'IT Management Data' `
               -DfsnPath
\\Reskit.Org\sharedata\IT\ITManagement | Out-Null
```

7. View replicated folders:

```
Get-DfsReplicatedFolder |
    Format-Table -Property GroupName, FolderName, DomainName,
                 DfsnPath
```

8. Set membership for `FSShareRG` replication group:

```
Set-DfsrMembership -GroupName FSShareRG
                   -FolderName ITData `
                   -ComputerName FS1
                   -ContentPath C:\It2 `
                   -PrimaryMembe $true -Force |
                                       Out-Null
Set-DfsrMembership -GroupName FSShareRG
                   -FolderName ItData `
                   -ComputerName FS2
                   -ContentPath c:\It2 `
                   -Force | Out-Null
Set-DfsrMembership -GroupName FSShareRG
                   -FolderName Sales `
                   -ComputerName FS1
                   -ContentPath C:\Sales `
                   -PrimaryMember $true -Force |
                                       Out-Null
Set-DfsrMembership -GroupName FSShareRG
                   -FolderName Sales `
                   -ComputerName FS2
                   -ContentPath c:\Sales `
                   -Force | Out-Null
Set-DfsrMembership -GroupName FSShareRG
                   -FolderName SalesHistorical `
                   -ComputerName FS1
```

```
                    -ContentPath C:\OldSales `
                    -PrimaryMember $true -Force |
                                           Out-Null
Set-DfsrMembership -GroupName FSShareRG `
                    -FolderName SalesHistorical `
                    -ComputerName FS2
                    -ContentPath c:\OldSales `
                    -Force | Out-Null
```

9. Set membership for DCShareRG replication group:

```
Set-DfsrMembership -GroupName DCShareRG `
                    -FolderName ITManagement `
                    -ComputerName DC1
                    -ContentPath C:\ITM `
                    -PrimaryMember $true -Force |
                                           Out-Null
Set-DfsrMembership -GroupName DCShareRG `
                    -FolderName ITManagement `
                    -ComputerName DC2
                    -ContentPath C:\ITM `
                    -Force | Out-Null
```

10. View DFSR membership of the two replication groups:

```
Get-DfsrMembership -GroupName FSShareRG `
                    -ComputerName FS1, FS2 |
     Format-Table -Property GroupName, ComputerName,
           ComputerDomainName, ContentPath, Enabled
Get-DfsrMembership -GroupName DCShareRG `
                    -ComputerName DC1, DC2 |
     Format-Table -Property GroupName, ComputerName,
           ComputerDomainName, ContentPath, Enabled
```

11. Add replication connections for both replication groups:

```
Add-DfsrConnection -GroupName FSShareRG `
        -SourceComputerName FS1 `
        -DestinationComputerName FS2 `
        -Description 'FS1-FS2 connection' `
        -DomainName Reskit.Org | Out-Null
Add-DfsrConnection -GroupName DCShareRG `
        -SourceComputerName DC1 `
        -DestinationComputerName DC2 `
        -Description 'DC1-DC2 connection' `
        -DomainName Reskit.Org  | Out-Null
Get-DfsrMember |
     Format-Table -Property Groupname, DomainName,
```

```
                           DNSName, Description
```

12. Update the DFSR configuration:

```
Update-DfsrConfigurationFromAD -ComputerName DC1,
                      DC2, FS1, FS2
```

13. Run a DfsrPropogationTest on FSShareRG:

```
Start-DfsrPropagationTest -GroupName FSShareRG `
                     -FolderName ITData `
                     -ReferenceComputerName FS1 `
                     -DomainName Reskit.Org
```

14. Create and review the output of DfsrPropagationReport:

```
Write-DfsrPropagationReport -GroupName FSShareRG `
                     -FolderName ITdata `
                     -ReferenceComputerName FS1 `
                     -DomainName Reskit.Org `
                     -Path C:\Foo\
$i = Get-Item -Path C:\Foo\Propagation*.Html |
    Sort-Object -Property LastWriteTime -Descending|
       Select-Object -First 1
Invoke-Item $i
```

15. Create and review the output of DfsrHealthReport:

```
Write-DfsrHealthReport -GroupName FSShareRG `
                     -ReferenceComputerName FS1 `
                     -DomainName Reskit.Org `
                     -Path C:\Foo
$i = Get-Item -Path C:\Foo\Health*.Html |
    Sort-object -property LastWriteTime |
       Select-Object -Last 1
Invoke-Item $i
```

How it works...

In *step 1*, you install the DFS-Replication feature. You need to install this on every server you plan to use in the replication. Depending on what other features you have already installed, the output can vary. Here is what the results should look like:

```
PS C:\> $Sb = {
        Add-WindowsFeature -Name FS-DFS-Replication `
                    -IncludeManagementTools
        }
PS C:\> Invoke-Command -ScriptBlock $sb `
            -ComputerName DC1, DC2, FS2, FS2, SRV1, SRV2 |
                Format-Table -Property PSComputername, FeatureResult, Success

PSComputerName FeatureResult       Success
-------------- -------------       -------
DC2            {DFS Replication}   True
DC1            {DFS Replication}   True
SRV2           {DFS Replication}   True
SRV1           {DFS Replication}   True
FS1            {DFS Replication}   True
FS2            {DFS Replication}   True
```

In *step 2*, you turn on the administrative shares on the servers involved. There is no output from this step. In *step 3*, you examine the DFS Replication cmdlets contained in the DFSR module. As you can see, after running *step 1*, you have the DFSR module, and that it contains 45 cmdlets, as follows:

```
PS C:\> Get-Module DFSR -ListAvailable

    Directory: C:\Windows\system32\WindowsPowerShell\v1.0\Modules

ModuleType Version  Name  ExportedCommands
---------- -------  ----  ----------------
Binary     2.0.0.0  DFSR  {New-DfsReplicationGroup, Get-DfsReplicationGroup, Set-DfsReplicationGroup, Remove-DfsReplicationGroup...}

PS C:\> Get-Command -Module DFSR | Measure-Object
Count    : 45
Average  :
Sum      :
Maximum  :
Minimum  :
Property :
```

With *step 4*, you create two replication groups: one for the shares on FS1 and FS2, the other for a share on DC1 and DC2, like this:

```
PS C:\> New-DfsReplicationGroup -GroupName FSShareRG `
                    -DomainName Reskit.Org `
                    -Description 'Replication Group for FS1, FS2 shares' |
                    Out-Null
PS C:\> New-DfsReplicationGroup -GroupName DCShareRG `
                    -DomainName Reskit.Org `
                    -Description 'Replication Group for DC1, DC2 shares' |
                    Out-Null
PS C:\> Get-DfsReplicationGroup | Format-Table -Property GroupName, DomainName, Description, State


GroupName DomainName  Description                             State
--------- ----------  -----------                             -----
FSShareRG Reskit.Org Replication Group for FS1, FS2 shares Normal
DCShareRG Reskit.Org Replication Group for DC1, DC2 shares Normal
```

In *step 5*, you add FS1 and FS2 to the replication group FSShareRG then define three replicated folders that relate to DFSN paths created by Configuring a DNS namespace recipe. In *step 6*, you add DC1 and DC2 to the DCShareRG replication group and define the replicated folder on those servers. There is no output from these steps.

In *step 7*, you view the DFSR replicated folders setup in the previous two steps, which look like this:

```
PS C:\> Get-DfsReplicatedFolder |
            Format-Table GroupName, FolderName, DomainName, DfsnPath

GroupName FolderName        DomainName DfsnPath
--------- ----------        ---------- --------
FSShareRG ITData            Reskit.Org \\Reskit.Prg\ShareData\IT\ITData
FSShareRG Sales             Reskit.Org \\Reskit.Org\ShareData\Sales\SalesData
FSShareRG SalesHistorical   Reskit.Org \\Reskit.Org\ShareData\Sales\SalesHistoric
DCShareRG ITManagement      Reskit.Org \\reskit.org\sharedata\IT\ITManagement
```

In *step 8* you set the DFS membership for the shares on FS1 and FS2. For each shared folder, you identify the content path which is a local folder on the respective servers and you identify the primary member. In *step 9*, you do the same thing for the folder shared on DC1 and DC2. There is no output for these steps.

In *step 10,* you view the membership of the two replication groups as follows:

```
PS C:\> Get-DfsrMembership -GroupName FSShareRG -ComputerName FS1, FS2 |
    Format-Table GroupName, ComputerName, ComputerDomainName, ContentPath, Enabled

GroupName ComputerName ComputerDomainName ContentPath Enabled
--------- ------------ ------------------ ----------- -------
FSShareRG FS1          Reskit.Org         C:\It2      True
FSShareRG FS2          Reskit.Org         c:\It2      True
FSShareRG FS1          Reskit.Org         C:\Sales    True
FSShareRG FS2          Reskit.Org         c:\Sales    True
FSShareRG FS1          Reskit.Org         C:\OldSales True
FSShareRG FS2          Reskit.Org         c:\OldSales True


PS C:\> Get-DfsrMembership -GroupName DCShareRG -ComputerName DC1, DC2 |
    Format-Table GroupName, ComputerName, ComputerDomainName, ContentPath, Enabled

GroupName ComputerName ComputerDomainName ContentPath Enabled
--------- ------------ ------------------ ----------- -------
DCShareRG DC1          Reskit.Org         C:\ITM      True
DCShareRG DC2          Reskit.Org         C:\ITM      True
```

In *step 11,* you create two DFS connections that DFS uses to perform the replication, producing no output. Then you review the members in the DFSR replication groups that you have defined, which looks like this:

```
PS C:\> Get-DfsrMember |
          Format-Table -Property Groupname, DomainName, DNSName, Description

GroupName DomainName DnsName         Description
--------- ---------- -------         -----------
FSShareRG Reskit.Org FS1.Reskit.Org  File Server members
FSShareRG Reskit.Org FS2.Reskit.Org  File Server members
DCShareRG Reskit.Org DC1.Reskit.Org  DC Server members
DCShareRG Reskit.Org DC2.Reskit.Org  DC Server members
```

In *step 13*, you initiate a DFS Replication propagation test. This test evaluates the propagation and health of the replicated folders you set up in this recipe. In *step 14*, you create and then view a propagation report in the browser which looks like this:

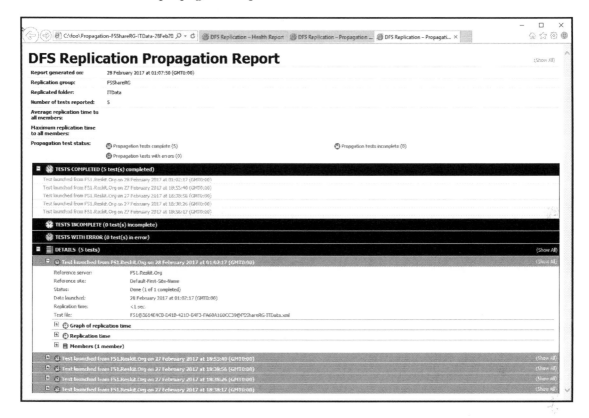

In *step 15,* you write then view a DFS health report. This report shows the health of your DFS service—in this case on server FS1. A neat feature of this report is the bandwidth savings achieved by DFS. The bandwidth used and the bandwidth saved figures are useful for capacity planning. The healthy report looks like this:

There's more...

In *step 2*, you turn on the administrative shares. This is a requirement for setting up DFS Replication. Once you have set up replication, you may wish to turn off these administrative shares.

In *step 8*, for each shared folder in the `FSShareRG` replication group, you identify a primary member. Should a document be changed different members in the replication group then, DFS considers the copy on the primary master as definitive.

In *step 11*, you set up simple DFS Replication connections. DFS enables you to manage rich replication topologies and supports your configuring replication schedules and bandwidth constraints.

The recipe sets up a simple set of replicated folders—four replicated folders on four servers based on the DFS Namespace created earlier. To extend this recipe, you could add other folders to the replication groups that were not part of the DFS Namespace.

DFS Replication is one way to replicate files in an organization. DFS was designed for use over lower-bandwidth networks, thus in larger networks, DFS replicas might be out of sync. Also, DFS only replicates a file after it has been closed.

With Server 2016, the **Storage Replica** (**SR**) feature is an alternative to DFSR. SR works at the block level unlike DFSR that operates at the file level. As a result SR can replicate the changes to open files.

For a comparison of DFS Replication and Storage Replica, see `https://www.petri.com/windows-server-2016-dfs-r-vs-storage-replica`.

10
Managing Internet Information Server

This chapter covers the following recipes:

- Installing IIS
- Configuring IIS for SSL
- Managing TLS cipher suites
- Configuring a central certificate store
- Configuring IIS bindings
- Configuring IIS logging and log files
- Managing applications and application pools
- Managing and monitoring network load balancing

Introduction

Internet Information Services (IIS) is a Windows feature that implements an extensible web server. IIS was first introduced as an add-on for Windows NT 4.0 and has been the focus of substantial development ever since. IIS version 10 is built into both Windows Server 2016 and Windows 10.

With IIS in Windows Server, you can host both internet facing public websites as well as sites on your internal intranet. You can integrate IIS with enterprise applications that include SharePoint, Exchange, and System Center. You can also use IIS on client operating systems including Windows 10.

IIS provides a platform for a variety of web-based applications. With IIS you can provide a simple HTML based static website as well as rich multi-tiered applications. You can combine the applications running on IIS with back end databases including Microsoft SQL Server.

Like other Windows Server features, you have PowerShell cmdlet coverage for IIS. The `WebAdministration` module, introduced in earlier versions of Windows Server, provides 79 cmdlets. Microsoft added a new module, `IISAdministration`, with Windows Server 2016 providing additional functionality.

This chapter covers how to install, configure, manage, and maintain IIS on Windows Server 2016. While you can load and use IIS in Windows 10, the focus in this chapter is on Windows Server 2016.

Installing IIS

Before you can use IIS, you must install it onto your host. Like other roles/features of Windows Server 2016 covered in this book, you install IIS by using the `Install-WindowsFeature` cmdlet. Once you have installed the web server, you take a look at the host after the installation is complete.

Getting ready

You run this recipe on `SRV1`, a member server running Windows Server 2016. This server is a server in the `Reskit.Org` domain.

How to do it...

1. Open a PowerShell console and install the `Web-Server` and all sub-features:

```
Install-WindowsFeature -Name Web-Server `
                       -IncludeAllSubFeature `
                       -IncludeManagementTools
```

2. See what web related features are installed on `SRV1`:

```
Get-WindowsFeature -Name Web* | Where-Object Installed
```

3. Check the `WebAdministration` module and discover how many commands are in the module:

```
Get-Module -Name WebAdministration -ListAvailable
Get-Command -Module webadministration |
    Measure-Object |
    Select-Object count
```

4. Check the `IISAdministration` module and discover how many commands are in the module:

```
Get-Module -Name IISAdministration -ListAvailable
Get-Command -Module IISAdministration |
Measure-Object |
Select-Object -Properties Count
```

5. Import the `WebAdministration` module:

```
Import-Module -Name WebAdministration
```

6. Look at the newly added `WebAdministration` PowerShell provider:

```
Get-PSProvider -PSProvider WebAdministration
```

7. View the top level of the `IIS:` drive:

```
Get-ChildItem -Path IIS:\
```

8. View what is in `IIS:\Sites`:

```
Get-ChildItem -Path IIS:\Sites
```

9. Look at the default website created by the web server installation:

```
$IE  = New-Object -ComObject InterNetExplorer.Application
$URL = 'http://srv1'
$IE.Navigate2($URL)
$IE.Visible = $true
```

How it works...

In *step 1* of this recipe, you install the `Web-Server` feature and all its sub-features as well as the management tools. The management tools include the `WebAdministration` module.

The output from this step looks like this:

```
PS C:\> Install-WindowsFeature -Name Web-Server
                              -IncludeAllSubFeature
                              -IncludeManagementTools

Success Restart Needed Exit Code   Feature Result
------- -------------- ---------   --------------
True    No             Success     {Application Development, Application Init...
```

In *step 2*, you view the `Web-Server` feature and its sub-features. As you can see, you have over 50 installed sub-features, with the output resembling this:

```
PS C:\> Get-WindowsFeature -Name Web*  | Where-Object installed

Display Name                                         Name                     Install State
------------                                         ----                     -------------
[X] Web Server (IIS)                                 Web-Server               Installed
    [X] Web Server                                   Web-WebServer            Installed
        [X] Common HTTP Features                     Web-Common-Http          Installed
            [X] Default Document                     Web-Default-Doc          Installed
            [X] Directory Browsing                   Web-Dir-Browsing         Installed
            [X] HTTP Errors                          Web-Http-Errors          Installed
            [X] Static Content                       Web-Static-Content       Installed
            [X] HTTP Redirection                     Web-Http-Redirect        Installed
            [X] WebDAV Publishing                    Web-DAV-Publishing       Installed
        [X] Health and Diagnostics                   Web-Health               Installed
            [X] HTTP Logging                         Web-Http-Logging         Installed
            [X] Custom Logging                       Web-Custom-Logging       Installed
            [X] Logging Tools                        Web-Log-Libraries        Installed
            [X] ODBC Logging                         Web-ODBC-Logging         Installed
            [X] Request Monitor                      Web-Request-Monitor      Installed
            [X] Tracing                              Web-Http-Tracing         Installed
        [X] Performance                              Web-Performance          Installed
            [X] Static Content Compression           Web-Stat-Compression     Installed
            [X] Dynamic Content Compression          Web-Dyn-Compression      Installed
        [X] Security                                 Web-Security             Installed
            [X] Request Filtering                    Web-Filtering            Installed
            [X] Basic Authentication                 Web-Basic-Auth           Installed
            [X] Centralized SSL Certificate Support  Web-CertProvider         Installed
            [X] Client Certificate Mapping Authentic... Web-Client-Auth       Installed
            [X] Digest Authentication                Web-Digest-Auth          Installed
            [X] IIS Client Certificate Mapping Authe... Web-Cert-Auth         Installed
            [X] IP and Domain Restrictions           Web-IP-Security          Installed
            [X] URL Authorization                    Web-Url-Auth             Installed
            [X] Windows Authentication               Web-Windows-Auth         Installed
        [X] Application Development                   Web-App-Dev              Installed
            [X] .NET Extensibility 3.5               Web-Net-Ext              Installed
            [X] .NET Extensibility 4.6               Web-Net-Ext45            Installed
            [X] Application Initialization           Web-AppInit              Installed
            [X] ASP                                  Web-ASP                  Installed
            [X] ASP.NET 3.5                          Web-Asp-Net              Installed
            [X] ASP.NET 4.6                          Web-Asp-Net45            Installed
            [X] CGI                                  Web-CGI                  Installed
            [X] ISAPI Extensions                     Web-ISAPI-Ext            Installed
            [X] ISAPI Filters                        Web-ISAPI-Filter         Installed
            [X] Server Side Includes                 Web-Includes             Installed
            [X] WebSocket Protocol                   Web-WebSockets           Installed
    [X] FTP Server                                   Web-Ftp-Server           Installed
        [X] FTP Service                              Web-Ftp-Service          Installed
        [X] FTP Extensibility                        Web-Ftp-Ext              Installed
    [X] Management Tools                             Web-Mgmt-Tools           Installed
        [X] IIS Management Console                   Web-Mgmt-Console         Installed
        [X] IIS 6 Management Compatibility           Web-Mgmt-Compat          Installed
            [X] IIS 6 Metabase Compatibility         Web-Metabase             Installed
            [X] IIS 6 Management Console             Web-Lgcy-Mgmt-Console    Installed
            [X] IIS 6 Scripting Tools                Web-Lgcy-Scripting       Installed
            [X] IIS 6 WMI Compatibility              Web-WMI                  Installed
        [X] IIS Management Scripts and Tools         Web-Scripting-Tools      Installed
        [X] Management Service                       Web-Mgmt-Service         Installed
```

In *step 3*, you look at the WebAdministration module. As you can see, there are 79 commands (which comprise 78 cmdlets and one function) in the module. The output looks like this:

```
PS C:\> Import-Module WebAdministration
PS C:\> Get-Module -Name WebAdministration -ListAvailable

    Directory: C:\Windows\system32\WindowsPowerShell\v1.0\Modules

ModuleType Version     Name                 ExportedCommands

---------- -------     ----                 ----------------

Manifest   1.0.0.0     WebAdministration    {Start-WebCommitDelay, Stop-WebCommitDelay, Get-WebConfigurationLock...}

PS C:\> Get-Command -Module webadministration |
          Measure-Object |
              Select-Object -Property Count

Count
-----
   79
```

In *step 4*, you look at the IISAdministration module. As you can see, there are 31 further cmdlets for you to use. The output of this step looks like this:

```
PS C:\> Get-Module -Name IISAdministration
PS C:\> Get-Command -Module IISAdministration |
          Measure-Object |
              Select-Object -Property Count

ModuleType Version     Name                 ExportedCommands

---------- -------     ----                 ----------------

Script     1.0.0.0     iisadministration    {Clear-IISCentralCertProvider, Clear-IISConfigCollection...

Count : 31
```

In *step 5*, you import the `WebAdministration` module manually. In addition to loading the cmdlets/functions contained in the module, importing the module also loads the `WebAdministration` PowerShell provider. This provider enables you to browse aspects of the web server, including the sites, application pools, and SSL bindings on the host. There is no output from loading the module. Once you have loaded the module, in *step 6* you get details of the provider, which looks like this:

```
PS C:\> Get-PSProvider -PSProvider WebAdministration


Name                    Capabilities    Drives
----                    ------------    ------
WebAdministration       ShouldProcess   {IIS}
```

In *step 7*, you look at the contents of the `IIS` drive. It contains just three folders as you can see from the output:

```
PS C:\> Get-ChildItem -Path IIS:\

Name
----
AppPools
Sites
SslBindings
```

In *step 8*, you take a look at the `Sites` folder in the `IIS` drive and you see details about any loaded websites on your server. Since you have just installed IIS, there is only one site, and the output of this step looks like this:

```
PS C:\> Get-Childitem -Path IIS:\Sites

Name              ID   State    Physical Path                      Bindings
----              --   -----    -------------                      --------
Default Web Site  1    Started  %SystemDrive%\inetpub\wwwroot      http *:80:
```

Finally, in *step 9*, you look at the default landing page for a newly installed IIS host, which looks like this:

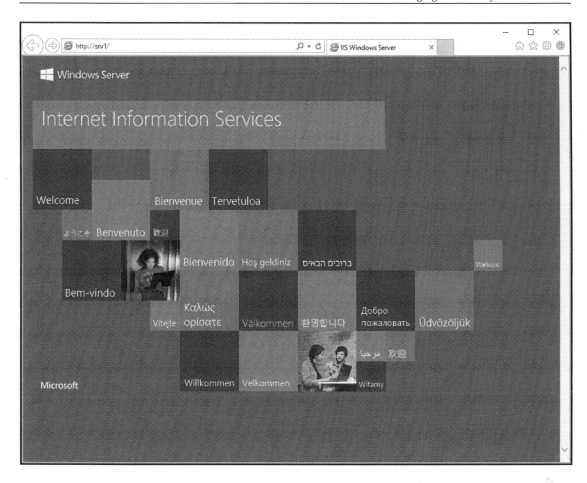

There's more...

In *step 1*, you installed the `Web-Server` and all of the sub-features. In most cases, many of these sub-features are ones you are not going to use.

In *step 5*, you import the module manually. If you are just going to use the cmdlets in this module, then PowerShell's module auto-load feature loads the module for you. Importing it implicitly ensures the correct module is loaded.

In *step 6* through *step 7*, you examine the provider. This provider can be very useful for some operations—for example creating an SSL binding as you see in the *Configure IIS for SSL* recipe.

In *step 9*, you open up **Internet Explorer** and navigate to the root of the default website on SRV1. This is, as you can see from the output, a standard landing page. This page is very useful for troubleshooting purposes, as it shows you IIS has been installed and is up and running.

Configuring IIS for SSL

Traffic between a web browser and a web server on the internet or even within a corporate intranet is open and can be intercepted. To avoid the data being compromised, you can make use of protocols built into your web browser and IIS to provide encryption as well as authentication.

In the 1990's, Netscape Communications developed a protocol that provided the necessary security, the **Secure Socket Layer** (**SSL**) protocol. SSL V1 was never commercially released, but SSL V2 and SSL V3 were developed, released, but are now deprecated as unsafe.

Transport Layer Security (**TLS**) was developed openly as the next version of SSL. TLS V1 is essentially SSL V3.1. In 2014, Google identified a serious vulnerability in both SSL V3 and TLS V1. That leaves TLS 2 as the best protocol to deploy and it is the only one installed by default with IIS in Windows Server 2013.

These days, SSL as a protocol is being deprecated in favour of TLS. Most major web sites no longer actually use the SSL protocol. Nevertheless we talk about such web sites as *having SSL* and we continue to use the HTTPS scheme since end-users can not explicitly choose between SSL and TLS.

When the user specifies a URL beginning with HTTPS: the browser contacts the server on port 443. The browser and server then negotiate which security protocol to use (for example TLS 1.2) and which cipher suite to use to protect the data being transferred. A cipher suite is a distinct set of algorithms to provide for key exchange and which encryption algorithms to use for both bulk encryption and hashing.

In this recipe, you setup your server to provide secure transfer of web pages. Strictly speaking, this recipe sets up IIS to use TLS 2.0 rather than SSL. In most references, we refer to this as *setting up SSL*, when in reality we are actually *setting up TLS*.

In order to set up IIS for secure transfer, you first need a certificate. The certificate identifies the server by name and specifies what the certificate can be used for. Associated with the certificate are public and private keys.

If you are setting up IIS as an internal web server, then you should use your internal **Certificate Authority (CA)** to create the web server certificate. If your web server is to be internet facing, you should get a certificate from a public CA. Remember that the certificate has to have been issued (and signed) by a CA that is explicitly trusted by any client accessing the secure site. Many public CAs around the world are automatically trusted by most modern browsers. Additionally, you can configure workstations and servers to enroll the root CA certificate for your internal CA automatically.

In this recipe, you use self-signed certificates. This works wonderfully in a test environment but should never be used in production. The technique you use in this recipe first generates a self-signed certificate. The recipe then copies this certificate into the local machine's trusted root store. This action makes the local machine trust the self-signed certificate.

Getting ready

In this recipe, you configure IIS on SRV1 for security. This recipe assumes you have setup IIS as shown in the *Install IIS* recipe.

How to do it...

1. Import the WebAdministration module:

   ```
   Import-Module -Name WebAdministration
   ```

2. Create a self-signed certificate in the local server's personal CERT store:

   ```
   $SSLCert = New-SelfSignedCertificate `
               -CertStoreLocation 'CERT:\LocalMachine\MY' `
               -DnsName 'SRV1.Reskit.Org'
   ```

3. Copy the certificate to the Root store on SRV1:

   ```
   $C = 'System.Security.Cryptography.X509Certificates.X509Store'
   $Store = New-Object -TypeName $C `
                       -ArgumentList 'Root','LocalMachine'
   $Store.Open('ReadWrite')
   $Store.Add($SSLcert)
   $Store.Close()
   ```

4. Create a new SSL binding on the `Default Website`:

```
New-WebBinding -Name 'Default Website' `
      -Protocol https -Port 443
```

5. Assign the `Cert` created earlier to this new binding:

```
$SSLCert | New-Item -Path IIS:\SslBindings\0.0.0.0!443
```

6. View the site using HTTPS:

```
$IE  = New-Object -ComObject InternetExplorer.Application
$URL = 'https://Srv1.Reskit.Org'
$IE.Navigate2($URL)
$IE.Visible = $true
```

How it works...

In *step 1*, you import the `WebAdministration` module, which ensures the `WebAdministration` provider you use later in this recipe is loaded. There is no output from this step.

In *step 2*, you create a self-signed certificate and store it in the local machine's personal certificate store (`Cert:\\LocalMachine\My`). There is no output from this step.

With *step 3*, you copy the self-signed certificate to the local machine's trusted `Root` certificate store. There is no output from this step.

In *step 4*, you create a new binding for IIS that binds port `443` to HTTPS. This tells IIS to use SSL/TLS for traffic coming into `SRV1` on that port. There is no output from this step.

In *step 5*, you update the SSL bindings to include which certificate to use. This step tells IIS to use the self-signed certificate for any HTTPS traffic coming into the default website. The output from this step looks like this:

```
PS C:\> $SSLCert | New-Item -Path IIS:\SslBindings\0.0.0.0!443

IP Address      Port   Host Name    Store   Sites
----------      ----   ---------    -----   -----
0.0.0.0         443                 MY      Default Web Site
```

In *step 6*, you use Internet Explorer to browse the default website using HTTPS. The output of this step is the default page for IIS, which looks like this:

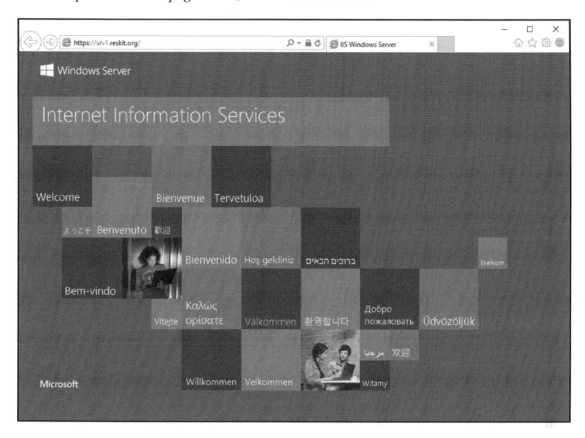

There's more...

In *step 3*, you use the .NET framework to copy the self-signed certificate into the local server's trusted Root cert store. This makes the self-signed certificate trusted by SRV1. You have to use .NET because the PowerShell certificate provider does not support a copy operation. Fortunately, the .NET framework provides that functionality. Alternatively, you could use the Export-Certificate and Import-Certificate to export the cert to a file and then re-import it.

The output shown for *step 6* is identical to the output *step 8* in the *Install IIS* recipe. Except you have retrieved it securely, over TLS.

Managing TLS cipher suites

With TLS, you are able to specify which cipher suite or suites your web server should support. A cipher suite is a specific set of methods or algorithms that provide functions including key exchange, bulk encryption, hashing and message digests, and authentication.

Once the browser connects to the server, the two parties negotiate and choose the *best* cipher suite that both sides can support. If the browser only asks for cipher suites that the web server does not support, then the server terminates the communication.

By default, Windows Server 2016 supports 31 cipher suites providing different algorithms and different key lengths. In this recipe, you retrieve the cipher suites on Windows Server 2016, and both enable and disable a specific cipher suite.

Getting ready

You run this recipe on the Windows Server 2016 server SRV1 on which you have loaded IIS (as per the *Install IIS* recipe) and configured secure HTTP (as per the *Configure IIS for SSL* recipe).

How to do it...

1. Get the cipher suites on SRV1 and display them:

```
Get-TlsCipherSuite |
  Format-Table Name, Exchange, Cipher, Hash, Certificate
```

2. Find cipher suites that support RC4:

```
Get-TlsCipherSuite -Name RC4 |
  Format-Table Name, Exchange, Cipher, Hash, Certificate
```

3. Disable RC4 based cipher suites:

```
Foreach ($P in (Get-TlsCipherSuite -Name 'RC4'))
  {Disable-TlsCipherSuite -Name $P.name}
```

4. Find cipher suites that support RC4:

```
Get-TlsCipherSuite RC4 |
  Format-Table -Property Name, Exchange, Cipher,
```

```
                                  Hash, Certificate
```

5. Re-enable the two cipher suites:

```
Enable-TlsCipherSuite -Name TLS_RSA_WITH_RC4_128_SHA
Enable-TlsCipherSuite -Name TLS_RSA_WITH_RC4_128_MD5
```

6. Find cipher suites that support RC4:

```
Get-TlsCipherSuite RC4 |
  Format-Table -Property Name, Exchange, Cipher,
                          Hash, Certificate
```

How it works...

In *step 1,* you use the Get-TlsCipherSuite cmdlet to return all the cipher suites that are supported on your server. The output looks like this:

```
PS C:\> Get-TlsCipherSuite |
            Format-Table Name, Exchange, Cipher, Hash, Certificate

Name                                        Exchange Cipher Hash   Certificate
----                                        -------- ------ ----   -----------
TLS_ECDHE_ECDSA_WITH_AES_256_GCM_SHA384     ECDH     AES           ECDSA
TLS_ECDHE_ECDSA_WITH_AES_128_GCM_SHA256     ECDH     AES           ECDSA
TLS_ECDHE_RSA_WITH_AES_256_GCM_SHA384       ECDH     AES           RSA
TLS_ECDHE_RSA_WITH_AES_128_GCM_SHA256       ECDH     AES           RSA
TLS_DHE_RSA_WITH_AES_256_GCM_SHA384         DH       AES           RSA
TLS_DHE_RSA_WITH_AES_128_GCM_SHA256         DH       AES           RSA
TLS_ECDHE_ECDSA_WITH_AES_256_CBC_SHA384
TLS_ECDHE_ECDSA_WITH_AES_128_CBC_SHA256     ECDH     AES    SHA256 ECDSA
TLS_ECDHE_RSA_WITH_AES_256_CBC_SHA384       ECDH     AES    SHA384 RSA
TLS_ECDHE_RSA_WITH_AES_128_CBC_SHA256       ECDH     AES    SHA256 RSA
TLS_ECDHE_ECDSA_WITH_AES_256_CBC_SHA        ECDH     AES    SHA1   ECDSA
TLS_ECDHE_ECDSA_WITH_AES_128_CBC_SHA        ECDH     AES    SHA1   ECDSA
TLS_ECDHE_RSA_WITH_AES_256_CBC_SHA          ECDH     AES    SHA1   RSA
TLS_ECDHE_RSA_WITH_AES_128_CBC_SHA          ECDH     AES    SHA1   RSA
TLS_DHE_RSA_WITH_AES_256_CBC_SHA            DH       AES    SHA1   RSA
TLS_DHE_RSA_WITH_AES_128_CBC_SHA            DH       AES    SHA1   RSA
TLS_RSA_WITH_AES_256_GCM_SHA384            RSA      AES           RSA
TLS_RSA_WITH_AES_128_GCM_SHA256            RSA      AES           RSA
TLS_RSA_WITH_AES_256_CBC_SHA256            RSA      AES    SHA256 RSA
TLS_RSA_WITH_AES_128_CBC_SHA256            RSA      AES    SHA256 RSA
TLS_RSA_WITH_AES_256_CBC_SHA               RSA      AES    SHA1   RSA
TLS_RSA_WITH_AES_128_CBC_SHA               RSA      AES    SHA1   RSA
TLS_RSA_WITH_3DES_EDE_CBC_SHA              RSA      3DES   SHA1   RSA
TLS_DHE_DSS_WITH_AES_256_CBC_SHA256
TLS_DHE_DSS_WITH_AES_128_CBC_SHA256        DH       AES    SHA256 DSA
TLS_DHE_DSS_WITH_AES_256_CBC_SHA           DH       AES    SHA1   DSA
TLS_DHE_DSS_WITH_AES_128_CBC_SHA           DH       AES    SHA1   DSA
TLS_DHE_DSS_WITH_3DES_EDE_CBC_SHA          DH       3DES   SHA1   DSA
TLS_RSA_WITH_NULL_SHA256                   RSA             SHA256 RSA
TLS_RSA_WITH_NULL_SHA                      RSA             SHA1   RSA
TLS_PSK_WITH_AES_256_GCM_SHA384
TLS_PSK_WITH_AES_128_GCM_SHA256            PSK      AES
TLS_PSK_WITH_AES_256_CBC_SHA384            PSK      AES    SHA384
TLS_PSK_WITH_AES_128_CBC_SHA256            PSK      AES    SHA256
TLS_PSK_WITH_NULL_SHA384                   PSK             SHA384
TLS_PSK_WITH_NULL_SHA256                   PSK             SHA256
TLS_RSA_WITH_RC4_128_SHA                   RSA      RC4    SHA1   RSA
TLS_RSA_WITH_RC4_128_MD5                   RSA      RC4    MD5    RSA
```

In *step 2*, you search for cipher suites that use *RC4*, a bulk encryption cipher. This makes use of the `-Name` parameter which is a wild card match. The output looks like this:

```
PS C:\> Get-TlsCipherSuite -Name RC4 |
    Format-Table Name, Exchange, Cipher, Hash, Certificate

Name                      Exchange Cipher Hash Certificate
----                      -------- ------ ---- -----------
TLS_RSA_WITH_RC4_128_SHA RSA      RC4    SHA1 RSA
TLS_RSA_WITH_RC4_128_MD5 RSA      RC4    MD5  RSA
```

In *step 3*, you disable the two cipher suites that use `RC4` although there is no output from this step. In *step 4*, which produces no output, you see that these two cipher suites are no longer available.

In *step 5*, you re-enable these two cipher suites (which produces no output) while in *step 6*, you verify that these two cipher suites are available. The output from this step looks like this:

```
PS C:\> Get-TlsCipherSuite -Name RC4 |
    Format-Table Name, Exchange, Cipher, Hash, Certificate

Name                      Exchange Cipher Hash Certificate
----                      -------- ------ ---- -----------
TLS_RSA_WITH_RC4_128_SHA RSA      RC4    SHA1 RSA
TLS_RSA_WITH_RC4_128_MD5 RSA      RC4    MD5  RSA
```

There's more...

In *step 2*, you look for cipher suites using RC4. Some security experts consider this cipher to have potential weaknesses that make deprecation appropriate. With *step 4*, you disable these two cipher suites. If you have, for example, Windows XP still in use, you may find that disabling *RC4* means these older OSs can no longer connect to your server. In *step 5*, you see how to re-enable them (should this be necessary).

It is important to record the names of the cipher suites that you disable. There is no cmdlet that can show you what cipher suites you have disabled—you can only see which ones are specifically enabled. BE CAREFUL!

Configuring a central certificate store

If you are hosting numerous secure servers on a variety of hosts (physical or virtual), you may find that certificate management can be challenging. Each time you add a new IIS host into your infrastructure, you need to ensure all the correct certificates are in place and the correct web binding (binding the certificates to IIS) is in place for each secure site. Additionally, you need to deal with certificate expiry and renewing certificates that expire across each IIS server that utilizes those certificates.

Windows Server 2012 added a new feature known as the **Central Certificate Store** (**CCS**). This feature allows certificates to be stored in a central location such as on an *SMB file share*. You then configure IIS to make use of the central store, rather than using the local certificate stores as you did in the *Configure IIS for SSL* recipe.

In this recipe, you are going to setup SRV1 to use a new share on DC1 to hold the central certificate share. You create the store, then create a new certificate for SRV1, and move the cert to the central certificate share on DC1.

Getting ready

This recipe uses SRV1 as an IIS server and DC1 to hold the SSL certificate central store. You should have both servers up and running. Also, this recipe assumes you have IIS at least partly loaded and setup for SSL (in other words, you have run the *Install IIS* and *Configure IIS for SSL* recipes. This recipe does check and ensure the needed features are added to SRV1. You should also load the AD cmdlets onto SRV1 if you have not already done so.

How to do it...

1. Remove existing certificates for SRV1:

```
Get-ChildItem -Path Cert:\localmachine\My |
    Where-Object Subject -Match 'SRV1.Reskit.Org' |
        Remove-Item -ErrorAction SilentlyContinue
Get-ChildItem Cert:\localmachine\root |
    Where-Object Subject -match 'SRV1.Reskit.Org' |
        Remove-Item
```

2. Remove SSL web bindings if any exist:

```
Import-Module -Name WebAdministration
Get-WebBinding | Where-Object protocol -EQ 'https' |
    Remove-WebBinding
Get-ChildItem -Path IIS:\SslBindings | Where-Object Port -eq 443 |
    Remove-Item
```

3. Create a shared folder and share it on DC1:

```
$sb = {
If (-Not (Test-Path C:\SSLCerts)) {
    New-Item  -Path C:\SSLCerts -ItemType Directory |
                    Out-Null}
New-SmbShare -Name 'SSLCertShare' -Path c:\SSLCerts `
            -FullAccess 'Everyone' `
            -Description 'SSL Certificate'
}
Invoke-Command -ScriptBlock $sb -ComputerName DC1
```

4. Add a new SSLCert and make it trusted locally:

```
$SSLCert = New-SelfSignedCertificate `
                -CertStoreLocation 'CERT:\LocalMachine\MY' `
                -DnsName 'SRV1.Reskit.Org'
$C = 'System.Security.Cryptography.X509Certificates.X509Store'
$Store = New-Object -TypeName $C `
                    -ArgumentList 'Root','LocalMachine'
$Store.Open('ReadWrite')
$Store.Add($SSLcert)
$Store.Close()
```

5. Export certificate to PFC file:

```
$Certpw   = 'SSLCerts101!'
$Certpwss = ConvertTo-SecureString -String $certpw `
                -Force -AsPlainText
Export-PfxCertificate -Cert $SSLCert `
                -FilePath 'C:\srv1.reskit.org.pfx' `
                -Password  $Certpwss
Move-Item -Path 'C:\srv1.reskit.net.pfx' `
            -Destination \\dc1\SSLCertShare\srv1.reskit.org.pfx `
            -Force
```

6. Install the CCS feature on SRV1:

```
Install-WindowsFeature Web-CertProvider | Out-Null
```

7. Create a new user for the certificate sharing:

```
$User        = 'Reskit\SSLCertShare'
$Password    = 'Pa$$w0rd'
$PasswordSS = ConvertTo-SecureString  -String $Password `
                -AsPlainText -Force
$NewUserHT   = @{AccountPassword       = $PasswordSS
                  Enabled              = $true
                  PasswordNeverExpires = $true
                  ChangePasswordAtLogon = $false
                  }
New-ADUser @NewUserHT `
            -SamAccountName SSLCertShare `
            -UserPrincipalName 'SSLCertShare@Reskit.Org' `
            -Name "SSLCertShare" `
            -DisplayName 'SSL Cert Share User'
```

8. Configure the SSLCertShare in the registry:

```
Set-ItemProperty -Path
HKLM:\SOFTWARE\Microsoft\IIS\CentralCertProvider\`
              -Name Enabled -Value 1
Set-ItemProperty -Path `
HKLM:\SOFTWARE\Microsoft\IIS\CentralCertProvider\`
              -Name CertStoreLocation -Value \\DC1\SSLCertShare
Enable-WebCentralCertProvider `
              -CertStoreLocation \\dc1\SSLCertShare `
              -UserName $user -Password $Password `
              -PrivateKeyPassword $Certpw
Set-WebCentralCertProvider -UserName $User -Password $password `
              -PrivateKeyPassword $Certpw
```

9. Setup SSL for default site:

```
New-WebBinding -Name 'Default Web Site' -Protocol https `
              -Port 443
$SSLcert | New-Item -Path IIS:\SslBindings\0.0.0.0!443
```

10. Remove the cert from SRV1:

```
Get-ChildItem -Path Cert:\LocalMachine\MY    |
   WHERE SUBJECT -MATCH 'SRV1.RESKIT.ORG' |
      Remove-Item -Force
```

11. Now view the website with SSL:

```
$IE  = New-Object -ComObject InterNetExplorer.Application
$URL = 'https://srv1.reskit.org/'
$IE.Navigate2($URL)
$IE.Visible = $true
```

How it works...

In *step 1*, you remove any existing certificates on SRV1—you create new ones later in this recipe. There is an output from this step.

In *step 2*, you remove any existing web bindings if they currently exist—you recreate these later in the recipe. There should be no output from this step.

In *step 3*, you create a script block and execute the script block on DC1. This script block creates the SSLCertificateShare). The output from this step shows the creation of the share on DC1, as follows:

```
PS C:\> $sb = {
If ( -NOT (Test-Path c:\SSLCerts)) {
    New-Item  -Path c:\SSLCerts -ItemType Directory
              -Name 'SSL Certificate Share'
New-SmbShare -Name 'SSLCertShare' -Path c:\SSLCerts
}
PS C:\> Invoke-Command -ScriptBlock $sb -ComputerName DC1

Name           ScopeName Path          Description PSComputerName
----           --------- ----          ----------- --------------
SSLCertShare * c:\SSLCerts             DC1
```

In *step 4*, you create a new certificate, and make it trusted. There is no output from this step.

In *step 5*, you export the self-signed certificate to a password protected .pfx file then move the file to the SSLCertShare on DC1.

In step 6, you install the centralized SSL certificate feature. There is no output from this step.

In *step 7*, you create a new AD user (`Reskit\SSLCertShare`) for use with IIS's centralized certificate share feature. There is no output from this step.

In *step 8*, you configure the centralized certificate share to point to the share on `DC1` and to use the new user created in *step 7*. There is no output from this step.

In *step 9*, you remove the self-signed certificate from `SRV1`, which also produces no output.

In *step 10*, you set web bindings for the default site on `SRV1` to use the self-signed certificate, producing no output.

In *step 11*, you navigate to the default website specifying HTTPS and see the default website on `SRV1`. This should look the same as that shown in the recipe *Configure IIS for SSL*.

Configuring IIS bindings

In IIS, a binding specifies how incoming connections to a web server should be handled.

A binding is a combination of a protocol (HTTP, HTTPS, and so on), an IP address, TCP/IP port, and host name. The binding thus tells Windows and IIS how to route requests inbound to your system.

Bindings allow you to run more than one website on a single host. There are a few ways to do this:

- Configure multiple IP addresses and create a binding for each IP address to a different website
- Configure a single IP addresses and multiple ports and point each to a different website
- Configure a single address and use the host header option that routes requests for a given write on the host.

If you use the multiple IP address option, you need to configure multiple IP addresses on the system and ensure that the DNS entries for each website point to the correct IP address. This approach requires extra overhead and uses more IP addresses.

Using a single IP address and multiple ports saves on IP addresses, but requires users specify the port number when connecting. This is OK for sites you want to *hide* from curious eyes.

The best option for supporting multiple websites is to use the host header feature. With host headers, the browser sends the name of the website as part of the request. IIS can read that header and use the appropriate binding to specify which site relates to that header and route accordingly. Thus, you could host `www.reskit.org` and `www2.reskit.org` on SRV1 and by using host headers you would need only a single IP address.

When you first install IIS, as you did in the *Install IIS* recipe, the setup creates a single binding that binds traffic inbound on port 80 to the default website using HTTP. In the recipe *Configure IIS for SSL*, you added a further binding for all traffic inbound to port 443 to the default website using HTTPS. So you have done some work with bindings already in this chapter.

Getting ready

You run this recipe on SRV1, where you have installed and configured IIS (as per the *Install IIS* and *Configuring IIS for SSL* recipes). This recipe also assumes you are using DC1.Reskit.Org as your domain controller and DNS server.

How to do it...

1. Import the `WebAdministration` module:

```
Import-Module -Name WebAdministration
```

2. Create and populate a new site:

```
$sitepath = 'C:\inetpub\www2'
New-Item -Path $sitepath -ItemType Directory
$page = @'
<!DOCTYPE html>
<html>
<head><title>Main Page for WWW2.Reskit.Org</title></head>
<body><p><center>
<b>HOME PAGE FOR WWW2.RESKIT.ORG</b></p>
This is the root page this site
</body>
</html>
'@
$PAGE | OUT-FILE -FilePath $sitepath\INDEX.HTML
```

3. Create a new website that uses host headers:

```
New-Website -PhysicalPath $sitepath -name www2 `
            -HostHeader 'www2.reskit.org'
```

4. Create a DNS record on DC1:

```
Invoke-Command -Computer DC1.Reskit.Org -ScriptBlock {
Add-DnsServerResourceRecordA -ZoneName 'Reskit.Org' `
                             -Name     'www2' `
                             -IpAddress 10.10.10.50
}
```

5. And show the page:

```
Start-Process 'http://www2.reskit.org'
```

How it works...

In *step 1*, you import the WebAdministration module. There is no output from this step.

In *step 2*, you create a new folder on SRV1 that holds the default landing page for a new website, www2.reskit.org. There is no output from this step.

In *step 3*, you create a new website, using the New-Website cmdlet. You specify the name of the site (www2) and the HostHeader that IIS uses to bind the name to the new website. The output from this step looks like this:

```
PS C:\> New-Website -PhysicalPath $sitepath -name www2 `
               -HostHeader 'www2.reskit.org'

Name   ID   State     Physical Path        Bindings
----   --   -----     -------------        --------
www2   2    Started   C:\inetpub\www2      http
                                           *:80:www2.reskit.org
```

Once you have set up the website and defined it in IIS, in *step 4*, you browse to the new site, which looks like the following:

There's more ...

By default, while you can have as many HTTP-based sites as you want on a given machine, you can only have one HTTPS site. This is because the details of which site the browser is asking for is inside the encrypted content, thus can only be action once decrypted.

To overcome this, a new feature was added to TLS called **Server Name Indication (SNI)**. SNI allows the name of the host name being contacted to be specified during the SSL/TLS handshake. This in turn enables IIS to support more than one secure site. To use SNI, the browser or web client as well as the web server must support SNI. Modern web browsers support SNI.

 More information on using SNI can be found at
http://en.wikipedia.org/wiki/Server_Name_Indication.

Configuring IIS logging and log files

Each time IIS receives a request from a client, it logs that request to a log file. This is the default behavior. With PowerShell, it's simple to modify this behavior, such as turning off logging, changing the logging frequency, or changing the folder where IIS stores its log files.

Log files are therefore great places to look when troubleshooting or to analyze the website's traffic. The logs can also be used for things such as capacity planning and can analyze the behavior of the traffic. Finding out where traffic is coming from can be invaluable.

By default, IIS creates a separate log file every day. This has advantages, but on a busy web server with many sites, managing log files can become a challenge. A web server that has been up and running for a month could have 30 separate log files. Changing the location of log files as well as how often to create a new log file can be appropriate.

You should also be aware that IIS has no built-in mechanism.

In this recipe, you configure logging in IIS using PowerShell and the provider contained in the WebAdministration module.

Getting ready

This recipe assumes you have installed IIS, as per the *Install IIS* recipe.

How to do it...

1. Import the WebAdministration module to ensure the IIS provider is loaded:

```
Import-Module WebAdministration
```

2. Look at where you are currently storing logfiles:

```
$LogfileLocation = (Get-ItemProperty
                        -Path'IIS:\Sites\Default Website' `
                        -Name logfile).directory
$LogFileFolder =
[System.Environment]::
ExpandEnvironmentVariables("$LogfileLocation")
Get-ChildItem -Path $LogFileFolder -Recurse
```

3. Change the folder to C:\IISLogs:

```
Set-ItemProperty -Path 'IIS:\Sites\Default Website' `
                    -Name logFile.directory `
                    -Value 'C:\IISLogs'
```

4. Change the type of logging done:

```
Set-ItemProperty -Path 'IIS:\Sites\Default Website' `
                 -Name logFile.logFormat `
                 -Value'W3C'
```

5. Change frequency of `logFile` changes:

```
Set-ItemProperty -Path 'IIS:\Sites\Default Website' `
                 -Name logFile.period `
                 -Value Weekly
```

6. Set a maximum size for the `logFile`:

```
Set-ItemProperty -Path 'IIS:\Sites\Default Website' `
                 -Name logFile.period `
                 -Value MaxSize
$Size = 1GB
Set-ItemProperty -Path 'IIS:\Sites\Default Website' 1
                 -Name logFile.truncateSize
                 -Value $Size
```

7. Disable logging for the default website:

```
Set-ItemProperty -Path 'IIS:\Sites\Default Website'
                 -Name logFile.enabled
                 -Value False
```

How it works...

In *step 1*, you import the `WebAdministration` module which produces no output. This recipe uses the provider as opposed to the cmdlets, contained in the module.

In *step 2*, you discover where, by default, IIS store its log files and view the log files available. The log file folder, by default, `%SystemDrive%\inetpub\logs\LogFiles`, is named using a system environment variable (`%SystemDrive%`). To convert the returned value into a full file system path, you use the ExpandEnvironmentVariables method of .NET `System.Environment`. The output of this step looks like this:

```
PS C:\> $LogfileLocation = (Get-ItemProperty 'IIS:\Sites\Default Web Site' -Name logfile).directory
PS C:\> $LogFileFolder = [System.Environment]::ExpandEnvironmentVariables("$LogfileLocation")
PS C:\> Get-ChileItem -Path $LogFileFolder -Recurse

    Directory: C:\inetpub\logs\LogFiles

Mode                LastWriteTime         Length Name
----                -------------         ------ ----
d-----        20/06/2017     16:54                W3SVC1

    Directory: C:\inetpub\logs\LogFiles\W3SVC1

Mode                LastWriteTime         Length Name
----                -------------         ------ ----
-a----        11/06/2017     16:39           1848 u_ex170611.log
-a----        15/06/2017     18:02            838 u_ex170615.log
-a----        20/06/2017     17:01           2217 u_ex170620.log
```

As you can see, there are three log files for this system—you may see different outputs depending on what requests you have sent to SRV1. If you are testing this recipe, consider viewing the contents of any log files generated. Using the provider, as you do in this step, generates no output.

In *step 3*, you use the provider to change the location of the IIS logs for the default website. You change the log file location to C:\IISLOGS. Of course, you can use any folder you choose! You may find it appropriate to put the log files on a separate disk. There is no output from this step.

In *step 4*, you change the output format for the log files. There are a number of different log file formats you can utilize (IIS, NCSA, W3C, and custom) in this step, which produces no output, to use the W3C format. Depending on your needs, and whether you have analysis software that prefers one format over the other, you can change the log file format. Log file formats you can specify include IIS, NCSA, and W3C.

In *step 5*, you change the frequency of log file changes. By default, IIS produces one file per day, but here you change it to a new file each week. Depending on the traffic, and how you plan to analyze it you might wish to change the defaults. You can set your log file changers to be: Hourly, Daily, Weekly, Monthly, or Maximum size.

In *step 6*, you update two IIS log file properties. The first sets the log file period to maximum size. The second sets the truncate size to a value (1 GB). These changes have the effect of having IIS log files both be a maximum size and to have IIS create a new log once the current log gets larger.

With *step 7*, you disable logging, in this case, for the default website. Best practice is to have a log file that describes the web requests sent to your IIS server and where they came from. But there may be cases where turning logging off may be useful. For example, if you use DSC, you may want to turn IIS logging off once your DSC environment is working. You could rely instead on DSC logging.

There's more...

In *step 3*, you adjusted the folder to hold the IIS logs. In production, you may choose to hold IIS log files on separate disks. As a best practice, you should consider having your IIS log files on a separate disk.

In *step 5*, you adjusted the log file format for IIS logging. You have several options for log file formats. See `https://docs.microsoft.com/en-us/iis/manage/provisioning-and-managing-iis/configure-logging-in-iis` for more information on IIS log file formats.

Here's more

You may want to keep your log files for longer time periods, say more than seven days. To avoid them from clogging up your web servers, you can write a simple script that copies each server's log files to a central repository. To achieve this, modify the recipe to use Move-Item to move the log files to a remote location instead of deleting them.

Managing applications and application pools

In earlier versions of IIS, all the web pages/sites on a given system ran in a single process. This meant that one application, if not written well could cause issues with other applications. An application could, for example, have a memory leak which would ultimately require a restart of IIS or even a reboot of the server.

In later versions of IIS, Microsoft adds the concept of web applications and application pools to IIS. With IIS, a web application is a set of one or more URLs (web pages) which you configure IIS to run inside independent worker processes. An application pool is a set of worker processes which IIS uses to run an application. You can run one or more applications within a given application pool. Technically a website and a web application are not the same, but in many cases, different websites end up being distinct applications.

The application pool feature provides application isolation, enabling you to run possibly badly-behaved applications independently of others. And since you can configure an application pool to run more than one worker process, application pools provide scalability. With application pools, IIS can spawn numerous threads in each worker which IIS runs in parallel. IIS can create and destroy worker processes on demand.

You can also set up the worker processes to have IIS recycle the process on a regular basis. Thus, if a badly-behaved application contains a memory leak (something quite possible using older ISAPI technologies for example), recycling the process returns the leaked resources back to the OS. Thus, even a very poorly-written application can run reasonably well inside IIS.

Another nice feature of application pools is that you can configure each application pool with separate credentials. Although is management of users to do, this approach provides increased security of IIS applications. For example, an HR application could run using the credentials `Reskit\HRApp` whilst you could configure an accounting web application to run as `Reskit\AccountApp`.

Web applications and application pools enable you to both scale a given web server and at the same time provide isolation between applications, which both improves security and minimizes disruptions caused by badly implemented applications.

With a web pool, you can also specify when to recycle the applications within the pool. Rich web applications can include executable code, written in a variety of languages. This code can have faults, resulting in resource leaks. One way to reduce the impact of such faults is to recycle the application—killing the worker process(s) running the pool and creating new ones. Any leaked resources are returned, although any state saved in the application pool's memory is lost.

There are a variety of conditions you can set to trigger recycling on an application pool. You can set a schedule of when to recycle, you can recycle if private memory exceeds a pre-determined value (For example 1 GB), or after a certain number of requests (recycle the application pool after 1 million hits).

For fuller details, see

`https://technet.microsoft.com/en-us/library/cc745955.aspx`

This page relates to IIS 7, but the details are still the same for IIS 10 included with Windows Server 2016 and Windows 10.

In this recipe, you create a new IIS web application. This new application is to be the single page WWW2 site you created in the Configure IIS bindings recipe. The recipe also creates and configures an application pool that hosts the new application.

Getting ready

This recipe assumes you have installed IIS, as per the *Install IIS* recipe. This recipe also makes use of the WWW2.Reskit.Org site you created in the *Configure IIS Bindings* recipe.

How to do it...

1. Import the WebAdministration module:

```
Import-Module WebAdministration
```

2. Create the new application pool:

```
New-WebAppPool -Name WWW2Pool
```

3. Create the new application in the pool:

```
New-WebApplication -Name WWW2 -Site www2 `
                   -ApplicationPool WWW2Pool `
                   -PhysicalPath C:\inetpub\www2
```

4. View the application pools on SRV1:

```
Get-IISAppPool
```

5. Set the application pool restart times:

```
Clear-ItemProperty -Path 'IIS:\AppPools\WWW2Pool' `
                   -Name Recycling.periodicRestart.schedule
$RestartAt = @('07:55', '19:55')
New-ItemProperty -Path 'IIS:\AppPools\WWW2Pool' `
                 -Name Recycling.periodicRestart.schedule `
                 -Value $RestartAt
```

6. Set the application pool maximum private memory:

```
Clear-ItemProperty IIS:\AppPools\WWW2Pool `
                   -Name Recycling.periodicRestart.privatememory
[int32] $PrivMemMax = 1GB
Set-ItemProperty -Path 'IIS:\AppPools\WWW2Pool' `
                 -Name Recycling.periodicRestart.privateMemory `
                 -Value $PrivMemMax
Get-ItemProperty -Path 'IIS:\AppPools\WWW2Pool' `
                 -Name Recycling.periodicRestart.privateMemory
```

7. Set the maximum number of requests before a recycle:

```
Clear-ItemProperty IIS:\AppPools\WWW2Pool `
                 -Name Recycling.periodicRestart.requests
[int32] $MaxRequests = 100000
Set-ItemProperty -Path 'IIS:\AppPools\www2POOL' `
                 -Name Recycling.periodicRestart.requests `
                 -Value $MaxRequests
Get-ItemProperty -Path 'IIS:\AppPools\www2POOL' `
                 -Name Recycling.periodicRestart.requests
```

8. View the application pool properties in IIS. Open the IIS management console, and view the application pool properties.

How it works...

In *step 1*, you import the `WebAdministration` module. This recipe uses the provider, so you should load it in advance. There is no output from this step.

In *step 2*, you create a new application pool (`WWW2Pool`). This has output that looks like this:

Once you have created the application pool, you can create a new web application that is to host the `WWW2` site created earlier. In step 3, you create an application within the just-created application pool. The output looks like this:

```
PS C:> New-WebApplication -Name WWW2 -Site www2 `
                     -ApplicationPool WWW2Pool `
                     -PhysicalPath C:\inetpub\www2

Name          Application pool   Protocols   Physical Path
----          ----------------   ---------   -------------
WWW2          WWW2Pool           http        C:\inetpub\www2
```

In *step 4*, you review the application pools, with output like this:

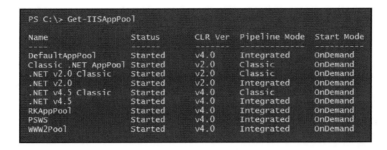

In *step 5*, you set the times when IIS is to recycle the application pool. You specify 7:55 in the morning and 19:55 in the evening. There is no output from this step.

In *step 6*, you specify a private memory maximum value of 1 GB. Setting the `privateMemory` property directs IIS to restart the application pool any time a worker process's private memory exceeds 1 GB. There is no output from this step.

In *step 7*, you open up the IIS console, click on the application pool node, then look at the advanced properties for the WWW2 application pool. As you can see in this output, the restart times, private memory maximum, and restart counts are all enabled:

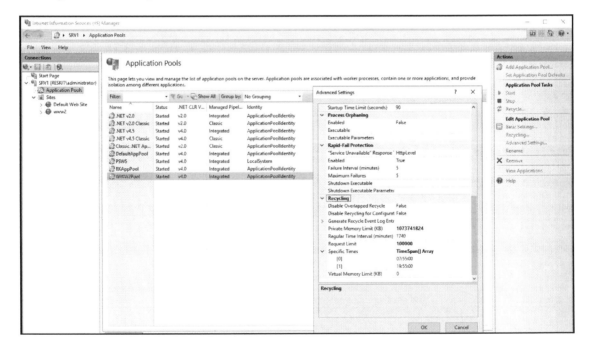

There's more...

In *step 2*, you create a new application pool, using the `New-WebAppPool` cmdlet. However, there is no `Get-WebAppPool` cmdlet—to view the application pools, as you see in *step 4*, you have to use the `Get-IISAppPool` cmdlet. That's because the `Get-IISAppPool` comes from the `IISAdministration` module and is new in Server 2016.

In *step 4*, you can see a variety of existing web pools. These show the IIS application pools created both by default and by other recipes in this book. The application pool is an important feature to enable you to run multiple web applications on a single server and avoid application interference. As part of deploying IIS, you might consider removing all but the necessary application pools.

In *step 5*, *step 6*, and *step 7*, you configure the application pool properties. You achieve this by setting item properties within the IIS provider. Where you want to configure pool properties, you set the relevant item property on the application pool item for the pool. These steps make use of the `WebAdministration` provider. The *item properties* you set are translated by the provider into the XML that drives IIS. For more information on the `WebAdministration` provider, see
https://technet.microsoft.com/en-us/library/ee909471(v=ws.10).aspx.

Managing and monitoring network load balancing

Network Load Balancing (**NLB**) is a feature of Windows and IIS that allows multiple hosts to host the same website. The NLB cluster distributes all traffic to the cluster to the individual hosts.

NLB provides both scalability and fault tolerance. If you add additional nodes, the cluster is able to handle more traffic. And if a node should fail, the other remaining nodes take the traffic, albeit at a potentially lower performance level.

NLB is a versatile feature. You can use NLB to load balance web, FTP, firewall, proxy, and VPN traffic. Performance is acceptable although many users prefer to use hardware load balancers.

In this recipe, you create a new NLB cluster (`ReskitNLB`) which loads balances between two hosts (`NLB1`, `NLB2`). The recipe creates a simple single page site on each system and load balances the site.

In this recipe, the single document site differs on each server, which is useful to show which server accepted and processed any given request. In production, you would want all nodes to have the same content, providing a seamless experience.

You run the core of this recipe on NLB1. Once you have the NLB cluster up and running, you can view it from another host (in this case DC1).

Getting ready

This recipe uses two previous servers, NLB1 and NLB2, as well as DC1. DC1 is the domain controller in the Reskit.Org domain and is also a DNS server for the domain. You must set static IP addresses on both servers, otherwise you see an error attempting to create the NLB cluster.

The two new servers should have the default setup, with IIS loaded. After you install the two servers, you can add IIS as follows:

```
Install-WindowsFeature -Name Web-Server `
                       -IncludeManagementTools
Install-WindowsFeature -Name Web-Server `
                       -IncludeManagementTools `
                       -ComputerName NLB2
```

How to do it...

1. Install NLB locally on NLB1, them remotely on NLB2:

```
Install-WindowsFeature -Name NLB `
                       -IncludeManagementTools
Install-WindowsFeature -Name NLB `
                       -IncludeAllSubFeature `
                       -IncludeManagementTools `
                       -ComputerName NLB2
```

2. Confirm NLB and Web-Server features are loaded on both systems:

```
Invoke-Command -ScriptBlock {Get-WindowsFeature Web-Server, NLB} `
               -ComputerName NLB1, NLB2 |
   Format-table -Property DisplayName,PSComputername,Installstate
```

3. Create the NLB cluster, initially on NLB1:

```
New-NlbCluster -InterfaceName Ethernet `
               -ClusterName 'ReskitNLB' `
               -ClusterPrimaryIP 10.10.10.55 `
               -SubnetMask 255.255.255.0 `
               -OperationMode Multicast
```

4. Add NLB2 to the ReskitNLB cluster:

```
Add-NlbClusterNode -NewNodeName NLB2 `
                   -NewNodeInterface 'Ethernet' `
                   -InterfaceName 'Ethernet'
```

5. Create a network firewall rule:

```
Invoke-Command -ComputerName NLB2   {
    Set-NetFirewallRule -DisplayGroup 'File and
    Printer Sharing' `
                        -Enabled True
}
```

6. Create a default document—differently on each machine:

```
'NLB Cluster: Hosted on NLB1' |
    Out-File  -FilePath C:\inetpub\wwwroot\index.html
'NLB Cluster: Greetings from NLB2' |
    Out-File  -FilePath \\nlb2\c$\inetpub\wwwroot\index.html
```

7. Add a DNS A record for the cluster:

```
$sb = {
Add-DnsServerResourceRecordA -Name ReskitNLB `
                             -IPv4Address 10.10.10.55 `
                             -zonename Reskit.Org}
Invoke-Command -ComputerName DC1 -ScriptBlock $sb
```

8. View the NLB site (do this on DC1):

```
Start-Process 'http://ReskitNLB.reskit.org'
```

9. Stop one node (the one that responded in *step 8*!):

```
Stop-NlbClusterNode -HostName NLB1
```

10. Then view the site again:

```
$IE  = New-Object -ComObject InterNetExplorer.Application
$URL = 'http://ReskitNLB.reskit.org'
$IE.Navigate2($URL)
$IE.Visible = $true
```

How it works...

In the *Getting ready* phase of this recipe, you create two servers in the Reskit.Org domain that are to host the NLB cluster. In this recipe, you are adding and configuring NLB on these two new servers.

In *step 1*, you add the NLB feature to your two hosts:

```
PS C:\> Install-WindowsFeature -Name NLB `
              -IncludeManagementTools

Success Restart Needed Exit Code    Feature Result
------- -------------- ---------    --------------
True    No             Success      {Network Load Balancing, Remote Server Adm...

PS C:\> Install-WindowsFeature -Name NLB `
                -IncludeManagementTools `
                -ComputerName NLB2

Success Restart Needed Exit Code    Feature Result
------- -------------- ---------    --------------
True    No             Success      {Network Load Balancing, Remote Server Adm..
```

In *step 2*, you confirm that you have loaded both the NLB and Web-Server features to both NLB1, and NLB2, which looks like this:

```
PS C:\> Invoke-Command -ScriptBlock {Get-WindowsFeature Web-Server, NLB} `
             -ComputerName NLB1, NLB2 |
   Format-Table -Property DisplayName,PSComputername,InstallState


DisplayName              PSComputerName InstallState
-----------              -------------- ------------
Web Server (IIS)         NLB2           Installed
Network Load Balancing   NLB2           Installed
Web Server (IIS)         NLB1           Installed
Network Load Balancing   NLB1           Installed
```

With the necessary features loaded, in *step 3*, you create the NLB cluster named ReskitNLB. The output of this step looks like this:

```
PS C:\> New-NlbCluster -InterfaceName ethernet `
              -ClusterName 'ReskitNLB' `
              -ClusterPrimaryIP 10.10.10.55 -SubnetMask 255.255.255.0 `
              -OperationMode Unicast

Name       IPAddress    SubnetMask     Mode
----       ---------    ----------     ----
ReskitNLB 10.10.10.55 255.255.255.0 MULTICAST
```

The previous step creates a one node NLB cluster. In *step 4*, you add the second node, NLB2, to the ReskitNLB load balancing cluster. The output from this step looks like this:

```
PS C:\> Add-NlbClusterNode -NewNodeName NLB2 `
                  -NewNodeInterface 'Ethernet' `
                  -InterfaceName 'Ethernet'

Name State               Interface HostID
---- -----               --------- ------
NLB2 Converged(default) Ethernet  2
```

In *step 5*, you add a simple firewall rule to allow file and printer sharing to be allowed. There is no output from this step.

In *step 6*, you create default documents for each server in the NLB cluster. This step generates different default documents for each of the two NLB hosts, which helps you see which host is servicing the request. There is no output from this step.

To complete the setup of the cluster, in *step 7*, you add a DNS A record pointing to the NLB Cluster IP address (10.10.10.55). This enables you to use a DNS host name (ReskitNLB.Reskit.Org) to access the cluster. There is no output from this step.

With the cluster setup, in *step 8* you view the site, using the new DNS name. You run this step on any host except the two NLB nodes, for example, DC1, using the full DNS name of the NLB cluster (ReskitNLB.Reskit.Org). When you do so, the output looks like this:

In *step 9*, which you run on NLB1 or NLB2, you stop the node that processed the previous reply to simulate a node failure. Assuming NLB1 previously responded, this step stops the NLB node on NLB1. The output looks like this:

With the NLB1 host now stopped, in *step 10*, you re-view the site (from the same computer you used in *step 8*, for example DC1). The output looks like this:

There's more...

This recipe uses two new servers (NLB1, NLB2). You could also run this recipe on other servers as appropriate—for example SRV1 and SRV2 used elsewhere in this book.

In *step 3*, you create the NLB cluster. Because NLB1 and NLB2 have just one network adapter, you create the cluster with an operation mode of Multicast. Had you used Unicast, Windows would have effectively killed off the normal connection to these systems.

In *step 9*, you stop a node in the ReskitNLB load balancing cluster. You could view the status of the nodes in the cluster by using the Get-NlbClusterNode cmdlet. After stopping the NLB1 node, the output when viewing ReskitNLB.Reskit.Org is that you see the default document on NLB2. This shows that the cluster is operational even if a node is not. You might make use of this during a maintenance window. You could take one node down and the cluster continues whilst you maintain the node. Of course, this means the overall cluster is less performant, but that is a fact to consider when setting any maintenance windows.

In *step 8*, *step 9*, and *step 10*, you view the operation of the NLB cluster. If you are testing this, you may find NLB2 responds to the initial request (*step 8*)—if so, then in step 9, shut down NLB2 instead. If you run these tests on either of the cluster members, NLB resolves the cluster to the local site. So running this from NLB1 would always pick NLB1, whereas from another host, such as DC1, you see the desired behavior.

11
Managing Hyper-V

In this chapter, we cover the following recipes:

- Installing and configuring Hyper-V feature
- Using Windows PowerShell Direct
- Securing Hyper-V host
- Creating a virtual machine
- Configuring VM hardware
- Configuring Hyper-V networking
- Implementing nested Hyper-V
- Managing VM state
- Configuring VM and storage movement
- Configuring VM replication
- Managing VM checkpoints
- Monitoring Hyper-V utilization and performance
- Creating a Hyper-V health report

Introduction

Hyper-V is Microsoft's virtual machine hypervisor. Both Windows Server 2016 and Windows 10 include Hyper-V as an option you can install. The Hyper-V feature is included in all versions of Windows Server 2016, as well as in the Enterprise, Professional, and Education editions of Windows 10. Nested Hyper-V, the ability to run Hyper-V inside a Hyper-V VM, is available in both Windows 10 Anniversary Update and Windows Server 2016. Additionally, Microsoft has made the Microsoft Hyper-V Server available as a free version of the Hyper-V hypervisor. The Hyper-V Server runs virtual machines with no GUI. You configure and manage remotely.

Hyper-V was first released with Server 2008. Successive versions of Windows brought improvements in features, hardware support, and scalability. The first version did not include PowerShell cmdlet support, but that was rectified in later releases. With Server 2016 there is good PowerShell coverage. This chapter focuses solely on Hyper-V inside Windows Server 2016 although you can manage Hyper-V Server using the tools used in this chapter's recipes.

Hyper-V's management tools enable you to configure and manage both the Hyper-V service and configure and manage virtual machines and the resources they utilize. This chapter starts with installing and configuring the Hyper-V Server role. Later in the chapter, you create and manage virtual machines. The chapter ends with looking at high availability for Hyper-V Servers and Hyper-V VMs, host resource protection, and PowerShell Direct.

Installing and configuring Hyper-V feature

To install Hyper-V on Windows Server 2016, you install the Hyper-V feature. In this recipe, you do the set up remotely from a client machine using the Hyper-V cmdlets and PowerShell's remoting capabilities.

Getting ready

For this recipe, you need to have the host computers on which you install Hyper-V. This recipe uses two servers, HV1 and HV2. Each server is a member of the domain on which you have added no additional services. As an alternative to having two systems running, you could use embedded Hyper-V and create the two VMs inside a third.

To demonstrate remote configuration, you perform this recipe from a third computer, CL1 running Windows 10 (Anniversary Update). This recipe makes use of a second hard disk, an H: drive on the HV1 and HV2 systems that you use to store Hyper-V VMs and virtual disks.

You need the Hyper-V tools on CL1—add them using the Enable-WindowsOptionalFeature and use the -Online switch, as follows:

```
# Add windows optional feature for CL1
Enable-WindowsOptionalFeature `
          -FeatureName Microsoft-Hyper-V-All `
          -Online -NoRestart
Restart-Computer -Computername CL1 -Force
```

If you are using Windows 10 to test these recipes, you can install Hyper-V features assuming you have the Professional, Enterprise, or Educational editions. If you install Hyper-V on either Windows 10 or Server 2016, you need to reboot the host computer before proceeding.

How to do it...

This recipe shows how to install Hyper-V:

1. From CL1, install the Hyper-V feature on HV1, HV2:

```
$Sb = {
  Install-WindowsFeature -Name Hyper-V `
                          -IncludeManagementTools }
Invoke-Command -ComputerName HV1, HV2 `
               -ScriptBlock $Sb
```

2. Reboot the servers to complete the installation:

```
Restart-Computer -ComputerName HV1, HV2 -Force `
                  -Wait -For -PowerShell
```

3. Create and set the location for VMs and VHDs on HV1 and HV2, then view results:

```
$Sb = {
    New-Item -Path H:\Vm      -ItemType Directory -Force |
        Out-Null
    New-Item -Path H:\Vm\Vhds -ItemType Directory -Force |
        Out-Null
    New-Item -Path H:\Vm\VMs  -ItemType Directory -force |
        Out-Null
  Get-ChildItem -Path H:\Vm  }
Invoke-Command -ComputerName HV1, HV2 -ScriptBlock $Sb
```

4. Set default paths for Hyper-V VM hard disks and VM configuration information:

```
Set-VMHost -ComputerName HV1,HV2 `
           -VirtualHardDiskPath 'H:\Vm\Vhds'
Set-VMHost -ComputerName HV1,HV2 `
           -VirtualMachinePath  'H:\Vm\VMs'
```

5. Setup NUMA spanning:

```
Set-VMHost -ComputerName HV1,HV2 -NumaSpanningEnabled $true
```

6. Set up `EnhancedSessionMode`:

```
Set-VMHost -ComputerName HV1,HV2 `
            -EnableEnhancedSessionMode $true
```

7. Setup host resource metering on HV1, HV2:

```
$RMInterval = New-TimeSpan -Hours 0 -Minutes 15
Set-VMHost -CimSession HV1, HV2 -ResourceMeteringSaveInterval
$RMInterval
```

8. Review key VMHost settings:

```
Get-VMHost -ComputerName HV1, HV2 |
    Format-List -Property Name, MemoryCapacity,
                        Virtual*Path, NumaSpanningEnabled,
                        EnableEnhancedSessionMode,
                        ResourceMeteringSaveInterval
```

How it works...

In *step 1,* you used PowerShell remoting to invoke a script block on the two Hyper-V Servers. The script block contains the command to install the Hyper-V feature on the server. PowerShell runs the script in parallel on both computers. Once complete, as you can see in the following screenshot, you need to reboot before proceeding:

```
PS C:> $Sb = {
        Install-WindowsFeature -Name Hyper-V `
                        -IncludeManagementTools}
PS C:> Invoke-Command -ComputerName HV1, HV2 `
            -ScriptBlock $Sb


PSComputerName : HV2
RunspaceId     : ae4a4853-631e-4d5c-a33d-e10886175ea3
Success        : True
RestartNeeded  : Yes
FeatureResult  : {Hyper-V, Hyper-V Module for Windows PowerShell, Hyper-V GUI Management Tools,
                 Remote Server Administration Tools...}
ExitCode       : SuccessRestartRequired
WARNING: You must restart this server to finish the installation process.

PSComputerName : HV1
RunspaceId     : 86417f8f-27c0-4755-bcfa-cc0113854628
Success        : True
RestartNeeded  : Yes
FeatureResult  : {Hyper-V, Hyper-V Module for Windows PowerShell, Hyper-V GUI Management Tools,
                 Remote Server Administration Tools...}
ExitCode       : SuccessRestartRequired
WARNING: You must restart this server to finish the installation process.
```

In *step 2*, you reboot the two servers. By using the `-Wait -For Powershell` parameters, you tell PowerShell to reboot HV1 and HV2 and wait until the servers are running and contactable. Once this cmdlet has finished, HV1 and HV2 are both in a state where you can continue to configure them using PowerShell remoting.

In *step 3*, you create a top-level folder (H:\Vm) and two sub-folders (H:\Vm\Vhds and H:\Vm\VMs). You can see the folders on the two Hyper-V hosts, as follows:

```
PS C:> $Sb = {
        New-Item -Path H:\Vm      -ItemType Directory -Force  | Out-Null
        New-Item -Path H:\Vm\Vhds -ItemType Directory -Force  | Out-Null
        New-Item -Path H:\Vm\VMs  -ItemType Directory -force  | Out-Null
        Get-ChildItem -Path H:\Vm
    }

Invoke-Command -ComputerName HV1, HV2 -ScriptBlock $Sb


    Directory: H:\Vm


Mode         LastWriteTime     Length Name    PSComputerName
----         -------------     ------ ----    --------------
d-----       01/03/2017  12:15        Vhds    HV1
d-----       01/03/2017  12:15        VMs     HV1
d-----       01/03/2017  12:16        Vhds    HV2
d-----       01/03/2017  12:16        VMs     HV2
```

In the next three steps, you set up some aspect of the two Hyper-V hosts. In *step 4*, you set the default paths for Virtual hard disks and Virtual Machines on the two Hyper-V hosts. In *step 5*, you enable NUMA spanning while in *step 6* you enable enhanced session mode. In *step 7*, you set the save interval for VM resource metering to 15 minutes. There is no output from these steps.

In *step 8*, you look at the settings you updated in this recipe, which looks like this:

```
PS C:\> Get-VMHost -ComputerName HV1, HV2 |
        Format-List -Property Name, MemoryCapacity,
                             Virtual*Path, NumaSpanningEnabled,
                             EnableEnhancedSessionMode,
                             ResourceMeteringSaveInterval


Name                         : HV1
MemoryCapacity               : 16776744960
VirtualHardDiskPath          : H:\vm\vhds
VirtualMachinePath           : H:\VM\VMs
NumaSpanningEnabled          : True
EnableEnhancedSessionMode    : True
ResourceMeteringSaveInterval : 01:30:00

Name                         : HV2
MemoryCapacity               : 16776744960
VirtualHardDiskPath          : H:\vm\vhds
VirtualMachinePath           : H:\VM\VMs
NumaSpanningEnabled          : True
EnableEnhancedSessionMode    : True
ResourceMeteringSaveInterval : 01:30:00
```

There's more...

In *step 1*, you installed the Hyper-V feature on two servers. You can only do this successfully if the host you are using supports the necessary virtualization capabilities and you have enabled them in your system's BIOS. To check if your system is capable, see this link: http://mikefrobbins.com/2012/09/06/use-powershell-to-check-for-processor-cpu-second-level-address-translation-slat-support/. Also you should double check the BIOS to ensure virtualization is enabled.

If your host is either misconfigured or incapable of supporting virtualization, you may see this message when you attempt to add the Hyper-V feature:

```
A prerequisite check for the Hyper-V feature failed.
1. Hyper-V cannot be installed: The processor does not have required virtualization capabilities.
    + CategoryInfo          : InvalidOperation: (Hyper-V:ServerComponentWrapper) [Install-WindowsFeature], Exception
    + FullyQualifiedErrorId : Alteration_PrerequisiteCheck_Failed,Microsoft.Windows.ServerManager.Commands.AddWindow
    sFeatureCommand
    + PSComputerName         : hv1
```

If you do encounter this message, then you need to find another host computer—yours is not ever going to run Hyper-V.

In *step 2*, you installed the Hyper-V features on the two Hyper-V hosts, and then in *step 3*, you rebooted the two servers. You could have allowed `Install-WindowsFeature` to have rebooted automatically by using the `-Restart` switch. In automation terms, this could have meant that the system started rebooting before the remote script has completed. This could cause the `Invoke-Command` to error out. The recipe avoids this by not rebooting after installation of the Hyper-V features, then rebooting in a controlled way. Once the `Reboot-Computer` command returns, your scripts can carry on managing the servers.

In each of *step 4* through *step 7*, you set up one aspect of the Hyper-V hosts. You could have combined these steps and just called `Set-VMHost` once with all of the properties specified.

You can find more information on some of the Hyper-V features used in this recipe (details of which are outside the scope of this book), as follows:

For more information on	See
Connecting to a VM, including enhanced session mode	https://technet.microsoft.com/en-us/windows-server- docs/compute/hyper-v/learn-more/use-local-resources-on-hyper-v-virtual-machine-with-vmconnect
Understanding the hard disk paths for VM and VHD information	https://blogs.msdn.microsoft.com/virtual_pc_guy/2010/03/10/understanding-where-your-virtual-machine-files-are-hyper-v/
Hyper-V and NUMA	https://technet.microsoft.com/en-us/library/dn282282%28v=ws.11%29.aspx?f=255MSPPError=-2147217396
Hyper-V Resource Metering	https://technet.microsoft.com/en- us/library/hh831661(v=ws.11).aspx

Using Windows PowerShell Direct

PowerShell Direct (**PSD**) is a new feature with Windows Server 2016 (and on Windows 10 Anniversary Update or later). PSD enables you to use PowerShell remoting to access a Hyper-V VM without needing to setup networking and firewall settings. With PSD, you use `Invoke-Command`, specifying either the VM's name or the VM's VMID (the VMID is a GUID used internally by Hyper-V to identify a VM). You can also use the VM name or VMID to enter a remote session using `Enter-PSSession`.

In previous versions of Hyper-V, you needed some sort of networking connection between your Hyper-V host and the guest OS in order to remote into the guest. This was often setting up firewall exceptions and establishing network connectivity. With PSD, you can use the VM's name or ID and remote straight in.

Getting ready

For this recipe, you need a Hyper-V Host running on either Windows 10 Anniversary Update (or later) or Windows Server 2016, with Hyper-V loaded and operational. Additionally, you need a VM running Windows Server 2016 (or Windows 10). You should name the VM `psdirect` and set the VM's guest OS hostname to `tiger`.

To ensure security, you need to specify credentials when you call `Invoke-Command` or `Enter- PSSession`. You can either specify the `-Credential` parameter or let either cmdlet prompt for credentials.

With Hyper-V, the VM name can be different to the hostname of the OS running inside the VM. In this example, you use a VM with a VM name of `psdirect` and a hostname of `tiger`.

How to do it...

Here is how you can use PowerShell Direct:

1. Create a credential object for `ReskitAdministrator`:

```
$RKAdmin = 'ReskitAdministrator'
$RKPass = ConvertTo-SecureString `
        -String 'Pa$$w0rd' `
        -AsPlainText `
        -Force
$RKCred = New-Object `
```

```
-TypeName System.Management.Automation.PSCredential
        -ArgumentList $RKAdmin,$RKPass
```

2. Display the details of the `psdirect` VM:

```
Get-VM -Name psdirect
```

3. Invoke a command on the VM, specifying VM name:

```
Invoke-Command -VMName psdirect `
            -Credential $RKCred `
            -ScriptBlock {hostname}
```

4. Invoke a command based on VMID:

```
$VMID = (Get-VM -VMName psdirect).VMId.Guid
Invoke-Command -VMid $VMID `
            -Credential $RKCred `
            -ScriptBlock {hostname}
```

5. Enter a PS remoting session with the `psdirect` VM:

```
Enter-PSSession -VMName psdirect -Credential $RKCred
Get-CimInstance -Class Win32_ComputerSystem
Exit-PSSession
```

How it works...

In *step 1*, you take a shortcut and directly create a credential object. Needless to say, it's not best practice, but for testing and learning, it is highly convenient.

In *step 2*, you use `Get-VM` to return information about the `psdirect` virtual machine, which looks like this:

```
PS C:\> Get-VM -Name psdirect

Name      State    CPUUsage(%) MemoryAssigned(M) Uptime              Status           Version
----      -----    ----------- ----------------- ------              ------           -------
psdirect  Running  0           1024              00:09:48.2910000    Operating normally 8.0
```

In *step 3*, you invoke a script block on the `psdirect` VM, specifying the VM by name. The script block just returns the name of the guest OS, as follows:

```
PS C:\> Invoke-Command -VMName psdirect `
                        -Credential $RKCred `
                        -ScriptBlock {hostname}
Tiger
```

In *step 4*, you invoke the same script block as in *step 3* but specifying the VM based on VMID. This property is a GUID that Hyper-V uses internally to address each VM. You get the VM's VMID from the object returned from `Get-VM`, and then use it as follows:

```
PS C:\> $VMID = (Get-VM -VMName psdirect).VMId.Guid
PS C:\> Invoke-Command -VMid $VMID `
                       -Credential $RKCred `
                       -ScriptBlock {hostname}
Tiger
```

In *step 5*, you enter a remote PowerShell session on the `psdirect` virtual machine. After entering the remote session, you use `Get-CimInstance` to return WMI information about the VM's operating system. You can see that the `psdirect` VM runs an OS whose hostname is `tiger`:

```
PS C:\> Enter-PSSession -VMName psdirect -Credential $RKCred

[psdirect]: PS C:\Users\administrator\Documents> Get-CimInstance -Class Win32_ComputerSystem

Name   PrimaryOwnerName         Domain       TotalPhysicalMemory  Model            Manufacturer
----   ----------------         ------       -------------------  -----            ------------
TIGER  Packt Recipe Book Reader Reskit.Org   1073270784           Virtual Machine  Microsoft Corporation

[psdirect]: Exit-PSSession
PS C:\>
```

There's more...

In *step 3* and *step 4*, you use the hostname console application to obtain the hostname. You could have displayed the environment variable `$env:COMPUTERNAME`.

In *step 5*, you enter a remote session directly into the `psdirect` VM. Notice that the prefix to the prompt changes to `[psdirect]`. And when you exit the remote session, the prompt changes back to `PS C:\>`. By changing the prompt, PowerShell helpfully reminds you of to the hostname that is to which is going to execute any command you type. Accidentally typing a command intended for the local host into the remote system instead is an all too common mistake.

Securing Hyper-V host

With server virtualization becoming more and more the norm, managing groups of Hyper-V Servers can be simplified by using VM groups. VM Groups are a new feature in Windows Server 2016 that allows you to create and use groups of servers. Server 2016 supports two different types of VM Groups: VM collection groups and management collection groups. A VM collection group is a collection of Hyper-V VMs. You can carry out tasks on the groups rather than on each individual VM. A management collection group is a collection of VM collection groups and other nested management collection groups. VM groups are especially useful for backups and for VM replication. In backup situations, a number of VMs making up a multi-tier application need to be backed up together.

In this recipe, you create a VM collection group containing two servers. Then you set the MAC addresses used by the two servers and you enable host resource protection.

Getting ready

This recipe assumes you have two servers on which you have installed Hyper-V, as set out in the *Installing and configuring Hyper-V feature* recipe. You run this recipe on server HV1. Note that this recipe is based on HV1 and HV2 being VMs.

How to do it...

Here is how you can secure your Hyper-V host:

1. Setup Hyper-V VM groups:

```
$VMGroup = New-VMGroup -Name HVServers `
                       -GroupType VMCollectionType
```

2. Create an array of members to add to the VM collection group:

```
$HVServers = 'HV1','HV2'
```

3. Add members to the VM group storage HVServers:

```
Foreach ($HVS in $HVServers) {
    $VM = Get-VM -Name $HVS
    Add-VMGroupMember -ComputerName HVServers -VM $VM}
```

4. Get and display VM group details:

```
Get-VMGroup |
    Format-Table -Property Name, GroupType, VMMembers
```

5. Get and display the VMs in the groups:

```
$Members = (Get-VmGroup -Name HVServers).VMMembers
$Members
```

6. Set up and view MAC addresses:

```
Set-VMhost -ComputerName HV1 -MacAddressMinimum 00155D017000 `
                            -MacAddressMaximum 00155D017099
Set-VMhost -ComputerName HV2 -MacAddressMinimum 00155D017100 `
                            -MacAddressMaximum 00155D017199
Get-VMhost -Computer HV1, HV2 |
    Format-Table -Property Name, MacAddressMinimum,
MacAddressMaximum
```

7. Stop any VMs that might be running in the HVServers VM group:

```
Stop-VM -VM (Get-VMGroup HVServers).VMMembers
```

8. Enable Hyper-V HostResourceProtection for VMs in the HVServer VM group:

```
Set-VMProcessor -VM (Get-VMGroup HVServers).VMMembers `
                -EnableHostResourceProtection $true
```

9. Start VMs in the HVServer VM group:

```
Start-VM -VM (Get-VMGroup HVServers).VMMembers
```

10. Observe the results of enabling `HostResourceProtection`:

```
Get-VMProcessor -VM (Get-VMGroup HvServers).VMMembers |
    Format-Table -Property VMName, OperationalStatus
```

How it works...

In *step 1*, you create a VM collection VM group called `HVServers`. In *step 2* and *step 3* you add the two Hyper-V VMs to the VM group. There is no output from these three steps.

In *step 4*, you use `Get-VMGroup` to return details of the VM groups on the server, like this:

```
PS C:\> Get-VMGroup |
           Format-Table -Property Name, GroupType, VMMembers

Name                GroupType        VMMembers
----                ---------        ---------
HVServers VMCollectionType {HV2, HV1}
```

In *step 5*, you retrieve details about the VMs in the `HVServers` VM group, as follows:

```
PS C:\> $Members = (Get-VmGroup -Name HVServers).VMMembers
PS C:\> $Members

Name State    CPUUsage(%) MemoryAssigned(M) Uptime                     Status              Version
---- -----    ----------- ----------------- ------                     ------              -------
HV2  Running 0            16000             21.04:47:26.3860000 Operating normally 8.0
HV1  Running 0            16000             21.02:39:38.7180000 Operating normally 8.0
```

In *step 6*, you set and then review the MAC addresses that Hyper-V uses on the two Hyper-V host servers, as follows:

```
PS C:\> Set-VMhost -ComputerName HV1 -MacAddressMinimum 00155D017000 `
                                     -MacAddressMaximum 00155D017099
PS C:\> Set-VMhost -ComputerName HV2 -MacAddressMinimum 00155D017100 `
                                     -MacAddressMaximum 00155D017199
PS C:\> Get-VMhost -ComputerName HV1, HV2 |
           Format-Table -Property Name, MacAddressMinimum,
                                  MacAddressMaximum

Name MacAddressMinimum MacAddressMaximum
---- ----------------- -----------------
HV1  00155D017000      00155D017099
HV2  00155D017100      00155D017199
```

In *step 7*, *step 8*, and *step 9*, you stop the VMs in the VM group, you enable `HostResourceProtection` on the Hyper-V hosts, and then you restart the VMs. There is no output from these steps. In *step 10*, once the VMs have restarted, you verify HV1 and HV2 are set to use `HostResourceProtection`, as follows:

```
PS C:\> Get-VMProcessor -VM (Get-VMGroup HvServers).VMMembers |
            Format-Table -Property VMName, OperationalStatus

VMName OperationalStatus
------ -----------------
HV2    {Ok, HostResourceProtectionEnabled}
HV1    {Ok, HostResourceProtectionEnabled}
```

There's more...

In *step 1* through *step 5*, you set up a VM group. This is meant to make dealing with groups of Hyper-V Servers easier. As you see in *step 7* through *step 10*, you use these VM groups to perform management functions on groups of servers.

The VMGroup feature is very useful, but unfortunately, none of the Hyper-V cmdlets support a – VMGroup parameter enabling a cmdlet to operate directly on the members of the VM group. Instead, you specify the VMs using the VM parameter like this, -VM (Get-VMGroup HvServers).VMMembers.

In *step 8*, you enable `HostResourceProtection`. In Server 2016 this is limited to CPU. setting `HostResourceProtection` ensures that the Hyper-V VMs do not use excessive resources (CPUs). You set resource protection settings for VMs in the next recipe.

If you are creating many VMs, you need to consider using the various deployment tools at your disposal. These tools include the commands in then DISM PowerShell modules as well as Windows deployment tools included in the **Windows Automated Installation Kit (WAIK)**. The details of deploying Windows is outside the scope of this recipe.

There are some third party tools, such as the free *Sysinternals* tool Disk2Vhd, that can assist. You can use Disk2VHD to create a VHDX file you can boot from, based on the WIM file on your Windows 2016 installation DVD image. You can download this tool from https://technet.microsoft.com/en- us/sysinternals/ee656415.aspx.

Create a virtual machine

You create Hyper-V virtual machines in several distinct steps. First, you need to create the VM itself—creating a virtual machine and the virtual hard drive and assign hardware such as memory, CPU cores, and DVD drives (and drive contents).

Once the VM is created, you need to work out how to install an OS into the VM. This process can be complex if you use native commands.

In this recipe, you create a simple VM that installs the OS into the VM based on GUI input. This recipe is therefore often the precursor to other configuration (that is you create a new VM and then add features and configure it per your requirements.
This is the same experience you would observe if you had a physical machine, with an empty C: drive that you boot from a Windows Server 2016 installation ISO.

Getting ready

For this recipe, you need a Hyper-V VM host—use HV1 which needs an H: drive. The H: drive is where you store the VM and virtual disks.

You also need the ISO image for Windows Server 2016. For testing purposes, you can download an evaluation edition from Microsoft. Navigate to https://www.microsoft.com/en- us/evalcenter/evaluate-windows-server-2016/ and download the ISO image. In order to download the ISO, you need to login to the TechNet website using a Microsoft ID.

How to do it...

Here is how to create a new VM:

1. Set up the VM name and paths for this recipe:

```
$VMname       = 'VM1'
$VMLocation   = 'H:\Vm\VMs'
$VHDlocation  = 'H:\Vm\Vhds'
$VhdPath      = "$VHDlocation\VM1.Vhdx"
$ISOPath      = 'C:\Builds\en_windows_server_2016_x64_dvd.iso'
```

2. Create a new VM:

```
New-VM -Name VM1 -Path $VMLocation -MemoryStartupBytes 1GB
```

3. Create a virtual disk file for the VM:

```
New-VHD -Path $VhdPath -SizeBytes 128GB -Dynamic
```

4. Add the virtual hard drive to the VM:

```
Add-VMHardDiskDrive -VMName $VMname -Path $VhdPath
```

5. Set ISO image in the VM's DVD drive:

```
Set-VMDvdDrive -VMName $VMName -ControllerNumber 1 `
                -Path $ISOPath
```

6. Start the VM:

```
Start-VM -VMname $VMname
```

7. View the results:

```
Get-VM -Name $VMname
```

How it works...

In *step 1*, you set variables that contain the VM name as well as the paths to the VM/VHDX locations, the VHDX file for this VM and to the Windows Server 2016 installation DVD image. There is no output from this step.

In *step 2*, you create a Hyper-V VM, which looks like this:

```
PS C:\> New-VM -Name VM1  -Path $VMLocation -MemoryStartupBytes 1GB

Name State CPUUsage(%) MemoryAssigned(M) Uptime    Status              Version
---- ----- ----------- ----------------- ------    ------              -------
VM1  Off   0           0                 00:00:00 Operating normally 8.0
```

In *step 3*, you create a dynamic VHDX file for the VM1 virtual machine. The output from this step looks like this:

```
PS C:\> New-VHD -Path $VhdPath -SizeBytes 128GB -Dynamic|

ComputerName            : HV1
Path                    : H:\Vm\Vhds\VM1.Vhdx
VhdFormat               : VHDX
VhdType                 : Dynamic
FileSize                : 4194304
Size                    : 137438953472
MinimumSize             :
LogicalSectorSize       : 512
PhysicalSectorSize      : 4096
BlockSize               : 33554432
ParentPath              :
DiskIdentifier          : E98F967A-0D2A-482B-99AF-7C05DFFA5912
FragmentationPercentage : 0
Alignment               : 1
Attached                : False
DiskNumber              :
Number                  :
```

In *step 4*, you add the VHD to the VM—there is no output from this step.

In *step5*, you add the ISO image to the VM, inserting the image into the VMs's DVD drive. There is no output from this step.

In *step 6*, you add the VHDX file to the VM. There is no output from this step.

Once you add the VHDX and ISO image to the VM, in *step 7*, you start the VM1 VM. There is no output from this step. However, you can observe, in *step 8*, that the VM has started, like this:

```
PS C:\> Get-VM -Name $VMname
Name State   CPUUsage(%) MemoryAssigned(M) Uptime         Status            Version
---- -----   ----------- ----------------- ------         ------            -------
VM1  Running 0           1024              00:00:53.2290000 Operating normally 8.0
```

Using the GUI tools (Hyper-V Manager and VMConnect), your new VM looks like this:

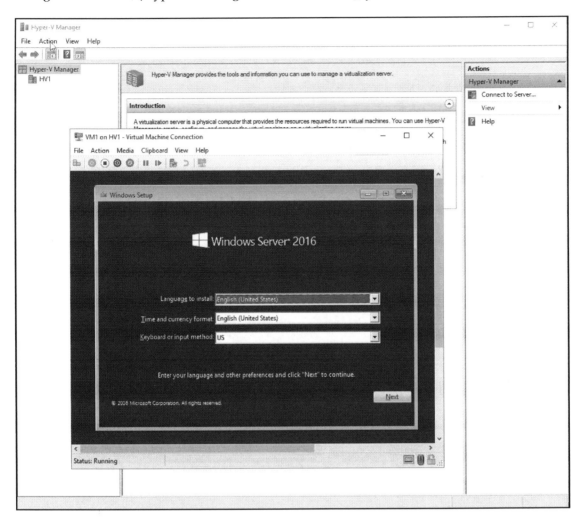

As you can see in this graphic, Windows 2016 has begun the installation process and is waiting for your input. This example was created using a **English (United States)** ISO image—if you use localized ISO images (for example, **English (United Kingdom)**), what you see when you do this recipe may differ from this example depending on the OS language you are using.

You use the VM in later recipes, so you should continue the installation, installing the Windows Server 2016 Enterprise edition with the desktop tools. After the installation has completed, log in to the new server (VM1) and use `Administrator` for your user id and `Pa$$w0rd` for the password.

There's more...

In *step 2*, you create a VM. The VM you create is not bootable as you have not added a hard disk or DVD drive. In *step 3*, you create a new VHDX and then in *step 4*, you add this VHDX to the VM1 VM. After completing this step, the VM is still not bootable. This recipe relies on you using the GUI to complete the installation. Of course, you could use any of the Windows deployment tools to automate the deployment of the VM.

Once you complete *step 6*, your new VM is created and running, but with no OS loaded. You then complete the installation of Windows 2016 in the VM before moving on to the next recipe. The next recipe assumes you have completed the installation of the VM, installing the OS using the *Enterprise* edition with the *Desktop Experience* and adding no additional features.

Configuring VM hardware

Configuring hardware in your virtual machine is very much like configuring a physical computer. With a physical computer, you can adjust the CPUs and BIOS settings. You can also adjust physical RAM, network interfaces, disk interfaces and disk devices, and DVD drives (with/without a loaded DVD), and so on. Each of these physical components is provided within a Hyper-V VM and the PowerShell cmdlets make it simple to adjust the virtual hardware in a VM.

In this recipe, you adjust the VM's BIOS, CPU count, memory, add a SCSI controller, and finally create and add a virtual disk to the SCSI controller. Just like in most commercial grade physical servers, not all of these components can be changed while the server is running. You run this recipe from HV1 and turn the VM1 VM off before configuring the virtual hardware.

This recipe does not cover the virtual NIC which you need in order to use the VM in your network. Configuring the VM's networking is covered in the *Configuring Hyper-V networking* recipe.

Getting ready

This recipe adjusts the virtual hardware inside the VM1 VM created in the *Creating a Virtual Machine* recipe.

How to do it...

Here is how to configure VM hardware on HV1 VM:

1. Turn off the VM1 VM:

```
Get-VM   -VMName VM1 -Verbose
Stop-VM -VMName VM1
Get-VM   -VMName VM1 -Verbose
```

2. Set the StartupOrder in the VM's BIOS:

```
Set-VMBios -VmName VM1 -StartupOrder ('IDE', 'CD',
          'LegacyNetworkAdapter', 'Floppy')
 Get-VMBios VM1
```

3. Set CPU count for VM1:

```
Set-VMProcessor -VMName VM1 -Count 2
Get-VMProcessor -VmName VM1
```

4. Set VM1 memory:

```
Set-VMMemory -VMName VM1 `
             -DynamicMemoryEnabled $true `
             -MinimumBytes 512MB `
             -StartupBytes 1GB `
             -MaximumBytes 2GB
Get-VMMemory -VMName VM1
```

5. Add a ScsiController to VM1:

```
Get-VMScsiController -VMName VM1
Add-VMScsiController -VMName VM1
Get-VMScsiController -VMName VM1
```

6. Restart the VM:

```
Start-VM -VMName VM1
Wait-VM -VMName VM1 -For IPAddress
```

7. Create a new VHDX file:

```
$VHDPath = 'H:\Vm\Vhds\VM1-D.VHDX'
New-VHD -Path $VHDPath -SizeBytes 8GB -Dynamic
```

8. Add the VHD to the ScsiController:

```
Add-VMHardDiskDrive -VMName VM1 -ControllerType SCSI `
                    -ControllerNumber 0 `
                    -ControllerLocation 0 `
                    -Path $VHDPath
```

How it works...

In *step 1*, you first examine the VM1 VM and you see it's running. You then shut down the VM. After it is shut down you observe its status like this:

```
PS C:\> Get-VM -VMName VM1
Name State    CPUUsage(%) MemoryAssigned(M) Uptime              Status              Version
---- -----    ----------- ----------------- ------              ------              -------
VM1  Running 0            1024              00:52:46.5730000 Operating normally 8.0
```

In *step 2*, you change the startup order, as follows:

```
PS C:\> Set-VMBios VM1 -StartupOrder ('IDE', 'CD', 'LegacyNetworkAdapter', 'Floppy')
PS C:\> Get-VMBios VM1

VMName StartupOrder                              NumLockEnabled
------ ------------                              --------------
VM1    {IDE, CD, LegacyNetworkAdapter, Floppy} False
```

In *step 3*, you change the VM to have two CPU (cores) and then display the CPUs available in the VM, as follows:

```
PS C:\> Set-VMProcessor -VMName VM1 -Count 2
PS C:\> Get-VMProcessor -VmName VM1

VMName Count CompatibilityForMigrationEnabled CompatibilityForOlderOperatingSystemsEnabled
------ ----- -------------------------------- --------------------------------------------
VM1    2     False                            False
```

In *step 4*, you update the memory settings for VM1. Then you display the memory settings for the VM, as follows:

```
PS C:\> Set-VMMemory -VMName VM1 `
            -DynamicMemoryEnabled $true `
            -MinimumBytes 512MB `
            -StartupBytes 1GB `
            -MaximumBytes 2GB

PS C:\> Get-VMMemory -VMName VM1

VMName DynamicMemoryEnabled Minimum(M) Startup(M) Maximum(M)
------ -------------------- ---------- ---------- ----------
VM1    True                 512        1024       2048
```

In *step 5*, you'll see you have two existing SCSI controllers, then you add a third, as you can see here:

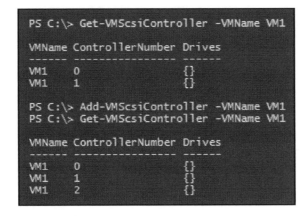

```
PS C:\> Get-VMScsiController -VMName VM1

VMName ControllerNumber Drives
------ ---------------- ------
VM1    0                {}
VM1    1                {}

PS C:\> Add-VMScsiController -VMName VM1
PS C:\> Get-VMScsiController -VMName VM1

VMName ControllerNumber Drives
------ ---------------- ------
VM1    0                {}
VM1    1                {}
VM1    2                {}
```

In *step 6*, you restart the VM1 VM. After the VM is restarted, in *step 7*, you create a new VHDX file on the HV1 system, like this:

```
PS C:\> $VHDPath = 'H:\Vm\Vhds\VM1-D.VHDX'
PS C:\> New-VHD -Path $VHDPath -SizeBytes 8GB -Dynamic

ComputerName              : HV1
Path                      : H:\Vm\Vhds\VM1-D.VHDX
VhdFormat                 : VHDX
VhdType                   : Dynamic
FileSize                  : 4194304
Size                      : 8589934592
MinimumSize               :
LogicalSectorSize         : 512
PhysicalSectorSize        : 4096
BlockSize                 : 33554432
ParentPath                :
DiskIdentifier            : E0555AA8-07C1-4615-A86B-434FCB396948
FragmentationPercentage   : 0
Alignment                 : 1
Attached                  : False
DiskNumber                :
Number                    :
```

Finally, in *step 8*, you add the newly created VHDX file as a disk on SCSI bus 0, location 0, which generates no output. In *step 9*, you view the disk in VM1, as follows:

```
PS C:\> Get-VMHardDiskDrive -VMName VM1

VMName ControllerType ControllerNumber ControllerLocation DiskNumber Path
------ -------------- ---------------- ------------------ ---------- ----
VM1    IDE            0                0                             H:\Vm\Vhds\VM1.Vhdx
VM1    SCSI           0                0                             H:\Vm\Vhds\VM1-D.VHDX
```

There's more...

In addition to the hardware components covered in this recipe, you can also manage a VM's COM ports and diskette drives. While you cannot directly connect a VM's COM port to the host's COM port, you can configure a VM to communicate with the physical computer via a named pipe on the host computer. A typical use for this is kernel debugging—probably something most IT Pros rarely ever do. For more information on named pipes, see https://msdn.microsoft.com/en-us/library/aa365590(v=vs.85).aspx.

You can also use a virtual floppy drive in a VM. There is no cmdlet support to create a virtual floppy drive file (a .vfd file) in the Hyper-V module. Nor is there support for mounting a VFD file in Windows. You can create VFD files using Hyper-V Manager and then use Set-VMFloppyDiskDrive to attach the VFD file as a floppy disk drive in the VM.

Configuring Hyper-V networking

In the *Creating a virtual machine* recipe, you created a VM, VM1. This virtual machine has, by default, a single network card that Hyper-V sets to acquire IP address details from DHCP. In this recipe, you assign the NIC to a switch and configure IP address details.

Getting ready

This recipe assumes you have created VM1 as per the *Creating a virtual machine* recipe. The recipe also makes use of a DHCP server running on DC1. You set this DHCP server up in the *Installing and authorizing a DHCP Server* recipe, and configured the DHCP server in the *Configure DHCP scopes recipe*, in Chapter 8, *Managing Windows Network Services*.

How to do it...

Here you see how to configure Hyper-V networking:

1. Get NIC details and any IP Address from the VM1 VM:

```
Get-VMNetworkAdapter -VMName VM1
```

2. Get VM networking details:

```
$user = 'Localhost\Administrator'
$pass =  ConvertTo-SecureString -String 'Pa$$w0rd' `
        -AsPlainText -Force
$cred = New-Object -TypeName `
            System.Management.Automation.PSCredential `
        -ArgumentList $user,$Pass
Invoke-Command -VMName VM1 `
            -ScriptBlock {Get-NetIPConfiguration |
                            Format-List} `
            -Credential $cred
```

3. Create a virtual switch on HV1:

```
New-VMSwitch -Name External -NetAdapterName 'Ethernet' `
            -Notes 'Created on HV1'
```

4. Connect VM1 to the switch:

```
Connect-VMNetworkAdapter -VMName  VM1 -SwitchName External
```

5. See VM networking information:

```
Get-VMNetworkAdapter -VMName VM1
```

6. With VM1 now in the network, observe the IP address in the VM:

```
Invoke-Command -VMName VM1 `
                -ScriptBlock {Get-NetIPConfiguration} `
                -Credential $cred
```

7. View the hostname on VM1:

```
Invoke-Command -VMName VM1 `
                -ScriptBlock {Hostname} `
                -Credential $cred
```

8. Change the name of the host:

```
$sb = {
Rename-Computer -NewName VM1 -Force}
Invoke-Command -VMName VM1 `
                -ScriptBlock $sb `
                -Credential $cred
```

9. Reboot and wait for the restarted VM:

```
Restart-VM -VMName VM1 -Wait -For IPAddress -Force
```

10. Get updated network configuration:

```
Invoke-Command -VMName VM1 `
                -ScriptBlock {Get-NetIPConfiguration} `
                -Credential $cred
```

11. Get hostname of the VM1 VM:

```
Invoke-Command -VMName VM1 `
                -ScriptBlock {Hostname} `
                -Credential $cred
```

How it works...

In step 1, you retrieve the Hyper-V networking adapter information for the VM1 VM, which looks like this:

```
PS C:\> Get-VMNetworkAdapter -VMName VM1

Name            IsManagementOs VMName SwitchName MacAddress    Status IPAddresses
----            -------------- ------ ---------- ----------    ------ -----------
Network Adapter False          VM1               00155D017001 {Ok}   {169.254.152.196,
                                                                     fe80::c413:c78b:ea9e:98c4}
```

In *step 2*, you first create a credential object for the VM. As noted here, the user is the new VM's administrator username (administrator) and the password (Pa$$w0rd). Then you invoke a script block on VM1 that retrieves the VM's IP configuration. As you can see, the NIC is not connected to any network. The output looks like this:

```
PS C:\> $user = 'VM1\Administrator'
PS C:\> $pass = ConvertTo-SecureString -String 'Pa$$w0rd' -AsPlainText -Force
PS C:\>$cred = New-Object -TypeName System.Management.Automation.PSCredential `
                         -ArgumentList $user,$Pass
PS C:\> Invoke-Command -VMName VM1 `
                       -ScriptBlock {Get-NetIPConfiguration | Format-List} `
                       -Credential $cred

InterfaceAlias       : Ethernet
InterfaceIndex       : 2
InterfaceDescription : Microsoft Hyper-V Network Adapter
NetAdapter.Status    : Disconnected
```

In *step 3*, you create a new virtual Hyper-V switch on your HV1 system. The switch, which you name External, is connected to an NIC on the HV1 computer. This allows VMs connected to this switch to network with both the Hyper-V host and any external networks to which you are connected. The output of this step looks like this:

```
PS C:\> New-VMSwitch -Name External -NetAdapterName 'Ethernet' `
                     -Notes 'Created on HV1'

Name     SwitchType NetAdapterInterfaceDescription
----     ---------- ------------------------------
External External   Microsoft Hyper-V Network Adapte
```

In *step 4*, you connect the VM's NIC to the Hyper-V switch you just created. There is no output from this step.

In *step 5*, you view the VM's networking information, which is updated as a result of connecting the NIC to the switch. Assuming that you have a DHCP server running on your network (the network the Hyper-V hosts connects to), you should see a DHCP assigned IP address, with output that looks like this:

```
PS C:\> Get-VMNetworkAdapter -VMName VM1

Name              IsManagementOs VMName SwitchName MacAddress   Status IPAddresses
----              -------------- ------ ---------- ----------   ------ -----------
Network Adapter   False          VM1    External   00155D017001 {Ok}   {10.10.10.157, fe80::c413:c78b:ea9e:98c4}
```

In *step 6*, you examine VM1 VM's IP address information, using the Get-NetIPConfiguration cmdlet run remotely, *inside* the VM. As you can see from the output, the VM has an IP address and has two configured DNS servers but with no default gateway:

```
PS C:\> Invoke-Command -VMName VM1 `
            -ScriptBlock {Get-NetIPConfiguration} `
            -Credential $cred

InterfaceAlias       : Ethernet
InterfaceIndex       : 2
InterfaceDescription : Microsoft Hyper-V Network Adapter
NetProfile.Name      : Reskit.Org
IPv4Address          : 10.10.10.157
IPv6DefaultGateway   :
IPv4DefaultGateway   :
DNSServer            : 10.10.10.10
                       10.10.10.11
PSComputerName       : VM1
```

In *step 7*, you retrieve the hostname of the VM1 virtual machine. The output looks like this:

```
PS C:\> Invoke-Command -VMName VM1 `
            -ScriptBlock {Hostname} `
            -Credential $cred
WIN-O5LPHTHBB5U
```

In *step 8*, you remotely update the VM's hostname to match the VM name (VM1). The only output from this step is a warning that the new name can only take affect once you reboot the machine. In *step 9*, you re-boot the machine and wait for the restarted VM. There is no output from the re-boot.

In *step 10*, you check the networking on the VM1 VM with output that looks like this:

```
PS C:\> Invoke-Command -VMName VM1 `
            -ScriptBlock {Get-NetIPConfiguration} `
            -Credential $cred

InterfaceAlias       : Ethernet
InterfaceIndex       : 2
InterfaceDescription : Microsoft Hyper-V Network Adapter
NetProfile.Name      : Reskit.Org
IPv4Address          : 10.10.10.157
IPv6DefaultGateway   :
IPv4DefaultGateway   :
DNSServer            : 10.10.10.10
                       10.10.10.11
PSComputerName       : VM1
```

In *step 11*, you remotely retrieve VM1 VM's hostname (VM1) as set earlier. The output looks like this:

```
PS C:\> Invoke-Command -VMName VM1 `
            -ScriptBlock {Hostname} `
            -Credential $cred
VM1
```

In *step 8* and *step 11*, you use the Hostname.exe console command to retrieve the hostname. There are other ways to get the hostname, including using WMI or using the environment variable env:ComputerName.

There's more...

In *step 1*, you use the Get-VMNetworkAdapter for the VM1 VM. The output from this step shows that the virtual NIC is not connected to any switch. It also shows that the VM has assigned an APIPA IP address to the NIC (169.254.152.96). Since the address chose by Windows is random, you may see a different address in the 169.254.0.0/16 network. And even though Windows has an IP address in mind for the NIC, since you have not connected the VM's NIC to a Hyper-V switch, no networking is possible with the VM, although subsequent steps fix that issue.

In *step 3*, you create a new switch. If you already have an `External` switch created on your Hyper-V host, you can use it in this recipe as opposed to the `External` switch created in this step.

In *step 5* and *step 6*, you examine the IP configuration of `VM1` VM's virtual NIC. Depending on the configuration of any DHCP server, you may see a different IP address. And if you do not have a working DHCP server on the network, you may see an APIPA address (that is, one in the `169.254.0.0/16` network). In *step 5*, you may see somewhat mangled output—you can always run *step 5* through `Format-Table` to tidy this up.

In *step 7*, you obtain the VM's configured hostname. Assuming you created the VM simply from the default installation via the product DVD, Windows automatically creates a hostname, in this case `WIN- O5LPHTHBB5U`. To complete the configuration of networking for the VM, you need to update the VM's hostname.

Implementing nested Hyper-V

Nested Hyper-V is a new feature in Windows 2016 and Windows 10 (Anniversary update and later). Nested Hyper-V enables a Hyper-V VM to host VMs which also have virtualization enabled. You could, for example, take a physical host (say, `HV1`) and on that host run a VM (say `VM1`). With nested Hyper-V, you could enable your `VM1` VM to host VMs and create a nested VM inside it called `Nested1`.

Nested VMs have a number of uses. First, nested MVs hosted in one VM are provided hardware isolation from nested VMs run in other VMs. This provides a further level of security for virtual machines. It's also useful for testing and education/training. In a training course, you could give a student one VM and enable him to create additional VMs as part of the course. And most IT pros just find it cool! You could, for example, run all the recipes in this chapter using Nested VMs.

Enabling nested Hyper-V is very simple. First, you must update the virtual CPU in the VM you want to support nesting. Therefore, in this recipe, you adjust the virtual CPU in the `VM1` VM to expose the virtualization extensions. This has to be done while the VM is turned off. After you restart the VM, you install the Hyper-V feature and create the `Nested1` nested VM. This recipe does not show the details of configuring the `Nested1` VM, which are left as an exercise for the reader.

Getting ready

This recipe uses the HV1 Hyper-V host, with an existing Hyper-V VM, VM1 available. The recipe assumes VM1 is set up as shown in the *Creating a virtual machine* recipe earlier in this chapter.

How to do it...

Here is how to implement nested Hyper-V:

1. Stop VM1 VM:

```
Stop-VM -VMName VM1
Get-VM -VMname VM1
```

2. Change the VM's processor to support virtualization:

```
Set-VMProcessor -VMName VM1 `
                -ExposeVirtualizationExtensions $true
Get-VMProcessor -VMName VM1 |
    Format-Table -Property Name, Count,
                           ExposeVirtualizationExtensions
```

3. Start the VM1 VM:

```
Start-VM -VMName VM1
Wait-VM -VMName VM1 -For Heartbeat
Get-VM -VMName VM1
```

4. Add Hyper-V into VM1:

```
$user = 'VM1\Administrator'
$pass =  ConvertTo-SecureString -String 'Pa$$w0rd' `
                                -AsPlainText -Force
$cred = New-Object -TypeName
System.Management.Automation.PSCredential `
                  -ArgumentList $user,$Pass
Invoke-Command -VMName VM1 `
               -ScriptBlock {Install-WindowsFeature `
               -Name Hyper-V -IncludeManagementTools} `
               -Credential $cred
```

5. Restart the VM to finish adding Hyper-V:

```
Stop-VM -VMName VM1
Start-VM -VMName VM1
Wait-VM -VMName VM1 -For IPAddress
Get-VM -VMName VM1
```

6. Create a nested VM:

```
$sb = {
    $VMname        = 'Nested11'
    New-VM -Name $VMname -MemoryStartupBytes 1GB}
Invoke-Command -VMName VM1 `
                -ScriptBlock $sb
```

How it works...

In *step 1*, you stop the VM1 VM, and then retrieve properties that show the VM has been turned off. The output looks like this:

```
PS C:\> Stop-VM -VMName VM1
PS C:\> Get-VM -VMname VM1

Name State CPUUsage(%) MemoryAssigned(M) Uptime   Status            Version
---- ----- ----------- ----------------- ------   ------            -------
VM1  Off   0           0                 00:00:00 Operating normally 8.0
```

In *step 2*, you change the VM's virtual processor(s) to expose the virtualization extensions to the VM's operating system. The output of this step looks like this:

```
PS C:\> Set-VMProcessor -VMName VM1 `
                        -ExposeVirtualizationExtensions $true
PS C:\> Get-VMProcessor -VMName VM1 |
            Format-Table -Property Name, Count,
                                   ExposeVirtualizationExtensions

Name       Count ExposeVirtualizationExtensions
----       ----- ------------------------------
Processor  1                                True
```

In *step 3*, you restart the VM. Once the VM is started, you wait until you get a heartbeat then examine the VM's properties, which looks like this:

```
PS C:\> Start-VM -VMName VM1
PS C:\> Wait-VM -VMName VM1 -For Heartbeat
PS C:\> Get-VM -VMName VM1

Name State   CPUUsage(%) MemoryAssigned(M) Uptime            Status             Version
---- -----   ----------- ----------------- ------            ------             -------
VM1  Running 2           1024              00:00:49.8890000  Operating normally 8.0
```

Once the VM is started, in *step 4*, you install the Hyper-V feature into the VM1 VM. As you can see in the following output, adding Hyper-V is both successful and requires you to reboot the VM:

```
PS C:\> $user = 'VM1\Administrator'
PS C:\> $pass = ConvertTo-SecureString -String 'Pa$$w0rd' `
                                       -AsPlainText -Force
PS C:\> $cred = New-Object -TypeName System.Management.Automation.PSCredential `
                           -ArgumentList $user,$Pass
PS C:\> Invoke-Command -VMName VM1 `
            -ScriptBlock {Install-WindowsFeature -Name Hyper-V `
                                                 -IncludeManagementTools} `
            -Credential $cred

Success Restart Needed Exit Code     Feature Result                PSComputerName
------- -------------- ---------     --------------                --------------
True    Yes            SuccessRest... {Hyper-V}                    VM1
WARNING: You must restart this server to finish the installation process.
```

In *step 5*, you restart the VM, wait for it to get an IP address assigned, and then retrieve the VM's details, as follows:

```
PS C:\> Stop-VM -VMName VM1
PS C:\> Start-VM -VMName VM1
PS C:\> Wait-VM -VMName VM1 -For IPAddress
PS C:\> Get-Vm -VMName VM1


Name State   CPUUsage(%) MemoryAssigned(M) Uptime            Status             Version
---- -----   ----------- ----------------- ------            ------             -------
VM1  Running 5           1024              00:01:43.6280000  Operating normally 8.0
```

Once the VM1 VM is started, in *step 6*, you create a nested VM Nested11. The Nested11 VM runs inside the VM1 VM, and the output looks like this:

```
$sb = {
    $VMname       = 'Nested11'
    New-VM -Name VM1 -MemoryStartupBytes 1GB}
Invoke-Command -VMName $VMName `
               -ScriptBlock $sb `
               -Credential $cred

Name     State CPUUsage(%) MemoryAssigned(M) Uptime   Status                  Version PSComputerName
----     ----- ----------- ----------------- ------   ------                  ------- --------------
Nested1  Off   0           0                 00:00:00 Operating normally 8.0          VM1
```

There's more...

In *step 2*, you look at the properties of the virtual CPU(s) in the VM1 VM. If you executed the *Configuring VM hardware* recipe previously, you may see a different CPU count.

In *step 5*, you stopped then started the VM. As an alternative, you could have used Restart-VM.

In *step 6*, you create a new VM but you have not loaded an operating system or configured the VM. Naturally, you can use the techniques in the chapter to configure your new VM as you need it. Also, in this step, you may be prompted for credentials. You can enter them using the prompt, or you could create a credential object and pass when you run this step.

Managing VM state

Managing the VM state involves stopping and starting or pausing and resuming a VM. You can also save and restore a VM.

Getting ready

This recipe uses the VM1 VM created in the *Creating a virtual machine* recipe. This recipe assumes the VM1 VM is stopped when you start this recipe. If this VM is running, then first stop it using Stop-VM.

How to do it...

Here is how to manage VM state:

1. Get the VM's state to check if it is off:

   ```
   Get-VM       -Name VM1
   ```

2. Start the VM, get its status, then wait until the VM has an IP address assigned and the networking stack is working, then examine the VM's state:

   ```
   Start-VM   -VMName VM1
   Get-Vm     -VMName VM1
   Wait-VM    -VMName VM1 -For IPAddress
   Get-VM     -VMName VM1
   ```

3. Suspend and resume a VM:

   ```
   Suspend-VM -VMName VM1
   Get-VM     -VMName VM1
   Resume-VM  -VMName VM1
   Get-VM     -VMName VM1
   ```

4. Save the VM and check status:

   ```
   Save-VM    -VMName VM1
   Get-VM     -VMName VM1
   ```

5. Resume the saved VM and view the status:

   ```
   Start-VM   -VMName VM1
   Get-Vm     -VMName VM1
   ```

6. Restart a VM:

   ```
   Get-VM     -VMname VM1
   Restart-VM -VMName VM1 -Force
   Get-VM     -VMName VM1
   Wait-Vm    -VMName VM1 -For IPaddress
   Get-VM     -VMName VM1
   ```

7. Hard power Off:

   ```
   Stop-VM    -VMName VM1 -TurnOff
   Get-VM     -VMname VM1
   ```

How it works...

In *step 1*, you retrieve VM1 VM's properties which show the VM as off. It should look like this:

```
PS C:\> Get-VM -Name VM1

Name State CPUUsage(%) MemoryAssigned(M) Uptime    Status             Version
---- ----- ----------- ----------------- ------    ------             -------
VM1  Off   0           0                 00:00:00  Operating normally 8.0
```

In *step 2*, you first start VM1 and retrieve its properties. You then wait for the VM to be assigned an IP address then re-retrieve the VM's properties, like this:

```
PS C:\> Start-VM -Name VM1
PS C:\> Get-VM -Name VM1

Name State   CPUUsage(%) MemoryAssigned(M) Uptime              Status             Version
---- -----   ----------- ----------------- ------              ------             -------
VM1  Running 0           1024              00:00:00.0740000    Operating normally 8.0

PS C:\> Wait-VM -VMName VM1 -For IPAddress
PS C:\> Get-VM -Name VM1

Name State   CPUUsage(%) MemoryAssigned(M) Uptime              Status             Version
---- -----   ----------- ----------------- ------              ------             -------
VM1  Running 1           1024              00:01:08.0590000    Operating normally 8.0
```

In *step 3*, you suspend and resume VM1. Notice that after suspending the VM, Hyper-V does not release the VM's memory. The output from this step looks like this:

```
PS C:\> Suspend-VM -VMName VM1
PS C:\> Get-VM      -VMName VM1

Name State  CPUUsage(%) MemoryAssigned(M) Uptime              Status             Version
---- -----  ----------- ----------------- ------              ------             -------
VM1  Paused 0           572               15:04:52.9640000    Operating normally 8.0

PS C:\> Resume-VM   -VMName VM1
PS C:\> Get-VM      -VMName VM1

Name State   CPUUsage(%) MemoryAssigned(M) Uptime              Status             Version
---- -----   ----------- ----------------- ------              ------             -------
VM1  Running 0           572               15:04:56.1310000    Operating normally 8.0
```

In *step 4*, you save the VM and check the VM's status. When you save a VM, the VM's state is written to disk, and the VM is stopped. The output looks like this:

```
PS C:\> Save-VM    -VMName VM1
PS C:\> Get-Vm     -VMName VM1

Name State CPUUsage(%) MemoryAssigned(M) Uptime    Status              Version
---- ----- ----------- ----------------- ------    ------              -------
VM1  Saved 0                 0           00:00:00 Operating normally  8.0
```

In *step 5*, you resume the saved VM then look at the VM's properties once the VM has restarted. The output looks like this:

```
PS C:\> Start-VM  -VMName VM1
PS C:\> Get-Vm    -VMName VM1

Name State   CPUUsage(%) MemoryAssigned(M) Uptime             Status             Version
---- -----   ----------- ----------------- ------             ------             -------
VM1  Running 3                572          00:00:04.2040000 Operating normally 8.0
```

In *step 6*, you forcibly restart VM1. In this step, you first view the running VM's properties then you stop it and re-view the VM properties. Then you restart the VM and wait for it to start up and get an IP address, then you re-view the properties to see that the VM is up and running. The output of this step looks like this:

```
PS C:\> Get-VM       -VMname VM1

Name State   CPUUsage(%) MemoryAssigned(M) Uptime             Status             Version
---- -----   ----------- ----------------- ------             ------             -------
VM1  Running 0                598          08:02:17.5450000 Operating normally 8.0

PS C:\> Restart-VM -VMName VM1 -Force
PS C:\> Get-VM       -VMName VM1

Name State   CPUUsage(%) MemoryAssigned(M) Uptime             Status             Version
---- -----   ----------- ----------------- ------             ------             -------
VM1  Running 8                1024         00:00:00.7290000 Operating normally 8.0

PS C:\> Wait-Vm     -VMName VM1 -For IPaddress
PS C:\> Get-VM       -VMName VM1

Name State   CPUUsage(%) MemoryAssigned(M) Uptime             Status             Version
---- -----   ----------- ----------------- ------             ------             -------
VM1  Running 4                1024         00:02:03.4850000 Operating normally 8.0
```

In *step 7*, you do a hard power off of VM1, and then you view the VM's properties, like this:

```
PS C:\> Stop-VM     -VMName VM1 -TurnOff
PS C:\> Get-VM      -VMname VM1

Name State CPUUsage(%) MemoryAssigned(M) Uptime    Status             Version
---- ----- ----------- ----------------- ------    ------             -------
VM1  Off   0           0                 00:00:00  Operating normally 8.0
```

There's more...

This recipe shows you how to manage state. In *step 1*, you view the properties of the VM that is not running. As you can see from the screenshot, VM1 is turned off and is not running (and has an up time of 00:00:00).

With *step 2*, you start the VM and retrieve the VM's status. Next, in *step 3*, you suspend then resume a VM. While the VM is suspended, the VM is not active and receives and sends no network traffic. The VM's memory is maintained as is the current state and the VM can be resumed at any moment, as you can see from this step.

With *step 4* and *step 5*, you save a VM, then restart it. When you save a VM, Hyper-V saves the VM's memory to disk and the VM's virtual disks are not used. Saving a VM is similar to saving it, except that with a saved VM, all the VM's memory is written to disk then released.

With *step 6*, you forcibly shut down the VM. This is equivalent to pulling the power from a running computer then restarting it or holding down the power button. When you do this, all state is lost, and it is possible to introduce corruption due to data being still in memory and not written to disk prior to the power off. While Windows and the most used Windows file systems (*NTFS* and *ReFS*) are fairly resilient to errors, you should avoid hard shutdown if possible.

Configuring VM and storage movement

Hyper-V enables you to both move a VM and to move the storage for a VM to a new location. Moving a VM and moving a VM's storage are two important features you can use to manage your Hyper-V hosts.

With live migration, you can move a Hyper-V VM to a different VM host with no downtime. This works best when the VM is held on shared storage (via a fiber channel SAN, iSCSI, or SMB). You can also move a VM's storage (that is any VHD/VHDX associated with the VM) to a different location. You can also combine these and move a VM supported by local storage to another Hyper-V host (moving both the VM and the underlying storage).

In this recipe, you first move the storage for the VM1 VM. You created this VM in the *Creating a virtual machine* recipe and stored the VM configuration and the VM's VHD on the H: drive. To move the storage, you create a new SMB share and then move the VM's storage to the new SMB share.

In the second part of this recipe, you do a live migration of the VM1 VM from HV1 to HV2 while the VM is running. This is possible since the VM is using shared storage (that is the SMB share you create).

Getting ready

In this recipe, you use the HV1 and HV2 systems (Windows 2016 Server with Hype-V loaded) as setup in the *Installing and configuring Hyper-V recipe* and the VM1 VM created in the *Creating a virtual machine* recipe.

In the first part of this recipe, you first move the storage for the VM1 VM. You created this VM in the *Creating a virtual machine* recipe and stored the VM configuration and the VM's VHD on the H: drive. You run all the steps in this recipe on HV1. You must have created the external switch on HV2, otherwise the following *step 8* fails.

How to do it...

Here is how you can configure a VM:

1. View the VM1 VM on HV1 and verify that it is turned off and not saved:

   ```
   Get-VM -Name VM1 -Computer HV1
   ```

2. Get the VM configuration location and VHD details:

   ```
   (Get-VM -Name vm1).ConfigurationLocation
   Get-VMHardDiskDrive -VMName VM1
   ```

3. Move the VM's storage to the `C:` drive:

```
Move-VMStorage -Name VM1 -DestinationStoragePath C:\VM1
```

4. View the configuration details after moving the VM's storage:

```
(Get-VM -Name VM1).ConfigurationLocation
Get-VMHardDiskDrive -VMName VM1
```

5. Get the VM details for VMs from HV2:

```
Get-VM -ComputerName HV2
```

6. Enable VM migration from both HV1 and HV2:

```
Enable-VMMigration -ComputerName HV1, HV2
```

7. Configure VM Migration on both hosts:

```
Set-VMHost -UseAnyNetworkForMigration $true `
           -ComputerName HV1, HV2
Set-VMHost -VirtualMachineMigrationAuthenticationType Kerberos `
           -ComputerName HV1, HV2
Set-VMHost `
   -VirtualMachineMigrationPerformanceOption Compression `
   -ComputerName HV1, HV2
```

8. Move the VM to HV2:

```
$start = Get-Date
Move-VM -Name VM1 `
        -ComputerName HV1.reskit.org `
        -DestinationHost HV2.reskit.org `
        -IncludeStorage `
        -DestinationStoragePath C:\VM1
$finish = Get-Date
```

9. Display the time taken to migrate:

```
"Migration took: [{0:n2}] minutes" `
                -f ($($finish-$start).totalminutes)
```

10. Check which VMs on are on HV1 and HV2:

```
Get-VM -ComputerName HV1
Get-VM -ComputerName HV2
```

11. Look at the details of the moved VM:

```
(Get-VM -Name VM1 -Computer HV2).ConfigurationLocation
Get-VMHardDiskDrive -VMName VM1 -Computer HV2
```

How it works...

In *step 1*, you view the basic details of the VM1 VM, running HV1. The output looks like this:

```
PS C:\> Get-VM -Name VM1

Name State   CPUUsage(%) MemoryAssigned(M) Uptime            Status            Version
---- -----   ----------- ----------------- ------            ------            -------
VM1  Running 1           4096              00:01:18.2620000 Operating normally 8.0
```

In *step 2*, you use the Get-VM cmdlet to display both the location of VM1 VM's configuration details and of VM1 VM's single virtual disk drive, with output like this:

```
PS C:\> (Get-Vm -VMName VM1).ConfigurationLocation
H:\Vm\VMs\VM1

PS C:\> Get-VMHardDiskDrive -VMName vm1

VMName ControllerType ControllerNumber ControllerLocation DiskNumber Path
------ -------------- ---------------- ------------------ ---------- ----
VM1    IDE            0                0                             H:\Vm\Vhds\VM1.Vhdx
```

In *step 3*, you move the VM's storage. You move the VM storage from the H: drive to C:\VM1. There is no output from this step. In *step 4*, you repeat the commands you used in *step 2* and observe that Hyper-V now stores the VM and the VHDX in C:\VM1. The output looks like this:

```
PS C:\> (Get-VM -Name VM1).ConfigurationLocation
C:\VM1

PS C:\> Get-VMHardDiskDrive -VMName VM1

VMName ControllerType ControllerNumber ControllerLocation DiskNumber Path
------ -------------- ---------------- ------------------ ---------- ----
VM1    IDE            0                0                             c:\VM1\Virtual Hard Disks\VM1.Vhdx
```

Next, this recipe looks at VM live migration. In *step 5*, you look at the VMs running on the two Hyper-V hosts. As you can see from the following output, HV1 is running only one VM (VM1) whilst HV2 runs no VMs:

```
PS C:\> Get-VM -ComputerName HV1

Name State    CPUUsage(%) MemoryAssigned(M) Uptime            Status              Version
---- -----    ----------- ----------------- ------            ------              -------
VM1  Running 0             4096                01:24:37.6100000 Operating normally 8.0

PS C:\> Get-VM -ComputerName HV2
```

In *step 6*, you enable VM migration from both HV1 and HV2. In *step 7*, you configure each VM host to support VM live migration. In this case, you configure both hosts to use their single NIC for migration, to authenticate using Kerberos and to compress the migration traffic. There is no output from these two steps.

In *step 8*, you live migrate VM1 from HV1 to HV2. There is no output from this step, but in *step 9*, you display how long the Move-VM cmdlet took to move the VM, like this:

```
PS C:\> "Migration took: [{0:n2}] seconds" `
                       -f ($($finish-$start).totalminutes)

Migration took: [7.49] minutes
```

Finally, in *step 10*, you look at the VMs running on HV1 and HV2 and observe that VM1 is now running successfully on HV2, like this:

```
PS C:\> Get-VM -ComputerName HV1

PS C:\> Get-VM -ComputerName HV2

Name State    CPUUsage(%) MemoryAssigned(M) Uptime            Status              Version
---- -----    ----------- ----------------- ------            ------              -------
VM1  Running 0             4096                00:18:09.1260000 Operating normally 8.0
```

There's more...

In this recipe, you moved the storage for a VM from one volume to another and you moved a running VM to a different machine. In *step 3*, you moved the storage for the VM. If you had a connection open to VM1, you would have seen the VM functioning normally. You may have seen a brief flicker as the storage movement completes and Hyper-V begins to use the new storage location.

In this case, you set up HV1 and HV2 as two non-clustered systems. In *step 8*, you move VM1 from HV1 to HV2. In this case, there is no shared storage involved with the VMs which means Hyper-V performs a storage migration and a VM migration from the old to the new VM host. Had you stored the VM on shared storage, moving a VM between cluster nodes would have been significantly faster.

At the completion of the VM movement in *step 8*, Hyper-V drops connectivity to the VM on HV1 and establishes it on HV2. This means that for a moment, you will lose connectivity. If you open a VM Connect window into VM1 before you move the VM, you can see that as the movement finishes, the VM **Connect** window stops showing the VM. After a few seconds, the VM **Connect** window should reappear with the VM running on HV2.

You could also open up a PowerShell window on another system, say DC1, and ping the VM continuously during the movement of the VM. You may notice a moment of dropped pings, before they pick up again once the live migration has completed.

Configuring VM replication

In Hyper-V, VM replication is a disaster recovery feature. It creates a replica of a VM on a remote Hyper-V Server and then keeps the replica up to date. The VM on the remote host is not active, but can be made active should the VM's host for some reason fail.

With Hyper-V replication, the source VM host bundles up any changes in a running VM's VHD file(s) and sends them to the replica server on a regular basis. The replica server then applies those changes to the dormant replica.

Once you have a replica established, you can test the replica to ensure it can start should you need that. Also, you can failover to the replica—bringing the replicated VM up based on the most recently replicated data. If the source VM host becomes inoperable before it can replicate changes on the source VM, there is a risk of those changes being lost.

In this recipe, you create and use a replica of a VM, VM1, that you have running on your HV1 server. The recipe sets up the replica on the HV2 server.

Getting ready

You created the HV1 and HV2 servers in the *Installing and configuring Hyper-V* recipe, and created VM1 in the *Creating a virtual machine recipe*. Should you have used the *Configuring VM and storage movement* recipe, you either need to move VM1 back to HV1, or run the recipe from HV2, not HV2, and adjust it as appropriate. This recipe also uses the AD cmdlets from DC1 to configure the HV1 and HV2 systems for delegation and assumes you have firewalls turned off. Also, if you moved the VM previously, you need to move the VM back to HV1.

How to do it...

Here is how to configure VM replication:

1. Configure HV1 and HV2 to be trusted for delegation in AD on DC1:

```
$sb = {
  Set-ADComputer -Identity HV1 `
                 -TrustedForDelegation $True}
Invoke-Command -ComputerName DC1 -ScriptBlock $sb
$sb = {
  Set-ADComputer -Identity HV2 `
                 -TrustedForDelegation $True}
Invoke-Command -ComputerName DC1 -ScriptBlock $sb
```

Reboot the HV1 and HV2:

```
Restart-Computer -ComputerName HV2
Restart-Computer -Force
```

2. Once both systems are restarted, from HV1, set up HV2 as a replication server:

```
Set-VMReplicationServer `
            -ReplicationEnabled $true `
            -AllowedAuthenticationType Kerberos `
            -KerberosAuthenticationPort 42000 `
            -DefaultStorageLocation 'C:\Replicas' `
            -ReplicationAllowedFromAnyServer $true `
            -ComputerName HV2
```

3. Enable VM1 on HV1 to be a replica source:

```
Enable-VMReplication -VMName 'VM1' `
                     -Computer HV1 `
                     -ReplicaServerName 'HV2' `
                     -ReplicaServerPort 42000 `
                     -AuthenticationType Kerberos `
                     -CompressionEnabled $true `
                     -RecoveryHistory 5
```

4. View the replication status of HV2:

```
Get-VMReplicationServer -ComputerName HV2
```

5. Check VM1 on HV2:

```
Get-VM -ComputerName HV2
```

6. Start the initial replication:

```
Start-VMInitialReplication -VMName VM1 -ComputerName HV2
```

7. Examine the initial replication state on HV1 just after you start the initial replication:

```
Measure-VMReplication -ComputerName HV1
```

8. Wait for replication to finish, then examine the replication status on HV1:

```
Measure-VMReplication -ComputerName HV1
```

9. Test VM1 failover to HV2:

```
$sb = {
    $VM1Test = Start-VMFailover -AsTest -VMName VM1 `
                                -Confirm:$false
    Start-VM $VM1test  }
Invoke-Command -ComputerName HV2 -ScriptBlock $sb
```

10. View the status of VMs on HV2:

```
Get-VM -ComputerName HV2
```

11. Stop the failover test:

```
$sb = {
        Stop-VMFailover -VMName VM1 }
Invoke-Command -ComputerName HV2 -ScriptBlock $sb
```

12. View the status of VMs on HV1 and HV2 after failover stopped:

```
Get-VM -ComputerName HV1
Get-VM -ComputerName HV2
```

13. Stop VM1 on HV1 prior to performing a planned failover:

```
Stop-VM VM1 -ComputerName HV1
```

14. Start VM failover from HV1:

```
Start-VMFailover -VMName VM1 -ComputerName HV2 `
                 -Confirm:$false
```

15. Complete the failover:

```
Complete-VMFailover -VMName VM1 -ComputerName HV2 `
                    -Confirm:$false
```

16. Start the replicated VM on HV2:

```
Start-VM -VMname VM1 -ComputerName HV2
```

17. See VMs on HV1 and HV2 after the planned failover:

```
Get-VM -ComputerName HV1
Get-VM -ComputerName HV2
```

How it works...

In *step 1*, you change the AD objects for computers HV1 and HV2 to enable the hosts as trusted for delegation. Then, in *step 2*, you reboot both HV1 and HV2. There is no output from either step.

In *step 2*, you reboot HV1 and HV2 to enable the updated computer settings. You see no output as such from this step, but both systems do reboot.

In *step 3*, you configure HV2 to accept inbound Hyper-V replication. You set this up to allow replication from any server. Then in *step 4*, you configure VM on HV1 as replication source, replicating VM1 to HV2. There is no output from these two steps.

In *step 5*, you look at the replication status on HV2, and the status of VM1 on HV2. You should see output like this:

```
PS C:\> Get-VMReplicationServer -ComputerName HV2

RepEnabled AuthType KerbAuthPort CertAuthPort AllowAnyServer
---------- -------- ------------ ------------ --------------
True       Kerb     42000        443          True

PS C:\> Get-VM -ComputerName HV2

Name State CPUUsage(%) MemoryAssigned(M) Uptime   Status             Version
---- ----- ----------- ----------------- ------   ------             -------
VM1  Off   0           0                 00:00:00 Operating normally 8.0
```

In *step 6*, you view the status of VM1 on the HV2 Hyper-V host, which looks like this:

```
#   STEP 6 -  Get VM1 Status on HV2:

PS C:\> Get-VM -ComputerName HV2

Name State CPUUsage(%) MemoryAssigned(M) Uptime   Status             Version
---- ----- ----------- ----------------- ------   ------             -------
VM1  Off   0           0                 00:00:00 Operating normally 8.0
```

With *step 7*, you start the initial replication of VM1 from HV1 to HV2. There is no output from this step. Once you have started the initial replication, in *step 8*, you can see the results. Once you start the initial replication, Measure-VMReplication returns output that looks like this:

```
#   STEP 6 -  Get VM1 Status on HV2:

PS C:\> Get-VM -ComputerName HV2

Name State CPUUsage(%) MemoryAssigned(M) Uptime   Status             Version
---- ----- ----------- ----------------- ------   ------             -------
VM1  Off   0           0                 00:00:00 Operating normally 8.0
```

Once Hyper-V has completed the initial replication, the output, from *step 9*, should look like this:

```
PS C:\> Measure-VMReplication -ComputerName HV1

VMName State      Health LReplTime              PReplSize(M) AvgLatency AvgReplSize(M) Relationship
------ -----      ------ ---------              ------------ ---------- -------------- ------------
VM1    Replicating Normal 12/07/2017 22:36:39 0.0039          00:00:31   628.29         Simple
```

In *step 10*, you start a test failover of VM1 from HV1 to HV2 with output that looks like this:

```
PS C:\> $sb = {
          $VM1Test = Start-VMFailover -AsTest -VMName VM1 `
                        -Confirm:$false
          Start-VM $VM1test}
PS C:\> Invoke-Command -ComputerName HV2 -ScriptBlock $sb

Name        State CPUUsage(%) MemoryAssigned(M) Uptime   Status              Version PSComputerName
----        ----- ----------- ----------------- ------   ------              ------- --------------
VM1 - Test  Off   0           0                 00:00:00 Operating normally  8.0     HV2
```

In *step 11*, you view the status of the VMs running on HV2. As you can see from the output, the replica of VM1 is still there, but now you have a new VM which Hyper-V created for you based on a checkpoint (which Hyper-V automatically creates) from the replicated VM1. The output for this step looks like this:

```
PS C:\> Get-VM -ComputerName HV2

Name       State   CPUUsage(%) MemoryAssigned(M) Uptime              Status              Version
----       -----   ----------- ----------------- ------              ------              -------
VM1        Off     0           0                 00:00:00            Operating normally 8.0
VM1 - Test Running 1           4096              00:00:22.4220000    Operating normally 8.0
```

In *step 12*, you stop the failover test. This removes the test VM and provides no output.

In *step 13*, you see the VMs running on both HV1 and HV2 after stopping the failover test, with output that looks like this:

```
PS C:\> Get-VM -ComputerName HV1

Name State   CPUUsage(%) MemoryAssigned(M) Uptime              Status              Version
---- -----   ----------- ----------------- ------              ------              -------
VM1  Running 2           4096              00:29:04.9700000    Operating normally 8.0

PS C:\> Get-VM -ComputerName HV2

Name State CPUUsage(%) MemoryAssigned(M) Uptime   Status              Version
---- ----- ----------- ----------------- ------   ------              -------
VM1  Off   0           0                 00:00:00 Operating normally 8.0
```

With *step 14*, you begin to look at bringing up VM1 on HV2—a real failover. In this step, you stop VM1. This step also ensures that the replica VM on HV2 is updated before Hyper-V stops VM1 on HV1, ensuring the replica is fully up to date. There is no output from this step.

In *step 15*, you start a formal failover, which you complete in *step 16*. Neither step produces output.

In *step 17*, you explicitly start VM1 on HV2 which produces no output.

In *step 18*, you view the VMs running on HV2 (and stopped on HV1), as follows:

```
PS C:\> Get-VM -ComputerName HV1

Name State  CPUUsage(%) MemoryAssigned(M) Uptime       Status              Version
---- -----  ----------- ----------------- ------       ------              -------
VM1  Off    0           0                 00:00:00     Operating normally  8.0

PS C:\> Get-VM -ComputerName HV2

Name State    CPUUsage(%) MemoryAssigned(M) Uptime       Status              Version
---- -----    ----------- ----------------- ------       ------              -------
VM1  Running 0            4096              00:01:13.3530000 Operating normally 8.0
```

There's more...

In *step 2*, you reboot both Hyper-V hosts (HV1 and HV2). Since you run this recipe from the HV1 machine, the second command in this step reboots the system you are working on. If you test this recipe, make sure you have any files saved before you reboot.

If you have loaded this recipe into the ISE, then after rebooting, the ISE can reload the scripts you had open before the reboot. This is a great feature of PowerShell!

In *step 3*, you configure HV2 to accept inbound replication from any Hyper-V system. If you have not configured the host firewalls (or turned them off) you may see errors trying to invoke replication. You may also wish to configure HV2 to accept replication only from a specific server, such as HV1. To do this, you would have to set up the replication server to not accept replication from any server. Then, you use the Hyper-V cmdlet New-VMReplicationAuthorizationEntry to specify that HV2 can only receive replicas from the HV1 server. To set this up, you would do the following:

```
Set-VMReplicationAuthorizationEntry `
    -AllowedPrimaryServer HV1 `
    -ReplicaStorageLocation C:\Replica `
    -ComputerName HV2
```

In *step 7*, you begin the initial replication of VM1 to HV2. The `Measure- VMReplication` command does not show you progress information with respect to the initial replication. However, if you use the Hyper-V MMC console, you can see how much of the replica has been sent and received for a given VM. Looking at HV1 and HV2 whilst executing *step 8*, you might see something like this:

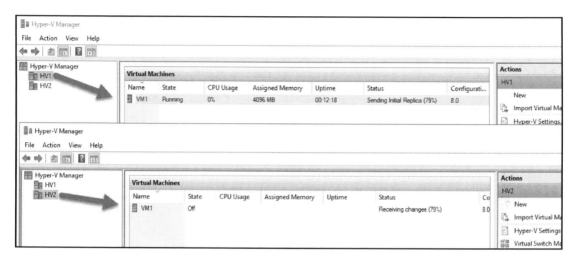

In *step 11*, you view the details of the test version of VM1 running. If you were to open up a VM **Connect** window on this test VM, you see that both the hostname and the IP address are not the same as the VM running on HV1 (where the hostname is VM1 and the IP address is 10.10.10.201). After *step 17*, if you looked inside VM1, running this time on HV2, you would find the same issue. The impact is that after a real life failover, you need to reset the computer/hostname for the computer and reset the IP configuration details. If you are using Hyper-V replica in production, it would be a great idea to develop a script to *fix* these two issues in an automated fashion.

In *Step 18*, you see that VM1 is running on HV2 and stopped on HV1. However, if you look inside VM1 inside HV2, you see it has a hostname that is *not* VM1 and has no networking setup. If you were to failover and wanted to run the failed over VM, you would need to deal with these two issues, which would involve re-booting VM1.

Managing VM checkpoints

With Hyper-V in Server 2016, a checkpoint captures the state of a VM into a restore point. Hyper-V then enables you to roll back a VM to a checkpoint. Windows Server 2008's version of Hyper-V provided this feature. With Server 2008, these restore points were called snapshots.

With Server 2012, Microsoft changed the name to checkpoint. This made the terminology consistent with System Center, and avoided confusion with respect to the **Volume Shadow Copy Service** (**VSS**) snapshots used by backup systems. Whilst the Hyper-V team did change the terminology, some of the cmdlet names remain unchanged. To restore a VM to a checkpoint, you use the `Restore-VMSnapShot` cmdlet.

When you create a checkpoint, Hyper-V temporarily pauses the VM. It then creates a new differencing disk (AVHD). Hyper-V then resumes the VM which writes all data to the differencing disk. You can create a variety of checkpoints for a VM.

Checkpoints are great for a variety of scenarios. It can be useful for troubleshooting. Get the VM to the point where some bug is triggered, take a checkpoint. Then try a fix—if it doesn't work, you can just roll back to the checkpoint and try some other fix. Checkpoints are also useful for training. You could create a VM for a course, and create a checkpoint after each successful lab. That way, the student can make a mistake in a lab, and skip forward to a later checkpoint and carry on.

Using checkpoints in production is a different matter. In general, you should avoid using checkpoints on your production systems for a number of reasons. If your servers use any sort of replication or transaction based applications, the impact of resetting the clock to an earlier time can be bad. Since checkpoints rely on differencing disks that feature constantly growing physical disk files, the use of checkpoints can result in poor performance. Checkpoints have their place—but should not be used as a backup strategy.

In this recipe, you create a snapshot of VM1, then you create a file. You take a further checkpoint and create a second file. Then you revert back to the first snapshot, observing that there are *no* files created. Then you roll forward to the second snapshot to see that the first file is there but not the second (because you created the second file *after* the snapshot was taken. Then you remove all the snapshots. After each key checkpoint operation, you observe the VHDX and AVHD files which support VM1.

Getting ready

This recipe assumes you have HV1 running the VM1 VM.

How to do it...

1. Create credentials for VM1:

```
$user = 'VM1\Administrator'
$pass =  ConvertTo-SecureString -String 'Pa$$w0rd' `
                                 -AsPlainText `
                                 -Force
$cred = New-Object -TypeName
System.Management.Automation.PSCredential `
                    -ArgumentList $user,$Pass
```

2. Look at C: in VM1 before we start:

```
$sb = { Get-ChildItem -Path C:\ }
Invoke-Command -VMName VM1 -ScriptBlock $sb `
               -Credential $cred
```

3. Create a snapshot of VM1 on HV1:

```
Checkpoint-VM -ComputerName HV1 `
              -VMName VM1 `
              -SnapshotName 'Snapshot1'
```

4. Look at the files created to support the checkpoints:

```
$Parent = Split-Path -Parent (Get-VM -Name VM1 |
              Select-Object
                   -ExpandProperty HARDDRIVES).PATH
Get-ChildItem -Path $Parent
```

5. Create some content in a file on VM1 and display it:

```
$sb = {
  $FileName1 = 'C:\File_After_Checkpoint_1'
  Get-Date | Out-File -FilePath $FileName1
  Get-Content -Path $FileName1}
Invoke-Command -VMName VM1 -ScriptBlock $sb `
               -Credential $cred
```

6. Take a second checkpoint:

```
Checkpoint-VM -ComputerName HV1 `
              -VMName VM1 `
              -SnapshotName 'Snapshot2'
```

7. Get the VM checkpoint details for VM1:

```
Get-VMSnapshot -VMName VM1
```

8. Look at the files supporting the two checkpoints:

```
Get-ChildItem -Path $Parent
```

9. Create and display another file in VM1 (after you have taken Snapshot2):

```
$sb = {
  $FileName2 = 'C:\File_After_Checkpoint_2'
  Get-Date | Out-File -FilePath $FileName2
  Get-ChildItem -Path C:\ -File
}
Invoke-Command -VMName VM1 -ScriptBlock $sb `
               -Credential $cred
```

10. Restore VM1 back to the checkpoint named Snapshot1:

```
$Snap1 = Get-VMSnapshot -VMName VM1 -Name Snapshot1
Restore-VMSnapshot -VMSnapshot $Snap1 -Confirm:$false
Start-VM -Name VM1
Wait-VM -For IPAddress -Name VM1
```

11. See what files we have now on VM1:

```
$sb = {Get-ChildItem -Path C:\}
Invoke-Command -VMName VM1 -ScriptBlock $sb `
               -Credential $cred
```

12. Roll forward to Snapshot2:

```
$Snap2 = Get-VMSnapshot -VMName VM1 -Name Snapshot2
Restore-VMSnapshot -VMSnapshot $Snap2 -Confirm:$false
Start-VM -Name VM1
Wait-VM -For IPAddress -Name VM1
```

13. Observe the files you now have on VM2:

```
$sb = {
  Get-ChildItem -Path C:\
}
Invoke-Command -VMName VM1 -ScriptBlock $sb `
                  -Credential $cred
```

14. Restore to Snapshot1 again:

```
$Snap1 = Get-VMSnapshot -VMName VM1 -Name Snapshot1
Restore-VMSnapshot -VMSnapshot $Snap1 -Confirm:$false
Start-VM -Name VM1
Wait-VM -For IPAddress -Name VM1
```

15. Check snapshots and VM data files again:

```
Get-VMSnapshot -VMName VM1
Get-ChildItem -Path $Parent
```

16. Remove all the snapshots from HV1:

```
Get-VMSnapshot -VMName VM1 |
      Remove-VMSnapshot
```

17. Check VM data files again:

```
Get-ChildItem -Path $Parent
```

How it works...

In *step 1*, you create a credential object to be used when invoking commands within the VM1 VM. There is no output from this step.

In *step 2*, you look at the files in the `C:\` drive within the VM1 VM, with output that looks like this:

```
PS C:\> $sb = { Get-ChildItem -Path C:\ }|
        Invoke-Command -VMName VM1 -ScriptBlock $sb `
                       -Credential $cred

    Directory: C:\

Mode         LastWriteTime    Length Name                      PSComputerName
----         -------------    ------ ----                      --------------
d-----    12/09/2016   12:36         Logs                      VM1
d-----    16/07/2016   14:23         PerfLogs                  VM1
d-r---    12/09/2016   12:35         Program Files             VM1
d-----    16/07/2016   14:23         Program Files (x86)       VM1
d-r---    13/07/2017   17:36         Users                     VM1
d-----    12/07/2017   10:49         Windows                   VM1
```

In *step 3*, you create an initial checkpoint, named `Snapshot1`, for the VM1 VM which produces no output.

In *step 4*, you examine the files that comprise the `C:` for the VM1 VM. As you can see, with output like this, there are two files—a base and a differencing drive:

```
PS C:\> $Parent = Split-Path -Parent (Get-VM -Name VM1 |
                  SELECT -ExpandProperty HARDDRIVES).PATH
PS C:\> Get-ChildItem -Path $Parent

    Directory: C:\vm1\Virtual Hard Disks

Mode         LastWriteTime       Length Name
----         -------------       ------ ----
-a----    15/07/2017   12:11   9969860608 VM1.Vhdx
-a----    15/07/2017   12:13    138412032 VM1_856D7A40-284A-4CFC-BF25-4D8B857254404.avhdx
```

In *step 5*, you create a file in VM1, and then display the contents, with output like this:

```
PS C:\> $sb = {
        $FileName1 = 'C:\File_After_Checkpoint_1'
        Get-Date | Out-File -FilePath $FileName1
        Get-Content -Path $FileName1}
PS C:\> Invoke-Command -VMName VM1 -ScriptBlock $sb `
                       -Credential $cred

15 July 2017 12:16:12
```

In *step 6*, you create a second checkpoint named `Snapshot2`. There is no output from this step.

In *step 7*, you view the details of the checkpoints (snapshots) you have taken so far for VM1, with output like this:

```
Get-VMSnapshot -VMName VM1


VMName  Name       SnapshotType CreationTime          ParentSnapshotName
------  ----       ------------ ------------          ------------------
VM1     Snapshot1  Standard     15/07/2017 12:12:01
VM1     Snapshot2  Standard     15/07/2017 12:17:39   Snapshot1
```

In *step 8*, you view the details of the files that Hyper-V creates to support the two checkpoints for VM1, with output like this:

```
PS C:\> Get-ChildItem -Path $Parent

    Directory: C:\vm1\Virtual Hard Disks

Mode            tWriteTime       Length Name
----            ----------       ------ ----
-a----    15/07/2017  12:11  9969860608 VM1.Vhdx
-a----    15/07/2017  12:17   196083712 VM1_856D7A40-284A-4CFC-BF25-4D8B57254404.avhdx
-a----    15/07/2017  13:57   272629760 VM1_E122EE41-1FD5-4EBD-BC0A-A84A290936C6.avhdx
```

With *step 9*, you create a second file in VM1, and display details of the two files created in VM1, like this:

```
PS C:\> $sb = {
    $FileName2 = 'C:\File_After_Checkpoint_2'
    Get-Date | Out-File -FilePath $FileName2
    Get-ChildItem -Path C:\ -File
}
Invoke-Command -VMName VM1 -ScriptBlock $sb `
              -Credential $cred

    Directory: C:\

Mode            LastWriteTime    Length Name                      PSComputerName
----            -------------    ------ ----                      --------------
-a----    15/07/2017  12:16          60 File_After_Checkpoint_1   VM1
-a----    15/07/2017  12:21          60 File_After_Checkpoint_2   VM1
```

In *step 10*, you restore VM1 back to the checkpoint Snapshot1. Then you start the restored VM and wait until it is starts up fully. This step generates no output, but can take 2 minutes to 3 minutes depending on the speed of your Hyper-V host.

In *step 11*, you look inside VM1 to see which of the two files created earlier now exists. As you should expect, since both files were created after the Snapshot1 checkpoint was taken, they do not exist in Snapshot1. The output of this step looks like this:

```
PS C:\> $sb = {Get-ChildItem -Path C:\}
PS C:\> Invoke-Command -VMName VM1 -ScriptBlock $sb `
              -Credential $cred


    Directory: C:\


Mode          LastWriteTime     Length Name                        PSComputerName
----          -------------     ------ ----                        --------------
d-----   12/09/2016   12:36            Logs                        VM1
d-----   16/07/2016   14:23            PerfLogs                    VM1
d-r---   12/09/2016   12:35            Program Files               VM1
d-----   16/07/2016   14:23            Program Files (x86)         VM1
d-r---   13/07/2017   17:36            Users                       VM1
d-----   12/07/2017   10:49            Windows                     VM1
```

In *step 12*, which generates no output, you roll forward to the Shapshot2 checkpoint. Remember that this checkpoint was after you created the first file (in *step 5*) but before you created the second file (in *step 9*).

In *step 13*, you look at the files that exist in VM1 which you have just restored to the Snapshot2 checkpoint. The output looks like this:

```
PS C:\> $sb = { Get-ChildItem -Path C:\}
PS C:\> Invoke-Command -VMName VM1 -ScriptBlock $sb `
              -Credential $cred


    Directory: C:\


Mode          LastWriteTime     Length Name                        PSComputerName
----          -------------     ------ ----                        --------------
d-----   12/09/2016   12:36            Logs                        VM1
d-----   16/07/2016   14:23            PerfLogs                    VM1
d-r---   12/09/2016   12:35            Program Files               VM1
d-----   16/07/2016   14:23            Program Files (x86)         VM1
d-r---   13/07/2017   17:36            Users                       VM1
d-----   12/07/2017   10:49            Windows                     VM1
-a----   15/07/2017   12:16         60 File_After_Checkpoint_1     VM1
```

In *step 14*, you revert back to the initial checkpoint, Snapshot1. Then you restart the VM1 VM. There is no output for this step.

With *step 15*, you again examine the checkpoints for VM1 and the files which Hyper-V maintains to support the checkpoints, with output like this:

```
PS C:\> Get-VMSnapshot -VMName VM1

VMName Name       SnapshotType CreationTime         ParentSnapshotName
------ ----       ------------ ------------         ------------------|
VM1    Snapshot1  Standard     15/07/2017 12:12:01
VM1    Snapshot2  Standard     15/07/2017 12:17:39  Snapshot1


PS C:\> Get-ChildItem -Path $Parent

    Directory: C:\vm1\Virtual Hard Disks

Mode            tWriteTime      Length Name
----            ----------      ------ ----
-a----   15/07/2017   12:11  9969860608 VM1.Vhdx
-a----   15/07/2017   12:17   196083712 VM1_856D7A40-284A-4CFC-BF25-4D8B57254404.avhdx
-a----   15/07/2017   13:57   272629760 VM1_E122EE41-1FD5-4EBD-BC0A-A84A290936C6.avhdx
```

With *step 16*, you remove all the snapshots for VM1, which generates no output.

In *step 17*, you view the Hyper-V is using to support VM1 showing all the snapshot files are gone, like this:

```
PS C:\> Get-ChildItem -Path $Parent

    Directory: C:\vm1\Virtual Hard Disks

Mode            LastWriteTime      Length Name
----            -------------      ------ ----
-a----   15/07/2017       13:58  9969860608 VM1.Vhdx
```

There's more...

In this recipe, you also examined the differencing files Hyper-V maintains to support the checkpoints. If you have a lot of checkpoints, the VM's performance can degrade, since Hyper-V needs to look in multiple AVHD files to support VM read requests to the VM's C: drive.

Monitoring Hyper-V utilization and performance

In `Chapter 6`, *Managing Performance*, you looked at performance counters and the **Performance Logs and Alerts** (**PLA**) feature of Windows Server 2016.

With PLA, applications, services, drivers, and OS components can expose operation data via counter sets and counters. A counter is a measurement of one specific value, such as the `%ProcessorTime` counter that measures how much CPU is being used at any given moment. Counters are grouped for convenience into counter sets. The `Processor` counter set contains the `%ProcessorTime` counter.

In this recipe, you examine some of the wide range of Hyper-V performance counters available to you. PLA in general, and Hyper-V in particular, expose a very large number of counter sets containing a wide range which Hyper-V exposes. It is very easy to get excited about the wealth of counters available. But most of the information provided is probably of little use to most IT professionals managing Hyper-V hosts and VMs.

A given Hyper-V host has a number of physical CPUs containing typically multiple cores. You can enable any given VM to utilize one or more of the cores as processors inside the VM. So, were you to have a dual processor 6-core system, you would have 12-cores which you can then divide up among your VMs.

One useful performance metric for your VM host is how much of the CPU is being used running VMs. The *Hyper-V* `Hypervisor Root Virtual Processor` counter set contains a counter (`% guest run time`) that provides that information.

If the Hyper-V host's guest run time is very high on an ongoing basis, it means your VMs are possibly being CPU bound. It may make sense on such a host to either increase the capacity of the host (adding more cores or moving to a more powerful server) or decreasing the workload by migrating a VM to another Hyper-V host.

Getting ready

In this recipe, you examine performance aspects of the VM host, VM1 (which you set up in the *Installing and Configuring Hyper-V* recipe), and the performance of VM1, the VM (created in the *Creating a virtual machine* recipe).

How to do it...

Here is how to example performance of your Hyper-V system:

1. Discover how many counter sets exist (on HV1):

```
$TotalCounters = Get-Counter -ListSet * | Measure-Object
"Total Counter sets           : [{0}]" -f $TotalCounters.Count
```

2. Discover how many counter sets exist for Hyper-V:

```
$Counters = Get-Counter -ListSet *
"Hyper-V Related Counter Sets : [{0}]" -F $Counters.Count
```

3. View counter set details for Hyper-V:

```
Get-Counter -ListSet * |
  Where-Object CounterSetName -match 'hyper'|
    Sort -Property CounterSetName |
        Format-Table -Property CounterSetName, Description
```

4. Determine how many individual counters exist in the Root Virtual Processor counter set:

```
$HVPCounters = Get-Counter -ListSet * |
  Where-Object CounterSetName -Match 'Root virtual Processor' |
        Select-Object -ExpandProperty Paths |
            Measure-Object
"Hyper-V RVP Counters           : [{0}]" -f $HVPCounters.count
```

5. Define some key counters in the Hypervisor Root Virtual Processor counter set:

```
$HVCounters = @("\\HV1\Hyper-V Hypervisor Root Virtual "+
                "Processor(*)\% Guest Run Time")
$HVCounters += @("\\HV1\Hyper-V Hypervisor Root Virtual "+
                "Processor(*)\% Hypervisor Run Time")
$HVCounters += @("\\HV1\Hyper-V Hypervisor Root Virtual "+
                "Processor(*)\% Remote Run Time")
$HVCounters += @("\\HV1\Hyper-V Hypervisor Root Virtual "+
                "Processor(*)\% Total Run Time")
```

6. Get counter samples for the counters defined:

```
$Samples = (Get-Counter -Counter $HVCounters).counterSamples |
    Where-Object Path -Like '*(_total)*'
```

7. Display the counter data returned:

```
"{0,-22} : {1:N3}" -f 'Counter', 'Value'
"{0,-22} : {1:N3}" -f '-------', '-----'
Foreach ($sample in $samples) {
  $countername = Split-Path -path $sample.path -leaf
  $counterdata = $sample.CookedValue
  "{0,-22} : {1:N3}" -f $countername, $counterdata  }
```

How it works...

In *step 1*, you discover how many total performance counter sets exist on your Hyper-V host, HV1. The output looks like this:

```
Total Counter sets          : [173]
```

In *step 2*, you discover how many of these counter sets on HV1 are Hyper-V related, with output like this:

```
Hyper-V Related Counter Sets : [31]
```

With *step 3*, you discover more details about the Hyper-V related counter sets, with output like this:

```
CounterSetName                                    Description
-------------                                     -----------
Hyper-V Configuration                             This counter set represents the statistics for HyperVStorage f...
Hyper-V Dynamic Memory Balancer                   This counter set represents the statistics for the Microsoft D...
Hyper-V Dynamic Memory Integration Service        This counter set represents the statistics for Dynamic Memory ...
Hyper-V Dynamic Memory VM                         This counter set represents the memory statistics for a Virtua...
Hyper-V Hypervisor                                Information on the hypervisor.
Hyper-V Hypervisor Logical Processor              Information on logical processors.
Hyper-V Hypervisor Partition                      Information on virtual machines
Hyper-V Hypervisor Root Partition                 Information on virtual machines
Hyper-V Hypervisor Root Virtual Processor         Information on virtual processors
Hyper-V Hypervisor Virtual Processor              Information on virtual processors
Hyper-V Legacy Network Adapter                    Performance counters for a virtual machine's Ethernet controller.
Hyper-V Replica VM                                This counter set represents the Hyper-V Replica statistics for...
Hyper-V Virtual IDE Controller (Emulated)         Performance counters for a virtual machine's IDE Controller.
Hyper-V Virtual Machine Bus                       This counter set represents the statistics for the virtual mac...
Hyper-V Virtual Machine Bus Pipes                 Per-Pipe statistics, for performance debugging.
Hyper-V Virtual Machine Bus Provider Pipes        Per-Pipe statistics, for performance debugging.
Hyper-V Virtual Machine Health Summary            This counter set represents the health summary statistics for ...
Hyper-V Virtual Network Adapter                   This counter set represents the statistics for the Microsoft H...
Hyper-V Virtual Network Adapter Drop Reasons      This counter set represents the drop reasons statistics for th...
Hyper-V Virtual Network Adapter VRSS              This counter set represents the statistics for the Microsoft H...
Hyper-V Virtual Storage Device                    This counter set represents the statistics for a virtual stora...
Hyper-V Virtual Switch                            This counter set represents the statistics for the Microsoft H...
Hyper-V Virtual Switch Port                       This counter set represents the statistics for the Microsoft H...
Hyper-V Virtual Switch Processor                  This counter set represents the statistics for the Microsoft H...
Hyper-V VM Live Migration                         Performance counters for a virtual machine's live migration.
Hyper-V VM Remoting                               Performance counters for a virtual machine's remoting system.
Hyper-V VM Save, Snapshot, and Restore            Performance counters for a virtual machine's save, snapshot, a...
Hyper-V VM Vid Numa Node                          The perf counters for a numa node.
Hyper-V VM Vid Partition                          These are the perf counters for a VID partition object.
Hyper-V VM Virtual Device Pipe IO                 Worker process per-pipe statistics, for performance debugging.
Hyper-V Worker Virtual Processor                  Performance counters for the virtual processor of a virtual ma...
```

In *step 4*, you determine how many counters exist in the counter set `Root Virtual Processor`. You should see output like this:

```
Hyper-V RVP Counters          : [146]
```

In *step 5*, you define several key CPU related counters. In *step 6*, you get sample values for each of these counters representing total values. There is no output from these two steps.

In *step 7*, you display key CPU counter values for a Hyper-V host. Depending on what load you are currently running, this step produces output that should look like this:

```
Counter                 : Value
-------                 : -----
% guest run time        : 1.223
% hypervisor run time   : 0.057
% remote run time       : 0.000
% total run time        : 1.280
```

There's more...

As you can see from *step 1*, a Hyper-V Server running Windows Server 2016 provides a large number of counter sets you can use to view an aspect of the server. These counter sets, as you can see in *step 2*, include a large number of Hyper-V related counters and you can see more details of these counter sets in *step 3*. With *step 4*, you can see that Hyper-V exposes a large number of individual counters in one counter set, the `Hyper-V Root Virtual Processor`.

It is quite probable that the vast majority of counter sets and counters are not of much use to most IT pros. But they are worth knowing about if you are chasing down a performance issue with Hyper-V or with Windows Server in general. You can easily spend hours (or longer) delving into the details of some of these counters. While the details of all the counters are not included here, you can use the techniques in this recipe to find other counters you may wish to investigate.

In *step 5*, you create an array of counter names that you obtain sample values for in *step 6*. In *step 7*, you display the sample values. Of course, depending on what load you are currently running, you may see different values.

Creating a Hyper-V health report

Any Hyper-V host that you deploy is a critical part of your IT infrastructure. If the Hyper-V host goes down or starts suffering performance or capacity issues, it can affect all the VMs running on that host. Your Hyper-V hosts are almost certainly *mission critical*.

If you deploy Hyper-V, it is important you report on and monitor the health of your Hyper-V host, as well as the health of the VMs. By monitoring the reports, you can detect issues, possibly before they become critical. If your VM host, for example, has a slowly increasing CPU load, you can consider moving a VM to another VM host.

Reports that you use to monitor the health of a Hyper-V host fall into two broad categories: the VM host itself, and the VMs running on that host. This recipe creates two *reports* to mirror this.

This recipe uses a variety of methods to obtain key performance and usage metrics and converts this information into an object. The recipe begins by defining a PowerShell hash table. The recipe then adds each of the measurements as a row in the hash table. At the end, the recipe emits an object with properties relating to the measurements

In this recipe, you first create a report object that contains details of the VM host. Then the recipe gets key information about each VM, and creates an object for each VM on the host, and adds it to an array. At the end of the recipe, you display the VM objects.

The technique used here is to create hash tables holding host and VM details then to turn these hash tables into fully-fledged objects. This enables you to sort and filter the objects to create whatever reporting you need.

Getting ready

This recipe runs on the Hyper-V host HV1. The host should be setup as per the *Installing and configuring Hyper-V feature* recipe. This host should be up and running and have one VM defined and running. The VM is VM1 which you created in the *Creating a virtual machine* recipe.

How to do it...

Here is how you can create a Hyper-V health report:

1. Create a basic report object hash table:

   ```
   $ReportHT = [Ordered]  @{}
   ```

2. Get the host details and add them to the Report object:

   ```
   $HostDetails          = Get-CimInstance `
                           -ClassName Win32_ComputerSystem
   $ReportHT.HostName = $HostDetails.Name
   $ReportHT.Maker    = $HostDetails.Manufacturer
   $ReportHT.Model    = $HostDetails.Model
   ```

3. Add the PowerShell version information:

   ```
   $ReportHT.PSVersion = $PSVersionTable.PSVersion.tostring()
   # Add OS information:
   $OS = Get-CimInstance -Class Win32_OperatingSystem
   $ReportHT.OSEdition    = $OS.Caption
   $ReportHT.OSArch       = $OS.OSArchitecture
   $ReportHT.OSLang       = $OS.OSLanguage
   $ReportHT.LastBootTime = $os.LastBootUpTime
   $Now = Get-Date
   $ReportHT.UpTimeDays = [float] ("{0:n3}" -f (($Now -
   $OS.LastBootUpTime).Totaldays))
   ```

4. Add a count of processors in the host:

```
$Proc = Get-CimInstance -ClassName MSvm_Processor `
                        -Namespace root/virtualization/v2
$ReportHT.CPUCount = ($Proc |
                      Where-Object elementname -match `
                         'Logical Processor').COUNT
```

5. Add the current host CPU usage:

```
$Cname      = '\\.\processor(_total)\% processor time'
$CPU = Get-Counter -Counter $Cname
$ReportHT.HostCPUUsage = $CPU.CounterSamples.CookedValue
```

6. Add the total host physical memory:

```
$Memory = Get-Ciminstance -Class Win32_ComputerSystem
$HostMemory       = [float] ( "{0:n2}" -f
($Memory.TotalPhysicalMemory/1GB))
$ReportHT.HostMemoryGB = $HostMemory
```

7. Add the memory allocated to VMs:

```
$Sum = 0
Get-VM | foreach {$sum += $_.MemoryAssigned + $Total}
$Sum = [float] ( "{0:N2}" -f ($Sum/1gb) )
$ReportHT.AllocatedMemoryGB = $Sum
```

8. Create and view the host report object:

```
$Reportobj = New-Object -TypeName PSObject `
                        -Property $ReportHT
$Reportobj
```

9. Create two new VMs to populate the VM report:

```
New-VM -Name VM2
New-VM -Name VM3
```

10. Get VM details on the local VM host and create a container array for individual VM related objects:

```
$VMs = Get-VM -Name *
$VMHT = @()
```

11. Get VM details for each VM into an object added to the hash table container:

```
Foreach ($VM in $VMs) {
  # Create VM Report hash table
  $VMReport = [ordered] @{}
  # Add VM's Name
  $VMReport.VMName     = $VM.VMName
  # Add Status
  $VMReport.Status     = $VM.Status
  # Add Uptime
  $VMReport.Uptime     = $VM.Uptime
  # Add VM CPU
  $VMReport.VMCPU      = $VM.CPUUsage
  # Replication Mode/Status
  $VMReport.ReplMode   = $VM.ReplicationMode
  $VMReport.ReplState = $Vm.ReplicationState
  # Create object from Hash table, add to array
  $VMR = New-Object -TypeName PSObject -Property $VMReport
  $VMHT += $VMR
}
```

12. Display the array of objects as a table:

```
$VMHT |
  Sort-Object -Property Uptime -Descending |
    Format-Table
```

How it works...

In *step1*, you create a hash table, $ReportHT. This hash table holds properties of the VM host which this recipe populates.

In *step 2*, you add details of the computer's hostname and the host's manufacturer and model.

In *step 3*, you add the PowerShell version and then in *step 4*, you obtain details about the OS running on the host and add it to the hash table.

With *step 5*, you add the count of CPUs in the host while in *step 6*, you add details of the CPU usage of the VM host.

In *step 7*, you add the host's total memory and in *step 8*, how much of that memory has been allocated to virtual machines.

These first 7 steps create no output.

In *step 9*, you create an object, $Reportobj based on the $ReportHT hash table. You then display the object, which looks like this:

```
PS C:\> $Reportobj = New-Object -TypeName PSObject -Property $report
PS C:\> $Reportobj

HostName          : HV1
Maker             : Microsoft Corporation
Model             : Virtual Machine
PSVersion         : 5.1.14393.0
OSEdition         : Microsoft Windows Server 2016 Datacenter
OSArch            : 64-bit
OSLang            : 1033
LastBootTime      : 15/07/2017 09:39:35
UpTimeDays        : 2.174
CPUCount          : 8
HostCPUUsage      : 31.61328927579385
HostMemoryGB      : 15.62
AllocatedMemoryGB : 4
```

In *step 10*, you create two new VMs simply to provide more VMs on which to report in the second part of this recipe. There is no output from this step.

In *step 11*, you get VM details by using the Get-VM cmdlet. Then you create an array to hold individual objects for each VM on the host. There is no output from this step.

In *step 12*, you iterate through each VM on the host and create an object that holds details about the VM. You then add the object to the array created in *step 11*. There is no output from this step.

Finally, in *step 13*, you display the detail array as follows:

```
PS C:\>   $vmht |
            sort-object -Property uptime -descending |
                Format-Table

VMName Status             Uptime              VMCPU ReplMode ReplState
------ ------             ------              ----- -------- ---------
VM1    Operating normally 2.01:50:10.1610000   12   None     Disabled
VM3    Operating normally 00:00:00              0   None     Disabled
VM2    Operating normally 00:00:00              0   None     Disabled
```

There's more...

This recipe presents two min-recipes to get the details of your Hyper-V host and the VMs deployed on the host.

In the first nine steps, you create a report object that contains information about the VM host. You could extend the report hash table/report to include information about network and I/O traffic.

Generating this report object produces a view in time of the server. You could extend this part of the recipe to create a measurement object say every hour, then once a day you can analyze it by reporting maximum and minimum CPU, memory usage, and generating alerts by email. You could use these daily reports and create richer capacity planning information as well.

In the second part of this recipe, you generate details about each of the VMs defined on the Hyper-V host. You could also extend these steps to capture more information about the VMs, including network and disk I/O traffic.

You may also find that, over time, the issues you need to keep an eye on evolve. Don't be afraid of re-visiting this recipe and improving it over time.

12
Managing Azure

In this chapter, we cover the following recipes:

- Using PowerShell with Azure
- Creating core Azure resources
- Exploring your storage account
- Creating and using an Azure SMB file share
- Creating and using Azure websites
- Creating and using Azure virtual machines

Introduction

Azure is Microsoft's cloud computing platform and is a competitor to Amazon's Amazon Web Services and other public cloud providers, Azure provides you with access to a huge range of features. Organizations can literally move their entire on-premises infrastructure into the cloud.

Azure features come at three levels:

- **Infrastructure as a service (IaaS)**
- **Platform as a service (PaaS)**
- **Software as a Service (SaaS)**

IaaS is, in effect, an instant computing infrastructure that you can provision, manage, and use over the internet or via a private network connection. IaaS includes the basic computing infrastructure components (servers, storage, networking, firewalls, and security) plus the physical plant required to run these components (power, air conditioning, and so on). In an IaaS environment, the servers are all Azure virtual machines (effectively Hyper-V VMs) and interact with the networking, security, and storage components.

PaaS is a complete deployment environment in the cloud, including the operating system, storage, and other infrastructure. One key PaaS offering in Azure is the Azure SQL Database. Things like the OS and SQL server patching, which you would have to deal with if you deploy SQL in an IaaS environment, are all managed by Azure. This provides a complete SQL service all managed by Azure. This of course means there are some things you can't do—actions that are reserved for the platform owner (that is Microsoft). For example, with SQL running inside and IaaS Azure VM, you can use database mirroring—the **SQL PaaS** service does not provide that feature for you to use.

With SaaS, you just use an application that the vendor has placed in the cloud. The key example of SaaS is **Office 365 (O365)**, which bundles Exchange Online, SharePoint Online, Skype For Business Online, OneDrive for Business, and Microsoft Teams.

Strictly speaking, Office 365 is not an Azure offering—you purchase directly from either the Office 365 web site or via a Microsoft Partner. In terms of purchase, O365 is a single offering with many different *plans* (combinations of services that also includes a downloadable version of the Office applications such as Word and Excel). In terms of using PowerShell to manage O365, each of the included applications has their own unique approach. With Exchange Online, for example, you use PowerShell Implicit Remoting to manage the exchange component of your O365 subscription.

To provide authentication for software running within Azure and for other SaaS applications, you can make use of **Azure Active Directory (AAD)**. With AAD you can create a cloud-only directory or you can synchronize the AAD with your on-premises Active Directory. AAD can also be used to provide authentication for a range of other third party SaaS applications. Full details of managing both AAD and Office 365 components are outside the scope of this chapter.

In this chapter, we begin with the first recipe: *Using PowerShell with Azure*. In this recipe, we look at setting up a basic environment with which to manage Azure and the O365 SaaS components. This recipe also shows how to download the AAD cmdlets.

The *Creating core Azure resources* recipe guides you through creating a few of the core resources you need to create and manage other Azure resources. These include a resource group and a storage account. Every Azure resource you create with the ARM API must be contained in a resource group. Also, any storage you may require, such as for VHD files for an Azure VM, you need a storage group. While the recipes in this chapter use a single resource group and a single storage account, large scale Azure deployments may require multiple instances of these key resources.

With the *Creating Azure storage* recipe, we look at setting up Azure storage using the storage account created earlier.

The *Creating and using an Azure SMB file share* recipe shows you how you can create an SMB file share that you can access from client applications across the internet. Instead of having an application point to an on-premises file share, you can now host the share in Azure. This might be useful if you use Azure IaaS VM to host an application that utilizes a shared folder for its data. You could also use it as a file share in the cloud.

The *Creating and using Azure websites* recipe shows how you can set up a simple website. The recipe sets up a WordPress blog using PowerShell. This feature enables you to setup a simple website, say for a short-term marketing campaign, as well as to build internet-scale web sites that you can have Azure scale dynamically according to load.

The next recipe, *Creating and using Azure virtual machines*, examines how to create an Azure VM and access it. This includes creating a virtual network and setting the VM up to enable you to manage it with PowerShell or connect via RDP.

This chapter is only a taster for using Azure with PowerShell. There is so much more that you can do that sadly would not fit into this book.

Using PowerShell with Azure

There are two key things you need to do before you can begin to manage Azure features using PowerShell. The first is to obtain an Azure subscription. The second is to get access to the cmdlets you need to be able to access Azure (and Office 365's features).

Azure is a commercial service—each feature you use has a cost attached. Azure charges are based on resource usage. With an Azure VM, for example, you would pay to have the VM running, with additional charges for the storage the VM uses and for any network traffic. The charges for Office 365, on the other hand, are user based—a given user can use lots of email, for example, without incurring any additional charges. For details on costs for Azure, see `https://azure.microsoft.com/en-us/pricing/`, and for details of Office 365 charges, see `https://products.office.com/en-us/business/compare-office-365-for-business-plans`.

To use Azure's IaaS and PaaS features, you need to have an Azure subscription. There are many ways you can get an Azure subscription, including via an MSDN subscription, an Action Pack subscription, or by outright purchase. Naturally, you need to ensure that any systems are properly licensed.

Microsoft also provides a one-month free trial subscription. This subscription provides you full access to Azure features up to a financial limit, which at the time of writing, is *US$200* or similar in other currencies. These limits may have changed by the time you read this book. Having said that, the trial subscription should be sufficient to enable you to learn how to use PowerShell with Azure.

If you do not have an existing subscription to Azure, navigate to `https://azure.microsoft.com/en-gb/free/` where you can create a trial subscription. Note that a free trial requires you to submit a credit card number. There is no charge for the subscription, the credit card number is used only to identify verification—plus it keeps the lawyers happier.

If you take out an Azure trial and you want to keep your Azure resources running after the trial expires, you have to move it to a pay as you go subscription. You receive an email shortly before the trial expires to transition it which prevents downtime if you using the trial for production.

To use PowerShell with Azure's various features requires you to obtain cmdlets that Microsoft does not provide in Windows Server 2016 or PowerShell 5.0/5.1. You get the relevant modules from the PowerShell Gallery using the cmdlets in the `PowerShellGet` module to find and download them.

It is important to note that the PowerShell Azure cmdlets are a wrapper around Azure's underlying API. Azure core API is REST based and involves a client sending various HTTP messages into Azure, as well as parsing the replies and dealing with errors—this is complex. Instead of using the underlying API you just use the cmdlets. In most cases, this is all very straightforward. But when you are troubleshooting, being able to see the detailed HTTP exchanges and the raw messages can help a great deal. You can obtain most of this information simply by using the -Verbose switch on the Azure cmdlets.

Over the years, Azure has implemented two APIs for Azure. The first API, known as the **Azure Service Management (ASM)** API, included a nice web based portal (known as the Classic Portal, at https://manage.windowsazure.com). To simplify things for the IT pro, this version came with a set of cmdlets. The cmdlet set is a work in progress and has grown significantly over time. As of the time of writing this chapter, ASM module contains 623 cmdlets.

Based on the feedback from the use of the ASM API, Microsoft did a fundamental re-design and implemented a new API, the **Azure Resource Management (ARM)** API. The ARM API is an improvement on the ASM API, and provides a wealth of new features that helps in the management of complex IaaS and PaaS deployments. The new API also supports templates to simplify deploying solutions within Azure. The Azure team also delivered a new and richer portal based on the ARM API (https://portal.azure.com). And like the ASM cmdlets, the ARM cmdlets in the new portal are also works in progress steadily growing over time. At the time of writing the AzureRM modules contain 1215 cmdlets.

While the new API provides lots of new features, there is some bad news. Unfortunately, the two APIs are essentially incompatible. Objects created with one API are not usable from the other API. Thus, if you create a VM using the ASM API (either the via the *Classic* portal or via the ASM cmdlets), you cannot manage it via the ARM API or the ARM portal.

Going forward, the ARM platform is where the Azure team is focusing and for that reason, the recipes in this chapter use the ARM API and the supporting cmdlets and on-line portal.

An issue related to the new API is the way in which cmdlets are developed and delivered. Historically, the Azure PowerShell team delivered just one module (Azure) which was dual-headed. It could manage either of the two API sets although not at the same time. This leads to a lot of confusion so (to make a long and complex story short) the team created separate modules for each of the API sets. The ASM cmdlets remain unchanged while the ARM cmdlets were renamed and repackaged. Today, there is one overarching Module (AzureRM) and a number of subsidiary modules (for example AzureRm.Websites, AzureRm.Tags, and so on).

One final point to bear in mind as you read and leverage the recipes in this chapter is that all of Azure is a work in progress. There are a large number of feature teams inside the Azure organization—each of which are working at what is often described as *Internet pace*. The new portal is updated on a regular basis—thus any screenshots of the portal are often out of date (almost instantly it sometimes appears). The cmdlets are more stable and breaking changes are usually pretty rare but regular updates are to be expected. If and when the Azure PowerShell team deem it necessary to do breaking changes, the affected modules are versioned and you can continue to use the older module until such times as you can update your scripts.

If this is the first time you've used `PowerShellGet`, you'll receive the following message which might be worth mentioning:

```
NuGet provider is required to continue
PowerShellGet requires NuGet provider version '2.8.5.201' or newer to
interact with NuGet-based repositories. The NuGet
 provider must be available in 'C:\Program
Files\PackageManagement\ProviderAssemblies' or
'C:\Users\JerryGarcia \AppData\Local\PackageManagement\ProviderAssemblies'.
You can also install the NuGet provider by
running 'Install-PackageProvider -Name NuGet -MinimumVersion 2.8.5.201 -
Force'. Do you want PowerShellGet to install
and import the NuGet provider now?
[Y] Yes [N] No [S] Suspend [?] Help (default is "Y"):
```

You need to accept install and import the NuGet provider in order to use PowerShell get in this recipe.

Getting ready

This recipe uses a Windows 10 Creator's Update computer, `CL1`, to manage the Azure account. You also need an Azure account, as noted earlier.

How to do it...

The steps for the recipe are as follows:

1. Find core Azure PowerShell modules:

```
Find-Module -Name Azure, AzureRM
```

2. Install the Azure ARM cmdlets:

```
Install-Module -Name AzureRM -Force
```

3. Discover what is in the Azure module:

```
$HT = @{ Label ='Cmdlets'}
$HT.Expression = {(Get-Command -Module $_.name).count}
Get-Module -Name Azure* -ListAvailable |
    Sort-Object -Property `
    {(Get-Command -Module $_.name).count} -Descending |
        Format-Table Name,Version,Author,$HT -AutoSize
```

4. Find `AzureAD` cmdlets:

```
Find-Module -Name AzureAD |
    Format-Table -AutoSize -Wrap
```

5. Download the `AzureAD` module:

```
Install-Module -Name AzureAD -Force
```

6. Discover the `AzureAD` module:

```
(Get-Command -Module AzureAD).count
Get-Module -Name AzureAD -ListAvailable |
Format-Table -AutoSize -Wrap
```

7. Log in to Azure:

```
$Subscription = Login-AzureRmAccount
```

8. Get Azure subscription details:

```
$SubID = $Subscription.CONTEXT.Subscription.SubscriptionId
Get-AzureRmSubscription -SubscriptionId $SubId |
        Format-List -Property*
```

9. Get Azure regions or locations:

```
Get-AzureRmLocation |
    Sort-Object -Property Location |
        Format-Table -Property Location, Displayname
```

How it works...

This recipe is all about getting started with Azure. Since there are no Azure cmdlets supplied with Windows Server 2016 or Windows 10 by default, you need to find them and install them on your local machine (for example CL1).

In *step 1*, you use the PowerShellGet module's `Find-Module` cmdlet to find the key Azure modules, as shown in the following screenshot:

```
PS C:\> Find-Module -Name Azure, AzureRM

Version    Name       Repository   Description
-------    ----       ----------   -----------
3.8.0      Azure      PSGallery    Microsoft Azure PowerShell - Service Management
3.8.0      AzureRM    PSGallery    Azure Resource Manager Module
```

As you can see, the first step displays the two core Azure modules. The `Azure` module is the one you use for accessing the ASM based Azure objects, while the `AzureRM` module provides access to the Azure ARM API and related objects. Since the recipes in this chapter only target Azure ARM, in *step 2*, you install the `AzureRM` module. This step produces no output.

In *step 3*, you use your discovery techniques to look at the Azure modules you just downloaded. You create a hash table (`$HT`) that calculates the number of cmdlets in each module, then you use that hash table to display the Azure modules, the module version number and how many cmdlets are contained in each module. The list is shown in the following screenshot:

```
PS C:\> $HT = @{ Label ='Cmdlets'}
PS C:\> $HT.Expression = {(Get-Command -Module $_.name).count}
PS C:\> Get-Module -Name Azure* -ListAvailable |
        Sort-Object -Property `
          {(Get-Command -Module $_.name).count} -Descending |
            Format-Table Name,Version,Author,$HT -AutoSize


Name                               Version     Author                Cmdlets
----                               -------     ------                -------
AzureRM                            3.8.0       Microsoft Corporation    1564
AzureRM.Network                    3.7.0       Microsoft Corporation     242
AzureRM.Compute                    2.9.0       Microsoft Corporation     155
AzureAD                            2.0.0.109   Microsoft Corporation     134
AzureRM.Sql                        2.8.0       Microsoft Corporation     113
AzureRM.ApiManagement              3.6.0       Microsoft Corporation      88
AzureRM.Automation                 2.8.0       Microsoft Corporation      70
AzureRM.Batch                      2.8.0       Microsoft Corporation      69
AzureRM.DataLakeStore              3.6.0       Microsoft Corporation      68
AzureRM.Resources                  3.8.0       Microsoft Corporation      67
AzureRM.SiteRecovery               3.7.0       Microsoft Corporation      62
Azure.Storage                      2.8.0       Microsoft Corporation      61
AzureRM.DataLakeAnalytics          2.8.0       Microsoft Corporation      50
AzureRM.LogicApp                   2.8.0       Microsoft Corporation      43
AzureRM.Websites                   2.8.0       Microsoft Corporation      41
AzureRM.OperationalInsights        2.8.0       Microsoft Corporation      40
AzureRM.HDInsight                  2.8.0       Microsoft Corporation      35
AzureRM.KeyVault                   2.8.0       Microsoft Corporation      35
AzureRM.ServiceBus                 0.2.0       Microsoft Corporation      34
AzureRM.DataFactories              2.8.0       Microsoft Corporation      29
AzureRM.Insights                   2.8.0       Microsoft Corporation      25
AzureRM.EventHub                   0.2.0       Microsoft Corporation      24
AzureRM.Cdn                        2.8.0       Microsoft Corporation      24
AzureRM.Backup                     2.8.0       Microsoft Corporation      24
AzureRM.StreamAnalytics            2.8.0       Microsoft Corporation      21
AzureRM.NotificationHubs           2.8.0       Microsoft Corporation      21
AzureRM.IotHub                     1.4.0       Microsoft Corporation      20
AzureRM.RecoveryServices.Backup    2.8.0       Microsoft Corporation      20
AzureRM.Scheduler                  0.13.0      Microsoft Corporation      17
AzureRM.RedisCache                 2.8.0       Microsoft Corporation      15
AzureRM.MachineLearning            0.13.0      Microsoft Corporation      14
AzureRM.AnalysisServices           0.2.0       Microsoft Corporation      14
AzureRM.TrafficManager             2.8.0       Microsoft Corporation      14
AzureRM.profile                    2.8.0       Microsoft Corporation      13
AzureRM.ServerManagement           2.8.0       Microsoft Corporation      13
AzureRM.Storage                    2.8.0       Microsoft Corporation      12
AzureRM.Dns                        2.8.0       Microsoft Corporation      11
AzureRM.DevTestLabs                2.8.0       Microsoft Corporation      10
AzureRM.Media                      0.5.0       Microsoft Corporation       9
AzureRM.RecoveryServices           2.8.0       Microsoft Corporation       7
AzureRM.CognitiveServices          0.6.0       Microsoft Corporation       7
AzureRM.PowerBIEmbedded            2.8.0       Microsoft Corporation       6
Azure.AnalysisServices             0.2.0       Microsoft Corporation       4
AzureRM.Tags                       2.8.0       Microsoft Corporation       3
AzureRM.UsageAggregates            2.8.0       Microsoft Corporation       3
AzureRM.Billing                    0.11.0      Microsoft Corporation       1
```

With *step 4*, you find the `AzureAD` module and display details as shown in the following screenshot:

```
PS C:\> Find-Module -Name AzureAD |
            Format-Table -Property Name,Version,Author `
                        -AutoSize -Wrap

Name     Version   Author
----     -------   ------
AzureAD  2.0.0.115 Microsoft Corporation
```

In *step 5*, you download and install the `AzureAD` module, which produces no output.

In *step 6*, you look in more detail at the `AzureAD` module which contains a wealth of commands to assist you with managing AAD. The output of this step is as shown in the following screenshot:

```
PS C:\> Get-Module -Name AzureAD -ListAvailable |
            Format-Table -Property Name,Version,Author, Description `
                -AutoSize -Wrap

Name     Version   Author                Description
----     -------   ------                -----------
AzureAD  2.0.0.115 Microsoft Corporation Azure Active Directory V2 General Availability
                                         Module.
                                         This is the General Availability release of Azure
                                         Active Directory V2 PowerShell Module.
                                         For detailed information on how to install and
                                         run this module from the PowerShell Gallery
                                         including prerequisites, please refer to https://m
                                         sdn.microsoft.com/powershell/gallery/readme
```

In *step 7*, you log in to Azure. You need to log in before you can use the modules you downloaded earlier. In this recipe's example, you use a Microsoft ID (previously a known as a Passport ID or a Live ID). Using a Microsoft ID is not an uncommon approach in some cases, such as when you are using an Azure trial subscription or using the Azure rights associated with an MSDN subscription. Using a Microsoft ID, you have to log in by entering your user id and password manually. Running *step 7* results in two pop-up dialog boxes. The first is requesting a user ID, as shown in the following screenshot:

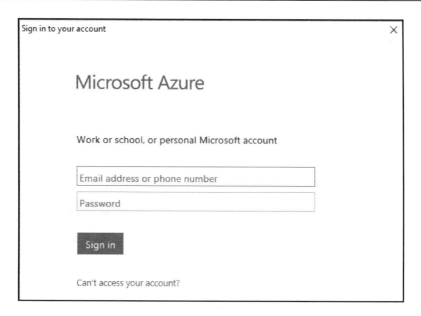

In the case of a Microsoft ID, you see the second dialog where you enter your password as shown in the following screenshot:

The `Login-AzureRmAccount` returns an object containing details of the Azure subscription, which the recipe saves in `$Subscription`. You use this variable in step 8 where you get and display details of your subscription, which is shown in the following screenshot:

```
PS C:\> $SubID = $Subscription.Context.Subscription.SubscriptionId
PS C:\> Get-AzureRmSubscription -SubscriptionId $SubId |
          Format-List -Property *

SubscriptionId            : 0bc29420-0222-4599-b91e-e8699f760742
SubscriptionName          : MSDN Platforms
State                     : Enabled
TenantId                  : c1a6d420-6960-42e1-9104-65669aabc420
CurrentStorageAccountName :
```

In *step 9*, you get the Azure Data Center regions. Later in this chapter, you use various IaaS resources, such as a Virtual Machine. When you create a resource like a VM, you create it in one of the regional data centers. The list of standard Azure data centers looks like this:

```
PS C:\> Get-AzureRmLocation | Sort-Object Location |
          Format-Table Location, Displayname

Location            DisplayName
--------            -----------
australiaeast       Australia East
australiasoutheast  Australia Southeast
brazilsouth         Brazil South
canadacentral       Canada Central
canadaeast          Canada East
centralindia        Central India
centralus           Central US
eastasia            East Asia
eastus              East US
eastus2             East US 2
japaneast           Japan East
japanwest           Japan West
koreacentral        Korea Central
koreasouth          Korea South
northcentralus      North Central US
northeurope         North Europe
southcentralus      South Central US
southeastasia       Southeast Asia
southindia          South India
uksouth             UK South
ukwest              UK West
westcentralus       West Central US
westeurope          West Europe
westus              West US
westus2             West US 2
```

In *step 10*, you get the set of Azure environments. Each environment is a separate cloud. At present, as the output shows, there are separate clouds in Germany, China, and for the US government. There may be additional environments which for security reasons Microsoft does not disclose. The list of environments is as shown in the following screenshot:

```
PS C:\> Get-AzureRmEnvironment |
    Format-Table -Property name, ManagementPortalURL

Name                ManagementPortalUrl
----                -------------------
AzureCloud          http://go.microsoft.com/fwlink/?LinkId=254433
AzureChinaCloud     http://go.microsoft.com/fwlink/?LinkId=301902
AzureUSGovernment   https://manage.windowsazure.us
AzureGermanCloud    http://portal.microsoftazure.de/
```

There's more...

In *step 1*, you find the two core modules for managing Azure: `Azure` and `AzureRM`. The Azure module is a single large monolithic module, while the `AzureRM` module actually has a number of sub-modules.

In *step 2*, you install the Azure RM modules (and the related subsidiary modules. By default, the PSGallery is not a trusted repository and the `Install-Module` prompts for permission to install from this untrusted repository. You avoid the prompt by using the –`Force` switch.

In *step 3*, you use a hash table to create a new column for use when displaying module information. This column just takes the module name and returns the number of cmdlets that are in that module. As you can see, there are a large number of small modules that make up the main `AzureRM` module. This approach makes it easier for the Azure PowerShell team to service and improve the individual sub-modules.

In *step 7*, you log into Azure. It would be nice if you could just pass a credential object to the `Login-AzureRMAccount`, but as Microsoft do not support this for Live IDs, you have to log in manually. This has been raised as an issue with the cmdlets, but Microsoft does not plan to fix this issue. For simple IaaS type applications, this means regular logins via a GUI.

Also in *step 7*, the first pop-up dialog box appears to allow you to enter both the userid and the password. The pop-up does not actually allow you to enter your password, instead you do that on the second pop-up.

Step 9 and *step 10* show you a bit of the breadth of Azure. The Azure cloud has, at the time of writing, 25 regional data centres, each of which are massive and more are planned, including in Africa. These regional data centers, such as those in Dublin, can span multiple physical buildings providing both scale and a degree of extra overall resilience. In addition to the main Azure public cloud, Microsoft has created separate cloud environments for China, Germany and the US Government as you can see in the output.

Creating Core Azure Resources

In the previous recipe, you created and used the basic Azure management environment by downloading the key cmdlets, logging in to Azure and having a brief look around. In this recipe, you create certain key Azure assets, including a resource group, a storage account, and tags. With Azure, all Azure resources are created within a resource group.

A storage account is a fundamental building block within Azure. ALL storage you use with any Azure feature always exists within a storage account. You create a storage account within one of the Azure regions you saw in the *Using PowerShell with the Azure* recipe. When you create your storage account, you also specify the level of resiliency and durability provided. There are several levels of replication provided within Azure which provide for multiple copies of the data that are replicated automatically in both the local Azure data center but also in other data centers. The extra resilience, which does come at a price, provides greater levels of recovery should the unthinkable happen and an entire data center somehow fails in a catastrophic way.

You can provision a storage account as either standard or premium. A standard storage account allows you to store any kind of data (as you see more in the *Exploring your storage account* recipe).

Getting Ready

This recipe requires you to have an Azure account and to have logged in, as done in the *Using PowerShell with Azure* recipe.

How to do it...

The steps for this recipe are as follows:

1. Set key variables:

```
$Locname    = 'uksouth'    # location name
$RgName     = 'packt_rg'   # resource group we are using
$SAName     = 'packt100sa' # Storage account name
```

2. Log in to your Azure account:

```
Login-AzureRmAccount
```

3. Create a new Azure resource group and tag it:

```
$RGTag  = [Ordered] @{Publisher='Packt'}
$RGTag +=           @{Author='Thomas Lee'}
$RG = New-AzureRmResourceGroup -Name $RgName -Location
$Locname -Tag $RGg
```

4. View resource group, with the tags:

```
Get-AzureRmResourceGroup -Name $RGName |
    Format-List -Property *
```

5. Create a new Azure storage account:

```
New-AzureRmStorageAccount -Name $SAName `
            -SkuName Standard_LRS `
            -ResourceGroupName $RgName -Tag $RGTag `
            -Location $Locname
```

How it works...

In *step 1*, you create a number of variables that define values for this recipe. This recipe creates a resource group (packt_rg) and a storage account (packt100sa) in the UK South Azure Region and the variables are setup accordingly.

In *step 2*, you log in to Azure. You saw details of how this works in the *Using PowerShell with Azure* recipe.

In *step 3*, you create a hash table, $RGTag, which contains tags (name/value pairs) then create a new Azure resource group, packt_rg, which is appropriately tagged. The step also has no output.

In *step 4*, you explore more new resource group's properties, with output as shown in the following screenshot:

```
PS C:\> Get-AzureRmResourceGroup -Name $RGName |
          Format-List -Property *

ResourceGroupName : packet_rg
Location          : uksouth
ProvisioningState : Succeeded
Tags              : {Publisher, Author}
TagsTable         :
                    Name        Value
                    =========   =========
                    Publisher   Packt
                    Author      Thomas Lee

ResourceId        : /subscriptions/0bc29420-0222-4599-b91e-e8699f760742/resourceGroups/packet_rg
```

In *step 5*, you create a new Azure storage account, named pact100sa, and tag it with the same tags as used for the resource group. The output is shown in the following screenshot:

```
PS C:\> New-AzureRmStorageAccount -Name $SAName `
            -SkuName Standard_LRS `
            -ResourceGroupName $RgName -Tag $RGTag `
            -Location $Locname

ResourceGroupName  : packet_rg
StorageAccountName : packt100_sa
Id                 : /subscriptions/0bc29420-0222-4599-b91e-e8699f760742/
                     resourceGroups/packet_rg/providers/Microsoft.Storage/storageAccounts/packt100_sa
Location           : uksouth
Sku                : Microsoft.Azure.Management.Storage.Models.Sku
Kind               : Storage
Encryption         :
AccessTier         :
CreationTime       : 11/05/2017 16:38:03
CustomDomain       :
LastGeoFailoverTime :
PrimaryEndpoints   : Microsoft.Azure.Management.Storage.Models.Endpoints
PrimaryLocation    : uksouth
ProvisioningState  : Succeeded
SecondaryEndpoints :
SecondaryLocation  :
StatusOfPrimary    : Available
StatusOfSecondary  :
Tags               : {[Author, Thomas Lee], [Publisher, Packt]}
Context            : Microsoft.WindowsAzure.Commands.Common.Storage.LazyAzureStorageContext
```

There's more...

In *step 1*, you set variables that hold key values for this recipe. In using this recipe, feel free to change these values. Depending on where you live, change the $Locname variable to hold the name of an Azure regional data center nearer to you.

With *step 5*, you create a storage account. In Azure, the storage account has to be globally unique. So if you were to try to create this storage account today it would fail as that name is already in use. To test whether a name (like a storage account) is available, you can use the Get-AzureRmStorageAccountNameAvailability cmdlet. Additionally, the storage account name must only contain lower case letters and numbers—so a storage account name of pact_sa or PactSA would not be allowed. Resource groups have less strict naming conventions.

Exploring your storage account

Many Azure resources use Azure storage. In the *Creating an Azure backup* recipe in Chapter 5, *Managing Server Backup*, you saw how to use Azure storage to hold server backups. When you create an Azure VM, you store the VHD file in Azure storage. Azure storage accounts can hold a variety of types of data, with different mechanisms for managing each data type. Additionally, the storage account provides both scalability and data durability and resiliency.

Azure storage manages five distinct types of data:

- Binary Large Object (Blob)
- Table
- Queue
- File
- Disk

A blob is unstructured data you store in Azure. Blob storage can hold any type of data in any form. This could include MP4 movies, ISO images, VHD drives, JPG files, etc. Individual blobs reside with blob containers which are equivalent to file store folders, but with no nesting capability.

Blobs come in three types: block blobs, append blobs, and page blobs. Block blobs are physically optimized for storing documents to the cloud and for streaming applications. Append blobs are optimized for append operations and are useful for logging. Page blobs are optimized for read/write operations—Azure VHDs, for example, are always of the page blob type. For more information about blob types see `https://azure.microsoft.com/en-gb/services/storage/blobs`).

An Azure table is a non-relational storage system utilizing key-value pairs. You use Azure tables for storing unstructured or semi-structured data. This contrasts with an SQL table that holds highly normalized data. A table consists of a grouping of entities. See `https://azure.microsoft.com/en-gb/services/storage/tables/` for more information about Azure tables.

An Azure queue is a durable message queuing feature used to implement scalable applications. With message queues, one part of an application can write a transaction to the queue for another part to process. The queues enable you to decouple application components for independent scaling and to provide greater resiliency. Queues allow the application to scale where needed in a simple and reliable way. For more details on Azure queues, see `https://azure.microsoft.com/en-gb/services/storage/queues/`.

The Azure file feature provides simple cross-platform file storage. This enables you to create and use SMB file shares in the cloud and access just like you would access on-premises SMB shares. Azure files support SMB 2.1 and 3.0 which makes it simple and easy for you to migrate legacy applications that rely on file shares. See for more information on Azure files, see `https://azure.microsoft.com/en-gb/services/storage/files/`.

Azure's disk storage provides persistent, highly secure disk options, particularly for Azure VMs. Azure disks are designed for low latency and high throughput. You can provision both traditional spinning disks as well as SSD disks that provide better I/O performance for I/O intensive applications. For more details on Azure disk storage see `https://azure.microsoft.com/en-gb/services/storage/unmanaged-disks/`.

Storage features continue to evolve with more options available as time goes by. For more details on Azure storage as a whole, see `https://docs.microsoft.com/en-us/azure/storage/storage-introduction`.

As noted earlier, you name your storage account based on a global naming scheme which is based on HTTPS URLs. The AZURE REST API relies on URLs to manage the Azure resources in your resource groups. All storage accounts are named specifying the storage account, data type, container name, and file name. The format for a blob is as shown in the following command:

```
https://<account>.<datatype>.core.windows.net/...
```

The account field is your storage account name, while the type field in the URL relates to the data type (blob, table, queue, file, or disk).

The storage account name must contain numbers and lower case letters only—this is an architectural restriction within Azure. Since the account name part of the URLs is processed by Azure, your storage account name must be unique globally. This means that you may need to experiment a bit in order to find a unique storage account name. The recipes in this chapter use the variable $SAName that contains the name packt100sa. At the time of writing, this storage account name is available but there is no guarantee that someone else may not use it in the meantime. When you are testing this recipe, you may need to change the name if for some reason the storage account has been taken by another customer.

When creating a storage account, you need to specify both the Azure region in which to create the account and what kind of replication you want Azure to perform on data stored in the storage account. You can create a storage account in any Azure region which supports the storage types you wish to utilize.

Azure's storage fabric stores all data multiple times to provide data durability. Azure replicates data based on the replication scheme you specify when you create the storage account. At present, there are five replication schemes you can use when creating a storage account:

- **Standard_LRS**: Azure maintains three copies of the data and all the data is stored in a single data centre in a region.
- **Standard_ZRS:** This scheme maintains three copies, but the copies are made asynchronously in different data centers within the region (or possibly another region). This provides greater durability than LRS replicated data at a price point lower than GRS. Azure restricts the use of ZRS data to block blobs.
- **Standard_GRS**: This scheme involves Azure maintaining six copies: three in the local data center (LRS) plus three in another region. Azure keeps all LRS/ZRS data up to date lock step—Azure's storage fabric only reports an I/O as completed once all three local copies have been written. Data replication to a different region is asynchronous.
- **Standard_RAGRS:** This is similar to Standard_GRS, but this replication scheme allows you to access the data in the remote location read only. You could, for example, store a SQL database in one region with Azure maintaining the data. You could then do reporting or analysis on the read/only copy.
- **Premium_LRS**: This is locally replicated data based on SSD technology that provides improved performance.

The Azure storage fabric maintains the local and remote copies automatically. Should one physical copy become unusable, Azure automatically removes the failed device and re-replicates the data.

It is important to note that while some of the replication options offer greater data durability, data replicated to another data center is done in an asynchronous manner. This involves a small delay, and it means that in the event of a local disaster, some data may not have been replicated.

This recipe explores the storage account and looks at some of the aspects of managing storage in Azure. In this recipe, you also create a blob container. Additionally, you create and display a file within the container. Later in this chapter, the recipe *Creating an Azure SMB file share* shows using the Azure file resources.

Getting ready

This recipe assumes you have an Azure account, and you have installed the Azure cmdlets, as shown in the *Using PowerShell with Azure* recipe. This recipe also relies on the resource group and storage account you created with the *Creating core Azure resources* recipe. To be on the safe side, you create these two resources if needed.

How to do it...

The steps for the recipe are as follows:

1. Define key variables:

```
$Locname    = 'uksouth'          # location name
$RgName     = 'packt_rg'         # resource group we are using
$SAName     = 'packt100sa'       # Storage account name
$CName      = 'packtcontainer'   # Container names
$CName2     = 'packtcontainer2'
```

2. Log in to your Azure account and ensure the $RG and $SA is created:

```
Login-AzureRmAccount
$RG = Get-AzureRmResourceGroup -Name $RgName `
                               -ErrorAction SilentlyContinue
if (-not $RG) {
  $RGTag  = [Ordered] @{Publisher='Packt'}
  $RGTag +=           @{Author='Thomas Lee'}
  $RG = New-AzureRmResourceGroup -Name $RgName `
```

```
                                      -Location $Locname `
                                      -Tag $RGTag
    "RG $RgName created"
}
$SA = Get-AzureRmStorageAccount -Name $SAName `
                                -ResourceGroupName $RgName `
                                -ErrorAction SilentlyContinue
if (-not $SA) {
    $SATag  = [Ordered] @{Publisher='Packt'}
    $SATag +=           @{Author='Thomas Lee'}
$SA = New-AzureRmStorageAccount -Name $SAName `
                                -ResourceGroupName $RgName `
                                -Location $Locname -Tag $SATag `
                                -SkuName 'Standard_LRS'
    "SA $SAName created"
}
```

3. Get and display the storage account key:

```
$Sak = Get-AzureRmStorageAccountKey -Name $SAName `
                                    -ResourceGroupName $RgName
```

4. Extract the first key's password:

```
$SakExtract the first key's 'password':
$Key = ($Sak | Select-Object -First 1).Value
```

5. Get the Storage account context:

```
$SACon = New-AzureStorageContext -StorageAccountName $SAName `
                                 -StorageAccountKey $Key
$SACon
```

6. Create two blob containers:

```
New-AzureStorageContainer -Name $CName `
                          -Context $SACon `
                          -Permission Blob
New-AzureStorageContainer -Name $CName2 `
                          -Context $SACon `
                          -Permission Blob
```

7. View blob containers:

```
Get-AzureStorageContainer -Context $SACon |
    Select-Object -ExpandProperty CloudBlobContainer
```

8. Create a blob:

```
'This is a small blob!!' | Out-File .\azurefile.txt
$Blob = Set-AzureStorageBlobContent -Context $SACon `
                                    -File .\azurefile.txt `
                                    -Container $CName
$Blob
```

9. Construct and display the blob name:

```
$BlobUrl = "$($Blob.Context.BlobEndPoint)$CName/$($Blob.name) "
$BlobUrl
```

10. View the URL via IE:

```
$IE  = New-Object -ComObject InterNetExplorer.Application
$IE.Navigate2($BlobUrl)
$IE.Visible = $true
```

How it works...

With *step 1*, you create variables to hold the names of the Azure objects that you create with this recipe. There is no output from this step.

Step 2 helps to ensure that you are logged into Azure and that the resource group and storage account both exist. If these do not exist, this step creates them.

In *step 3*, you get your storage account keys and display them. The output looks as shown in the following screenshot:

```
PS C:\> $Sak = Get-AzureRmStorageAccountKey -Name $SAName
                               -ResourceGroupName $RgName
PS C:\> $Sak

KeyName Value                                                                      Permissions
------- -----                                                                      -----------
key1    DhJnWVlT4flCN1hDSkTJ22pRPtfCSCOBVWB5LzIcJrtFb6vvfiAX52pCd3apziIPs420pSlosvJHP5Vevt/j7Q==    Full
key2    gKxqYQc+W4a3wf3jghI1RxNS4PVs/J8qOX59xQmzS5Unt1BYZJYT6PrAvAMO66iiGndcljtWpg/51KnNOroUeA==    Full
```

In *step 4*, you get the key value for the first key. There is no output for this step. In *step 5*, you get and display your storage account's storage context, which looks as shown in the following screenshot:

```
PS C:\> $SACon = New-AzureStorageContext -StorageAccountName $SAName
                                          -StorageAccountKey $Key
PS C:\> $SACon

StorageAccountName : packt100sa
BlobEndPoint       : https://packt100sa.blob.core.windows.net/
TableEndPoint      : https://packt100sa.table.core.windows.net/
QueueEndPoint      : https://packt100sa.queue.core.windows.net/
FileEndPoint       : https://packt100sa.file.core.windows.net/
Context            : Microsoft.WindowsAzure.Commands.Common.Storage.AzureStorageContext
Name               :
StorageAccount     : BlobEndpoint=https://packt100sa.blob.core.windows.net/;QueueEndpoint=https://packt100sa.queue.core.windows.net/;
                     TableEndpoint=https://packt100sa.table.core.windows.net/;FileEndpoint=https://packt100sa.file.core.windows.net/;
                     AccountName=packt100sa;AccountKey=[key hidden]
EndPointSuffix     : core.windows.net/
```

In *step 6*, you use the storage context and create two blob containers in your storage account. The output is as shown in the following screenshot:

```
PS C:\> New-AzureStorageContainer -Name $CName -Context $SACon -Permission Blob

CloudBlobContainer : Microsoft.WindowsAzure.Storage.Blob.CloudBlobContainer
Permission         : Microsoft.WindowsAzure.Storage.Blob.BlobContainerPermissions
PublicAccess       : Blob
LastModified       : 29/05/2017 15:10:31 +00:00
ContinuationToken  :
Context            : Microsoft.WindowsAzure.Commands.Common.Storage.AzureStorageContext
Name               : packtcontainer

PS C:\> New-AzureStorageContainer -Name $CName2 -Context $SACon -Permission Blob

CloudBlobContainer : Microsoft.WindowsAzure.Storage.Blob.CloudBlobContainer
Permission         : Microsoft.WindowsAzure.Storage.Blob.BlobContainerPermissions
PublicAccess       : Blob
LastModified       : 29/05/2017 15:13:03 +00:00
ContinuationToken  :
Context            : Microsoft.WindowsAzure.Commands.Common.Storage.AzureStorageContext
Name               : packtcontainer2
```

In *step 7*, you display details of the two blob containers, which is as shown in the following screenshot:

```
PS C:\> Get-AzureStorageContainer -Context $SACon |
   Select-Object -ExpandProperty CloudBlobContainer


   Blob End Point: https://packt100sa.blob.core.windows.net/

Name             Uri                                                        LastModified
----             ---                                                        ------------
packtcontainer   https://packt100sa.blob.core.windows.net/packtcontainer    30/05/2017 13:18:11 +00:00
packtcontainer2  https://packt100sa.blob.core.windows.net/packtcontainer2   30/05/2017 13:18:11 +00:00
```

In *step 8*, you create a file locally (`.\azurfile.txt`). This step then uploads this local file to an Azure blob. The output is as shown in the following screenshot:

```
PS C:\> 'This is a small blob!!' | Out-File .\Azurefile.txt
PS C:\> $Blob = Set-AzureStorageBlobContent -Context $SACon `
                                            -File .\Azurefile.txt `
                                            -Container $CName
PS C:\> $Blob

ICloudBlob         : Microsoft.WindowsAzure.Storage.Blob.CloudBlockBlob
BlobType           : BlockBlob
Length             : 50
ContentType        : application/octet-stream
LastModified       : 29/05/2017 15:14:10 +00:00
SnapshotTime       :
ContinuationToken  :
Context            : Microsoft.WindowsAzure.Commands.Common.Storage.AzureStorageContext
Name               : azurefile.txt
```

In *step 9*, you create and then display the URL for the Azure blob you just created, with output as shown in the following screenshot:

```
PS C:\> $BlobUrl = "$($Blob.Context.BlobEndPoint)$CName/$($Blob.name) "
PS C:\> $BlobUrl
https://packt100sa.blob.core.windows.net/packtcontainer/azurefile.txt
```

In *step 10*, you use Internet Explorer to download and display the contents of this data blob. It is as shown in the following screenshot:

There's more...

In *step 1* you define variables to hold the name of several different Azure resources that you create with this recipe. You may want to change these, for example if the storage account name is already in use, or if you want to create different names for these objects.

In *step 2*, you ensure that you are logged into Azure and that your resource group and storage account exist. If either of these is not present, then this step creates them. Note that if for some reason the storage account name is in use by some other Azure customer, you need to change the value of the $SAName variable in step 1.

In *step 3* you retrieve the storage account keys. Each key's value property is, in effect, a password for your Azure storage account. Having two keys enables you to regularly regenerate and rotate your key values. In step 4, you get this value for the first key.

In *step 5*, you get the storage account's storage context. This object encapsulates the details of the storage account, including the storage account key you created in the prior step.

In *step 6* and *step 7*, you create two blob containers and display their URLs. Containers are a single level folder like object that contains your blobs. In *step 8*, you create a simple blob and as you can see from the output, this is a block blob, with the contents just an octet stream.

In *step 9*, you display the URL to the Azure blob you create in step 8.

> The storage account name, container name, and filename are embedded into this URL.

Creating Azure an SMB File Share

Azure provides you with the ability to create SMB shares with an Azure storage account. These SMB shares act the same as local on-premises SMB shares you used in Chapter 9, *Managing Network Shares*. The key difference is how you create them and the credentials you use to access the shares.

Before an SMB client can access data held in an SMB share, the SMB client needs to authenticate with the SMB server. With Windows based shares, you either use a userid/password credential, or in a domain environment, the SMB client utilizes Kerberos to authenticate. With Azure, you use the storage account name as the userid and the storage account key as the password.

The storage account key provides you with two keys (imaginatively named key1 and key2). The value of either key is a valid password for Azure SMB file shares. You have two keys to enable you to do regular key rotation. If your application uses the value of key1, you can change the application to use the key2 value as the share's password then regenerate the key1 value. Sometime later you repeat—changing the application to use key1's value then regenerate key2. This provides you with immediate key update where you need it. Armed with the value of either key, you can easily create SMB shares that are directly addressed across the internet.

An Azure SMB share differs from Azure blobs with respect to how you access them. You access a blob via HTTP, whereas you access an Azure File share via the standard SMB networking commands you used in, for example, Chapter 9, *Managing Network Shares*. Blobs and files also differ in that with blobs you only have a single level of folder (the container). With Azure files, you can have as many folders as you wish or need.

From the point of view of SMB file sharing, remember that the account key is the password for the share, where the username is the storage account name. You should exercise caution when including the account key in code.

In this recipe, you use the resource group and storage account created earlier (in the *Create Core Azure resources* recipe). The recipe also checks to ensure these exist and creates them if they are not available just in case.

Getting ready

This recipe assumes you have an Azure account, and you have installed the Azure cmdlets, as shown in the *Using PowerShell with Azure* recipe. This recipe also relies on the resource group and storage account you created with the *Creating core Azure resources* recipe. To be on the safe side, you can create these two resources if needed.

How to do it...

The steps for the recipe are as follows:

1. Define variables:

```
$Locname    = 'uksouth'      # location name
$RgName     = 'packt_rg'     # resource group we are using
$SAName     = 'packt100sa'   # Storage account name
$ShareName  = 'packtshare'   # must be lower case!
```

2. Log in and ensure the resource group and storage account exist:

```
Login-AzureRmAccount
$RG = Get-AzureRmResourceGroup -Name $rgname `
                                -ErrorAction SilentlyContinue
if (-not $RG) {
  $RGTag  = [Ordered] @{Publisher='Packt'}
  $RGTag +=           @{Author='Thomas Lee'}
  $RG = New-AzureRmResourceGroup -Name $RgName `
                                 -Location $Locname `
                                 -Tag $RGTag
  "RG $RgName created"
   }
 $SA = Get-AzureRmStorageAccount -Name $SAName `
                                 -ResourceGroupName $RgName `
                                 -ErrorAction SilentlyContinue
if (-not $SA) {
  $SATag = [Ordered] @{Publisher='Packt'}
  $SATag += @{Author='Thomas Lee'}
  $SA = New-AzureRmStorageAccount -Name $SAName `
                                  -ResourceGroupName $RgName `
                                  -Location $Locname -Tag $SATag `
                                  -SkuName 'Standard_LRS'
  "SA $SAName created"
  }
```

3. Get the storage account key and storage account's context:

```
$Sak = Get-AzureRmStorageAccountKey -Name $SAName `
                                    -ResourceGroupName $RgName
$Key = ($Sak | Select-Object -First 1).Value
$SACon = New-AzureStorageContext -StorageAccountName $SAName `
                                 -StorageAccountKey $Key
```

4. Add credentials to the local store:

```
cmdkey /add:$SAName.file.core.windows.net/user:$SAName `
/pass:$Key
```

5. Create an Azure SMB share:

```
New-AzureStorageShare -Name $ShareName -Context $SACon
```

6. Ensure `Z:` is not in use then mount the Azure share as Z:

```
$Mount = 'Z:'
Get-Smbmapping -LocalPath $Mount -ErrorAction SilentlyContinue |
    Remove-Smbmapping -Force -ErrorAction SilentlyContinue
$Rshare = \\$SaName.file.core.windows.net\$ShareName
New-SmbMapping -LocalPath $Mount -RemotePath $Rshare `
                -UserName $SAName -Password $Key
```

7. View the share:

```
Get-AzureStorageShare -Context $SACon |
    Format-List -Property *
```

8. View local SMB mappings:

```
Get-SmbMapping
```

9. Now use the new share and create a file in the share:

```
New-Item -Path z:\foo -ItemType Directory | Out-Null
'Recipe 15-4' | Out-File -FilePath z:\foo\recipe.txt
```

10. Retrieve details about the share contents:

```
Get-ChildItem -Path z:\ -Recurse |
    Format-Table -Property FullName, Mode, Length
```

11. Get the content from the file:

```
Get-Content -Path z:\foo\recipe.txt
```

How it works...

In *step 1*, you define PowerShell variables that hold key Azure object names. In *step 2*, you log into Azure and ensure that the resource group and storage account exist (and create them if not). There is no output from either of these steps.

In *step 3*, you get the storage account keys for your storage account. You retrieve the key from the first password, then create a storage context object. There is no output from this step.

In *step 4*, you store the credentials for your storage account. Cmdkey is a console application that you use to store the userid and password that your SMB client uses when it connects to an SMB share. There is no output from this step.

In *step 5*, you create an Azure file share using the `New-AzureStorageShare` cmdlet, which produces output as shown in the following screenshot:

```
PS C:\> New-AzureStorageShare -Name $ShareName -Context $SACon


    File End Point: https://packt100sa.file.core.windows.net/

Name            LastModified
----            ------------
packtshare      29/05/2017 17:30:13 +00:00
```

In *step 6*, you initially ensure that the `Z:` drive is not mapped to a share (and remove it if the Z: drive exists). Then you create a mapping to your Azure file share. The output from this step looks like this:

```
PS C:\> $Mount = 'Z:'
PS C:\> Get-Smbmapping -LocalPath $Mount -ErrorAction SilentlyContinue |
         Remove-Smbmapping -Force -ErrorAction SilentlyContinue
PS C:\> $Rshare = "\\$SaName.file.core.windows.net\$ShareName"
PS C:\> New-SmbMapping -LocalPath $Mount -RemotePath $Rshare `
                       -UserName $SAName -Password $Key

Status Local Path Remote Path
------ ---------- -----------
OK     Z:         \\packt100sa.file.core.windows.net\packtshare
```

You view the Azure file share in *step 7*, where you see the following output that resembles the following:

```
PS C:\> Get-AzureStorageShare -Context $SACon |
         Format-List -Property *

ServiceClient : Microsoft.WindowsAzure.Storage.File.CloudFileClient
Uri           : https://packt100sa.file.core.windows.net/packtshare
StorageUri    : Primary = 'https://packt100sa.file.core.windows.net/packtshare';
                Secondary = ''
Name          : packtshare
Metadata      : {}
Properties    : Microsoft.WindowsAzure.Storage.File.FileShareProperties
```

In *step 8*, you view the local SMB mappings, which should look similar to this:

```
PS C:\> Get-SmbMapping

Status Local Path Remote Path
------ ---------- -----------
OK     Z:                   \\packt100sa.file.core.windows.net\packtshare
```

In *step 9*, you create a folder, foo, in your mapped Z: drive, then you create a new file in that folder (Z:\foo\recipe.txt). There is no output from this step. In *step 10*, you list the items in the Z: drive which look like this:

```
PS C:\> Get-ChildItem -Path z:\ -Recurse |
    Format-Table -Property FullName, Mode, Length

FullName            Mode   Length
--------            ----   ------
z:\foo              d-----
z:\foo\recipe.txt   -a---- 28
```

In the final step, *step 10*, you view the contents of the file stored in your Azure file share. The output is as follows:

```
PS C:\> Get-Content -Path z:\foo\recipe.txt
Recipe 15-4
```

There's more...

In *step 1*, you create variables to hold the names of the Azure objects you use in this recipe. The $Locname variable holds the name of the Azure region in which you create your storage account which you may wish to change to a more local Azure region.

In *step 3*, you create a storage context object. The context object encapsulates the credentials for your storage account.

You use cmdkey.exe in *step 4* to save credentials for Azure's storage account. You use cmdkey to store the userid and password which Windows should use to authenticate against a given computer or domain. For more details on cmdkey, see https://technet.microsoft.com/en-us/library/cc754243(v=ws.11).aspx. You can use the cmdkey utility to list all the stored credentials (cmdkey /list).

Creating and using websites

Azure provides a number of ways in which you can create rich web and mobile applications in the cloud. You could setup your own virtual machines, install IIS, and add your own web application. If your application needs to store data, you can create SQL Server VMs, or use Azure's SQL database feature—or any of the other database packages supported in Azure.

A simpler way is to create an Azure Web App. At one time, Azure offered what were termed websites. These were, as the name says, websites in which you could run your own application, or a host of others such as WordPress. These were single tier (possibly with a back-end database). However, Microsoft discontinued this feature and has replaced it with the more generic Web App feature.

Azure Web Apps enabled you to build, deploy, and manage rich websites and web applications. You can use frameworks such as .NET, Node.js, PHP, and Python in these applications and use any database software appropriate to your needs. These applications can be simple static HTML sites, or rich multi-tier applications that run on both web and mobile platforms.

In this recipe, you create a simple single tier website. You also create a very simple single page *application* and upload it and view the page.

Getting ready

This recipe assumes you have an Azure account, and you have installed the Azure cmdlets, as shown in the *Using PowerShell with Azure* recipe. This recipe also uses the resource group and storage account created with the *Creating Core Azure Resources recipe*. As with earlier recipes, if these objects do not exist, a step in the recipe creates them.

This recipe uses C:\ to hold files—but feel free to move the location of these files to any location on your system.

This recipe also needs a file, `C:\Index.htm`, containing the following HTML code:

```
<!DOCTYPE html>
<html>
<head>
<meta charset="utf-8" />
<title>New Azure Web Site</title>
</head><body></p>
<br>
<center>
<b>This is the start page for the really cool NEW Azure Web App</b>
</p>
A page created by PowerShell in Microsoft Azure
</body>
</html>
```

This recipe creates an Azure web app and uploads this file to Azure. Feel free to add code (or additional pages) appropriate.

How to do it...

The steps for the recipe are as follows:

1. Define key object variables:

```
$Locname     = 'uksouth'      # location name
$RgName      = 'packt_rg'     # resource group we are using
$AppSrvName  = 'packt100'
$AppName     = 'packt100'
$Locname     = 'uksouth'
```

2. Log in to your Azure Account and ensure the RG and SA is created:

```
Login-AzureRmAccount
$RG = Get-AzureRmResourceGroup -Name $rgname `
                              -ErrorAction SilentlyContinue
if (-not $RG) {
  $RGTag  = [Ordered] @{Publisher='Packt'}
  $RGTag +=           @{Author='Thomas Lee'}
  $RG = New-AzureRmResourceGroup -Name $RgName `
                                -Location $Locname `
                                -Tag $RGTag
   "RG $RgName created"
 }
    $SA = Get-AzureRmStorageAccount -Name $SAName `
                                   -ResourceGroupName $RgName `
```

```
                                       -ErrorAction SilentlyContinue
if (-not $SA) {
    $SATag  = [Ordered] @{Publisher='Packt'}
    $SATag +=           @{Author='Thomas Lee'}
    $SA = New-AzureRmStorageAccount -Name $SAName `
                                -ResourceGroupName $RgName `
                                -Location $Locname `
                                 -Tag $SATag `
                                -SkuName 'Standard_LRS'
    "SA $SAName created"
}
```

3. Create the app service plan:

```
New-AzureRmAppServicePlan -ResourceGroupName $RgName `
                          -Name $AppSrvName `
                          -Location $Locname -Tier Free |
                              Out-Null
```

4. View the service plan:

```
Get-AzureRmAppServicePlan -ResourceGroupName $RGname
                          -Name $AppSrvName
```

5. Create the new Azure web app:

```
New-AzureRmWebApp -ResourceGroupName $RgName `
                  -Name $AppSrvName `
                  -AppServicePlan $AppSrvName `
                  -Location $Locname |
                      Out-Null
```

6. View application details:

```
$WebApp = Get-AzureRmWebApp -ResourceGroupName $RgName
                            -Name $AppSrvName
$WebApp
```

7. Now see the web site:

```
$SiteUrl = "https://$($WebApp.DefaultHostName)"
$IE  = New-Object -ComObject InterNetExplorer.Application
$IE.Navigate2($SiteUrl)
$IE.Visible = $true
```

8. Get the publishing profile XML and extract FTP upload details:

```
$x = [xml](Get-AzureRmWebAppPublishingProfile `
                    -ResourceGroupName $RgName `
                    -Name $AppSrvName `
                    -OutputFile c:\pdata.txt)
$x.publishData.publishProfile[1]
```

9. Extract the credentials and site details from the publishing profile:

```
$UserName = $x.publishData.publishProfile[1].userName
$UserPwd  = $x.publishData.publishProfile[1].userPWD
$Site     = $x.publishData.publishProfile[1].publishUrl
```

10. Create ftp client:

```
$Ftp          = [System.Net.FtpWebRequest]::Create("$Site/Index.Html")
$Ftp.Method   = [System.Net.WebRequestMethods+Ftp]::UploadFile
$Ftp.Credentials = New-Object `
                    -TypeNameSystem.Net.NetworkCredential `
                    -ArgumentList $UserName,$UserPwd
$Ftp.UseBinary   = $true
$Ftp.UsePassive  = $true
```

11. Get the contents of the file to upload as a byte array:

```
$Filename = 'C:\Index.htm'
$Content = [System.IO.File]::ReadAllBytes($fileName)
$Ftp.ContentLength = $Content.Length
```

12. Get the ftp request stream and write the file to the web site:

```
$Stream = $Ftp.GetRequestStream()
$Stream.Write($Content, 0, $Content.Length)
```

13. Close the connection and dispose of the stream object:

```
$Stream.Close()
$Stream.Dispose()
```

14. Now look at the site:

```
$SiteUrl = https://$($WebApp.DefaultHostName)
$IE  = New-Object -ComObject InterNetExplorer.Application
$IE.Navigate2($SiteUrl)
$IE.Visible = $true
```

How it works...

As in previous recipes, in *step 1*, you create variables to hold key object names. This produces no output. You use *step 2* to ensure that the resource group and storage account exist—if not this step creates them but does not produce output.

In *step 3*, you create an Azure web application service plan, to define the location and type of host that you wish to use to run your web application. There is no output from this step. In *step 4*, you get and display the new application service plan and the output of this step looks like this:

```
PS C:\> Get-AzureRmAppServicePlan -ResourceGroupName $RGname -Name $AppSrvName

Sku                        : Microsoft.Azure.Management.WebSites.Models.SkuDescription
ServerFarmWithRichSkuName  : packt100
WorkerTierName             :
Status                     : Ready
Subscription               : 0bc29420-0222-4599-b91e-e8699f760742
AdminSiteName              :
HostingEnvironmentProfile  :
MaximumNumberOfWorkers     : 1
GeoRegion                  : UK South
PerSiteScaling             : False
NumberOfSites              : 1
ResourceGroup              : packet_rg
Id                         : /subscriptions/0bc29420-0222-4599-b91e-e8699f760742/resourceGroups/packet_rg/
                             providers/Microsoft.Web/serverfarms/packt100
Name                       : packt100
Location                   : UK South
Type                       : Microsoft.Web/serverfarms
```

With *step 5*, you create the web application which you wish to run on top of the previously created application service plan. This step produces no output.

In *step 6*, you then can display the web app, which as shown in the following screenshot:

```
PS C:\> $WebApp = Get-AzureRmWebApp -ResourceGroupName $RgName -Name $AppSrvName
$WebApp


SiteName                     : packt100
State                        : Running
HostNames                    : {packt100.azurewebsites.net}
RepositorySiteName           : packt100
UsageState                   : Normal
Enabled                      : True
EnabledHostNames             : {packt100.azurewebsites.net, packt100.scm.azurewebsites.net}
AvailabilityState            : Normal
HostNameSslStates            : {packt100.azurewebsites.net, packt100.scm.azurewebsites.net}
ServerFarmId                 : /subscriptions/0bc29250-0222-4599-b91e-e8aa9f760794/resourceGroups/
                               packt_rg/providers/Microsoft.Web/serverfarms/pack
                               t100
LastModifiedTimeUtc          : 30/05/2017 13:39:41
SiteConfig                   : Microsoft.Azure.Management.WebSites.Models.SiteConfig
TrafficManagerHostNames      :
PremiumAppDeployed           :
ScmSiteAlsoStopped           : False
TargetSwapSlot               :
HostingEnvironmentProfile    :
MicroService                 : WebSites
GatewaySiteName              :
ClientAffinityEnabled        : True
ClientCertEnabled            : False
HostNamesDisabled            : False
OutboundIpAddresses          : 51.140.37.134,51.140.39.0,51.140.36.48,51.140.39.192
ContainerSize                : 0
MaxNumberOfWorkers           :
CloningInfo                  :
ResourceGroup                : packt_rg
IsDefaultContainer           :
DefaultHostName              : packt100.azurewebsites.net
Id                           : /subscriptions/0bc29250-0222-4599-b91e-e8aa9f760794/resourceGroups/
                               packt_rg/providers/Microsoft.Web/sites/packt100
Name                         : packt100
Location                     : UK South
Type                         : Microsoft.Web/sites
Tags                         :
```

With *step 7*, you see the basic website which Azure created. This is not the final site, but does show you that the web application is up and running, which looks like this:

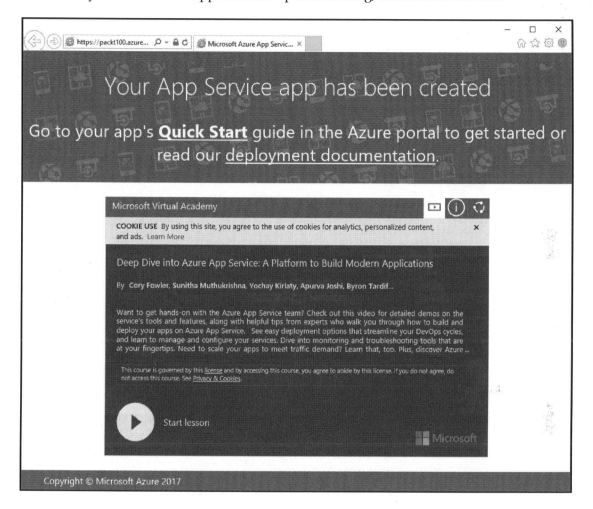

In *step 8*, you retrieve the web publishing profile. This is an XML document that describes details about the app site. The publishing profile includes the details you need in order to upload content to your site via FTP. In *step 9*, you extract the website name and the user credentials for the site. With *step 10*, you use this information and create an FTP client. In *step 11*, you get the web page (Index.htm) and encode it into a byte array which, in *step 12*, you up load to the FTP site. With *step 13*, you close the FTP site. There is no output from *step 8* through *step 13*.

In *step 14*, you display your web site, as shown in the following screenshot:

There's more...

In *step 3*, you create the web application service plan. In effect this defines the location and size of the host that Azure assigns to run your web application.

With *step 4*, you crate the new Azure application. Azure creates some default content, which you view in *step 7*. It's useful to see this default content so you can ensure the web app is up and running prior to loading any content.

When you create an Azure web app, Azure creates an FTP web site you can use to upload your content. Azure provides the details you need (the FTP server name and the userid and password for this FTP site) via the web app publishing profile which you download and view in *step 8*. In *step 9*, you pull out the host and user information from the XML returned in *step 8*, and then create an FTP client (*step 10*).

In *step 11* through *step 13*, you use the FTP client to upload the contents of your web site (i.e. the single page held at `C:\Index.htm`). In most production scenarios, you would probably have a number of files to upload - you would adjust *step 11* and *step 12* to upload all the relevant files for your web application.

Creating and using Azure virtual machines

An Azure VM is essentially a Hyper-V VM that you run within Azure. There are some differences between Hyper-V VMs you create within Server 2016 (or Windows 10) and Azure VMs but they are minor. The ARM based cmdlets you use are a little different in style to Hyper-V cmdlets which may mean a bit of a learning curve.

At the time of writing, you can only use the VHD format for your virtual hard disks in an Azure VM although like many things in Azure this may change at some point in the future. Should you wish to move a Hyper-V VM into Azure that uses a VHDX hard disk file, you would need to convert the disk type to be a VHD.

In this recipe, you first create a virtual network. Your VM can have both a public IP address and a private VLAN based IP address. At the end of this recipe, you access the VM via the VM's public IP address. In a later recipe, you create a VPN and connect to the VM using the VPN addresses. You also create a NIC and give it a public IP address.

Azure VMs are locked down by default. In order to enable any traffic into or out of the VM, you create a **Network Security Group (NSG)** and create network security rules, allowing traffic in or out of the VM. In this recipe, you set traffic rules to allow RDP and PowerShell remoting inbound.

With your network and network created, you next create a new `PSVirtualMachine` object. This object holds the configuration settings for your VM. Once you create the object, you can then set properties around things like OS type, VHD names, network adapters, etc. Finally, once you have fully populated the `PSVirtualMachine` object, you pass it to `New-AzureRmVM` to create the VM.

The `PSVirtualMachine` object holds the details of your VM prior to creating the VM. An important property of this object is the image to use when creating the VM. An image is effectively a syspreped OS image (with or without additional applications).

You can choose between a large number of pre-existing images from a variety of vendors. These images can contain different operating systems (Windows or Linux), different applications, and can be very differently set up. In this recipe, you create a basic Windows Server 2016 VM with nothing else added.

Once you have the `PSVirtualMachine` object created, you pass this to Azure when you create the VM. Creating a new VM can take time as Azure needs to create a new disk holding your image as well as the VM itself and then start the VM.

Once your VM is up and running the VM, you can access it via its public IP address. If you also want to link the VM with your corporate network, you can create a VPN to link your Azure cloud subnet with your on-premises network or allow a single client to access hosts on the cloud subnet. In this recipe, you create the Azure Virtual network and a VM in that network. In the next recipe, *Creating and using an Azure VPN*, you create the VPN gateway and access the Virtual Machine via a P2S VPN.

Getting ready

This recipe assumes you have an Azure account, and you have installed the Azure cmdlets, as shown in the *Using PowerShell with Azure* recipe. This recipe also uses the resource group and storage account created with the *Creating core Azure resources recipe*. As with earlier recipes, if these objects do not exist, a step in the recipe creates them.

How to do it...

The steps for the recipe are as follows:

1. Define key variables

```
$Locname = 'uksouth'              # location name
$RgName  = 'packt_rg'             # resource group name
$SAName  = 'packt100sa'           # Storage account name
$NSGName = 'packt_nsg'            # NSG name
$FullNet = '10.10.0.0/16'         # Overall networkrange
$CLNet   = '10.10.2.0/24'         # Our cloud subnet
$GWNet   = '192.168.200.0/26'     # Gateway subnet
$DNS     = '8.8.8.8'              # DNS Server to use
$IPName  = 'Packt_IP1'            # Private IP Address name
$VMName  = "Packt100"             # the name of the vm
$CompName = "Packt100"            # the name of the VM host
```

2. Just in case, log in to Azure and ensure the resource group and storage account exist:

```
Login-AzureRmAccount
$RG = Get-AzureRmResourceGroup -Name $RgName `
                              -ErrorAction SilentlyContinue
if (-not $rg) {
$RGTag  = @{Publisher='Packt'}
$RGTag += @{Author='Thomas Lee'}
$RG = New-AzureRmResourceGroup -Name $RgName `
                              -Location $Locname `
                              -Tag $RGTag
}
$SA = Get-AzureRmStorageAccount -Name $SAName `
                              -ResourceGroupName
$RgName -ErrorAction SilentlyContinue
if (-not $SA) {
  $SATag  = [Ordered] @{Publisher='Packt'}
  $SATag +=           @{Author='Thomas Lee'}
  $SA = New-AzureRmStorageAccount -Name $SAName `
```

```
                                        -ResourceGroupName $RgName `
                                        -Location $Locname `
                                        -Tag $SATag `
                                        -skuname 'Standard_LRS'
    }
```

3. Create subnet network config objects:

```
$SubnetName    = 'CloudSubnet1'
$CloudSubnet   = New-AzureRmVirtualNetworkSubnetConfig `
                        -Name $SubnetName -AddressPrefix $CLNet
$GWSubnetName  = 'GatewaySubnet'
$GWSubnet      = New-AzureRmVirtualNetworkSubnetConfig `
                        -Name $GWSubnetName -AddressPrefix $GWNet
```

4. Create the virtual network, and tag it—this can take a while

```
$VnetName = "Packtvnet"
$PackVnet = New-AzureRmVirtualNetwork -Name $VnetName `
                        -ResourceGroupName $RgName `
                        -Location $Locname `
                        -AddressPrefix $fullnet,'192.168.0.0/16' `
                        -Subnet $CloudSubnet,$GWSubnet `
                        -DnsServer $DNS `
                        -Tag @{Owner='PACKT';Type='VNET'}
```

5. Create a public IP address and NIC for our VM to use:

```
$PublicIp = New-AzureRmPublicIpAddress -Name $IPName `
                    -ResourceGroupName $RgName `
                    -Location $Locname -AllocationMethod Dynamic `
                    -Tag @{Owner='PACKT';Type='IP'}
  $PublicIp | Format-Table `
        -Property Name, IPAddress,ResourceGroup*,
                Location, *State
```

6. Create the Azure VM NIC:

```
 $NicName = "VMNic1"
 $Nic = New-AzureRmNetworkInterface -Name $NicName `
        -ResourceGroupName $RgName `
        -Location $Locname `
        -SubnetId $Packvnet.Subnets[0].Id `
        -PublicIpAddressId $PublicIp.Id `
        -Tag @{Owner='PACKT';Type='NIC'}
#Create network security rule to allow RDP inbound:
$NSGRule1 = New-AzureRmNetworkSecurityRuleConfig `
            -Name RDP-In -Protocol Tcp `
```

```
            -Direction Inbound -Priority 1000 `
            -SourceAddressPrefix *  -SourcePortRange * `
            -DestinationAddressPrefix * -DestinationPortRange 3389 `
            -Access Allow
```

7. Create network security rule to allow RDP inbound:

```
$NSGRule1 = New-AzureRmNetworkSecurityRuleConfig `
            -Name RDP-In -Protocol Tcp `
            -Direction Inbound -Priority 1000 `
            -SourceAddressPrefix * -SourcePortRange * `
            -DestinationAddressPrefix * `
            -DestinationPortRange 3389 `
            -Access Allow
```

8. Create an NSG with one NSG rule:

```
$PacktNSG = New-AzureRmNetworkSecurityGroup `
            -ResourceGroupName $RgName `
            -Location $Locname `
            -Name $NSGName `
            -SecurityRules $NSGRule1
```

9. Configure subnet:

```
Set-AzureRmVirtualNetworkSubnetConfig `
    -Name $SubnetName `
    -VirtualNetwork $PackVnet `
    -NetworkSecurityGroup $PacktNSG `
    -AddressPrefix $CLNet | Out-Null
```

10. Set the Azure virtual network based on prior configuration steps:

```
Set-AzureRmVirtualNetwork -VirtualNetwork $PackVnet | Out-Null
```

11. Create and display an Azure VM Configuration object:

```
$VM = New-AzureRmVMConfig -VMName $VMName -VMSize 'Standard_A1'
$VM
```

12. Create the credential for VM Admin:

```
$VMUser = 'tfl'
$VMPass = ConvertTo-SecureString 'J3rryisG0d!!'-AsPlainText -Force
$VMCred = New-Object System.Management.automation.PSCredential `
                -ArgumentList $VMUser, $VMPass
```

13. Set OS information for the VM and display the VM configuration object:

```
$VM = Set-AzureRmVMOperatingSystem -VM $VM `
                -Windows -ComputerName $CompName `
                -Credential $VMCred `
                -ProvisionVMAgent -EnableAutoUpdate
$VM
```

14. Determine which image to use and get the offer:

```
$Publisher = 'MicrosoftWindowsServer'
$OfferName = 'WindowsServer'
$Offer  = Get-AzureRmVMImageoffer -Location $Locname
                                  -PublisherName $Publisher |
          Where-Object Offer -eq $Offername
```

15. Then get the SKU/Image:

```
$SkuName = '2016-Datacenter'
$SKU = Get-AzureRMVMImageSku -Location $Locname `
                             -Publisher $Publisher `
                             -Offer $Offer.Offer |
       Where-Object Skus -eq $SkuName
$VM = Set-AzureRmVMSourceImage -VM $VM `
                               -PublisherName $publisher `
                               -Offer $Offer.offer `
                               -Skus $sku.Skus `
                               -Version "latest"
$VM
```

16. Add the NIC to the VM config object:

```
$VM = Add-AzureRmVMNetworkInterface -VM $VM -Id $Nic.Id
```

17. Identify the page blob to hold the VM Disk:

```
$StorageAcc = Get-AzureRmStorageAccount -ResourceGroupName
$RgName -Name $SAName
$BlobPath = "vhds/Packt100.vhd"
$OsDiskUri = $storageAcc.PrimaryEndpoints.Blob.ToString() +
$BlobPath
$DiskName = 'PacktOsDisk'
$VM = Set-AzureRmVMOSDisk -VM $VM -Name $DiskName `
                         -VhdUri $OsDiskUri `
                         -CreateOption FromImage
$VM
```

18. Create the VM—this can take some time to provision:

```
$VM      = New-AzureRmVM -ResourceGroupName $RgName `
                        -Location $Locname `
                 -VM $VM -Tag @{Owner='Packt'}
```

19. Get the Public IP address of the VM's NIC:

```
$VMPublicIP = Get-AzureRmPublicIpAddress -Name $IPName `
                        -ResourceGroupName $RgName
```

20. Open an RDP session on our new VM:

```
$IPAddress = $VMPublicIP.IpAddress
mstsc /v:$ipaddress
```

21. Once the RDP client opens, logon using `pact100\tfl` as your user id and a password of `J3rryisG0d!!` (omitting of course, the quotes!).

How it works...

In *step 1*, you define PowerShell variables that hold key Azure object names. In *step 2*, you log in to Azure and ensure that the resource group and storage account exist (and create them if not). There is no output from either of these steps.

In *step 3*, you create two new virtual subnets (one for the gateway you use in the Create and use Azure VPN recipe) and the other a cloud based subnet. Then in *step 4* you create the virtual network. There is no output from either *step 3* or *step 4*.

In *step 5*, you create an Azure public IP address which you use later in this recipe. Then you display the IP address details, as shown in the following screenshot:

```
PS C:\> $Pip = New-AzureRmPublicIpAddress -Name $IPName `
                   -ResourceGroupName $RgName `
                   -Location $Locname -AllocationMethod Dynamic `
                   -Tag @{Owner='PACKT';Type='IP'}
WARNING: The output object type of this cmdlet will be modified in a future release.

PS C:\> $Pip  | FT Name, IPAddress,ResourceGroup*, Location, *State

Name      IpAddress     ResourceGroupName Location ProvisioningState
----      ---------     ----------------- -------- -----------------
Packt_IP1 Not Assigned packt_rg            uksouth  Succeeded
```

With *step 6*, you create an Azure network interface. You configure the NIC to have the public IP address you created in *step 5*. There is no output from this step.

In *step 7*, you create NSG rules to enable RDP traffic inbound which generates no output.

In *step 8*, you create and display the NSG using the two NSG rules ($NSGRule1, $NSGRule2) previously defined, which also produces no useful cmdlet output. You should see the warning message similar to the one in *step 5*.

In *step 9*, you continue the configuration of your Azure subnet and assign the NSG to this subnet. There is no output from this step.

You complete the configuration of your Azure network in *step 10* where you set your network to use the virtual network you just created, which produces no output.

With the network created, you now turn to creating your Azure VM. In *step 11*, you start this process by creating and displaying the VM Config object, as shown in the following screenshot:

```
PS C:\> $VM = New-AzureRmVMConfig -VMName $VMName -VMSize "Standard_A1"
PS C:\> $VM

Name             : Packt100
HardwareProfile : {VmSize}
```

In *step 12*, you create a credential object that defines the first user in our VM. There is no output from this step. In *step 13*, you set the details of your VM, including the computer name, then display the VM config object, as shown in the following screenshot:

```
PS C:\> $VM = Set-AzureRmVMOperatingSystem -VM $VM `
                    -Windows -ComputerName $CompName `
                    -Credential $VMCred `
                    -ProvisionVMAgent -EnableAutoUpdate
PS C:\> $VM

Name              : Packt100
HardwareProfile   : {VmSize}
OSProfile         : {ComputerName, AdminUsername, AdminPassword, WindowsConfiguration}
```

In *step 14*, you find Azure images of `WindowsServer` published by Microsoft Window server. This step, which has no output, finds the offers that exist in the Azure region you are using for your VM.

In *step 15*, you find the specific Image SKU and update the VM configuration object with the details of the specific image for your VM. Then you display the configuration object as shown in the following screenshot:

```
PS C:\> $SkuName = '2016-Datacenter'
PS C:\> $SKU = Get-AzureRMVMImageSku -Location $Locname `
                                -Publisher $Publisher `
                                -Offer $Offer.Offer |
            Where-Object Skus -eq $SkuName
PS C:\> $VM = Set-AzureRmVMSourceImage -VM $VM -PublisherName $publisher `
                                -Offer $Offer.offer `
                                -Skus $sku.Skus `
                                -Version "latest"
$VM

Name              : Packt100
HardwareProfile   : {VmSize}
OSProfile         : {ComputerName, AdminUsername, AdminPassword, WindowsConfiguration}
StorageProfile    : {ImageReference}
```

In *step 16*, you add the network interface to the VM configuration object. There is no output from this step.

In *step 17*, you define the file to hold your VM's disk image, in effect the VM's `C:` drive. This file is a page blob you create in your storage account. The output is as shown in the following screenshot:

```
PS C:\> $StorageAcc = Get-AzureRmStorageAccount -ResourceGroupName $RgName -Name $SAName
PS C:\> $BlobPath  = "vhds/Packt100.vhd"
PS C:\> $OsDiskUri = $storageAcc.PrimaryEndpoints.Blob.ToString() + $BlobPath
PS C:\> $DiskName  = 'PacktOsDisk'
PS C:\> $VM        = Set-AzureRmVMOSDisk -VM $VM -Name $DiskName -VhdUri $OsDiskUri -CreateOption FromImage
PS C:\> $VM

Name                : Packt100
HardwareProfile     : {VmSize}
NetworkProfile      : {NetworkInterfaces}
OSProfile           : {ComputerName, AdminUsername, AdminPassword, WindowsConfiguration}
StorageProfile      : {ImageReference, OsDisk}
NetworkInterfaceIDs : {/subscriptions/0bc29420-0222-4599-b91e-e8699f760742/resourceGroups/
                      packt_rg/providers/Microsoft.Network/networkInterfaces/VMNic1}
```

In *step 18*, you use the VM configuration object ($VM) to create the actual VM. This step takes some time and generates no output.

Once your VM is up and running, you can move on to *step 19*, where you retrieve the details of the Public IP address object. The object returned from Get-AzureRmPublicIpAddress contains details about the public IP object you created earlier and assigned to your VM's NIC including the actual IP address.

Using the IP address, in *step 20*, you make a Remote Desktop connection to your VM, via the public IP address. Once you logon, you can see your VM. You need to specify the userid and password, as shown in the following screenshot:

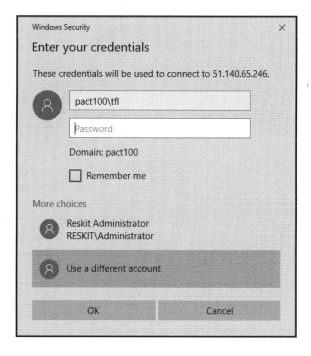

Assuming you entered the userid and password correctly, the RDP connection then presents a security dialog, like the one in the following screenshot:

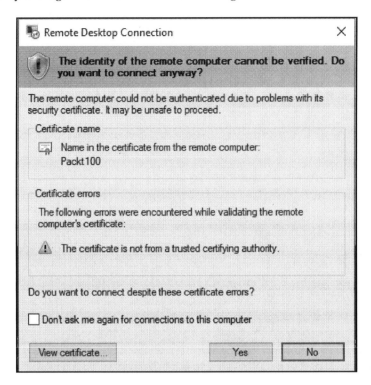

If you plan to use the VM often, you can click in the **Don't ask me again for connections to this computer** check box to avoid seeing this dialog box in future. Once the connection has completed, you can see your VM, like this:

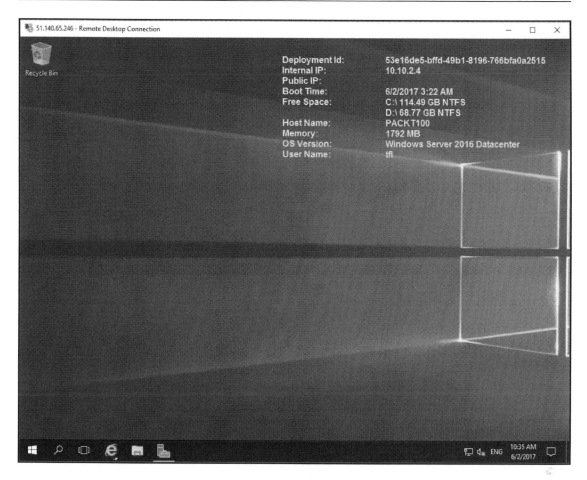

There's more...

In *step 4*, you define a new Azure virtual network. As you can see from the output, the `New-AzureRmVirtualNetwork` cmdlet returns a warning message stating that *The output object type of this cmdlet will be modified in a future release*. Other Azure RM networking cmdlets issue this waning, although at present there is no action to take.

In this recipe, you just allowed two protocols (RDP and PowerShell Remoting) inbound. In practice you may need to create additional network security rules. You should also create outbound network security rules as well.

In several of the steps, you pipe the output of an Azure cmdlet to `Out-Null` which eliminates the cmdlet's output. Several of the Azure cmdlets you use in this recipe display a long JSON document describing various objects. In most automation scenarios, this extra output is not necessary. But as you work through this recipe, consider removing the `Out-Null` statements to see the extra output.

In *step 18*, you use the VM configuration object created earlier to create the VM. The creation process takes quite a while since Azure has to create the VHD blob, copy the image to this VHD, then spin up the VM and go through the post Sysprep process.

In *step 19*, you retrieved the public IP address resource, `Packt_IP1`, that you created in *step 5*. When Azure starts your new VM, the Azure networking fabric allocates an actual public IP address. The public IP address object contains two useful properties. The first is `ProvisioningState`. When the VM is running, the provisioning state should be `Succeeded`. The second property is a string, `IPAddress`. This string is the public facing IP address for the VM.

In *step 20*, you use that string to create an RDP connection to the public IP address of your VM, and in *step 21*, you can log in to the VM using the credentials specified in *step 5*. Given that this is a publicly addressable, internet facing VM, that password should be long and complex. You should consider what additional security measures to take against inevitable attack.

Once you complete *step 21* and log in to your Azure VM, you see the VM's desktop!

13
Using Desired State Configuration

In this chapter, we will cover the following recipes:

- Using DSC and built-in resources
- Parameterizing DSC configuration
- Finding and installing additional DSC resources
- Using DSC with PSGallery resources
- Configuring Local Configuration Manager
- Implementing a SMB pull server
- Implementing a DSC web-based pull server
- Using DSC partial configuration

Introduction

Desired State Configuration (**DSC**) is management platform within Windows Server and is implemented with Windows PowerShell. DSC enables you to define a computer's desired state declaratively and have PowerShell ensure the computer is configured accordingly and remains so. This is simpler than writing complex scripts to configure a given computer. Microsoft added DSC with PowerShell and delivered improvements V5 and V/5.1 and Server 2016.

With DSC, you define a configuration that describes the details of how a given node (computer) is to be configured. The configuration defines a series of resources to be invoked on the node and how these resources should be configured. A DSC resource is PowerShell code and executable that knows to configure a given object residing on a node. Resources primarily exist as PowerShell modules and you need them both on the computer on which you author DSC configurations and on the target node.

For example, you could define a node and specify that the `WindowsFeature` resource should be configured to ensure that `Web-Server` feature (a subset of the full installation of **Internet Information Server** (**IIS**) is installed, or that the `File` resource ensures a set of files, available from somewhere in your network or the internet, are present on the target node. This could dramatically simplify the process of configuring a web farm and ensuring it stays configured properly.

Resources come from a variety of sources. Microsoft has a few resources built in and these ship inside Windows Server 2016. But you can also get additional DSC resources from the internet. And of course, you can also develop your own DSC resources. For more information on developing DSC resources, refer to `https://docs.microsoft.com/en-us/ powershell/dsc/authoringresource`.

The first step in `DSC` is defining a configuration statement. A configuration statement, which is not dissimilar to a function, defines the desired state of a node. It states how you wish certain resources on the target node to be configured. After you define the configuration, you compile it by executing the configuration statement. This is a lot like functions in PowerShell.

You can parameterize configuration statements to make it simple to create different **Managed Object Format** (**MOF**) files based on the parameter values. For example, a configuration statement could take a node name and the name of a Windows feature that should be present on the node. When you run the configuration, you specify values for the node name (for example `DC1`), and the name of the Windows feature you want loaded (for example `Web-Server`). The generated MOF file instructs DSC to ensure the `Web-Server` feature is present on `DC1`.

When you run the configuration statement, you in effect compile it. The compilation process converts the configuration statement into an actual PowerShell function. When you run this generated function, PowerShell creates a MOF file based on the specified configuration. A MOF file tells PowerShell precisely how the resource is to be configured on a specific node.

Microsoft chose to use the MOF file in addition to the configuration statement to define the configuration. MOF is standardized and well supported, albeit more complex in terms of syntax and content. Separating the specification of the configuration from the details of deploying it can feel like additional overhead (create the PowerShell configuration statement then create and deploy the MOF file).

Microsoft envisaged that someone could create a DSC workbench type product that enabled you to use a GUI and define the configuration graphically. Then at the click of a button this as yet unbuilt tool would generate the necessary MOF file and deploy it automatically. Even though this GUI has never been built, the approach does allow you to define security boundaries between defining a configuration and deploying it.

Once you have generated the MOF files, you deploy the configuration. DSC uses the MOF file to ensure that the specified DSC resources are correctly configured on the target node. Subsequently. you can check that the node is correctly configured, with the service and files in place, and remedy any unapproved changes to the target node, referred to as configuration drift.

You can also use DSC to have a node pull configuration details from a centralized pull server. The pull server is a server that makes DSC configuration files (that is the MOF files) and the resources available to target nodes. A target node is set up to regularly contact the pull server and pull configuration information (and any required resources) from the pull server. You can have two types of pull server—a web pull server or an SMB pull server. The latter is simpler to set up.

With a pull server, you configure the target node's **Local Configuration Manager** (LCM) with a GUID and the location of the pull server. The LCM uses that GUID to locate the configuration information you want to be applied to the node on the pull server. This enables you to configure multiple servers, for example a multi-node web farm, identically by just giving them the same GUID.

A DSC partial configuration is a configuration statement that defines part of a node's overall configuration. This enables you to combine different configuration statements and have DSC add them together as it configures the node. In larger organizations, different teams can determine a part of a node's configuration independently. Partial configurations allow you to deploy the partial configurations from the different teams to the relevant nodes.

In this chapter, you first look at the built-in resources and the basics of DSC deployment. You then look at how you get more resources, how you set up a pull server, and finally how you implement partial configurations.

Using DSC and built-in resources

Windows Server 2016 comes with a limited set of built-in DSC resources. In this recipe, you explore the built-in DSC resources and then write and deploy a simple configuration to a single node. The recipe also examines changes in configuration.

Getting ready

In this recipe, you examine the Windows Server 2016 built-in resources and use these to create and compile a configuration statement on server SRV1. You use this configuration statement to then deploy the Web-Server feature on a second server, SRV2.

This recipe relies on two files being created and shared from DC1. The two files are Index.Htm, and Page2.Htm. These two files are created and shared as \\DC1\ReskitApp. The first file, Index.HTM contains the following:

```
<!DOCTYPE html>
<html>
<head><title>Main Page - ReskitApp Application</title></head>
<body><p><center>
    <b>HOME PAGE FOR RESKITAPP APPLICATION</b></p>
    This is the root page of the RESKITAPP application<b>
    Pushed via DSC</p><br><hr>
<a href="http://srv2/reskitapp/page2.htm">
Click to View Page 2</a>
</center>
<br><hr></body></html>
```

The second file, Page2.Htm contains the following:

```
<!DOCTYPE html>
<html><head><title>Page 2 </title></head>
<body><p><center><b>My Second Page</b></p>
Enjoy<br>
Second page - pushed out by DSC.<br><hr>
<br><a href="http://srv2/reskitapp/Index.htm">Clck herer to go back
home!</a>
</center></body></html>
```

This recipe does not set up a web application—all this recipe does it to copy two files across from DC1 to SRV1.

How to do it...

1. Discover the built-in DSC resources on SRV1:

   ```
   Get-DscResource
   ```

2. Examine the DSC resource File:

   ```
   Get-DscResource -Name File | Format-List -Property *
   ```

3. Get the syntax for the DSC resource File:

   ```
   Get-DscResource -Name File -Syntax
   ```

4. Create/compile a configuration block to copy files to SRV2 by executing:

   ```
   Configuration PrepareSRV2
   {
     Import-DscResource `
     -ModuleName 'PSDesiredStateConfiguration' `
     Node SRV2
   {
     File BaseFiles
     {
        DestinationPath = 'C:\ReskitApp\'
        SourcePath      = '\\DC1\ReskitApp\'
        Ensure          = 'Present'
        Recurse         = $True
     }
   }
   }
   ```

5. View configuration function:

   ```
   Get-Item Function:\PrepareSRV2
   ```

6. Create the MOF output folder:

   ```
   New-Item -Path C:\DSC -ItemType Directory `
                        -ErrorAction SilentlyContinue
   ```

7. Run the configuration and produce a MOF file:

```
PrepareSRV2 -OutputPath C:\DSC `
            -Wait  -Verbose
```

8. View the generated MOF file:

```
Get-Content -Path C:\DSC\SRV2.mof
```

9. Start the DSC configuration:

```
Start-DscConfiguration -Path C:\DSC\ `
                        -Wait -Verbose
```

10. Observe results of DSC configuration:

```
Invoke-Command -Computer SRV2 `
      -ScriptBlock {Get-Childitem C:\ReskitApp}
```

11. Introduce a change to the configuration:

```
Invoke-Command -Computer SRV2 `
    -ScriptBlock {  Remove-Item -Path C:\ReskitApp\Index.htm
                     Get-Childitem -Path C:\ReskitApp }
```

12. Reapply the configuration manually:

```
Start-DscConfiguration -Path C:\DSC\ `
                        -Wait -Verbose
```

13. Observe the results of reapplying the DSC configuration when no configuration drift is present:

```
Invoke-Command -Computer SRV2 `
    -ScriptBlock { Get-Childitem -Path C:\ReskitApp }
```

How it works...

In *step 1*, you examine the resources on SRV1. This server has only the default DSC resources installed as part of a default installation of Windows Server 2016. This list looks like this:

```
PS C:\> Get-DscResource

ImplementedAs   Name                     ModuleName                     Version   Properties
-------------   ----                     ----------                     -------   ----------
Binary          File                                                              {DestinationPath, Attributes, Checksum, Content...
Binary          SignatureValidation                                               {SignedItemType, TrustedStorePath}
PowerShell      Archive                  PSDesiredStateConfiguration    1.1       {Destination, Path, Checksum, Credential...}
PowerShell      Environment              PSDesiredStateConfiguration    1.1       {Name, DependsOn, Ensure, Path...}
PowerShell      Group                    PSDesiredStateConfiguration    1.1       {GroupName, Credential, DependsOn, Description...}
Composite       GroupSet                 PSDesiredStateConfiguration    1.1       {DependsOn, PsDscRunAsCredential, GroupName, En...
Binary          Log                      PSDesiredStateConfiguration    1.1       {Message, DependsOn, PsDscRunAsCredential}
PowerShell      Package                  PSDesiredStateConfiguration    1.1       {Name, Path, ProductId, Arguments...}
Composite       ProcessSet               PSDesiredStateConfiguration    1.1       {DependsOn, PsDscRunAsCredential, Path, Credent...
PowerShell      Registry                 PSDesiredStateConfiguration    1.1       {Key, ValueName, DependsOn, Ensure...}
PowerShell      Script                   PSDesiredStateConfiguration    1.1       {GetScript, SetScript, TestScript, Credential...}
PowerShell      Service                  PSDesiredStateConfiguration    1.1       {Name, BuiltInAccount, Credential, Dependencies...
Composite       ServiceSet               PSDesiredStateConfiguration    1.1       {DependsOn, PsDscRunAsCredential, Name, Startup...
PowerShell      User                     PSDesiredStateConfiguration    1.1       {UserName, DependsOn, Description, Disabled...}
PowerShell      WaitForAll               PSDesiredStateConfiguration    1.1       {NodeName, ResourceName, DependsOn, PsDscRunAsC...
PowerShell      WaitForAny               PSDesiredStateConfiguration    1.1       {NodeName, ResourceName, DependsOn, PsDscRunAsC...
PowerShell      WaitForSome              PSDesiredStateConfiguration    1.1       {NodeCount, NodeName, ResourceName, DependsOn...}
PowerShell      WindowsFeature           PSDesiredStateConfiguration    1.1       {Name, Credential, DependsOn, Ensure...}
Composite       WindowsFeatureSet        PSDesiredStateConfiguration    1.1       {DependsOn, PsDscRunAsCredential, Name, Ensure...}
PowerShell      WindowsOptionalFeature   PSDesiredStateConfiguration    1.1       {Name, DependsOn, Ensure, LogLevel...}
Composite       WindowsOptionalFeatureSet PSDesiredStateConfiguration   1.1       {DependsOn, PsDscRunAsCredential, Name, Ensure...}
PowerShell      WindowsPackageCab        PSDesiredStateConfiguration    1.1       {Ensure, Name, SourcePath, DependsOn...}
PowerShell      WindowsProcess           PSDesiredStateConfiguration    1.1       {Arguments, Path, Credential, DependsOn...}
```

In *step 2*, you view the details of the DSC resource `File`. The output looks like this:

```
PS C:\> Get-DscResource -Name File | Format-List -Property *

ResourceType   : MSFT_FileDirectoryConfiguration
Name           : File
FriendlyName   : File
Module         :
ModuleName     :
Version        :
Path           :
ParentPath     : C:\Windows\system32\Configuration\Schema\MSFT_FileDirectoryConfiguration
ImplementedAs  : Binary
CompanyName    :
Properties     : {DestinationPath, Attributes, Checksum, Contents...}
```

In *step 3*, you use `Get-DSCResource` to obtain the syntax of the `File` resource, which looks like this:

```
PS C:\> Get-DscResource -Name File -Syntax
File [String] #ResourceName
{
    DestinationPath = [string]
    [Attributes = [string[]]{ Archive | Hidden | ReadOnly | System }]
    [Checksum = [string]{ CreatedDate | ModifiedDate | SHA-1 | SHA-256 | SHA-512 }]
    [Contents = [string]]
    [Credential = [PSCredential]]
    [DependsOn = [string[]]]
    [Ensure = [string]{ Absent | Present }]
    [Force = [bool]]
    [MatchSource = [bool]]
    [PsDscRunAsCredential = [PSCredential]]
    [Recurse = [bool]]
    [SourcePath = [string]]
    [Type = [string]{ Directory | File }]
}
```

In *step 4*, you create a DSC configuration. To this, you execute the configuration block. When you run the configuration block, much like running a function block, you get no output from the compilation process. The configuration block relies on the two files created and shared from DC1.

In *step 5*, you examine the Function: drive and look at the function that DSC created when you ran the Configuration block. Again, much like running a function block, when you execute the Configuration block, PowerShell creates a function, complete with a function definition. The output looks like this:

In *step 6*, you ensure the output folder for the MOF file exists, and in *step 7*, you ensure the folder to hold the ReskitApp files exists on SRV2. Both these steps produce no output.

In *step 7*, you create a MOF file by executing the compiled configuration. When you specify the -Wait and -Verbose parameters, DSC shows what it is doing and the script does not continue until after the DSC operation is complete. The output from this step is like this:

In *step 8*, you view the resultant MOF file, which looks like this:

```
PS C:\> Get-Content -Path C:\DSC\SRV2.mof
/*
@TargetNode='SRV2'
@GeneratedBy=administrator
@GenerationDate=04/06/2017 14:20:02
@GenerationHost=SRV1
*/
instance of MSFT_FileDirectoryConfiguration as $MSFT_FileDirectoryConfiguration1ref
{
ResourceID = "[File]basefiles";
  Ensure = "Present";
  DestinationPath = "c:\\reskitapp\\";
  ModuleName = "PSDesiredStateConfiguration";
  SourceInfo = "::6::5::File";
  Recurse = True;
  SourcePath = "\\\\dc1\\ReskitApp\\";
  ModuleVersion = "1.0";
  ConfigurationName = "PrepareSRV2";
};
instance of OMI_ConfigurationDocument
                    { Version="2.0.0";
                      MinimumCompatibleVersion = "1.0.0";
                      CompatibleVersionAdditionalProperties= {"Omi_BaseResource:ConfigurationName"};
                      Author="administrator";
                      GenerationDate="04/06/2017 14:20:02";
                      GenerationHost="SRV1";
                      Name="PrepareSRV2";
                    };
```

In *step 9*, you run `Start-DscConfiguration` with the `-Verbose` switch. This switch when combined with `-Wait` creates additional output that shows you what actions DSC is taking as it executes.

The output shows that SRV2 has received a LCM which has received a method call from SRV1. LCM cannot find the folder, so it creates the folder. Then, you see that the LCM cannot find the two files, and copies those files to the specified location:

```
PS C:\> Start-DscConfiguration -Path C:\dsc\ `
                   -Wait -Verbose
VERBOSE: Perform operation 'Invoke CimMethod' with following parameters,
  ''methodName' = SendConfigurationApply,
  'className' = MSFT_DSCLocalConfigurationManager,'namespaceName' = root/Microsoft/Windows/DesiredStateConfiguration'.
VERBOSE: An LCM method call arrived from computer SRV1 with user sid S-1-5-21-715049209-2702507345-667613206-500.
VERBOSE: [SRV2]: LCM:  [ Start  Set      ]
VERBOSE: [SRV2]: LCM:  [ Start  Resource ] [[File]basefiles]
VERBOSE: [SRV2]: LCM:  [ Start  Test     ] [[File]basefiles]
VERBOSE: [SRV2]:                            [[File]basefiles] The system cannot find the file specified.
VERBOSE: [SRV2]:                            [[File]basefiles] The related file/directory is: c:\reskitapp.
VERBOSE: [SRV2]:                            [[File]basefiles] The network name cannot be found.
VERBOSE: [SRV2]:                            [[File]basefiles] The related file/directory is: \\dc1\ReskitApp.
VERBOSE: [SRV2]:                            [[File]basefiles] Building file list from cache.
VERBOSE: [SRV2]: LCM:  [ End    Test     ] [[File]basefiles]  in 2.3430 seconds.
VERBOSE: [SRV2]: LCM:  [ Start  Set      ] [[File]basefiles]
VERBOSE: [SRV2]:                            [[File]basefiles] The system cannot find the file specified.
VERBOSE: [SRV2]:                            [[File]basefiles] The related file/directory is: c:\reskitapp.
VERBOSE: [SRV2]:                            [[File]basefiles] The network name cannot be found.
VERBOSE: [SRV2]:                            [[File]basefiles] The related file/directory is: \\dc1\ReskitApp.
VERBOSE: [SRV2]:                            [[File]basefiles] Building file list from cache.
VERBOSE: [SRV2]:                            [[File]basefiles] Copying file \\dc1\ReskitApp\Index.htm to c:\reskitapp\Index.htm.
VERBOSE: [SRV2]:                            [[File]basefiles] Copying file \\dc1\ReskitApp\Page2.htm to c:\reskitapp\Page2.htm.
VERBOSE: [SRV2]: LCM:  [ End    Set      ] [[File]basefiles]  in 0.4690 seconds.
VERBOSE: [SRV2]: LCM:  [ End    Resource ] [[File]basefiles]
VERBOSE: [SRV2]: LCM:  [ End    Set      ]
VERBOSE: [SRV2]: LCM:  [ End    Set      ]  in  43.0380 seconds.
VERBOSE: Operation 'Invoke CimMethod' complete.
VERBOSE: Time taken for configuration job to complete is 45.014 seconds
```

In *step 10*, you see the two files in the C:\ReskitApp folder, like this:

```
Invoke-Command -Computer SRV2 `
    -ScriptBlock {Get-Childitem C:\reskitapp}

    Directory: C:\reskitapp

Mode           LastWriteTime     Length Name          PSComputerName
----           -------------     ------ ----          --------------
-a----    05/01/2017    11:50      472 Index.htm     SRV2
-a----    05/01/2017    11:52      383 Page2.htm     SRV2
```

In *step 11*, you introduce configuration drift by removing one of the two files copied previously in *step 10*. The output looks like this:

```
PS C:\> Invoke-Command -Computer SRV2 `
    -ScriptBlock {  Remove-Item -Path C:\ReskitApp\Index.htm
                    Get-Childitem -Path C:\ReskitApp }

    Directory: C:\ReskitApp

Mode           LastWriteTime     Length Name          PSComputerName
----           -------------     ------ ----          --------------
-a----    05/01/2017    11:52      383 Page2.htm SRV2
```

As you can see, there is only one file remaining in the ReskitApp folder on SRV2. To remedy that manually, in *step 12*, you re-apply the configuration by re-running Start-DscConfiguration, like this:

```
PS C:\> Start-DscConfiguration -Path C:\dsc\ `
                -Wait -Verbose
VERBOSE: Perform operation 'Invoke CimMethod' with following parameters, ''methodName' = SendConfigurationApply,
'className' = MSFT_DSCLocalConfigurationManager,'namespaceName' = root/Microsoft/Windows/DesiredStateConfiguration'.
VERBOSE: An LCM method call arrived from computer SRV1 with user sid S-1-5-21-715049209-2702507345-667613206-500.
VERBOSE: [SRV2]: LCM:  [ Start  Set      ]
VERBOSE: [SRV2]: LCM:  [ Start  Resource ]  [[File]basefiles]
VERBOSE: [SRV2]: LCM:  [ Start  Test     ]  [[File]basefiles]
VERBOSE: [SRV2]:                            [[File]basefiles] The network name cannot be found.
VERBOSE: [SRV2]:                            [[File]basefiles] The related file/directory is: \\dc1\ReskitApp.
VERBOSE: [SRV2]:                            [[File]basefiles] Building file list from cache.
VERBOSE: [SRV2]: LCM:  [ End    Test     ]  [[File]basefiles]  in 0.0310 seconds.
VERBOSE: [SRV2]: LCM:  [ Start  Set      ]  [[File]basefiles]
VERBOSE: [SRV2]:                            [[File]basefiles] The network name cannot be found.
VERBOSE: [SRV2]:                            [[File]basefiles] The related file/directory is: \\dc1\ReskitApp.
VERBOSE: [SRV2]:                            [[File]basefiles] Building file list from cache.
VERBOSE: [SRV2]:                            [[File]basefiles] Copying file \\dc1\ReskitApp\Index.htm to c:\reskitapp\Index.htm.
VERBOSE: [SRV2]:                            [[File]basefiles] The destination object was found and no action is required.
VERBOSE: [SRV2]: LCM:  [ End    Set      ]  [[File]basefiles]  in 0.0310 seconds.
VERBOSE: [SRV2]: LCM:  [ End    Resource ]  [[File]basefiles]
VERBOSE: [SRV2]: LCM:  [ End    Set      ]
VERBOSE: [SRV2]: LCM:  [ End    Set      ]  in  0.7350 seconds.
VERBOSE: Operation 'Invoke CimMethod' complete.
VERBOSE: Time taken for configuration job to complete is 2.112 seconds
```

As you can see, the folder was found, but one file was not. The `File` resource restores the file to SRV2.

In *step 13*, you run where the configuration has not changed. The `File` resource tests to see that the files and the folder exist, and since they do, the `File` resource take no further action, like this:

```
PS C:\> Start-DscConfiguration -Path C:\dsc\ `
                             -Wait -Verbose
VERBOSE: Perform operation 'Invoke CimMethod' with following parameters, ''methodName' = SendConfigurationApply,
'className' = MSFT_DSCLocalConfigurationManager,'namespaceName' = root/Microsoft/Windows/DesiredStateConfiguration'.
VERBOSE: An LCM method call arrived from computer SRV1 with user sid S-1-5-21-715049209-2702507345-667613206-500.
VERBOSE: [SRV2]: LCM:  [ Start  Set      ]
VERBOSE: [SRV2]: LCM:  [ Start  Resource ] [[File]basefiles]
VERBOSE: [SRV2]: LCM:  [ Start  Test     ] [[File]basefiles]
VERBOSE: [SRV2]:                            [[File]basefiles] The network name cannot be found.
VERBOSE: [SRV2]:                            [[File]basefiles] The related file/directory is: \\dc1\ReskitApp.
VERBOSE: [SRV2]:                            [[File]basefiles] Building file list from cache.
VERBOSE: [SRV2]:                            [[File]basefiles] The destination object was found and no action is required.
VERBOSE: [SRV2]: LCM:  [ End    Test     ] [[File]basefiles]  in 0.0080 seconds.
VERBOSE: [SRV2]: LCM:  [ Skip   Set      ] [[File]basefiles]
VERBOSE: [SRV2]: LCM:  [ End    Resource ] [[File]basefiles]
VERBOSE: [SRV2]: LCM:  [ End    Set      ]
VERBOSE: [SRV2]: LCM:  [ End    Set      ]  in  0.1840 seconds.
VERBOSE: Operation 'Invoke CimMethod' complete.
VERBOSE: Time taken for configuration job to complete is 0.269 seconds
```

As you can see in *step 10*, *step 12*, and *step 13*, if you use the `-Verbose` switch, the cmdlet produces a trace of what it is doing. In *step 10*, you can see DSC creating the folder and copying the two files over. In *step 12*, DSC just copies the missing file, whilst in *step 13*, DSC takes no action since it finds the configuration of SRV2 to conform to the desired state.

There's more...

The resources you see in *step 1* come from the `PSDesiredStateConfiguration` module. Since DSC resources are PowerShell code, you can read and view what each built-in resource does. You can also view the inner workings of any DSC resource you download.

In *step 6*, you store the MOF file to `C:\DSC`. In a production environment, you would need to create tight configuration control over the generated MOF files (and the configuration statements that relate). You should put all DSC resoruces and MOF files under source control, such as GIT.

In *step 12* and *step 13*, you induce then correct a change in the configuration of the system—in this case, a given file being removed. In this case, you are rectifying the configuration manually.

When DSC applies the configuration, by default, it just makes sure that the files that existed on \\DC1\ReskitApp the first time you pushed the configuration still exist on SRV2. Should the application grow to include additional files, DSC does not copy them if you re-apply the configuration. To achieve that, you add the line MatchSource = $true to the configuration of the File resource you developed in *step 4* (and redeploy the configuration).

Also, the recipe does not correct another type of configuration drift—a file on SRV2 exists, but is different to the file of the same name on \\DC1\ReskitApp. To ensure that the files on SRV2 are identical and remain identical to those on \\DC1\ReskitApp, you add another line to the configuration of the File resource, in *step 4*: Checksum = 'SHA-256'. This directive causes the File resource to create a checksum of each file in the source folder and compare it with the checksum of the file on SRV2. If the checksums do not match, the File resource overwrites the file with a copy from \\DC1\ReskitApp. In production, specifying both of these two properties would be good, but if there are large numbers of files there is a speed impact. You could also specify SHA-1 or SHA-512 as checksum algorithms, although the use of SHA-1 is no longer best practice.

This recipe used just one of the built-in DSC resources in Windows Server 2016. The built-in resources are just a subset of the resources you might need to use DSC in a rich production environment, but enough to get you started. In later recipes, you use an internet repository, the PowerShell Gallery, to provide additional DSC resources.

In this recipe, you utilized the push approach to DscConfiguration. You created a configuration document and the MOF file on SRV1, then pushed it to the target node (SRV2). As an alternative, you could setup a node to pull configuration information and the DSC resources from a central pull server. Later recipes in this chapter examine how you can set up and configure DSC to use a pull server.

Parameterizing DSC configuration

As with functions, you can create configuration blocks with parameters. These enable you to produce different MOF files by varying the parameter values used when you execute the configuration.

For example, suppose you wanted to add a feature to a node. You could create a specific configuration where you hard code the feature name and the node name. This is not dissimilar to how you copied specific files from DC1 to SRV1 in the use DSC and built-in resources recipe.

Alternatively, you could create a configuration that takes the node name and the service name as parameters and when you run the configuration, PowerShell creates a MOF file that adds the specified service to the specified node. This recipe demonstrates that approach.

One challenge this approach throws up is that, by default, you can only send a single MOF file to a given node. Thus, if you used the earlier recipe and copied files to SRV2, attempting to send a second MOF file to the system results in an error. There are three solutions to this.

The first approach is to have a single MOF file generated for each target node. This means larger MOF files and those for larger organizations sometimes require hard to achieve co-ordination between the different groups that create the overall configuration for a node.

The second approach is to use DSC partial configurations, a feature added with PowerShell V5 and improved in V5.1. This feature enables you to send multiple partial configurations to a node. You configure the node to pull different configuration blocks from potentially multiple DSC pulls servers then the LCM combines then applies them. The recipe *Using DSC partial configuration* shows you how to use partial configurations.

Getting ready

In this recipe, you create a configuration block on server SRV1 that adds a Windows feature to a node. The feature and node names are both specified as parameters. You also remove any previous configuration details from the server before adding the feature. Also, this recipe assumes no firewall is running on the systems.

How to do it...

1. Check the status of the DNS feature on SRV2:

```
Get-WindowsFeature DNS -ComputerName SRV2
```

2. Create parameterized configuration:

```
Configuration ProvisionServices
{
param (
  [Parameter(Mandatory=$true)]  $NodeName,
  [Parameter(Mandatory=$true)]  $FeatureName)
  Import-DscResource -ModuleName 'PSDesiredStateConfiguration'
Node $NodeName
```

```
      {
       WindowsFeature $FeatureName
        {
           Name                  = $FeatureName
           Ensure                = 'Present'
           IncludeAllSubFeature  = $true
        }
      }
    }
```

3. Ensure an empty DSC folder exists on SRV1:

```
New-Item -Path C:\DSC -ItemType Directory `
        -ErrorAction SilentlyContinue | Out-Null
Get-ChildItem -Path C:\DSC | Remove-Item -Force | Out-Null
```

4. Clear any existing configuration documents on SRV2:

```
Invoke-Command -ComputerName SRV2 {
    Remove-Item -Path 'C:\Windows\System32\configuration\*.mof' `
            -ErrorAction SilentlyContinue
}
```

5. Now create the MOF file on SRV1:

```
ProvisionServices -OutputPath  C:\DSC `
                  -NodeName    SRV2 `
                  -FeatureName DNS
```

6. View the generated MOF file:

```
Get-Content -Path C:\DSC\SRV2.mof
```

7. Configure SRV2 with DNS:

```
Start-DscConfiguration -Path C:\DSC -Wait -Verbose
```

8. Check the results of installing the DNS feature on SRV2:

```
Get-Service -Name DNS -ComputerName SRV2
```

How it works...

In *step 1*, you check the status of the DNS feature on SRV2; as you can see, DNS is not installed on this system:

```
PS C:\> Get-WindowsFeature -Name DNS -ComputerName SRV2

Display Name          Name       Install State
------------          ----       -------------
[ ] DNS Server        DNS            Available
```

In *step 2*, you create a new configuration document, ProvisionDNS. As in previous recipes, running this code produces no output, but this does compile the configuration document.

In *step 3*, you ensure that C:\DSC exists on SRV1 and that it is empty. In *step 4*, you remove any existing MOF files from SRV2. Neither of these steps produce any output. The first time you run this step, the folder is empty. But if you run this multiple times, then you want to ensure the C:\DSC folder is empty.

In *step 5*, you run the configuration function, specifying both a node name (SRV2) and a feature to add (DNS). As you can see, running the configuration produces a new MOF file for SRV2:

```
PS C:\> ProvisionServices -OutputPath C:\DSC
                          -NodeName   SRV2
                          -FeatureName DNS
    Directory: C:\DSC

Mode              LastWriteTime         Length Name
----              -------------         ------ ----

-a----      12/04/2017     13:04          1914 SRV2.mof
```

In *step 6*, you view the MOF file created by *step 5*, which looks like this:

```
PS C:\> Get-Content -Path C:\DSC\SRV2.mof
/*
@TargetNode='SRV2'
@GeneratedBy=administrator
@GenerationDate=04/12/2017 13:07:03
@GenerationHost=SRV1
*/
instance of MSFT_RoleResource as $MSFT_RoleResource1ref
{
ResourceID = "[WindowsFeature]DNS";
 IncludeAllSubFeature = True;
 Ensure = "Present";
 SourceInfo = "::9::3::WindowsFeature";
 Name = "DNS";
 ModuleName = "PSDesiredStateConfiguration";
ModuleVersion = "1.0";
 ConfigurationName = "ProvisionServices";
};

instance of OMI_ConfigurationDocument
{
 Version="2.0.0";
 MinimumCompatibleVersion = "1.0.0";
 CompatibleVersionAdditionalProperties= {"Omi_BaseResource:ConfigurationName"};
 Author="administrator";
 GenerationDate="04/12/2017 13:07:03";
 GenerationHost="SRV1";
 Name="ProvisionServices";
};
```

Finally, in *step 7*, you start the `DscConfiguration`. DSC finds that the DNS feature does not exist on SRV2 and so installs this feature, as follows:

```
PS C:\> Start-DscConfiguration -Path C:\DSC -Wait -Verbose
VERBOSE: Perform operation 'Invoke CimMethod' with following parameters,
''methodName' = SendConfigurationApply,'className' = MSFT_DSCLocalConfigurationManager,
'namespaceName' = root/Microsoft/Windows/DesiredStateConfiguration'.
VERBOSE: An LCM method call arrived from computer SRV1 with user sid S-1-5-21-715049209-2702507345-667613206-500.
VERBOSE: [SRV2]: LCM:  [ Start  Set     ]
VERBOSE: [SRV2]: LCM:  [ Start  Resource ]  [[WindowsFeature]DNS]
VERBOSE: [SRV2]: LCM:  [ Start  Test    ]  [[WindowsFeature]DNS]
VERBOSE: [SRV2]:                            [[WindowsFeature]DNS] The operation 'Get-WindowsFeature' started: DNS
VERBOSE: [SRV2]:                            [[WindowsFeature]DNS] The operation 'Get-WindowsFeature' succeeded: DNS
VERBOSE: [SRV2]: LCM:  [ End    Test    ]  [[WindowsFeature]DNS]  in 12.4460 seconds.
VERBOSE: [SRV2]: LCM:  [ Start  Set     ]  [[WindowsFeature]DNS]
VERBOSE: [SRV2]:                            [[WindowsFeature]DNS] Installation started...
VERBOSE: [SRV2]:                            [[WindowsFeature]DNS] Continue with installation?
VERBOSE: [SRV2]:                            [[WindowsFeature]DNS] Prerequisite processing started...
VERBOSE: [SRV2]:                            [[WindowsFeature]DNS] Prerequisite processing succeeded.
VERBOSE: [SRV2]:                            [[WindowsFeature]DNS] Installation succeeded.
VERBOSE: [SRV2]:                            [[WindowsFeature]DNS] Successfully installed the feature DNS.
VERBOSE: [SRV2]:                            [[WindowsFeature]DNS]  in 80.3970 seconds.
VERBOSE: [SRV2]: LCM:  [ End    Set     ]  [[WindowsFeature]DNS]
VERBOSE: [SRV2]: LCM:  [ End    Resource ]  [[WindowsFeature]DNS]
VERBOSE: [SRV2]: LCM:  [ End    Set     ]
VERBOSE: [SRV2]: LCM:  [ End    Set     ]  in 94.2100 seconds.
VERBOSE: Operation 'Invoke CimMethod' complete.
VERBOSE: Time taken for configuration job to complete is 94.554 seconds
```

In *step 8*, you use the `Get-Service` cmdlet to check that the DNS service is up and running:

There's more...

In *step 2*, you create a simple parameterized configuration statement. This configuration block takes two parameters: a node name and a feature name. The configuration adds the feature to the node.

In *step 4*, you clear any previously created MOF files from SRV2. If you delete a previously pushed MOF file, the configuration set by those configuration MOF files does not change. This does allow you to use a server, such as SRV2, to test different configurations (or multiple DSC recipes).

Finding and installing DSC resources

A DSC resource is a specially created PowerShell module that enables DSC to configure various aspects of a node. The `WindowsFeature` DSC resource, for example, enables you to ensure that a particular node of a particular Windows feature installed. You could also specify that a particular Windows feature should not be present.

As you have seen in this chapter so far, Windows comes with a few DSC resources built in. But these do not provide broad coverage. For example, you can use the built-in `File` resource to copy the source files for a small web application onto a new server. But the built-in resources do not allow you to specify the application's settings (what the application name is, which application pool it runs in, and so on) which is where add-on DSC resources come in.

The community, which includes various Microsoft teams, has been busy since the release of DSC with PowerShell V4 and has created a large range of additional resources. These resources are free to download—and many were developed by the Windows PowerShell team. And of course, if you can't find a resource, you can always build your own.

With PowerShell V5, Microsoft provided a much-simplified approach to building your own resources, using the `Class` feature. And this accelerated the creation of additional resources.

DSC resources are PowerShell modules which you can download and use. While there are a number of sources for DSC resource modules, the key source is the PowerShell Gallery (`PSGallery`). You find and download DSC resources from the `PSGallery` using PowerShell's `PowerShellGet` module, as shown in this recipe.

Community provided resources (and the containing modules) are meant to obey a naming convention. If the resource/module name begins with *x*, it is considered experimental (despite having been authored by the PowerShell team). Community authored resources may begin with a *c*. Recently, however, guidance from Microsoft now suggests the *c* prefix should no longer be used (see `http://stevenmurawski.com/powershell/2015/06/dsc-people-lets-stop-using-c-now`). Of course, you are free to rename any resource to suit any naming convention you may have.

In this recipe, you download the `xWebAdministration` module that contains a number of IIS related DSC resources. This recipe focuses on obtaining additional DSC resources from `PSGallery`. In a later recipe in this chapter, Use DSC with `PSGallery` resources, you use these additional resources to configure a web application.

Getting ready

In this recipe, you find, download, and install DSC resources on `SRV1` and `SRV2`. This recipe looks at just the `PSGallery` repository, but there are many other places you can find DSC resources. And of course, you can always create your own customized resources.

How to do it...

1. Discover the DSC repositories available:

```
Get-PSRepository
```

2. Discover the DSC resources available from `PSGallery`:

```
Find-DscResource -Repository 'PSGallery'
```

3. See what IIS resources might exist:

```
Find-DscResource | Where-Object ModuleName -Match 'IIS'
```

4. Examine the xWebAdministration resource:

```
Find-DscResource |
    Where-Object ModuleName -eq 'xWebAdministration'
```

5. Install the xWebAdministration module (on SRV1):

```
Install-Module -Name 'xWebAdministration' -Force
```

6. See local module details:

```
Get-Module -Name xWebAdministration -ListAvailable
```

7. See what is in the module:

```
Get-DscResource -Module xWebAdministration
```

How it works...

In *step 1*, you view the registered DSC repositories. By default, only one repository, PSGallery, is supported, although there are other repositories, such as Chocolatey that you can also use.

The PSGallery repository is run by Microsoft and contains a wealth of PowerShell add-in modules and scripts many of which were created by Microsoft product teams. These add-ins include modules that provide DSC resources for you to download.

The repository list generated by *step 1* looks like this:

```
PS C:\foo> Get-PSRepository

Name            InstallationPolicy   SourceLocation
----            ------------------   --------------
PSGallery       Untrusted            https://www.powershellgallery.com/api/v2/
```

The PSGallery contains a large number of resources and in *step 2*, you discover DSC resources available in this repository using Find-DscResource. The (truncated) output looks like this:

```
PS C:\> Find-DscResource -Repository 'PSGallery'

Name                         Version  ModuleName                       Repositor
----                         -------  ----------                       ---------
Archive                      2.5.0.0  PSDscResources                   PSGallery
Environment                  2.5.0.0  PSDscResources                   PSGallery
Group                        2.5.0.0  PSDscResources                   PSGallery
GroupSet                     2.5.0.0  PSDscResources                   PSGallery
Registry                     2.5.0.0  PSDscResources                   PSGallery
Script                       2.5.0.0  PSDscResources                   PSGallery
Service                      2.5.0.0  PSDscResources                   PSGallery
ServiceSet                   2.5.0.0  PSDscResources                   PSGallery
User                         2.5.0.0  PSDscResources                   PSGallery
WindowsFeature               2.5.0.0  PSDscResources                   PSGallery
WindowsFeatureSet            2.5.0.0  PSDscResources                   PSGallery
WindowsOptionalFeature       2.5.0.0  PSDscResources                   PSGallery
WindowsOptionalFeatureSet    2.5.0.0  PSDscResources                   PSGallery
WindowsPackageCab            2.5.0.0  PSDscResources                   PSGallery
WindowsProcess               2.5.0.0  PSDscResources                   PSGallery
ProcessSet                   2.5.0.0  PSDscResources                   PSGallery
Carbon_EnvironmentVariable   2.4.1    Carbon                           PSGallery
Carbon_FirewallRule          2.4.1    Carbon                           PSGallery
Carbon_Group                 2.4.1    Carbon                           PSGallery
Carbon_IniFile               2.4.1    Carbon                           PSGallery
...
```

With such a large number of DSC resources, finding a specific one can be challenging but your favorite search engine should help. In this recipe, you download the xWebAdministration module which you use to set up an IIS web application. One simple way to discover DSC resources related to IIS is to look for a module with a module name containing IIS in *step 3*. The output looks like this:

```
PS C:\>Find-DscResource | Where-Object Name -match 'IIS'

Name                         Version   ModuleName                       Repositor
----                         -------   ----------                       ---------
xIisFeatureDelegation        1.17.0.0  xWebAdministration               PSGallery
xIisHandler                  1.17.0.0  xWebAdministration               PSGallery
xIisLogging                  1.17.0.0  xWebAdministration               PSGallery
xIisMimeTypeMapping          1.17.0.0  xWebAdministration               PSGallery
xIisModule                   1.17.0.0  xWebAdministration               PSGallery
IisLogging                   0.1.0.0   WebAdministrationDsc             PSGallery
xIISWebBinding               1.0.0.1   xIISWebBinding                   PSGallery
xIISCertSBinding             1.0.0.1   xIISCertSBinding                 PSGallery
xIISApplicationPoolIdentityType 1.0.0.2 xIISApplicationPoolIdentityType PSGallery
xIISMachineKey               1.0.0.1   xIISMachineKey                   PSGallery
xIISMail                     1.0.0.1   xIISMail                         PSGallery
cIISSharedConfig             1.0.37    cCogito                          PSGallery
cAspNetIisRegistration       1.0.0     cAspNetIisRegistration           PSGallery
xIISSession                  1.0.0.0   xIISSession                      PSGallery
```

As you can see from this output, there are several modules that could be useful, but the `xWebAdministration` module looks potentially useful. In *step 4*, you look at the DSC resources included in the `xWebAdministration` module, which looks like this:

```
PS C:\>Find-DscResource | Where-Object ModuleName -eq 'xWebAdministration'

Name                   Version     ModuleName           Repository
----                   -------     ----------           ----------
xIisFeatureDelegation  1.17.0.0    xWebAdministration   PSGallery
xIisHandler            1.17.0.0    xWebAdministration   PSGallery
xIisLogging            1.17.0.0    xWebAdministration   PSGallery
xIisMimeTypeMapping    1.17.0.0    xWebAdministration   PSGallery
xIisModule             1.17.0.0    xWebAdministration   PSGallery
xSSLSettings           1.17.0.0    xWebAdministration   PSGallery
xWebApplication        1.17.0.0    xWebAdministration   PSGallery
xWebAppPool            1.17.0.0    xWebAdministration   PSGallery
xWebAppPoolDefaults    1.17.0.0    xWebAdministration   PSGallery
xWebConfigKeyValue     1.17.0.0    xWebAdministration   PSGallery
xWebsite               1.17.0.0    xWebAdministration   PSGallery
xWebSiteDefaults       1.17.0.0    xWebAdministration   PSGallery
xWebVirtualDirectory   1.17.0.0    xWebAdministration   PSGallery
```

In *step 5*, you use the `Install-Module` cmdlet to download and install the `xWebAdministration` module. There is no output from the installation of this module. In *step 6*, you examine the module on `SRV1`—the output looks like this:

```
PS C:\> Get-Module -Name xWebAdministration -ListAvailable

    Directory: C:\Program Files\WindowsPowerShell\Modules

ModuleType Version   Name                    ExportedCommands
---------- -------   ----                    ----------------
Manifest   1.17.0.0  xWebAdministration
```

In the final step, *step 7*, you get the DSC resources contained in the `xWebAdministration` module, which looks like this:

```
PS C:\> Get-DscResource -Module xWebAdministration

ImplementedAs Name                  ModuleName          Version   Properties
------------- ----                  ----------          -------   ----------
PowerShell    xIisFeatureDelegation xWebAdministration  1.17.0.0  {OverrideMode, SectionName, DependsOn, PsDscRun...
PowerShell    xIisHandler           xWebAdministration  1.17.0.0  {Ensure, Name, DependsOn, PsDscRunAsCredential}
PowerShell    xIisLogging           xWebAdministration  1.17.0.0  {LogPath, DependsOn, LogFlags, LogFormat...}
PowerShell    xIisMimeTypeMapping   xWebAdministration  1.17.0.0  {Ensure, Extension, MimeType, DependsOn...}
PowerShell    xIisModule            xWebAdministration  1.17.0.0  {Name, Path, RequestPath, Verb...}
PowerShell    xSSLSettings          xWebAdministration  1.17.0.0  {Bindings, Name, DependsOn, Ensure...}
PowerShell    xWebApplication       xWebAdministration  1.17.0.0  {Name, PhysicalPath, WebAppPool, Website...}
PowerShell    xWebAppPool           xWebAdministration  1.17.0.0  {Name, autoShutdownExe, autoShutdownParams, aut...
PowerShell    xWebAppPoolDefaults   xWebAdministration  1.17.0.0  {ApplyTo, DependsOn, IdentityType, ManagedRunti...
PowerShell    xWebConfigKeyValue    xWebAdministration  1.17.0.0  {ConfigSection, Key, WebsitePath, DependsOn...}
PowerShell    xWebsite              xWebAdministration  1.17.0.0  {Name, ApplicationPool, ApplicationType, Authen...
PowerShell    xWebSiteDefaults      xWebAdministration  1.17.0.0  {ApplyTo, AllowSubDirConfig, DefaultApplication...
PowerShell    xWebVirtualDirectory  xWebAdministration  1.17.0.0  {Name, PhysicalPath, WebApplication, Website...}
```

There's more...

The `PSGallery` repository contains over 200 modules that in turn contain over 800 DSC resources. Some of these are just updates of the in-box resources although there is a huge range of additional resources for you to leverage.

It is worth noting that the source code for the Microsoft resources can be found on GitHub: `https://github.com/PowerShell/DscResources`. If you find areas that can be improved, the team is happy to accept pull requests that resolve errors or that improve the resource.

In *step 3*, you used one method of discovery—searching for a module containing some subject—in this case `IIS`. You could also search for DSC resources with a subject. Be creative in searching. And you can use the `-ModuleName` parameter and call the cmdlet like this: `Find-DscResource -ModuleName *IIS*`.

Using `Find-DscResource` with no parameters returns a large set of DSC resource objects. This takes both time and bandwidth. If you are looking for resources using your discovery skills, consider assigning the output of `Find-DscResource` to a variable and carry out discovery type searching using the in-memory variable. It's a lot faster.

In *step 5*, you use the `Install-Module` cmdlet to download and install the `xWebadministration` module on `SRV1`. The `Install-Module` cmdlet produces no output by default. You can get more information about details of what the cmdlet does by using the `-Verbose` parameter.

Using DSC with PSGallery resources

In the *Finding and installing DSC resources* recipe, you downloaded a module, `xWebAdministration`, which contains a number of DSC resources. In this recipe, you use the resources in this module to create an IIS web application. You create and run this recipe from `SRV1` to configure a web application on `SRV2`. You obtain the source files for the web application from `DC1`.

Getting ready

With this recipe, you configure IIS on SRV2 to support a simple web application—a similar application. To test this recipe, you need two source files, which you store on the ReskitApp share on your DC1 computer. The first, Index.Htm contains the following:

```
<!DOCTYPE html>
<html>
<head><meta charset="utf-8" />
<title>Main Page of The ReskitApp Application</title>
</head>
<body></p>
<br>
<center>
<b>Home Page for ReskitApp Application</b></p>
The home page of the ReskitApp application pushed by DSC to SRV2
</p><hr><br>
<a href="Http://SRV2/ReskitApp/Page2.Htm">
A reference to a second page - click to view page 2</a></center>
</body>
</html>
```

The second file, Page2.html, looks like this:

```
<!DOCTYPE html>
<html>
<head><meta charset="utf-8" />
<title>Page 2 of ReskitApp application</title>
</head>
<body>
<p><br><center>
<b>The Second Page</b>
</p>
The second page of the ReskitApp application pushed out by DSC to SRV2.
</p><hr><br>
<a href="HTTP://SRV2/ReskitApp/Index.htm">Click here to go back home!</a>
</center>
</body>
</html>
```

DSC requires that resources must be on both the computer you use to create the MOF file and on the target node. In this recipe, the module containing the resources used in the configuration statement, xWebAdministration, must be on SRV1 when you create the MOF file, and on SRV2 when you deploy the DSC configuration. If you attempt to configure the target node with resources that are not available on the target node, you see an error message like this:

```
PS C:\Windows\system32> Start-DscConfiguration -Path C:\DSC  -Verbose -Wait
VERBOSE: Perform operation 'Invoke CimMethod' with following parameters, ''methodName' = SendConfigurationApply,
'className' = MSFT_DSCLocalConfigurationManager,'namespaceName' = root/Microsoft/Windows/DesiredStateConfiguration'.
VERBOSE: An LCM method call arrived from computer SRV1 with user sid S-1-5-21-715049209-2702507345-667613206-500.
VERBOSE: [SRV2]: LCM:  [ Start  Set      ]
VERBOSE: [SRV2]: LCM:  [ End    Set      ]
The PowerShell DSC resource MSFT_xWebAppPool from module <xWebAdministration,1.17.0.0> does not exist at the PowerShell
module path nor is it registered as a WMI DSC resource.
    + CategoryInfo          : InvalidOperation: (root/Microsoft/...gurationManager:String) [], CimException
    + FullyQualifiedErrorId : DscResourceNotFound
    + PSComputerName        : SRV2

VERBOSE: Operation 'Invoke CimMethod' complete.
VERBOSE: Time taken for configuration job to complete is 1.841 seconds
```

You downloaded the xWebAdministration module in the *Finding and installing DSC resources* recipe. For this recipe, copy the module from SRV1 to SRV2 like this:

```
# on SRV1
Copy-Item -Path 'C:\Program
Files\WindowsPowerShell\Modules\xWebAdministration\' `
  -Destination '\\SRV2\C$\Program Files\WindowsPowerShell\Modules\' `
  -Recurse
```

Also, consider modifying the firewall on SRV2, like this:

```
Invoke-Command -ComputerName SRV2 {
   Set-NetFirewallRule -DisplayGroup 'File and Printer Sharing' `
                       -Enabled True}
```

How to do it...

1. Create and compile this configuration document:

```
Remove-Item '\\SRV2\c$\Windows\System32\configuration\*.mof' `
    -ErrorAction SilentlyContinue
Configuration  RKAppSRV2
{Remove-Item '\\SRV2\c$\Windows\System32\configuration\*.mof' `
          -ErrorAction SilentlyContinue
 Import-DscResource -ModuleName xWebAdministration
                                PSDesiredStateConfiguration
Node SRV2
{
 Windowsfeature IISSrv2
     { Ensure      = 'Present'
       Name        = 'Web-Server' }
 Windowsfeature IISSrvTools
     { Ensure      = 'Present'
       Name        = 'Web-Mgmt-Tools'
       DependsOn   = '[WindowsFeature]IISSrv2' }
 File   RKAppFiles
     { Ensure      = 'Present'
       Checksum    = 'ModifiedDate'
       Sourcepath  = '\\DC1\ReskitApp\'
       Type        = 'Directory'
       Recurse     = $true
       DestinationPath = 'C:\ReskitApp\'
       MatchSource = $true }
 xWebAppPool ReskitAppPool
     {  Name       = 'RKAppPool'
        Ensure     = 'Present'
        State      = 'Started'
        DependsOn  = '[File]RKAppFiles' }
 xWebApplication ReskitAppPool
     {  Website     = 'Default Web Site'
        WebAppPool  = 'RKAppPool'
        Name        = 'ReskitApp'
        PhysicalPath = 'C:\ReskitApp\'
        Ensure      = 'Present'
        DependsOn   = '[xWebAppPool]ReskitAppPool' }
 }
} # End of Config
```

2. Remove any old MOF files on both computers, then run the configuration block:

```
Remove-Item C:\DSC\* -Rec -Force
Remove-Item `
    '\\SRV2\c$\Windows\System32\configuration\*.mof' `
            -ErrorAction SilentlyContinue
RKAppSRV2 -OutputPath C:\DSC  | Out-Null
```

3. Deploy the configuration to SRV2:

```
Start-DscConfiguration -Path C:\DSC  -Verbose -Wait
```

4. Test result:

```
Start-Process 'http://SRV2/ReskitApp/'
```

How it works...

In *step 1*, you create and execute a configuration document RKAppSRV2. This configuration block configures SRV2 with two Windows features (Web-Server and Web-Mgmt-Tools), copies the application's source files from DC1 to SRV2, creates an application pool, RKAppPool, and finally creates an IIS web application, ReskitApp.

This step demonstrates the dependency mechanism in DSC. A dependency allows you to state that a particular resource configuration can only be performed after some other resource configuration has completed. For example, this configuration does not create a ReskitApp application until the RKAppPool application pool exists, and does not do either until the WindowsFeature resource has completed installing IIS.

In *step 2*, you run the configuration and create the relevant MOF file. *Step 2* generates no output.

In *step 3*, you deploy this configuration to SRV2. Assuming this is the first time you've run this configuration then the output looks like this:

```
PS C:\> Start-DscConfiguration -Path C:\DSC -Verbose -Wait
VERBOSE: Perform operation 'Invoke CimMethod' with following parameters, ''methodName' = SendConfigurationApply,
'className' = MSFT_DSCLocalConfigurationManager,'namespaceName' = root
/Microsoft/Windows/DesiredStateConfiguration'.
VERBOSE: An LCM method call arrived from computer SRV1 with user sid S-1-5-21-715049209-2702507345-667613206-500.
VERBOSE: [SRV2]: LCM:  [ Start  Set      ]
VERBOSE: [SRV2]: LCM:  [ Start  Resource ] [[WindowsFeature]IISSrv2]
VERBOSE: [SRV2]: LCM:  [ Start  Test     ] [[WindowsFeature]IISSrv2]
VERBOSE: [SRV2]:                            [[WindowsFeature]IISSrv2] The operation 'Get-WindowsFeature' started: Web-Server
VERBOSE: [SRV2]:                            [[WindowsFeature]IISSrv2] The operation 'Get-WindowsFeature' succeeded: Web-Server
VERBOSE: [SRV2]: LCM:  [ End    Test     ] [[WindowsFeature]IISSrv2] in 2.1870 seconds.
VERBOSE: [SRV2]: LCM:  [ Start  Set      ] [[WindowsFeature]IISSrv2]
VERBOSE: [SRV2]:                            [[WindowsFeature]IISSrv2] Installation started...
VERBOSE: [SRV2]:                            [[WindowsFeature]IISSrv2] Continue with installation?
VERBOSE: [SRV2]:                            [[WindowsFeature]IISSrv2] Prerequisite processing started...
VERBOSE: [SRV2]:                            [[WindowsFeature]IISSrv2] Prerequisite processing succeeded.
VERBOSE: [SRV2]:                            [[WindowsFeature]IISSrv2] Installation succeeded.
VERBOSE: [SRV2]:                            [[WindowsFeature]IISSrv2] Successfully installed the feature Web-Server.
VERBOSE: [SRV2]: LCM:  [ End    Set      ] [[WindowsFeature]IISSrv2] in 97.0810 seconds.
VERBOSE: [SRV2]: LCM:  [ End    Resource ] [[WindowsFeature]IISSrv2]
VERBOSE: [SRV2]: LCM:  [ Start  Resource ] [[WindowsFeature]IISSrvTools]
VERBOSE: [SRV2]: LCM:  [ Start  Test     ] [[WindowsFeature]IISSrvTools]
VERBOSE: [SRV2]:                            [[WindowsFeature]IISSrvTools] The operation 'Get-WindowsFeature' started: Web-Mgmt-Tools
VERBOSE: [SRV2]:                            [[WindowsFeature]IISSrvTools] The operation 'Get-WindowsFeature' succeeded: Web-Mgmt-Tools
VERBOSE: [SRV2]: LCM:  [ End    Test     ] [[WindowsFeature]IISSrvTools] in 3.7500 seconds.
VERBOSE: [SRV2]: LCM:  [ Start  Set      ] [[WindowsFeature]IISSrvTools]
VERBOSE: [SRV2]:                            [[WindowsFeature]IISSrvTools] Installation started...
VERBOSE: [SRV2]:                            [[WindowsFeature]IISSrvTools] Continue with installation?
VERBOSE: [SRV2]:                            [[WindowsFeature]IISSrvTools] Prerequisite processing started...
VERBOSE: [SRV2]:                            [[WindowsFeature]IISSrvTools] Prerequisite processing succeeded.
VERBOSE: [SRV2]:                            [[WindowsFeature]IISSrvTools] Installation succeeded.
VERBOSE: [SRV2]:                            [[WindowsFeature]IISSrvTools] Successfully installed the feature Web-Mgmt-Tools.
VERBOSE: [SRV2]: LCM:  [ End    Set      ] [[WindowsFeature]IISSrvTools] in 33.2590 seconds.
VERBOSE: [SRV2]: LCM:  [ End    Resource ] [[WindowsFeature]IISSrvTools]
VERBOSE: [SRV2]: LCM:  [ Start  Resource ] [[File]RKAppFiles]
VERBOSE: [SRV2]: LCM:  [ Start  Test     ] [[File]RKAppFiles]
VERBOSE: [SRV2]:                            [[File]RKAppFiles] The system cannot find the file specified.
VERBOSE: [SRV2]:                            [[File]RKAppFiles] The related file/directory is: C:\ReskitApp.
VERBOSE: [SRV2]:                            [[File]RKAppFiles] The network name cannot be found.
VERBOSE: [SRV2]:                            [[File]RKAppFiles] The related file/directory is: \\DC1\ReskitApp.
VERBOSE: [SRV2]:                            [[File]RKAppFiles] Building file list without using cache.
VERBOSE: [SRV2]: LCM:  [ End    Test     ] [[File]RKAppFiles] in 0.2650 seconds.
VERBOSE: [SRV2]: LCM:  [ Start  Set      ] [[File]RKAppFiles]
VERBOSE: [SRV2]:                            [[File]RKAppFiles] The system cannot find the file specified.
VERBOSE: [SRV2]:                            [[File]RKAppFiles] The related file/directory is: C:\ReskitApp.
VERBOSE: [SRV2]:                            [[File]RKAppFiles] The network name cannot be found.
VERBOSE: [SRV2]:                            [[File]RKAppFiles] The related file/directory is: \\DC1\ReskitApp.
VERBOSE: [SRV2]:                            [[File]RKAppFiles] Building file list without using cache.
VERBOSE: [SRV2]:                            [[File]RKAppFiles] Copying file \\DC1\ReskitApp\Index.htm to C:\ReskitApp\Index.htm.
VERBOSE: [SRV2]:                            [[File]RKAppFiles] Copying file \\DC1\ReskitApp\Page2.htm to C:\ReskitApp\Page2.htm.
VERBOSE: [SRV2]: LCM:  [ End    Set      ] [[File]RKAppFiles] in 0.0650 seconds.
VERBOSE: [SRV2]: LCM:  [ End    Resource ] [[File]RKAppFiles]
VERBOSE: [SRV2]: LCM:  [ Start  Resource ] [[xWebAppPool]ReskitAppPool]
VERBOSE: [SRV2]: LCM:  [ Start  Test     ] [[xWebAppPool]ReskitAppPool]
VERBOSE: [SRV2]:                            [[xWebAppPool]ReskitAppPool] Application pool "RKAppPool" was not found.
VERBOSE: [SRV2]:                            [[xWebAppPool]ReskitAppPool] The "Ensure" state of application pool "RKAppPool" does not match the desired state.
VERBOSE: [SRV2]:                            [[xWebAppPool]ReskitAppPool] The target resource is not in the desired state.
VERBOSE: [SRV2]: LCM:  [ End    Test     ] [[xWebAppPool]ReskitAppPool] in 2.4550 seconds.
VERBOSE: [SRV2]: LCM:  [ Start  Set      ] [[xWebAppPool]ReskitAppPool]
VERBOSE: [SRV2]:                            [[xWebAppPool]ReskitAppPool] Performing the operation "Set-TargetResource" on target "RKAppPool".
VERBOSE: [SRV2]:                            [[xWebAppPool]ReskitAppPool] Application pool "RKAppPool" was not found.
VERBOSE: [SRV2]:                            [[xWebAppPool]ReskitAppPool] Creating application pool "RKAppPool".
VERBOSE: [SRV2]:                            [[xWebAppPool]ReskitAppPool] Application pool "RKAppPool" was found.
VERBOSE: [SRV2]: LCM:  [ End    Set      ] [[xWebAppPool]ReskitAppPool] in 1.2330 seconds.
VERBOSE: [SRV2]: LCM:  [ End    Resource ] [[xWebAppPool]ReskitAppPool]
VERBOSE: [SRV2]: LCM:  [ Start  Resource ] [[xWebApplication]ReskitAppPool]
VERBOSE: [SRV2]: LCM:  [ Start  Test     ] [[xWebApplication]ReskitAppPool]
VERBOSE: [SRV2]:                            [[xWebApplication]ReskitAppPool] Web application "ReskitApp" is absent and should not absent.
VERBOSE: [SRV2]: LCM:  [ End    Test     ] [[xWebApplication]ReskitAppPool] in 0.2030 seconds.
VERBOSE: [SRV2]: LCM:  [ Start  Set      ] [[xWebApplication]ReskitAppPool]
VERBOSE: [SRV2]:                            [[xWebApplication]ReskitAppPool] Creating new Web application "ReskitApp".
VERBOSE: [SRV2]: LCM:  [ End    Set      ] [[xWebApplication]ReskitAppPool] in 0.5890 seconds.
VERBOSE: [SRV2]: LCM:  [ End    Resource ] [[xWebApplication]ReskitAppPool]
VERBOSE: [SRV2]: LCM:  [ Start  Resource ] [[Log]Completed]
VERBOSE: [SRV2]: LCM:  [ Start  Test     ] [[Log]Completed]
VERBOSE: [SRV2]: LCM:  [ End    Test     ] [[Log]Completed] in 0.0000 seconds.
VERBOSE: [SRV2]: LCM:  [ Start  Set      ] [[Log]Completed]
VERBOSE: [SRV2]:                            [[Log]Completed] Finished running the RKAPP DSC against SRV2
VERBOSE: [SRV2]: LCM:  [ End    Set      ] [[Log]Completed] in 0.0000 seconds.
VERBOSE: [SRV2]: LCM:  [ End    Resource ] [[Log]Completed]
VERBOSE: [SRV2]: LCM:  [ End    Set      ]
VERBOSE: [SRV2]: LCM:  [ End    Set      ] in 147.5190 seconds.
VERBOSE: Operation 'Invoke CimMethod' complete.
VERBOSE: Time taken for configuration job to complete is 148.871 seconds.
```

Once the DSC configuration has been pushed successfully to SRV2, you can use the new web application. In *step 4*, you generate an `Internet Explorer` object, navigate the object to the root of the web application, then show the root page, which looks like this:

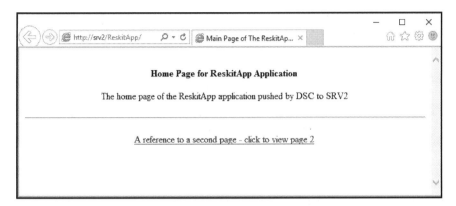

If you click on the link at the bottom of this page, you bring up the application's second page:

There's more...

This recipe uses the push model for DSC deployment. In this recipe, you manually copied the xWebAdministration to SRV2 as part of the recipe setup. If you use a pull server model to deploy DSC, target nodes can download the necessary resources from the pull server, which greatly simplifies deployment of DSC resources. The two recipes later in this chapter (Implement an SMB pull server and Implement a DSC web pull server) show how to configure a pull server.

The configuration you create in *step 1* uses the dependency mechanism in DSC. A dependency allows you to state that a particular resource configuration can only be performed after some other resource configuration has completed. For example, this configuration does not create a `ReskitApp` application until the `RKAppPool` application pool exists, and does not do either until the `WindowsFeature` resource has completed installing IIS.

Configuring Local Configuration Manager

The LCM is a key component of DSC that initially shipped within PowerShell V4. LCM is a Windows service that runs on each DSC target node and is responsible for receiving configuration information and ensuring the node is configured in the desired state (and remains that way).

The LCM has two mechanisms for desired state delivery: *push* and *pull*. The earlier recipes in this chapter demonstrate the push model: you create a configuration and its related MOF file on one node, and push that configuration to another node. In the pull model, you configure the node with details of where and how to find a pull server. Once configured, a node can pull configurations from the configured pull server.

With this recipe, which you run on SRV2, you configure the LCM based on PowerShell V5/5.1. PowerShell V4 used a different approach to configuring the LCM. In this recipe, you configure the LCM on SRV2 and set up SRV2 to use SRV1 as an SMB pull server. You setup SRV1 itself in the next recipe, *Implement and SMB pull server*.

Getting ready

In this recipe, you use a special type of configuration known as a meta-configuration. You use the meta-configuration statement to configure DSC on a node. You run this recipe on the target node, SRV2.

If you have already used any DSC configuration against SRV2, for example, based on other recipes in this chapter, you should clear the DSC configuration. To do this, do the following on SRV2:

```
Remove-Item -Path 'C:\Windows\System32\configuration\*.mof'
```

You should also create and two local folders on SRV1, C:\DSC (\\SRV1\DSC), and C:\DSCResouruce (\\SRV1\DSCResource) which are references in the following *step 1*.

How to do it...

1. Create and run the meta-configuration for LCM on SRV2:

```
[DSCLocalConfigurationManager()]
Configuration LCMConfig
{
    Node localhost
    {
      Settings
        {
            ConfigurationModeFrequencyMins = '30'
            ConfigurationMode = 'ApplyAndAutoCorrect'
            RebootNodeIfNeeded = $true
            ActionAfterReboot = 'ContinueConfiguration'
            RefreshMOde = 'Pull'
            RefreshFrequencyMins = '45'
            AllowModuleOverwrite = $true
            ConfigurationID = '5d79ee6e-0420-4c98-9cc3-
            9f696901a816'
        }
    ConfigurationRepositoryShare PullServer
        {
            SourcePath = '\\SRV1\DSCConfiguration'
        }

    ResourceRepositoryShare ResourceServer
        {
            SourcePath = '\\SRV1\DSCResource'
        }
    }
 }
```

2. Create the meta-configuration MOF on SRV2:

```
New-Item -Path c:\DSC -ErrorAction SilentlyContinue
Remove-Item C:\DSC -Recurse | Remove-Item -Force
LCMConfig -OutputPath C:\DSC
```

3. Configure `SRV2`:

```
Set-DscLocalConfigurationManager -Path C:\DSC
```

4. Examine LCM configuration:

```
Get-DscLocalConfigurationManager
```

5. Examine pull server information:

```
Get-DscLocalConfigurationManager |
    Select-Object -ExpandProperty
ConfigurationDownloadManagers
Get-DscLocalConfigurationManager |
    Select-Object -ExpandProperty ResourceModulemanagers
```

How it works...

In *step 1*, you create a meta-configuration block that defines the LCM configuration for `SRV2`. The meta-configuration defines `SRV2` to be configured using an SMB share for both the download of configuration statements and for the download of resources not on the target node. This configuration checks every 45 minutes to see if the checksum file has changed and if so it re-applies the updated MOF file. The configuration block downloads resources from `\\SRV1\DSCResource` and specifies that the LCM updates DSC resource modules updated on `SRV1`. There is no output from this step.

In *step 2*, you ensure that `SRV2` has local `C:\DSC` folder, then compile the meta-configuration. As you can see here, the output file is `C:\DSC\SRV2.meta.mof`:

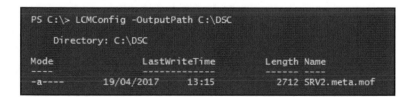

In *step 3*, you use the `Set-DscLocalConfigurationManager` cmdlet to set the LCM configuration on `SRV2`. This step generates no output.

In *step 4*, you use the `Get-DscLocalConfigurationManager` to review the LCM settings. The output of this cmdlet looks like this:

```
PS C:\Windows\system32> Get-DscLocalConfigurationManager

ActionAfterReboot                : ContinueConfiguration
AgentId                          : 9CE04E83-1AE3-11E7-836B-B187B8E24E90
AllowModuleOverWrite             : True
CertificateID                    :
ConfigurationDownloadManagers    : {[ConfigurationRepositoryShare]PullServer}
ConfigurationID                  : 5d79ee6e-0420-4c98-9cc3-9f696901a816
ConfigurationMode                : ApplyAndAutoCorrect
ConfigurationModeFrequencyMins   : 30
Credential                       :
DebugMode                        : {NONE}
DownloadManagerCustomData        :
DownloadManagerName              :
LCMCompatibleVersions            : {1.0, 2.0}
LCMState                         : Idle
LCMStateDetail                   :
LCMVersion                       : 2.0
StatusRetentionTimeInDays        : 10
SignatureValidationPolicy        : NONE
SignatureValidations             : {}
MaximumDownloadSizeMB            : 500
PartialConfigurations            :
RebootNodeIfNeeded               : True
RefreshFrequencyMins             : 45
RefreshMode                      : Pull
ReportManagers                   : {}
ResourceModuleManagers           : {[ResourceRepositoryShare]ResourceServer}
```

You can also run this cmdlet before *step 3* so as to see the difference before and after applying the local configuration.

In *step 5*, you expand the object returned from `Get-DSCLocalConfigurationManager` to discover the source path settings for DSC resources and DSC configurations, as follows:

```
PS C:\> Get-DscLocalConfigurationManager |
          Select-Object -ExpandProperty ConfigurationDownloadManagers

ResourceId    : [ConfigurationRepositoryShare]PullServer
SourceInfo    : ::22::6::ConfigurationRepositoryShare
Credential    :
SourcePath    : \\SRV1\DSCConfiguration

PS C:\> Get-DscLocalConfigurationManager |
          Select-Object -ExpandProperty ResourceModulemanagers

ResourceId    : [ResourceRepositoryShare]ResourceServer
SourceInfo    : ::27::6::ResourceRepositoryShare
Credential    :
SourcePath    : \\SRV1\DSCResource
```

There's more...

This recipe just configures the LCM on a single node, in this case SRV2. Unless you setup the pull server on SRV1, this recipe has no real effect on SRV2.

 For information on the settings you can configure when you setup the LCM on a node, see this MSDN article:
`https://msdn.microsoft.com/en-us/powershell/dsc/metaconfig`.

Implementing a SMB pull server

There are two different types of DSC pull server you implement: SMB-based and web-based. The SMB-based pull server approach is most useful on a private routable network, one where all nodes can reach the centralized configuration and resource pull server shares. For high availability, you could set up an SMB pull server on a scale out file server.

In DSC, MOF files are used to communicate the desired state to a node. The LCM on that node, in effect, does anything the MOF file says. MOF files are ,at rest, just plain text documents and are not encrypted or signed. If your private network is secure, then the SMB pull server is easier to set up and configure. If security is an issue, consider using the web server pull server approach and configure it with HTTPS.

In the previous recipe, *Configuring Local Configuration Manager*, you configured a node, SRV2 to pull configurations from a DSC pull server. In this recipe, you configure another node, SRV1, to be the pull server. This recipe also creates a new configuration for use in the pull server scenario and tests using the pull server to apply the new configuration.

When you configure a node to pull from an SMB-based pull server, you configure that node with both a GUID (`ConfigurationID`) and a SMB share path where the LCM can find configuration MOF files. The MOF file that you deploy to a node is named using the GUID (that is `<guid>.mof`).

In the earlier recipe, *Configuring Local Configuration Manager*, you configured SRV2 with a ConfigurationID `5d79ee6e-0420-4c98-9cc3-9f696901a816` and you specified that LCM pull configurations from the SMB pull server located at `\\SRV1\DSCConfiguration`. Based on this, the LCM on SRV2 would therefore look for the file `\\SRV1\DSCConfiguration\5d79ee6e-0420-4c98-9cc3-9f696901a816.mof` plus the related checksum file.

Getting ready

This recipe is run on SRV1 and provides a DSC configuration for SRV2. SRV2 was previously setup to use SRV1 as its pull server in the *Configuring Local Configuration Manager* recipe. You also need the xSmbShare resource installed on SRV1.

How to do it...

1. Create and execute the configuration for SRV1:

```
{
Import-DscResource -ModuleName PSDesiredStateConfiguration,
                                  xSmbShare
File ConfigFolder
    { DestinationPath = 'C:\DSCConfiguration'
      Type = 'Directory'
      Ensure = 'Present' }
File ResourceFolder
    { DestinationPath = 'C:\DSCResource'
      Type = 'Directory'
      Ensure = 'Present' }
xSmbShare DscConfiguration
    { Name = 'DSCConfiguration'
      Path = 'C:\DSCConfiguration\'
      DependsOn = '[File]ConfigFolder'
      Description = 'DSC Configuration Share'
      Ensure = 'Present' }
xSmbShare DscResource
    { Name = 'DSCResource'
      Path = 'C:\DSCResource'
      DependsOn = '[File]ResourceFolder'
      Description = 'DSC Resource Share'
      Ensure = 'Present' }
}
```

2. Remove existing MOF files then create the MOF file:

```
New-Item -Path C:\DSC -ItemType Directory `
         -ErrorAction SilentlyContinue | Out-Null
Get-ChildItem -Path C:\DSC | Remove-Item -Force | Out-Null
Remove-Item '-Path C:\Windows\System32\configuration\*.mof' `
           -ErrorAction SilentlyContinue
PullSrv1 -OutputPath C:\DSC
```

3. Configure the local host:

```
Start-DscConfiguration -Path C:\DSC -Wait -Verbose
```

4. Get the SMBShares on SRV1:

```
Get-SMBShare -Name DSC*
```

5. Create the new configuration for SRV2:

```
Configuration TelnetSRV2
  {
Import-DscResource -ModuleName 'PSDesiredStateConfiguration'
  Node SRV2
    { WindowsFeature TelnetSRV2
    { Name = 'Telnet-Client'
      Ensure = 'Present' }}}
```

6. Compile the configuration:

```
TelnetSRV2 -OutputPath C:\DSCConfiguration
```

7. Rename the MOF file with the GUID name:

```
$Guid = '5d79ee6e-0420-4c98-9cc3-9f696901a816'
Rename-Item -Path 'C:\DSCConfiguration\SRV2.mof' `
            -NewName "C:\DSCConfiguration\$Guid.mof"
```

8. Create the MOF checksum file:

```
New-DscChecksum -Path C:\DSCConfiguration
```

9. View the MOF and checksum files:

```
Get-ChildItem C:\DSCConfiguration
```

10. Check the presence of the Telnet-Client on SRV2:

```
Get-WindowsFeature -Name Telnet-Client `
                   -ComputerName SRV2
```

How it works...

In *step 1*, you create and execute a configuration block on SRV1. The configuration block ensures two folders exist (C:\DSCConfiguration and C:\DSCResource) and they are both shared folders. This configuration uses the File and xSMBShare resources (which you downloaded and installed on SRV1 prior to running this step, which generates no output.

In *step 2*, you ensure you have the C:\DSC folder created and that it's empty, then run the configuration which creates a MOF file to configure SRV1 as per the configuration statement in *step 1*. This step produces output like this:

In *step 3*, you apply the configuration to SRV1, setting up the two DSC folder shares. The output is like this:

```
PS C:\> Start-DscConfiguration -Path C:\DSC -Wait -Verbose
VERBOSE: Perform operation 'Invoke CimMethod' with following parameters, ''methodName' = SendConfigurationApply,
'className' = MSFT_DSCLocalConfigurationManager, 'namesp
aceName' = root/Microsoft/Windows/DesiredStateConfiguration'.
VERBOSE: An LCM method call arrived from computer SRV1 with user sid S-1-5-21-715049209-2702507345-667613206-500.
VERBOSE: [SRV1]: LCM:  [ Start  Set      ]
VERBOSE: [SRV1]: LCM:  [ Start  Resource ]  [[File]ConfigFolder]
VERBOSE: [SRV1]: LCM:  [ Start  Test     ]  [[File]ConfigFolder]
VERBOSE: [SRV1]:                            [[File]ConfigFolder] The system cannot find the file specified.
VERBOSE: [SRV1]:                            [[File]ConfigFolder] The related file/directory is: C:\DSCConfiguration.
VERBOSE: [SRV1]: LCM:  [ End    Test     ]  [[File]ConfigFolder]  in 0.0000 seconds.
VERBOSE: [SRV1]: LCM:  [ Start  Set      ]  [[File]ConfigFolder]
VERBOSE: [SRV1]:                            [[File]ConfigFolder] The system cannot find the file specified.
VERBOSE: [SRV1]:                            [[File]ConfigFolder] The related file/directory is: C:\DSCConfiguration.
VERBOSE: [SRV1]: LCM:  [ End    Set      ]  [[File]ConfigFolder]  in 0.0310 seconds.
VERBOSE: [SRV1]: LCM:  [ End    Resource ]  [[File]ConfigFolder]
VERBOSE: [SRV1]: LCM:  [ Start  Resource ]  [[File]ResourceFolder]
VERBOSE: [SRV1]: LCM:  [ Start  Test     ]  [[File]ResourceFolder]
VERBOSE: [SRV1]:                            [[File]ResourceFolder] The system cannot find the file specified.
VERBOSE: [SRV1]:                            [[File]ResourceFolder] The related file/directory is: C:\DscResource.
VERBOSE: [SRV1]: LCM:  [ End    Test     ]  [[File]ResourceFolder]  in 0.0000 seconds.
VERBOSE: [SRV1]: LCM:  [ Start  Set      ]  [[File]ResourceFolder]
VERBOSE: [SRV1]:                            [[File]ResourceFolder] The system cannot find the file specified.
VERBOSE: [SRV1]:                            [[File]ResourceFolder] The related file/directory is: C:\DscResource.
VERBOSE: [SRV1]: LCM:  [ End    Set      ]  [[File]ResourceFolder]  in 0.0160 seconds.
VERBOSE: [SRV1]: LCM:  [ End    Resource ]  [[File]ResourceFolder]
VERBOSE: [SRV1]: LCM:  [ Start  Resource ]  [[xSmbShare]DscConfiguration]
VERBOSE: [SRV1]: LCM:  [ Start  Test     ]  [[xSmbShare]DscConfiguration]
VERBOSE: [SRV1]:                            [[xSmbShare]DscConfiguration] Share with name DSCConfiguration does not exist
VERBOSE: [SRV1]: LCM:  [ End    Test     ]  [[xSmbShare]DscConfiguration]  in 0.5620 seconds.
VERBOSE: [SRV1]: LCM:  [ Start  Set      ]  [[xSmbShare]DscConfiguration]
VERBOSE: [SRV1]:                            [[xSmbShare]DscConfiguration] Creating share DSCConfiguration to ensure it is Present
VERBOSE: [SRV1]: LCM:  [ End    Set      ]  [[xSmbShare]DscConfiguration]  in 0.1260 seconds.
VERBOSE: [SRV1]: LCM:  [ End    Resource ]  [[xSmbShare]DscConfiguration]
VERBOSE: [SRV1]: LCM:  [ Start  Resource ]  [[xSmbShare]DscResource]
VERBOSE: [SRV1]: LCM:  [ Start  Test     ]  [[xSmbShare]DscResource]
VERBOSE: [SRV1]:                            [[xSmbShare]DscResource] Share with name DSCResource does not exist
VERBOSE: [SRV1]: LCM:  [ End    Test     ]  [[xSmbShare]DscResource]  in 0.0150 seconds.
VERBOSE: [SRV1]: LCM:  [ Start  Set      ]  [[xSmbShare]DscResource]
VERBOSE: [SRV1]:                            [[xSmbShare]DscResource] Creating share DSCResource to ensure it is Present
VERBOSE: [SRV1]: LCM:  [ End    Set      ]  [[xSmbShare]DscResource]  in 0.0620 seconds.
VERBOSE: [SRV1]: LCM:  [ End    Resource ]  [[xSmbShare]DscResource]
VERBOSE: [SRV1]: LCM:  [ End    Set      ]
VERBOSE: [SRV1]: LCM:  [ End    Set      ]  in  2.1920 seconds.
VERBOSE: Operation 'Invoke CimMethod' complete.
VERBOSE: Time taken for configuration job to complete is 2.652 seconds
```

In *step 4*, you examine the SMBShares created by *step 3* with output like this:

```
PS C:\> Get-SMBShare -Name DSC*

Name                 ScopeName Path                   Description
----                 --------- ----                   -----------
DSCConfiguration     *         C:\DscConfiguration    DSC Configuration Share
DSCResource          *         C:\DscResource         DSC Resource Share
```

In *step 5*, you create a new configuration block, TelnetSRV, which installs the telnet client on SRV2. Executing this configuration block produces no output. In *step 6*, you execute the configuration, which generates a MOF file like this:

```
PS C:\> TelnetSRV2 -OutputPath C:\DSCConfiguration

    Directory: C:\DSCConfiguration

Mode                LastWriteTime         Length Name
----                -------------         ------ ----
-a----    19/04/2017      21:32             1858 SRV2.mof
```

In *step 7*, you rename the MOF file, using the configuration ID (the GUID) that you specified when configuring SRV2 to pull from SRV1. The MOF file generated in *step 6*, is renamed to 5d79ee6e-0420-4c98-9cc3-9f696901a816.mof. Then, in *step 8*, you create the MOF checksum file, which generates no output. In *step 9*, as follows:

```
PS C:\> Get-ChildItem C:\DSCConfiguration

    Directory: C:\DSCConfiguration

Mode        LastWriteTime   Length Name
----        -------------   ------ ----
-a----   19/04/2017  20:56    1858 5d79ee6e-0420-4c98-9cc3-9f696901a816.MOF
-a----   19/04/2017  21:23      64 5d79ee6e-0420-4c98-9cc3-9f696901a816.MOF.checksum
```

Once you have placed the two files (the MOF file and the checksum file), you need to wait for the target server to pull the configuration. In the earlier recipe, you set the refresh time to 45 minutes, thus you may need to wait that long before SRV2 pulls the configuration from SRV1 and installs the telnet client. Once this time period has elapsed, you can check on SRV2 to see that DSC has installed the telnet client.

There's more...

If, in *step 1*, you had not downloaded the xSMBShare module (containing the xSMBShare resource), running the PullSrv1 configuration block would generate an error indicating that the resource cannot be found.

Implementing a DSC web-based pull server

Deploying a DSC web-based pull server is more complex than deploying an SMB pull server. The SMB-based pull server is simple: just create a couple of shares and place the relevant files on that share. The web server approach requires you to also load IIS, install the DSC service, and configure the service, as well as placing the MOF files, resources, and any relevant checksums on the web server. Of course, in both cases, you need to configure each node's LCM.

You deploy a web based pull server to provide a pull client with both resources and configuration MOF files. Unlike an SMB-based pull server, a web-based pull server also provides reporting capabilities enabling a pull client to report status back to the reporting server. Reporting is not available using an SMB-based pull server.

To simplify the creation of a web-based DSC pull server, you can use the xPSDesiredStateConfiguration module DSC resource. You download this resource from PSGallery. This resource greatly simplifies configuring a node to be a DSC pull server and to be a reporting server.

As with SMB-based pull servers, once you have set up a DSC web pull server, you need to configure the clients to pull configurations/resources from the pull server and send reporting information to the report servers.

Setting up a DSC web based pull server changed between PowerShell V4 and V5. This recipe is based on PowerShell V5.

Getting ready

This recipe uses two servers: SRV1 and SRV2. SRV1 is the pull server—this recipe configures the DSC web service on SRV1 and configures SRV2 to pull configurations and resources from the pull server.

Before using this recipe, you need to download the xPSDesiredStateConfigurtion module from the PSGallery, as follows:

```
Install-Module -Name xPSDesiredStateConfiguration
```

How to do it...

1. Create a self-signed certificate for SRV1:

```
$DscCert = New-SelfSignedCertificate `
                -CertStoreLocation 'CERT:\LocalMachine\MY' `
                -DnsName 'SRV1'
```

2. Copy the certificate to the root store on SRV2:

```
$Sb = {
  Param ($Rootcert)
  $C = 'System.Security.Cryptography.X509Certificates.X509Store'
  $Store = New-Object -TypeName $C `
                      -ArgumentList 'Root','LocalMachine'
  $Store.Open('ReadWrite')
  $Store.Add($Rootcert)
  $Store.Close()
}
Invoke-Command -ScriptBlock $Sb -ComputerName SRV2 `
                -ArgumentList $DscCert -Verbose
```

3. Check the certificate on SRV2:

```
Invoke-Command -ScriptBlock {Get-ChildItem `
 -Path Cert:\LocalMachine\root |
                    Where-Object Subject -Match 'SRV1'} `
                -ComputerName SRV2
```

4. Create and compile DSCService configuration:

```
Configuration WebPullSrv1 {
Param ([String] $CertThumbPrint)
Import-DscResource -Module PSDesiredStateConfiguration,
                           xPSDesiredStateConfiguration
Node SRV1 {
    File DSCConfig-Folder{
        DestinationPath = 'C:\DSCConfiguration'
          Ensure = 'Present'
          Type = 'Directory' }
```

```
        File DSCResource-Folder{
            DestinationPath = 'C:\DSCResource'
            Ensure = 'Present'
            Type = 'Directory' }
        WindowsFeature DSCService {
            Ensure = 'Present'
            Name = 'DSC-Service' }
        xDscWebService WebPullSRV1 {
            Ensure = 'Present'
            EndpointName = 'PSDSCPullServer'
            Port = 8080
            PhysicalPath = 'C:\inetpub\wwwroot\PSDSCPullServer'
            CertificateThumbPrint = $CertThumbPrint
            ConfigurationPath = 'C:\DSCConfiguration'
            ModulePath = 'C:\DSCResource'
            State = 'Started'
            DependsOn = '[WindowsFeature]DSCService'
            UseSecurityBestPractices = $true }
        File RegistrationKeyFile {
            Ensure = 'Present'
            Type = 'File'
            DestinationPath =
'C:\ProgramFiles\WindowsPowerShell\DscService\RegistrationKeys.txt'
            Contents = '5d79ee6e-0420-4c98-9cc3-9f696901a816'
            }}}
```

5. Remove existing MOF files then create the MOF file:

```
New-Item -Path C:\DSC -ItemType Directory `
        -ErrorAction SilentlyContinue | Out-Null
Get-ChildItem -Path C:\DSC -File | Remove-Item -Force | Out-Null
Remove-Item -Path 'C:\Windows\System32\configuration\*.mof' `
        -ErrorAction SilentlyContinue
WebPullSrv1 -OutputPath C:\DSC `
        -CertThumbPrint $DscCert.Thumbprint
```

6. Add the web service to SRV1:

```
Start-DscConfiguration -Path C:\DSC -Wait -Verbose
```

7. Check on the results:

```
$IE = New-Object -ComObject InterNetExplorer.Application
$Uri = 'https://SRV1:8080/PSDSCPullServer.svc/'
$IE.Navigate2($Uri)
$IE.Visible = $TRUE
```

8. Create a configuration to make SRV2 pull from SRV1:

```
[DSCLocalConfigurationManager()]
Configuration SRV2WebPull {
param ([string] $Guid)
Node SRV2 {
 Settings
    { RefreshMode = 'Pull'
      ConfigurationID = $guid
      RefreshFrequencyMins = 30
      RebootNodeIfNeeded = $true }
 ConfigurationRepositoryWeb DSCPullSrv
    { ServerURL = 'https://SRV1:8080/PSDSCPullServer.svc' }
 ResourceRepositoryWeb DSCResourceSrv
    { ServerURL = 'https://SRV1:8080/PSDSCPullServer.svc' }
 ReportServerWeb DSCReportSrv
    { ServerURL = 'https://SRV1:8080/PSDSCPullServer.svc' }
 }
}
```

9. Create MOF to configure DSC LCM on SRV2:

```
Remove-Item C:\DSC\* -Recurse -Force
$Guid = '5d79ee6e-0420-4c98-9cc3-9f696901a816'
SRV2WebPull -Guid $Guid -OutputPath C:\DSC
```

10. Configure LCM on SRV2:

```
Set-DscLocalConfigurationManager -ComputerName SRV2 `
                                 -Path C:\DSC `
                                 -Verbose
```

11. Create and compile a configuration that ensures the telnet client is installed on SRV2:

```
Configuration TelnetSRV2
{
Import-DscResource -ModuleName 'PSDesiredStateConfiguration'
Node SRV2
  {
    WindowsFeature TelnetClient
    { Name = 'Telnet-Client'
      Ensure = 'Present' }
  }
}
```

12. Create the MOF file for this configuration:

```
Remove-Item -Path C:\DSCConfiguration -Recurse -Force
TelnetSRV2 -OutputPath C:\DSCConfiguration
```

13. Rename the file and create the checksum files:

```
Rename-Item -Path C:\DSCConfiguration\SRV2.mof `
            -NewName C:\DSCConfiguration\$Guid.MOF
New-DscChecksum -Path C:\DSCConfiguration
Get-ChildItem C:\DSCConfiguration
```

14. Update the configuration on SRV2 (based on pulling from SRV1):

```
Update-DscConfiguration -ComputerName SRV2 -Wait -Verbose
```

15. Review details of the DSC configuration on SRV2:

```
$Session = New-CimSession -ComputerName SRV2
Get-DscConfiguration -CimSession $Session
```

How it works...

In *step 1*, you create a self-signed certificate with a subject name of SRV1. The New-SelfSignedCertificate creates this certificate in the local machine's MY folder. There is no output from this step, but the certificate is stored in the $DscCert variable for use in the next step. This recipe uses this certificate to provide SSL access to the DSC web service.

In *step 2*, you copy the certificate to the root store on SRV2. Unfortunately, the certificate provider in PowerShell does not support copying a certificate from one store to another, so you need to dip down into the .NET framework to add the self-signed certificate held in $DscCert to the SRV2 server's local machine trusted root store. This has the effect of enabling SRV2 to trust the SSL certificate from SRV1 during DSC operations (for example, downloading configurations).

In *step 3*, you check to see that the certificate is now contained in the trusted root store for the local machine's store on SRV2. The output looks like this:

```
PS C:\> Invoke-Command -ScriptBlock {Get-ChildItem -Path Cert:\LocalMachine\root |
          Where Subject -Match 'SRV1'} -ComputerName SRV2

  PSParentPath: Microsoft.PowerShell.Security\Certificate::LocalMachine\root

Thumbprint                                Subject    PSComputerName
----------                                -------    --------------
57BEA3F06B515B15C8CB97F4DD2861F80840CA39  CN=SRV1    SRV2
```

In *step 4*, you create and compile a DSC configuration block, WebPullSrv1, to configure SRV1 to be a DSC web-based pull server. There is no output from this step.

After removing any old MOF files, in *step 5* you create a MOF file for the WebPullSrv1 configuration block. The output looks like this:

```
PS C:\> New-Item -Path C:\DSC -ItemType Directory `
                  -ErrorAction SilentlyContinue | Out-Null
PS C:\> Get-ChildItem -Path C:\DSC | Remove-Item -Force | Out-Null
PS C:\> Remove-Item -Path 'C:\Windows\System32\configuration\*.mof' `
                  -ErrorAction SilentlyContinue
PS C:\> WebPullSrv1 -OutputPath C:\DSC

    Directory: C:\DSC

Mode        LastWriteTime    Length  Name
----        -------------    ------  ----

-a----      20/04/2017 4:20    4104  SRV1.mof
```

Once the MOF file has been created, in *step 6*, you add the DSC pull web service to SRV1. The output looks like this:

```
PS Cert:\LocalMachine\my> Start-DscConfiguration -Path C:\DSC -WAIT -Verbose
VERBOSE: Perform operation 'Invoke CimMethod' with following parameters, ''methodName' = SendConfigurationApply,
'className' = MSFT_DSCLocalConfigurationManager,'name
spaceName' = root/Microsoft/Windows/DesiredStateConfiguration'.
VERBOSE: An LCM method call arrived from computer SRV1 with user sid S-1-5-21-715049209-2702507345-667613206-500.
VERBOSE: [SRV1]: LCM:  [ Start  Set      ]
VERBOSE: [SRV1]: LCM:  [ Start  Resource ]  [[WindowsFeature]DSCService]
VERBOSE: [SRV1]: LCM:  [ Start  Test     ]  [[WindowsFeature]DSCService]
VERBOSE: [SRV1]:                            [[WindowsFeature]DSCService] The operation 'Get-WindowsFeature' started: DSC-Service
VERBOSE: [SRV1]:                            [[WindowsFeature]DSCService] The operation 'Get-WindowsFeature' succeeded: DSC-Service
VERBOSE: [SRV1]: LCM:  [ End    Test     ]  [[WindowsFeature]DSCService] in 3.3520 seconds.
VERBOSE: [SRV1]: LCM:  [ Skip   Set      ]  [[WindowsFeature]DSCService]
VERBOSE: [SRV1]: LCM:  [ End    Resource ]  [[WindowsFeature]DSCService]
VERBOSE: [SRV1]: LCM:  [ Start  Resource ]  [[xDSCWebService]WebPullSRV1]
VERBOSE: [SRV1]: LCM:  [ Start  Test     ]  [[xDSCWebService]WebPullSRV1]
VERBOSE: [SRV1]:                            [[xDSCWebService]WebPullSRV1] Check Ensure
VERBOSE: [SRV1]:                            [[xDSCWebService]WebPullSRV1] The Website PSDSCPullServer is not present
VERBOSE: [SRV1]: LCM:  [ End    Test     ]  [[xDSCWebService]WebPullSRV1] in 0.8750 seconds.
VERBOSE: [SRV1]: LCM:  [ Start  Set      ]  [[xDSCWebService]WebPullSRV1]
VERBOSE: [SRV1]:                            [[xDSCWebService]WebPullSRV1] Create the IIS endpoint
VERBOSE: [SRV1]:                            [[xDSCWebService]WebPullSRV1] Setting up endpoint at - https://SRV1:8080/PSDSCPullServer.svc
VERBOSE: [SRV1]:                            [[xDSCWebService]WebPullSRV1] Verify that the certificate with the provided thumbprint exists in CE
RT:\LocalMachine\MY\
VERBOSE: [SRV1]:                            [[xDSCWebService]WebPullSRV1] Checking IIS requirements
VERBOSE: [SRV1]:                            [[xDSCWebService]WebPullSRV1] Delete the App Pool if it exists
VERBOSE: [SRV1]:                            [[xDSCWebService]WebPullSRV1] Remove the site if it already exists
VERBOSE: [SRV1]:                            [[xDSCWebService]WebPullSRV1] Create the bin folder for deploying custom dependent binaries require
d by the endpoint
VERBOSE: [SRV1]:                            [[xDSCWebService]WebPullSRV1] Adding App Pool
VERBOSE: [SRV1]:                            [[xDSCWebService]WebPullSRV1] Set App Pool Properties
VERBOSE: [SRV1]:                            [[xDSCWebService]WebPullSRV1] Add and Set Site Properties
VERBOSE: [SRV1]:                            [[xDSCWebService]WebPullSRV1] p11
VERBOSE: [SRV1]:                            [[xDSCWebService]WebPullSRV1] Enabling firewall exception for port 8080
VERBOSE: [SRV1]:                            [[xDSCWebService]WebPullSRV1] Disable Inbound Firewall Notification
VERBOSE: [SRV1]:                            [[xDSCWebService]WebPullSRV1] Add Firewall Rule for port 8080
VERBOSE: [SRV1]:                            [[xDSCWebService]WebPullSRV1] Set values into the web.config that define the repository later than
BLUE OS
VERBOSE: [SRV1]:                            [[xDSCWebService]WebPullSRV1] Only ESENT is supported on Windows Server 2016
VERBOSE: [SRV1]:                            [[xDSCWebService]WebPullSRV1] Pull Server: Set values into the web.config that indicate the locatio
n of repository, confi
guration, modules
VERBOSE: [SRV1]: LCM:  [ End    Set      ]  [[xDSCWebService]WebPullSRV1] in 9.7930 seconds.
VERBOSE: [SRV1]: LCM:  [ End    Resource ]  [[xDSCWebService]WebPullSRV1]
VERBOSE: [SRV1]: LCM:  [ Start  Resource ]  [[File]RegistrationKeyFile]
VERBOSE: [SRV1]: LCM:  [ Start  Test     ]  [[File]RegistrationKeyFile]
VERBOSE: [SRV1]:                            [[File]RegistrationKeyFile] The system cannot find the path specified.
VERBOSE: [SRV1]:                            [[File]RegistrationKeyFile] The related file/directory is: C:\ProgramFiles\WindowsPowerShell\DscSer
vice\RegistrationKeys.
txt.
VERBOSE: [SRV1]: LCM:  [ End    Test     ]  [[File]RegistrationKeyFile] in 0.0160 seconds.
VERBOSE: [SRV1]: LCM:  [ Start  Set      ]  [[File]RegistrationKeyFile]
VERBOSE: [SRV1]:                            [[File]RegistrationKeyFile] The system cannot find the path specified.
VERBOSE: [SRV1]:                            [[File]RegistrationKeyFile] The related file/directory is: C:\ProgramFiles\WindowsPowerShell\DscSer
vice\RegistrationKeys.
txt.
VERBOSE: [SRV1]: LCM:  [ End    Set      ]  [[File]RegistrationKeyFile] in 0.0470 seconds.
VERBOSE: [SRV1]: LCM:  [ End    Resource ]  [[File]RegistrationKeyFile]
VERBOSE: [SRV1]: LCM:  [ End    Set      ]
VERBOSE: [SRV1]: LCM:  [ End    Set      ]  in 16.1180 seconds.
VERBOSE: Operation 'Invoke CimMethod' complete.
VERBOSE: Time taken for configuration job to complete is 16.256 seconds
```

In *step 7*, you use Internet Explorer to view the details of the DSC web service you just set up. If the computer on which you run this step trusts the certificate you generated in *step 1*, then the output from *step 7* looks like this:

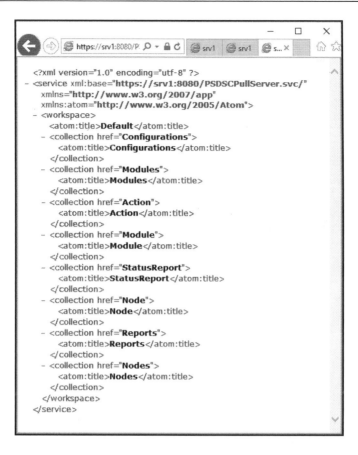

In *step 8*, you create and compile a configuration to make SRV2 pull DSC configurations and resources from the website on SRV1. As with compiling any DSC configuration, this step generates no output.

With *step 9*, you create the MOF file DSC needs to configure the LCM on SRV2 to pull configuration and resources from SRV1. The output looks like this:

```
PS C:\> Remove-Item -Path C:\DSC\* -Recurse -Force
PS C:\> $Guid = '5d79ee6e-0420-4c98-9cc3-9f696901a816'
PS C:\> SRV2WebPull -Guid $Guid -OutputPath C:\DSC


    Directory: C:\DSC


Mode                LastWriteTime         Length Name
----                -------------         ------ ----
-a----        22/04/2017     20:28           1988 SRV2.meta.mof
```

In *step 10*, you send the meta-configuration to SRV2 that configures SRV2 to be a pull server and to pull from SRV1. The output looks like this:

```
PS C:\Users\administrator.RESKIT\Documents> Set-DscLocalConfigurationManager -ComputerName SRV2 `
                              -Path C:\DSC `
                              -Verbose
VERBOSE: Performing the operation "Start-DscConfiguration: SendMetaConfigurationApply" on target
"MSFT_DSCLocalConfigurationManager".
VERBOSE: Perform operation 'Invoke CimMethod' with following parameters,
''methodName' = SendMetaConfigurationApply,'className' = MSF
T_DSCLocalConfigurationManager,'namespaceName' = root/Microsoft/Windows/DesiredStateConfiguration'.
VERBOSE: An LCM method call arrived from computer SRV1 with
user sid S-1-5-21-715049209-2702507345-667613206-500.
VERBOSE: [SRV2]: LCM:  [ Start  Set       ]
VERBOSE: [SRV2]: LCM:  [ Start  Resource  ]  [MSFT_DSCMetaConfiguration]
VERBOSE: [SRV2]: LCM:  [ Start  Set       ]  [MSFT_DSCMetaConfiguration]
VERBOSE: [SRV2]: LCM:  [ End    Set       ]  [MSFT_DSCMetaConfiguration]  in 0.0310 seconds.
VERBOSE: [SRV2]: LCM:  [ End    Resource  ]  [MSFT_DSCMetaConfiguration]
VERBOSE: [SRV2]: LCM:  [ End    Set       ]
VERBOSE: [SRV2]: LCM:  [ End    Set       ]  in  0.0940 seconds.
VERBOSE: Operation 'Invoke CimMethod' complete.
VERBOSE: Set-DscLocalConfigurationManager finished in 1.291 seconds.
```

In *step 11*, you create and compile a meta-configuration that configures SRV2 server's LCM. This configuration is a pull configuration that you store on SRV1, and which SRV2 then pulls from SRV1 using the web service on SRV1. There is no output from this step.

With *step 12*, you create the MOF file for the configuration you compiled in *Step 11*, and looks like this:

```
PS C:\> Remove-Item -Path C:\DSC\* -Rec -Force
PS C:\> TelnetSRV2 -OutputPath C:\DSCConfiguration

    Directory: C:\DSCConfiguration

Mode                LastWriteTime         Length Name
----                -------------         ------ ----
-a----        22/04/2017     20:51          1850 SRV2.mof
```

Because you are using the GUID naming convention for configuration statements, in *step 13*, you rename the file and create the checksum in the appropriate folder. The output looks like this:

```
PS C:\> Rename-Item -Path    C:\DSC\SRV2.mof `
                    -NewName C:\DSC\$Guid.MOF
PS C:\> New-DscChecksum  -Path c:\DSC
PS C:\> Get-ChildItem -Path C:\DSC

    Directory: C:\DSC

Mode                LastWriteTime         Length Name
----                -------------         ------ ----
-a----        22/04/2017     20:51          1850 5d79ee6e-0420-4c98-9cc3-9f696901a816.MOF
-a----        22/04/2017     20:52            64 5d79ee6e-0420-4c98-9cc3-9f696901a816.MOF.checksum
```

In *step 14*, you use the `Update-DscConfiguration` cmdlet to update SRV2. Based on the setup you have done in this recipe, SRV2 pulls the configuration block from SRV1, verifies that the checksum is valid, then applies the new configuration (which ensures the telnet client is present on SRV2. The output looks like this:

```
PS C:\> Update-DscConfiguration -ComputerName SRV2 -Wait -Verbose
VERBOSE: Perform operation 'Invoke CimMethod' with following parameters,
''methodName' = PerformRequiredConfigurationChecks,'className' = MSFT_DSCLocalConfigurationManager,
'namespaceName' = root/Microsoft/Windows/DesiredStateConfiguration'.
VERBOSE: An LCM method call arrived from computer SRV1 with user sid S-1-5-21-715049209-2702507345-667613206-500.
VERBOSE: [SRV2]:                          [] Executing Get-Action with configuration 5d79ee6e-0420-4c98-9cc3-9f696901a816's
checksum: E342D86BD10FBD2C027AF5D5A667136485AFBA3F56DCC4D7AFF638699D5D5845.
VERBOSE: [SRV2]:                          [] Executing Get-Action with configuration 's checksum returned result status: GetConfiguration.
VERBOSE: [SRV2]:                          [] Checksum is different. LCM will execute GetConfiguration to pull configuration .
VERBOSE: [SRV2]:                          [] Executing GetConfiguration succeeded. Configuration  was pulled from server.
VERBOSE: [SRV2]:                          [] Applying the new configuration(s) pulled.
VERBOSE: [SRV2]: LCM:  [ Start  Resource ]  [WindowsFeature]TelnetClient
VERBOSE: [SRV2]: LCM:  [ Start  Test     ]  [WindowsFeature]TelnetClient
VERBOSE: [SRV2]:                             [WindowsFeature]TelnetClient  The operation 'Get-WindowsFeature' started: Telnet-Client
VERBOSE: [SRV2]:                             [WindowsFeature]TelnetClient  The operation 'Get-WindowsFeature' succeeded: Telnet-Client
VERBOSE: [SRV2]: LCM:  [ End    Test     ]  [WindowsFeature]TelnetClient  in 1.0930 seconds.
VERBOSE: [SRV2]: LCM:  [ Start  Set      ]  [WindowsFeature]TelnetClient
VERBOSE: [SRV2]:                             [WindowsFeature]TelnetClient  Installation started...
VERBOSE: [SRV2]:                             [WindowsFeature]TelnetClient  Continue with installation?
VERBOSE: [SRV2]:                             [WindowsFeature]TelnetClient  Prerequisite processing started...
VERBOSE: [SRV2]:                             [WindowsFeature]TelnetClient  Prerequisite processing succeeded.
VERBOSE: [SRV2]:                             [WindowsFeature]TelnetClient  Installation succeeded.
VERBOSE: [SRV2]:                             [WindowsFeature]TelnetClient  Successfully installed the feature Telnet-Client.
VERBOSE: [SRV2]: LCM:  [ End    Set      ]  [WindowsFeature]TelnetClient  in 23.2420 seconds.
VERBOSE: [SRV2]: LCM:  [ End    Resource ]  [WindowsFeature]TelnetClient]
VERBOSE: Operation 'Invoke CimMethod' complete.
VERBOSE: Time taken for configuration job to complete is 25.194 seconds
```

In the final step, *step 15*, you create a CIM session on SRV2 (from SRV1) and over that session, you run the `Get-DscConfiguration` cmdlet that shows the impact of *step 14* on SRV2, like this:

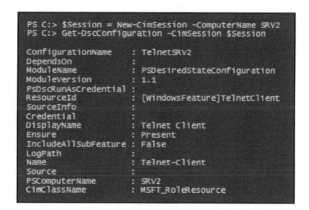

```
PS C:> $Session = New-CimSession -ComputerName SRV2
PS C:> Get-DscConfiguration -CimSession $Session

ConfigurationName    : TelnetSRV2
DependsOn            :
ModuleName          : PSDesiredStateConfiguration
ModuleVersion       : 1.1
PsDscRunAsCredential :
ResourceId          : [WindowsFeature]TelnetClient
SourceInfo          :
Credential          :
DisplayName         : Telnet Client
Ensure              : Present
IncludeAllSubFeature : False
LogPath             :
Name                : Telnet-Client
Source              :
PSComputerName      : SRV2
CimClassName        : MSFT_RoleResource
```

There's more...

In *step 7*, you viewed output from the SRV1 server's DSC web service. If the system, that is, SRV2, on which you run this step trusts the certificate, you see the page as shown earlier. However, if you run the step on another computer, say SRV1, then you are going to see a certificate error since the computer does not trust the self-signed certificate. If you save the self-signed certificate you created in *step 1* to the trusted root store of a computer, then that computer trusts the certificate (and you see no errors in your browser).

In *step 14*, you used the Update-DscConfiguration cmdlet to force SRV2 to pull any required configuration from SRV1. As an alternative, you could have waited until the refresh time (which you set in step to be 30 minutes) to allow SRV2 to pull the updated configuration.

Using DSC partial configurations

PowerShell V5 introduced a new feature with DSC: partial configurations. A partial configuration, as the name suggests, is part of the configuration you wish to see applied to a given node.

Partial configurations allow you to share the configuration of a node between multiple teams. For example, you might want the central IT team to define the basic configuration of a node. Another team could be responsible for deploying a web application to that same node. With PowerShell 4, you would have needed to put all the configuration components into a single configuration document/MOF file and deploy that to the node.

To support partial configurations, you must configure each node's LCM to define the partial configurations, and how they are to be deployed. Each partial configuration can be either pushed or pulled. Thus, you can deploy partial configurations that direct the node to pull the basic host configuration for an IT central configuration server and to pull the application details from a separate and independent server. You can also have some partial configurations pulled by the node, with other configurations pushed to the node. This gives you considerable flexibility in deploying DSC partial configurations.

Defining partial configurations is broadly the same as defining full configurations. On each node, you define which partial configurations the node pulls and from what server, as well as any partial configurations you plan to push to the node. The node's LCM takes these different partial configurations (each partial configuration is a MOF file) and creates a single composite configuration and applies the composite to the node.

Getting ready

In this recipe, you use two servers, SRV1 and SRV2. SRV1 serves as the DSC pull server with SRV2 the node you configure using two partial DSC configurations. You create the pull server using a downloadable module xPSDesiredStateConfiguration. This module contains a number of DSC resources you use in the recipe. You downloaded and distributed it using an earlier recipe. Normally you can use the Install-Module cmdlet to install this module on both SRV1 and SRV2. Or you can install it on one server, then copy it to any target servers that need the module, as you do in this recipe.

How to do it...

1. Create a self-signed certificate on SRV1, copy it to the local machine's root store, and then display it:

```
Get-ChildItem -Path Cert:LocalMachine\My |
    Where-Object Subject -eq 'CN=SRV1' |
        Remove-Item -Force
$DscCert = New-SelfSignedCertificate `
                -CertStoreLocation 'CERT:\LocalMachine\MY' `
                -DnsName 'SRV1'
$C = 'System.Security.Cryptography.X509Certificates.X509Store'
$Store = New-Object -TypeName $C -ArgumentList
'Root','LocalMachine'
$Store.Open('ReadWrite')
$Store.Add($Dsccert)
$Store.Close()
$DscCert
```

2. Copy the certificate to the root store on SRV2 and ensure it's the only one:

```
$Sb = {
  Param ($Rootcert)
  Get-ChildItem Cert:LocalMachine\Root |
      Where Subject -eq 'CN=SRV1' | Remove-Item -Force
  $C = 'System.Security.Cryptography.X509Certificates.X509Store'
  $Store = New-Object -TypeName $C `
                        -ArgumentList 'Root','LocalMachine'
  $Store.Open('ReadWrite')
  $Store.Add($Rootcert)
  $Store.Close()}
Invoke-Command -ScriptBlock $Sb -ComputerName SRV2 -Verbose `
                                -ArgumentList $DscCert
```

3. Display the certificate on SRV2:

```
$sb = {Get-ChildItem Cert:\LocalMachine\root |
        Where Subject -Match 'SRV1' }
Invoke-Command -ScriptBlock $sb `
                -ComputerName SRV2
```

4. Check that the xPsDesiredStateConfiguration module is installed on both SRV1 and SRV2:

```
$ModPath = Join-Path `
        -Path 'C:\Program Files\WindowsPowerShell\Modules' `
        -ChildPath 'xPSDesiredStateConfiguration'
Copy-Item -Path $ModPath `
        -Destination '\\SRV2\C$\Program
Files\WindowsPowerShell\Modules' `
        -Recurse -ErrorAction SilentlyContinue
Get-Module xPSDesiredStateConfiguration -ListAvailable
Invoke-Command -ComputerName SRV2 `
    -ScriptBlock {
        Get-Module xPSDesiredStateConfiguration `
            -ListAvailable}
```

5. Create and compile the DscService configuration block for SRV1:

```
Configuration WebPullSrv1 {
Param ([String] $CertThumbPrint)
Import-DscResource -Module PSDesiredStateConfiguration,
                        xPSDesiredStateConfiguration
$Regfile=Join-Path `
    -Path 'C:\Program Files\WindowsPowerShell\DscService' `
    -Childpath 'RegistrationKeys.txt'
Node SRV1 {
    File DSCConfig-Folder{
        DestinationPath = 'C:\DSCConfiguration'
        Ensure = 'Present'
        Type = 'Directory' }
    File DSCResource-Folder{
        DestinationPath = 'C:\DSCResource'
        Ensure = 'Present'
        Type = 'Directory' }
    WindowsFeature DSCService {
        Ensure = 'Present'
        Name = 'DSC-Service' }
    xDscWebService WebPullSRV1 {
        Ensure = 'Present'
        EndpointName = 'PSDSCPullServer'
```

```
            Port = 8080
            PhysicalPath = 'C:\inetpub\PSDSCPullServer'
            CertificateThumbPrint = $CertThumbPrint
            ConfigurationPath = 'C:\DSCConfiguration'
            ModulePath = 'C:\DSCResource'
            State = 'Started'
            DependsOn = '[WindowsFeature]DSCService'
            UseSecurityBestPractices = $true }
        File RegistrationKeyFile {
            Ensure = 'Present'
            Type = 'File'
            DestinationPath = $Regfile
            Contents = '5d79ee6e-0420-4c98-9cc3-9f696901a816'}}}
```

6. Remove existing MOF files then create an MOF file for SRV1:

```
Get-ChildItem -Path C:\DSC -ErrorAction SilentlyContinue |
    Remove-Item -Force | Out-Null
Remove-Item -Path 'C:\Windows\System32\configuration\*.mof' `
        -ErrorAction SilentlyContinue
WebPullSrv1 -OutputPath C:\DSC -CertThumbPrint
$DscCert.Thumbprint
```

7. Add the DSC web service to SRV1:

```
Start-DscConfiguration -Path C:\DSC -Wait -Verbose
```

8. Check on the results of adding the web server:

```
$IE = New-Object -ComObject
InterNetExplorer.Application
$Uri = 'https://SRV1:8080/PSDSCPullServer.svc/'
$IE.Navigate2($Uri)
$IE.Visible = $true
```

9. Create a meta-configuration to make SRV2 pull from SRV1:

```
[DSCLocalConfigurationManager()]
Configuration SRV2WebPullPartial {
Node Srv2 {
  Settings
      { RefreshMode = 'Pull'
          ConfigurationModeFrequencyMins = 30
          ConfigurationMode = 'ApplyandAutoCorrect'
          RefreshFrequencyMins = 30
          RebootNodeIfNeeded = $true
          AllowModuleOverwrite = $true }
  ConfigurationRepositoryWeb DSCPullSrv
      { ServerURL = 'https://SRV1:8080/PSDSCPullServer.svc'
          RegistrationKey = '5d79ee6e-0420-4c98-9cc3-9f696901a816'
          ConfigurationNames = @('TelnetConfig','TFTPConfig') }
  PartialConfiguration TelnetConfig
      { Description = 'Telnet Client Configuration'
          Configurationsource =
@('[ConfigurationRepositoryWeb]DSCPullSrv')}
  PartialConfiguration TFTPConfig {
          Description = 'TFTP Client Configuration'
          Configurationsource =
@('[ConfigurationRepositoryWeb]DSCPullSrv')
          DependsOn = '[PartialConfiguration]TelnetConfig'}
  }
}
```

10. Create a MOF to configure DSC LCM on SRV2:

```
Remove-Item -Path C:\DSCConfiguration\* -Recurse -Force
Remove-Item -Path `
'\\SRV2\C$\Windows\System32\Configuration\*.mof'
SRV2WebPullPartial -OutputPath C:\DSC | Out-Null
```

11. Configure the LCM on SRV2:

```
$CSSrv2 = New-CimSession -ComputerName SRV2
Set-DscLocalConfigurationManager -CimSession $CSSrv2 `
                                 -Path C:\DSC `
                                 -Verbose
```

12. Create/compile the `TelnetConfig` partial configuration and build the MOF file:

```
$Guid = '5d79ee6e-0420-4c98-9cc3-9f696901a816'
$ConfigData = @{
   AllNodes = @(
      @{ NodeName = '*' ; PsDscAllowPlainTextPassword = $true},
      @{ NodeName = $Guid }
   )
}
Configuration TelnetConfig {
Import-DscResource -ModuleName PSDesiredStateConfiguration
Node $Allnodes.NodeName {
  WindowsFeature TelnetClient
    { Name = 'Telnet-Client'
      Ensure = 'Present' }
    }
}
TelnetConfig -ConfigurationData $ConfigData `
            -OutputPath C:\DSCConfiguration | Out-Null
Rename-Item -Path "C:\DSCConfiguration\$Guid.mof" `
            -NewName 'C:\DSCConfiguration\TelnetConfig.Mof'
```

13. Create and compile the `TFTPConfig` partial configuration:

```
$Guid = '5d79ee6e-0420-4c98-9cc3-9f696901a816'
$ConfigData = @{
   AllNodes = @(
      @{ NodeName = '*' ; PsDscAllowPlainTextPassword = $true},
      @{ NodeName = $Guid }
   )
}
Configuration TFTPConfig {
Import-DscResource -ModuleName 'PSDesiredStateConfiguration'
Node $AllNodes.NodeName {
WindowsFeature TFTPClient
    { Name = 'TFTP-Client'
      Ensure = 'Present' }
    }
}
TFTPConfig -ConfigurationData $ConfigData -OutputPath
TFTPConfig -ConfigurationData $ConfigData `
          -OutputPath 'C:\DSCConfiguration\' | Out-Null
Rename-Item -Path "c:\DSCConfiguration\$Guid.mof" `
            -NewName 'TFTPConfig.Mof'
```

14. Create checksum files for these two partial configurations:

```
New-DscChecksum -Path C:\DSCConfiguration
```

15. Observe configuration documents and checksum:

```
Get-ChildItem -Path C:\DSCConfiguration
```

16. Update the LCM on SRV2 and test to see if it configured per the desired state:

```
Update-DscConfiguration -ComputerName SRV2 -Wait -Verbose
Test-DSCConfiguration -ComputerName SRV2
```

17. Induce the configuration drift:

```
Remove-WindowsFeature -Name tftp-client, telnet-client `
                    -ComputerName SRV2 |
        Out-Null
```

18. Test the DSC configuration:

```
Test-DscConfiguration -ComputerName SRV2
```

19. Fix the configuration drift:

```
Start-DscConfiguration -UseExisting -Verbose -Wait `
                    -ComputerName SRV2
```

20. Test to check SRV2 is in compliance with the desired state:

```
Get-WindowsFeature -Name Telnet-Client, TFTP-Client `
                    -ComputerName SRV2
```

How it works...

In *step 1*, you create a self-signed certificate. You drop this certificate both in the `LocalMachine\My` folder and in the `LocalMachine\Root` folder. In effect, this creates a trusted certificate on `SRV1` that you can use with IIS. Creating the certificate produces no output, but the final command in this step looks like this:

```
PS C:\> $DscCert

    PSParentPath: Microsoft.PowerShell.Security\Certificate::LocalMachine\MY

Thumbprint                                Subject
----------                                -------
FCE666DED34214D913141246506E5AA3B34F0FA9  CN=SRV1
```

Once you have this certificate on `SRV1`, you can copy it to the trusted root store on `SRV2`. This step works by running a script block on the remote machine to make the certificate trusted on `SRV2`. There is no output from *step 2*.

In *step 3*, you display the root certificate added to `SRV2` server's trusted root store, which looks like this:

```
PS C:\> Invoke-Command -ScriptBlock {Get-ChildItem -Path Cert:\LocalMachine\root |
            Where-Object Subject -Match 'SRV1'} -ComputerName SRV2

    PSParentPath: Microsoft.PowerShell.Security\Certificate::LocalMachine\root

Thumbprint                                Subject      PSComputerName
----------                                -------      --------------
FCE666DED34214D913141246506E5AA3B34F0FA9  CN=SRV1      SRV2
```

This recipe uses the `xPSDesiredStateConfiguration` module which contains DSC resources you use to setup DSC. This module is one you need to download using the `Install-Module` cmdlet. In *step 4*, you copy the module to `SRV2` (and ignore any errors that might occur if the module exists on `SRV2`.

The output, checking you have the same versions of xPSDesiredStateConfiguration on SRV1 and SRV2 looks like this:

```
PS C:\> Get-Module xPSDesiredStateConfiguration -ListAvailable

    Directory: C:\Program Files\WindowsPowerShell\Modules

ModuleType Version  Name                          ExportedCommands
---------- -------  ----                          ----------------
Script     6.2.0.0  xPSDesiredStateConfiguration  {Publish-MOFToPullServer, Publish-DSCModuleAndMof,
                                                   Publish-ModuleToPullServer}
PS C:\> Invoke-Command -ComputerName SRV2
            -ScriptBlock {Get-Module xPSDesiredStateConfiguration -ListAvailable}

    Directory: C:\Program Files\WindowsPowerShell\Modules

ModuleType Version  Name                          ExportedCommands                                          PSComputerName
---------- -------  ----                          ----------------                                          --------------
Script     6.2.0.0  xPSDesiredStateConfiguration  {Publish-ModuleToPullServer, Publish-MOFToPullServer,     SRV2
                                                   Pu...}
```

With *step 5*, you create a configuration block to configure SRV1 to be a DSC pull server. This includes creating two folders for pull clients to find configuration details and DSC resources—you ensure the DSC service is running, then use the xDscWebService resource to configure the DSC service. Finally, this step creates a registration file needed to enable pull clients to authenticate to the pull server. As with other DSC configuration blocks, running this block of code generates no output.

Once you compile the configuration block, you have to create the related MOF file, which you do in *step 6*. The output looks like this:

```
PS C:\> Get-ChildItem -Path C:\DSC -ErrorAction SilentlyContinue |
            Remove-Item -Force | Out-Null
PS C:\> Remove-Item -Path 'C:\Windows\System32\configuration\*.mof' `
            -ErrorAction SilentlyContinue
PS C:\> WebPullSrv1 -OutputPath C:\DSC  -CertThumbPrint $DscCert.Thumbprint

    Directory: C:\DSC

Mode                LastWriteTime      Length Name
----                -------------      ------ ----
-a----       03/05/2017     19:35        5536 SRV1.mof
```

In *step 7*, you apply the `WebPullSrv1` configuration to `SRV1`. Using the `-Wait` and `-Verbose` parameters, you view the actions taken by DSC on `SRV1`, which looks like this:

```
PS C:\> Start-DscConfiguration -Path C:\DSC -Wait -Verbose
VERBOSE: Perform operation 'Invoke CimMethod' with following parameters,
  'methodName' = SendConfigurationApply,'className' = MSFT_DSCLocalConfigurationManager,
  'namespaceName' = root/Microsoft/Windows/DesiredStateConfiguration'.
VERBOSE: An LCM method call arrived from computer SRV1 with user sid S-1-5-21-715049209-2702507345-667613206-500.
VERBOSE: [SRV1]: LCM:  [ Start  Set      ]
VERBOSE: [SRV1]: LCM:  [ Start  Resource ]  [[File]DSCConfig-Folder]
VERBOSE: [SRV1]: LCM:  [ Start  Test     ]  [[File]DSCConfig-Folder]
VERBOSE: [SRV1]:                             [[File]DSCConfig-Folder]
VERBOSE: [SRV1]:                             [[File]DSCConfig-Folder] The system cannot find the file specified.
VERBOSE: [SRV1]:                             [[File]DSCConfig-Folder] The related file/directory is: C:\DSCConfiguration.
VERBOSE: [SRV1]: LCM:  [ End    Test     ]  [[File]DSCConfig-Folder]  in 0.0160 seconds.
VERBOSE: [SRV1]: LCM:  [ Start  Set      ]  [[File]DSCConfig-Folder]
VERBOSE: [SRV1]:                             [[File]DSCConfig-Folder] The system cannot find the file specified.
VERBOSE: [SRV1]:                             [[File]DSCConfig-Folder] The related file/directory is: C:\DSCConfiguration.
VERBOSE: [SRV1]: LCM:  [ End    Set      ]  [[File]DSCConfig-Folder]  in 0.0000 seconds.
VERBOSE: [SRV1]: LCM:  [ End    Resource ]  [[File]DSCConfig-Folder]
VERBOSE: [SRV1]: LCM:  [ Start  Resource ]  [[File]DSCResource-Folder]
VERBOSE: [SRV1]: LCM:  [ Start  Test     ]  [[File]DSCResource-Folder]
VERBOSE: [SRV1]:                             [[File]DSCResource-Folder]
VERBOSE: [SRV1]:                             [[File]DSCResource-Folder] The system cannot find the file specified.
VERBOSE: [SRV1]:                             [[File]DSCResource-Folder] The related file/directory is: C:\DSCResource.
VERBOSE: [SRV1]: LCM:  [ End    Test     ]  [[File]DSCResource-Folder]  in 0.0160 seconds.
VERBOSE: [SRV1]: LCM:  [ Start  Set      ]  [[File]DSCResource-Folder]
VERBOSE: [SRV1]:                             [[File]DSCResource-Folder] The system cannot find the file specified.
VERBOSE: [SRV1]:                             [[File]DSCResource-Folder] The related file/directory is: C:\DSCResource.
VERBOSE: [SRV1]: LCM:  [ End    Set      ]  [[File]DSCResource-Folder]  in 0.0310 seconds.
VERBOSE: [SRV1]: LCM:  [ End    Resource ]  [[File]DSCResource-Folder]
VERBOSE: [SRV1]: LCM:  [ Start  Resource ]  [[WindowsFeature]DSCService]
VERBOSE: [SRV1]: LCM:  [ Start  Test     ]  [[WindowsFeature]DSCService]
VERBOSE: [SRV1]:                             [[WindowsFeature]DSCService]
VERBOSE: [SRV1]:                             [[WindowsFeature]DSCService] The operation 'Get-WindowsFeature' started: DSC-Service
VERBOSE: [SRV1]:                             [[WindowsFeature]DSCService] The operation 'Get-WindowsFeature' succeeded: DSC-Service
VERBOSE: [SRV1]: LCM:  [ End    Test     ]  [[WindowsFeature]DSCService]  in 0.9530 seconds.
VERBOSE: [SRV1]: LCM:  [ Start  Set      ]  [[WindowsFeature]DSCService]
VERBOSE: [SRV1]:                             [[WindowsFeature]DSCService] Installation started...
VERBOSE: [SRV1]:                             [[WindowsFeature]DSCService] Continue with installation?
VERBOSE: [SRV1]:                             [[WindowsFeature]DSCService] Prerequisite processing started...
VERBOSE: [SRV1]:                             [[WindowsFeature]DSCService] Prerequisite processing succeeded.
VERBOSE: [SRV1]:                             [[WindowsFeature]DSCService] Installation succeeded.
VERBOSE: [SRV1]:                             [[WindowsFeature]DSCService] Successfully installed the feature DSC-Service.
VERBOSE: [SRV1]: LCM:  [ End    Set      ]  [[WindowsFeature]DSCService]  in 106.2660 seconds.
VERBOSE: [SRV1]: LCM:  [ End    Resource ]  [[WindowsFeature]DSCService]
VERBOSE: [SRV1]: LCM:  [ Start  Resource ]  [[xDSCWebService]WebPullSRV1]
VERBOSE: [SRV1]: LCM:  [ Start  Test     ]  [[xDSCWebService]WebPullSRV1]
VERBOSE: [SRV1]:                             [[xDSCWebService]WebPullSRV1] Check Ensure
VERBOSE: [SRV1]:                             [[xDSCWebService]WebPullSRV1] Check Port
VERBOSE: [SRV1]:                             [[xDSCWebService]WebPullSRV1] Check Physical Path property
VERBOSE: [SRV1]:                             [[xDSCWebService]WebPullSRV1] Physical Path of Website PSDSCPullServer does not match the desired state.
VERBOSE: [SRV1]: LCM:  [ End    Test     ]  [[xDSCWebService]WebPullSRV1]  in 1.8000 seconds.
VERBOSE: [SRV1]: LCM:  [ Start  Set      ]  [[xDSCWebService]WebPullSRV1]
VERBOSE: [SRV1]:                             [[xDSCWebService]WebPullSRV1] Create the IIS endpoint
VERBOSE: [SRV1]:                             [[xDSCWebService]WebPullSRV1] Setting up endpoint at - https://SRV1:8080/PSDSCPullServer.svc
VERBOSE: [SRV1]:                             [[xDSCWebService]WebPullSRV1] Verify that the certificate with the provided thumbprint exists in CERT:\LocalMachine\MY\
VERBOSE: [SRV1]:                             [[xDSCWebService]WebPullSRV1] Checking IIS requirements
VERBOSE: [SRV1]:                             [[xDSCWebService]WebPullSRV1] Delete the App Pool if it exists
VERBOSE: [SRV1]:                             [[xDSCWebService]WebPullSRV1] Remove the site if it already exists
VERBOSE: [SRV1]:                             [[xDSCWebService]WebPullSRV1] pll
VERBOSE: [SRV1]:                             [[xDSCWebService]WebPullSRV1] Create the bin folder for deploying custom dependent binaries required by the endpoint
VERBOSE: [SRV1]:                             [[xDSCWebService]WebPullSRV1] Adding App Pool
VERBOSE: [SRV1]:                             [[xDSCWebService]WebPullSRV1] Set App Pool Properties
VERBOSE: [SRV1]:                             [[xDSCWebService]WebPullSRV1] Add and Set Site Properties
VERBOSE: [SRV1]:                             [[xDSCWebService]WebPullSRV1] pll
VERBOSE: [SRV1]:                             [[xDSCWebService]WebPullSRV1] Enabling firewall exception for port 8080
VERBOSE: [SRV1]:                             [[xDSCWebService]WebPullSRV1] Disable Inbound Firewall Notification
VERBOSE: [SRV1]:                             [[xDSCWebService]WebPullSRV1] Add Firewall Rule for port 8080
VERBOSE: [SRV1]:                             [[xDSCWebService]WebPullSRV1] Set values into the web.config that define the repository later than BLUE OS
VERBOSE: [SRV1]:                             [[xDSCWebService]WebPullSRV1] Only ESENT is supported on Windows Server 2016
VERBOSE: [SRV1]:                             [[xDSCWebService]WebPullSRV1] Pull Server: Set values into the web.config that indicate the location of repository, configuration, mo
dules
VERBOSE: [SRV1]: LCM:  [ End    Set      ]  [[xDSCWebService]WebPullSRV1]  in 12.7870 seconds.
VERBOSE: [SRV1]: LCM:  [ End    Resource ]  [[xDSCWebService]WebPullSRV1]
VERBOSE: [SRV1]: LCM:  [ Start  Resource ]  [[File]RegistrationKeyFile]
VERBOSE: [SRV1]: LCM:  [ Start  Test     ]  [[File]RegistrationKeyFile]
VERBOSE: [SRV1]:                             [[File]RegistrationKeyFile] The destination object was found and no action is required.
VERBOSE: [SRV1]: LCM:  [ End    Test     ]  [[File]RegistrationKeyFile]  in 0.0320 seconds.
VERBOSE: [SRV1]: LCM:  [ Skip   Set      ]  [[File]RegistrationKeyFile]
VERBOSE: [SRV1]: LCM:  [ End    Resource ]  [[File]RegistrationKeyFile]
VERBOSE: [SRV1]: LCM:  [ End    Set      ]  in 124.8960 seconds.
VERBOSE: Operation 'Invoke CimMethod' complete.
VERBOSE: Time taken for configuration job to complete is 127.37 seconds
```

In *step 8*, you check the DSC web service by using the `Internet Explorer COM` object. The step navigates to the DSC service endpoint on SRV1, which looks like this:

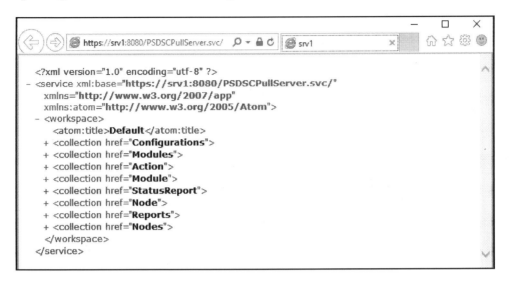

Once you have configured the DSC pull server on SRV1, you need to configure the pull client, SRV2, to be a pull client. In *step 9*, you create and compile a meta-configuration that configures the LCM on SRV2. This meta-configuration specifies details of the pull server and specifies that SRV2 should pull two partial configurations from the pull server on SRV1. Running this step produces no output.

In *step 10*, you run this configuration to create the necessary MOF file. There is no output from this step.

With *step 11*, you deploy the LCM configuration to SRV2. Using the –Verbose parameter enables you to see what DSC is doing as it applies the configuration to SRV2, which looks like this:

```
PS C:\> $CSSrv2 = New-CimSession -ComputerName SRV2
PS C:\> Set-DscLocalConfigurationManager -CimSession $CSSrv2 `
                          -Path C:\DSC `
                          -Verbose
VERBOSE: Performing the operation "Start-DscConfiguration:
SendMetaConfigurationApply" on target "MSFT_DSCLocalConfigurationManager".
VERBOSE: Perform operation 'Invoke CimMethod' with following parameters,
''methodName' = SendMetaConfigurationApply,'className' = MSFT_DSCLocalConfigurationManager,
'namespaceName' = root/Microsoft/Windows/DesiredStateConfiguration'.
VERBOSE: An LCM method call arrived from computer SRV2 with user
         sid S-1-5-21-715049209-2702507345-667613206-500.
VERBOSE: [SRV2]: LCM:  [ Start  Set       ]
VERBOSE: [SRV2]: LCM:  [ Start  Resource  ]  [MSFT_DSCMetaConfiguration]
VERBOSE: [SRV2]: LCM:  [ Start  Set       ]  [MSFT_DSCMetaConfiguration]
VERBOSE: [SRV2]: LCM:  [ End    Set       ]  [MSFT_DSCMetaConfiguration]  in 0.0150 seconds.
VERBOSE: [SRV2]: LCM:  [ End    Resource  ]  [MSFT_DSCMetaConfiguration]
VERBOSE: [SRV2]:                          [] Registration of the Dsc Agent with the
         server https://SRV1:8080/PSDSCPullServer.svc was successful.
VERBOSE: [SRV2]: LCM:  [ End    Set       ]
VERBOSE: [SRV2]: LCM:  [ End    Set       ]  in 25.0200 seconds.
VERBOSE: Operation 'Invoke CimMethod' complete.
VERBOSE: Set-DscLocalConfigurationManager finished in 25.203 seconds.
```

In *step 12* and *step 13*, you create two partial configurations (TelnetConfig and TFTPConfig). Each partial configuration defines a Windows feature that DSC should ensure exists on SRV2. You run the configurations and store the MOF file on where the DSC Pull server can deliver it to SRV2 when requested. Note that each configuration is renamed. There is no output from these steps.

DSC requires that each configuration MOF file has an accompanying checksum to avoid issues with data corruption. In *step 14* You use the New-DscCheksum cmdlet to create the checksum file. This cmdlet scans the target path and creates checksums for all MOF files contained in the folder. There is no output from this step.

In *step 15*, you observe the two partial configuration MOF files and their related checksum files, which looks like this:

```
PS C:\> Get-ChildItem -Path C:\DSCConfiguration

    Directory: C:\DSCConfiguration
Mode                LastWriteTime     Length Name
----                -------------     ------ ----
-a----        03/05/2017     20:29       1936 TelnetConfig.Mof
-a----        03/05/2017     20:29         64 TelnetConfig.Mof.checksum
-a----        03/05/2017     20:29       1920 TFTPConfig.Mof
-a----        03/05/2017     20:29         64 TFTPConfig.Mof.checksum
```

In *step 16*, you use the `Update-DscConfiguration` cmdlet to update the DSC configuration on SRV2. As you can see from the following output, this ensures that the two partial configurations are applied and that the DSC installs the two Windows features described in the configuration MOF files. In this step, you also test to see if the DSC configuration on SRV2 is correct, as follows:

```
PS C:\> Update-DscConfiguration -ComputerName SRV2 -Wait -Verbose
VERBOSE: Perform operation 'Invoke CimMethod' with following parameters,
''methodName' = PerformRequiredConfigurationChecks,'className' = MSFT_DSCLocalConfigurationManager,'name
spaceName' = root/Microsoft/Windows/DesiredStateConfiguration'.
VERBOSE: An LCM method call arrived from computer SRV1 with user sid S-1-5-21-715049209-2702507345-667613206-500.
VERBOSE: [SRV2]:                         [] Executing Get-Action with configuration 's checksum returned result status: GetConfiguration.
VERBOSE: [SRV2]:                         [] Checksum is different. LCM will execute GetConfiguration to pull configuration .
VERBOSE: [SRV2]:                         [] Executing GetConfiguration succeeded. Configuration TelnetConfig was pulled from server.
VERBOSE: [SRV2]:                         [] Executing GetConfiguration succeeded. Configuration TFTPConfig was pulled from server.
VERBOSE: [SRV2]:                         [] Applying the new configuration(s) pulled.
VERBOSE: [SRV2]: LCM:  [ Start  Resource ] [[WindowsFeature]TelnetClient]
VERBOSE: [SRV2]: LCM:  [ Start  Test     ] [[WindowsFeature]TelnetClient]
VERBOSE: [SRV2]:                         [[WindowsFeature]TelnetClient] The operation 'Get-WindowsFeature' started: Telnet-Client
VERBOSE: [SRV2]:                         [[WindowsFeature]TelnetClient] The operation 'Get-WindowsFeature' succeeded: Telnet-Client
VERBOSE: [SRV2]: LCM:  [ End    Test     ] [[WindowsFeature]TelnetClient]  in 0.9530 seconds.
VERBOSE: [SRV2]: LCM:  [ Start  Set      ] [[WindowsFeature]TelnetClient]
VERBOSE: [SRV2]:                         [[WindowsFeature]TelnetClient] Installation started...
VERBOSE: [SRV2]:                         [[WindowsFeature]TelnetClient] Continue with installation?
VERBOSE: [SRV2]:                         [[WindowsFeature]TelnetClient] Prerequisite processing started...
VERBOSE: [SRV2]:                         [[WindowsFeature]TelnetClient] Prerequisite processing succeeded.
VERBOSE: [SRV2]:                         [[WindowsFeature]TelnetClient] Installation succeeded.
VERBOSE: [SRV2]:                         [[WindowsFeature]TelnetClient] Successfully installed the feature Telnet-Client.
VERBOSE: [SRV2]: LCM:  [ End    Set      ] [[WindowsFeature]TelnetClient]  in 32.4180 seconds.
VERBOSE: [SRV2]: LCM:  [ End    Resource ] [[WindowsFeature]TelnetClient]
VERBOSE: [SRV2]: LCM:  [ Start  Resource ] [[WindowsFeature]TFTPClient]
VERBOSE: [SRV2]: LCM:  [ Start  Test     ] [[WindowsFeature]TFTPClient]
VERBOSE: [SRV2]:                         [[WindowsFeature]TFTPClient] The operation 'Get-WindowsFeature' started: TFTP-Client
VERBOSE: [SRV2]:                         [[WindowsFeature]TFTPClient] The operation 'Get-WindowsFeature' succeeded: TFTP-Client
VERBOSE: [SRV2]: LCM:  [ End    Test     ] [[WindowsFeature]TFTPClient]  in 2.1090 seconds.
VERBOSE: [SRV2]: LCM:  [ Start  Set      ] [[WindowsFeature]TFTPClient]
VERBOSE: [SRV2]:                         [[WindowsFeature]TFTPClient] Installation started...
VERBOSE: [SRV2]:                         [[WindowsFeature]TFTPClient] Continue with installation?
VERBOSE: [SRV2]:                         [[WindowsFeature]TFTPClient] Prerequisite processing started...
VERBOSE: [SRV2]:                         [[WindowsFeature]TFTPClient] Prerequisite processing succeeded.
VERBOSE: [SRV2]:                         [[WindowsFeature]TFTPClient] Installation succeeded.
VERBOSE: [SRV2]:                         [[WindowsFeature]TFTPClient] Successfully installed the feature TFTP-Client.
VERBOSE: [SRV2]: LCM:  [ End    Set      ] [[WindowsFeature]TFTPClient]  in 21.9150 seconds.
VERBOSE: [SRV2]: LCM:  [ End    Resource ] [[WindowsFeature]TFTPClient]
VERBOSE: Operation 'Invoke CimMethod' complete.
VERBOSE: Time taken for configuration job to complete is 71.607 seconds

PS C:\> Test-DscConfiguration -ComputerName srv2
True
```

To test DSC ability to ensure DSC configurations remain in place and to correct any configuration drift, in *step 17*, you remove the two network clients from SRV2. There is no output from this step.

In *step 18*, now that you have induced configuration drift on SRV2 (by removing the two Windows features), you use `Test-DscConfiguration` to test the DSC configuration of SRV2, which produces the following output:

```
PS C:\> Test-DscConfiguration -ComputerName SRV2
False
```

To resolve the configuration drift induced earlier, you can either wait for DSC regular consistency check to correct the issue or as you use the `Start-DscConfiguration` cmdlet, using the `-UseExisting` parameter as you do in *step 19*. This parameter instructs the LCM (on SRV2) to use the current LCM configuration and to correct any drift. The output from this step looks like this:

```
PS C:\> Start-DscConfiguration -UseExisting -Verbose -Wait -ComputerName srv2
VERBOSE: Perform operation 'Invoke CimMethod' with following parameters,
 ''methodName' = ApplyConfiguration,'className' = MSFT_DSCLocalConfigurationManager,'namespaceName' = roo
t/Microsoft/Windows/DesiredStateConfiguration'.
VERBOSE: An LCM method call arrived from computer SRV1 with user sid S-1-5-21-715049209-2702507345-667613206-500.
VERBOSE: [SRV2]:                              [] Starting consistency engine.
VERBOSE: [SRV2]:                              [] Checking consistency for current configuration.
VERBOSE: [SRV2]: LCM:  [ Start  Resource ]   [[WindowsFeature]TelnetClient]
VERBOSE: [SRV2]: LCM:  [ Start  Test     ]   [[WindowsFeature]TelnetClient]
VERBOSE: [SRV2]:                              [[WindowsFeature]TelnetClient] The operation 'Get-WindowsFeature' started: Telnet-Client
VERBOSE: [SRV2]:                              [[WindowsFeature]TelnetClient] The operation 'Get-WindowsFeature' succeeded: Telnet-Client
VERBOSE: [SRV2]: LCM:  [ End    Test     ]   [[WindowsFeature]TelnetClient]  in 0.4840 seconds.
VERBOSE: [SRV2]: LCM:  [ Start  Set      ]   [[WindowsFeature]TelnetClient]
VERBOSE: [SRV2]:                              [[WindowsFeature]TelnetClient] Installation started...
VERBOSE: [SRV2]:                              [[WindowsFeature]TelnetClient] Continue with installation?
VERBOSE: [SRV2]:                              [[WindowsFeature]TelnetClient] Prerequisite processing started...
VERBOSE: [SRV2]:                              [[WindowsFeature]TelnetClient] Prerequisite processing succeeded.
VERBOSE: [SRV2]:                              [[WindowsFeature]TelnetClient] Installation succeeded.
VERBOSE: [SRV2]:                              [[WindowsFeature]TelnetClient] Successfully installed the feature Telnet-Client.
VERBOSE: [SRV2]: LCM:  [ End    Set      ]   [[WindowsFeature]TelnetClient]  in 24.0370 seconds.
VERBOSE: [SRV2]: LCM:  [ End    Resource ]   [[WindowsFeature]TelnetClient]
VERBOSE: [SRV2]: LCM:  [ Start  Resource ]   [[WindowsFeature]TFTPClient]
VERBOSE: [SRV2]: LCM:  [ Start  Test     ]   [[WindowsFeature]TFTPClient]
VERBOSE: [SRV2]:                              [[WindowsFeature]TFTPClient] The operation 'Get-WindowsFeature' started: TFTP-Client
VERBOSE: [SRV2]:                              [[WindowsFeature]TFTPClient] The operation 'Get-WindowsFeature' succeeded: TFTP-Client
VERBOSE: [SRV2]: LCM:  [ End    Test     ]   [[WindowsFeature]TFTPClient]  in 1.7030 seconds.
VERBOSE: [SRV2]: LCM:  [ Start  Set      ]   [[WindowsFeature]TFTPClient]
VERBOSE: [SRV2]:                              [[WindowsFeature]TFTPClient] Installation started...
VERBOSE: [SRV2]:                              [[WindowsFeature]TFTPClient] Continue with installation?
VERBOSE: [SRV2]:                              [[WindowsFeature]TFTPClient] Prerequisite processing started...
VERBOSE: [SRV2]:                              [[WindowsFeature]TFTPClient] Prerequisite processing succeeded.
VERBOSE: [SRV2]:                              [[WindowsFeature]TFTPClient] Installation succeeded.
VERBOSE: [SRV2]:                              [[WindowsFeature]TFTPClient] Successfully installed the feature TFTP-Client.
VERBOSE: [SRV2]: LCM:  [ End    Set      ]   [[WindowsFeature]TFTPClient]  in 16.4280 seconds.
VERBOSE: [SRV2]: LCM:  [ End    Resource ]   [[WindowsFeature]TFTPClient]
VERBOSE: [SRV2]:                              [] Consistency check completed.
VERBOSE: Operation 'Invoke CimMethod' complete.
VERBOSE: Time taken for configuration job to complete is 42.861 seconds
```

You complete this recipe, in *step 20*, by using the `Get-Windows` feature cmdlet to check if the two network clients are installed on SRV2 (which they are). This step produces output like this:

```
PS C:\> Get-WindowsFeature -Name Telnet-Client, TFTP-Client -ComputerName SRV2

Display Name                    Name                   Install State
------------                    ----                   -------------
[X] Telnet Client               Telnet-Client          Installed
[X] TFTP Client                 TFTP-Client            Installed
```

There's more...

In *step 1*, you create a self-signed certificate that you make trusted on SRV1 and in *step 2* you make this certificate trusted on SRV2. In an ideal world, you should create an enterprise **Certificate Authority (CA)**, then issue certs signed by that CA. With an enterprise CA, your root certificates can be auto-published, making SRV1 server's certificate trusted by everyone.

In *step 2*, you use a bit of .NET magic to copy the certificate to SRV2. Sadly, the certificate provider in PowerShell does not support a copy operation, allowing you to use Copy-Item to copy the certificate between certificate stores on SRV1 and to SRV2.

With *step 3*, you view the certificate contained in SRV2 server's trusted root store. Note the thumbprint is the same as the thumbprint shown in step 2. In effect, what you have done is to make the certificate in the local machine's personal certificate store trusted on SRV2 (and via *step 1*, on SRV1).

Note you could set DSC up to not use SSL (and thus require certificates). This is, in general, not a good idea as it does not protect from a man in the middle attack. It also means the MOF documents transmitted from a pull server are in plain text. For configurations that contain credentials or other internal *secrets*, best practice always suggests you use SSL. Creating a self-signed and trusted cert for a lab experiment is much easier, and simple to automate.

In *step 4*, you ensure the resource you needed (xPSDesiredStateConfiguration module) was copied to SRV2. You could also have placed it on the pull server (SRV1) to enable the pull client to download it. This is probably a better approach for production use—just put all the resources in one place, and let nodes pull that module when necessary.

In *step 5*, you run/compile a DSC configuration, which produces no console output. You can use the Get-Command cmdlet, or look in the Function: drive on SRV1 to see the results of compiling the configuration.

In *step 11*, you configure the LCM on SRV2 to pull configuration details from SRV1. There are several ways to do this—the recipe creates a CIM session to SRV2 and then updates the LCM on SRV2 over the CIM session. The key point is that with some of the cmdlets you use in the recipe, you can use the -ComputerName parameter and name the target computer, whilst with others you need to use a CIM session.

In *step 12*, you create and compile a partial configuration which allows an empty password. In practice, this is not a great idea and you should be using a real password.

Index